Foreword by Jean-François Dugas

When the time comes to write the foreword for a guide like this one, it means the game is done and we're now planning for some serious vacation time (so that, by the time you read these lines, we'll already be started on creating something new.)

Reviving the Deus Ex franchise established by Warren Spector and his team at Ion Storm wasn't an easy task, but it has been an honor and a labor of love, really. I hope this will be quite evident as you experience the game and, using this guide as your companion, root out all the secrets, details, and different possibilities crafted by our passionate team.

Building a world as rich as the one found in Deus Ex: Human Revolution required a great deal of research, trial and error, and most importantly, passion. I don't quite know the exact moment I felt it, but I remember the game coming alive at some point during production when we caught ourselves talking about the characters and locations as if they were real people, real places. Looking back at what we created, it's hard to believe that we were able to infuse so much lore, secrets, and storytelling into the final product.

It is mostly impossible to experience the game in its entirety through one playthrough or without the help of this beautiful guide for the completionists out there.
Speaking of the guide, I've always believed that strategy guides should be more than just a collection of solutions for a game. They should increase your immersion in the game itself, making you go deeper in every possible aspect.

I've seen many guides in my 14 years in the biz and I can say with confidence that Future Press outdid itself with this Deus Ex: Human Revolution guide. They work with the same passion as we do. It's beautifully crafted, with such painstaking detail and so much information that reading it becomes a whole experience in itself. You will look at the game with a different eye after digging into this guide. And the guide itself will become a much treasured collection piece, even after you're done with the game. Mark my words!

So, crack a bottle open, sit comfortably, don't forget your game guide, and immerse yourself in the game to enjoy the mysteries and secrets that Deus Ex: Human Revolution has to offer!

Jean-François Dugas – Game Director

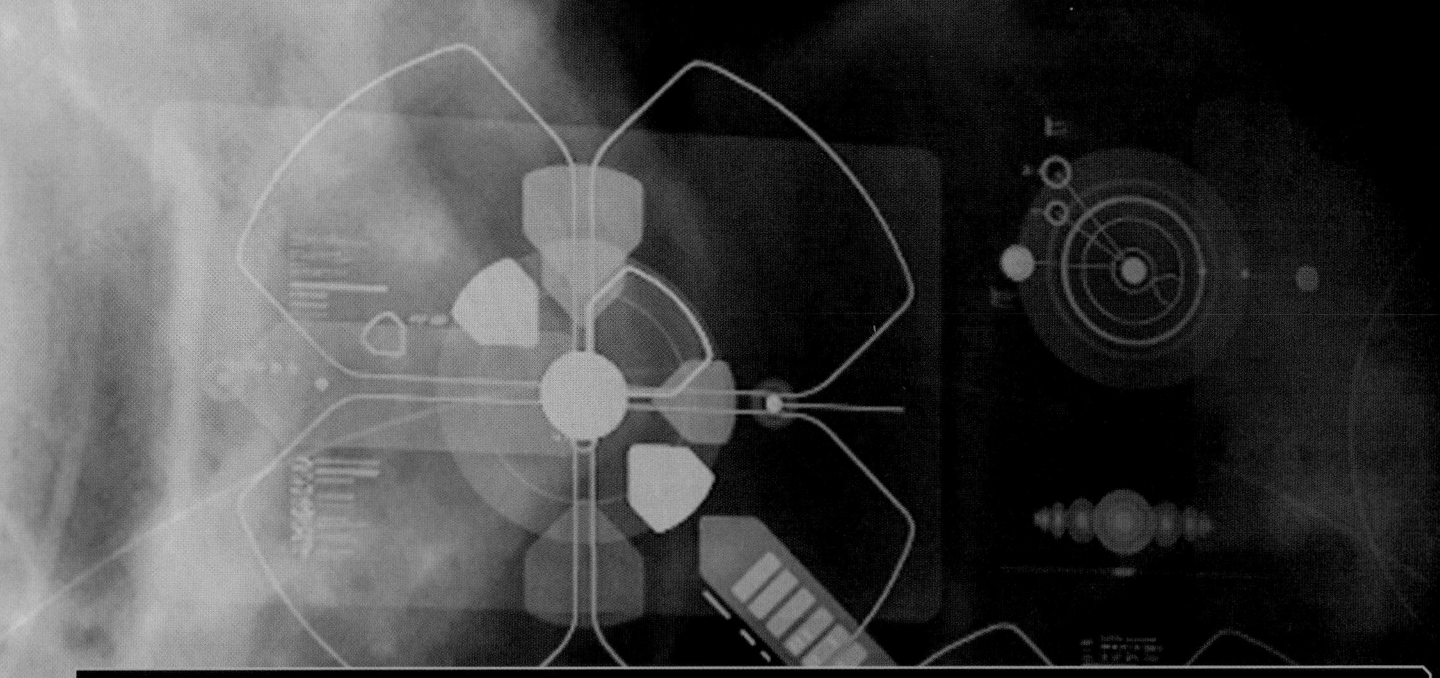

USING THIS GUIDE

Welcome to your most valuable Augmentation

After six months of intensive sneaking, shooting and hacking, the production of our Deus Ex: Human Revolution guide has come to an end. We've long since lost count of the number of different ways we have guided Adam Jensen through his adventure. Why? Because we didn't want to cover just the 'most effective', 'quickest' or 'most XP rewarding' route. This game can be played in so many possible ways – none of which are right or wrong – and providing a single guideline of how to get through the game would have required you to play 'our' way. Taking such an approach wouldn't have done justice to the many gameplay choices the game has to offer. On the other hand, we did have to consider the guide's page count and find a structure that makes multiple routes easy to follow. So we eventually decided to include the three most likely ways to play the game: pure stealth, pure combat and a mixture of both, using the environment and the tools available at any given point – the developers call this approach "adaptive".

We believe that no matter what type of player you are, there is something for you inside this guide that will ultimately enrich your gaming experience (which is the ultimate goal of every Future Press game guide). So we hope you'll find this guide to be indeed "the most valuable Augmentation".

Allow us to express our very special thanks to the fine folks over at Eidos Montréal right here: without their precious support, this guide wouldn't be nearly as good as it is. Thanks, guys!

CHAPTERS

The guide is separated into seven chapters to make the information you're looking for much easier to locate. Here we'll give a brief overview of the purpose of these chapters and what you'll find within each of them.

01 SYSTEM BASICS

The opening chapter is home to all of the basic information that you'll need when getting started in Deus Ex: Human Revolution. If you want to know about the game's controls, menus or basic mechanics then this is the place to look.

02 AUGMENTATIONS

You can Augment Jensen in any way you want, but it'll cost you precious Praxis Points to do so. This chapter gives you all the details on each Augmentation, so you can be fully informed about your potential purchases in advance, and ensure that not a single Praxis point is wasted.

03 WEAPONS & UPGRADES

As the name suggests, we've gathered all of the information about the game's weapons and upgrades in one place. Want to know which weapon is best to spend the upgrade you just got on? Or which weapons make good combinations to maximise your inventory space and killing potential? This is the place to go.

04 OPPONENTS

This is where you'll come to arm yourself with all the knowledge you need to take down the game's toughest bad guys. If a particular enemy is causing you problems you can check this chapter to easily find the best ways to deal with them.

05 WALKTHROUGH

The Walkthrough chapter provides you with three separate route types through almost every part of the game, with maps describing each one. This ensures that you can play the game the way you want and still find the help you need to get past any point using your desired approach.

06 SIDE QUESTS

This chapter is dedicated to exposing the location of every Side Quest and guiding you through each of them. You'll find full walkthroughs for all Side Quests with all rewards detailed in advance.

07 EXTRAS

Here you'll find a full rundown of the game's story and a detailed guide to unlocking every Achievement/Trophy in a single play through the game. We've also included other bonus sections here, including a shop and item list and a list of the many references to be found in the game.

TABLE OF CONTENTS

About Future Press Video Codes

Video Codes are a special feature of selected Future Press game guides. Many strategies, techniques and tricks are tagged with a Video Code consisting of a five-digit number. Enter this number on our website and a video will pop up, allowing you to see the referenced topic in motion. For an even simpler experience, download our brand new Video Code app with your iOS or Android device at www.future-press.com/app and simply scan the codes with the integrated QR reader. Note that our QR codes do not work with other QR readers.

The Video Code feature is a free service that any owner of the game guide can enjoy. Here's how:

1) Create an account at future-press.com or via our app (if you haven't already).

2) Connect your guide to your profile: Log in and click on MY PROFILE. Enter the answer to the unique question that only owners of the guide could answer. Your guide is now connected with your account (you only need to do this once).

3) Enter the number into the VIDEO CODE field on

CH01 System Basics

Deus Ex: Human Revolution is a very complex game that includes many different mechanics and systems for players to get familiar with. This chapter is designed to make everything clear, and ensure that any questions you may have about the game's basic elements are all answered in a single place.

GETTING STARTED

This section will cover the real basics, such as the controls and the in-game menus. We'll also detail the various HUD elements in this section to ensure that each of their functions is clear.

CONTROLS

First we'll go over the controls for each platform. The console versions of Deus EX: Human Revolution doesn't allow you to change specific control functions or layouts, but the default control setup follows a standard that should make it very easy to use.

Function	Xbox 360
Cover	LT
Sprint	LB
Movement	Left Stick
Crouch	Click Left Stick
Activate Cloak	↑
Activate Silent Movement	←
Activate Typhoon	→
Activate Smart Vision	↓

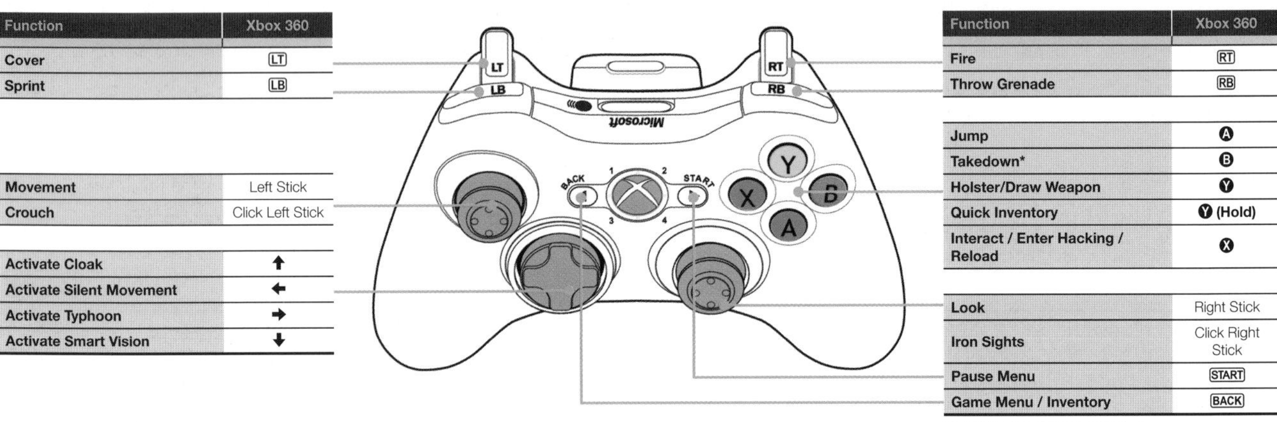

Function	Xbox 360
Fire	RT
Throw Grenade	RB
Jump	A
Takedown*	B
Holster/Draw Weapon	Y
Quick Inventory	Y (Hold)
Interact / Enter Hacking / Reload	X
Look	Right Stick
Iron Sights	Click Right Stick
Pause Menu	START
Game Menu / Inventory	BACK

*Tap for non-lethal, hold for lethal

Function	PS3
Sprint	L2
Cover	L1
Activate Cloak	↑
Activate Smart Vision	↓
Activate Silent Movement	←
Activate Typhoon	→
Movement	Left Stick
Crouch	L3

Function	PS3
Throw Grenade	R2
Fire	R1
Jump	⊗
Takedown*	◎
Holster/Draw Weapon	△
Quick Inventory	△ (Hold)
Interact / Enter Hacking / Reload	□
Look	Right Stick
Iron Sights	R3
Pause Menu	START
Game Menu / Inventory	SELECT

*Tap for non-lethal, hold for lethal

QUICK BAR

The PC version of the game makes use of a Quick Bar to more easily select weapons. You can very quickly scroll though and select any weapon or usable item you currently have, all of which are shown in this bar at the bottom of the HUD.

Function	PC
Movement	W,A,S,D or Arrow Keys
Look	Mouse
Jump	Space Bar
Interact/Enter Hacking	E
Crouch	C
Quick Inventory	–
Reload	R
Holster/Draw Weapon	H
Fire	Left Mouse Button
Cover	Right Mouse Button

Function	PC
Throw Grenade	G
Takedown*	Q
Sprint	Left Shift
Iron Sights	Middle Mouse Button or Right Shift
Activate Cloak	F1
Activate Typhoon	F2
Activate Silent Movement	F3
Activate Smart Vision	F4
Game Menu/Inventory	Tab
Pause Menu	Esc

*Tap for non-lethal, hold for lethal

MAIN MENU

Next we'll go over the options available to you in the game's main menu. Here you can load your game or change the options to suit your preferences.

Continue

Once a save file has been made, this will become the default option from the Main Menu. Selecting Continue will instantly load up your most recent save file and take you straight into the game.

New Game

This is what you'll need to select in order to start a new play through the game from the beginning. If you have no save files at all then this will be your only option to begin playing. If you already have existing save data then selecting a New Game will overwrite your last Auto Save file, so ensure that you have a manual save file from your previous progress before proceeding. Upon selecting New Game you'll be asked to select your desired difficulty level.

Load

This option lets you choose from all of your previously saved game states, as well as the two most recent Auto Saves that were created. You'll see some info about each save file available on the right of the screen including the area of the game and the date and time the save was created which will help you to identify which save file you want to load up.

Options

The Options menu contains a few different sub-menus, each of which leads to a group of settings that can change aspects of the game. We'll go through each of these sub-menus in turn here.

Video

» The two options in this menu are Subtitles and Luminosity. Subtitles can be turned on to let you read the game's dialog, while luminosity will allow you to brighten the game to suit your display and viewing conditions.

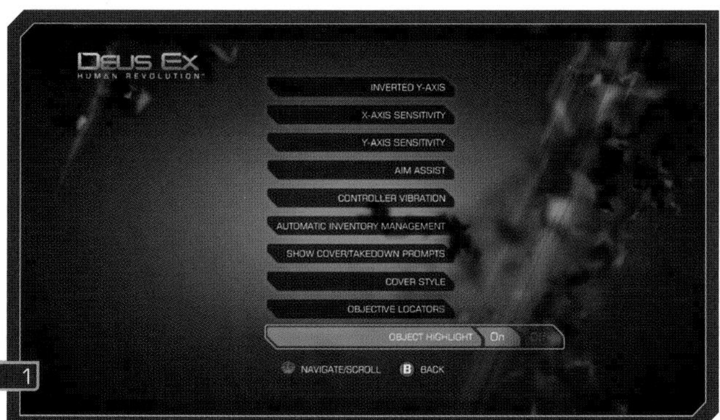

Audio

» Here you'll have separate volume controls for the three elements that make up the game's soundtrack: Music, Dialog and SFX. You can tweak each of these to get the balance you like, or simply turn the background music off completely.

Controls

» Selecting this option will simply bring up a diagram of the controller with the control configuration displayed. You can't change the game's controls, so this menu is only for information purposes.

Gameplay

» There are many useful tweaks you can make inside this menu that allow you to tailor the game to your liking. Some of the more standard ones include changing the X- or Y-Axis sensitivity and inverting the Y-Axis. You can also toggle Aim Assist and controller vibration and turn the HUD's objective indicators and the Cover and Takedown prompts on or off.

The other options are more unique to Deus Ex: Human Revolution. First there's the Automatic Inventory Management, which is on by default, and will arrange the items in your inventory to take full advantage of the space available. Next is the Cover Style option, which you can set to Hold or Toggle. The default is Hold, which means you'll need to hold the Cover button down in order to remain attached to cover. Finally there's the Object Highlight option, which toggles the gold outline you can see around items that you can interact with. [→☐ 1]

Storage

» Here you can simply select the storage device you wish to save to or load from. This will only be useful if you want to load or save files from multiple storage devices, effectively increasing the amount of possible save files you can make.

Tutorials

This option leads to a menu that lists various game elements. Selecting one of these categories will play a short movie designed to explain the subject to you. These are the same moves you'll have the chance to watch when playing through the very beginning of the game.

Credits

Choosing this option will instantly start the game's credits sequence playing. You can exit this by pressing Start at any point and choosing "skip". This is the staff credits only, and does not include the game's ending or any potential spoilers.

GAME MENU

Pressing the Game Menu button will bring up a tabbed menu that contains all of the information you'll need when playing Deus Ex: Human Revolution. Here we'll go through everything you can do in these tabs.

Item Management Tab

In the Game Menu, navigating to the Inventory Tab will allow you to view and manage all of the items and weapons you've picked up or purchased [→□ 1]. These are split into two categories: Inventory items and Quest items. Quest items can be viewed separately, and can only be used automatically at certain points in the game.

Inventory items need to be managed and used manually, and must fit into the inventory space available (which can be increased through Augmentations). By default the game will automatically sort your inventory items so that they take fit into the space you have. For each item you have a few actions you can perform when you select it. You can move them around the inventory space, use or equip them, combine them with other items, examine them or drop them. Examining weapons will let you see their stats and any upgrades that have been applied to them. [→□ 2]

Mission Log Tab

This tab in the Game Menu provides you with a rundown of all missions you've accepted or completed. This includes main mission and side quests, and by pressing the Interact button you can set the selected mission to be either active or inactive. This helps to keep your current objectives clear, as only those selected will appear as Objective Indicators on your HUD. You'll also find some useful information about the each objective here just in case you've forgotten what you're doing. [→□ 3]

Media Log Tab

The Media Log tab keeps track of all emails you've read while playing. These can be from Pocket Secretaries or personal Terminals and are all sorted according to the location you found them in. To switch which location's log you wish to view, press the Interact button and select your desired location from the list.

POCKET SECRETARIES

Pocket Secretaries are small, single-use PDAs that may contain emails or other documents and are found in the environment. These often contain useful information or passwords and codes. When you pick up a Pocket Secretary pressing the Game Menu button straight away will bring up its contents without you having to go through the usual menus to get to the Media Log.

Augmentations Tab

Once you start earning or buying Praxis Points you'll be able to unlock more powerful Augmentations and upgrade existing ones using the Augmentations Tab. Each Major Augmentation type has its own upgrade tree, which means you must unlock certain ones before you can get others [→□ 4]. Most new Augmentations will require two Praxis Points to unlock, and then the remaining Augmentations in that tree will generally only require a single Point.

Map Tab

The Map Tab features a simple interactive map of your surroundings. This map is split into separate floors that you can switch between at will. The yellow arrowhead icon represents your current position and direction. Active mission objectives are displayed as a flashing "X" [→□ 5]. You have a limited ability to zoom in, and some useful items such as elevators, stairs and toilets are marked on the map as icons. Using this map can be very helpful at times when you're not sure exactly how to reach the current mission objective.

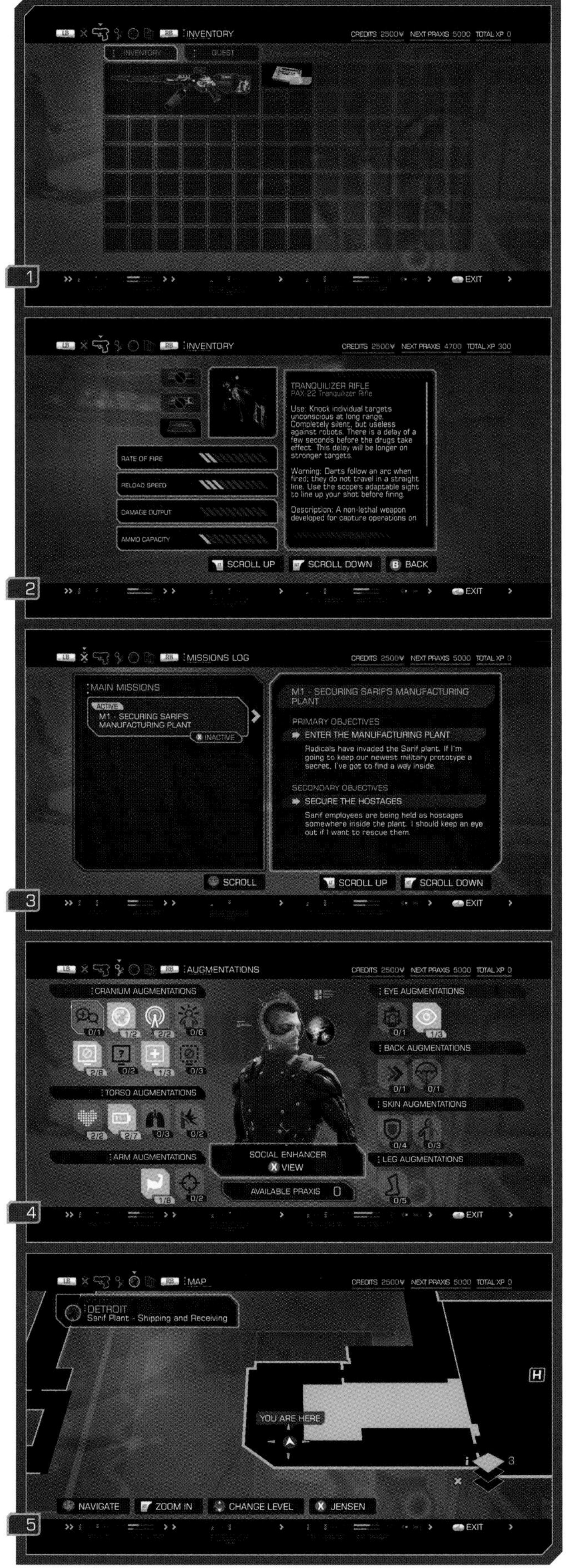

ON-SCREEN DISPLAY

The HUD in Deus Ex: Human Revolution will change according to the Augmentations you choose to unlock. There are, however, some basic elements that Jensen always has access to, and we'll go over those here.

Health Indicator
Your health meter can be found at the top right of the HUD, represented as a line of arrowheads. You'll see a second grayed-out line beneath this that you can fill up by consuming items when already at maximum health.

Crosshair
The central element of your on-screen display is always the crosshair. The crosshair is a direct representation of where your currently equipped weapon is aiming. It's shown as a tiny dot when not holding a weapon, but once you draw your weapon it will change to that weapon's appropriate crosshair type automatically.

Energy Indicator
You'll need to expend Energy in order to power any activated Augmentations you use, and this display tells you how much energy you have in the form of batteries. You'll start with two batteries available, but can upgrade your supply by spending Praxis Points.

Auto-Highlighting
Objects in the game environment that you can pick up or interact with will be highlighted with a gold outline when Object Highlighting is turned on.

Radar System
The Radar is shown in the bottom left of the screen, with a yellow triangle at its center that represents you. The Radar only picks up people (both enemies and friendly), robots and security cameras, all of which are displayed as different colored triangles. See the Radar section later in this chapter for full details.

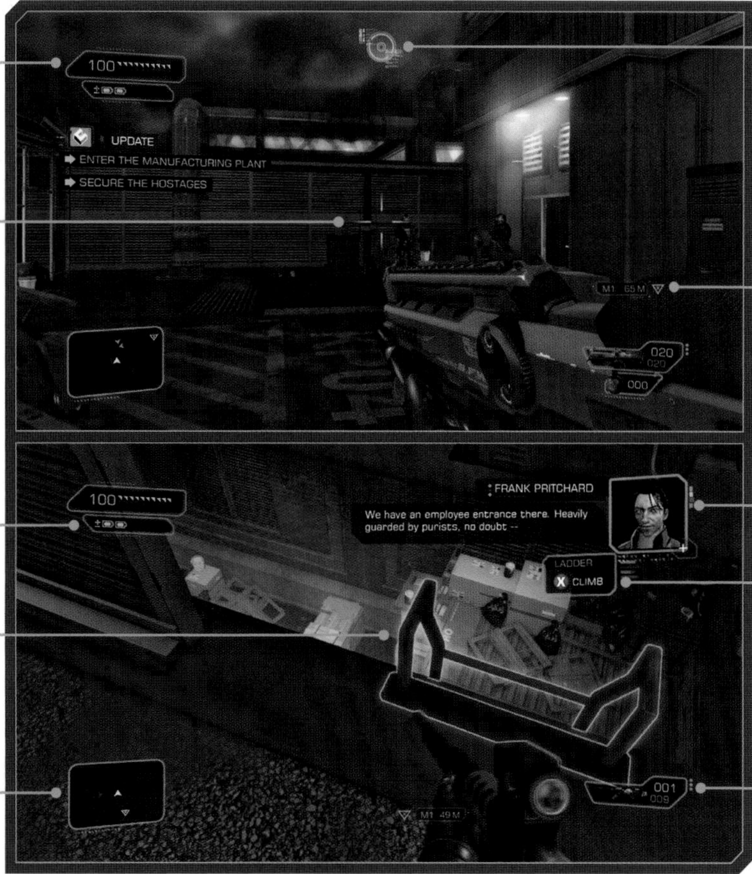

Auto Save Icon
This icon will appear at the top of the screen whenever the game is being saved. This usually happens when you enter a new area, but it cannot occur during combat situations.

Objective Indicator
The Objective Indicator will appear on screen if you have at least one currently active mission. It displays the distance in meters to your next required location. If multiple missions are active you'll have multiple Objective Indicators on-screen at once.

Infolink
When Sarif or Pritchard need to contact you they will use the Infolink, which will be displayed in the top right of the screen. These messages are often critical to your mission and as such cannot be skipped.

Interact Prompt
This will appear any time you get close enough to an object or item that you can interact with. Pressing the Interact button will cause you to pick up, use or inspect the object in question.

Weapon & Grenade Counter
The bottom left of the HUD is home to the weapon and grenade counter. You'll see a small picture of your currently equipped weapon and grenade or mine type, along with the current ammo value for each of them.

GAME FLOW

This section explains the things that make up the game's overall flow. From saving and item management to taking damage and how the difficulty settings work, there's a lot to learn about the systems that underlie the gameplay in Deus Ex: Human Revolution.

DIFFICULTY SETTINGS

Difficulty Changes

	Easy	Normal (Base Value)	Hard
Player Health	150%	100% (100)	75%
Player Health Regen	115%	100% (4 pt/sec)	85%
Player Health Regen Delay	75%	100% (6.5s)	115%
Energy Regen	150%	100% (1 pt/sec)	75%
Energy Regen Delay	75%	100% (10)	125%
Enemy Accuracy	60%	100% (Per Enemy)	125%
Enemy Health	75%	100% (Per Enemy)	125%

1

Deus Ex: Human Revolution features three selectable difficulty settings. There are named as follows: Tell Me a Story, Give Me a Challenge, and Give Me Deus Ex and they represent Easy, Normal and Hard modes, respectively [→□ 1]. The table here shows how each setting affects your character's health and energy, as well as the enemy's health and accuracy. There are no changes to the enemy AI behavior between the difficulty settings. The number of health displayed in the game (100) does not change across difficulty settings.

XP AND LEVELING UP

Most of the things you do while playing Deus Ex: Human Revolution can award you with XP. There are two main types of XP you'll gain: Awards and Bonuses. The most common ways you'll get XP Awards are for completing missions, hacking, or exploring. Bonuses are given for completing missions under certain requirements, usually without being seen by any enemies or not triggering any alarms. The possible Awards and Bonuses are listed in the tables here. You will also earn XP for incapacitating or killing enemies, and the amount awarded is based on the enemy type and the way in which you take them out.

The bonuses you are awarded for combat can stack on top of each other, leading to much higher totals for taking out enemies in certain ways. For example, if you incapacitate an enemy with a headshot from the Tranquilizer Rifle, you'll receive the Man Down award, the Merciful Soul award, and the Marksman award, resulting in total of 40 XP for taking out a single enemy. [→□ 2]

2

Getting Things Done Awards	
Completing an easy primary objective.	Variable (Up to 1000 XP)
Completing a challenging primary objective.	Variable (Up to 1750 XP)
Completing a difficult primary objective.	Variable (Up to 2500 XP)
Completing an easy secondary objective.	Variable (Up to 500 XP)
Completing a challenging secondary objective.	Variable (Up to 750 XP)

Completionist Awards	
Completing an easy side quest objective.	100 XP
Completing a challenging side quest objective.	300 XP
Completing a difficult side quest objective.	750 XP
Completing an easy secondary side quest objective.	100 XP
Completing a challenging secondary side quest objective.	300 XP
Completing a difficult secondary side quest objective.	750 XP

Mission Bonuses

Name	Requirement	Award
Ghost (main missions)	Not being seen.	500 XP
Smooth Operator (main missions)	No alarm triggered.	250 XP

Combat Bonuses

Name	Requirement	Award
Man Down	Incapacitating an enemy.	10 XP
Merciful Soul	Incapacitating an enemy without killing them.	20 XP
Marksman	Incapacitating an enemy with a headshot.	10 XP
Expedient	Incapacitating an enemy using a Takedown.	20 XP
Two Against One	Incapacitating two enemies at once using a multiple Takedown.	45 XP
Hunk of Junk	Disabling a Medium Sentry.	45 XP
Hunk of Junk	Disabling a Box Guard.	750 XP

Hacking Awards

Name	Requirement	Award
Script Kiddie	Successfully hacking a device with a level of difficulty of 1.	25 XP
Grey Hat	Successfully hacking a device with a level of difficulty of 2.	50 XP
Black Hat	Successfully hacking a device with a level of difficulty of 3.	75 XP
L33t Sk1llz	Successfully hacking a device with a level of difficulty of 4.	100 XP
Master Hacker	Successfully hacking a device with a level of difficulty of 5.	125 XP

Exploration Awards

Name	Requirement	Award
Traveler	Finding a level 0 secret area.	100 XP
Explorer	Finding a level 1 secret area.	200 XP
Pathfinder	Finding a level 2 secret area.	300 XP
Trailblazer	Finding a level 3 secret area.	400 XP

Other Awards

Name	Requirement	Award
Silver Tongue	Successfully convincing an NPC.	1000 XP
Life Lesson	Pissing off an NPC.	100 XP
Scholar	Reading one of Hugh Darrow's eBooks	200 XP

HEALTH & DAMAGE

Base Health Value	100
Maximum Health Value	200
Health Regeneration Rate	4 points per second (25 seconds for full regeneration from 1 health point)
Health Regeneration Delay	6.5seconds

Taking damage from enemy fire will result in the screen turning ever more red until you are eventually killed. You have 100 hit points by default, and you'll die as soon as all of these hit points run out. Unless you've been caught completely in the open there's a good chance that you can get behind cover before losing the last of your hit points. After a short delay from the time that you received the damage (6.5 seconds, during which the Sentinel implant calculates the appropriate response) healing systems will kick in and you will start to see the value rise back up to 100.

Any time you sustain damage you will also see the health value flash red to give you an additional indication. Through artificial means such as Painkillers it is also possible to increase your body's resistance to damage, and thus increase your overall health value to a maximum of 200. The normal color of the health display is orange, but if you increase your health above the normal levels it will become green to show the effect.

Auto Saving

Deus Ex: Human Revolution uses an Auto Save system like most other modern games. This means that your progress is saved automatically at certain points in the game. You can also make manual save files at any point outside of full-on combat, and these are always separate from your Auto Save files, so if something goes wrong you can choose to load either a manual save or an Auto Save (and should generally choose whichever one is more recent, so that you loose less of your progress).

Pause Menu

While playing you can bring up the Pause Menu at any time by pressing Start. Here you can save, load and change the game's options. You can exit back to the game either by selecting Resume or by pressing or the Cancel button.

Resume	Takes you back to regular gameplay.
Load	Load a save file or Auto Save.
Save	Create a new manual save file.
Options	Access the standard Options Menu.
Exit to Main Menu	Return to the game's Main Menu.

GAME ELEMENTS

This section deals with all of the major elements that make up Deus Ex: Human Revolution's gameplay. The game features many separate elements that you'll need to get used to, but none are too complex on their own and all are explained in full here.

WEAPONS

Weapons play a central role in the game. Even though you can choose to avoid using them almost entirely you'll still be faced with armed opponents at every turn and must learn to deal with them. Even if it's only as a last resort, you should always have a weapon available to use. When talking to friendly characters you'll need to keep your weapon holstered, or they will be very reluctant to deal with you. The Weapon Switch button lets you draw or put away your weapon instantly, so you can react quickly if things suddenly get hostile.

Lethal & Non-Lethal

Near the beginning of the game you'll get to choose between a lethal or non-lethal weapon, and you'll be able to find other examples of both types as you progress [→☐ 3]. Which you choose depends on how you want to play, with non-lethal weapons being more limited in use but offering slightly better XP bonuses. Non-lethal weapons are also generally better for stealth purposes, while lethal weapons offer more firepower if you want to clear out entire groups of enemies.

3

Acquiring Weapons

You can search the bodies of enemies you've incapacitated and take their weapon, ammo and items by aiming at them and pressing the Interact button. The weapon will very often be lying close to the enemy's body and sometime underneath it. Scavenging like this will be your primary source of new weapons and ammo, but you can also buy them from vendors whenever you come across ones that have the type you want in stock.

> **SELECTING WEAPONS**
>
> Pressing the Weapon Switch button will draw or put away your currently equipped weapon. Holding this button down will bring up the Quick Inventory menu, from which you can quickly equip any weapon or explosive type you currently have.

BUYING/SELLING

Most things you do in Deus Ex: Human Revolution will earn you some money. You'll get it most commonly for talking to characters and by searching the environment. Money takes the form of Credit Chips, all of which are added to your total and do not take up any space in your inventory [→□ 1]. You'll find merchants buying and selling goods, as well as some characters who want money in exchange for information, so there will always be something to spend your money on.

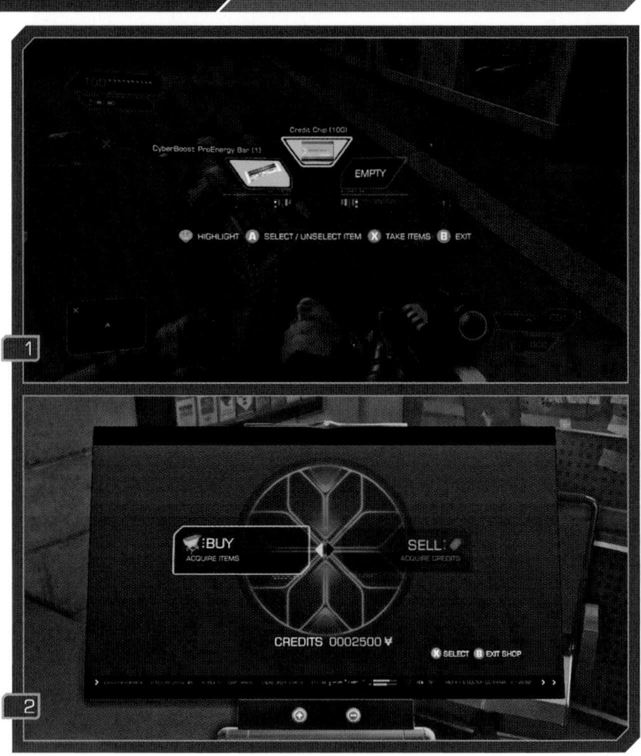

LIMB Clinics

These Clinics specialize in Augmentations, and sell a range of Augmentation related products. This includes Praxis Kits, which will grant you an instant Praxis Point. Their supply of these is very limited, however, so you shouldn't hesitate to buy them whenever they are available. You can also buy Typhoon ammo here, which is very hard to come by elsewhere.

Weapon Dealers

There are quite a few merchants in the world of Deus Ex: Human Revolution who will be eager to take your money in exchange for goods, or take your goods in exchange for considerably less money [→□ 2]. When you find one you'll need to talk to them first, and then use their Terminal to view what they are selling and see how much they will pay for your unwanted items. All transactions are final, so if you buy something you don't actually want you'll need to reload from an earlier save file to undo your mistake.

AUGMENTATIONS

Jensen's Augmentations are what set him apart and grant him his impressive abilities. Some Augmentations are available by default as soon as Jensen returns to work at the beginning of the game. These are all passive Augmentations, most of which provide the HUD functions and basic hacking abilities. You can see which Augmentations you have at any point by selecting the Augmentations Tab from the Game Menu. For the full details on all of these, see the "Augmentations" chapter.

USABLE ITEMS

You'll come across many items in the environment or from vendors that you can pick up and use, consume or otherwise ingest. These all go into your inventory and can be added to your Quick Inventory menu for easy use. Most of these items are used to increase Jensen's health or energy, though some are not entirely beneficial. Alcoholic beverages will imbue the drinker with a small increase in damage resistance above the normal maximum. Each additional beverage consumed will increase this effect. Adverse effects will include blurred vision. These effects last for certain durations, and the stronger the drink the longer the effect will last.

Name	Size	Buy	Sell	Effect
CyberBoost ProEnergy Bar	1x1	100	20	Extra 50 Energy
CyberBoost ProEnergy Pack	2x1	200	40	Extra 100 Energy
CyberBoost ProEnergy Jar	2x2	300	60	Extra 150 Energy
Painkillers	1x1	200	40	Increase Health by 25%
Stim Pack	2x2	400	80	Increase Health by 50%
Mahara Jah Hot Devil Ale (bottle)	1x1	10	2	Extra 5 hit points
Paul Neumann's Pilsner (bottle)	1x1	10	2	Extra 5 hit points
Nanbao Beer (bottle)	1x1	10	2	Extra 5 hit points
Mahara Jah Hot Devil Ale (can)	1x1	10	2	Extra 5 hit points
Paul Neumann's Pilsner (can)	1x1	10	2	Extra 5 hit points
Nanbao Beer (can)	1x1	10	2	Extra 5 hit points
Aiswine Rice Liquor (bottle)	1x1	20	4	Extra 10 hit points
Zhenchuan Moutai (bottle)	1x1	20	4	Extra 10 hit points
Extreme Crimson Premium Vodka (bottle)	1x1	50	10	Extra 20 hit points
Tango Foxtrot Tasty Whiskey (bottle)	1x1	75	15	Extra 25 hit points
Great Wall Red Chardonnay	1x1	35	7	Extra 10 hit points
Nohname Cabernet Sauvignon	1x1	35	7	Extra 15 hit points
Ernest Oaks Chardonnay	1x1	35	7	Extra 15 hit points

HACKING

Throughout the game you will come across many different types of device that you are capable of hacking, and this Augmentation is your gateway into them. Hacking will not only give you access to the personal terminals of many characters so that you can delve deeper into the story, but it will often be one the main tools at your disposal for getting into restricted areas.

	Node	Description
	Diagnostic Subroutine	This is where the networks trace will originate from and it will work its way back from there to the I/O Port that you accessed to begin the hack. Accessing this Node at any time will also result in a successful hack, and will also unlock all Datastores.
	Registry	These are your primary goals during any hack and you will need to capture all of them to be successful.
	I/O Port	This is your entry point into the system and where your hack begins. If the security system manages to capture this Node, you will be ejected from the system.
	Datastore	Datastores are caches of items or rewards that are contained with a system. If you successfully manage to capture the Node you will be able to unlock the rewards inside. These can vary from additional XP or Credits, to useful Virus programs.
	API	API Nodes are useful programs within the system that can have beneficial effects on other Nodes that are adjacent to it. There are four different types of API Node that you will come across and the type will always be labeled on the Node so that you know which one you are accessing. **Soften:** lowers the rating of adjacent Nodes by 1 **Transfer:** this will transfer 2 points to a random adjacent Node. If it is a Node you have captured the rating will increase, if you have not then it will decrease. **Spam:** this decreases the rating of the Diagnostic Subroutine Node, making it easier to capture.
	Directory	These Nodes hold no tactical value and only serve as a means of reaching your goal.

Bridge	Description
Unidirectional	These Bridges appear as dotted lines and only allow travel in the direction indicated by the arrows accompanying them. Always pay close attention to the direction of the arrows to make sure that you do not follow a path that leads to a dead end.
Bidirectional	These Bridges appear as solid lines and allow travel in any direction.

Hacking Basics

To hack a device, simply walk up close to it and target it, and then press the Interaction button when the prompt appears on screen [→□ 3]. Once the interface pops up, you will be offered the chance to put in a password or code if you have it or you can press the Quick Inventory button to initiate a hack. Your Capture Augmentation will then perform a quick analysis and give you a report on the security rating of the device, along with the number of attempts you have to hack it [→□ 4]. If you choose to carry on with the hack you will be brought to a visual representation of the access nodes within the device and you can look over the system before you begin hacking and try to work out the best route possible.

To begin hacking, move your cursor over any Node adjacent to the I/O Port and then hold down the Interaction button to bring up the Selection Wheel. You need to keep holding down the Interaction button while you choose what to do from the Selection Wheel or else it will close. In the Selection Wheel there are four things you can choose from: Capture Program, Stop! Worm, Fortify Program and Nuke Virus.

The Capture Program option at the top is the main thing that you will be selecting while hacking since it is your means of capturing a Node. Once highlighted, the Capture Program will show you the probability of being detected after capturing the Node so you can decide if you

want to continue. The Nuke Virus on the left will only be highlighted if you have any Nuke Viruses in your inventory, and once selected it will automatically capture a Node, regardless of its rating, with no chance of being detected.

To reach either the Registry or Diagnostic Subroutine you will need to travel along Bridges, through other Nodes to your destination. The Bridges, which are normally gray, can also be used to track your progress. As soon as you select a Node to Capture, the Bridge will begin to turn blue as your program closes in. The Nodes, which are also gray by default, will then begin gradually turning blue as they are being captured. Similarly, as the Diagnostic Subroutine runs its trace program, you can keep an eye on which Nodes it is heading for by watching the Bridges turn red. [→□ 5]

STOP! AND NUKE

The Stop! Worm and the Nuke Virus are two extremely useful tools you can use to make hacking much easier. You only have a limited supply of each, so you'll need to find more after using up your existing ones. The Stop! Worm halts the progress of the Diagnostic Subroutine for 5 seconds with each use, and will only highlight if you have one available. The Nuke Virus automatically captures whichever single node you use it on.

Item Name	Size	Buy	Sell
Stop! Worm	1x1	250	50
Nuke Virus	1x1	250	50

Successful Hacking

To complete a hacking attempt, you need to reach either the Registry Node or the Diagnostic Subroutine Node before the trace reaches the I/O Port or the timer expires. If you just reach the Registry you will complete the hack with whatever Datastores you picked up along the way. If, however, you manage to get to the Diagnostic Subroutine, you will automatically unlock all of the Datastore Nodes and receive their contents as well.

Reaching the Diagnostic Subroutine is usually more difficult than reaching the Registry, and sometimes there is no way to reach it at all, but if you want to get the contents of the Datastores it can work out quicker and safer in the long-run. Devices can often have more than one Registry or Diagnostic Subroutine so you should always make sure to look over the system before beginning a Hack and have your route planned out ahead of time.

API Nodes

Most of the Nodes you will come across will be Directories, which are simply there to serve as a step towards your goal. Occasionally you will come across API Nodes, and these can be worth going after to slow down the trace [→☐ 1]. Similar to the security level of a device, each Node is assigned a rating from 1-5 and this is used as a general indication of how long it will take you to capture it. Lower rated Nodes will be captured very quickly, with higher rated ones taking much longer. API Nodes can often reduce the rating on Nodes adjacent to it and thus speed up your progress. Conversely, as the Diagnostic Subroutine captures Nodes, their rating will increase, making things more difficult for you.

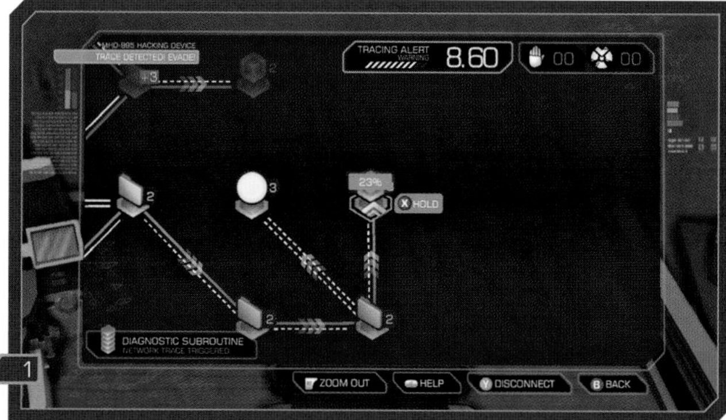

1

DOMINATION

Hacking can lead to more than just access to areas or computers; it can also be used to take control of security cameras and turrets. Camera Domination is unlocked by default, so any time you hack a Security Hub Terminal you'll be able to turn any cameras in the area off. Once you unlock the Turret and Robot Domination Augmentations you can also either turn these deadly machines off or set them to attack your enemies.

PERSUASION SYSTEM

At various points throughout the story you'll encounter characters that Jensen will need to argue with in order to persuade them to help him or let him proceed. During these conversations you'll need to pay attention to what the character is saying and then try to judge the best response from the available options. Conversations usually take place over two or three rounds, and your combined answers from these rounds will be used to decide if you've been convincing enough. If you have you'll often be rewarded with an easier route or a better outcome for the character, so it's well worth trying to "win" these conversations.

Each conversation is covered in full in the "Walkthrough" chapter. Some conversations are entirely optional and don't affect the story at all [→☐ 2]. These mini-conversations reward thorough players with extra dialog that may reveal details about the history and motives of various characters.

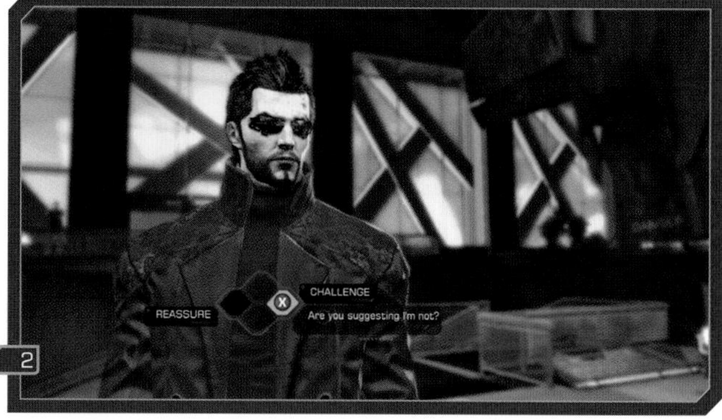

2

EXPLORATION

Exploration plays a major part in Deus Ex: Human Revolution. The game is designed to reward exploration at every point and players that take the time to search their surroundings thoroughly will very often find far more than they initially suspected.

Multiple Routes

Deus Ex games are all about giving the player choice, and this is especially true with regards to the way forward at any point. Most parts of the game are non-linear, offering multiple ways to approach from and many possible routes to take. Some routes will be great for stealth, while others may be much quicker (though not necessarily easier) if you want to head through guns blazing. For the most part, the routes are interchangeable and you can choose your own path and style of play at any point.

Side Quests

At certain points during the game you'll talk to character that may offer you an optional quest that you can choose to take on. These characters aren't always to be found in obvious places, so you'll need to explore a lot in order to find them all. Once you've found one and accepted the quest you'll be able to set it as active, just like main missions, but the objective markers for side quests will appear on your HUD in blue.

Note that most side quests are only available for a defined period within the game, and this period only lasts until you head to the next major area. It is therefore advisable to accept a side quest as soon as you're offered it if you don't want to risk missing it. For a whole lot more on this, see the "Side Quests" chapter.

Environmental Objects

There are lots of objects in the environment that you can interact with, and many of them can lead to finding interesting items or places. Most boxes and crates you see can easily be picked up, and there can sometimes be useful items hidden underneath them. Heavier objects can also be picked up and moved with the use of the right Augmentation, and these can sometimes open the way to new areas.

You will sometimes come across damaged walls, indicated by a barely visible crack. These walls can be destroyed, though it may take quite a bit of firepower to do so. Using the Punch Through Walls Augmentation will make this much easier, and will also highlight all of these walls if Auto Highlighting is turned on. You'll also find that some locked doors that would otherwise need to be hacked can actually be destroyed if you shoot them enough.

Destroyable Objects

Category	Weak	Medium	Hard
Breakable Walls	100 HP	100 HP	100 HP
Cardboard Crates	21 HP	42 HP	63 HP
Wooden Crates	21 HP	42 HP	63 HP
Doors	150 HP (weak armor)	150 HP (medium armor)	150 HP (strong armor)

EBOOKS/NEWSPAPERS

While exploring you'll come across eBooks and newspapers that you can read. You won't keep hold of these, so you don't need to worry about inventory space when reading them. They will generally contain information about the game world, and in the case of newspapers this will often reflect the actions you've taken when playing. Some eBooks (those written by Hugh Darrow) will award you with XP when read, and will count towards an Achievement/Trophy.

STEALTH & COMBAT

This section looks at the real meat of the game; how you'll deal with the many enemies you'll need to get past. There's no "best way" to deal with enemies in a Deus Ex game; you simply handle things the way you want to, but you'll need to know all your options for doing so.

THE RADAR

RADAR ICON LEGEND

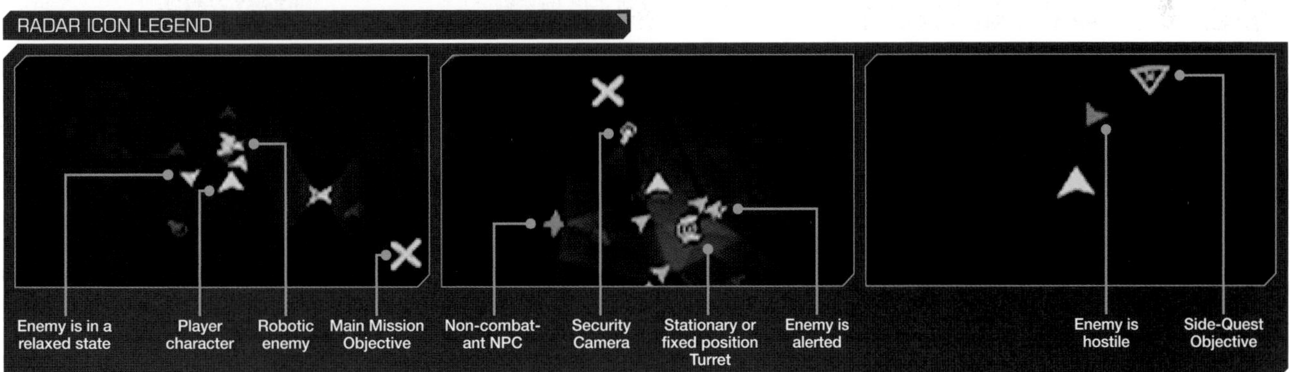

The radar is one of your most important tools for both combat and stealth purposes. You will be able to take advantage of the Radar System as soon as you enter combat for the first time after becoming augmented. It is displayed in the bottom left-hand corner of the screen and is used to keep track of, or show the position of, a variety of different things within the game.

Each enemy within range is represented by a small triangular marker. The color of this marker is used to show the current status of the enemy so that you can see at a glance how they will act. If the marker is gray, the enemy is at ease and currently unaware that anything is wrong. If it is yellow, then the enemy is investigating either a partial sighting of you, or a suspicious noise. An orange marker means the enemy is in an alerted state and is actively searching for you or investigating the area.

When the marker turns red it means you have been discovered and the enemies will begin engaging you on sight. As well as humanoid enemies, your radar will also display robotic enemies such as Boxguards and Turrets, or even other key security features such as Security Cameras. Like with humanoid enemies, you can use the marker on the radar to tell which direction a camera is facing before you move out.

As well as all of the combat related benefits, the radar will also display waypoints for all current mission objectives. Main mission markers are shown in an orange color, and those relating to side-quests are in light blue. The actual marker used will change depending on your height in relation to the objective. If you are on the same level as it, the marker will be a large cross mark, if you are above the objective the marker will change to a downwards facing triangle with a small cross inside it. Being below the objective will cause the marker to become an upwards-facing triangle, again with a small cross inside it [→□ 3]. By looking at these markers you will quickly be able to tell your relative height to the objective and know whether you will have to ascend or descend in order to reach it.

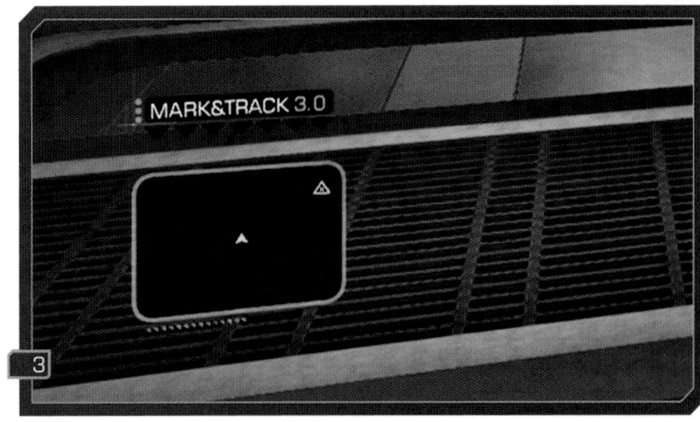

MOVEMENT

Careful movement is important to stealth, combat and exploration. You'll need to move slowly through the environment to avoid alerting enemies you didn't even know were there. Even when you're willing to enter combat it's better to always take your enemies by surprise.

Crouching

Crouching is extremely important in stealth play, as it greatly reduces the sound you make and the chance of enemies spotting you. Crouching and movingly slowly will give you the best chance of getting by undetected in any situation. It does leave you a little more vulnerable, but it's often the best option until combat breaks out. You must also crouch in order to enter any of the many vents found in the game. [→☐ 1]

Sprinting

Sprinting is only useful for getting between locations quickly, unless you need to retreat in a hurry. You can only sprint for a limited time before Jensen tires, which is represented by the sprint bar at the top left of the HUD. You'll need to wait a few seconds before you can begin sprinting again. You can increase the time you can sprint for through the use of Augmentations.

Jumping

Jumping is very useful in exploration, and can often lead to reaching alternate routes that might avoid combat. This is often the case when you need to jump in order to reach a vent, and can be the key to a perfect stealth route. Upgrading your jumping height through Augmentations can lead to reaching even more places, and make even more potential routes available to you.

STEALTH BASICS

Here we'll cover some of the basics you'll need to know for successful stealth play. Stealth play can mean sneaking past enemies or distracting them, but generally it's about not being spotted at all.

Hiding Bodies

After incapacitating an enemy you will need to hide their body in a place where the other enemies in the area won't look. This means checking the patrol routes of all enemies in the area before engaging any of them. To hide a body you'll need to drag it, which you can do by getting close to it and holding down the Interact button. [→☐ 2]

Noise Awareness

Controlling the amount of noise you make is crucial to stealth play. Every action you take will produce at least a little noise, unless you're using the Silent Movement Augmentations to suppress sound. Generally, you'll want to move as slowly as possible and avoid knocking over objects in the environment or firing loud weapons. If you're picking up an object, you can avoid making too much noise when putting it back down by crouching and aiming at the ground.

Distractions

Using sound to your advantage can be another useful tool for stealth. You can create noise at any point by moving objects around or simply jumping on the spot. Noises like these can be used to distract enemies while you move to another position, or to lure a single enemy to your current position so that you can use a Takedown without other enemies becoming alerted.

COMBAT BASICS

Here we'll go through the basics of combat, detailing the simple tips and tricks that may be familiar to shooter veterans, but which will improve the skills of anyone who applies them.

Shooting

Aiming your weapon works much like in other shooting games, but shooting from out in the open is almost never a good idea. You should always try to be attached to cover before firing, as this allows you to line up your shot perfectly before popping out. Aiming for headshots is essential when going up against basic human enemies. Rising from cover with an instant headshot is by far the best way to take out single opponents safely. [→☐ 3]

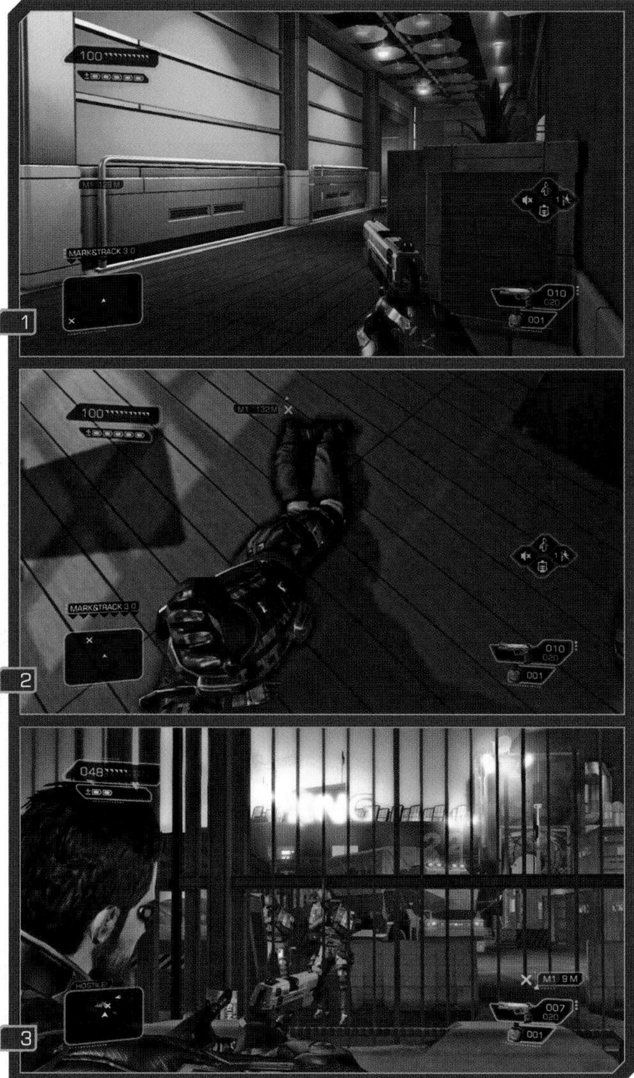

AIM MODE

Aim Mode uses the weapon's specific iron sights or scope to gain a steadier aim and a zoomed view. This is most important with scoped weapons, as you'll gain a greatly increased level of zoom and can fire your shot much more precisely. For weapons with a laser sight Upgrade attached, you'll usually be better off avoiding Aim Mode, as the laser sight will be enough to ensure perfect accuracy.

Explosives

There are two types of explosives in Deus Ex: Human Revolution: Grenades and Mines. These each have their own unique uses and neither should be neglected, especially when playing a combat heavy style. Grenades can be thrown safely into rooms, potentially taking out groups of enemies at once.

Takedowns

When you get close to an enemy, pressing the Takedown button will take the view into third-person mode and you'll see a sequence in which Jensen incapacitates the enemy. Doing this consumes one full battery of Energy, which means you won't be able to use Takedowns unless you have enough Energy.

USING COVER

Cover is an essential part of both stealth and combat play, as it offers protection during combat and gives the stealth player a way to safely survey upcoming areas. For these reasons, no matter how you choose to play, it'll be wise to use cover as often as possible.

Almost any flat wall or object in the game that is big enough to provide you with adequate cover can be attached to using the Cover button. Doing so will change the view to third-person mode and allow you some control over the camera. This lets you attach to cover near a corner and then use the camera control to see what's around the corner without exposing yourself.

Short Cover Swap

Pressing the Interact button and the direction of the nearest available cover will make you very quickly move across the gap and take cover at the new position (if it's close enough).

Long Cover Swap (Roll)

Again, pressing the Interact button along with the direction of your desired cover destination will cause you to move between the two positions. If the gap between these positions is fairly large, however, Jensen will perform a slow roll to minimize his vulnerability whilst moving.

Rounding Cover

When taking cover at a corner, pressing the Jump button will cause you to round the corner while remaining attached to the cover.

CH02 Augmentations

The Augmentations you choose to use will have a large impact on how you interact with the world of Deus Ex: Human Revolution, with many of them opening up new avenues of exploration or combat tactics. Through this chapter, we aim to provide you with in-depth knowledge about the performance and abilities that each Augmentation brings with it, so that can choose those best suited to your play-style.

INTRODUCTION TO AUGMENTATION

After you first become augmented in the game, you will have a number of Augmentations already unlocked and ready to use, but those are just the start. Hidden within Jensen's body are numerous dormant Augmentations that are just waiting to be unlocked as he becomes more familiar with his new body, and that is where Praxis Points come in. Praxis Points are what you will need to use every time you wish to improve an existing Augmentation, or open up an entirely new system.

Praxis Points can be acquired in numerous ways, but the most common one is when you reach a 5000XP milestone. Each time you accumulate 5000XP you will be awarded with one Praxis Point to use any way you see fit. In addition to these milestones, you can also gain Praxis Points by finding Praxis Kits. These kits can be received as rewards for successfully completing a mission, or they can be sometimes found in hidden areas scattered through the game. Because unlocking Augmentations relies entirely on Praxis Points, you shouldn't pass up an opportunity to acquire additional XP, and make sure to search areas thoroughly for any bonus kits.

Most Augmentations contain a group of linked systems that must be unlocked in sequence. As such, planning how you will spend your Praxis Points is extremely important to ensure that you do not use any going down a path that does not benefit your play-style. Similarly, you may have to spend points unlocking things that do not seem too important to you, but opens the path to something that may aid you greatly.

//-CH 02 AUGMENTATIONS

CRANIUM AUGMENTATIONS

SOCIAL ENHANCER

Augmentation Name
Unlock Requirements
Social Enhancer
2 Praxis Points
Emotional Intelligence Enhancer
Automatically unlocked after acquiring the Social Enhancer
PERSUASION LEVEL
PERSONALITY TYPE
ALPHA BETA OMEGA
1

The Computer Assisted Social Interaction Enhancer, or CASIE, is a group of systems designed to give the user an advantage during social interactions with other people. These systems monitor the behavior patterns of a subject, checking for subtle inflections in their language and facial expressions to gauge their emotional state, while also building up a psychological profile. With this information, users of this system can, with reasonable certainty, predict how a person is likely to respond and thus temper their actions accordingly.

Activation	Cost
Automatic	None

Emotional Intelligence Enhancer

The Emotional Intelligence Enhancer Augmentation works in conjunction with the normal conversation system within the game. Anytime you enter a conversation after activating this Augmentation it will start gathering information immediately and this will all be fed back to you through on-screen displays. The main systems you will see at work are the Optical Polygraph, the Personality Analyzer and the Synthetic Pheromone Propagator.

The Optical Polygraph is displayed in the top left-hand corner of the screen just under the Energy Core display, and is shown as a series of dots constantly scrolling across a small field that can change color [→□ 1]. The color of the field, along with the position of the dots will change to give an indication of how well received your response was in a conversation. If you gave a response that the person is happy with, the dots will rise up and the color of the field will turn green.

If they were unhappy with your response, however, the dots will lower and the field will turn red. Because characters in the game can react in many different ways to being questioned, it is not always easy to gauge how well you are doing in a conversation until it is too late. This extra level of feedback will allow you to alter your line of questioning almost immediately if you are not getting the desired results so that you can attempt to steer the conversation back onto a more favorable track.

The Personality Analyzer works in conjunction with the Polygraph to give you further insights into the psyche of the person you are talking too by providing a personality profile containing valuable information about the subject. The profile, along with a number of key personality traits is displayed on the right side of the screen and the details they provide, can aid you in selecting the correct response to get the information you need. [→☐ 2]

The psychological profile contains valuable information on how the person you are speaking with is likely to react in different situations, and gives clues as to how you should deal with some of their reactions ahead of time. This information gives you another layer of details to think about when choosing a response in a conversation, and can often help steer you to a more appropriate choice.

The final part of this system is the Synthetic Pheromone Propagator, which actively profiles the person you are speaking with and, through their responses, can determine which of the three main personality types the person is. Just below the Polygraph on the left-hand side of the screen you will be able to see this system at work during conversations and you will need to pay close attention to it, so that you know which personality type the person is. [→☐ 3]

The three personality types are Alpha, Beta and Omega and just below there names are a series of small boxes. During the conversation these boxes will light up to show what state of mind the person is in, and as more boxes begin to fill you will be able to get a feel for which type is the person's dominant personality. At different points within each conversation you will then see a button prompt appear on-screen giving you the option to activate the Pheromone Propagator.

Once pressed, you will be given a choice of three responses as usual, each one designed to work on a specific personality type; providing you select the correct response, it will nearly always result in a successful outcome. One or two characters in the game will become aware if you try to use the CASIE on them, but these will always be pointed out during the conversation portions of the walkthrough.

Play-style Suggestion

If you are the kind of player that is looking to see all possible dialog options then you will want to acquire this as soon as possible to get the maximum benefits. Since there are also a number of Achievement/Trophies tied to conversations, this Augmentation will also make things easier for players looking to unlock them, there are even ones that cannot be unlocked without it. Alternatively, if you are having trouble winning conversations, this Augmentation can provide an invaluable means of still coming out of the conversations with a favorable outcome and receiving the Silver Tongue XP Bonus.

RADAR SYSTEM

In combat, the radar will display the positions of any enemies that are within range, along with their status. Each enemy is assigned a positional marker on the display, the tip of which is used to show which direction the enemy is currently facing [→☐ 4]. While the radar system is unlocked by default, you can choose to upgrade it to a second level, granting double the normal area coverage at the cost of 1 Praxis Point.

Activation	Cost
Automatic	None

Augmentation Level	Range
Radar 1	25m
Radar 2	50m

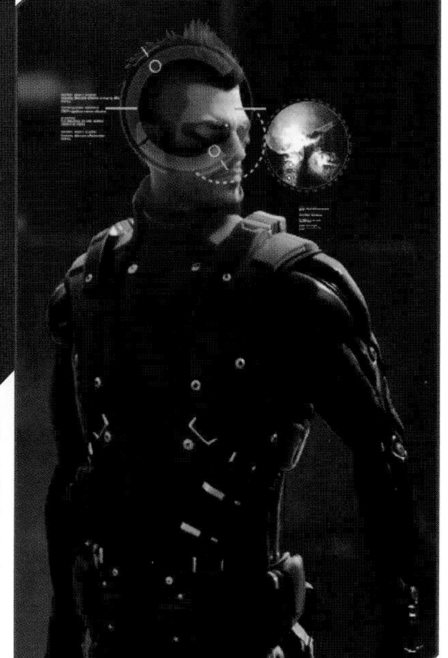

Play-style Suggestion

For players choosing to play stealthily, or using long-range weapons such as the Sniper Rifle, upgrading the radar to its maximum range is highly recommended. With the increased range, enemies will show up on the radar while you are still a safe distance away, and you can begin planning your routes, or getting into firing positions much earlier than normal [→□ 1]. If you often find yourself actively engaging the enemy at close range, then you will find no real need to upgrade the radar.

INFOLINK

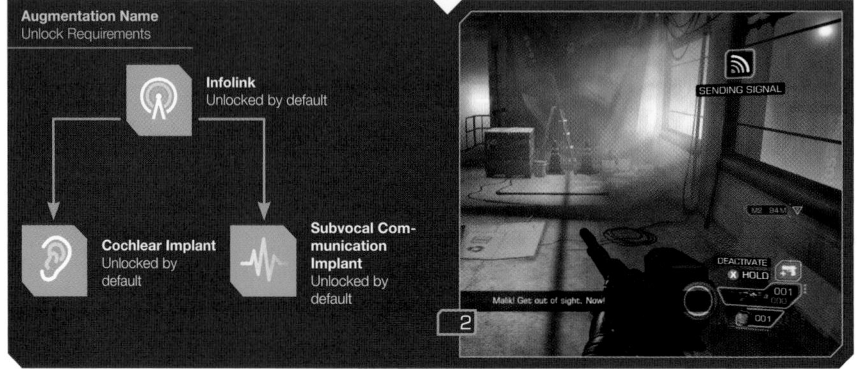

Activation	Cost
Automatic	None

The Infolink is an Augmentation that allows the user to wirelessly communicate anywhere in the world without generating any audible sound. Through this device you will be able to send and receive critical mission information to different character throughout the game without alerting anyone to your presence. Any time you are about to send or receive a transmission, you will see an icon pop-up in the top right-hand corner of the screen to give you some warning. [→□ 2]

If it is an incoming transmission, once it starts the signal icon will be replaced by an image of the sender if it a known person, along with a dialog box to help you keep track of the conversation. You cannot manually activate the Infolink, and Jensen will only send out transmissions when there are mission specific details to discuss. Most of the time this system will be used for receiving transmissions from characters who will update you on mission details or give you clues on where to go next.

STEALTH ENHANCER

08_010

The Augmentations that can be unlocked through the Stealth Enhancer are, as the name suggests, geared towards improving your ability to stealthily make your way through the game. All of these systems are designed to give you additional layers of feedback regarding your position in relation to an enemy, while also giving you a better indication of their movements.

Noise Feedback

Once you have acquired the Stealth Enhancer, information regarding your ambient noise level will start being received and displayed in your radar. Any time you make a noise you will be able to see a grey circle emanating from your positional marker in the radar every time a noise is made. The larger this circle becomes, the more noise is currently being generated.

Activation	Cost
Automatic	None

Actions such as performing a normal jump or jogging at a moderate pace only generate a small amount of noise so the circle generated is small as well. Sprinting on the other hand causes a large amount of almost continuous noise due to the frequency of your steps so you will see a large number of circles rapidly emanating from the marker. Firing your weapons or throwing heavy objects will naturally generate the most noise and result in the circle filling the entire radar most of the time. [→□ 3]

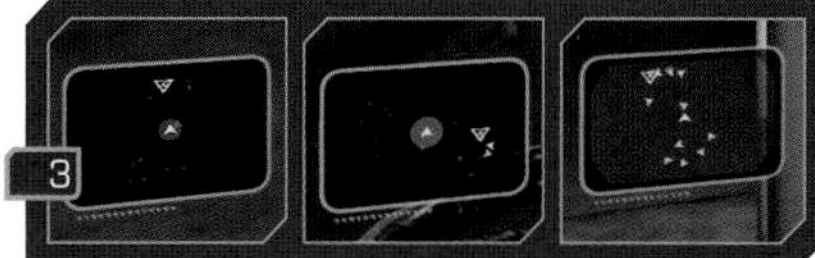

Through this feedback you can easily tell when you are moving stealthily, which will make it easier to stay undetected in the long run. This is especially important when trying to move in for Takedowns or sneak past guards where staying quiet is extremely important. Using the different levels of sound, and getting used to the ranges at which they can be heard will also allow you to better set up traps and ambushes for guards. Sound is one of the best means you have of getting an enemy's attention and will allow you to break them out of their normal patrol patterns and lure them into a favorable location.

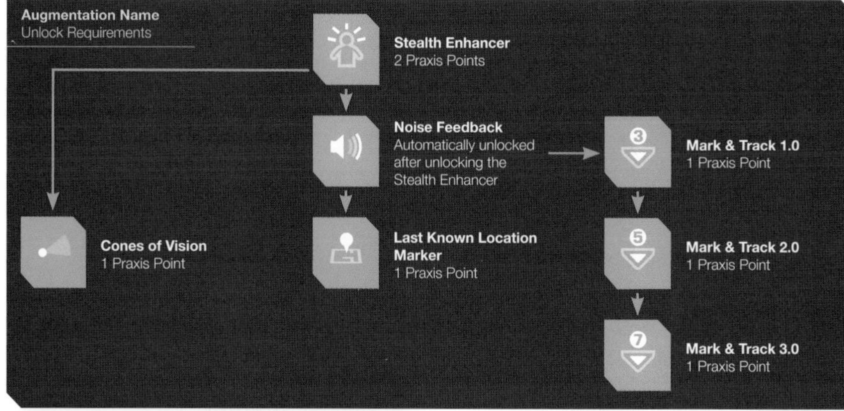

Activation	Cost
Automatic	None

Cones of Vision

Activating this Augmentation will allow the Stealth Enhancer implant to actively track the positions and movement of each individual enemy's head and relay that information back to your visual implants. This information is displayed in your radar in the form of an approximate vision cone extending from the tip of an enemy's positional marker. The color of the cone is always the same as the position marker, which can make it even easier to keep track of an enemy's Alert status. Not only will this Augmentation show you the cone of vision for humanoid enemies, but it will also do the same for any robotic enemies, so nothing will catch you by surprise.

The size of the cone will also change depending on the enemy's status. If they are in a Relaxed state the cone will generally be narrow to reflect this. If, however, they are alerted, the cone will become much wider because they are actively scanning for you; once an enemy becomes Hostile, and is engaging you, the cone will become even wider. [→☐ 4/5/6]

Using the information these cones of vision provide makes it much easier for you to plan routes around enemy patrols and take advantage of hiding spots. You can also use them to ensure that you are always out of one enemy's line of sight while you are taking out another. If you couple this with the enhanced radar you can start to get an excellent tactical view of the area that can make planning your approach much easier.

Activation	Cost
Automatic	None

Last Known Location Marker

Unlike the other stealth systems which are designed to help keep you out of trouble, the Last Known Location Marker is designed to help you escape it if you do find yourself being hunted down. Any time you are spotted by an enemy, and then break their line of sight, this system will automatically calculate the position that they are expecting you to be in. The position is then displayed in your normal field of view, rather than in the radar, in the form of an orange circular target on the ground with a marker pointing down in the center. [→☐ 7]

What this system does is allow you to know exactly where enemies' search patterns will be focused so that you can better plan your escape route, or flank around the enemy to engage them from a more advantageous position. You can even use it to set traps with mines since you know the exact positions the enemy will be investigating [→☐ 8]. The marker will stay in place until the enemy loses their Alert status and resumes their normal activities. It is also worth remember that you not only have to break the line of sight of the enemy that initially saw you, but all enemies or NPCs; if even one can see you the system won't activate.

Mark & Track

Level of Augmentation	No. of enemies tracked
Mark & Track 1.0	3
Mark & Track 2.0	5
Mark & Track 3.0	7

Activation	Deactivation	Cost
Place the reticule over a target, and then hold the Interaction button briefly	Move the reticule over the target once again and then hold the Interaction button until the marker disappears	None

The Mark & Track system allows you to place a marker above a target's head that appears in your normal field of vision, rather than on the radar. To accomplish this, simply hover the targeting reticule over any NPC and hold down the Interaction button for a short period of time until you see the marker appear above their head [→□ 1]. As long as the target is in your field of view you will be able to mark them, so you can safely do it from behind cover without being spotted.

This marker conveys all of the same information as the one found on your radar, with the interior of it changing color to indicate the target's status. Directly above the marker there is also a distance counter that shows you exactly how far away the target is from your current position [→□ 2]. In fact, with this Augmentation you will be able to keep track of a target's position far beyond the range of even a fully augmented radar. Where as the radar has a limit of 50m, this system will keep functioning all the way back to 100m away, giving you double the range. As long as the target is within the 100m range, you can mark them at any time, even through the scope of a weapon, which is ideal for weapons such as the Sniper Rifle or Tranquilizer Rifle.

The markers and distance counter will always remain in your normal field of view, no matter where the enemy goes in the area and no matter how many walls are between you. Because the markers are in your normal field of view, you can get a much better sense of where the enemy actually is in the world, allowing you to plan your actions even more precisely. The distance markers also provide an extra level of information that you are otherwise unable to obtain, and knowing the exact range of an enemy can be crucial with some weapons.

The usefulness of these markers is not limited to solely keeping track of enemies, however; they're equally useful in helping you navigate through larger areas. Because you can mark any NPC, you can easily use this system to highlight Shopkeepers, or other NPCs that wouldn't normally be highlighted on your radar as part of a quest [→□ 3]. Marking these key NPCs can make finding your way around some of the cities much easier, especially if the NPC is in an out of the way location and you know you will be in the area for a while.

Play-style Suggestion

All of the systems in this Augmentation branch are designed for players that like to have as much tactical information as possible before heading into any area. They are predominantly geared towards players adopting a mainly stealth approach, but the Last Known Location and Mark & Track systems can be equally useful for someone taking a more combat heavy approach. If you are the type of the player that is incorporating lots of Takedowns for the extra XP they offer, then the Noise Feedback and Cones of Vision systems can prove very useful.

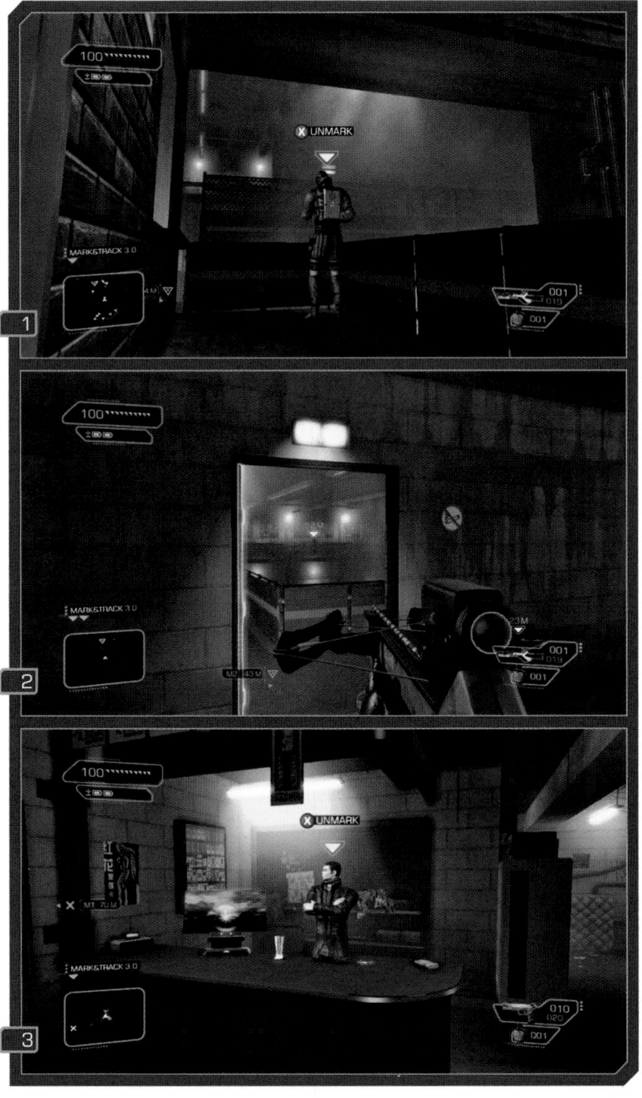

HACKING: CAPTURE

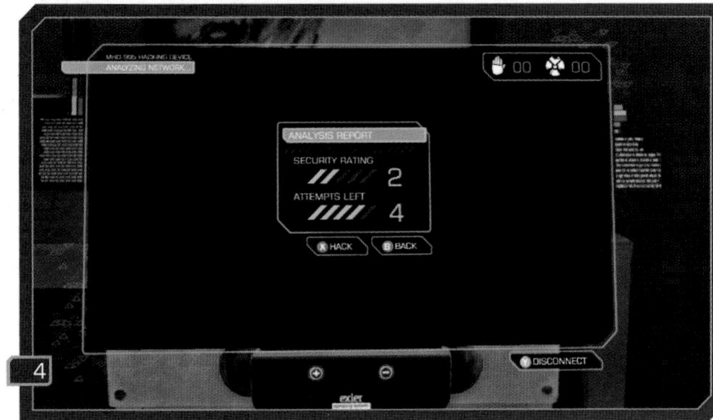

Gates and doors will often use dedicated terminals to restrict access, and hacking them to get past will normally be one of the quickest ways to get through an area. Security Hubs can also be hacked if you come across them and they will allow you to turn off many different types of security features. Disabling the security devices in an area will give you a lot more freedom of movement in the area, which can open up new tactical avenues for assaulting or sneaking past enemies.

Activation	Cost
Automatic	None

Capture 1-5

Every device that can be hacked in the game has a security rating of 1-5, and to be able to attempt a hack on that device, you will need to have a corresponding or higher level of Capture Augmentation. Lower level devices have very slow response times, so if you are detected you will have plenty of time to complete the hack before the trace reaches the

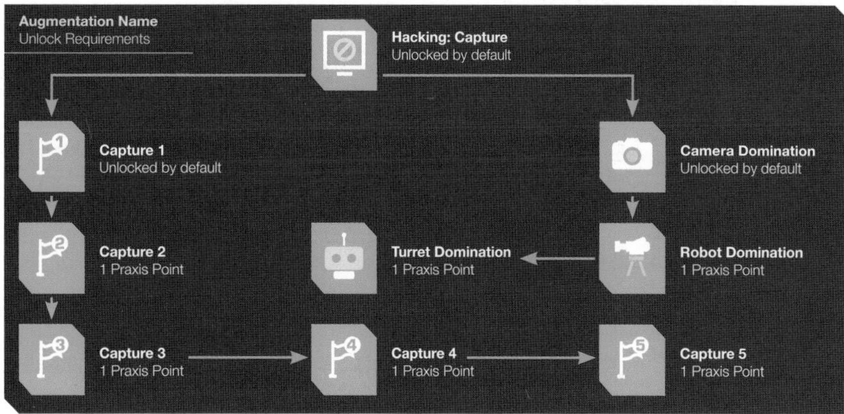

IO Port. As the security level of a device rises, so does its response time, which means at the highest level you will have very little time in which to complete a hack if you are detected. [→☐ 4]

Each device also has a total number of hacking attempts that you can use before being locked out of the device temporarily. Each time you are detected you will lose one of these attempts and be locked out of the system for 30 seconds; once the lockout timer has run down you can attempt another hack if you are able [→☐ 5]. You can choose to disconnect from the system at any time if it looks like you are running out of time by pressing the Quick Inventory Button.

The number of attempts is also linked to the security rating of the device, with lower level devices giving more attempts and the highest level devices often only allowing one attempt before an alarm is sounded. Having a higher level Capture Augmentation than a device requires will also give you some added bonuses. For each level that your capture software is above the device you are trying to hack, you will receive a 10% reduction in the possibility of being detected when capturing a Node.

So, for example, if you are trying to hack a device with a security rating of 3, and have Capture software level 5, you will be 20% less likely to be detected when attempting to capture a Node. For Nodes that have a very high rating, however, their detection chance can actually exceed the listed 100% so you may not see a reduction on those Nodes.

Activation	Cost
Automatic	None

Camera Domination

Camera Domination is unlocked by default, and it allows you to take control over Security Cameras after you have gained access to a Security Hub. Once you are in the hub you will see any cameras that are connected to it displayed in a small window underneath the main viewing screen. You can select any of the cameras by highlighting them and then pressing the Interaction Button, which will change the display on the main screen to that of the selected camera. [→☐ 6]

While a camera is on the main screen you will be able to see everything that comes into its field of vision as it sweeps across the area, allowing you to scout ahead for potential threats. Once you have seen everything that a camera has to offer, you can then choose to deactivate it by pressing the Jump button, turning it off for good without setting off any alarms. Since your other means of disabling cameras are all either short-term or will set off an alarm, this more permanent and safe solution is a much better option.

Activation	Cost
Automatic	None

Turret Domination

Turret Domination gives you another option that you can use after successfully hacking a Security Hub. To the left of the main viewing screen you will be able to see a tab marked Turrets; if there are Turrets linked to this hub you will be able to select it by pressing the Interaction button, if not, it will say "None Connected" and you will not be able to select it.

Once the tab has been selected you will be presented with three options that you can choose from in the bottom of the tab: Default, Disable and Enemies [→☐ 7]. Default will simply keep the Turret acting normally so it will fire at you on sight, and Disable will deactivate the Turret so that it becomes inert and will no longer fire at anything. If you select Enemies, you will reprogram the Turret to fire on any enemies that pass in front of its sights, while also allowing you to pass safely. What choice you take will largely depend on how you are playing because selecting the Enemies option will usually result in an alarm being triggered, which could be the last thing you want.

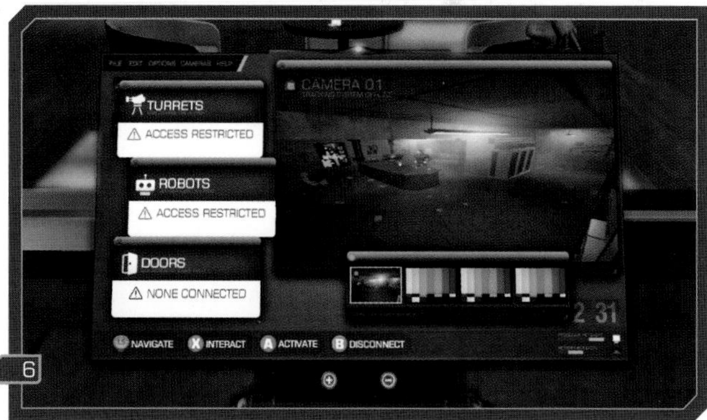

6

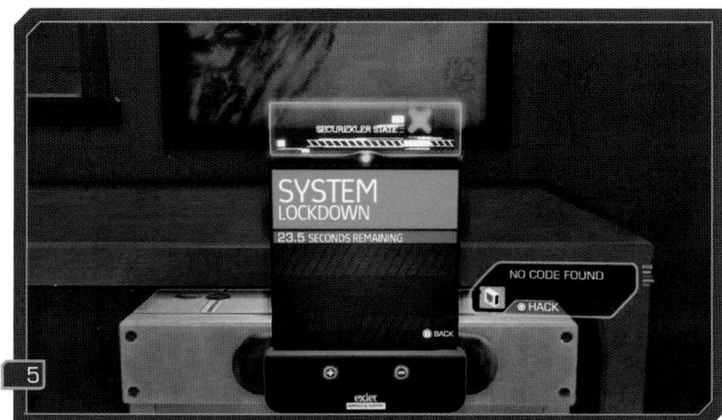

5

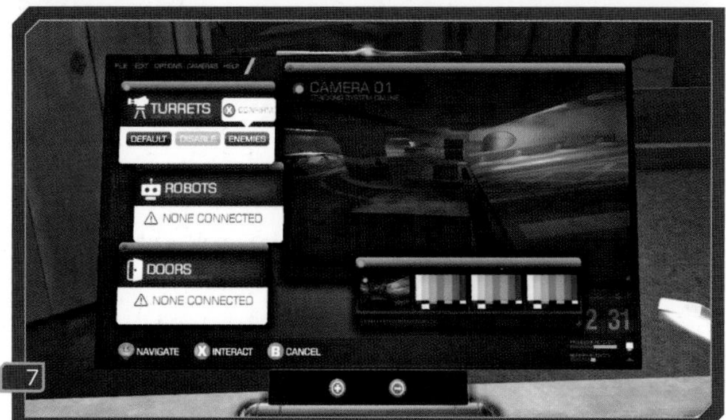

7

If you are not playing stealthily, however, selecting Enemies will make things considerably easier for you since Turrets can often take out large numbers of enemies before being destroyed. Stealthy players may wish to simply disarm them, however, to make sure they do not arouse any suspicions.

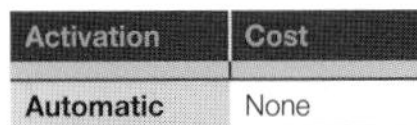

Activation	Cost
Automatic	None

Robot Domination

Robot Domination works in the exact same way as Turret Domination, but allows you to assume direct control over any of the robotic enemies such as the Boxguards. If you select the Enemies option with robots, however, and the hub is connected to Medium Sentries that are currently deactivated and in storage areas, they will activate straight away and begin patrolling [→☐ 1]. This can bring you unwanted attention if you are still in the area, so always plan ahead before activating any robots.

Play-style Suggestion

There are many different dedicated terminals that can be found along your travels and these can often be linked to storage units containing valuable caches of weapons or items. Hacking is also a very valuable XP acquiring resource, since not only do you get XP for successfully completing any level of device, but you can also secure extra XP from Datastore Nodes found while hacking. Other useful items such as Nuke and Stop! Worms can often be found while hacking, and these can be extremely useful in getting past higher level devices.

Generally, getting the Capture Augmentation to level 3 will allow you to be able to get past most mission related obstacles. Devices with a rating of 4 or 5 are normally reserved for the personal terminals of very import characters or items caches. As such, unlocking the higher Capture levels is mainly recommended for players who like to explore everywhere and experience everything.

HACKING ANALYZE ADD-ON

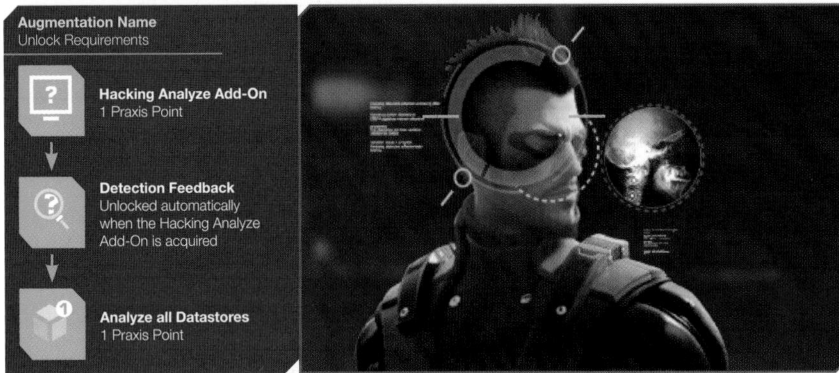

Augmentation Name
Unlock Requirements
Hacking Analyze Add-On
1 Praxis Point
Detection Feedback
Unlocked automatically when the Hacking Analyze Add-On is acquired
Analyze all Datastores
1 Praxis Point

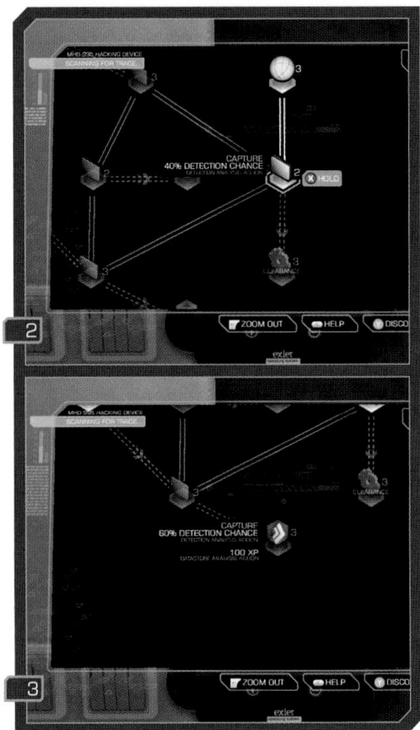

The Hacking Analyze Add-On Augmentation allows you acquire much more information about how the Nodes within a network will behave before you even start hacking. With this added information you will be able to better plan your routes to ensure the most efficient path is take to your goal, or valuable Datastores.

Activation	Cost
Automatic	None

Detection Feedback

With the Detection Feedback Augmentation you will be able to see the chance of being detected from capturing any Nodes within a network, not just ones that are adjacent to your position [→☐ 2]. Because of this, you will be able to survey every Node in a network before you even begin hacking and see the exact percentage of detection it has. This extra knowledge can save you valuable time during the hacking process because you will already know ahead of time whether you will be able to capture a Node as normal, or if you will need to make use of a Stop! Worm or Nuke Virus.

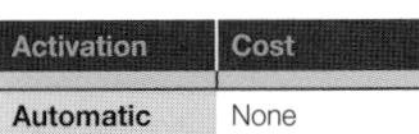

Activation	Cost
Automatic	None

Analyze all Datastores

This Augmentation builds on its predecessor and allows you to see exactly what is contained with the Datastores of any network [→☐ 3]. With this information, coupled with knowing the likelihood of being detected along the way, you can work out whether or not you feel the content of the Datastore is worth trying to capture. This will become especially important on some of the networks with higher security ratings where you have very little time once you actually begin hacking. Knowing that a Datastore only contains a small amount of credits, which you may not need, can save you a lot of time since you will not have to actually get to the Datastore to find that out; this can easily mean the difference between the success or failure of a hacking attempt.

Play-style Suggestion

These Augmentations can only really be recommended to players who are having a difficult time completing hacks early in the game. After you have spent a while in the game and have performed a reasonable amount of hacks you will start to build up a general knowledge base for how likely you are to get detected from any Node's given rating. This accumulative knowledge will serve the same purpose as the first part of this Augmentation and thus render it less useful as you progress. Similarly, the more you hack the better you will get at it and the more Stop! Worms or Nukes you will build up, which will also make getting to any Datastore relatively easy, no matter what the contents may be.

HACKING: FORTIFY

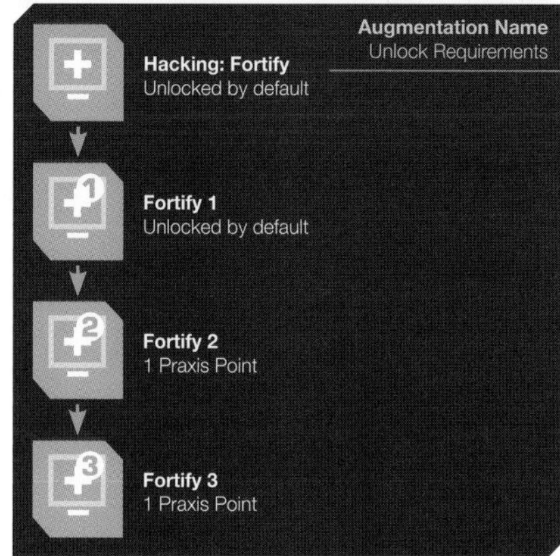

Activation	Cost
Automatic	None

Aug. Level	Description
Fortify 1	Adds 1 point to the rating of a Node
Fortify 2	Adds 2 points to the rating of a Node
Fortify 3	Adds 3 points to the rating of a Node

The Hacking: Fortify Augmentation allows you to bolster the defensive capabilities of any Nodes that you have already captured, thus slowing down the progress of the trace once it reaches that Node. Each level of the Fortify Augmentation will add an extra point onto the rating of a Node, so at its highest level you can add 3 points to it. These points can go above the normal maximum rating of 5, so you can potentially end up with a Node that has a rating of 8 [→□ 4]. Nodes with these exceptionally high ratings will take the trace a long time to break through, so you can ensure that your IO Port will be secure.

Once a captured Node becomes fortified it will take on a gold color instead of the usual blue so that you can easily identify it [→□ 5]. If you fortify a Node in a position that is in the direct path of the trace system at the time, you will also receive a small increase in the overall time you have to complete the hack. This time increase is stackable, so if you keep fortifying Nodes in its path you can keep gaining more time as the trace gets progressively slower because of your countermeasures.

The benefits of fortifying a Node do not come without risk, however, since fortifying has a much higher detection rate than capturing. Your chances of being detected after fortifying a Node will always be 20% higher than they were to initially capture it, up to a maximum detection rate of 100%. Because of this elevated detection rate you will need to choose carefully which Nodes to fortify. Also, it is difficult to plan ahead when fortifying because the trace does not always follow the most obvious route, meaning you won't often begin fortifying until you have already been detected.

Play-style Suggestion

Similar to the Analyze Add-On Augmentation, this one is geared towards helping players who are having difficulty with hacking during the early stages of the game. The most important thing to remember with this Augmentation is that if you do not fortify a Node in the trace's direct path you will not receive any real tangible benefits. On many of the larger hacking fields you can often complete the hack without going anywhere near the route that the trace system is using, so unless it gets near your IO Port you will not need to fortify anything.

It is this major downside, along with the increased detection rate, that can sometimes actually make hacking more difficult because of the time you spend to fortify a Node could be spent moving to the next one and continuing your progress. This is especially true the further you progress in the game when you start getting consistently more devices with higher security ratings. Even if you use a Stop! Worm to gain some time, that time could still be used to capture other Nodes.

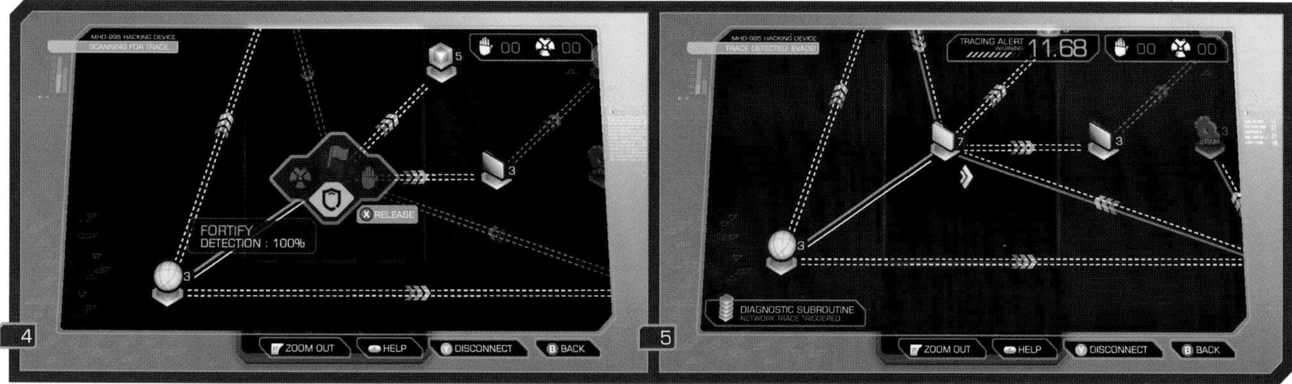

HACKING: STEALTH

Activation	Cost
Automatic	None

Aug. Level	Description
Stealth 1	Lowers the chance of being detected while Capturing a Node by 15%
Stealth 2	Lowers the chance of being detected while Capturing a Node by 30%
Stealth 3	Lowers the chance of being detected while Capturing a Node by 45%

The Hacking: Stealth Augmentation actively sends out packets of junk information to slow down the response time of the security measures within a network, reducing the chance that you will be detected when capturing a Node. At its highest level, this Augmentation will reduce this detection chance by almost half, which is an extremely significant decrease. This reduction applies to every type of node, so it doesn't matter if you are capturing a Datastore or a Diagnostic Subroutine, you will still be able to reap the benefits.

Augmentation Name
Unlock Requirements
Hacking: Stealth
1 Praxis Point
Stealth 1
Unlocked automatically when you acquire Hacking: Stealth
Stealth 2
1 Praxis Point
Stealth 3
1 Praxis Point

With higher levels of this Augmentation, many Nodes will be reduced to a detection chance of only 15% so you can often complete hacking attempts without ever being detected, even when collecting Datastores [→☐ 1]. In fact, if a Node has a 0 rating, either naturally or through use of an API Node it will have a 0% chance of detecting you. Using this Augmentation will almost certainly make all of your hacking attempts go much smoother, and since you will not be detected as often, you will also be able to save valuable Stop! Worms and Nuke Viruses. This means that when you are detected on a high rated system, you will always have plenty of them available to use and can easily get out of trouble.

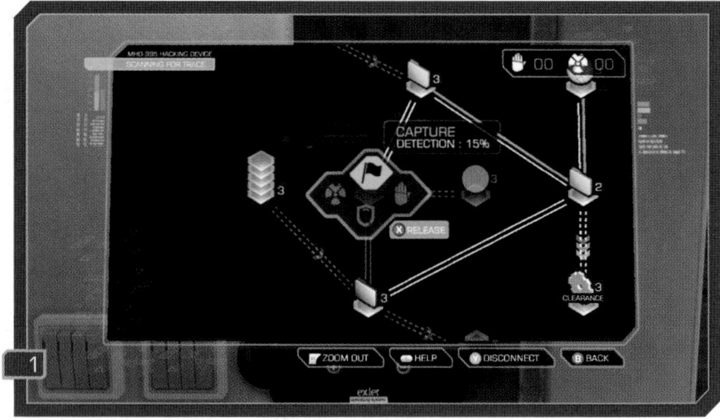

1

Play-style Suggestion

This Augmentation is worth getting for all players since its effects are immediate and remains beneficial all the way through the game. Even players who do not intend on doing a lot of hacking will be able to make use of it in the areas where they will need to hack a device. If you spend points on this, you will not need to spend any points on the other defensive hacking Augmentations such as Fortify or the Analyze Add-On, allowing you to spend them on other abilities.

Also more than those other Augmentations, this one will help players who are having trouble with hacking at any point in the game, but especially early on when Stop! Worm and Nuke Virus supplies are low. Since it only costs 1 Praxis Point to get the first level of this Augmentation, it is well worth getting at the start of the game so that you can begin getting the benefits straight away.

TORSO AUGMENTATIONS

SENTINEL RX HEALTH SYSTEM

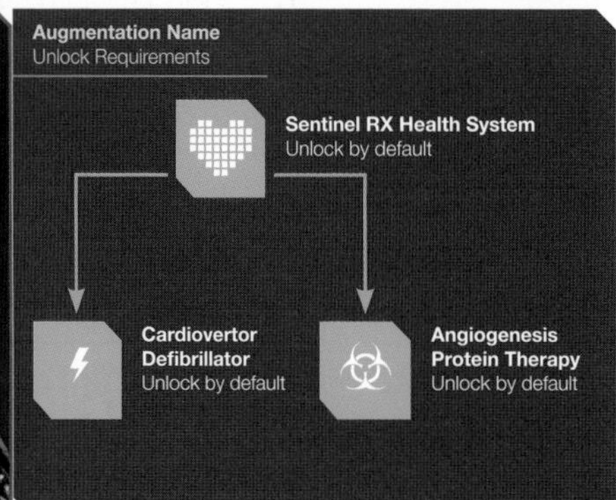

2

Activation	Cost
Automatic	None

The Sentinel Health System was one of the key Augmentations Jenson received during his surgery, and even though you have no direct interaction with it, it is one of the most important ones in the game. The Sentinel system constantly tracks and analyzes biomedical data from within Jensen's body and anytime even the slightest damage is detected, secondary systems are activated to stimulate and accelerate the body's natural healing process. This biomedical data is represented in your normal field of vision as an overall health value found in the top left-hand corner.

The normal value indicated in this area is 100, which means you are in perfect health; if any time the number drops below this it means that you have sustained damage. Along with the numerical representation of your health, there is also a series of small triangles, which serve as a secondary means of checking your health status. Each of these triangles is equivalent to 10 points in the numerical value so if only see half of them illuminated, you know you are at roughly half health. [→☐ 2]

SARIF SERIES 8 ENERGY CONVERTER

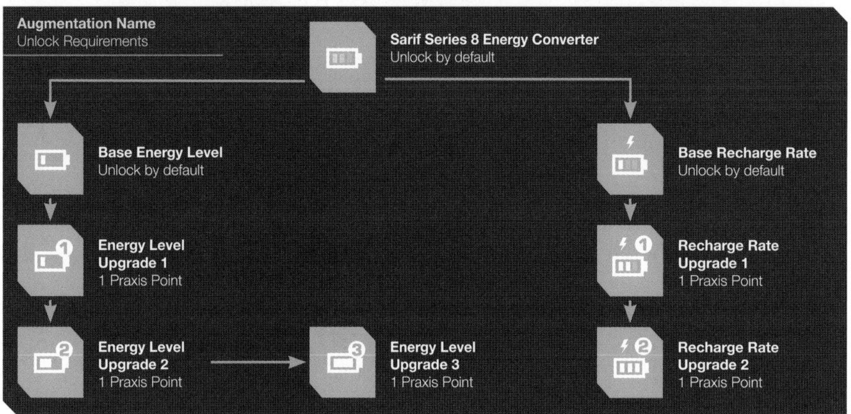

The Sarif Series 8 Energy Converter takes everyday nutrients and converts them into electrochemical energy, which then gets stored in dedicated cells for use by many different Augmentation systems. Without this system in place, many other Augmentations would simply be unable to function, and their continued usage is strictly dependent on the energy provided by this augmentation.

Energy Level

Energy Units per Cell	30

	No. of cells added	Total
Base Energy Level	2	2
Energy Level Upgrade 1	1	3
Energy Level Upgrade 2	1	4
Energy Level Upgrade 3	1	5

Your overall energy level is conveyed as a series of cells, which is displayed just underneath the health display on the left of the screen. When an energy cell is full, both the outline and the interior will be green in color; as the energy contained within a cell is used, you will see the interior portion start to drop until it is empty. An empty cell is then displayed as an empty red outline. To begin with you will only have access to two energy cells, but as you upgrade this Augmentation you can eventually get a maximum of five.

Additional energy cells allow you to employ energy-heavy Augmentations such as the Cloaking System or Smart Vision for longer, often allowing you to accomplish things that would otherwise impossible. They can even allow for multiple Takedowns in quick succession without the need to stop and ingest some nutrients in the middle of a battle. Combinations of these Augmentations are also made easier with additional cells, such as using the Cloak to cross a long corridor so that you can use a Takedown on a guard at the end.

	Recharge Rate	Recharge Delay
Base Recharge Rate	1 unit per second	10 seconds
Recharge Rate Upgrade 1	1.2 units per second	5 seconds
Recharge Rate Upgrade 2	1.5 units per second	1 second

Recharge Rate

The Recharge Rate system directly controls how long it takes an energy cell to build up its charge after it has been drained, or any active Augmentations are turned off. As soon as there is no more energy being drained, the system will begin searching for additional nutrients with which to recharge the cell, and this is the Recharge Delay; as soon as the delay is over, the cell will begin to recharge.

The first energy cell will always recharge if it has been totally drained of energy, but all additional cells will require extra nutrients to fill if they have been emptied. As long as you do not empty one of the additional cells fully, however, it will recharge back up to its maximum; if possible, always disengage any active Augmentations before a cell empties so that you can allow it to recharge without additional nutrients.

Once a cell starts to recharge you will see it start flashing gold with every pulse of new energy it stores; the speed of these pulses depends on the recharge rate. At the base level, it would take a full 30 seconds to recharge one cell, and with an additional 10 seconds on top for the delay you can be waiting a long time between uses. Upgrading this system to its maximum, however, will allow you to cut down the delay almost entirely, and allow you to recharge a cell in only 20 seconds. Cutting the recharge time in half like this can have a dramatic impact on how you approach areas. It will allow you to stagger the usage of stealth Augmentations such as the Cloaking System, using them for short bursts between cover points, behind which the energy can quickly recharge. [→□ 3]

Play-style suggestion

Both systems within this Augmentation are perfectly geared towards different game play styles. If you find yourself using energy heavy Augmentations for extended periods of time then you will want to invest in additional energy cells to facilitate this, just ensure that you have plenty of nutritional supplements to refill the additional cells [→□ 4]. Alternatively, if you predominantly use energy for Takedowns or the Typhoon, increasing the Recharge rate should be of greater importance to cut down on the time between uses.

IMPLANTED REBREATHER

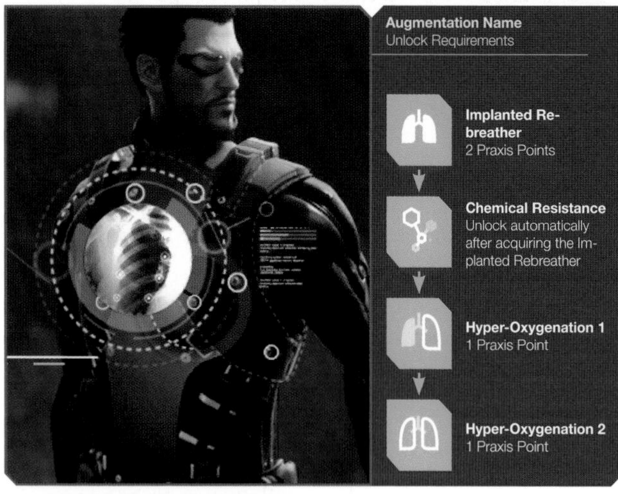

Augmentation Name
Unlock Requirements
Implanted Rebreather
2 Praxis Points
Chemical Resistance
Unlock automatically after acquiring the Implanted Rebreather
Hyper-Oxygenation 1
1 Praxis Point
Hyper-Oxygenation 2
1 Praxis Point

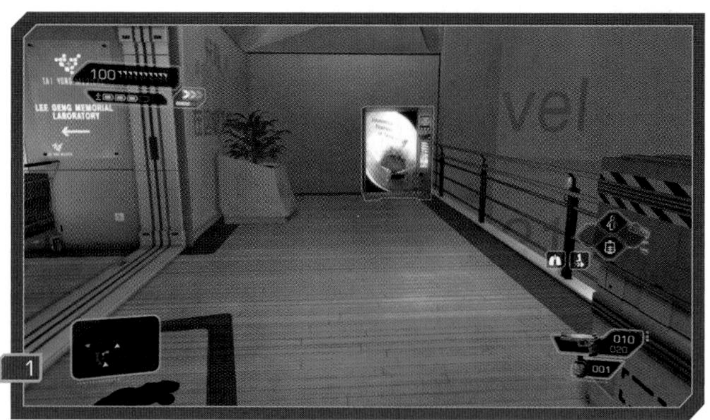

Activation	Cost
Automatic	None

Chemical Resistance

One of the main systems within the Rebreather is its ability to provide the user with resistance to all forms of airborne toxins and poisons. This system automatically activates as soon as anything potentially harmful is detected within the air, and allows the user to continue to breathe normally in their presence without the need for a gas mask. There is no limit on the duration of the effect provided by this Augmentation, and you can stay within the gas cloud for as long as is necessary. The damage that can be inflicted by these toxins in the game is significant, and without this additional resistance it would only be possible to survive in them for a few seconds.

Augmentation Level	Sprint Duration
Base level	2.5 seconds
Hyper-Oxygenation 1	5 seconds
Hyper-Oxygenation 2	7.5 seconds

Activation	Cost
Automatic	None

Hyper-Oxygenation

This system works in harmony with the cybernetic leg prosthesis to increase the amount of time that you can spend sprinting. Once this Augmentation has been acquired, you will see a small icon appear on the right hand side of the screen every time you sprint to show that it is active [→☐ 1]. The extended sprint duration this Augmentation provides will allow you cover ground much faster, enabling you to reach objectives or cover points much easier than normal.

From a combat perspective, you will be able to take advantage of cover positions that are further away than normal because of the ability to maintain sprinting speed to reach it quickly. Also, if you are detected by enemies, this Augmentation will allow you to quickly retreat back further to break the enemy's line of sight and set up a counter-attack. Couple this with other systems such as the Cloaking System, Sprint Enhancement and Run Silently and you will be able to cross a large amount of space very quickly while remaining undetected, perfect for stealthy Takedowns.

While it does extend the amount of time you are able to sprint for, it does not speed up the cool down time between sprints. As with normal sprinting, once you begin you will see a small stamina bar appear next to your health display showing the amount of time remaining that you can spend sprinting. With this Augmentation that bar will go down much slower than normal, but it will also take longer to fill back up again once you have finished sprinting. Like with normal sprinting, however, you can still stop and start at any time and do not have to wait for the stamina bar to refill fully.

Play-style Suggestion

If you intend to spend a lot of time exploring the game world, it can be worth investing points in this Augmentation system, purely so that you can navigate around the areas quicker. When you consider the size of some of the cities and areas, the amount of time you will be able to save is quite significant. There are also a number of areas throughout the game that are filled with poisonous gas and this Augmentation is your only means of accessing them.

If you are looking to scout out all of the possible ways through an area, or find all of the items, you will need this Augmentation. Some enemies will also make use of Gas Grenades and having the Chemical Resistance will make fighting them much easier since you will not have to flee the area if they throw one in your direction.

TYPHOON EXPLOSIVE SYSTEM

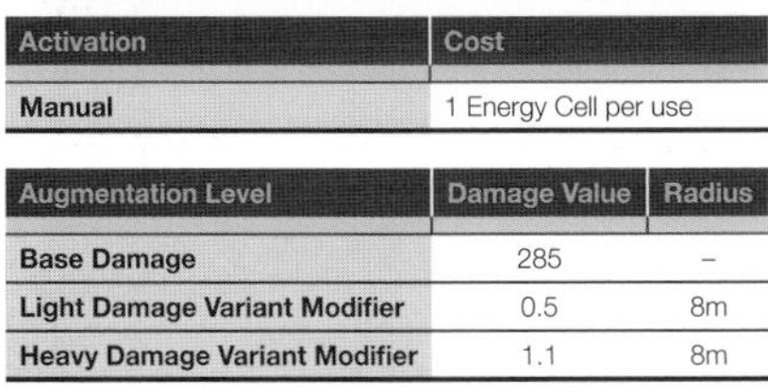

Activation	Cost
Manual	1 Energy Cell per use

Augmentation Level	Damage Value	Radius
Base Damage	285	–
Light Damage Variant Modifier	0.5	8m
Heavy Damage Variant Modifier	1.1	8m

Augmentation Name
Unlock Requirements

Typhoon Explosive System
2 Praxis Points

Light Damage Variant (1)
Unlocked when you acquire the Typhoon System

Heavy Damage Variant (2)
1 Praxis Point

The Typhoon Explosive Augmentation is a state of the art system designed for close range tactical engagements. Once activated, the system uses a series of repulsion field generators to fire off pockets of small ball bearings in a 360 degree radius around the user. Each usage of the Typhoon system requires one full ammo pack, along with 1 energy cell. Ammo Packs for the Typhoon are a lot rarer than ammunition for conventional weapons because of how new the system is, but they can still be acquired through LIMB clinics, or occasionally picked up in the world.

Once activated, the camera will pull back in a cinematic style to give you a view of the surrounding area and enemies before the system activates [→☐ 2]. During this time you will be totally invulnerable to any damage, including any incoming gunfire or effects of toxic gas. Because of this invulnerability, the Typhoon also works as an excellent means of getting out of trouble if an enemy manages to flank around you or surprises you.

Time will also dilate slightly to better show the system in action, and it will remain slow until the final ball bearings have made impact. Although time is slowed down, however, it is still moving and enemies will attempt to move out of the way before the blast activates. Try to make sure that you are as close as possible to your target, and that no potential solid cover that they can use is in the way.

At its base level with the Light Damage Variant, the Typhoon is capable of killing any human enemy caught within the radius instantly. Once upgraded to the Heavy Damage Variant, however, it will also be capable of destroying even the most robust augmented foe or even Boxguards in a single use. To ensure that the maximum damage is always inflicted, you should try to be as close to the target as possible before you trigger the system, since the damage does decrease the further away from the epicenter they are. At the very edge of its range, however, the Typhoon will simply knock over the enemy rather than kill them. Even the toughest Bosses in the game can only stand up to a few hits from the Typhoon!

As well as its uses against enemies, the Typhoon can also cause significant damage to the environment and objects in it. What this means is that you could use the Typhoon to destroy a vehicle that enemies are using for cover, or destroy a door that you otherwise could not get past. You can also use it to destroy the same weak walls that you are able to destroy using the Punch through Walls Augmentation; if you can identify the tell-tale cracks in the walls you will still be able to get through them even without that ability [→☐ 3]. All of this environmental damage becomes possible with just the base level of the Typhoon system, so you will not even have to upgrade it fully if you do not wish.

In general combat use, the Typhoon is most effective when dealing with multiple opponents at the same time, since it allows the user to take them all out simultaneously and instantly. Because the blast extends around the user in all directions, this system also eliminates the need for any additional aiming, which is another bonus when dealing with multiple enemies.

Play-style Suggestion

Because of its sheer versatility, the Typhoon Augmentation can be effectively used by all players. If you are focusing more on combat you will be able to bring its extremely lethal firepower into many different engagements, and know that the Typhoon will be able to get you out of any trouble. Even in those instances where the game surrounds you with enemies and you would normally have to run or seek cover, using the Typhoon you would be able to take them all out in an instant. The only limitations to its uses is the amount of ammunition you have available so always make sure to buy any that you come across.

Of course, since there isn't a non-lethal option for the Typhoon, if you are playing in a manner that avoids unnecessary combat, the potential uses for the Augment are slightly diminished, but no less important. Since it is likely that using this play-style you will not have the same arsenal (or Augments to go with them) on hand as a more combat focused style, the Typhoon may be even more important in Boss battles. If you rely on the Typhoon to get you through any of the Boss encounters it will avoid having to carry additional weapons just for those encounters. The Typhoon is more than capable of taking out each of the Bosses extremely quickly so even just for this reason, it is worth upgrading.

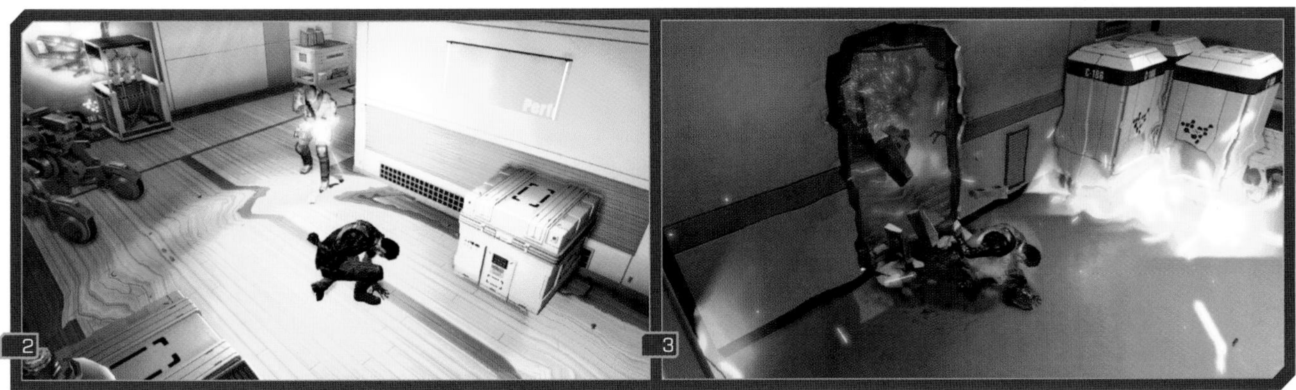

ARM AUGMENTATIONS

08 013

CYBERNETIC ARM PROSTHESIS

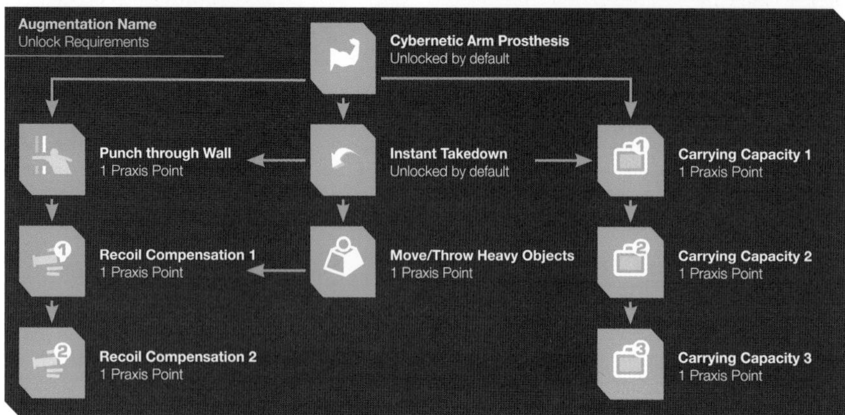

The Cybernetic Arm Prosthesis is a replacement for normal organic limbs that are capable of greatly exceeding the functions of a normal human body. A number of different systems are governed by the strength of the arms and as such they are one of the most diverse Augmentation paths.

Activation	Cost
Contextual	1 Energy Cell per use

Instant Takedown

The Instant Takedown is a contextual action that you are able to perform anytime you are in close proximity to an enemy or most NPCs. When you are within range, a prompt will appear in the bottom half of the screen to let you know that you can use a Takedown whenever you are ready. Tapping the button will result in a non-lethal Takedown that simply knocks out the target, whereas holding the button down for longer will result in a lethal version, killing the target instantly.

A Takedown is strong enough to bring down every humanoid enemy short of a major Boss, so it is an extremely strong technique; non-lethal Takedowns are also virtually silent so are perfect for stealthy players [→☐ 1]. Within each type of Takedown there are also a number of different possible animations that can take place. For each side that you grab an enemy from, there are a number of different possible Takedowns that may get used, but you never know exactly which one will happen until it has started.

For the most part the different animations have no effect on actual gameplay and are purely cosmetic; the only real difference is how they cause the body to fall to the ground. Try to make sure when you use a Takedown on an enemy that the body will not drop down into the line of sight of other enemies in the area. Since the specific Takedown that happens is largely random, all directions should ideally be taken into account.

Each Takedown requires a full energy cell, so their use is only limited by the amount of energy you have available. If you are in an area where you envision using a lot of Takedowns, it is worth making use of the free recharge from the first energy cell each time you use them, rather than using lots of valuable items to refill the other cells.

1

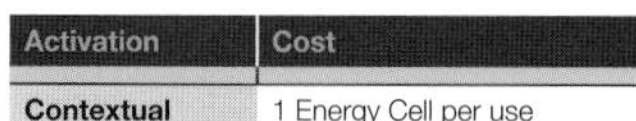

Activation	Cost
Contextual	1 Energy Cell per use

Punch Through Wall

Thanks to the shock buffers and superior strength and density of the artificial bone structure with the cybernetic arms, it is possible to punch through numerous structurally weak walls that can be found throughout the game [→☐ 2]. Before acquiring this Augmentation you would have to scour each area looking for the small telltale cracks in the wall and then either use the Typhoon or expend a lot of ammunition to break through them; using this system all it will cost you is a single energy cell and that is all.

2

On top of saving ammo, this Augmentation will also make spotting the weak walls easier by placing a bright orange outline around them in your normal field of vision [→☐ 3]. Spotting the small cracks can be extremely difficult and time consuming when you are first scouring an area looking for them, so having them highlighted can save you a lot of time, and even show you ones you may have missed.

Another benefit to this system is that if there happens to be an enemy on the other side of the weak wall at the time you punch through it, you will automatically move into a unique Takedown animation to incapacitate them. This move is highly lethal, however, so those players looking to avoid killing anyone will need to be very careful. Using other Augmentations such as the Smart Vision can aid greatly when you want to find out if there are any enemies behind a wall, allowing you to time your actions accordingly.

Augmentation Level	Recoil Reduction
Recoil Compensation 1	50%
Recoil Compensation 2	100%

Activation	Cost
Automatic	None

Recoil Compensation

The Recoil Compensation Augmentation takes advantage of special buffers built within the elbow and wrist of the Cybernetic Arm to greatly reduce the amount recoil given off when discharging a weapon. For most weapons in the game, each successive shot will cause the barrel of the weapon to rise slightly, taking it off the target you were aiming at. This is issue becomes increasingly severe as the weapon's rate of fire increases, with fully automatic weapons suffering the most from recoil issues. As such, they are also the weapon types that benefit the most from this Augmentation. At the first level of this Augmentation you will be able to see a slight decrease in the recoil generated by fully automatic weapons, but will feel only marginal reduction in semi-automatic ones.

At the second level of this Augmentation, however, all recoil related barrel movement is gone so you will see a significant difference with all weapons. Normally with weapons such as the Combat Rifle and Heavy Rifle you have to compensate for the recoil during extended firing by constantly aiming down as the barrel starts to rise, this greatly reduces their effective accuracy. With the highest level of this Augmentation, however, those weapons suddenly become a lot more accurate thanks to stable barrel. Even successive shots with weapons such as the Pistol or Revolver will be a lot more accurate since you do not have to readjust your aim every time; once your crosshairs are on target they will remain there for every shot until you decide to move.

Activity	Energy Usage
Moving Heavy Objects	0.5 units per second
Throwing Heavy Objects	10 units

Activation	Cost
Contextual	Low

Move/Throw Heavy Objects

Acquiring this Augmentation will allow you to move around all of the many heavy objects that you will come across throughout the game. These can be anything from a vending machine to a large crate, or even an enemy Turret. Being able to move these objects will often open up new paths that you would otherwise be unable to take advantage of, including revealing hidden vent access points.

Additional defensive tactics are also available after you have this Augmentation since you will be able to use the large crates to block off areas, funneling enemies into locations of your choosing. You will even be able to set up additional large cover points that you can take advantage of during shootouts. Heavy items can also be very effective weapons when thrown at enemies, with most enemies only being able to take one or two hits before being incapacitated. Being able to pick up Turrets also allows for some very effective combat avenues to be explored, because you will be able to carry Turrets between areas and use them to take out enemies for you. [→□ 4]

All of these benefits do not come without cost, however, and any action you take with a heavy object will cost you energy. While the drain from simply carrying a heavy item is relatively small, throwing them can drain it very quickly, especially when you consider the other downside of heavy objects. Anytime you are carrying one of these items your movement speed will be greatly reduced, so you will often want to throw the item simply to speed up movement, which will cause you to expend energy rapidly.

Augmentation Level	Inventory Capacity
Base Inventory	8x7
Carrying Capacity 1	10x7
Carrying Capacity 2	12x7
Carrying Capacity 3	14x7

Carrying Capacity

The Carrying Capacity Augmentation takes advantage of the extra strength that comes from the Cybernetic Arms to allow you to carry even more items. Each level of this Augmentation opens up an additional two columns within your inventory, which can lead to a significant increase. While the initial inventory size may seem fine at the beginning of the game, as you progress and acquire more weapons and other items you will find inventory management to become more troublesome. The additional space that comes from this Augmentation makes carrying those additional weapons and explosives much simpler and takes away a lot of the need to swap items in and out depending on the situation.

Play-style Suggestion

There is something in this Augmentation tree that can benefit players of all styles, with a lot of them being universally helpful. Punch Through Walls and Move Heavy Objects are almost essential tools for players that like to explore the environments, but they also aid combat focused players by opening up new tactical positions [→□ 5]. The only purely combat focused Augmentation is the Recoil Compensation, and because you need to acquire both Punch Through Walls and Move Heavy Objects to get it, the price is quite steep. The benefits, however, are also significant for anyone using fully automatic weapons and for them it will be well worth the cost.

AIM STABILIZER

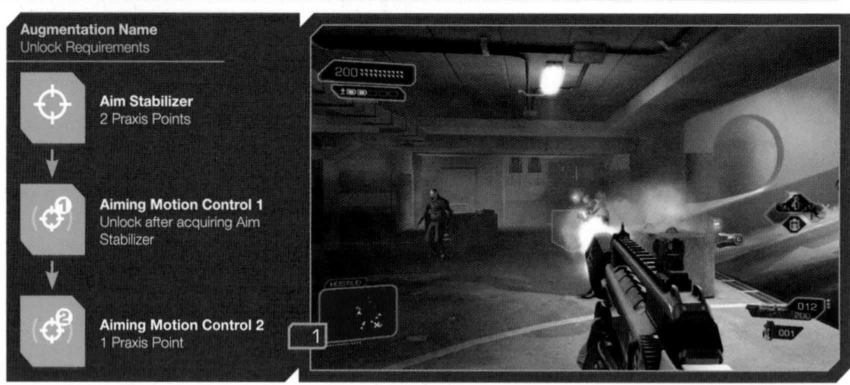

Augmentation Level	Reticule Growth Reduction
Aiming Motion Control 1	50%
Aiming Motion Control 2	100%

Activation	Cost
Automatic	None

Every weapon in the game suffers an accuracy penalty if fired while moving; if you are moving slowly this penalty will be relatively small, but the faster you move, the larger it becomes. This loss in accuracy is depicted on screen by showing the targeting reticule spread further apart the faster you move. The exact size of the penalty also varies from weapon to weapon with some, such as the Pistol, suffering a big drop in accuracy, while others like the Shotgun see only a small drop. This Augmentation is geared towards lowering, and eventually whipping out this penalty altogether so that all weapons can be fired while on the move and still retain 100% of their accuracy.

Another hidden bonus to this Augmentation is the fact that it also stabilizes the barrel of all weapons that make use of optical scopes. What this means is that, at its highest level, there will be no barrel sway at all when using the scope on weapons such as the Sniper Rifle or Tranquilizer Rifle. Clearly this makes those weapons much deadlier because lining up shots, especially at long range, will be a much simpler and faster process.

Play-style Suggestion

This system is clearly designed for the more combat focused player since it has the largest impact on all of the lethal weapons. With this system you will be able to fire effectively while moving between cover points, without slowing down to center your aim. This can free you up a great deal in combat since you will not be as inclined to stick behind single cover positions and you will be able to take out targets on the move, while moving to a different position to flank other enemies. [→☐ 1].

When used in conjunction with other systems such as the Recoil Compensation, you can also drastically increase the effectiveness of circle strafing around enemies. While moving around the enemy you will be able to avoid a lot of their gunfire, and with these two systems in place your shots will always remain accurate. Because of the benefits to scoped weapons, however, there are also some benefits for stealth players using the Tranquilizer Rifle. Taking away the sway of the barrel while using the scope will not only allow you to be more accurate with your shots, but also line them up faster, which can be extremely important when trying to remain undetected.

EYE AUGMENTATIONS

SMART VISION

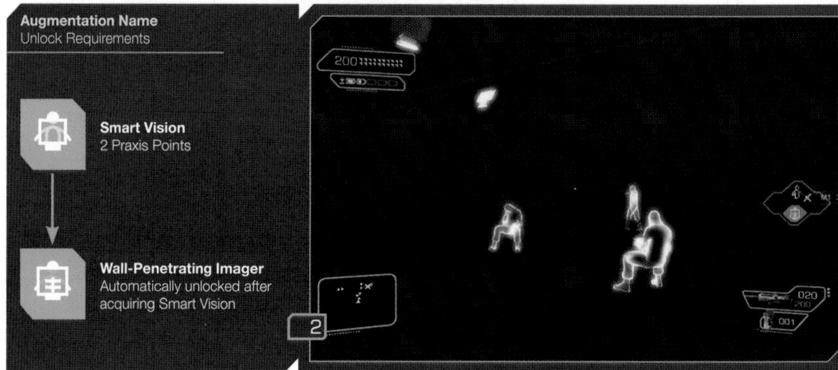

Augmentation Name
Unlock Requirements
Smart Vision
2 Praxis Points
Wall-Penetrating Imager
Automatically unlocked after acquiring Smart Vision
2

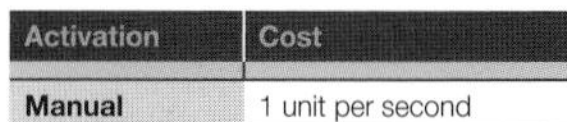

Activation	Cost
Manual	1 unit per second

The Smart Vision Augmentation is an upgrade for the Eye-Know Retinal Prosthesis that allows you to see through nearly any object in the game to see what lies on the other side. Activating this system will cause an additional lens filter to cover your field of vision and nearly all color will drain from the picture, leaving everything only with a slight orange hue. Any object that can be detected by the system will then have a bright illuminated orange glow around the edges so that it stands out. Many different things can be picked up by this system, including all enemies and NPCs, security devices such as cameras and Turrets, and also hackable interfaces such as computers and terminals. [→☐ 2]

Activating this system will also cause a constant energy drain until the time it is turned off, but thankfully this drain is relatively slow so it is easy to switch off before fully draining an Energy Cell so that it can recharge. There is also a 20m range within which the system will detect objects and highlight them, so it is only really useful for checking the immediate vicinity. As you move beyond this range, any targets will begin to fade until they are no longer visible. While you are inside this range, however, walls and other objects will be obscured from your vision for the most part, so you will need to take care while navigating through an area.

When you are looking at an enemy behind cover while this Augmentation is active, your targeting reticule will behave as if you have direct line of sight over the target. This means that it will turn red if you hover it over a Hostile enemy, even if they are behind cover; always make sure to disengage the imager before firing to ensure that the enemy is actually in view to avoid alerting them to your presence. Other systems that rely on the reticule to function, such as Track & Mark can also be used while this Augmentation is active, so you can mark targets even if they are behind a wall or cover.

Play-style Suggestion

This is another Augmentation that can suit all different play styles because of its useful applications in and out of combat. For stealthy players, this will be an almost essential system to have, as it will allow you to scout ahead past walls and doors to spot enemy positions on the other side. This information can then be used to better time your movements so that you can either avoid them, or take them down at an opportune moment. It can also be used to keep an eye on the movements of a security camera that is out of direct line of sight so that you can time your route past it.

For combat focused players, this system will allow you to know exactly when an enemy is about to round a corner so that you can preemptively have your crosshairs perfectly lined up to take them out before they can start firing. It also allows you to take advantage of weapons that have any form of splash damage such as Frag Grenades or an upgraded Revolver. Those weapon types, coupled with this system will allow you to effectively take out enemies while they are behind cover, as you will know exactly where to throw or shoot to ensure they are caught in the blast radius.

RETINAL PROSTHESIS

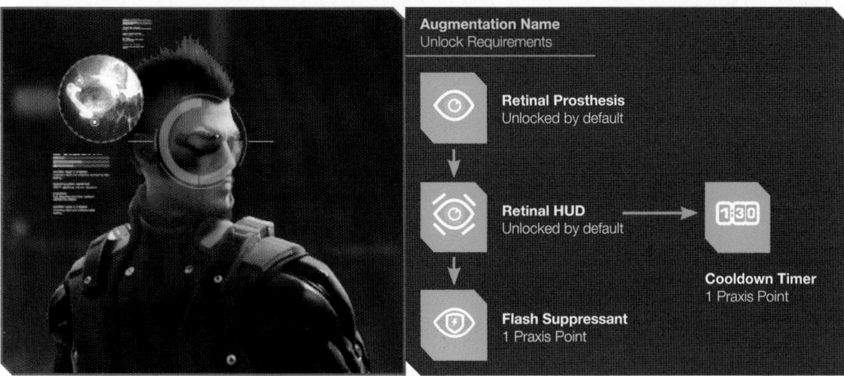

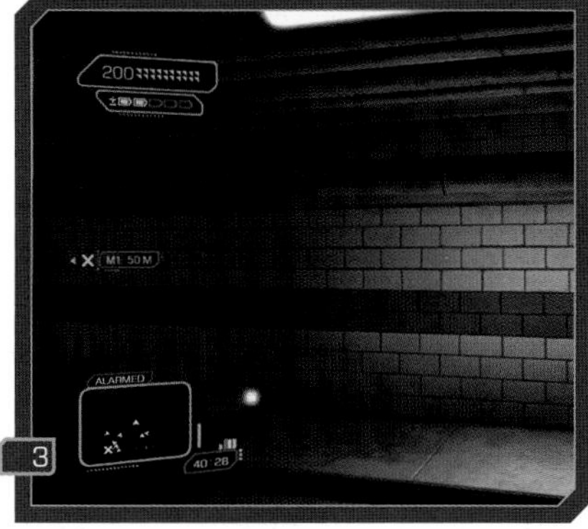

The Eye-Know Retinal Prosthesis is responsible for projecting all of the digital information gathered by your other Augmentation systems into your Head-Up Display. Everything from the biomedical data to radar information is only so user friendly because of this Retinal Prosthesis, and it also houses other unique systems that can be unlocked.

Activation	Cost
Automatic	None

Cooldown Timer

If you happen to be detected by an enemy they will go into a Hostile state for as long as you remain in their line of sight. If you break this line of sight the enemies will go into an Alarmed state, during which they will begin actively searching the area for you. If you remain hidden for long enough the enemies will eventually give up searching for you and start moving back towards their normal patrol routes, but they will still be an Alarmed state and ready to react quickly.

Once this system is in place, a small countdown timer, along with a gradually lowering bar, will appear next to the radar in your normal field of vision as soon as the enemies call off their search [→☐ 3]. Both of these displays are used to let you know exactly how long it will be until the enemies have returned to their normal patrol routes and have dropped out of their Alert status. Like some of the other visual Augmentations, you have to be within 20m of the enemies for the system to be able to calculate their movements and predict the remaining time.

Activation	Cost
Automatic	None

Flash Suppressant

Under normal circumstances, if you are caught within the blast radius of a Concussion Grenade or Mine the screen will turn white and you will lose all vision. After acquiring this system your Retinal Prosthesis can compensate and adjust much faster, reducing the time in which your vision is impaired.

Later in the game when facing better-equipped enemies that make use of Concussion Grenades to try to flush you out, losing your vision can be deadly. With this system in place you will be able to hold your ground and not try to avoid any incoming Concussion Grenades while still being able to deal with any enemies that try to advance.

Play-style Suggestion

The Cooldown Timer is helpful for players who use distractions to lure enemies from their normal routes. This allows you to know exactly how long you have left to either move through the area or set up a trap for when enemies return to a position. Most enemies, however, take around the same amount of time (80 seconds) to drop out of Alert status, so once you have a feel for this time, you can accomplish the same thing without this system.

The Flash Suppressant is suited for players who engage in open combat often. If used along with the EMP shielding and Chemical Resistance Augmentations, you'll be totally immune to most grenades used by enemies, so you'll only have to look out for Frag Grenades.

BACK AUGMENTATIONS

REFLEX BOOSTER

Activation	Cost
Contextual	1 Energy Cell per use

The Reflex Booster is a system that greatly increases the reaction time so that it is possible to safely engage more than one opponent in close quarters combat. Once you have acquired this system, you will be able to simultaneously Takedown two opponents at the same time providing they are within close proximity to each other [→☐ 1]. The actual range between the enemies is quite generous, so they do not have to be standing exactly side-by-side.

All of the same rules that applied to the single target Takedown still apply to the multi Takedown. You still have the lethal and non-lethal variations that you can use, and there are many different variations depending on where you initiate it from, and it will still only cost you a single energy cell to take down both opponents.

Play-style Suggestion

The biggest benefit to this system is that it enables you to instantly, and quietly incapacitate two enemies at the same time. When you are playing through an area stealthily, this ability will come in extremely useful and will often save you having to spend the time luring one enemy away. Another benefit is that you receive a number of XP bonuses for doing a multi Takedown, especially a non-lethal one so it is a good way to build experience.

08_015

ICARUS LANDING SYSTEM

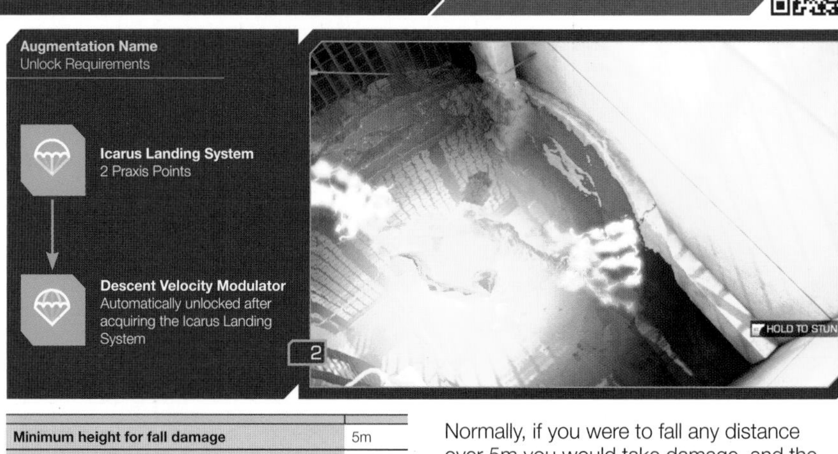

Minimum height for fall damage	5m
Maximum height for fall damage	9.9m
Minimum height before Icarus system activates	5m

Activation	Cost
Automatic	None

Normally, if you were to fall any distance over 5m you would take damage, and the amount of damage you take would increase the further you fall up to 10m, at which point you would receive a fatal injury [→☐ 2]. With the Icarus Landing System, anytime you fall further than 5m an electromagnetic field is generated automatically from within the Augmentation to slow the descent down to safe levels. This system works from any height, even above 10m, so you can safely fall from any distance and not have to worry about receiving damage.

As soon as the system activates you will lose any control over your movement, so if you were trying to jump across a high gap you will lose any forward momentum and float down to the ground below. As well as being able to land safely, however, you can also turn this system into an offensive weapon. When you near the bottom of your descent you have the option to press the Fire button to change the normally soft landing into an attack. The ensuing impact form the attack has similar effects to that of a Concussion Grenade in that it will knock all enemies in the vicinity off their feet and disorientate them for a short time. [→□ 3]

Play-style Suggestion

There are many tall shafts that you can access throughout the game that either lead to new routes through an area or to item caches, and the only way you can safely get down them is through the use of this system. Because of the many option routes you can reach, this Augmentation is perfect for those players that will also acquire the Punch Through Walls and similar Augmentations to ensure all possible approaches are explored.

3

The Landing system is also a perfect safety net when you're exploring high-up ledges or along rooftops where one false step would normally mean death; with this system in place you are able to take a lot more risks than you otherwise would. The attack that you can do while landing can also be used as a very effective combat tool in certain situations. Anytime you can get above a group of enemies you can use the Landing System to drop down between them and deliver an attack to disorientate them, allowing you to quickly finish them off.

SKIN AUGMENTATIONS

DERMAL ARMOR

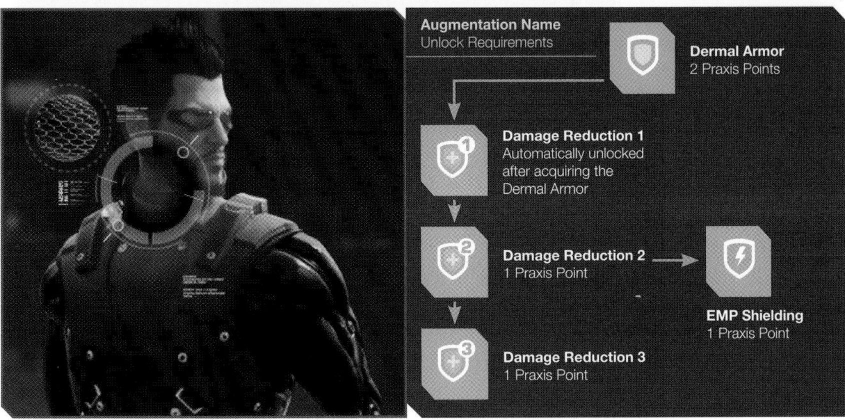

Dermal Armor consists of a series of thin phased composite material sections placed underneath the skin and over cybernetic limbs. The impact force from anything striking an area covered in this material is immediately deflected or dissipated to greatly reduce any possible damage it may cause.

Damage Reduction

The Damage Reduction system is the main draw with Dermal Armor as it allows you to take significantly less damage from any enemy attacks, be they from firearms, explosives of simply blunt trauma. The only things it does not protect you from are the effects of toxic gas or falling from a great height. The large reduction in received damage will allow you to survive in open combat much longer than normal, or ensure that you survive an encounter with an enemy that catches you by surprise.

Augmentation level	Damage Reduced
Damage Reduction 1	15%
Damage Reduction 2	30%
Damage Reduction 3	45%

Activation	Cost
Automatic	None

4

Activation	Cost
Automatic	None

EMP Shielding

EMP Shielding is a secondary system that you can activate within the Dermal Armor, but it is no less important than the Damage Reduction. There are many sections of floor that have been electrified due to broken power lines, and if you were to walk onto them normally they would inflict a large amount of damage [→□ 4]. With this system active you will be able to walk over any of them like normal without taking any damage. Electrified areas often contain item caches or alternate routes through areas that can lead you to advantageous positions.

You will also be immune to the effects of enemies' EMP Grenades or Mines, which means you will not have to move out of the way to protect yourself, potentially exposing yourself to incoming enemy fire. This is especially important since EMP Grenades will cause your entire system to reboot, leaving you without any active Augmentations, and also drain your entire energy reserve.

Play-style Suggestion

The Dermal Armor Augmentation is primarily a combat focused system and players who are spending a lot of time in open combat will see the biggest benefits. The extra damage you will be able to sustain during combat will mean you are able to spend more time returning fire on enemies before having to duck down behind cover. It also allows you to rush enemy positions more effectively to take advantage of close range weapons such as the Shotgun.

Similarly, the EMP Shielding is a very effective defensive measure in combat, especially later in the game when the enemies are more prone to throwing grenades. The EMP Shielding can also be very useful for stealthy players, however, as it does allow the exploration of many areas that would otherwise be inaccessible. There are also certain mandatory battles where having electrical shielding can be very beneficial and will make players of all styles' lives much easier.

08_016

CLOAKING SYSTEM

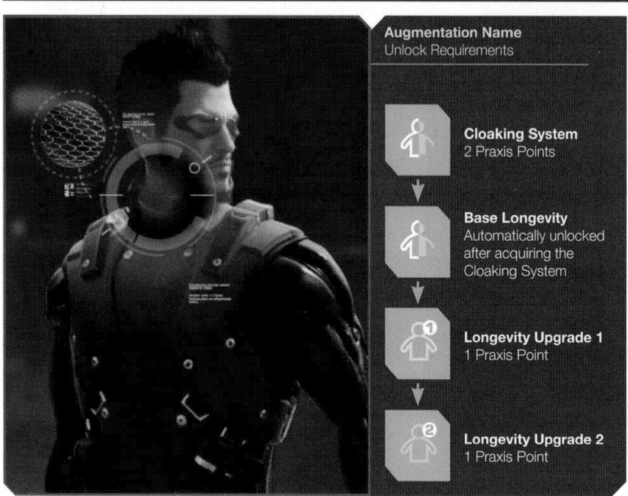

Aug. Level	Energy Drain
Base Longevity	10 units per second (3seconds of active time per energy cell)
Longevity Upgrade 1	6 units per second (5seconds of active time per energy cell)
Longevity Upgrade 2	4.285 units per second (7seconds of active time per energy cell)

Activation	Cost
Manual	High

The Glass Shield Cloaking System is an Augmentation that bends light around the user to render them practically invisible. When you activate this system you will see Jensen's body and the weapon he is holding, become almost fully translucent, just visible enough for you to keep track of your movements. While this Augmentation is active, no enemy in the game will be able to visually identify you, no matter what range you are at, which allows you to easily move past guards on their patrol routes with no real risk of detection. [→☐ 1]

You are able to perform nearly all of the normal actions available to you in-game and still remain cloaked, the only exception to this are Takedowns. During the Takedown animation you will become visible again for a brief period of time, and then instantly cloak again once it is complete. Since Takedowns occur at accelerated speeds, enemies will not be able to react to your presence even if you are in their line of sight. They will of course react to the body caused by the Takedown and will likely start firing at that location.

1

Not only are you rendered invisible to organic enemies, but you will also be unable to be seen by any security cameras, robots or turrets, meaning you can safely walk past cameras instead of timing your movements. Also, because the beams used in the security laser fields are part of the visual spectrum, you can pass straight through them without fear of triggering the alarm. With all of the benefits offered by the Cloaking System, there has to be a limiting factor, and that comes in the form of extremely heavy energy drain. No other system will drain your energy cells as fast as the Cloaking System so always make sure to have sufficient energy to keep it active before you move; dropping out of being cloaked in the middle of an enemy group could have dire consequences.

It is worth remembering, however, that while you are invisible to enemies, they can still hear you if you make too much noise, but this can be used to your advantage. Even if there is no conventional cover available, with this system you can still lure an enemy into an area using sound, and then cloak yourself to move in for an easy Takedown [→☐ 2]. As well as noise, enemies will also react to you if you get too close to them, and most of the time they will become hostile straight

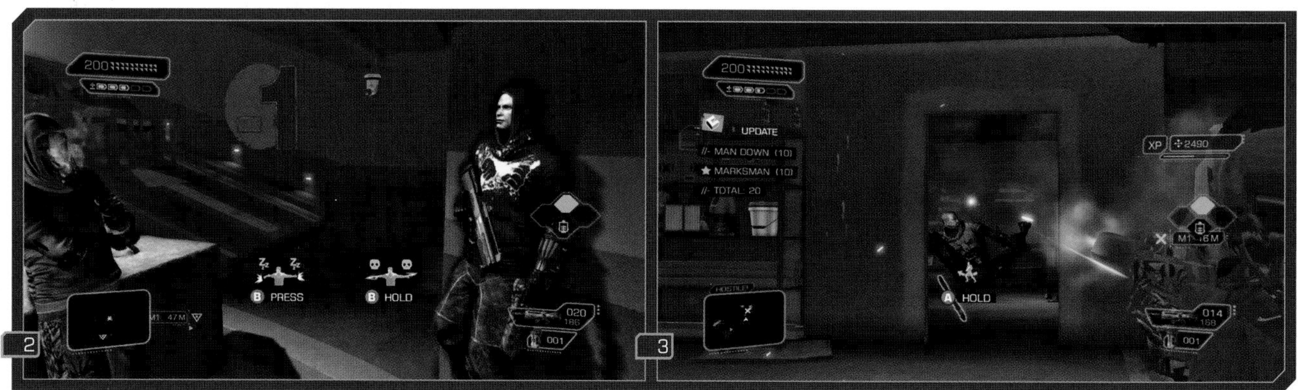

2
3

away when this happens. You will need to take care not to get too close to anyone when moving around multiple enemies or risk setting off unnecessary alarms.

Play-style Suggestion

Although it may seem like an Augmentation geared toward stealth, the Cloaking System actually can be a very effective aid in open combat. Anytime you are behind cover and looking to pop out and return fire, if you have the Cloak active you will be able to do so at a greatly reduced risk. The enemies will not be able to see you come out from behind cover so they will not immediately open fire [→☐ 3]. This allows you to safely get your shot off and then drop back into cover before the remaining enemies open fire. If you are using close range weapons it will also allow you to close in on enemies safely so that you can engage them at optimum range.

For players either playing pure stealth or stealth combat, the Cloaking System can literally be a life saver. You will often come across groups of enemies whose patrol routes leave no real gap for you to sneak through. With the Cloak you will often be able to find a solution or safely incapacitate without being detected. Whether it is moving to an advantageous position you would have otherwise been unable to reach, or simply moving through an enemy group and continuing on, the Cloaking System opens up new possibilities.

Heavy reliance on the Cloaking System is, of course totally dependent on having the energy to sustain it. For combat use where you will only be switching it on and off briefly for the most part, the base level Cloak will be sufficient, in conjunction with increases to the energy recharge rate to allow for more frequent use. For stealthy players, however, where more prolonged use is often called for, investing in as many energy cells as possible is all but essential, as is upgrading the Cloak as high as possible. With the maximum number of energy cells and a fully upgraded Cloak you will have over 30 seconds of invisibility time, which is more than enough to get past most enemy groups. Just make sure to stock up on energy bars.

LEG AUGMENTATIONS

CYBERNETIC LEG PROSTHESIS

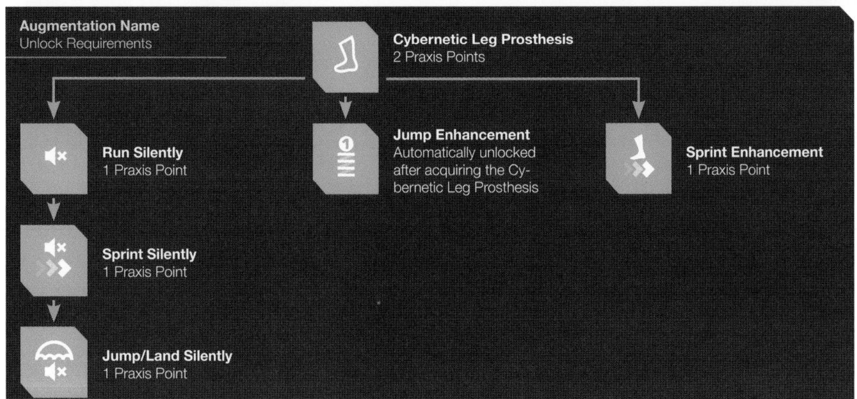

The Cybernetic Leg Prosthesis is built using the same advanced materials that are used in Cybernetic Arms, and as such are capable of a similar level of performance. Nearly all functions that you use your legs for in the game can be heightened through extended training in the use of this prosthesis.

Jump Enhancement

Base Jump Height	1.1m
Enhanced Jump Height	3m

Activation	Cost
Automatic	None

The Jump Enhancement Augmentation is another in the line of extremely important tools that help you navigate through the game. Like Punch Through Walls, there are many areas that you will only be able to access through use of this ability and others, which are made much easier through its use. This is especially true early in the game when you are first deciding where to spend the crucial first few Praxis Points. The Jump Enhancement will allow you to reach areas in early missions such as the alleyway next to the police station, or Tindall's Apartment, that would otherwise require multiple different Augmentations. [→☐ 4]

Outside of access areas within missions, the Jump Enhancement also gives you much more freedom in exploring the city streets. A lot of useful item caches can be reached through the use of this Augmentation, such as the on top of the gas station in Detroit. Because of the extra jump distance you will be able to leap across the high rooftops in Shanghai, or between catwalks in Detroit with greater ease and safety. Because of the ease of reaching these higher areas, it is important to remember that this Augmentation does nothing to protect you if you fall. Even the seemingly harmless act of jumping up onto a fence and then jumping off will often lead to you taking damage; investing in the Icarus Landing System shortly after this Augmentation is highly recommended.

Sprint Enhancement

Base Sprint Speed	6.5m per second
Enhanced Sprint Speed	7.5m per second

Activation	Cost
Automatic	None

The Sprint Enhancement allows you to exceed the normal base sprinting speed by taking full advantage of the functions within the Cybernetic Leg Prosthesis. One extra meter per second may not sound like much, but even with the base sprint duration it can often be enough to allow you to reach a cover point without having to run the last couple of meters. If you have the Hyper-Oxygenation Augmentation as well you can dramatically increase the amount of ground you can cover in a single sprint.

Silent Movement

Activation	Cost
Manual	Low

Energy Drain	2 units per second

The Silent Movement group of Augmentations are a manually activated system that allows you to make otherwise noisy activities such as running and jumping into virtually silent ones. This system first comes available to you when you acquire the Silent Running Augmentation that allows you to either walk or run silently. As soon as the system is active that movement type will instantly stop generating sound until you either run out of energy or choose to turn the system off. Sprinting and then the Jump/Land system can then be added on to also allow those movements to become silent.

The energy drain remains constant at 2 units per second no matter how many movement types you are making silent, which makes getting them all very enticing. Having direct control over when you want to make yourself silent is actually a very usual tactical option. With manual control you have the ability to silently move through and area, and then disengage the system just as you reach a good cover position to lure an enemy if you wish.

Play-style Suggestion

The Jump and Sprint Enhancements are useful for all types of players for the advantages they bring to movement and exploration. The Silent Movement systems are very useful for stealthy players, or those that like to set up traps, but can be made even more effective when combined with other Augmentations, primarily the Cloaking System. Because the Cloak drains energy very rapidly, being able to cover as much ground as possible is crucial, and these systems will enable that. Not only will you be able to sprint further while cloaked, but you can also do so silently so that there is no chance of alerting a guard if you don't want to.

RECOMMENDED UPGRADE PATHS

There are many different ways to play through Deus Ex, each suiting different types of player and playing styles. In this section we will provide suggested Augmentation upgrade paths for several different playstyles that will take players through their first 20 Praxis Points. These upgrade suggestions take into account the different factors that different approaches to the game require and give you a reference point as for what Augmentations may be beneficial to your way of playing. Like the routes provided in the Walkthrough Chapter, however, you should always feel free to experiment by mixing and matching your Augmentations to find a balanced approach that works best for you.

Before going ahead with any new Augmentation for the first time, it is recommended that you save your game so that if it does not suit your play style, you can re-load and go down a different path. Anytime that Save is used in the Recommended Augmentation field it means that you should hold onto it until you get another point, and is generally used when opening up entirely new systems.

Stealth

With pure stealth, the emphasis is on avoiding combat where possible, and as such, the early focus is on acquiring all of the Augmentations that allow you to make use of alternate routes through areas. With these systems in place you will have a great deal more options available to you in any given area, increasing your chances of avoiding enemies. At this early point in the game, it can also be worth investing in the Social Enhancer Augmentation if you are having trouble getting through conversations positively, and it will continue to be useful all the way through the game.

To make moving through areas easier, it is a good idea to invest in the Cloaking System and some additional energy to keep it going for longer. The Smart Vision will also give you a significant advantage in keeping track of enemies so that you can avoid them [→☐ 1]. If you are not having a problem sneaking past enemies, then you may want to purchase the EMP Shielding instead. There are some additional areas that this will allow you access to, and it also comes in very handy during some of the Boss fights.

The Silent Movement systems will allow you to move through areas much faster than you would otherwise be able while cloaked, and then with both systems active you will need additional energy to keep them going. This point in the game is also generally a good time to start increasing your Capture software if you are doing a lot of hacking, and maybe even investing in Hacking: Stealth Augmentation. Finally, increasing the longevity of the Cloak will be extremely useful for navigating through the more challenging areas later in the game.

Praxis Point No.	Recommended Augmentation
1	Capture 2
2	Save
3	Cybernetic Leg Prosthesis
4	Punch Through Wall
5	Move/Throw Heavy Objects
6	Save
7	Icarus Landing System
8	Save
9	Cloaking System
10	Energy Level Upgrade 1
11	Recharge Rate Upgrade 1
12	Save
13	Smart Vision
14	Run Silently
15	Sprint Silently
16	Jump/Land Silently
17	Energy Level Upgrade 2
18	Recharge upgrade Rate 2
19	Cloaking System Longevity Upgrade 1
20	Cloaking System Longevity Upgrade 2

Stealth Combat

The Stealth Combat approach is all about silently taking down as many enemies as possible without being detected and maximizing the potential amount of XP gained in any situation. As usual, getting Capture 2 early will quite literally open a lot of doors, and since this play style is about gathering XP, you will undoubtedly be doing a lot of hacking. The Cybernetic Leg Prosthesis remains as important as ever early in the game so is definitely worth saving for as soon as possible.

Because you will be moving around in close proximity to enemies often, rather than avoiding them with this style, purchasing the Cloaking System will help greatly, especially when moving in for Takedowns

[→□ 2]. With this style you will generally only employ the Cloak for short durations, so the one extra energy cell is generally sufficient and the recharge rate is arguably more important, especially with this Takedown focused class.

Praxis Point No.	Recommended Augmentation
1	Capture 2
2	Save
3	Cybernetic Leg Prosthesis
4	Save
5	Cloaking System
6	Recharge Rate Upgrade 1
7	Energy Level Upgrade 1
8	Capture 3
9	Hacking: Stealth
10	Save
11	Reflex Booster
12	Save
13	Smart Vision
14	Punch Through Walls
15	Move/Throw Heavy Objects
16	Save
17	Typhoon Explosive System
18	Carrying Capacity
19	Recharge Rate 2
20	Hacking: Stealth 2

Increasing the Capture software, along with acquiring the Hacking: Stealth Augmentation will make gathering all of the bonus XP form hacks much simpler. At this time it can even be worth spending the next couple of Praxis Points to max out the Capture software so that it is out of the way, which will then make most hacks relatively straightforward. Getting the Multiple Takedown system at around this point will make dealing with small groups of enemies much easier, and give you a nice XP boost.

The Smart Vision Augmentation is an extremely important tool for this style of play as you will often be using noise to set traps for enemies and need to know exactly when they are approaching. It also allows you to keep an eye on enemy movements on the other side of cover or a wall, so you know exactly when to move in for a Takedown. The next few points should ideally be spent on opening up additional routes through areas so that you have more options as enemy patterns get more complex. [→□ 3]

The Typhoon is a worthy purchase at around this time to give you an easy means of dealing with Bosses or robots. The extra Carrying Capacity will also come in handy to accommodate all of the energy refill items this style requires, as well as any potential weapons for Boss encounters. Finally, another increase to the recharge rate of your energy will be useful for coping with the drain of both the Smart Vision and Cloak, and the extra hacking: Stealth will help deal with the more difficult hacks later in the game.

Open Combat

Although a more combat focused style will generally not be doing much in the way of hacking, getting Capture 2 out of the way early will ensure you can get through all of the mission related hacks. To compensate for the increased risk associated with this style of play, investing in the Dermal Armor early is all but essential. Also, to allow for the carrying of additional weapons and the ammo for them, increasing your Carrying Capacity early can be very useful.

Praxis Point No.	Recommended Augmentation
1	Capture 2
2	Save
3	Dermal Armor
4	Carrying Capacity 1
5	Move/Throw Heavy Objects
6	Punch Through Wall
7	Recoil Compensation 1
8	Recoil Compensation 2
9	Recharge Rate Upgrade 1
10	Damage Reduction 2
11	EMP Shielding
12	Damage Reduction 3
13	Save
14	Typhoon Explosive System
15	Save
16	Aim Stabilizer
17	Aiming Motion Control 2
18	Flash Suppressant
19	Save
20	Implanted Rebreather

Being able to move the heavy objects such as large crates or vending machines will allow you to use them as very effective makeshift weapons, along with enabling you to create your own cover points [→□ 4]. The Punch Through Walls system isn't really essential to this style of play, but getting it opens the path to the Recoil Reduction system which is arguably one of the most important when you are relying heavily on automatic weapons.

There isn't a heavy reliance on energy with this style of play, so additional cells are not really necessary; increasing the recharge rate, however, will allow you to use more Takedowns which is very useful. The next points are wisely spent acquiring the rest of the systems within the Dermal Armor Augmentation to ensure your defensive capabilities are as high as possible. The extra defense will then allow you to make effective use of the Typhoon system to move in and take out large groups of enemies instantly.

To increase your offensive capabilities it is worth spending the next few points maxing out the Aim Stabilizer so that you can fire while on the move more effectively. Finally you should consider rounding out your defensive abilities by making yourself immune to the Concussion or Gas Grenades that enemies later in the game tend to use.

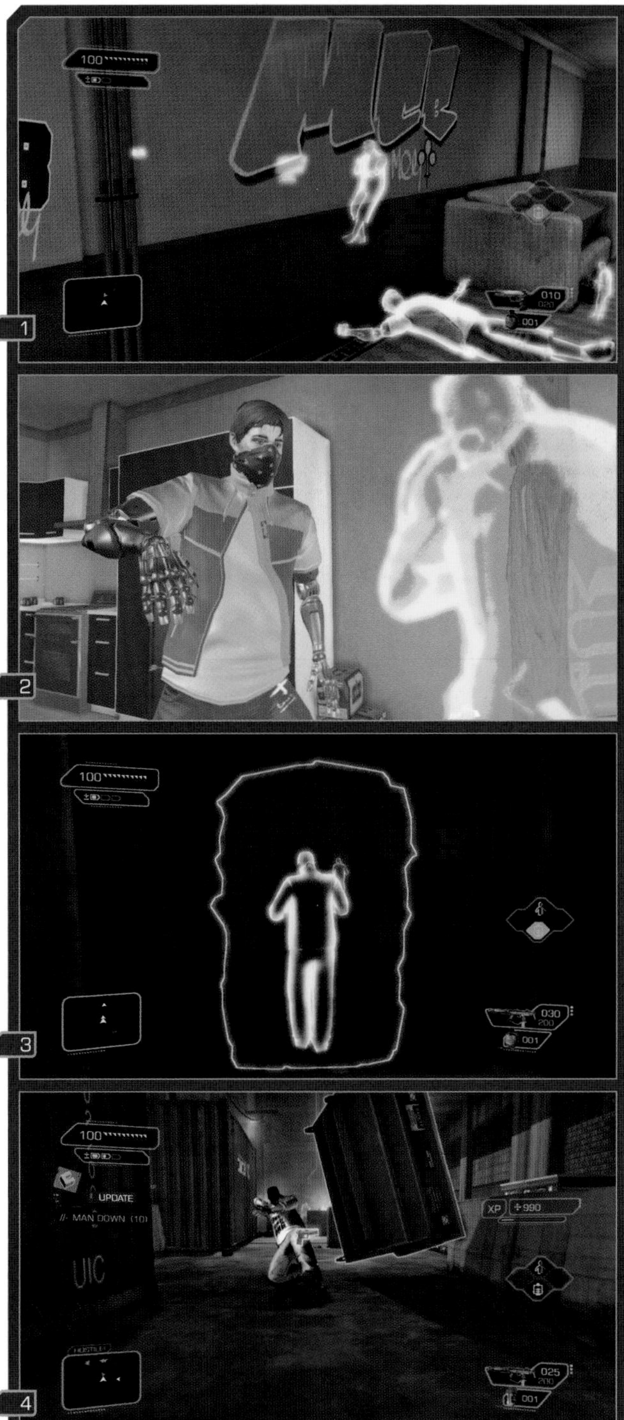

CH03 Weapons and Upgrades

The majority of your interaction with the game world is achieved through the use of weapons. Whether you're going for stealth or a run-and-gun approach, the use of firearms and explosives is paramount to success. Knowing how to use each weapon, where to spend upgrades and how to supplement your weapons with Augmentations is essential. Detailed usage tips for both stealth and aggression, and technical data for each weapon down to the last detail will be covered on the following pages.

WEAPON LOADOUTS

There are several ways to approach combat in Deus Ex: Human Revolution. You can choose to avoid direct confrontation either by stealthily taking out your enemy while unseen or from outside their range of detection. Or you could take a more hands-on approach, destroying anything in your path and relying on massive firepower. While you may find yourself switching between several styles of play during the course of the game, it is still very important to have an over-arching gameplan in regards to inventory management. If you find yourself favoring one style of play over another, it is vital that you choose the right weapon loadout for the job, or else you will quickly find that you are carrying weapons that you never use, are inadequate for the task at hand, or worse, you simply run out of inventory space.

This section will give you some ideas for weapon loadouts and styles that may suit you. Remember that these are just some tried and tested recipes that have proven to be effective, and you shouldn't hesitate to continue to innovate and create your own style if you should so choose.

BALANCED

Recommended Weapons | 10mm Pistol, Combat Rifle, Shotgun/Double-Barrel Shotgun, Sniper Rifle/Silenced Sniper Rifle, Plasma Rifle, Revolver, Stun Gun, Crossbow, Tranquilizer Rifle, Laser Rifle

Recommended Augmentations | Typhoon Explosive System Augmentations, Hacking Augmentations, Carrying Capacity Augmentations, Cloaking System, Social Enhancer, Punch Through Walls, Silent Running/Sprinting

The Balanced play style can't specialize too much in any one area, for fear of running out of inventory space. However, with a few smart weapon and Augmentation choices, the Balanced player can deal with every situation fairly well.

The balance between power, range, and stealth comes with the 10mm Pistol, Combat Rifle and Shotgun combination. Silencing and upgrading the 10mm Pistol will make it your go-to weapon when you want to deal with enemies quickly and silently, while the Combat Rifle helps in more intense entanglements that require slightly more firepower. This can later be swapped out for the Plasma Rifle for the tougher enemies you will encounter. The Shotgun, Revolver and Typhoon Augmentation loadout will help you in Boss fights and against armored and robotic enemies [→☐ 1]. And if you are willing to cut down on healing items and explosives, you can make room for the Sniper Rifle, giving you another option for stronger enemies you would rather deal with from a distance. If you would prefer to take out your enemies stealthily from afar, then the Crossbow or Tranquilizer Rifle is also a good fit. All three ranged weapons are clunky, however, so one of the three should be more than enough. The Stun Gun can give you a temporary option against robotic threats and is a useful, non-lethal close range option. When you eventually get the Laser Rifle, its power, range and precision can make it the go-to weapon for a lot of situations.

Augmentations

Since automatic weapons and weapons prone to reticule enlargement during movement are heavily featured in this play style, the Aim Stabilizer and Recoil Reduction Augmentations should definitely be considered. The Typhoon will help greatly in many situations, especially against Bosses. The Dermal Plating Augmentations should also be purchased, as they will help when stealth is no longer an option. As a minimum, the Cloaking System should be purchased for stealth purposes, and the Silent Running Augmentation should also be considered.

Since this play style utilizes many weapons, you should definitely consider purchasing all the inventory size increase Augmentations. Buying a few Hacking Augmentations can help you find alternate paths around an area, giving the Balanced player yet another option. For general exploration and alternate solutions and paths, you should also consider the Social Enhancer and Punch Through Wall Augmentations [→☐ 2]. The Balanced play style should always be about having multiple ways to deal with a given situation, combat or otherwise.

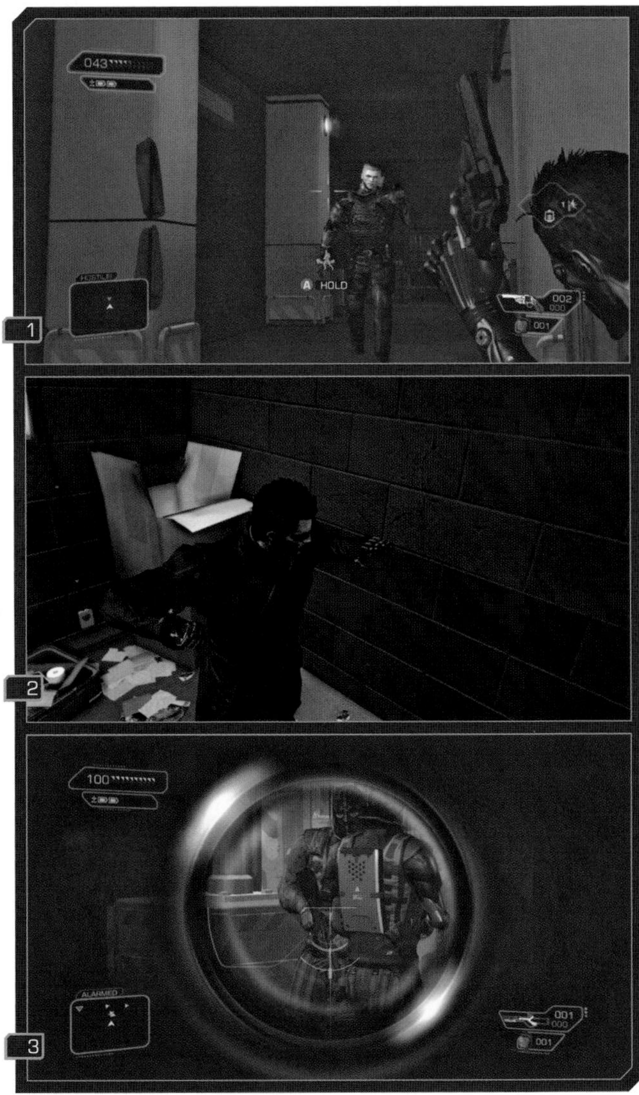

STEALTH

Recommended Weapons | Silenced Sniper Rifle, Crossbow, Tranquilizer Rifle, Stun Gun, 10mm Pistol, Machine Pistol, Revolver, Shotgun/Double-Barrel Shotgun

Recommended Augmentations | Cloaking System, Sarif Series 8 Energy Converter Augmentations,Various Hacking Augmentations, Jump/Run/Sprint Silently, Social Enhancer, Noise Feedback, Wall Penetrating Imager, Radar 2,Move/Throw Heavy Objects

Stealth is usually the best approach to take in most situations you will encounter. This means avoiding a problem as much as dealing with it silently. The rewards for doing so are great, and much safer than tackling a situation head on. Thankfully, there are plenty of tools to help you accomplish this, especially in terms of Augmentations.

First, your arsenal. It will be composed largely of silent weapons that are effective at various ranges, namely the 10mm Pistol or Machine Pistol for close to mid-range, and the Silenced Sniper Rifle, Crossbow or Tranquilizer Rifle for mid to long-range [→☐ 3]. The standard Sniper Rifle doesn't really work here, as the inability to silence it will be very counter-productive to your stealthy endeavors. You will also need to carry at least one powerful weapon for Bosses, or when you are forced to fight. The Revolver and Shotgun fit well here, thanks to their small inventory footprints compared to other heavy weapons. The Stun Gun will also give you another option when ammo is low or you wish to go for a non-lethal approach. The ethos of the Stealth user should always be to avoid confrontation where possible, so fire your weapon as a last resort.

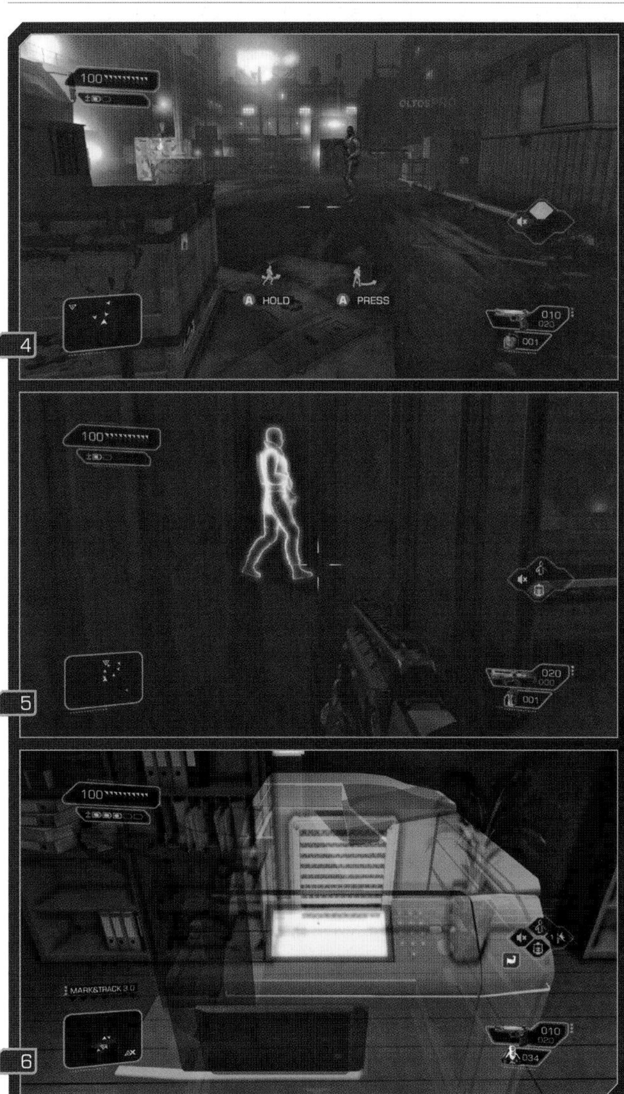

Augmentations

What will really determine your success as a Stealth user will be your Augmentations. It is no understatement to say that this style of play is the most Augmentation-hungry, and planning your upgrade route beforehand is an absolute must. Every Praxis Kit you spend will be precious.

As a bare minimum, you have to invest in the Cloaking System and Silent Running Augmentations. They will be your biggest aids in moving around unseen [→☐ 4]. You will also need something to keep these energy-hungry Augmentations fed, so go for the Sarif Series 8 Energy Converter Augmentations ASAP. After that, you can be a bit more selective in what you choose to upgrade. It's worth investing in some Hacking upgrades, since you will be hacking often, either to find an alternate safer route, or to disable security devices. Also, in order to stay hidden, you'll need to know where your enemies are at all times. For this reason, it's worth investing in the Wall-Penetrating Imager and Radar 2 Augmentations, so you can keep an eye on enemy patrol routes as you move about. [→☐ 5]

Another aid in helping you establish stealthy movements is the Noise Feedback Augmentation, which will let you know how far your footstep sounds are traveling, helping you to avoid disturbing a guard. Also, it might be worth considering the Lift/Throw Heavy Objects Augmentation. Many of the hidden vents that will take you through hazardous areas are concealed by large vending machines or other large objects that can only be moved once you have this Augmentation [→☐ 6]. It is also worth having for the massive increase in throwing distance you will gain, which is very handy for distracting enemies while you sneak past.

CLOSE COMBAT

Recommended Weapons | Shotgun/Double-Barrel Shotgun, PEPS, Revolver, 10mm Pistol, Heavy Rifle, Plasma Rifle

Recommended Augmentations | Dermal Plating Upgrades, Icarus Landing System, Typhoon Explosive System, Move/Throw Heavy Objects, Hyper-Oxygenation Upgrades, Multiple Takedown, Punch Through Walls

This author's personal favorite, the Close Combat play style is as much about using Augmentations to get close to the enemy as what you will do when you get there. To this end, your Augmentations should be based around speedy freedom of movement that will allow you to close the distance quickly, and then strike with deadly efficiency when you do.

A great asset of this style of play is that it allows you to keep your inventory relatively free of large, cumbersome weapons (except for the Heavy Rifle), allowing you to pack extra health and hacking items, as well as extra explosives. The basis of this style is of course the Shotgun. Concentrating on this weapon with upgrades will keep it strong enough to be useful and potent throughout the game, especially once you add the Burst Round System unique upgrade. The Revolver and 10mm Pistol can give you a little more range, with one adding some power and the other some precision, depending on your needs. The PEPS can also help clear a group of close enemies, giving you time to take them out while they're down with your Shotgun, or giving you time to escape.

While the Heavy Rifle actually has good range, its accuracy seriously deteriorates the further the target is. So it's absolutely devastating at close range; a no-brainer for this style. You will also be making a lot of use of explosives, for flushing out enemies in cover while you make your way closer, or for finishing off a group of enemies you have shepherded together [→□ 1]. When you eventually get the Plasma Rifle, its great power and short range will complement the rest of your arsenal.

Augmentations

The Augmentations you should go for should help you to accentuate movement options, and help you take the enemy out once you're actually close. Going for the Dermal Plating Augmentations, Damage Reduction 1 and 2 is an obvious choice, as it will help you survive longer out in the open, which is where you will be most of the time. The Icarus Landing System is also quite useful, as there are many places in the game where you will be able to drop down next to an unsuspecting enemy. Either landing on the enemy or using the ILS's built-in attack by pressing the Fire button will allow you to immediately incapacitate the enemy [→□ 2]. It is also useful for general exploration purposes, which is important for this style, as it offers you another path to catch the enemy unawares for a Takedown. The Punch Through Walls Augmentation works in a similar way, as it will open up paths for you, and allow you to take out any enemy that is on the other side of the wall you are punching through.

The Typhoon will obviously be useful here, since you will be spending a lot of time in the thick of the action surrounded by enemies. Move/Throw Heavy Objects serves a few purposes here. The obvious one is to throw large objects at the enemy. The other is to use the large object as portable cover, helping you to move in safely. Hyper-Oxygenation is also important, as you will need to close the distance as fast as possible, so you'll need to sprint often. And finally, definitely one of the most satisfying Augmentations you can get, the Multiple Takedown Augmentation. This will come into play more often than you think, as a quick means of disposing multiple enemies when you are surrounded, or even taking out two patrolling guards that happen to be standing next to each other.

HEAVY GUNNER

Recommended Weapons | Machine Pistol, Combat Rifle, Heavy Rifle, Plasma Rifle, Rocket Launcher/Grenade Launcher, Laser Rifle, PEPS

Recommended Augmentations | Dermal Plating, Typhoon Explosive System, Recoil Compensation, Aim Stabilizer, Jump Enhancement, Chemical Resistance, Flash Suppressant, EMP Shielding, Carrying Capacity Augmentations

The most simple and yet possibly most effective play style, the Heavy Gunner makes no qualms about what he means to do. Essentially, this style is about never having to worry about ammo, stealth, hacking or even accuracy, and just laying waste to everything in the area with heavy weapons.

The weapons in this loadout are all designed to allow you to fortify a strong position, and eliminate everything in the area. They share some similarities; they are almost all automatic, and they all have ammo readily available for them at different stages of the game. The Machine Pistol is the best backup sidearm to use here, you will always have ammo available for it should you need to fall back to it. The Laser Rifle and Rocket Launcher are a bit more difficult to acquire ammo for, but they are best reserved for robots and Bosses.

Once you first enter an area, the first order of business should be finding an area from which you can fire from cover, see the rest of the room and have walls around so enemies cannot flank you. Usually this will be the corner of the room, although if you can get a height advantage, this is even more desirable. If you can herd the enemies into a choke point, everything in front of the barrel of your gun will become a killing field. Once you are set up, simply select one of your automatic weapons, such as the Combat, Heavy or Plasma Rifles, and go to work [→□ 3]. For enemies that stay in cover, you have the options of using explosives or employing the sizeable splash damage of the Rocket or Grenade Launchers. The Laser Rifle can also pierce through thin cover, giving you another option. Inevitably, there will be times when you won't be able to take out all the enemies near you in time, or an inopportune reload will occur at a critical moment, and before you know it, enemies will be swarming down on your fortified position.

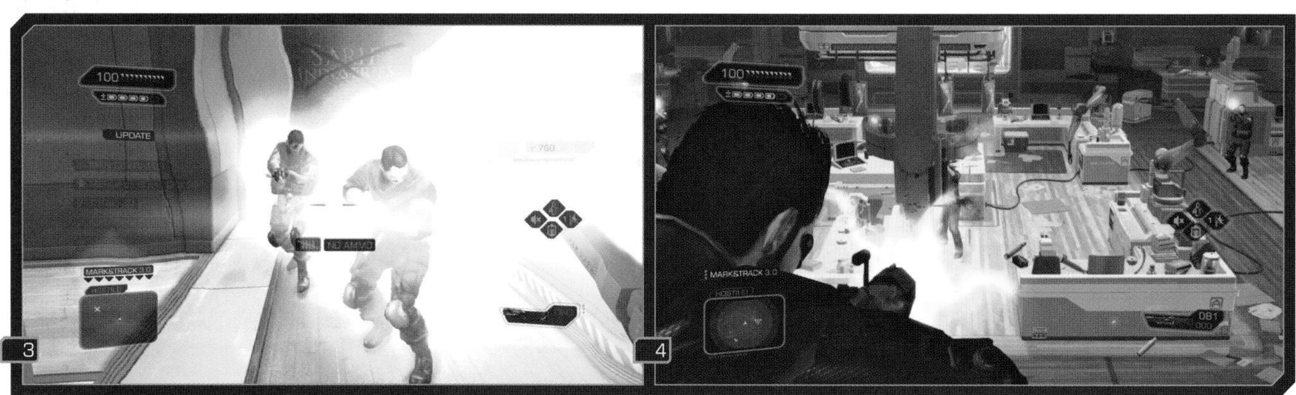

At times like these, it is very handy to have the PEPS with you, to clear the space around you and give you some breathing room. [→☐ 4]

Augmentations

Since this style is about mostly staying put and fortifying a position, you have to be ready to take a lot of fire, as well as a lot of explosives being hurled in your direction. To this end, the Dermal Plating, Chemical Resistance, Flash Suppressant and EMP Shielding Augmentations will make you a defensive tank, protecting you against all status effect explosives and making you harder to kill. The Typhoon can be used if an enemy does manage to make it through your wall of fire and close the distance. All these heavy weapons and explosives will take up a lot of inventory space, so upgrading your carrying capacity is a must. The Aim Stabilizer and Recoil Reduction series of Augmentations will greatly help here, since you will be dealing mostly with automatic weapons. Finally, going for Jump Enhancement will help you get to those high vantage points, where you will have a serious tactical advantage over your enemies. [→☐ 5]

5

SNIPER

Recommended Weapons | Heavy Rifle, Sniper/Silenced Sniper Rifle, Tranquilizer Rifle, Crossbow, Rocket Launcher, 10mm Pistol, Laser Rifle

Recommended Augmentations | Cloaking System, Jump Enhancement, Hacking Augmentations, Turret Domination, Cones of Vision, Last Known Location Marker, Mark and Track Augmentations, Radar 2, Wall-Penetrating Imager

The mainstays of this loadout will of course be the long-range weapons. The Sniper/Silenced Sniper Rifle, Tranquilizer Rifle and Crossbow. You can do without the Tranquilizer Rifle unless you are adamant about not killing your foes. You can also choose to omit the Crossbow, if you are confident in your ability to tackle all enemies from outside their range of audible detection. The Rocket Launcher is actually the weapon with the longest range, and fills multiple roles here. If you can establish a great enough range and can group your enemies together (most easily done by luring them toward a specific spot using the sound of the impact of a Tranquilizer dart or Crossbow bolt), you can take them all out with one well-placed rocket, hundreds of meters away [→☐ 6]. It is also a potent weapon for dealing with robotic enemies and Bosses. The Laser Rifle can also double as a great Boss-killing weapon, while having great range and power, and offering penetrative abilities to boot. Finally, the 10mm Pistol is simply a backup weapon, or an option when there is absolutely no way to establish longer range.

Augmentations

There are plenty of Augmentations that must be used to help establish long-range dominance. The Cloaking System is useful for when you're not quite out of audible range, and need to be hidden when firing a loud shot. Hacking Augmentations and Jump Enhancement are there to allow you to move more freely, and get to that perfect long-range position, often high up from a group of enemies. Turret Domination will allow you to turn a Turret against its masters, perhaps the ultimate form of long range fighting, since you won't even have to be in the room when the Turret does its work [→☐ 7]! However, the crux of the play style comes down to the Stealth Enhancer series of Augmentations. These will allow you to completely control the battlefield, and find the perfect range and location from which to begin your attack.

Cones of Vision is important to help make sure you know the maximum range at which you can be spotted by the enemy, helping you stay at the perfect range. The Mark and Track Augmentations will be useful in cluttered areas where patrolling guards are moving in and out of sight [→☐ 8]. Keeping them tracked will help you plan your sequence of shots. Keeping sight of your opponents is vital, so to that end the Radar 2 and Wall-Penetrating Imager Augmentations should be purchased. The Imager will also be perfect for use with the Laser Rifle, allowing you to pierce the enemy through thin obstacles. And when you do fire that first shot, the Last Known Location Marker will show you where the enemy will be heading towards, allowing you to immediately relocate after firing the shot, the most important tenet of a sniper.

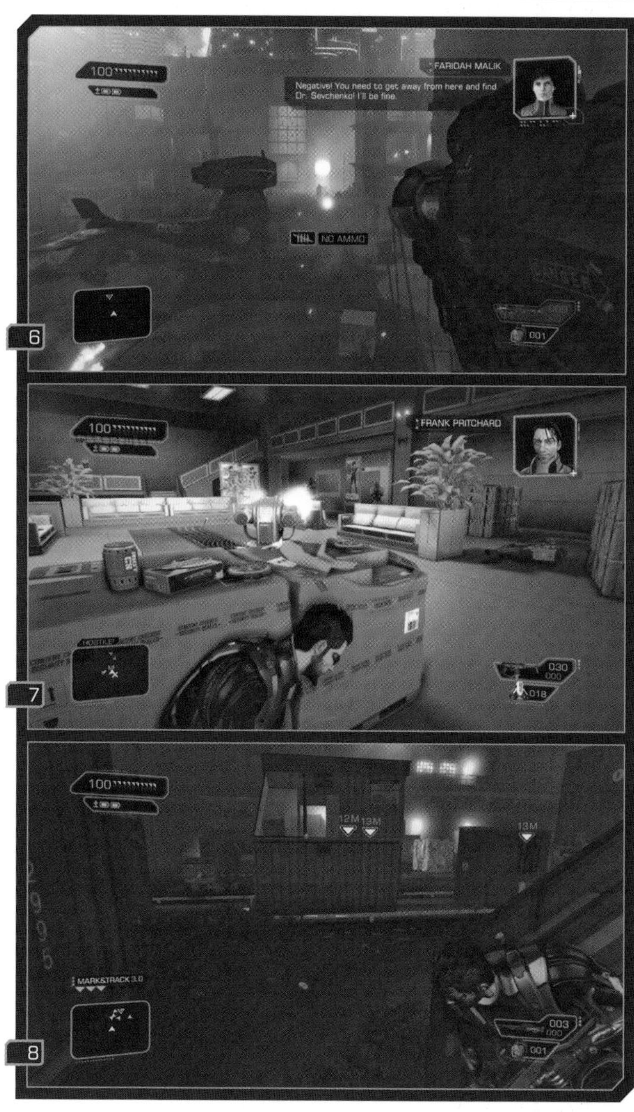

6
7
8

UPGRADES

Throughout the course of the game, you will come across upgrade kits for your weapons. They can be found in the game world, while some of the more common ones can also be purchased from vendors. See the table for some basic data for them.

Upgrades Stats

Regular Upgrades	Quick Description	Size	Buy	Sell
Rate of Fire	Increases the number of bullets fired per second.	2x2	750	150
Reload Speed	Increases the weapon's reload speed.	2x2	750	150
Ammo Capacity	Adds a few bullets to the weapon's magazine.	2x2	750	150
Damage	Increases the weapon's damage.	2x2	750	150

Unique Upgrades	Compatibility	Quick Description	Size	Buy	Sell
Fragmenting Explosive Rounds	Revolver	Fires exploding rounds that do considerable damage.	4x2	3000	600
Armor Penetration	10mm Pistol	Allows shots fired to ignore the enemy's armor modifier.	4x2	3000	600
Flechette Navigation System	Machine Pistol, Combat Rifle	Gives shots fired a limited homing ability.	4x2	3000	600
Cooling System	Heavy Rifle, Plasma Rifle	Decreases cooldown time for weapons after extended use.	4x2	3000	600
Burst Round System	Shotgun	Fire 2 shots at once.	4x2	3000	600
Scope with Leading Software	Crossbow, Tranquilizer Rifle	Compensates for target's movement and gives optimum firing location.	4x2	3000	600
Heat Targeting System	Rocket Launcher	Allows rockets to home in on heat signatures after locking on.	4x2	3000	600

Attachments	Quick Description	Size	Buy	Sell
Laser Targeting System	Attaches a laser sight to the weapon for easier targeting.	2x1	750	150
Silencer	Reduces the noise made by the weapon.	2x1	750	150

REGULAR UPGRADES

These upgrades are the most common, and while still hard to find, can be used more liberally than the Unique Upgrades. However, they must still be used with an overall plan in mind, and spending them on weapons you will rarely use, or on weapons where they will have little effect, can still be detrimental.

Rate of Fire

Standard Rate Increment Upgrade Package for Weapons
Manufacturer: Kaiga Systems Ltd.

The Rate of Fire upgrade will systematically increase the firing rate of your standard bullet-based firearms. There are a few things you should take into account before spending this upgrade on a weapon. Firstly, you will not see a hugely noticeable change in the ROF until you spend at least 2 of these upgrades on a weapon. Taking this into account, it is better to spend these on weapons that already have a decent firing rate, as using them on a slow weapon in an attempt to change it into something it's not is a futile endeavor. It's best to quash those dreams of a rapid-firing shotgun out of your head now. Increasing the fire rate of an already quick gun will help improve the main strength of said gun, for example the Machine Pistol [→□ 1]. You should be wary of weapons with small ammo capacities however, as using this upgrade will burn through them even faster.

Optimal Weapons: Machine Pistol, Combat Rife, Heavy Rifle

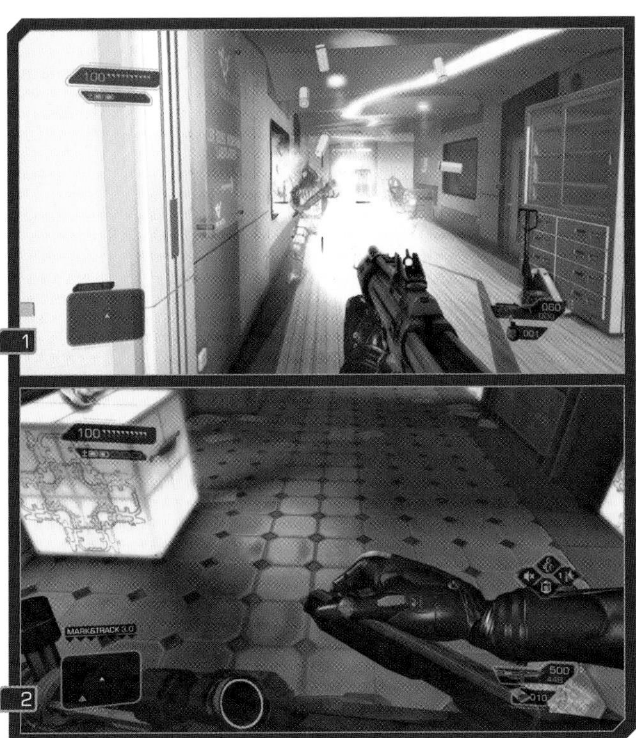

1

2

Reload Speed

QuickFire Reload Upgrade Kit for Weapons
Manufacturer: Sea-Tec

The Reload Speed upgrade is versatile and useful in many weapon types. The actual reduction in reload time is the same for every weapon and at every level of upgrade: each time you use it you will shave off 0.3 seconds of the weapon's reload time. This is a decent amount of time, but won't really affect slow-loading weapons too much unless you are willing to invest multiple upgrades into a single weapon. For example, the Laser Rifle takes 6 seconds to reload [→☐ 2]. After using the Reload Speed upgrade 3 times on it, you can bring the time down to 5.1 seconds. While significantly quicker, a 5 second reload time is still a slow reload time. With this in mind, it is really down to your own discretion whether you want to pursue the path of investing multiple upgrades into a single slow weapon, or making a quick weapon slightly quicker. Either method can yield good returns in terms of damage per second inflicted.

Optimal Weapons: 10mm Pistol and Revolver (single use), Rocket Launcher, Shotgun, Laser Rifle (multiple use)

Ammo Capacity

Extended Magazine Upgrade Modification for Weapons
Manufacturer: Kaiga Systems Ltd.

The Ammo Capacity upgrade is essential for keeping those ammo-hungry automatic weapons fed. You will see the best returns from this upgrade on weapons that already have large clips, such as the Heavy Rifle and Laser Rifle, while weapons with small clips and single shot firing mechanisms will only see increases in single unit increments [→☐ 3]. The Revolver and Sniper Rifle for example will only increase their clip sizes by 1 for each Ammo Upgrade used on them.

This upgrade really proves its worth when used in conjunction with other upgrades to power up a single weapon. Combine this with a few Rate of Fire upgrades on a Combat Rifle or Machine Pistol, along with a Damage upgrade and watch as your damage per second skyrockets.

Optimal Weapons: Heavy Rifle, Laser Rifle

Damage

ShotClock Damage Upgrade Kit for Weapons
Manufacturer: Sea-Tec

The Damage upgrade will probably be your most important upgrade, and deciding what to spend it on is no easy task. An important thing to consider is damage per second inflicted; even a small increase in power would yield great results when added to a weapon that can fire quickly. However, the potency of a few single shots fired with massive force behind them cannot be denied.

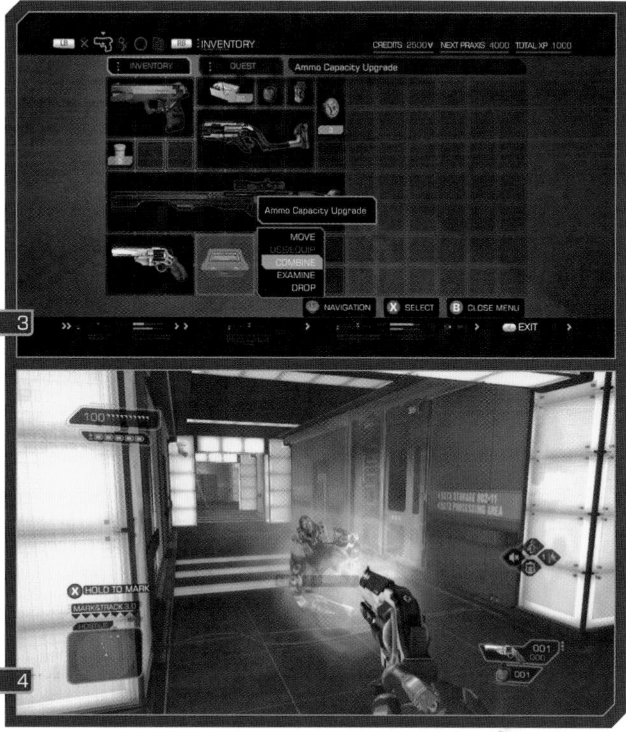

3
4

The decision boils down to the type of play style you have decided on. If you find yourself in intense firefights often, then attaching this to quick firing automatic weapons with large ammo clips is the answer. However, if small skirmishes are simple for you to handle, but Bosses or Box Guards are giving you trouble; it is worth spending the upgrade on beefing up your existing power weapons, such as the Revolver or Rocket Launcher [→☐ 4]. If, however, you prefer either a stealthy, silent single shot kill, or if you prefer engaging the enemy from long range and want to make sure that they'll go down in one hit, then you should invest these upgrades into the 10mm Pistol or Sniper Rifle.

Optimal Weapons: Combat Rifle, Revolver, 10mm Pistol, Crossbow, Sniper Rifle

ATTACHMENTS

Attachments are small items that can add to some weapons to improve their functionality. While not as widely compatible with most weapons as the Regular Upgrades, they nonetheless play a vital role.

Laser Targeting System

Spectra-Point Laser Targeting Attachment
Manufacturer: Kaiga Systems Ltd.

The Laser Targeting System is not just for visual effect, it actually provides a substantial accuracy boost to any weapon it is compatible with, reducing the spread of bullets drastically. It also has the effect of removing your reticule and replacing it with a laser dot [→☐ 1]. This has the added benefit of removing any reticule enlargement due to movement (since there is no reticule), effectively removing movement penalties to accuracy. Also, when out of range of your target, there will be no red targeting dot displayed, letting you know exactly how close you need to be to your target.

Optimal Weapons: 10mm Pistol, Plasma Rifle, Machine Pistol

Silencer

Hush Sound Suppressor Attachment
Manufacturer: Sea-Tec

By far your most important tool when trying to maintain stealth, the silencer is absolutely vital. Best used in conjunction with a powerful single shot weapon to bring your target down quickly and silently allowing you to escape to cover immediately after. Attaching this to the 10mm Pistol, along with several damage upgrades and laser sight, makes it one of the best weapons in the game. [→☐ 2]

Optimal Weapons: 10mm Pistol

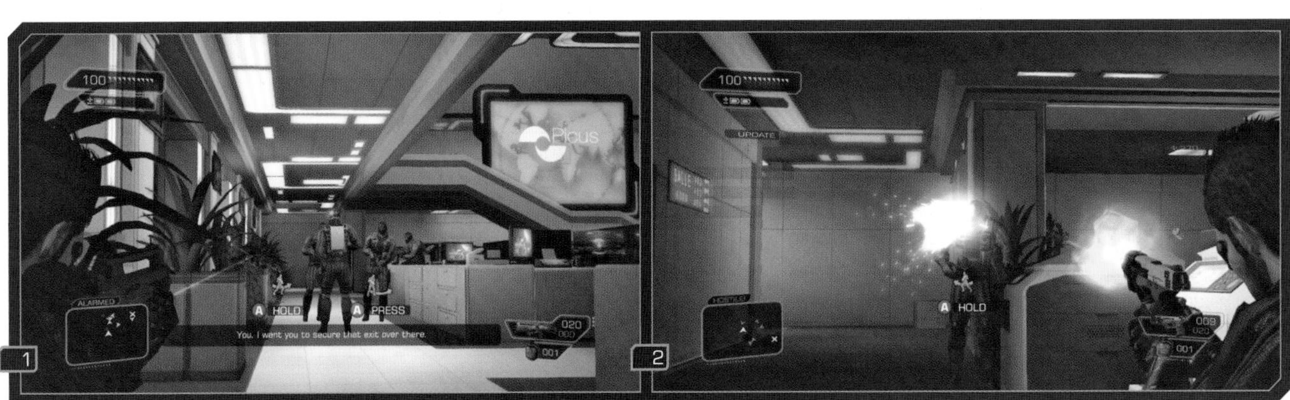

HOW TO USE THE WEAPONS SECTION

If anything in the following pages is anything but perfectly clear then we have surely failed. To account for this possibility we'll describe here exactly what each drop of information on the weapons pages ahead actually means and how it can be used. There's a lot of information to cover, so we've linked it all to an example page just to be extra clear.

Weapon Details
Here you'll see the weapon's basic details, such as its name, manufacturer and ammunition type. There are also some brief contextual details about the weapon's origins and combat uses.

Upgrade Compatibility
Here you'll see a visual display where each normal upgrade type is listed. Any types that the weapon in question is compatible with will be ticked, and the maximum amount of times you can use the upgrade on the weapon will be shown.

Usage
All of the weapon's most interesting traits and uses are described here, alongside any weaknesses it may have. If you want to know the best ways to employ the weapon in combat, this is the place to look.

Useful Augmentations
This text describes any specific Augmentations that work particularly well in combination with the weapon.

Recommended Upgrades
The table here displays the exact effect that every upgrade you apply to a weapon will have. This is split across the number of possible upgrade levels, so you can see what is actually gained each time. The accompanying text will recommend the best upgrade path for the weapon based on the data and most likely in-game applications.

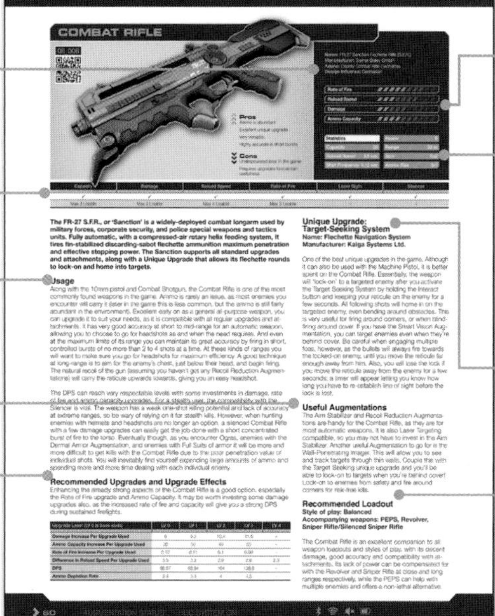

Quick Stats
The bars here display the relative strengths of the weapon in the various categories that you can upgrade. Orange bars show the weapon's base rating, and if the attribute can be upgraded then light grey bars represent the potential gain from fully upgrading it.

Statistics
This table reveals all of the weapon's in-game attributes as values. These include its ammunition capacity, reload time in seconds, and shot frequency, which is the amount of time between each shot rather than an overall rate of fire value. The power value given is per bullet, unless otherwise specified. To know what the actually power will be against specific enemies, you'll need to compare this value to those given in the 'Opponents' chapter for each enemy's armor value. The size values denote how much space both the weapon and its ammo take up in your inventory.

Unique Upgrades
If the weapon has one or more unique upgrades available for it, everything about those upgrades is covered here. Sometimes a unique upgrade can be applied to two different weapons, in which case recommendations will be given for which of the weapons gains the most from it.

Recommended Loadout
Here we describe the best combinations of weapon to use alongside the one in question. This is based somewhat on the recommended Style of Play section at the start of this chapter, and is designed to maximize inventory space and help you decide which weapons to carry.

WEAPON CATEGORIES

Within the Weapons section we've grouped the weapons into seven categories to make it a little easier to find the one you want. The categories are based on the type of weapon, so the Long-Range category includes the expected Sniper Rifles and the Explosive Weapons category includes a much less expected Rocket Launcher.

Rifles and Shotguns
The bulk of the most common weapons will fall into this category. While generally large and taking up a lot of inventory space, Rifles and Shotguns also have the advantages of generally having large clips, decent firing rates and good damage. Ammo is also plentiful, and usually weapons in this category are compatible with all regular upgrades.

Long-Range
A very powerful strategy in any game, the advantages of dealing with your enemies from long-range are just as apparent in Deus Ex: Human Revolution. Offering several silenced, lethal options, you have a multitude of choices of how to deal with your enemies at range. While it is difficult to rely solely on long-range weapons in every situation, they are great as a first option in many scenarios.

Explosive Weapons
The Rocket and Grenade Launcher are interesting weapons. Incredibly powerful with huge splash damage, they will let you take out any foe in the game. The cost for this explosive power is ammo rarity, big inventory footprints and slow firing and reload rates.

Pistols
The main advantage of Pistols is their relatively small inventory space requirement. The 10mm Pistol, Machine Pistol and Revolver all require very little space, and are excellent backup weapons to bolster your main arsenal. While all three have very different strengths and uses on the battlefield, their balance between power, speed and range means you are spoilt for choice when making your selection.

Energy Weapons
Energy Weapons in Deus Ex: Human Revolution are very specialized, and have very specific features and uses. While they are very rare, and the ammo is very hard to come by, they can do things no other weapons in the game can.

Non-Lethal
The two main non-lethal options you have in Deus Ex are the Tranquilizer Rifle for long-range engagements, and the Stun Gun for those who want to deal with things in a more 'up-close and personal' fashion. Whatever you choose, you will be picking a very useful, silent weapon.

Explosives
Explosives in Deus Ex fall into one of two categories, Grenades or Mines. They are the third option you have in the trio of offensive capabilities that are available to you, along with your main weapons and Augments. As such, they are an important part of your arsenal and should always be considered for use in any situation.

COMBAT RIFLE

08_017
Pros
Ammo is abundant
Excellent unique upgrade
Very versatile
Highly accurate in short bursts
Cons
Underpowered later in the game
Requires upgrades to maintain usefulness

Name: FR-27 Sanction Flechette Rifle [S.F.R.]
Manufacturer: Steiner-Bisley GmbH
Ammo: Osprey Combat Rifle Flechettes
Design Influence: Germasian

Statistics			
Capacity	20	Power	8
Reload Speed	3.5 sec	Range	50 m
Shot Frequency	0.12 sec	Size	5x2
		Ammo Size	3x1

Capacity	Damage	Reload Speed	Rate of Fire	Laser Sight	Silencer
✓	✓	✓	✓	✓	✓
Max 3 Usable	Max 3 Usable	Max 4 Usable	Max 3 Usable	–	–

The FR-27 S.F.R., or 'Sanction' is a widely-deployed combat longarm used by military forces, corporate security, and police special weapons and tactics units. Fully automatic, with a compressed-air rotary helix feeding system, it fires fin-stabilized discarding-sabot flechette ammunition maximum penetration and effective stopping power. The Sanction supports all standard upgrades and attachments, along with a Unique Upgrade that allows its flechette rounds to lock-on and home into targets.

Usage

Along with the 10mm pistol and Combat Shotgun, the Combat Rifle is one of the most commonly found weapons in the game. Ammo is rarely an issue, as most enemies you encounter will carry it (later in the game this is less common, but the ammo is still fairly abundant in the environment). Excellent early on as a general all-purpose weapon, you can upgrade it to suit your needs, as it is compatible with all regular upgrades and attachments. It has very good accuracy at short to mid-range for an automatic weapon, allowing you to choose to go for headshots as and when the need requires. And even at the maximum limits of its range you can maintain its great accuracy by firing in short, controlled bursts of no more than 2 to 4 shots at a time. At these kinds of ranges you will want to make sure you go for headshots for maximum efficiency. A good technique at long-range is to aim for the enemy's chest, just below their head, and begin firing. The natural recoil of the gun (assuming you haven't got any Recoil Reduction Augmentations) will carry the reticule upwards towards, giving you an easy headshot.

The DPS can reach very respectable levels with some investments in damage, rate of fire and ammo capacity upgrades. For a stealth user, the compatibility with the Silencer is vital. The weapon has a weak one-shot killing potential and lack of accuracy at extreme ranges, so be wary of relying on it for stealth kills. However, when hunting enemies with helmets and headshots are no longer an option, a silenced Combat Rifle with a few damage upgrades can easily get the job done with a short concentrated burst of fire to the torso. Eventually though, as you encounter Ogres, enemies with the Dermal Plating Augmentation, and enemies with Full Suits of armor it will be more and more difficult to get kills with the Combat Rifle due to the poor penetration value of individual shots. You will inevitably find yourself expending large amounts of ammo and spending more and more time dealing with each individual enemy.

Recommended Upgrades and Upgrade Effects

Enhancing the already strong aspects of the Combat Rifle is a good option, especially the Rate of Fire upgrade and Ammo Capacity. It may be worth investing some damage upgrades also, as the increased rate of fire and capacity will give you a strong DPS during sustained firefights.

Upgrade Level (LV 0 is base stats)	LV 0	LV 1	LV 2	LV 3	LV 4
Damage Increase Per Upgrade Used	8	9.2	10.4	11.6	–
Ammo Capacity Increase Per Upgrade Used	20	30	40	50	–
Rate of Fire Increase Per Upgrade Used	0.12	0.11	0.1	0.09	–
Difference in Reload Speed Per Upgrade Used	3.5	3.2	2.9	2.6	2.3
DPS	66.67	83.64	104	128.9	–
Ammo Depletion Rate	2.4	3.3	4	4.5	–

Unique Upgrade: Target-Seeking System

Name: Flechette Navigation System
Manufacturer: Kaiga Systems Ltd.

One of the best unique upgrades in the game. Although it can also be used with the Machine Pistol, it is better spent on the Combat Rifle. Essentially, the weapon will 'lock-on' to a targeted enemy after you activate the Target Seeking System by holding the Interact button and keeping your reticule on the enemy for a few seconds. All following shots will home in on the targeted enemy, even bending around obstacles. This is very useful for firing around corners, or when blind-firing around cover. If you have the Smart Vision Augmentation, you can target enemies even when they're behind cover. Be careful when engaging multiple foes, however, as the bullets will always fire towards the locked-on enemy, until you move the reticule far enough away from him. Also, you will lose the lock if you move the reticule away from the enemy for a few seconds; a timer will appear letting you know how long you have to re-establish line of sight before the lock is lost.

Useful Augmentations

The Aim Stabilizer and Recoil Reduction Augmentations are handy for the Combat Rifle, as they are for most automatic weapons. It is also Laser Targeting compatible, so you may not have to invest in the Aim Stabilizer. Another useful Augmentation to go for is the Wall-Penetrating Imager. This will allow you to see and track targets through thin walls. Couple this with the Target Seeking unique upgrade and you'll be able to lock-on to targets when you're behind cover! Lock-on to enemies from safety and fire around corners for risk-free kills.

Recommended Loadout

Style of play: Balanced
Accompanying weapons: PEPS, Revolver, Sniper Rifle/Silenced Sniper Rifle

The Combat Rifle is an excellent companion to all weapon loadouts and styles of play, with its decent damage, good accuracy and compatibility with attachments. Its lack of power can be compensated for with the Revolver and Sniper Rifle at close and long ranges respectively, while the PEPS can help with multiple enemies and offers a non-lethal alternative.

SHOTGUN
08_018
Pros
Very large spread makes aiming easier
Ammo is easy to find
Good for crowd control in early stages of the game
Cons
Ineffective against armored opponents you will encounter later
Useless at mid-range or further

Name: Widowmaker TX Shotgun
Manufacturer: Military Arms of Ostrava
Ammo: Halfbacks Special Edition Shotgun Cartridges
Design Influence: Amerussian

Rate of Fire
Reload Speed
Damage
Ammo Capacity

Statistics			
Capacity	6	Power	45
Reload Speed	4 sec	Range	30 m
Shot Frequency	0.8 sec	Size	5x2
		Ammo Size	2x1

Capacity	Damage	Reload Speed	Rate of Fire	Laser Sight	Silencer
✓	✓	✓	✓	–	–
Max 3 Usable	Max 4 Usable	Max 3 Usable	Max 3 Usable	–	–

The wide spread of the buckshot from the Widowmaker TX Shotgun makes it the weapon of choice when it comes to room clearance, riot control, and police actions. The poor reload speed and accuracy at mid-range and further are the cost of the high stopping power. Firing pellet loads from 12 gauge cartridges in an underbarrel helical magazine, the Widowmaker TX Shotgun supports all standard upgrade packages, but no attachments. A special two-round burst attachment is also available, firing 2 shots with a single pull of the trigger.

Usage

The Widowmaker shotgun is easy to find, as many enemies carry it. However, there are usually better options available no matter where you are. Decent firing speed and massive spread mean you can rely on it in crowded, tight situations, but beyond that, its effectiveness is limited. While still decently accurate even at mid-range, the damage output drops exponentially outside of anything other than extreme close quarters. Even with damage upgrades and the Burst Round System, nothing can stave off the rapid drop in damage it receives outside of close range.

As you might imagine, the Shotgun doesn't have a lot of use in terms of stealth. It is handy as a backup weapon for when a stealth Takedown has failed, as chances are good that you will be right next to your target when they detect you, and you must dispose of them quickly before they raise the alarm. It is also worth using from cover via blind fire, as its wide area of effect will drastically increase your chances of hitting your target. [→☐ 1]

Recommended Upgrades and Upgrade Effects

The Shotgun's devastating damage at close range is its main strength, and enhancing this is a good tactic if you really want to go toe-to-toe with the tougher enemies in the game later. It is also a good idea to use a few Reload Speed upgrades on it, as it can really improve your DPS in a sustained firefight, against a Boss for example.

Upgrade Level (LV 0 is base stats)	LV 0	LV 1	LV 2	LV 3	LV 4
Damage Increase Per Upgrade Used	45	49.5	54	58.5	63
Ammo Capacity Increase Per Upgrade Used	6	8	10	12	–
Rate of Fire Increase Per Upgrade Used	0.8	0.7	0.6	0.5	–
Difference in Reload Speed Per Upgrade Used	4	3.7	3.4	3.1	–
DPS	56.25	70.71	90	117	126
Ammo Depletion Rate	4.8	5.6	6	6	–

Unique Upgrade: Burst Round System

Name: Automatic Dual Burst System
Manufacturer: Military Arms of Ostrava

A simple upgrade that can only be used with the Shotgun, essentially it allows you to fire 2 rounds at once. The upgrade can be activated and deactivated by holding the Interact button, allowing you to conserve ammo for enemies that can be dealt with in a single round. This is a decent upgrade, but even with the added power, and in conjunction with standard damage upgrades, it still isn't that effective against armored opponents, both human and otherwise. Considering that the shotgun is powerful enough to kill unarmored foes in 1 shot even when unmodified, this makes this upgrade somewhat redundant.

Useful Augmentations

Augmentations that aid accuracy aren't necessary with the shotgun, but it may be worth considering using the Damage Reduction Augmentations, since you will be fighting up-close often and can expect to take a lot of fire [→☐ 2]. Another aid in close range battles is the Typhoon Explosive System, which can help when you are being attacked and the shotgun isn't quite cutting it.

Recommended Loadout

Style of play: Close Quarters
Accompanying weapons: Stun Gun, 10mm Pistol, Rocket Launcher/Grenade Launcher

The Shotgun is the foundation of the Close Quarters Combatant's offense, and is the go-to weapon in open combat. When stealth is desired, the pistol can take care of that, with the Stun Gun offering a non-lethal approach. And when the damage output isn't quite high enough with the shotgun, the Rocket Launcher is there to back you up.

DOUBLE-BARREL SHOTGUN (BONUS DLC)

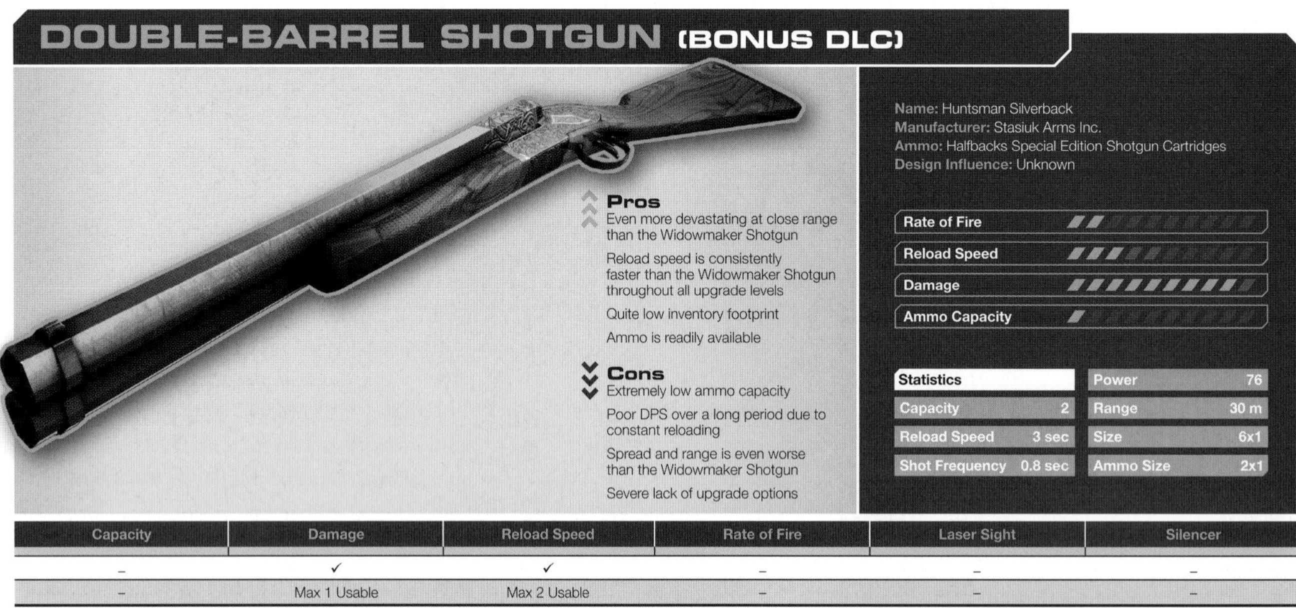

Name: Huntsman Silverback
Manufacturer: Stasiuk Arms Inc.
Ammo: Halfbacks Special Edition Shotgun Cartridges
Design Influence: Unknown

Pros
- Even more devastating at close range than the Widowmaker Shotgun
- Reload speed is consistently faster than the Widowmaker Shotgun throughout all upgrade levels
- Quite low inventory footprint
- Ammo is readily available

Cons
- Extremely low ammo capacity
- Poor DPS over a long period due to constant reloading
- Spread and range is even worse than the Widowmaker Shotgun
- Severe lack of upgrade options

Rate of Fire
Reload Speed
Damage
Ammo Capacity

Statistics			
Capacity	2	Power	76
Reload Speed	3 sec	Range	30 m
Shot Frequency	0.8 sec	Size	6x1
		Ammo Size	2x1

Capacity	Damage	Reload Speed	Rate of Fire	Laser Sight	Silencer
–	✓	✓	–	–	–
–	Max 1 Usable	Max 2 Usable	–	–	–

A smoothbore dual-barrel shotgun with break-action loading, the Huntsman Silverback is a timeless weapon, used primarily for hunting small game or birds. It can also be used for sport shooting such as clay pigeon shooting, trap shooting or skeet shooting. While clunky and difficult to use compared to its modern cousin, the Huntsman Silverback is even more devastating thanks to its ability to fire both barrels at once. The Huntsman Silverback supports increased damage and reload speed upgrades, but isn't compatible with sound suppressors or laser targeting system add-ons.

Usage

The DLC exclusive Double-Barrel Shotgun is an old-school, no nonsense weapon. The base damage is much higher than the standard Shotgun, and is practically unmatched until you get to explosive weapons. However, the trade-off is even greater spread of bullets than the Shotgun, meaning that the effective range is less [→☐ 1]. You will literally need to be more or less point-blank with your target to take advantage of the tremendous power available to you. It is also of course extremely loud and cannot be upgraded much. In addition, you will be reloading very often, as there are only 2 rounds available per clip, which you could blow in one shot thanks to the double-barrel firing mechanism. This feature also allows you to selectively choose the power you wish to use in each shot, expending one barrel for weaker unarmored enemies, while unloading both barrels on tougher enemies.

However, the biggest reason you should try to keep the Double-Barrel Shotgun with you at all times is its frankly tiny inventory requirement. For the kind of power it brings, the inventory cost is paltry. Also, thanks to it taking the same ammo as the standard Shotgun, ammo will be readily available at all times. This makes it a very useful one-shot kill weapon. For example, taking out tougher enemies quickly in situations where stealth is no longer an option, such as after you have been spotted and must deal with several armored foes, and of course against Bosses. [→☐ 2]

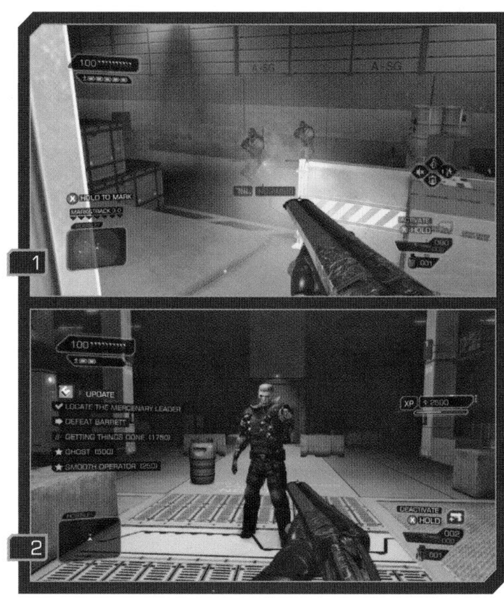

Recommended Upgrades and Upgrade Effects

The Double-Barrel Shotgun is not widely compatible with upgrades, and not with any attachments at all. The inability to increase ammo capacity is a real problem, but increasing the Reload Speed is a decent option, as you will be reloading very often.

Upgrade Level (LV 0 is base stats)	LV 0	LV 1	LV 2	LV 3	LV 4
Damage Increase Per Upgrade Used	76	79.8	–	–	–
Ammo Capacity Increase Per Upgrade Used	2	–	–	–	–
Rate of Fire Increase Per Upgrade Used	3.8	–	–	–	–
Difference in Reload Speed Per Upgrade Used	3	2.7	2.4	–	–
DPS	20	21	–	–	–
Ammo Depletion Rate	7.6	–	–	–	–

Unique Upgrade: None

The Double-Barrel Shotgun does not have a unique upgrade.

Useful Augmentations

Much like the regular Shotgun, Damage Reduction is a good option to use with the Double-Barrel Shotgun. The Typhoon is also great to have, as you will be in close quarters often. Also, it might be worth investing in the Cloaking System, as the short time you will be invisible will be enough to take out an enemy with a quick double-barreled shot and retreat to cover. While nearby enemies will be alerted to the noise, they won't see you, and you can reload, recharge your energy and plan your next attack while safely in cover.

Recommended Loadout

Style of play: Various
Accompanying weapons: Combat Rifle, 10mm Pistol, Sniper Rifle / Silenced Sniper Rifle, Tranquilizer Rifle, Machine Pistol

The Double-Barrel Shotgun is an excellent accompaniment to most loadouts and play styles. Its low inventory cost means it can fit in almost anywhere. Stealth users can use it as an excellent backup and Boss-killing weapon, snipers can use it for up-close situations, and more balanced play styles will be able to use when they need more power to support their arsenal.

HEAVY RIFLE

08_019

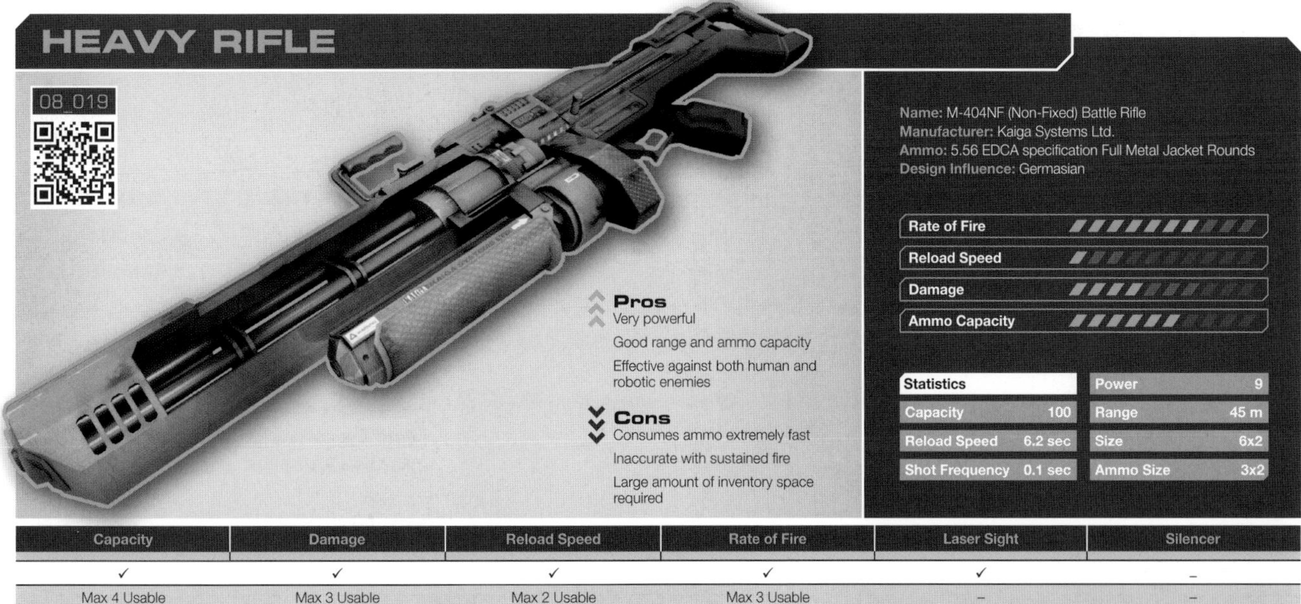

Pros
Very powerful
Good range and ammo capacity
Effective against both human and robotic enemies

Cons
Consumes ammo extremely fast
Inaccurate with sustained fire
Large amount of inventory space required

Name: M-404NF (Non-Fixed) Battle Rifle
Manufacturer: Kaiga Systems Ltd.
Ammo: 5.56 EDCA specification Full Metal Jacket Rounds
Design Influence: Germasian

Rate of Fire
Reload Speed
Damage
Ammo Capacity

Statistics		Power	9
Capacity	100	Range	45 m
Reload Speed	6.2 sec	Size	6x2
Shot Frequency	0.1 sec	Ammo Size	3x2

Capacity	Damage	Reload Speed	Rate of Fire	Laser Sight	Silencer
✓	✓	✓	✓	✓	–
Max 4 Usable	Max 3 Usable	Max 2 Usable	Max 3 Usable	–	–

One of the most powerful projectile firearms available, the M-404NF is a military-specification support weapon typically deployed with ground infantry units. Capable of delivering a hail of fully-automatic fire, it is suitable for suppressing enemy positions or attacking armored targets. While the Battle Rifle provides excellent damage delivery, and has great range, ammunition capacity, and rate of fire, its large mass and inherent instability during sustained fire make it suitable only for area attack options: laying down heavy fire to suppress the enemy. Reloading is cumbersome and time consuming. The M-404NF Battle Rifle supports all standard upgrades, as well as a special Internal Coolant Enhancement (ICE) package that can prevent the weapon from overheating during sustained firing.

Usage

Massive, loud and powerful, the Heavy Rifle is a costly weapon in more ways than one. It can decimate anything in its path, thanks to the ridiculous firing rate and massive capacity per clip. You won't have to reload very often, and ammo is more and more readily available as you progress through the game as the opponents you encounter become better equipped. It is also effective against practically every enemy type, including armored humans and Augmentations, and even robotic enemies (although fighting a Box Guard still isn't recommended!). It also can be upgraded quite heavily, and has excellent range and good accuracy for a substantial portion of that range.

The Heavy Rifle's drawbacks are plentiful, however. First, stealth can be forgotten as soon as you draw the weapon, as every enemy in the game will hear you fire it, no matter where they are. It depletes ammo very rapidly, and while the large ammo capacity can stave off the need to reload, your ammo reserves will get chewed through very quickly. The long wind-up of the barrel means you won't be able to fire immediately in situations where you'll have to react quickly. This can be compensated for somewhat when firing from cover, as you can pre-spin the barrel before popping out to begin firing [→☐ 3]. It will also overheat quickly, and will in fact overheat faster when you add some rate of fire upgrades to it, resulting in you being able to fire fewer shots before it overheats the more upgrades you pile on! None of this, however, takes away from the fact that it is the easiest to find and most readily available heavy weapon in the game.

Recommended Upgrades and Upgrade Effects

Ammo Capacity upgrades spent on the Heavy Rifle will see massive returns, as you can see from the table, reaching a huge 200 round clip at level 4. The Damage and Reload Speed upgrades don't affect either stat enough to justify their use. The Rate of Fire upgrade is a double-edged sword. While it will allow your shot frequency to reach unprecedented levels, it will also make the weapon overheat much faster. However, if you can get the Cooling System unique upgrade and a Laser Sight, the Heavy Rifle will produce an accurate torrent of lead-based punishment.

Upgrade Level (LV 0 is base stats)	LV 0	LV 1	LV 2	LV 3	LV 4
Damage Increase Per Upgrade Used	9	9.9	10.8	11.7	–
Ammo Capacity Increase Per Upgrade Used	100	125	150	175	200
Rate of Fire Increase Per Upgrade Used	0.1	0.09	0.08	0.07	–
Difference in Reload Speed Per Upgrade Used	6.2	5.9	5.6	–	–
DPS	90	110	135	167.1	195
Ammo Depletion Rate	10	11.25	12	12.25	12

3

Unique Upgrade: Cooling System

Name: Internal Coolant Enhancement (ICE) package for Weapons
Manufacturer: Connaught Technologies

The unique upgrade for the Heavy Rifle adds a cooling system to the gun, stopping it from overheating. This completely eliminates one of the major weaknesses of the gun, making it much more viable.

Useful Augmentations

The Heavy Rifle can benefit significantly from the Aim Stabilizer and Recoil Reduction Augmentations. Since the maximum range of the gun is quite substantial, you will want to reduce the spread of bullets as much as possible. It is also worth going for the Dermal Plating Augmentations, Damage Reduction 1 and 2, as you will be quite exposed when laying down sustained fire.

Recommended Loadout

Style of play: Heavy Gunner
Accompanying weapons: Machine Pistol, Plasma Rifle, PEPS

The Heavy Rifle forms the cornerstone of the Heavy Gunner style of play, as you can use it most situations against most enemies, without having to worry about ammo or accuracy. The Machine Pistol and Plasma Rifle can be used against weaker and stronger enemies respectively, while the PEPS can help in crowded situations or when ammo has finally run dry.

SNIPER RIFLE

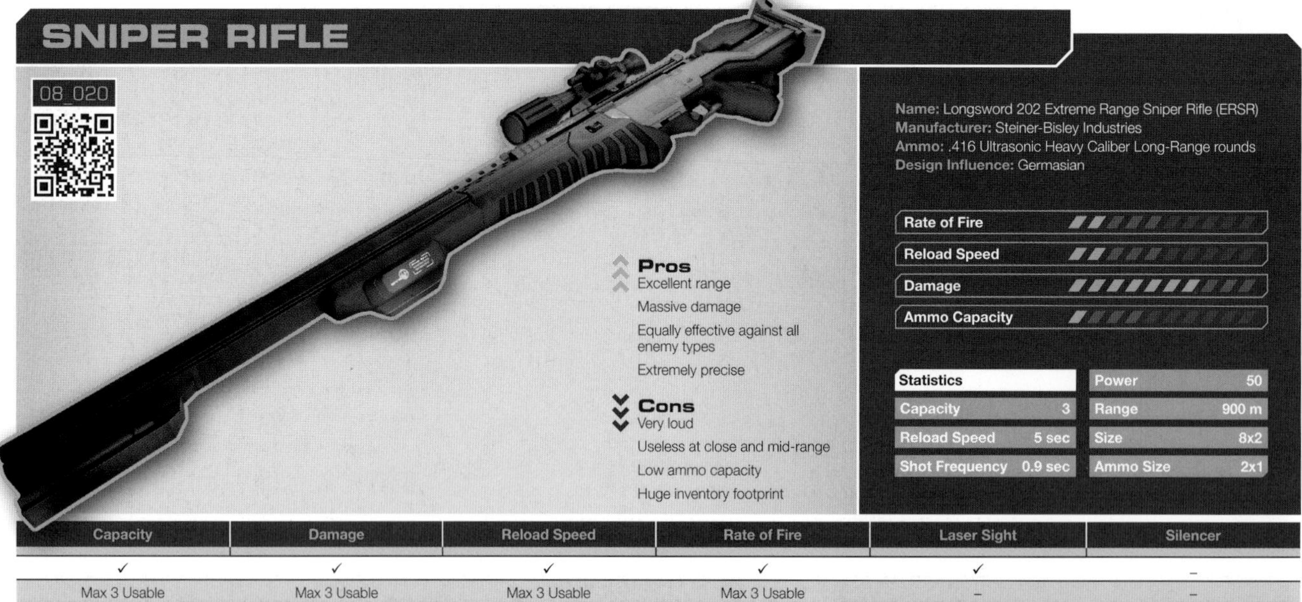

Capacity	Damage	Reload Speed	Rate of Fire	Laser Sight	Silencer
✓	✓	✓	✓	✓	–
Max 3 Usable	Max 3 Usable	Max 3 Usable	Max 3 Usable	–	–

A long-range, semi-automatic, high-caliber rifle used by law enforcement and military specialists, the Longsword is a marksman's weapon. While it possesses a small magazine capacity, the rifle's extreme accuracy against distant targets allows it to send large caliber rounds exactly where needed. The Longsword's accuracy is balanced by its ineffectiveness at short and medium ranges. This weapon is upgradeable and does support laser targeting system add-ons. The Longsword 202 ERSR supports all standard upgrade packages and can be equipped with the Spectra-Point Laser Targeting Attachment to dramatically boost its accuracy. The weapon is not compatible with sound suppressor add-ons, however.

Usage

Like most Sniper Rifles, this is a deadly weapon at long-range. When zoomed in, you will see the distance to your target in meters next to the centre of the reticule [→□ 1]. With a maximum range of 900m, as long as you can see your target, you will be able to hit them. However, the weapon is extremely loud, making it difficult to use as a stealth weapon. Even at the most extreme ranges, the loud bang will attract attention. If you are at a far enough distance, you won't be spotted immediately, and instead nearby enemies will head in your direction. You can use this to your advantage to lure enemies towards you.

A headshot will kill any human or Augmentation with one shot as long as they're not wearing a helmet, even Ogres. If they are wearing a helmet, you'll have to target a different area of the body, in which case the actual damage value of the gun will come into play (which is still quite respectable at 50 base damage per shot) . The Sniper Rifle can also be effective against Bosses, if you can incapacitate them for a moment and get a few headshots off, you can inflict massive damage in a relatively short amount of time.

These perks come at a significant cost, however. For one, the inventory space taken up by the Sniper Rifle is enormous. This will present a serious problem in your overall arsenal plan, as you won't be able to carry as much with the Sniper Rifle in tow. Also, the ammo capacity and reload times are terrible. The inability to attach a Silencer also puts a major dent in its usability, since nearby enemies will immediately be alerted to the gunshot, crippling its usefulness as both a stealth weapon and in situations where there are multiple enemies nearby. And if enemies DO get close, you won't have a chance at close proximity with the Sniper Rifle. These attributes make the Sniper Rifle a highly specialized weapon that has to have a good weapon loadout supporting it.

Recommended Upgrades and Upgrade Effects

Upgrade Level (LV 0 is base stats)	LV 0	LV 1	LV 2	LV 3	LV 4
Damage Increase Per Upgrade Used	50	55	60	65	–
Ammo Capacity Increase Per Upgrade Used	3	4	5	6	–
Rate of Fire Increase Per Upgrade Used	0.9	0.8	0.7	0.6	–
Difference in Reload Speed Per Upgrade Used	5	4.7	4.4	4.1	–
DPS	55.56	68.75	85.71	108.3	–
Ammo Depletion Rate	2.7	3.2	3.5	3.6	–

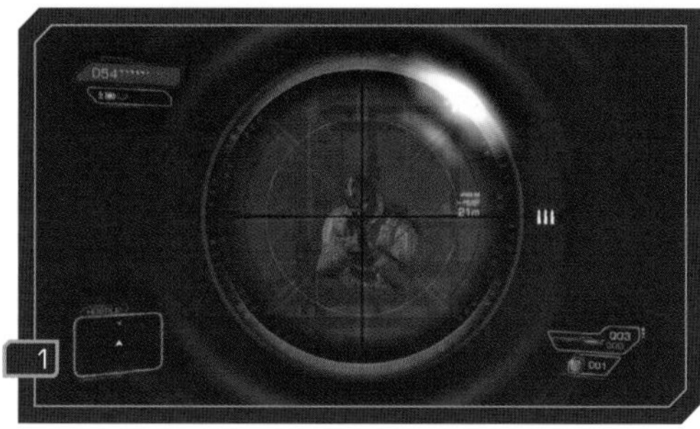
1

The strength of the Sniper Rifle comes from its one-shot killing potential, but this really comes from headshots. Damage increases won't really affect it in this regard, and it will still be weak against enemies with helmets. So in the end, you will probably benefit more from spending your upgrades elsewhere.

Unique Upgrade: None

The Sniper Rifle does not have a unique upgrade.

Useful Augmentations

Stealth Augmentations can greatly help when using the Sniper Rifle, since there is no Silencer available for it. In particular, the Cloaking System Augmentation will help when the enemies look in the direction of the gunshot you fire . It may also be worth investing in some Cybernetic Leg Prosthesis Augmentations, such as Run Silently and Sprint Silently, as these will help you avoid detection. The Aim Stabilizer Augmentation can also help for zoomed in shots, as it will stop your sight from swaying and make your aim much steadier.

Recommended Loadout

Recommended Styles of play: Sniper, Balanced
Accompanying weapons: PEPS, Revolver, Tranquilizer Rifle, Crossbow, 10mm Pistol, Laser Rifle

The Sniper Rifle's power and huge range are beneficial to many styles of play. You can center your whole gameplan around the Sniper approach, or use it to bolster your long-range offense in other play styles.
It fits in well with the Balanced Agent play style also, giving you another option when the power or range of the Combat Rifle and 10mm Pistol might be lacking.

SILENCED SNIPER RIFLE (BONUS DLC)

Name: Longsword Whisperhead Suppressed Extreme Range Sniper Rifle (SERSR)
Manufacturer: Steiner-Bisley Industries
Ammo: .416 Ultrasonic Heavy Caliber Long-Range rounds
Design Influence: Germasian

Rate of Fire
Reload Speed
Damage
Ammo Capacity

Statistics			
Capacity	5	Power	30
Reload Speed	5 sec	Range	900 m
Shot Frequency	0.9 sec	Size	8x2
		Ammo Size	2x1

Pros
- Built-in Silencer makes it one of the best stealth weapons in the game
- Excellent range
- Extremely precise

Cons
- Low damage and penetration relative to normal Sniper Rifle
- Bolt action means firing rate is very slow
- Lack of upgradeability
- Huge inventory footprint

Capacity	Damage	Reload Speed	Rate of Fire	Laser Sight	Silencer
✓	–	✓	✓	✓	–
Max 3 Usable	–	Max 3 Usable	Max 2 Usable	–	–

A military Spec-Ops variant of the standard Longsword 202 "ERaSeR" sniper rifle, this highly accurate long-range, bolt-action weapon features a built-in sound suppression system that renders it virtually silent, making the shooter in cover almost undetectable at long-range. In addition, the rifle's extreme accuracy against distant targets allows it to send large caliber rounds exactly where needed; it is the ultimate "one-shot, one-kill" weapon. The Longsword Whisperhead SERSR supports all standard upgrade packages except the ShotClock Damage Upgrade Kit. It can also be equipped with the Spectra-Point Laser Targeting Attachment.

Usage

The Silenced Sniper Rifle is similar to the standard one, and can be used in most of the same situations. The Silencer makes it a far superior weapon, however. Be careful of firing it too close to other enemies, though, as despite the Silencer, it still makes some slight noise. But by and large, it is essentially a silent weapon. However, if a Silenced Sniper Rifle sounds too good to be true, it might just be.

First, the power of the Silenced Sniper Rifle is significantly lower than that of the Sniper Rifle. While this doesn't affect the one shot killing potential of the weapon too much due to headshots, it can still be an issue against tougher enemies, or if you accidentally hit an area other than the head. It also employs a bolt action system, requiring you to load every shot individually [→□ 2]. This means if you miss a shot and your target becomes suspicious, it will be a second or two before you can fire again. There is also a serious lack of upgrade options available, with no Damage upgrades available at all. Couple this with the existing problems of the Sniper Rifle, the huge inventory footprint and ineffectiveness at close and mid-ranges, and the initial appearance of an overpowered weapon is somewhat mitigated. Despite these drawbacks, it is still a great weapon and should definitely be used over the standard Sniper Rifle when possible.

Recommended Upgrades and Upgrade Effects

Since you cannot help raise the quite low damage output of the Silenced Sniper Rifle, you should try to rectify its other major weakness; its slow firing rate.

Upgrade Level (LV 0 is base stats)	LV 0	LV 1	LV 2	LV 3	LV 4
Damage Increase Per Upgrade Used	30	–	–	–	–
Ammo Capacity Increase Per Upgrade Used	5	6	7	8	–
Rate of Fire Increase Per Upgrade Used	0.9	0.8	0.7	–	–
Difference in Reload Speed Per Upgrade Used	5	4.7	4.4	4.1	–
DPS	33.33	–	–	–	–
Ammo Depletion Rate	4.5	4.8	4.9	–	–

Unique Upgrade: None

There is no unique upgrade for the Silenced Sniper Rifle.

Useful Augmentations

Since you won't really have to worry about stealth with the Silenced Sniper Rifle, you can instead consider Augmentations that will help you spot and keep track of your targets. The Stealth Enhancer Augmentations, Mark and Track 1, 2 and 3 can help you track potential targets, see their patrol routes and plan your sequence of attack to ensure none of the enemies get suspicious as you take them out one by one. Also, the Cybernetic Leg Prosthesis Augmentation, Jump Enhancement, can be very useful, as it can help you gain a high vantage point over your enemies, an excellent advantage for any marksman. [→□ 3]

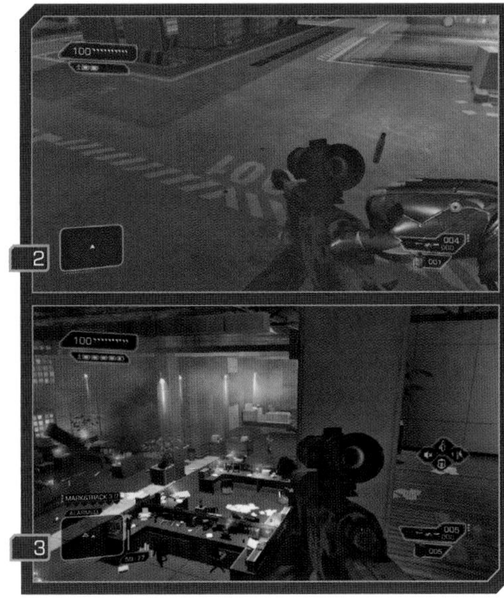

Recommended Loadout

Style of play: Balanced, Sniper, Stealth
Accompanying weapons: 10mm Pistol, Combat Rifle, Revolver, Tranquilizer Rifle, PEPS, Stun Gun, Laser Rifle

The Silenced Sniper Rifle fits in well the Balanced and Sniper play styles, but also has a place amongst players using the Stealth play style thanks to the silencer. Remember that the large inventory footprint will limit what else you can carry.

CROSSBOW

Name: HawkEye Xbow XH-II
Manufacturer: Stasiuk Arms Inc.
Ammo: Guillaume Tell Golden Arrows
Design Influence: Amerussian

Rate of Fire
Reload Speed
Damage
Ammo Capacity

Statistics			
Capacity	1	Power	60
Reload Speed	4 sec	Range	See Note
Shot Frequency	2 sec	Size	5x2
% Chance of bolt breaking upon collection			70%

Pros
- Completely silent
- Powerful against unarmored opponents
- Very accurate
- Ammo is reusable

Cons
- Only 1 shot at a time
- Very slow reloading speed
- Range is difficult to gauge
- Ammo is rare

Capacity	Damage	Reload Speed	Rate of Fire	Laser Sight	Silencer
–	✓	✓	–	–	–
–	Max 2 Usable	Max 3 Usable	–	–	–

The crossbow has been around in one form or another for centuries, thanks to the simplicity and effectiveness of its basic design: with few moving parts, the weapon can operate in near-silence and in almost any conditions. The HawkEye XH-II version is a lightweight, single-shot crossbow with a built-in optical sight. This improves the weapon's accuracy, but reload time is slow, as each bolt must be hand-loaded. The HawkEye XH-II does support some standard upgrade packages. It can also make use of a special package called the LeadFire Targeting Suite. This upgrade relies on scope-leading software to predict a target's movements, improving the accuracy of shots.

Usage

Although very rare, the Crossbow has some unique properties that make it invaluable. It is more or less completely silent, with only the impact of the bolts making a sound. As long as you can reach your bolt after firing it, you can collect it and use it again, meaning that potentially it can have unlimited ammo. There is a 70% chance of the bolt breaking upon attempting to recollect however, however. Against unarmored opponents, one shot to the torso or head is enough for a kill, and if you're close enough to your target, you can skewer them to a surface, making the retrieval of spent bolts easier.

The built-in scope makes it a good ranged weapon, and a decent alternative to the Sniper Rifle, especially considering it has a smaller inventory footprint. Be wary of firing it from great distances, however, as the crossbow bolt will lose speed and dip, eventually falling to the ground. While this means the range is excellent, it can be very difficult to gauge the arc at which the bolt will fall. It can also be a useful distraction tool, as firing it at a wall or floor near an enemy will cause him to investigate the sound of bolt striking, usually giving you enough time to slip past or go for a Takedown.

While the Crossbow is very effective against unarmored and basic vest-wearing enemies, it is very ineffective against fully suited and Augmented enemies, and practically useless against robotic enemies. It also has a very slow firing rate, due to the need to individually load each bolt. There is also quite a lengthy reload time, and the lack of upgrade options cannot help these problems for the most part. The general slowness of the weapon means that outside specific sniping and stealth kill scenarios, it doesn't have much use. It is however, very effective when used in the aforementioned scenarios.

Recommended Upgrades and Upgrade Effects

There are not many upgrade options available, but the 2 damage upgrade levels available can give you a big damage boost. Increasing the reload speed can be useful, since you will need to reload constantly after every fired shot.

Upgrade Level (LV 0 is base stats)	LV 0	LV 1	LV 2	LV 3	LV 4
Damage Increase Per Upgrade Used	60	80	100	–	–
Ammo Capacity Increase Per Upgrade Used	1	–	–	–	–
Rate of Fire Increase Per Upgrade Used	2	–	–	–	–
Difference in Reload Speed Per Upgrade Used	4	3.7	3.4	3.1	–
DPS	30	40	–	–	–
Ammo Depletion Rate	2	–	–	–	–

Unique Upgrade: Target Leading Software

Name: LeadFire Targeting Suite
Manufacturer: Connaught Technologies

The Target Leading Software will allow the Crossbow to calculate the best possible place to fire your shot against a moving target, compensating for erratic movements [→☐ 1]. Generally, you won't be using this too much, you'll often be undetected when aiming this weapon and targeting a stationary enemy. However, if an enemy is moving during a patrol and you need to make the shot quickly, or you have been spotted and you need to take out a fast approaching target, this upgrade can prove invaluable.

Useful Augmentations

Stealth Augmentations such as the Cloaking System and Silent Running are very handy when using the crossbow, as they will help you stay hidden when silently taking out enemies, and help you get into favorable positions for taking your shots.

Recommended Loadout

Style of play: Sniper, Stealth
Accompanying weapons: Tranquilizer Rifle, 10mm Pistol, Stun Gun, Sniper Rifle/Silenced Sniper Rifle, Laser Rifle

The Crossbow can be used in a lot of weapon loadouts, as its power, silenced capabilities and range are invaluable tools that can strengthen any arsenal. As such, it should be considered for most inventories, especially if you are planning to specialize in stealth or ranged offense. The fairly low inventory cost is also another reason to keep with you when you can.

ROCKET LAUNCHER

08_022
MPRS
Pros
Extremely powerful
Huge range
Tremendous blast radius
Cons
Massive inventory footprint
Projectile travels slowly
Inaccurate
Ammo is rare
Low capacity and slow reload

Name: 329-Series Man-Portable Rocket System (MPRS)
Manufacturer: Steiner-Bisley GmbH
Ammo: High Explosive Dual Purpose (HEDP) Semi-Smart Rocket
Design Influence: Amerussian

Rate of Fire
Reload Speed
Damage
Ammo Capacity

Statistics			
Capacity	1	Power	160
Reload Speed	6 sec	Range	1000 m
Shot Frequency	1 sec	Size	8x3
Blast Radius	5 m	Ammo Size	2x3

Capacity	Damage	Reload Speed	Rate of Fire	Laser Sight	Silencer
–	–	✓	–	–	–
–	–	Max 4 Usable	–	–	–

A heavy weapon used primarily against installations, armored targets, or a large numbers of enemies, the 329-Series Rocket Launcher is slow to reload but has a very powerful impact footprint, creating a wide area of 'splash damage' around the target. Keep in mind, however, that at close range, the blowback from a rocket hit can injure the weapon's operator as well as its target. The 329-Series MPRS supports standard reload speed upgrades. It can also be upgraded using the RedHot Thermal Targeting Kit, a unique heat targeting system that is capable of locking-on to a target's heat signature to ensure the accuracy of shots.

Usage

The Rocket Launcher is a very specialized weapon. It is the ultimate robot and Boss-killing weapon, with its devastating power and impressive splash radius. It is also useful for dealing with a large group of enemies, or for those critical situations where you have a patrol of Ogre's bearing down on you and no cover in sight. The Rocket Launcher can deal with them in one well-placed shot. Using a thrown object to lure a bunch of guards into one place is an effective strategy. It's practically limitless range means you can also take out that pesky Turret or that group of unsuspecting guards from well outside their range. The gunshot is exceptionally loud, however, so expect them to come to investigate. The Rocket Launcher also has incredible range, so if you can spot your target from far enough way, and can ensure that they won't move, you can take them out from a huge distance away. And even if you don't quite take out all your enemies, the big blast radius means you will likely stagger them, allow you to finish them off with another weapon.

All this power and range comes at a hefty cost. The slow velocity of the rocket after it is launched means fast moving targets may well move out of the way before it hits, making it more effective against Turrets or Box Guards, or an unsuspecting group of enemies. The rocket also follows an erratic flight path, often wobbling unsteadily after being fired. This presents quite a risk if firing it in a cluttered environment, as it could clip something and explode prematurely. Ammo is also very hard to come by, making a wasted shot truly costly.

Its single shot nature means that you will have to make sure each shot counts, as the reload time is quite poor. But the real problem is its size. The 8x3 inventory cost means you have to sacrifice a lot of other weapons that might have been able to fit with a smaller weapon alongside them. This is really the biggest question that needs to be asked when deciding to wield the Rocket Launcher: Is the huge power worth the massive inventory cost? More often than not, the answer will be no, but if you play a specific style and Augmentation build, it can fit in very well to a well thought out weapon loadout.

Recommended Upgrades and Upgrade Effects

Upgrade Level (LV 0 is base stats)	LV 0	LV 1	LV 2	LV 3	LV 4
Damage Increase Per Upgrade Used	160	–	–	–	–
Ammo Capacity Increase Per Upgrade Used	1	–	–	–	–
Rate of Fire Increase Per Upgrade Used	1	–	–	–	–
Difference in Reload Speed Per Upgrade Used	6	5.7	5.4	5.1	4.8
DPS	160	–	–	–	–
Ammo Depletion Rate	1	–	–	–	–

The only thing that can be upgraded here is the Reload Speed. However, the Rocket Launcher is essentially a 'one-and-done' weapon anyway, and more often than not a single shot will get the job done.

Unique Upgrade: Target-Seeking System

Name: Heat Targeting System
Manufacturer: Kaiga Systems Ltd.

After activating the Heat Targeting System by holding the Interact button, your zoomed in view will allow you to lock-on to certain targets. All humanoid enemies can be locked-on to, as can Box Guards and Medium Sentries. Stationary Turrets and security cameras cannot be locked-on to. Once you are locked to your target, you can move your reticule away or exit zoom and keep the lock on maintained for about 7 seconds, before losing the lock. The best use of this upgrade is to lock-on to your target, and then move into cover, before quickly firing your rocket into the sky or around the corner from the safety of cover before the lock is lost. This way you can ensure you will hit your target without being seen.

Useful Augmentations

If you're going to carry the Rocket Launcher, you will have to invest in several Carrying Capacity upgrades to compensate for the space it will take up in your inventory. It's also worth thinking about getting the Throw/Move Heavy Objects Augmentation, as being able to throw an object further will be very useful when trying to lure a group of enemies into one place.

Recommended Loadout

Style of play: Heavy Gunner, Sniper
Accompanying weapons: 10mm Pistol, Tranquilizer Rifle, Machine Pistol, Combat Rifle, Crossbow, PEPS, Stun Gun

The Rocket Launcher can fit in well with loadouts that require a single heavy-hitting weapon to tackle tougher enemies, especially if the rest of your arsenal is made up of weaker weapons. It's useful as a ranged weapon for groups of enemies that you can spot from far away, or a robotic obstacle that needs to be dealt with quickly. Remember that keeping it with you means sacrificing a lot of space that potentially could have taken up with other weapons.

GRENADE LAUNCHER (BONUS DLC)

Pros
Great Range
Excellent capacity in relation to its power
Good firing rate
Great splash radius
Low inventory footprint for such a powerful weapon
Cons
Projectile arc makes accurate long-range shots difficult
Slow reload time
Ammo is rare

Name: Linebacker G-87 MSGL (Multiple Shot Grenade Launcher)
Manufacturer: Steiner-Bisley GmbH
Ammo: 40x46m HE Grenade cartridges
Design Influence: Unknown

Rate of Fire
Reload Speed
Damage
Ammo Capacity

Statistics			
Capacity	6	Power	160
Reload Speed	5 sec	Range	See note
Shot Frequency	1 sec	Size	4x3
Blast Radius	4 m	Ammo Size	2x1

Capacity	Damage	Reload Speed	Rate of Fire	Laser Sight	Silencer
–	–	✓	✓	–	–
–	–	Max 2 Usable	Max 2 Usable	–	–

The G-87 is a multi-shot shoulder-arm low velocity grenade launcher with a gravity-fed magazine containing six 40x46mm high explosive grenade cartridges. The weapon delivers impact-detonation rounds over a ballistic arc to the objective point. Designed for military use against enemy personnel or armored targets, the 'Linebacker' operates as a powerful force multiplier for any small offensive troop unit. The G-87 supports rate-of-fire and reload speed upgrades. However, it isn't compatible with sound suppressors or laser targeting system add-ons.

Usage

This is a great weapon, and superior to the Rocket Launcher in almost every way. The power is exactly the same, while the DPS is much, much higher thanks to its great ammo capacity and decent firing rate. This allows you to decimate any enemy in the game in seconds when armed with a full clip. The blast radius is also good, if not quite as good as the Rocket Launcher. While the grenades do arc, this only really affects accuracy at long ranges. The grenade is propelled at great velocity and will most often hit where your reticule is aiming before the dipping nature of the shot can affect accuracy. But the biggest strength of the Grenade Launcher is its relatively tiny inventory footprint. It will only take up 4x3 blocks in your inventory, the same size as the Machine Pistol! All that power for a Machine Pistol-sized weapon is too good to pass up.

The Grenade Launcher does not have many weaknesses. You will be buying most of your ammo, as finding it is a difficult task. This can end up being a very costly endeavor. It's a little harder to use at extreme ranges compared to the Rocket Launcher. This is due to the dipping nature of the projectiles, similar to the arc of the Crossbow and Tranquilizer Rifle shots [→☐ 1]. There is also no zoom functionality on the Grenade Launcher, or even a set of sights, so all your shots must be done from the hip, making accuracy even more of an issue at range.

Recommended Upgrades and Upgrade Effects

The Grenade Launcher is quite potent at its base upgrade levels, however increasing the Rate of Fire and Reload Speed levels will push the already great DPS even higher. Be wary of burning through the already precious ammo even faster though.

Upgrade Level (LV 0 is base stats)	LV 0	LV 1	LV 2	LV 3	LV 4
Damage Increase Per Upgrade Used	160	–	–	–	–
Ammo Capacity Increase Per Upgrade Used	6	–	–	–	–
Rate of Fire Increase Per Upgrade Used	1	0.9	0.8	–	–
Difference in Reload Speed Per Upgrade Used	5	4.7	4.4	–	–
DPS	160	–	–	–	–
Ammo Depletion Rate	6	–	–	–	–

Unique Upgrade: None

The Grenade Launcher does not have a unique upgrade.

Useful Augmentations

A lot of the same Augmentations that work well with the Rocket Launcher also work well here, but you don't have to go out of your way to get the Carrying Capacity upgrades since the Grenade Launcher is fairly small. It may be worth investing in Dermal Amor, since this weapon promotes a very aggressive, high-risk play style, you will often be exposed and under heavy fire.

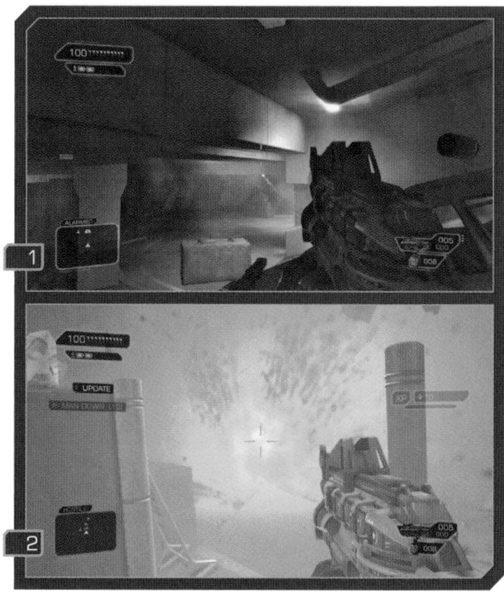

Recommended Loadout

Style of play: Various
Accompanying weapons: PEPS, Sniper/Silenced Sniper Rifle, 10mm Pistol, Machine Pistol, Combat Rifle, Heavy Rifle, Shotgun, Tranquilizer Rifle, Crossbow, Plasma Rifle, Stun Gun

The incredible power and small inventory footprint means the Grenade Launcher can fit into most arsenals well. It can work well for Stealth builds as a Boss killing weapon, or to get you out of a tight situation [→☐ 2]. In this capacity it works in well in most loadouts as the power weapon to take out robotic enemies or Bosses. Its range is very good, so the Sniper can still use it for long-range demolitions. The Heavy Gunner can use it as a replacement for the Rocket Launcher and save on space quite considerably.

10MM PISTOL

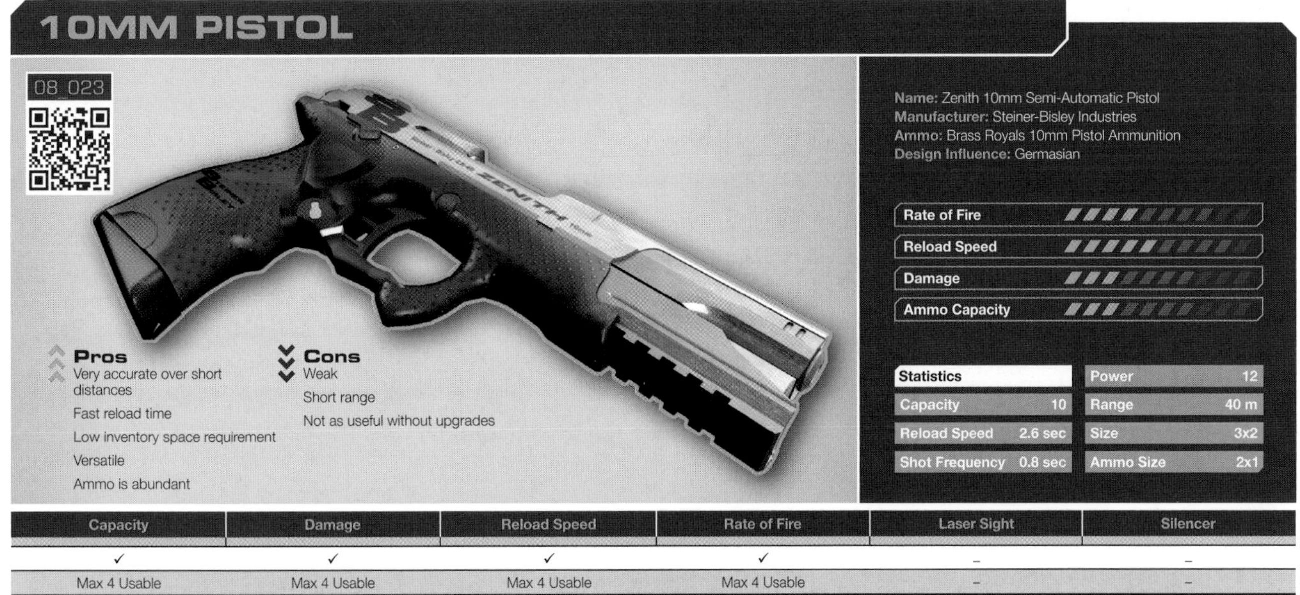

Capacity	Damage	Reload Speed	Rate of Fire	Laser Sight	Silencer
✓	✓	✓	✓	–	–
Max 4 Usable	Max 4 Usable	Max 4 Usable	Max 4 Usable	–	–

A widely available 'jack-of-all-trades' pistol used by everyone from gang-bangers to generals, the Zenith 10mm Pistol is a lightweight, semi-automatic handgun with a short effective range but quick rate-of-fire, average ammunition capacity, standard reloading time, and regular damage capability. The gun supports all standard upgrades, plus one that's all its own: a specialized armor-piercing barrel modification. The gun also supports add-ons such as silencers and laser targeting systems.

Usage

One of the most useful weapons in the game, the 10mm Pistol can fulfill almost any role you need it to thanks to its versatility and compatibility with upgrades. Not only that, but its tiny inventory space requirements and the abundance of ammo available for it mean it's worth keeping for the entire game. If you pile enough Damage and Rate of Fire upgrades into it, it can reach a very respectable DPS level. Each single shot also has decent stopping power, which only becomes even more effective when adding Damage upgrades to it. Couple this with excellent short-range accuracy and it is a force to be reckoned with at short to mid-range. Take this stopping power, add a Silencer and a few headshots, and you have arguably the best stealth weapon in the game.

If you don't mind taking your opponents down in lethal fashion, you'll be hard pressed to beat the 10mm Pistol at close to mid-range. It's even better than the Crossbow at these ranges, since if the enemy does survive your initial shot, the rate of fire is good enough that you can have a few more attempts to silence him before the alarm is raised. It also has very good reload speed and decent capacity, all of which can be upgraded the maximum of four times to make it even faster. Watching a guard's patrol route from cover and lining up a headshot before popping out to fire is incredibly effective, quick, and with a Silencer, very quiet.

There are a couple of drawbacks to this weapon, however. It suffers from quite heavy reticule enlargement during movement, but generally you should never have to fire it while moving anyway. Any armored foe will present a serious problem for the 10mm Pistol, and if they are equipped with a helmet, there is practically no chance of a one-shot kill. This can be alleviated somewhat with Damage upgrades and the Armor-Piercing System unique upgrade, but against some of the tougher Augmented enemies it still won't be enough. Generally, you will find it less and less useable as you continue through the game, making it best used as a support weapon later on, or reserved for unarmored opponents.

Recommended Upgrades and Upgrade Effects

Upgrade Level (LV 0 is base stats)	LV 0	LV 1	LV 2	LV 3	LV 4
Damage Increase Per Upgrade Used	12	13	14	15	16
Ammo Capacity Increase Per Upgrade Used	10	13	16	19	22
Rate of Fire Increase Per Upgrade Used	0.5	0.45	0.4	0.35	0.3
Difference in Reload Speed Per Upgrade Used	2.6	2.3	2	1.7	1.4
DPS	24	28.89	35	42.86	56.33
Ammo Depletion Rate	5	5.85	6.4	6.65	6.6

Adding a few Damage upgrades to the 10mm Pistol is a very prudent choice, as are rate of fire upgrades. When these are applied along with the Silencer, the 10mm Pistol becomes a deadly, silent killing machine. Adding a laser targeting system to the pistol is useful as it will help you identify the maximum range from which you can take out an opponent

Unique Upgrade: Armor-Piercing System

Name: Quantum Tunneling Armor-Piercing (Q-Tap) System
Manufacturer: Sea-Tec

This gives all bullets fired from the pistol an armour-piercing property, complete with blue muzzle flash. This won't really improve its killing potential, but helps with its one-shot stealth kill capacity, as you will now be able to kill enemies with helmets with one headshot. Later in the game, however, it will require subsequent Damage upgrades to maintain its one-shot killing power.

Useful Augmentations

The 10mm Pistol suffers from reticule enlargement during movement, to the point where it becomes practically useless. The Aim Stabilizer will rectify this, although the weapon should primarily be used while stationary, while either going for headshots or popping out from cover. To aid this, the Wall-Penetrating Imager will greatly benefit you in knowing when an enemy will expose himself as he passes a corner.

Recommended Loadout

Style of play: Various
Accompanying weapons: PEPS, Revolver, Sniper/Silenced Sniper Rifle, Shotgun/Double-Barrel Shotgun, Combat Rifle, Plasma Rifle, Laser Rifle, Heavy Rifle

The 10mm Pistol can literally fit in anywhere, but especially benefits Stealth and Balanced play styles. It can fill the role of an easy to obtain stealth weapon or close range precision weapon in any loadout. The Balanced and Stealth play styles can use it as the cornerstone of their stealth tactics, and even the Close Range style can use it as an alternative to the Shotgun. You will need some accompanying heavy weapons to deal with tougher threats, and automatic weapons that can be used as staples in firefights.

REVOLVER

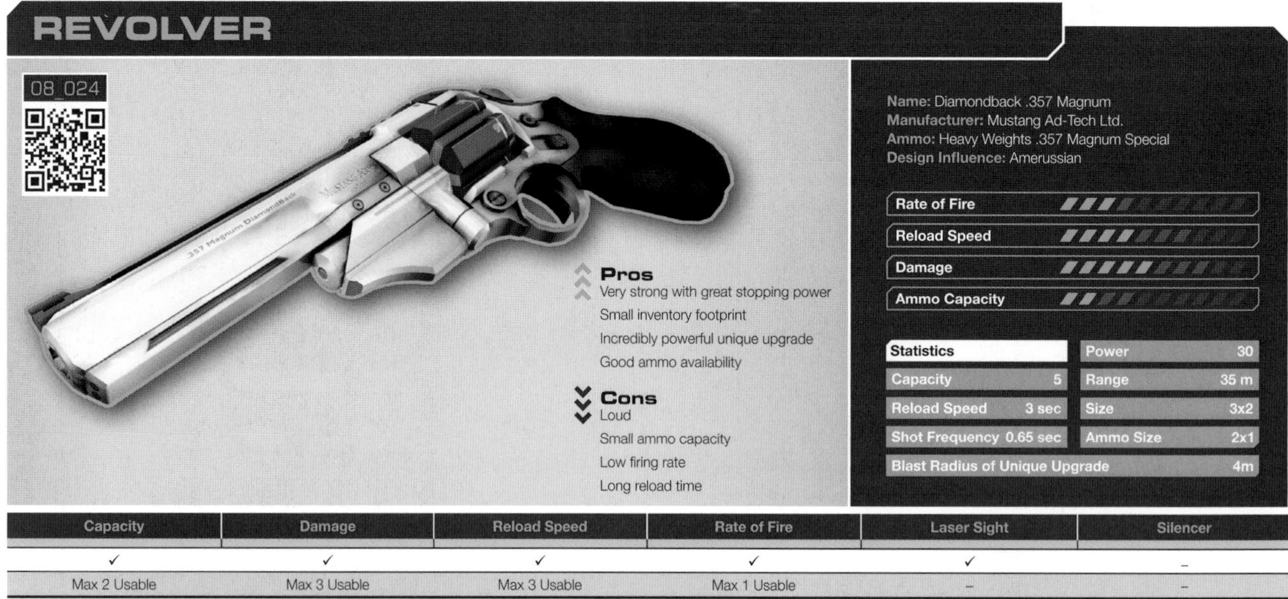

Capacity	Damage	Reload Speed	Rate of Fire	Laser Sight	Silencer
✓	✓	✓	✓	✓	–
Max 2 Usable	Max 3 Usable	Max 3 Usable	Max 1 Usable	–	–

Often used as back-up weapons by corporate security agents or law enforcement officers, the Diamondback .357 Magnum is a heavyweight, double-action revolver with a swing-out cylinder. Its compact but dense frame makes it a powerful weapon, but its short effective range and low ammunition capacity are the trade-off for the damage it delivers. The Diamondback supports all standard upgrades as well as a unique one: the revolver's barrel can be enhanced to launch ammunition as explosive, delayed-action, fragmenting rounds, thus adding area effect to the weapon's normal damage-to-target ratio. The gun does not support a sound suppressor, but it is compatible with laser targeting systems.

Usage

A very powerful weapon within its somewhat limited range, the DiamondBack Magnum Revolver is no joke. If you don't have another strong close to mid-range weapon, like the Shotgun or Heavy Rifle (which could very well be the case if you prefer to fight from long-range and use a lot of Sniper Rifles or non-lethal weapons), then the Revolver is an excellent backup weapon when things get hairy. It's also an excellent tool for fighting Bosses, and once you get your hands on the unique upgrade and a few Damage upgrades, your enemies will be laid to waste. Only the Ogre class of enemy and fully armored Riot Cops will be able to last for more than 2 or 3 shots.

It has a small inventory footprint, a common feature of pistols, and its power in relation to the minimal space it takes up is a great bargain. While only Thug type enemies will carry this gun, ammo for it is readily available in the environment, and since each shot packs such a punch, you won't have to fire many shots in most situations. The upgrade compatibility is also very good, with only the Silencer being incompatible.

The range is a little misleading. While it is listed at 35m, outside of 15-20m, shots will become very erratic and inaccurate, so don't rely on it for long-range precision. The unique upgrade helps in this regard, thanks to the splash damage of the explosion. Hitting fast moving targets is also a problem, as any missed shots can be very costly due its slow firing rate. You should also forget all notions of stealth if you use this weapon, as it is incredibly loud. While still a great, compact and powerful weapon, its inclusion in your arsenal will depend on what the rest of your weaponry consists of.

Recommended Upgrades and Upgrade Effects

The Revolver is destined to be a low-capacity, slow firing weapon, and no amount of upgrades will change that fact, so don't bother using them. However, what you can enhance is the already devastating power and quick reload speeds, making the Revolver excellent for tougher enemies you will encounter later in the game.

Upgrade Level (LV 0 is base stats)	LV 0	LV 1	LV 2	LV 3	LV 4
Damage Increase Per Upgrade Used	30	33	36	39	–
Ammo Capacity Increase Per Upgrade Used	5	6	7	–	–
Rate of Fire Increase Per Upgrade Used	0.65	0.5	–	–	–
Difference in Reload Speed Per Upgrade Used	3	2.7	2.4	2.1	–
DPS	46.15	66	72	–	–
Ammo Depletion Rate	3.25	3	–	–	–

Unique Upgrade: Exploding Rounds Package

Name: Fragmenting Explosive Rounds
Manufacturer: Mustang Ad-Tech Ltd.

This gives all rounds fired from the Revolver an explosive property. These explosions have a blast radius of around 4 metres, and are very handy for taking out enemies behind cover. You can also take out multiple enemies grouped together with a few well-placed shots. The splash damage isn't great, however, even with a few damage upgrades. The explosion itself can also stagger practically any humanoid enemy in the game, forcing them to their knees, if it does not kill them outright. This can be very useful to temporarily stagger tougher enemies such as Ogres by firing near them, then taking them out before they recover with headshots. You can stagger them again if need be, until the job is done.

Useful Augmentations

The Wall-Penetrating Imager can be useful here, as it will help you spot where enemies are behind cover. Once you have the unique upgrade, you can use the splash damage to take out enemies behind it. Dermal Plating is also viable, since you'll probably be engaged in serious firefights when using the Revolver. The Revolver suffers from significant recoil and reticule enlargement problems, so the Aim Stabilizer and Recoil Reduction Augmentations should be considered.

Recommended Loadout

Style of play: Balanced Agent, Close Quarters, Stealth
Accompanying weapons: Tranquilizer Rifle, 10mm Pistol, Machine Pistol, Combat Rifle, Shotgun, Stun Gun, PEPS, Plasma Rifle

There are a few roles that the Revolver can play in a weapon loadout. As a compact, high-impact backup weapon, the Revolver has no equal thanks to its small inventory footprint and decent availability of ammo. While there are more powerful options, the Revolver is also a very good Boss killing tool, and great for taking care of tougher normal enemies. The Stealth user will probably want to carry this to save on space in order to be able to carry the more space-hungry long-range weapons, as will the Balanced player. For Close Quarters, this can be a good alternative to the Shotguns.

MACHINE PISTOL

Capacity	Damage	Reload Speed	Rate of Fire	Laser Sight	Silencer
✓	✓	✓	✓	✓	✓
Max 4 Usable	Max 2 Usable	Max 4 Usable	Max 3 Usable	–	–

Beloved by gangbangers everywhere, but also the choice of special ops agents and tank crews, the Machine Pistol is a smaller variant in the submachine-type class of weapons. Lightweight, with a good ammunition capacity, the Hurricane TMP-18 throws out round bursts at a devastating rate of fire. Its positive traits are balanced out by its negative ones, though: The weapon is less precise than other, larger and more stable firearms, and its rapid firing means ammo is quickly depleted. Chambered in 9x19mm caliber, the fully upgradeable Hurricane is also compatible with sound suppressors and the Spectra-Point Laser Targeting Attachment. It can also be outfitted with a special Target-seeking Flechette system.

Usage

Sort of a poor man's Combat Rifle, the Machine Pistol shares many of the same traits, including being readily available due to being carried by the gang members you encounter on the streets. It is also compatible with every common upgrade. However, unlike the Combat Rifle, its accuracy is worse, with its very wide reticule becoming a huge liability at max range [→□ 1]. Couple this with the fact that you will only put out any kind of decent damage if you land all your shots in a sustained burst, and the weapon really only becomes usable at close to mid-range (although the unique upgrade can alleviate its accuracy issues somewhat).

It does have an amazing rate of fire, so at close ranges where accuracy is of less important, it can do a lot of damage quickly. It can still be useful early on due to being so easy to obtain, but not worth spending too many upgrades on, except a rate of fire increase to really take advantage of its already impressive damage per second output. Of the 3 available sidearms, this also takes up the most inventory space, putting it behind both the 10mm Pistol and Revolver in terms of overall usefulness.

While the Machine Pistol is indeed compatible with the Silencer, and headshots with it do more damage, its inherent weakness means eventually it will no longer kill with one shot. Add to this its very poor accuracy at around the 20 – 30 meter mark, and you won't find many uses for it as a stealth weapon.

Recommended Upgrades and Upgrade Effects

The incredible firing rate of the Machine Pistol is something worth investing in, if you insist on using it. You will burn through ammo at an alarming rate, so a few Ammo Capacity and Reload Speed upgrades also wouldn't go amiss. Don't bother spending a Damage upgrade on it.

Upgrade Level (LV 0 is base stats)	LV 0	LV 1	LV 2	LV 3	LV 4
Damage Increase Per Upgrade Used	7	7.6	8.2	–	–
Ammo Capacity Increase Per Upgrade Used	30	40	50	60	70
Rate of Fire Increase Per Upgrade Used	0.1	0.09	0.08	0.07	–
Difference in Reload Speed Per Upgrade Used	3.1	2.8	2.5	2.2	1.9
DPS	70	84.44	102.5	117.1	–
Ammo Depletion Rate	3	3.6	4	4.2	4.2

1

Unique Upgrade: Target-Seeking System

Name: Flechette Navigation System
Manufacturer: Kaiga Systems Ltd.

The tremendous Target Seeking System is also usable here. However, we would highly recommend spending it on the Combat Rifle if you have to choose between the two. While the Machine Pistol has serious accuracy problems that this upgrade can help with, its lack of power and range make it a waste here.

Useful Augmentations

If there's one weapon that sees serious benefits from the Recoil Reduction Augmentation, it's the Machine Pistol. The Aim Stabilizer can also help, but you're probably better off attaching a Laser Sight. If you do use the Target Seeking unique upgrade with it, it is also handy to have the Wall-Penetrating Imager. As with the Combat Rifle, it will allow you to lock-on to targets from behind cover.

Recommended Loadout

Style of play: Stealth, Heavy Gunner
Accompanying weapons: PEPS, Stun Gun, Heavy Rifle, Combat Rifle, Plasma Rifle, Laser Rifle, Rocket Launcher, Sniper/Silenced Sniper Rifle, Crossbow, Tranquilizer Rifle

The Machine Pistol is a backup sidearm designed to support your main arsenal, making it fit in well with the Stealth and Heavy Gunner styles. When silenced, it can take out most unarmored enemies quickly with a short burst at close range. Due to the abundance of ammo, it is a good fallback weapon for the Heavy Gunner if ammo starts to run dry.

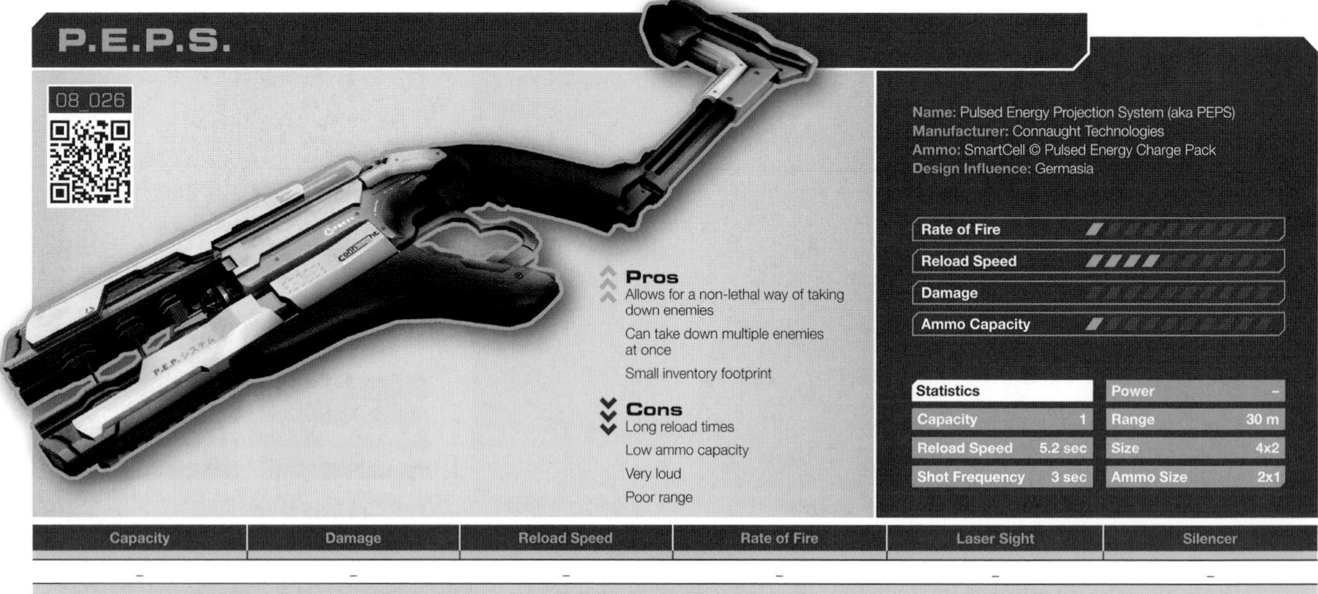

Capacity	Damage	Reload Speed	Rate of Fire	Laser Sight	Silencer
–	–	–	–	–	–
–	–	–	–	–	–

An experimental weapon design, recently introduced to the marketplace, the Pulsed Energy Projection System is a single-shot, non-lethal firearm capable of generating an immensely powerful, conical 'blast wave' of concussive force that will knock down enemy combatants and displace small or medium-weight objects in its firing range. It is most often used in military scenarios where threat forces must be disarmed and casualties kept to a minimum. Bear in mind, though, that the weapon has a long firing cycle, a short operational range, and a lengthy reload time. The PEPS does not support standard upgrade packages.

Usage

The PEPS is an oddity. It fires a concussive blast towards enemies in the form of a short-range wave of energy. This has the effect of knocking down human foes, and stunning robot ones for a short while. When you use it on a human target, they will drop their weapons, and either fall over temporarily and then get back up again, or be knocked out. This essentially means the PEPS is an excellent tool for going for no-kill runs and racking up experience bonuses. It's also a great of dealing with a group of enemies bunched together. A secondary feature of the gun is that can also knock away small to medium sized objects with incredible force, even into other enemies. Also, its inventory footprint is quite small, giving you the option of keeping it with you most of the time.

However, it isn't all sunshine and roses with the PEPS. Ammo is hard to come by, and the ammo capacity itself is stuck at 1 round per reload, so you had better make sure you hit your target. It isn't a massively loud weapon, but unless you can take out all the enemies near you, other enemies in the immediate vicinity will be alerted by the sound. There's also the long reload time, which cannot be improved via upgrades. The range is also quite short, meaning you'll need to be close to your targets when firing your shot. The wave-like nature of the projectile doesn't have a massive radius either, so enemies must be very closely grouped together. The random factor to the weapon can also be a serious liability, as you never immediately know if you have stunned your target or actually knocked them out. And none of these limitations can be compensated for via upgrades, as the PEPS is not compatible with any of them.

All these features equate to a very specialized weapon. On the one hand, it is incredibly loud, alerting everyone to your presence the moment you use it. However, if you can ensure that you hit all the enemies in the nearby vicinity in one shot, you will remain undetected and can then take them out with a close-range weapon while they recover, or use Takedowns. It is one of the best ways to deal with multiple enemies grouped together. The low inventory footprint and lack of upgrade compatibility means it's a low maintenance weapon that you can essentially forget about, and equip to use in those unique situations that only the PEPS can address.

Recommended Upgrades and Upgrade Effects

The PEPS is not compatible with any upgrades.

Upgrade Level (LV 0 is base stats)	LV 0	LV 1	LV 2	LV 3	LV 4
Damage Increase Per Upgrade Used	–	–	–	–	–
Ammo Capacity Increase Per Upgrade Used	1	–	–	–	–
Rate of Fire Increase Per Upgrade Used	3	–	–	–	–
Difference in Reload Speed Per Upgrade Used	5.2	–	–	–	–
DPS	–	–	–	–	–
Ammo Depletion Rate	3	–	–	–	–

Unique Upgrade: None

There is no unique upgrade for the PEPS.

Useful Augmentations

The PEPS is best used on a group of enemies, or to disrupt a particularly bothersome robotic obstacle. As such, you will want the means to get close to an enemy or enemies without being seen or heard. To this end, the Cloaking System and Silent Movement Augmentations are your best bet. You should also get the Multiple Takedown Augmentation, which will be useful to finish enemies off quickly after they have been knocked down by the PEPS.

Recommended Loadout

Style of play: Balanced, Close Combat, Heavy Gunner
Accompanying weapons: 10mm Pistol, Shotgun/Double-Barrel Shotgun, Heavy Rifle, Plasma Rifle, Rocket/Grenade Launcher, Combat Rifle, Revolver

If you're not particularly concerned about stealth, the PEPS can go well with several play styles. Whatever your primary method of play, the PEPS will generally serve the same purpose: to clear the immediate vicinity of enemies. Whether this is done to give you some space in a tight situation, help you take out all the unsuspecting guards in an area at once, or to give you time to move in on your helpless foes, the Balanced, Heavy Gunner and Close Combat styles will be well served. The accompanying weapons can be varied, and are generally designed for taking out your enemies quickly while they are stunned.

PLASMA RIFLE

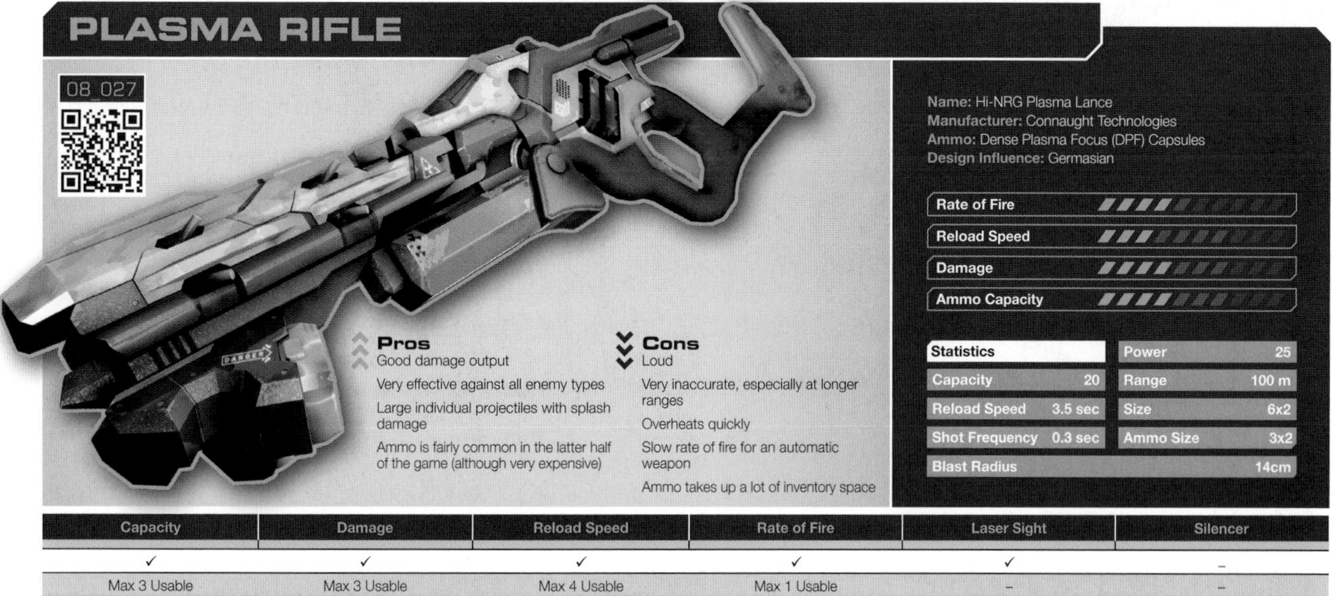

08_027

Name: Hi-NRG Plasma Lance
Manufacturer: Connaught Technologies
Ammo: Dense Plasma Focus (DPF) Capsules
Design Influence: Germasian

Rate of Fire
Reload Speed
Damage
Ammo Capacity

Pros
- Good damage output
- Very effective against all enemy types
- Large individual projectiles with splash damage
- Ammo is fairly common in the latter half of the game (although very expensive)

Cons
- Loud
- Very inaccurate, especially at longer ranges
- Overheats quickly
- Slow rate of fire for an automatic weapon
- Ammo takes up a lot of inventory space

Statistics			
Capacity	20	Power	25
Reload Speed	3.5 sec	Range	100 m
Shot Frequency	0.3 sec	Size	6x2
		Ammo Size	3x2
Blast Radius			14cm

Capacity	Damage	Reload Speed	Rate of Fire	Laser Sight	Silencer
✓	✓	✓	✓	✓	–
Max 3 Usable	Max 3 Usable	Max 4 Usable	Max 1 Usable	–	–

A next-generation weapon, the Plasma Lance is perhaps the most advanced battlefield weapon of the 2020s, a high-tech firearm that projects a 'bolt' or 'pulse' of superheated plasma down an ionized path toward its target. It can deliver heavy damage against medium and heavily-armored targets - enough to actually disintegrate some of them - but only at limited range and at a slow rate of fire. Sustained operation can also result in temporary shutdown due to overheating. The weapon supports all standard upgrades, as well as a special Internal Coolant Enhancement (ICE) package that can prevent it from overheating during sustained firing. It is also compatible with laser targeting systems.

Usage

The final evolution in the common rifle type weapons carried by enemies, the Plasma Rifle is a powerful weapon. This power is also equally effective versus all enemy types, armored or augmented, and will take out practically any humanoid enemy before a full clip runs out as long as they are direct shots, and that's before any Damage upgrades are applied. Ammo is hard to come by at first, but becomes more and more common near the later stages of the game. You can also buy it, but it is the most expensive ammo to buy.

It is compatible with every upgrade except the Silencer, and the Laser Targeting System especially helps accuracy. The reload speed is not the fastest, but is fairly quick. The projectiles themselves are quite large, making it more likely that you will hit your target. They also cause a small explosion on impact, not enough for you to rely on this feature, but large enough that if you spot an exposed foot from an enemy hiding behind cover, you can use the splash damage to take him out.

The Plasma Rifle is very loud, meaning it has practically no use as a stealth weapon. The accuracy is also quite poor. While it doesn't suffer from huge amounts of recoil, it does suffer significant reticule enlargement during movement. The reticule is already quite large to begin with, further demonstrating the weapon's inherent instability and tendency for shots to stray. And at anything other than close range, the shots will stray very far from their intended targets. Add to this the slow projectiles, and it means hitting a moving target is a herculean task. There is also the overheating issue, which is a massive problem when you have to deal with multiple enemies and don't have time to wait for the cooldown. The firing rate is also quite poor, and when each shot contributes towards overheating, it is costly to miss any shots. The ammo is also quite bulky, so the total inventory footprint is quite big.

Recommended Upgrades and Upgrade Effects

The Plasma Rifle benefits most from Ammo Capacity upgrades, especially once you apply the Cooling System. Be wary of upgrading the rate of fire too much, as this will just cause you to overheat quicker. Also, you should apply a Laser Targeting System attachment to the weapon as soon as possible, to alleviate some of the accuracy issues.

Upgrade Level (LV 0 is base stats)	LV 0	LV 1	LV 2	LV 3	LV 4
Damage Increase Per Upgrade Used	25	27.5	30	32.5	–
Ammo Capacity Increase Per Upgrade Used	20	30	40	50	–
Rate of Fire Increase Per Upgrade Used	0.3	0.25	–	–	–
Difference in Reload Speed Per Upgrade Used	3.5	3.2	2.9	2.6	2.3
DPS	83.33	110	120	130	–
Ammo Depletion Rate	6	7.5	–	–	–

Unique Upgrade: Cooling System

Name: Internal Coolant Enhancement (ICE) package for Weapons
Manufacturer: Connaught Technologies

The Cooling System is absolutely vital to the Plasma Rifle, as it will completely eliminate overheating. For sheer power and effectiveness against all enemy types, the Plasma Rifle is worth investing the upgrade into. However, you should definitely try get two of this upgrade and use it on both weapons if they are both in your arsenal.

Useful Augmentations

If you don't want to use a laser targeting system on the Plasma Rifle, it's a good idea to use the Aim Stabilizer series of Augmentations to try to help accuracy problems. This is a weapon designed for end-game firefights, and as such you will need the Dermal Amour series of Augmentations to survive for long. The Wall-Penetrating Imager can also be handy to see enemies hiding behind corners and then take them out with splash damage.

Recommended Loadout

Style of play: Balanced, Heavy Gunner
Accompanying weapons: 10mm Pistol, Sniper/Silenced Sniper Rifle, Crossbow, Tranquilizer Rifle, the PEPS, Rocket/Grenade Launcher

The Plasma Rifle can fill the role of a powerful automatic weapon late in the game. The rest of your arsenal should be designed to compensate for its lack of range, accuracy and stealth. The 10mm Pistol and various ranged weapons can give you quieter and more long-range options, while the Rocket Launcher also gives you significant power and range, compensating for the need for accuracy with a huge blast radius.

LASER RIFLE

Capacity	Damage	Reload Speed	Rate of Fire	Laser Sight	Silencer
✓	✓	✓	–	–	–
Max 4 Usable	Max 3 Usable	Max 3 Usable	–	–	–

A next-generation firearm, the LS-66 Laser Rifle is a prototype, constant-beam, battlefield laser weapon, designed for engagements against enemy infantry and light armor. The weapon has limited range and a long reload time, and is somewhat cumbersome compared to ballistic weapons. However, the rifle's single, constant beam of powerful energy can penetrate low-density obstacles and cover to deliver damage directly to concealed targets. Still an experimental first-block prototype, the LS-66 Sabre Directed Energy Rifle is not compatible with sound suppressors or laser targeting system add-ons. It does, however, accept upgrades for reload speed, damage output, and ammo capacity.

Usage

The prototype Laser Rifle is a one-of-a-kind weapon that you can only get in one place in the game. This is quite late in the campaign, so you won't get to enjoy the significant advantages the Laser Rifle offers until quite late. And what a set of advantages...

The Laser Rifle is the only weapon that can pierce obstacles, such as thin walls and pieces of cover that your enemies might hide behind. Combine this with the Wall-Penetrating Imager Augmentation, and you have a weapon that your enemies can never hide from. The weapon also packs absolutely devastating power, outputting it in a steady beam form. This allows it to have the highest DPS in the game, wrecking any enemy after a few seconds of sustained use. You can also afford to be a bit more liberal in its use, keeping the beam going and strafing it across several foes, preferably near the head area to get even faster kills.

The massive capacity of each clip allows you to keep the beam going for as long as necessary, with no risk of overheating. Being a pinpoint laser, the weapon is incredibly precise, as you would expect. There is no targeting reticule, but it does have a scope for more precise shots. The zoomed view will indicate the distance to a target once you have them lined up in your sights. Going for headshots on enemies on the other side of a wall using the Wall-Penetrating Imager is a very powerful tactic. It also does not suffer from recoil or reticule enlargement in any way whatsoever. Just like the Plasma Rifle, the Laser Rifle is also very effective against all enemy types.

The Laser Rifle, while still an incredible weapon, has some problems. The lack of a targeting reticule when firing from the hip is a problem, usually causing you to fire once to see exactly where your beam is going. It is also quite loud, so while you can still fire from the other side of a wall to attack your foes, they will immediately head towards your location. This can be used to your advantage, however, to lay traps. For example, hiding in a room and firing at some enemies on the other side of the wall in the corridor will immediately grab their attention. While they head towards the room to investigate, you will have ample time to lay a Frag or Gas Mine and hide. The ammo availability is also quite poor, and you will either have to pay a lot to purchase the ammo from a vendor, or try to conserve ammo as much as possible.

Recommended Upgrades and Upgrade Effects

The first thing you should do is upgrade the already impressive capacity of the Laser Rifle to its maximum level, which will grant you an insane 900 round clip. Upgrading the power is the next step, making each one of those 900 rounds incredibly potent. Bosses and Box Guards will crumble at the mere sight of the powerhouse you wield.

Upgrade Level (LV 0 is base stats)	LV 0	LV 1	LV 2	LV 3	LV 4
Damage Increase Per Upgrade Used	50	55	60	65	–
Ammo Capacity Increase Per Upgrade Used	500	600	700	800	900
Rate of Fire Increase Per Upgrade Used	0.012	–	–	–	–
Difference in Reload Speed Per Upgrade Used	6	5.7	5.4	5.1	–
DPS	50	55	60	65	–
Ammo Depletion Rate	6	7.2	8.4	9.6	10.8

Unique Upgrade: None

The Laser Rifle does not have a unique upgrade.

Useful Augmentations

The most important Augmentation to use here is the Wall-Penetrating Imager. Having the ability to see through walls while using a weapon that can penetrate said walls is a no-brainer. It is also worth getting the Cloaking System. Since using the Laser Rifle is a loud activity, you want to be gone when nearby enemies come to investigate. The Noise Feedback Augmentation can also give you an idea of how far the noise of your laser bursts is traveling, allowing you to be at the optimal range to remain undetected.

Recommended Loadout

Style of play: Balanced, Heavy Gunner, Sniper
Accompanying weapons: 10mm Pistol, Machine Pistol, Combat Rifle, Heavy Rifle, Crossbow, Tranquilizer Rifle, Plasma Rifle

The Laser Rifle should have a home in any arsenal. The capabilities it brings to the table are too good to pass up. However, it is of particular benefit to the Heavy Gunner and Sniper play styles. In the middle of an intense firefight while you are laying down suppressing fire with your automatic weapons, the Laser Rifle will be invaluable to take out enemies that have fled for cover. The Sniper can make use of the great range and accuracy, not to mention using the Wall-Penetrating Imager, to snipe foes from behind cover. The incredible power of the weapon also makes it a perfect Boss killing weapon.

STUN GUN

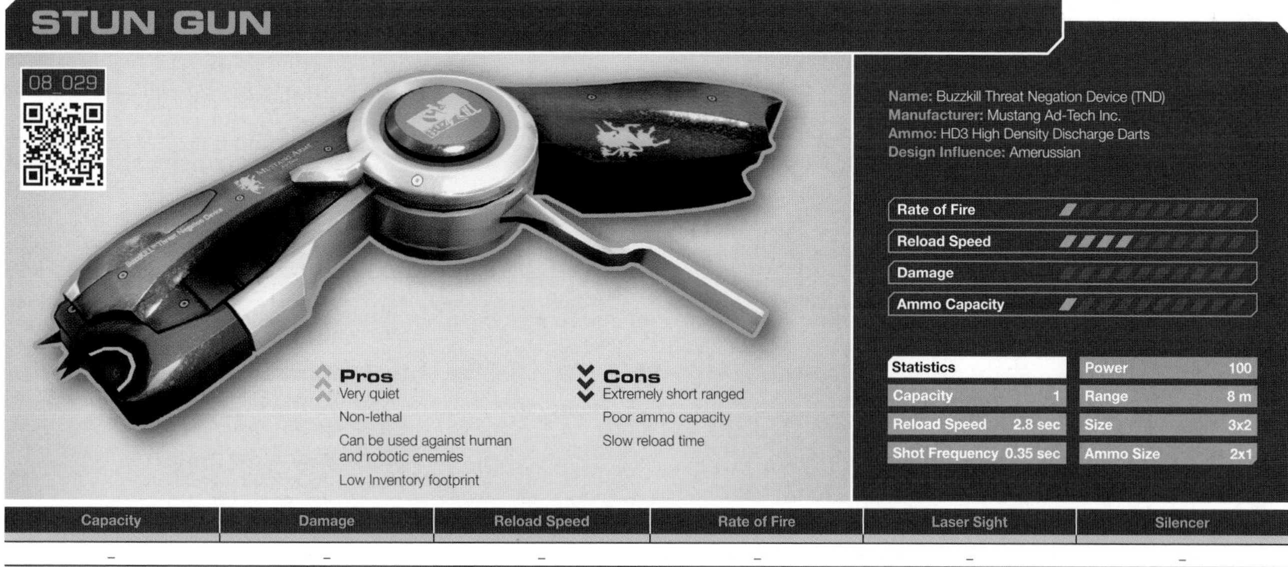

Capacity	Damage	Reload Speed	Rate of Fire	Laser Sight	Silencer
–	–	–	–	–	–
–	–	–	–	–	–

The Buzzkill Threat Negation Device is a single-shot, non-lethal firearm that uses an intense electroshock discharge to render targets unconscious. While easy to conceal, the weapon has a short range, slow firing cycle, and lengthy reload time. It is primarily for use against organic targets, but is also effective in temporarily disabling security cameras, Turrets and robots. The Buzzkill Threat Negation Device cannot be upgraded.

Usage

The Stun Gun can be acquired very early on in the game if chosen by the player. It comes in handy throughout the game, allowing you to take out the most dangerous of human and Augmented human opponents with a single shot. In many ways, it's the weapon equivalent of a melee Takedown; a silent, close range non-lethal way to take down your enemy. The very small inventory footprint is also great, as more often than not you can just chuck it into your inventory and forget about it until you need it. It is also useable against robotic enemies, temporarily stunning them. This is quite risky, however, and if you are close enough to use it and have not yet been seen, you're probably better off sneaking past.

In a desperate firefight against a Box Guard, the few seconds the Stun Gun can buy could save your life. Against groups of humanoid opponents, you can still use the weapon effectively despite the need to be close to your enemy. Get into cover near your first target and pop out to take him down with the Stun Gun. Other enemies nearby will see the prone body of the first and come to wake him. Take this opportunity to pop out and take out the curious guard [→□ 1]. You can quickly take out an entire patrol this way as long as you are careful (and have enough ammo!).

The real problem with the Stun Gun is its extremely short range. You will have to execute the sometimes extremely dangerous task of getting close to your opponent before you can do anything. And then you have to ensure you are not spotted by anyone else as you pop out to take your shot. And if someone else did spot you, you won't be taking them out in a hurry, as the single shot capacity means you will be reloading after one use, and the reload time is long enough to make this a serious problem. A lot of the time, a simple non-lethal Takedown can perform the same job, at the cost of energy that will automatically come back. However, the Stun Gun can still be handy against robotic enemies.

Recommended Upgrades and Upgrade Effects

The Stun Gun is not compatible with any upgrades.

Upgrade Level (LV 0 is base stats)	LV 0	LV 1	LV 2	LV 3	LV 4
Damage Increase Per Upgrade Used	100	–	–	–	–
Ammo Capacity Increase Per Upgrade Used	1	–	–	–	–
Rate of Fire Increase Per Upgrade Used	0.35	–	–	–	–
Difference in Reload Speed Per Upgrade Used	2.8	–	–	–	–
DPS	285.7	–	–	–	–
Ammo Depletion Rate	0.35	–	–	–	–

Unique Upgrade: None

The Stun Gun does not have a unique upgrade.

Useful Augmentations

You will need to get close to your enemies without being seen, so the Cloaking System and Silent Movement Augmentations are a must. In fact, if your gameplan is primarily stealth and the Stun Gun is your weapon of choice, you will need to be cloaked and silent often, so purchasing the getting the Sarif Series 8 Energy Converter Augmentations would be a wise purchase, particularly the Energy Level Upgrade Augmentations. You will also be in close quarters constantly, and should something go wrong, having the Multiple Takedown Augmentation ready to go at a tap of a button will be very useful.

Recommended Loadout

Style of play: Balanced, Stealth
Accompanying weapons: Tranquilizer Rifle, 10mm Pistol, Crossbow, Revolver, Combat Rifle, Plasma Rifle

The Stun Gun is a great weapon to have around when you want to go for non-lethal stealth. The experience bonuses for dealing with enemies in this way are good, so you'll probably want to do it often. While the Stealth user should be more concerned with trying to avoid engaging the enemy, the Stun Gun is a great second alternative. It is also a low inventory cost stealth option for the Balanced style, where inventory management is vital. The rest of your arsenal should have better range or more lethality, with something for dealing with Bosses.

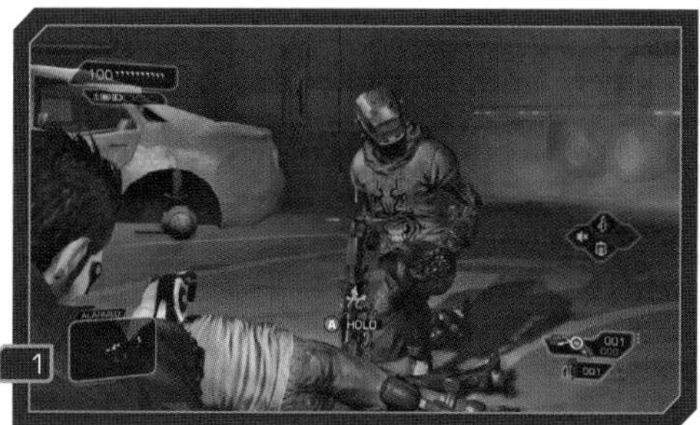

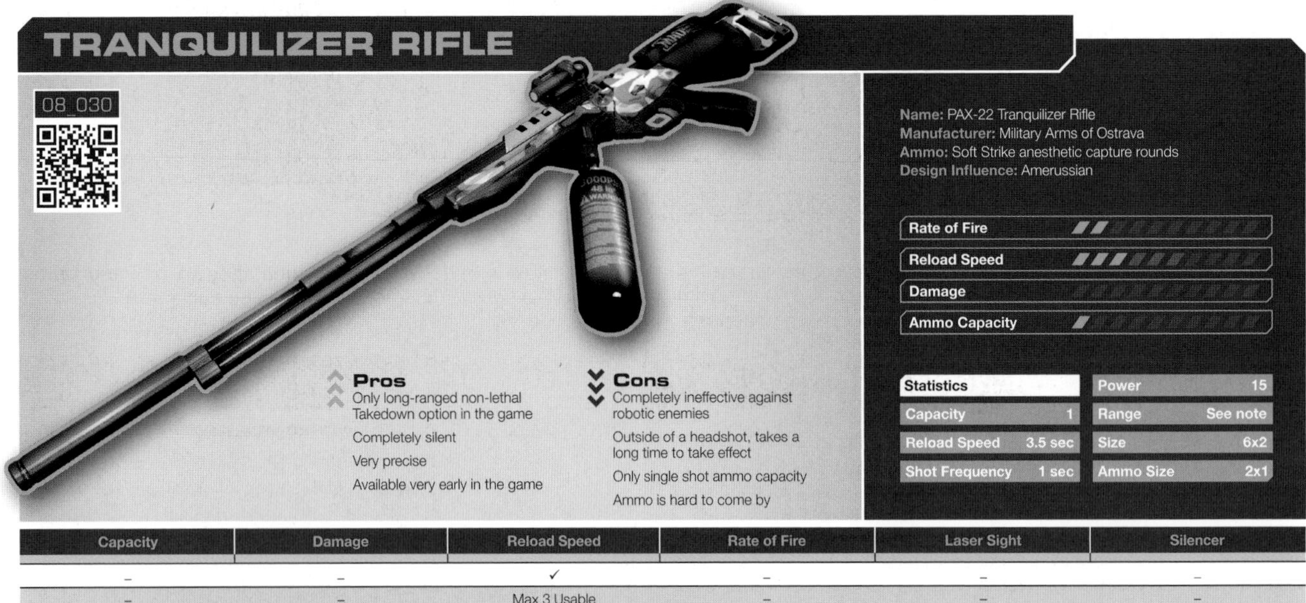

Capacity	Damage	Reload Speed	Rate of Fire	Laser Sight	Silencer
–	–	✓	–	–	–
–	–	Max 3 Usable	–	–	–

A non-lethal weapon developed for capture operations on wildlife and other organic targets, the PAX-22 Tranquilizer Rifle is very accurate at long-range, extremely precise, and virtually silent; however, it can fire only a single round at a time and its reloading action is slow. The weapon's drug load induces torpor and unconsciousness, but has no effect on non-organic targets. The PAX-22 supports standard reload speed upgrades. It also has a targeting scope built in to its design; therefore, accuracy can be improved via the LeadFire Targeting Suite, a special upgrade package that uses scope-leading software to predict a target's movements.

Usage

You can get the Tranquilizer Rifle more or less at the start of the game if you so choose. This gives you access to a very handy silent weapon early on. The high zoom and the non-lethal nature of the weapon make it excellent for racking up experience points from the relative safety of long-range, as you can score Marksman and non-lethal Takedown experience bonuses in one shot. The Tranquilizer Rifle also shares some similarities with the Crossbow, in that it employs the same physics-based system to determine the range and arc of darts fired. This means that the weapon has practically limitless range, but you will have to compensate for the dip of the dart. Also like the Crossbow, you can use the sound of the impact of the darts hitting a solid surface as a distraction tool to lure enemies away.

It also shares some of the Crossbow's more negative traits. The single round capacity and bolt action nature of the weapon mean you will be reloading after every shot,; very dangerous if the anesthetic doesn't take effect immediately. Which it won't if you don't land a headshot. Landing a dart anywhere else means it will take much longer to knock the enemy out. Also, it is much less effective against armored and augmented foes, and completely useless against robots. And of course you will still need a lethal option against Bosses.

Ammo is more rare than for some of the other weapons, as none of the enemies you encounter will carry it, meaning you will have to rely on finding it or buying it. It also has almost no compatibility with upgrades, save for Reload Speed ones. Add this to the fact that you will only be knocking your enemies out, which means that there is a chance they could be revived by their allies (although this can also be a useful tactic to employ, by using the unconscious body of one enemy to lure another one in, then taking him out too). And finally, the inventory footprint is fairly large, so serious consideration should be paid before committing to the Tranquilizer Rifle.

Recommended Upgrades and Upgrade Effects

Upgrade Level (LV 0 is base stats)	LV 0	LV 1	LV 2	LV 3	LV 4
Damage Increase Per Upgrade Used	15	–	–	–	–
Ammo Capacity Increase Per Upgrade Used	1	–	–	–	–
Rate of Fire Increase Per Upgrade Used	1	–	–	–	–
Difference in Reload Speed Per Upgrade Used	3.5	3.2	2.9	2.6	–
DPS	15	–	–	–	–
Ammo Depletion Rate	1	–	–	–	–

The Tranquilizer Rifle only actually supports one standard upgrade: Reload Speed. However, it is worth investing in, since you will be reloading often, and sometimes you will need to fire multiple rounds to ensure your target goes down as fast as possible.

Unique Upgrade: Target Leading Software

Name: LeadFire Targeting Suite
Manufacturer: Connaught Technologies

The aforementioned Target Leading Software can also be used on the Tranquilizer Rifle, as well as the Crossbow. Using it here will reap benefits in similar situations as the Crossbow, and where you spend it will come down to which weapon you use more. There is slightly more chance you will find it more useful here though. When an enemy spots his ally unconscious and runs over to him to wake up, you will only have a short time to take him out before he revives his ally. The Targeting Suite can help out here, allowing you to take out the new enemy before he ever gets to his unconscious buddy.

Useful Augmentations

Being both an effective long-range weapon and a good stealth weapon, there are several Augmentations that can aid you here. Mark and Track, Jump Enhancement and the Wall-Penetrating Imager can help you spot your enemies, get the drop on them and get into advantageous positions more easily. On the stealth side, Silent Running and the Cloaking System can help you stay hidden as you carry out your attacks.

Recommended Loadout

Style of play: Stealth, Sniper
Accompanying weapons: Sniper Rifle /Silenced Sniper Rifle, Crossbow, 10mm Pistol, Laser Rifle

The Tranquilizer Rifle fits in well with both the Stealth and Sniper play styles, much like the Crossbow. It essentially can give you either a non-lethal option or a silenced option, filling whichever hole you may have in your loadout.

EXPLOSIVES

Explosives in Deus Ex fall into one of two categories, Grenades or Mines. They are the third option you have in the trio of offensive capabilities that are available to you, along with your main weapons and Augmentations. As such, they are an important part of your arsenal and should always be considered for use in any situation.

GRENADES

Grenades are commonly found dotted around the game world, and can be purchased from vendors. By and large, they are incredibly useful, as they take up a tiny amount of inventory space, and can potentially clear a group of enemies, human or robotic, lethally or non-lethally. The drawbacks are their inherent inaccuracy and the need to be relatively close to your target, but they are very important tools that should have a place in every inventory.

General Usage

Depending on your style of play, you will find yourself using some grenades more than others, although they can all be useful in certain situations. There are a few general guidelines that apply to all grenades that you should be mindful of.

Grenades can be held, but not 'cooked' like other FPS games. What this essentially means is that holding the Secondary Weapon button will prepare to throw the grenade, but not start its timer, so you can hold it indefinitely until you choose to release the button. It will then explode after a set time of around 3 seconds. The timer only starts once the grenade comes to a rest on the floor, so you can throw it a great distance and the grenade will still wait for 3 seconds before it explodes after it comes to a rest. This timer is the same for all grenades.

You'll obviously want to match the grenade to the job. Don't feel as if you have to wait for a cluster of enemies before you are compelled to use one. If a particular enemy or electrical obstacle is giving you trouble, don't hesitate to use a grenade if it will solve the problem. They are quite plentiful and easy to obtain. Also remember that when throwing a grenade, enemies are drawn towards the source of the throw, i.e. you, not the sound of the explosion [→☐ 1]. You won't be able to use the explosion as a means of luring the enemy to where you want them.

1
2

There are plenty of other ways to group your enemies together. Use the sound of a Crossbow bolt or Tranquilizer dart to send your enemies to a specific location, or throw a small object [→☐ 2]. Remember that until you purchase the specific Augmentations, you are susceptible to your own grenades, and that your EMP grenades will work on Augmented humans, not just cameras and bots. However, Gas Grenades will not have any effect on mechanical enemies, nor will Concussion Grenades. Your Frag Grenades are equally potent against all enemy types, so remember that you have them when you go toe-to-toe with a Boss.

MINES

3

There are a few ways of acquiring mines in Deus Ex: Human Revolution. You can purchase them from vendors, or find, disarm and collect them in the game world. Finally, you can also create your own mines, by combining a grenade with a Mine Template item, which will subsequently give you the mine of the type of grenade you used.

General Usage

The big advantage of mines is that you can be anywhere you want when they go off. Setting off a Fragmentation Mine, while making the enemy alert, will not send them instantly in your direction. If you lay the mine further along the route of the enemy you are targeting while out of sight, you'll never be seen. Waiting for your enemy to stumble into the path of the mine also gives you ample time to get into an advantageous position and switch to another weapon, so you can immediately finish off your enemy [→☐ 3]. For example, waiting for a group of guards to walk towards a Concussion Mine while you wait in cover with a Heavy Rifle primed is a deadly scenario for your enemies. Mines also have some use in more direct firefights. Since they are thrown and immediately stick to the first surface they hit (not including the actual bodies of enemies), you can throw them at the feet of particularly quick or hard to find enemies, like Shifters [→☐ 1]. Unlike a grenade, there's no risk of you missing with the mine, as it will only go off once the enemy walks near it.

You can also choose to set the mine off yourself, by firing at it. If an enemy has walked by but isn't quite close enough to set the mine off, shooting it yourself can still detonate it. You can also detonate enemy mines this way, saving you the hassle of having to first disarm them and then lay them again. Remember not long after you set the mine, you yourself are also susceptible to setting it off, so clear the vicinity immediately. You will also want to be careful when laying the mine, as the sound of the impact of the mine landing is actually a little noisy, and can alert nearby enemies. Although, chances are that if they were close enough to hear it, it will probably be the last sound they ever hear.

In terms of inventory space, mines are something of a double-edged sword. On the one hand, they take up 2 inventory blocks each, twice as much as a grenade, however, they make up for this in a big way by being stackable, a feature they enjoy over Grenades. They also require an extra item, a Mine Template, if you are planning to make them yourself. This means multiple mines of the same type will only take up the same 2 inventory blocks, up to a maximum set of 3 (if you are carrying more than three mines of the same type, they will take up another set of 2 inventory blocks). The Remote Detonated Explosive Device is also stackable, up to a maximum of 2 per set of inventory blocks.

Disarming Mines

Once you've actually spotted an enemy mine in the wild, you'll most likely want to disarm it so you can collect it and use it yourself. Doing so is simple. Just approach the mine very slowly, at walking pace (crouch if you need to). Once you are close enough, you can disarm it and collect it by highlighting it with your targeting reticule and then pressing the Interact button [→☐ 2]. Remember that you can always just choose it from a distance if you want instead.

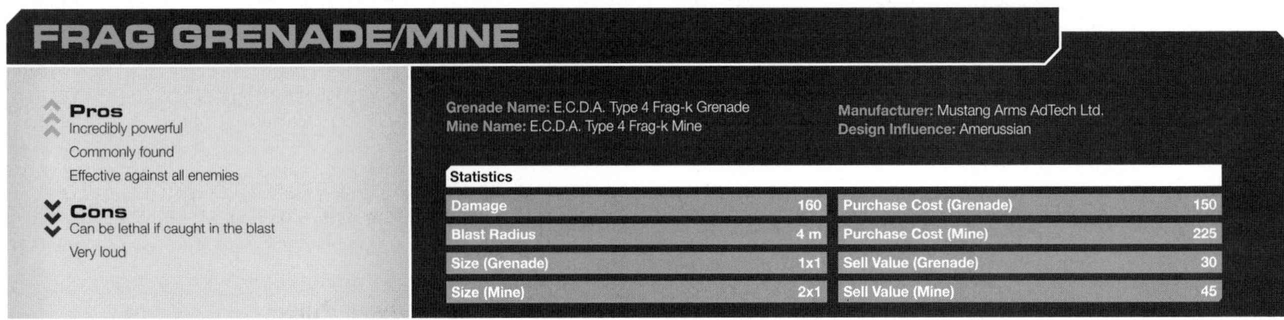

FRAG GRENADE/MINE

Pros
Incredibly powerful
Commonly found
Effective against all enemies

Cons
Can be lethal if caught in the blast
Very loud

Grenade Name: E.C.D.A. Type 4 Frag-k Grenade
Mine Name: E.C.D.A. Type 4 Frag-k Mine

Manufacturer: Mustang Arms AdTech Ltd.
Design Influence: Amerussian

Statistics			
Damage	160	Purchase Cost (Grenade)	150
Blast Radius	4 m	Purchase Cost (Mine)	225
Size (Grenade)	1x1	Sell Value (Grenade)	30
Size (Mine)	2x1	Sell Value (Mine)	45

A basic but effective hand-thrown explosive device, the Type 4 Frag-k is typical of most fragmentation grenade designs in use in combat zones around the world. Modern polymers, high-density explosives, and configured shrapnel elements make this a singularly deadly weapon, especially when used against unarmored targets at close range. The Type 4 cannot be upgraded, but it is configured for modular use: combining it with the Mark 87 Tactical Munition Mine Template will turn it into a highly effective 'fragmentation mine'. The Fragmentation Mine is a static anti-personnel munition; a modular variant of the E.C.D.A. Type 4 Frag-k Grenade, made possible by the Mark 87 Tactical Munition Mine Template (TMMT). The mine is sensitive to vibrations from approaching targets and, when triggered, immediately sends high-velocity shrapnel exploding outward. It can be attached to most surfaces and is active within seconds of deployment.

Usage

The basic Frag Grenade is an incredibly powerful tool, even taking out Box Guards in a few grenades. It's also great for Bosses. The good blast radius will damage and stagger enemies if it does not kill them outright, giving you the opportunity to finish them off [→☐ 3]. This makes it a great tool for flushing enemies out of cover. It's also a good option for taking out a security camera or Turret from outside their range. Be careful when blind throwing it from cover, however, or when throwing it in a tight confined space. It isn't very bouncy, so if it hits a wall or other surface it will come to a rest quickly, and getting caught in the blast will probably equal death.

In mine form it is not quite as useful. It wont have much use as a stealth tool as it still incredibly loud, and it is difficult to get multiple enemies to walk into the path of the mine at the same time, meaning you will only be able to take out a single enemy. It can still be used as a somewhat makeshift grenade by throwing it towards fast moving enemies in a firefight, and either detonating it manually with gunfire or letting the enemy do it. [→☐ 4]

Recommended Style of Play

The Frag Grenade and Mine definitely promote an aggressive style, but their devastating power can also help in other ways. As such, it can benefit all styles, but especially the Heavy Gunner and Stealth styles. The enemy will often take cover when you lay down heavy suppressing fire, so using Frag Grenades to flush them out is a good tactic. The great power of the Frag Grenade is useful when you don't have many other hard hitting or powerful weapons, so it can help out Stealth loadouts by taking out Bosses. This is a good enough reason for all styles to carry it, and all inventories should carry a few for Box Guards, Ogres and Bosses.

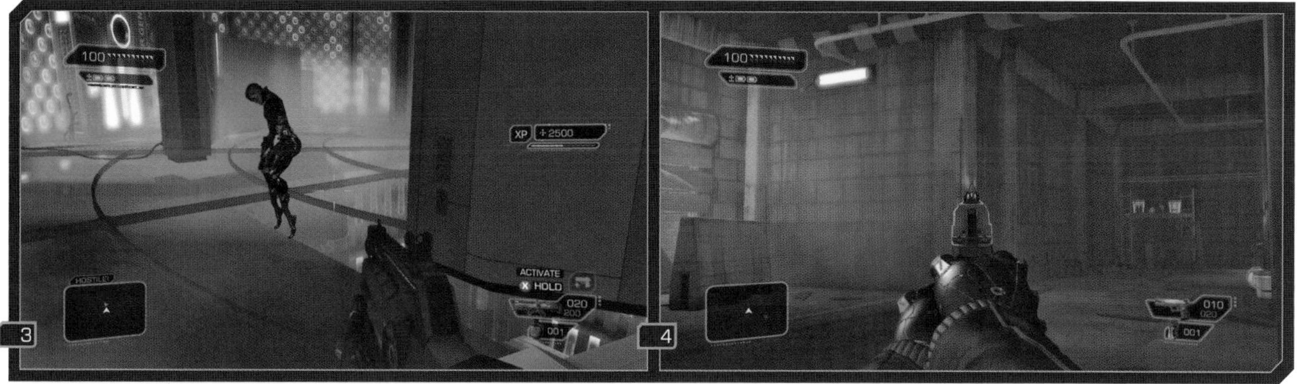

CONCUSSION GRENADE/MINE

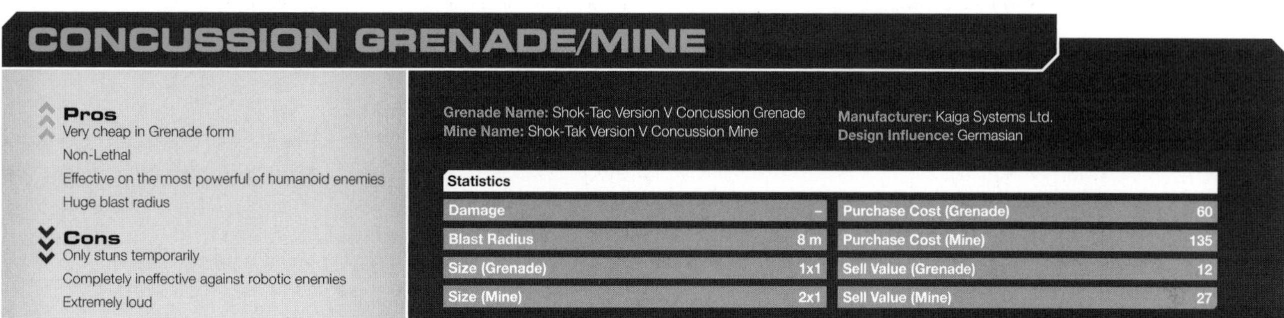

Pros
- Very cheap in Grenade form
- Non-Lethal
- Effective on the most powerful of humanoid enemies
- Huge blast radius

Cons
- Only stuns temporarily
- Completely ineffective against robotic enemies
- Extremely loud

Grenade Name: Shok-Tac Version V Concussion Grenade
Mine Name: Shok-Tak Version V Concussion Mine
Manufacturer: Kaiga Systems Ltd.
Design Influence: Germasian

Statistics			
Damage	–	Purchase Cost (Grenade)	60
Blast Radius	8 m	Purchase Cost (Mine)	135
Size (Grenade)	1x1	Sell Value (Grenade)	12
Size (Mine)	2x1	Sell Value (Mine)	27

The Shok-Tac Concussion Grenade is a non-fragmenting, hand-thrown munition that uses explosive overpressure to damage and disorient targets at close range. The Version V combines the common function of a concussion grenade with the noise/flash capability of a diversionary device (or 'flashbang') for a 'one-two-three punch'. It is most effective against organic targets at close quarters in a confined environment, but has zero effect on robots. The Shok-Tac Version V cannot be upgraded, but is configured for modular use. Combining it with the Mark 87 Tactical Munition Mine Template will turn the grenade into a highly effective 'concussion mine'. The Concussion Mine is a static diversionary ordnance; a modular variant of the Shok-Tac Version V Grenade, made possible by the Mark 87 Tactical Munition Mine Template (TMMT). Sensitive to vibrations from approaching targets, this non-fragmenting mine damages and disorients combatants with a concussive detonation and sensory overload upon explosion. It can be attached to most surfaces and is active within seconds of deployment.

Usage

The biggest reason to use the Concussion Grenade is because it is so cheap. It is readily available from most vendors for a paltry sum. As such, you can be much more liberal with its use. It is still a very loud explosive however, even more so than the Frag Grenade, so stealth isn't really a viable option when using it. It is also useful at practically every stage of the game, since it will work on every humanoid enemy, augmented or not, even the deadly Ogres [→☐ 5]. This can give you ample time to run in and finish them off with a Takedown or other close range weapon, or to escape the area. It also has the biggest effective blast radius of all explosives, meaning you are likely to stun most of the enemies in the area if you throw it into the center. The huge blast radius means that you are also likely to be caught in its effects, so turn away from the explosive before it detonates to stop that from happening. Failing that, you can also purchase the Flash Suppressant Augmentation.

You are probably better off avoiding using the Concussion explosive in mine form, as it is far more useful as a grenade. In a closely guarded corridor, it can stun a patrolling guard long enough for you to run past, or run in for a Takedown.

Recommended Style of Play

The Concussion Grenade is loud and can buy you valuable time in a firefight. The Close Quarter style in particular benefits from it, as the stun time is long enough for you to run in and take out all your helpless foes. Throwing the explosive from cover will keep you shielded from its effects, and as soon as it has gone off you can run in from out of cover and move closer. [→☐ 6]

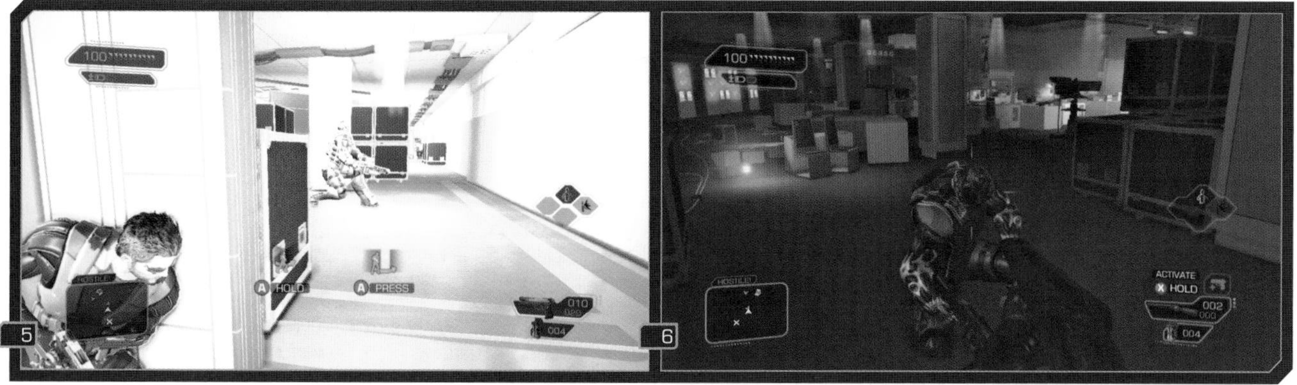

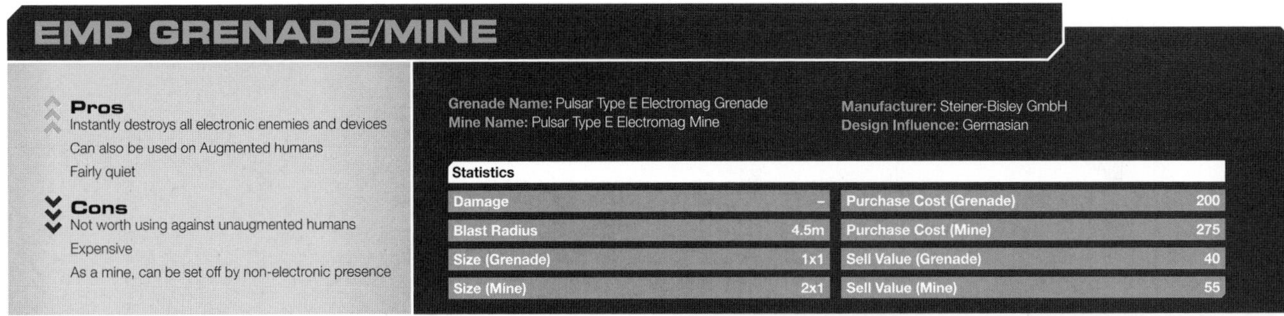

EMP GRENADE/MINE

Pros
- Instantly destroys all electronic enemies and devices
- Can also be used on Augmented humans
- Fairly quiet

Cons
- Not worth using against unaugmented humans
- Expensive
- As a mine, can be set off by non-electronic presence

Grenade Name: Pulsar Type E Electromag Grenade
Mine Name: Pulsar Type E Electromag Mine
Manufacturer: Steiner-Bisley GmbH
Design Influence: Germasian

Statistics			
Damage	–	Purchase Cost (Grenade)	200
Blast Radius	4.5m	Purchase Cost (Mine)	275
Size (Grenade)	1x1	Sell Value (Grenade)	40
Size (Mine)	2x1	Sell Value (Mine)	55

A hand-thrown device, the Pulsar Type E Electomag Grenade is a specialized anti-systems grenade, capable of generating a localized electromagnetic field pulse that renders nearby electronic circuitry inoperative. While it has no effect against organic targets, the grenade is extremely useful in disabling robots, augmented humans, security cameras, and automated defensive Turrets. The Pulsar Type E cannot be upgraded, but can be turned into a highly effective 'EMP mine' when combined with the Mark 87 Tactical Munition Mine Template. The EMP Mine is a static anti-systems munition; a modular variant of the Pulsar type E Electromag Grenade, made possible by the Mark 87 Tactical Munition Mine Template (TMMT). Sensitive to vibrations from approaching targets, the mine generates an electromagnetic pulse field upon detonation that renders nearby electronic circuitry inoperative. It is especially useful for disabling robots and augmented combatants. The mine is active within seconds of deployment and can be attached to most surfaces.

1

Usage

The EMP Grenade is an absolutely invaluable tool for taking out electronic obstacles. Powerful enough that it can take out a Box Guard in a single blast, it also works on security cameras, Turrets and Medium Sentries. It can also temporarily stagger augmented humans, not as long as a Concussion Grenade would, but enough for you to find cover or try to escape. It is great to use on stationary electrical devices like cameras and turrets from outside of their range, so you can take them out without much hassle. The explosions themselves are also relatively quiet for explosives, as long as you detonate it around 5 meters away from a nearby enemy, you will go unheard. [→☐ 1]

The EMP explosive does have some decent utility as a mine. Patrolling Medium Sentries can prove to be difficult to deal with, an EMP Mine can deal with them handily [→☐ 2]. However, you will have to be careful when placing it, as it can actually be set off by non-augmented humans, essentially wasting it.

Recommended Style of Play

The EMP explosives should be used with every style, since you will always have to deal with robotic threats no matter how you play. They fit in well with Stealth styles, since they are fairly quiet and can deal with solitary threats like cameras to help keep you hidden. The Sniper can also use them from long-range to deal with Box Guards from well outside their range.

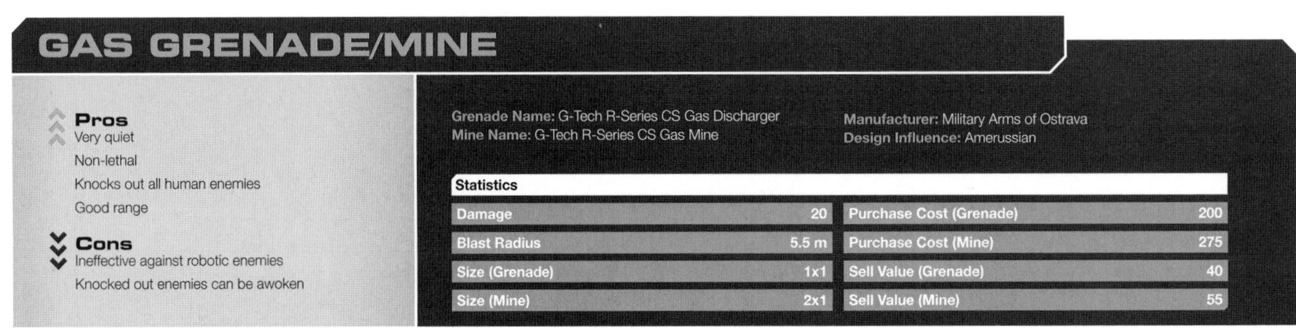

GAS GRENADE/MINE

Pros
- Very quiet
- Non-lethal
- Knocks out all human enemies
- Good range

Cons
- Ineffective against robotic enemies
- Knocked out enemies can be awoken

Grenade Name: G-Tech R-Series CS Gas Discharger
Mine Name: G-Tech R-Series CS Gas Mine
Manufacturer: Military Arms of Ostrava
Design Influence: Amerussian

Statistics			
Damage	20	Purchase Cost (Grenade)	200
Blast Radius	5.5 m	Purchase Cost (Mine)	275
Size (Grenade)	1x1	Sell Value (Grenade)	40
Size (Mine)	2x1	Sell Value (Mine)	55

The R-Series CS Gas Discharger is a standard tactical anti-personnel gas grenade, capable of discharging CS gas (also known as tear gas) over a defined radius. A hand-thrown device, the grenade has no effect against inorganic targets or targets equipped with sealed environment masks or rebreather augmentations; however, against unprotected organic targets, the discharge cloud causes temporary loss of vision and a nausea reaction. The gas grenade is not upgradeable, but can be turned into a very effective 'gas mine' when combined with the Mark 87 Tactical Munition Mine Template. The Gas Mine is a static anti-personnel tear gas delivery system; a modular variant of the G-Tech R-Series CS Gas Discharger, made possible by the Mark 87 Tactical Munition Mine Template (TMMT). The mine is sensitive to vibrations from approaching targets and active within seconds of deployment. Upon detonation, it releases a cloud of CS (tear) gas, which incapacitates unprotected targets. It can be attached to most surfaces.

Usage

Arguably the best explosive device in the game, the Gas Grenade is excellent for a multitude of reasons. It is very quiet so you can maintain stealth while using it, and the blast radius is very good. It also works very quickly putting enemies to sleep almost instantly, even tougher Augmentations like Ogres [→☐ 3]. The fact that you dealt with your enemies non-lethally means it is great for harvesting experience points.

As a mine, it is also excellent. Thanks to it being relatively quiet, you can set a trap for a patrolling enemy and move on without having to worry about it. Also, if multiple guards patrol the same path, after one is taken out you can wait nearby while his companion comes to wake him and use the opportunity to take him out too.

Recommended Style of Play

Obviously, the gas-related explosives are excellent for Stealth play styles. It's worth carrying a few all the time, but they are quite rare, so be selective in where you choose to use them. It's important to note Gas Grenades don't end Boss fights. Instead, some bosses will start coughing in the gas cloud in a semi stunned state leaving the player an opportunity to carefully line up their shots without fear of counter attack.

REMOTE DETONATED EXPLOSIVE DEVICE (BONUS DLC)

Pros
- Can be picked up again if misplaced or unused
- Very powerful
- Stackable

Cons
- Loud
- Takes up as twice as much inventory space as a Frag Grenade
- Does not stick to surfaces

Name: M-28 Utility Remote-Detonated Explosive Device (UR-DED)

Manufacturer: Steiner-Bisley GmbH
Design Influence: Unknown

Statistics			
Damage	160	Purchase Cost	200
Blast Radius	4m	Sell Value	40
Size	2x1		

A next-generation iteration of the venerable 'satchel charge' demolition/anti-armor device, the M-28 is a user-deployed explosive twinned to a handheld short-range wireless radio detonator. The M-28 is versatile, capable of working alone against a single target, or being slaved to other M-28 devices to create simultaneous explosions over a large area. Detonation is equally versatile, using either direct-fire targeting, environmental triggers like pressure or temperature, or a remote trigger.

Usage

The Remote Detonated Explosive Device is essentially a Frag Mine that does not stick to surfaces and can be manually detonated. This makes it quite versatile. If you lay it as a trap for an approaching enemy, you can detonate it at the perfect moment instead of running the risk of having him walk past it without detonating it like a Frag Mine. In a firefight, you can use it much like a conventional Frag Grenade, throwing it and then immediately holding the button to detonate it quickly mid-flight, ensuring your enemies cannot move away from the blast. [→☐ 4]

The fact that you can detonate all the explosives at once means you have access to the single most powerful attack you can execute. Piling up several in one place before detonating them can result in devastating damage, enough to take out any Boss in the game [→☐ 5]. The manual detonation also makes it a more versatile trap tool than standard mines. Laying one for a group of enemies then luring them towards it can work much better with the Remote Detonated Explosive Device since you can wait until multiple enemies are in the correct position before detonating.

Recommended Style of Play

The Remote Detonated Explosive Device is an effective tool in any build. The Sniper can make great use of it, planting the explosives and then moving back out of range before detonating them, then picking off any alerted enemies in the ensuing confusion.

CH04 Opponents

There are many classes and types of enemy throughout the game, each with different weapon loadouts, armor types and health values. This chapter will break down their A.I. tendencies and give detailed statistics on each of them. In addition, it will also contain detailed information and strategies for each of the Bosses in the game, giving multiple strategies to defeat each one.

STEALTH A.I.

The A.I. of every enemy you encounter in the game other than Bosses can be broken down into 2 main forms: Stealth and Combat. These are the algorithms that the game will process to decide what steps each enemy will take in relation to your actions. A thorough understanding of this system will allow you to manipulate the A.I. and play Deus Ex to the highest level.

The Stealth aspect of the A.I. is the initial state that all non-playable characters in the game start off in, and determines whether they can detect, and then what they will do depending on the severity of the detection.

DETECTION

When you see an enemy out in the wild, he will begin in the Relaxed state [→☐ 1]. Then, depending on your interaction with the enemy, they will move onto one of 5 other states. There are three categories of detection that an NPC can employ to interact with the player. Each of these categories of detection are then further subdivided into whether they were Major or Minor events. All these things are taken into account to determine which state the enemy will then change to. The categories of detection are as follows

1

2

3

Visual Detection

Visual detection involves anything the enemy sees in relation to something the player does, whether that is the player himself or something that is related to the player's presence, like a dead or unconscious body, or a door opening [→☐ 2]. A visual detection incident is much more likely to lead to a serious and aggressive reaction. The Minor and Major visual detection incidents that enemies can pick up on are:

Minor Incidents
Being briefly spotted peeking from cover
Being briefly spotted in plain sight
A door opening of its own accord

Major Incidents
Player in plain sight (Enemy acknowledges the threat)
Enemy finds a dead body
Enemy finds an unconscious body
Enemy sees an object being thrown
Enemy sees an object move by itself
Enemy sees a grenade or the explosion
Enemy finds a broken camera
Enemy sees a comrade being killed
Enemy finds a broken door
Enemy finds a hole in the wall that the player has made
Enemy finds a broken window destroyed by the player
Enemy sees player fire a weapon

Audio Detection

Audio detection can occur much more often than Visual detection, since almost every activity makes some kind of noise. Compared to visual detection incidents, there are many more minor ways to be detected, but they lead to only a slightly suspicious or investigative reaction [→☐ 3]. The Minor and Major audio detection incidents are as follows:

Minor Incidents
Hearing the player running
Hearing the player sprinting
Hearing the player landing (from a jump or fall)
Hearing a thrown object landing
Hearing the player punch through a wall
Hearing the impact of a bullet hitting a surface
Hearing a grenade landing (NOT detonating)
The activation of an environmental object, like a faucet or toilet flush
An object breaking, such as a crate or window

Major Incidents
If another enemy hears his comrade identify you and call for help
If you use a lethal Takedown in audio range of another enemy
Enemy hears a weapon fired
Hearing an explosive detonation

Collision Detection

A collision detection incident will occur when you physically interact with an enemy. There aren't many instances of this that will cause a minor reaction as you might imagine, so avoid doing this at all costs. The Minor and Major collision detection incidents are:

Minor Incidents
Enemy is hit by Tranq dart

Major Incidents
Directly touching an enemy
Landing on an enemy
Injuring but not killing an enemy
Enemy is hit by an object thrown by a player or bumps into an object being held by the player

REACTION

If you cause any of these Minor or Major detection incidents in the detectable vicinity of an enemy, they will then proceed to move into a reaction state. These can vary from a simple curious glance to a full blown search. The diagram shows how the different Minor and Major incidents are linked to the Reaction states, and how each state transitions to the next. Knowing what the enemy will do in each state and how to stay hidden during each one is vital.

Relaxed

The Relaxed state is the state all enemies and other NPC's are in by default. Unless you interact with them in some way via the aforementioned detection incidents, they will permanently remain in this state. This is the state you will encounter the majority of the time. In this state, the NPC will be doing one of the following things:

Guard Post: In this mode, the enemy will remain stationary, sporadically looking around for enemies but never moving from his assigned spot. If the enemy returns to the Relaxed state they will return to their post and resume their duties. [→☐ 4]

Focused Patrol: These are casual pre-determined search patterns that follow a designated route with no real urgency. Enemies are not actively looking for you here, just looking. Enemies will move at a slow, steady pace and look from side to side.

Activity: This can refer to several things an NPC may be doing. Chatting with a colleague, watching a T.V., and just generally neglecting their duties. This is an easier state to avoid an enemy in, since they will be pre-occupied and not actively looking around. When this activity ends, they will go into one of the two previously mentioned states. [→☐ 5]

Suspicious

This is the most non-threatening state an enemy can enter after encountering a detection incident. This is the state they will enter after you cause a Minor detection, and it leads to one A.I. pattern, the Investigation Patrol. Upon investigation, if nothing suspicious is discovered, the enemy will return to the Relaxed state.

Investigation Patrol: This is more of a curious investigation than an out and out search. The enemy will turn towards the source of the Minor detection and perhaps say something. This can also attract the attention of an enemy nearby. The enemy (or enemies) will then proceed to slowly and deliberately walk towards the source of the detection incident and look around. Should they find nothing, they will return to whatever they were doing in their Relaxed state. [→☐ 6]

Alarmed

Enemies will enter the Alarmed state following a Major detection incident. This is designed to punish the player for a more grievous lapse in stealth, so expect to take extra measures when trying to stay hidden during the enemy patrol. If entering this state, enemies will also attempt to activate an alarm panel. The enemy that tries to activate is usually the one that registered the Major detection incident, so if you can stop him before he gets there, the alarm won't immediately sound. [→☐ 7/8]

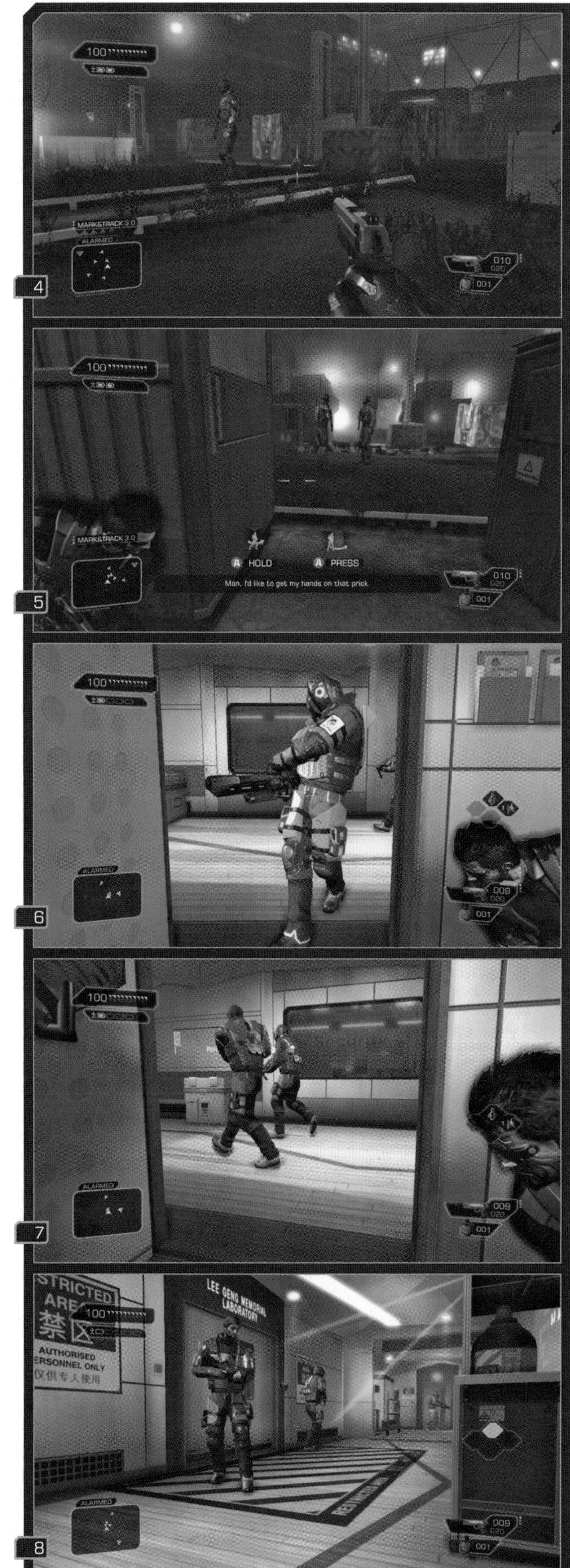

Alarm Patrol: The Alarm Patrol is the stance enemies will take when they have experienced a Major detection incident but have not outright spotted and identified you. This is a serious and aggressive A.I. state. The enemy will activate alarms in the area if they are nearby. They will then proceed to conduct an aggressive and thorough search of the area of the Major disturbance and outlying areas, including all unlocked rooms and corridors. They will be ready to react to anything and have their guns poised, moving quickly and with purpose [→☐ 1]. They will also attempt to conduct this search in a group if possible. If the enemies don't find you after the pre-determined time, they will enter the Cautious state. If the enemy registers any other Major or Minor detection incidents, they will remain in the Alarmed state longer while they go to investigate the source of the detection incident.

Hostile

The Hostile state is only activated when an enemy has identified and spotted you. He will initiate combat, and the resulting actions he takes will be dictated by the combat A.I., which will be explained later. If the enemy enters the Hostile state, but then loses sight of you, after a certain period of time they will enter the Agitated state. [→☐ 2]

Agitated

The enemy will enter the Agitated state if they first entered the Hostile state after spotting you and then subsequently lost you. This is the most dangerous search type state, and the enemy will ruthlessly search for you. Even after completing the search, they will transition into the Alarmed state, where they will conduct the Alarm Patrol, prolonging the time needed to stay hidden.

Search Patrol: This is a very aggressive patrol, similar to the Alarm Patrol. However, this patrol is more focused, and is centered on the last known location of the player. The enemy will actively search areas near to where you were last spotted during the Hostile state, and will constantly be moving and searching with their weapon drawn and ready to fire. Multiple enemies will also join in on this search. The focused search will mean enemies will look for you in areas that they wouldn't during other patrols, such as up ladders or into a vent. This will mean that you will have to leave the immediate area to avoid being seen, as simply hiding won't save you.

Cautious

The Cautious state is only entered after the designated cooldown period for the Alarm state has finished. This is similar to the Relaxed state, and the enemy will conduct whatever they would normally do in that state, such as guarding a post or resuming a focused patrol. If they were previously engaged in an activity, then they will instead enter the Post-Alarm Patrol.

Post-Alarm Patrol: This patrol only comes into play if the enemy was in the middle of an activity during his relaxed state. The enemy will instead perform a variation of the Focused Patrol, concentrating on a critical area.

COMBAT A.I.

The Combat A.I. is only initiated when the enemy has turned Hostile towards you. There are several processes that the enemy will go through when entering combat, and there are various circumstances which you can influence that determine what actions he will take. Understanding and controlling these can give you the edge in combat.

THE COMBAT AREA

As the diagram shows, the Combat Area is the area immediately surrounding the player. A hostile enemy's position in relation to the Combat Area will dictate many of his actions.

The zones in the diagram are different depending on the weapon the enemy is wielding. An enemy wielding a sniper rifle will have a Preferred Combat Range that is much further away from the player than an enemy wielding a shotgun [→☐ 3]. Knowing this will help you dictate the pace of the fight, and let you move in and out of the preferred range of the enemy.

Maximum Combat Range

This represents the limit of the range at which an enemy will actively attack you and attempt to seek cover. This maximum range isn't wildly different for the majority of enemies you will face, and only drastically changes when battling an enemy using a sniper rifle. If you move further than this range, the enemy will only fire sporadically with suppressive fire as he attempts to close the distance and get into range, and sometimes may not attack at all.

Dead Zone (Far)

This is a passive A.I. algorithm that is also dependent on the enemy's weapon. The Dead Zone is a range too far for the weapon to be effective, so this A.I. pattern asks the enemy to move into the Preferred Combat Range when it is convenient. This means, should you be laying down suppressive fire, the overwhelming priority for the enemy will be to survive and find immediate cover, rather than move out of the Dead Zone. This can be exploited to force your enemy to stay at a range where his weapon will do minimal damage (forcing a shotgun wielding enemy to stay far away, for example). [→□ 4]

Preferred Combat Range

This is the optimal range at which the enemy wishes to initiate combat, and is again different depending on the weapon. The priority for the enemy will be to find cover within this zone, and once they do, they will not move from cover unless you force them to. Moving so this range changes, and throwing a grenade or mine so the enemy reacts to it are a few ways to force your enemy to move out this preferred cover point. [→□ 5]

Preferred Combat Zone

This is an area that is actually the same distance from the player as the Preferred Combat Range, but is in front of your cone of vision, as indicated by the diagram. The difference between an enemy being in the Preferred Combat Range and Preferred Combat Zone is the way they'll react to your presence, since what you can see dictates which cover point the enemy will select. [→□ 6]

Dead Zone (Near)

This works the same as the far Dead Zone, in that it is not a preferred area for combat, based on the weapon the enemy is wielding. Again, the top priority for the enemy will be survival, but when it is convenient, he will attempt to take cover within the Preferred Combat Range.

Minimum Combat Range

This is an absolute no-entry zone for the enemy, forcing him to IMMEDIATELY back away from you to create distance. The enemy will still fire at you from this distance, but will do so while moving away quickly. This can be an excellent, albeit gutsy, tactic to force the enemy out of cover, of particular use in the Close Combat style of play. [→□ 7]

COMBAT AREA

△ Player

Preferred Combat Zone

Dead Zone (near)

Preferred Combat Range

Dead Zone (far)

Maximum Combat Range

Minimum Combat Range

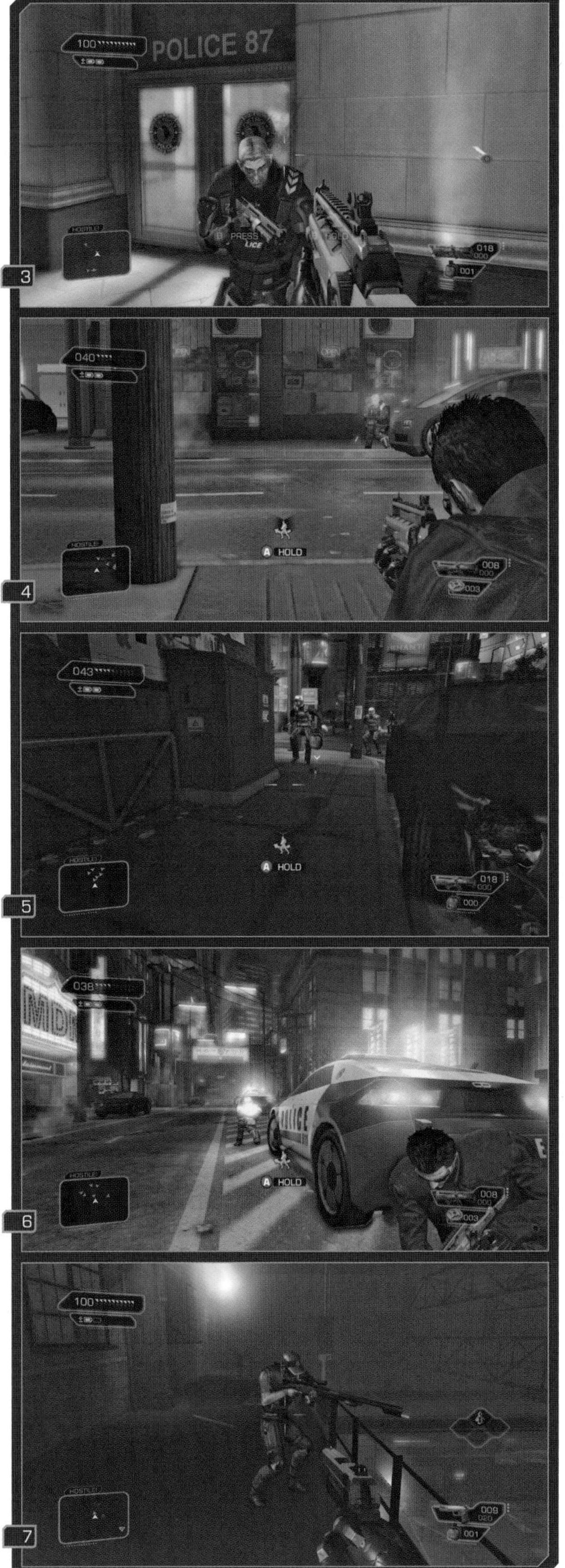

ENTERING THE COMBAT AREA

An enemy will enter into the Combat Area by attempting to run into cover as close to the Preferred Combat Range as possible, while firing at the player if it is safe to do so and if he has a clear line of sight. If it isn't convenient to do so, he will enter into cover in the far Dead Zone, with the ultimate goal of moving into the preferred range. If there are no nearby cover points to move into, the enemy will lay down suppressive fire while he moves to the nearest one inside the Combat Area.

Remembering these rules can help you exploit an enemy's tendency to seek preferential cover at certain distances. Once you identify the type of weapon they are carrying, it is an effective strategy to move the different zones of the Combat Area to encourage enemies to leave cover.

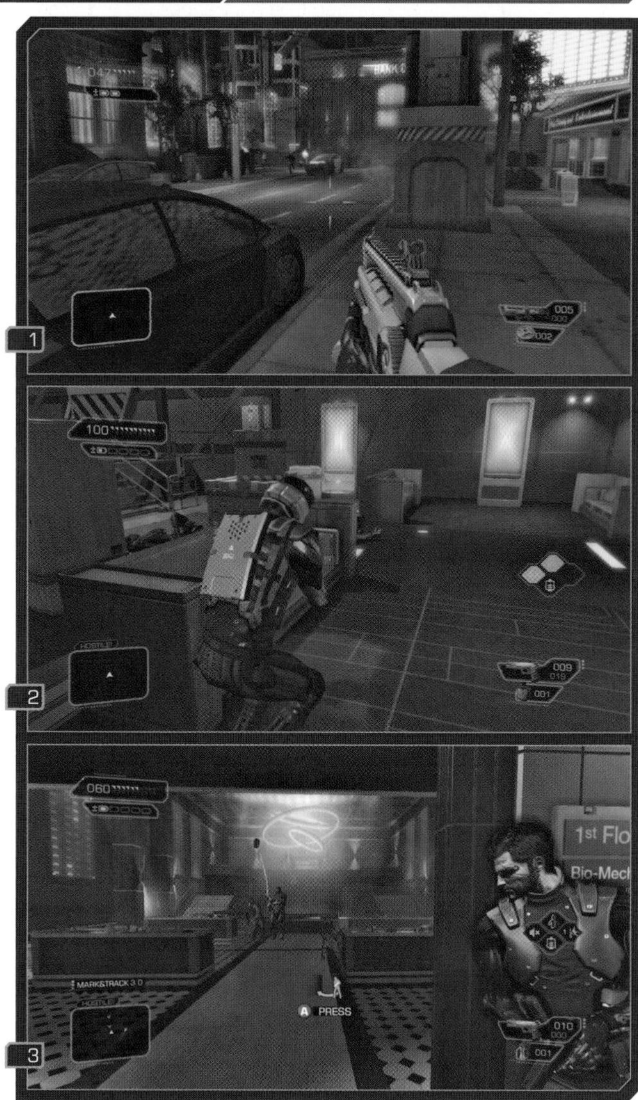

FLOW OF COMBAT

The flow of combat as indicated earlier is dictated by the enemy's desire to move into cover in a preferred zone of the Combat Area. From then on, the enemy will either stay in the cover they have found if it's inside the Preferred Combat Range, or he will move when it is convenient and safe to do so. He can also be forced out with a grenade or mine thrown near him, or by drastically reducing or increasing the range between you and him, thus either forcing the enemy into the Minimum Combat Range which he will have to immediately move out of, or moving him out of the Combat Area completely and forcing him to catch up. [→□ 1]

COMBAT VISION

The Combat Vision zone in front of an enemy dictates the area in which they can see you. This cone is much larger than when an enemy is outside the Hostile state and has not yet initiated combat. However, as the diagram demonstrates, even when Hostile, enemies still have a blind spot that can be exploited if you can escape their sight for a few seconds and get round to their backs. [→□ 2]

COVER-LESS COMBAT

As mentioned earlier, an enemy's priority is to fire from the safety of cover. However, in situations where this is not possible, such as when there are no suitable cover points around, when the enemy is moving to a cover point, or when you have forced the enemy to move either by moving the Combat Area or by forcing the enemy to move with a grenade or mine, the enemy will initiate Cover-Less Combat. While not preferred, the enemy will still be able to perform all his actions in Cover-Less Combat, such as:

Firing at the player
The enemy will still fire at the player outside of cover, and in most zones of the Combat Area, regardless of weapon type. However, this leaves them very vulnerable and is an excellent opportunity for you to take the enemy out, before he gets into cover to fortify his position.

Throwing a Grenade
The enemy will tend to throw a grenade when you are in cover or hiding for a prolonged period of time. Stay aware of your enemy's actions and take advantage of this by killing him before the lengthy grenade throwing animation finishes. [→□ 3]

Using suppressive fire
When you are in cover or the enemy does not have a clear shot, or when he is well outside the Preferred Combat Range of his weapon, he will lay down suppressive fire, to help keep you in place, cover his movements and those of his allies and help to get himself into a better position. If you can recognize that the enemy is using suppressive fire rather than a focused burst from a strong firing position, you can take this opportunity to fire back with minimal risk and take him out.

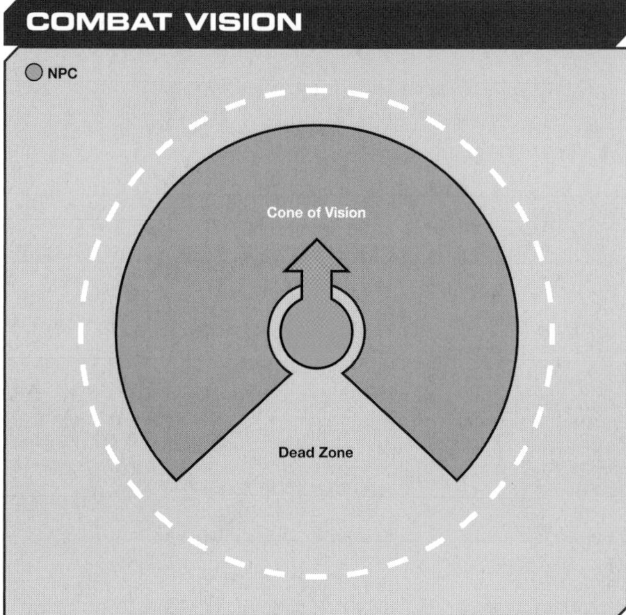

Encroaching on the player's position and moving to a closer cover point is their aim. When entering the Combat Area, enemies will always try to move into their Preferred Combat Range, and encroach on a player to help improve their line of sight and give themselves the optimal firing range for their weapon. [→□ 4]

Making sure the player remains in his line of sight

If you move out of an enemy's line of sight, he will attempt to re-establish it by cautiously moving around while remaining in the Preferred Combat Range [→□ 5]. If this is not possible, he will first try to re-establish line of sight before improving his position in the Combat Area. Remember, just going into cover is not enough to break line of sight, as the enemy will still lay down suppressive fire and grenades to flush you out.

Crouching to give the player a smaller target

If there is a lack of suitable cover points available, the enemy can sometimes move into a crouched position to give you a smaller target and lay down more focused fire.

COVER COMBAT

If possible, the enemy will always try to get to a cover point inside the Preferred Combat Range. If there is not a suitable cover position available, the enemy will continue to use Cover-Less Combat. In order for a cover point to be valid, it must be inside the Combat Area, outside the Minimum Combat Range, and provide sufficient cover so as to not leave the enemy exposed to the player. Taking these conditions into account, it is possible to force an enemy out of cover.

By increasing the distance between yourself and the enemy, you will eventually put the enemy outside the Combat Area altogether, forcing the cover point to become invalid and thus causing the enemy to exit it and expose himself. Likewise, closing the distance enough so the enemy has breached the Minimum Combat Range will force him to immediately get out of cover and move away from you. Also, if you can flank an enemy's position while he is in cover so the cover is no longer protecting him, essentially exposing him, this will make the cover point invalid, again forcing him to move [→□ 6]. If a mine is placed near a cover point, it will be recognized by the enemy and no longer be considered a viable cover option, very useful for closing your enemies off and herding them into position. Finally, if a Gas Grenade or Mine has detonated and the resulting gas cloud has engulfed a cover point, it will also render the cover point invalid, another method to force your enemies away from an area.

PEEKING

While in cover, there are a few parameters that decide whether an enemy will peek out to begin shooting at you. If you are currently firing, or have fired upon the enemy or his position within the last second or two, the enemy will not peek out. Also, throwing a grenade or mine near the enemy will immediately cause him to stop peeking and choose a different course of action (usually to run far away). The enemy will also not peek out to fire unless their weapon is fully loaded, so after a sustained burst you have an opportunity to take action. Also, if his health is low, he will be very hesitant to leave cover or peek.

SWITCHING COVER

Should the enemy be forced to leave his cover point due to your actions, he will either move towards the next valid cover point by moving sideways while firing at you, or while heading directly to it as fast as possible while ignoring you (this is more likely if he has allies laying down suppressive fire while he moves). The distance to the next cover point is the major decider as to which method will be used. Should it be fairly far away, the enemy will run to it, while if it is fairly close he will strafe and shoot. [→□ 7]

Make a quick mental note of viable cover locations in the Combat Area that the enemy will likely use, and be ready to head him off should he choose to move from one to the other.

WEAPONS FIRE

When the enemy begins firing, he won't stop until his pre-determined weapon burst has come to an end, or you force him to stop. There are a few conditions under which the enemy will stop firing. If a friendly NPC is in the path of fire between you and the enemy, the enemy will not fire. This is a VERY useful technique in crowded situations and when you are caught without cover. Maneuvering yourself so an enemy is between you when engaged in a firefight ensures you will only

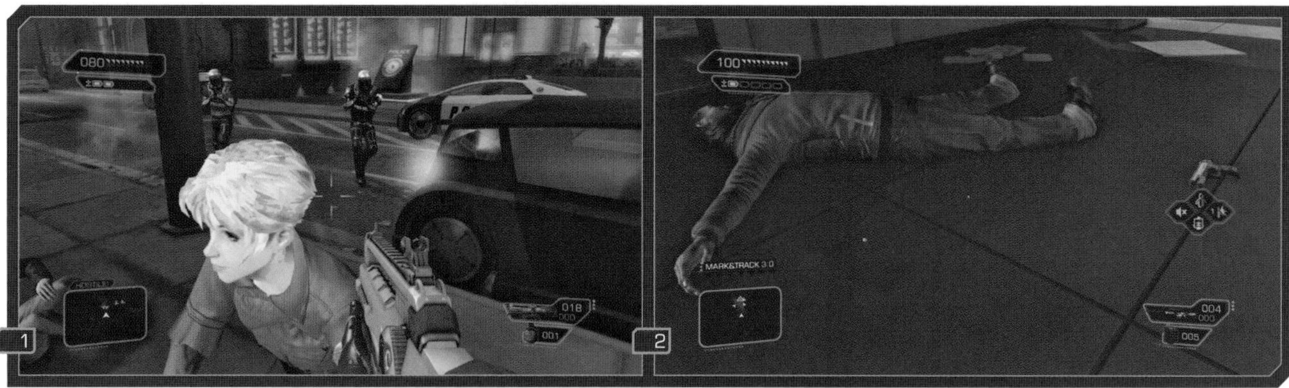

have to deal with one target firing at you at any one time. [→☐ 1]. This is also useful when battling police, as placing civilians in the line of fire will ensure they never open fire until they get a clear shot.

Depending on the weapon the enemy is wielding, the amount of bullets fired and the length of the burst in each firing sequence is different. The firing patterns for enemies holding each of the following weapons are:

Pistol	Enemy will fire frequently, emptying about half a clip in each burst.
Revolver	Fires infrequently, with single or 2 shots at a time.
Machine Pistol	Enemy will fire infrequently, in a long burst of around 10 rounds each time.
Combat Rifle	Fires frequently, enemy will use short controlled bursts of around 3 rounds each time.
Shotgun	When in range, the enemy will fire frequently with single shots.
Heavy Rifle	While fired infrequently, the bursts will be extremely long.
Sniper Rifle	Fires infrequently, in single shot bursts.

In addition to firing patterns, the base accuracy of each weapon is affected by the action and manner in which the enemy fires his weapon. When in a stationary or crouched position, or when firing after peeking out of cover, the enemy's weapon accuracy is unaffected. However, if firing during movement, the accuracy will drop. And if using suppressive fire, the accuracy will drop drastically.

DROPPING WEAPONS

When you knock an enemy unconscious, they will drop their primary weapon [→☐ 2]. All enemies are equipped with both a primary and secondary weapon, and upon dropping their primary, they will equip the secondary. Note that knocking the enemy down temporarily is not enough to make them drop their primary weapon, they must be knocked unconscious. The enemy will make an effort to retrieve their primary weapon if they can.

AUTOMATED DEFENSES

In addition to the various enemies and Bosses you encounter, you will also frequently come across various automated defense systems and traps.

SECURITY CAMERAS

Security Cameras are found frequently in the various secure locations you will find yourself infiltrating. They show up on your radar with a unique icon. They also emit two lines of green light that indicate the area they are looking at as they rotate [→☐ 3]. Should you cross into this cone of vision, the camera will focus on you and the lights will turn yellow. You now have a few seconds before the camera confirms you as a threat to get out of the range of the camera and hide. If you stay in the camera's sight for too long, the lights will eventually turn red and an alarm will be raised. All nearby enemies will then head to your location.

Most cameras can be slipped past quite easily by keeping an eye on the cone of light they emit. The Cloaking Augmentation will also shield you from its sight, and an EMP explosive will completely destroy it, as will conventional gunfire. You can sometimes also hack a nearby computer to gain access to a camera and see what it sees, useful for scouting ahead.

LASER SYSTEMS

Laser grids are dotted throughout some secure facilities you will find yourself in. Stepping across them will immediately put nearby enemies into the Alarmed State, and they will rush to your location.

Using the Cloaking Augmentation completely nullifies the Lasers, and allows you to walk through them undetected. If you have the Increased Jump Height Augmentation, you can also use that to vault over the Laser grid, if you are confident in your leaping abilities.

SECURITY TURRETS

Turrets are stationary gun emplacements that fire upon any perceived threat, I.E. you. They have long range and good accuracy, so if you do get sighted, you'd better find cover quickly or its guns will make short work of you. Like security cameras, the Turret can also sometimes be hacked from a nearby computer and made to work for you. Also, Turrets are considered movable objects, so it is possible to pick them up once you have the Move/Throw Heavy Objects Augmentation [→☐ 4]. This can allow for some interesting tactics, such as first hacking a Turret and then picking it up and throwing it into a room full of enemies, and watching the carnage ensue. While durable, the Turret can still be destroyed with conventional weapons fire or EMP explosives.

4

ARMOR

Throughout the game, the various enemies you encounter will occasionally come equipped with armor. This armor can vary from the basic helmet and vest, to a full body battle suit. These pieces of armor will affect the impact of certain weapons more than others, and the table shows how each weapon is affected. The Multiplier heading refers to how the base damage of the weapon is affected assuming a clean shot. 1.00 is the base damage, anything higher than this is extra damage and anything under this number equates to less damage.

Table Key

Example of effectiveness	Multiplier
Very Effective	1.25
Effective	1.00
Weak	0.50
Very Weak	0.25

	No Armor	Vest	Vest & Helmet	Full Suit	Dermal Plating	Medium Sentry	Box Guard	Barrett	Fedorova	Namir
Revolver	1.25	1.25	1.25	1.00	0.50	0.50	0.50	0.50	0.50	0.50
10mm Pistol	1.25	1.00	1.00	0.50	0.25	0.40	0.25	0.25	0.25	0.25
Machine Pistol	1.25	1.00	1.00	0.50	0.25	0.40	0.25	0.25	0.25	0.25
Combat Rifle	1.25	1.00	1.00	0.50	0.25	0.40	0.25	0.25	0.25	0.25
Heavy Rifle	1.25	1.25	1.25	1.00	0.50	0.50	0.25	0.50	0.50	0.50
Tactical Shotgun	1.25	1.25	1.25	0.50	0.25	0.40	0.25	0.25	0.25	0.25
Sniper Rifle	1.25	1.25	1.25	1.00	0.50	0.50	0.50	0.50	0.50	0.50
Crossbow	1.25	1.00	1.00	0.50	0.25	0.40	0.25	0.25	0.25	0.25
Tranq Gun	1.00	1.00	1.00	1.00	1.00	1.00	1.00	1.00	1.00	1.00
Rocket Launcher	1.25	1.00	1.00	1.00	1.33	1.33	1.25	1.00	1.00	1.00
Plasma Rifle	1.25	1.25	1.25	1.25	1.00	1.00	1.00	1.00	1.00	1.00
Laser Rifle	1.25	1.25	1.25	1.25	1.00	1.00	1.00	1.00	1.00	1.00
PEPS	1.00	1.00	1.00	1.00	1.00	1.00	1.00	1.00	1.00	1.00
Stun Gun	1.00	1.00	1.00	1.00	1.00	1.00	1.00	1.00	1.00	1.00
Frag Grenade	1.25	1.00	1.00	1.00	1.33	1.33	1.25	1.00	1.00	1.00
Concussion Grenade	1.00	1.00	1.00	1.00	1.00	1.00	1.00	1.00	1.00	1.00
Gas Grenade	1.00	1.00	1.00	1.00	1.00	1.00	1.00	1.00	1.00	1.00

BASIC ENEMY TYPES

All the enemies you encounter in the game will fall into one of several archetypes, which are then subsequently differentiated further with specific classes. While you may find enemies that appear different from one another, as long they belong to the same class, they will behave the same and have the same base statistics and equipment loadout. They will all be listed here, along with specific weapon resistance data for each enemy, showing how many shots it will take for them to go down with each weapon.

POLICE OFFICERS

Versions: Detroit, Hengsha

The Policemen are found throughout the streets of the two major cities you will find yourself in, Detroit and Hengsha. Generally well armed, the very powerful Riot Cop variation will be out in force during the riot events. The powerful SWAT variation is rarely seen except during special scripted events and areas. These enemies are neutral, and will not attack you unless you attack them first, or flagrantly break the law in front of them. They are also rarely alone, and will quickly call for backup. The Police Station area is where you will find the weakest variation, the Desk Cop. The Street and Riot variations are well armed, and decently well armored. No Policeman variation possesses any Augmentations.

Class	Street Cop	Riot Cop/SWAT	Desk Cop
Health	70	250	30
Armor	Bullet Proof Vest, Helmet, Gas Mask	Full Body Armor	None
Possible Primary Weapons	Combat Rifle	Shotgun	Pistol
Backup Weapon	Pistol	Pistol	Pistol
Usable Grenades	Concussion Grenade	Gas	None
Augmentations	None	None	None

Riot Cop

Street Cop

The Street Cop is the most common variation of the Policemen class that you will encounter. Rarely alone and packing a decent weapon in the Combat Rifle, the Street Cop also has good armor, and can take a fair few hits. The helmet will also make headshots less effective He is also armed with a Concussion Grenade to disorient you. Best avoided altogether, it is rarely if ever worth aggravating him.

Riot Cop/SWAT

The Riot/SWAT Class is incredibly dangerous, and the decision to engage him should not be made lightly. Outdone only by the Ogres and Bosses in sheer toughness, they will take an immense amount of punishment before going down, having the highest base health value in the game for a non-boss humanoid opponent. Their lack of the Dermal Armor Augmentation doesn't make them quite as durable as Ogres however. If you absolutely must engage them in combat, try to go for a Takedown, as any other weapon other than an energy based one will be quite ineffective, and costly in terms of ammo. When using a non-lethal weapon like the Stun Gun or Tranquilizer Rifle, remember that he won't go down in one shot, so you may be spotted and the alarm may be raised before he goes down.

Desk Cop

The Desk Cop is only encountered in the Police Station. While not difficult to put down, they are present in massive numbers, and can create serious problems for you if they raise the alarm and subsequently summon their tougher comrades.

Street Cop

	Minimum Body Shots			Minimum Headshots		
Weapon	Street Cop	Riot Cop/SWAT	Desk Cop	Street Cop	Riot Cop/SWAT	Desk Cop
Revolver	1	2	3	1	1	1
10mm Pistol	2	5	15	1	2	1
Machine Pistol	4	8	26	1	3	1
Combat Rifle	3	7	23	1	2	1
Heavy Rifle	3	5	10	1	2	1
Tactical Shotgun	1	1	4	1	1	1
Sniper Rifle	1	1	2	1	1	1
Crossbow	1	1	3	1	1	1
Tranq Gun (sec)	2	4	6	1	1	1
Rocket Launcher	1	1	1	1	1	1
Plasma Rifle	1	2	3	1	1	1
Laser Rifle	1	1	2	1	1	1
Stun Gun	1	1	1	1	1	1
Frag Grenade	1	1	1	1	1	1
Gas Grenade (sec)	2	3	5	1	1	1

SECURITY GUARDS

Versions: Belltower, Sarif Security, Bodyguards, Hive Bouncers

The Security Guard Archetype is a mid-level opponent, representing more of a threat than your average thug but not quite as tough as militarily trained special forces. They are present in many areas of the game, particularly in the employ of powerful individuals and corporations rather than military installations. The most powerful class, the Heavy Security Guard, is a very perilous opponent similar to an Ogre, although not quite as dangerous. They also have the versatility of the Sniper class, giving them good range to back up good front line capabilities.

Class	Light	Medium	Heavy	Sniper
Health	30	50	90	40
Armor	Bullet Proof Vest	Bullet Proof Vest, Helmet	Full Body Armor	None
Possible Primary Weapons	Pistol	Combat Rifle, Machine Pistol, Shotgun	Heavy Rifle	Sniper Rifle
Backup Weapon	Pistol	Pistol	Pistol	Pistol
Usable Grenades	Concussion, Frag, Gas, EMP	Concussion, Frag, Gas, EMP	Concussion, Frag, Gas, EMP	None
Augmentation	None	None	None	None

Light Security Guard

Light
The weakest iteration of the Security Guard, the Light class is found in many places, in such variations as Bodyguards and Door Guards [→☐ 1]. They will be in places of low importance, but important enough to still require some degree of security. The further you progress in an area, the higher the level of security you can expect, and as such, expect to find this level of Security Guard early on.

Medium
A considerable step up from the Light variation, the real problem when dealing with the Medium Security Guard is his helmet. This makes stealthy headshots much less likely early on. Thankfully, he still has quite low health, so a few shots of a silenced automatic weapon will still put him down quickly and quietly.

Heavy
The Heavy Security Guard is assigned to guard the most sensitive of secure locations. His Full Suit of armor makes conventional weapons fire ineffective, but also reduces his mobility. It is strongly recommended to use a Takedown, as he is not equipped with the Ogre's Typhoon Augmentation at close range. His lack of the Dermal Armor Augmentation also leaves him vulnerable to a well placed Frag Grenade or Mine. [→☐ 2]

Sniper
The Sniper is designed to supplement a squad of Security Guards that are patrolling area. Once the rest of the squad have spotted and engaged you in combat, it is the Sniper's job to take you out quickly and accurately. When entering an area, check high balconies or other elevated positions . Thankfully he has no armor and very low health, so taking him out first with a long range headshot can help you deal with the rest of the enemies in an area much more easily.

Heavy Security Guard

	Minimum Body Shots				Minimum Headshots			
Weapon	Light	Medium	Heavy	Sniper	Light	Medium	Heavy	Sniper
Revolver	1	2	3	2	1	1	1	1
10mm Pistol	2	5	15	3	1	2	3	1
Machine Pistol	4	8	26	5	1	3	5	1
Combat Rifle	3	7	23	4	1	2	5	1
Heavy Rifle	3	5	10	4	1	2	2	1
Tactical Shotgun	1	1	4	1	1	1	1	1
Sniper Rifle	1	1	2	1	1	1	1	1
Crossbow	1	1	3	1	1	1	1	1
Tranq Gun (sec)	2	4	6	3	1	1	2	1
Rocket Launcher	1	1	1	1	1	1	1	1
Plasma Rifle	1	2	3	2	1	1	1	1
Laser Rifle	1	1	2	1	1	1	1	1
Stun Gun	1	1	1	1	1	1	1	1
Frag Grenade	1	1	1	1	1	1	1	1
Gas Grenade (sec)	2	3	5	2	1	1	1	1

THUGS

Versions: Detroit Gangers, Hengsha Thugs, Harvesters, Merchants, Purity First

Throughout the vibrant cities you traverse during the course of the game, you will inevitably encounter the seedy underbelly of society in the form of the Thug archetype. Designed to provide a basic and straightforward obstacle to the player, Thugs can be numerous in number, but go down quickly and easily, having only rudimentary weapons, no armor and very low health in all Classes.

Class	Lowlife	Show Off	Striker	Lieutenant
Health	20	20	30	30
Armor	None	None	None	None
Possible Primary Weapons	Machine Pistol, Shotgun, Revolver, Pistol	Machine Pistol, Shotgun, Revolver, Pistol	Machine Pistol, Shotgun, Revolver, Pistol	Machine Pistol, Shotgun, Revolver, Pistol
Backup Weapon	Pistol	Pistol	Pistol	Pistol
Usable Grenades	Concussion, Frag	Concussion, Frag	Concussion, Frag	Concussion, Frag
Augmentation	None	None	None	None

DRB Thug

Lowlife
The weakest enemy in the game, the Lowlife can still pose a threat when he is equipped with the Machine Pistol or Shotgun. This class of enemy populates the streets and gang hideouts you will encounter, and is designed to be more of a hindrance than an actual threat. Practically every weapon will take him out in 1 or 2 shots, so taking him out quickly is a viable option no matter the situation. [→☐ 1]

Show Off
The Show Off doesn't add much to the Lowlife other than the possibility of a having a Shotgun. They still share the same low health, and can be dealt with just as quickly and easily.

Striker
Slightly healthier than the previous two classes, the Striker still won't pose much more of a threat, and can really be regarded as just another Thug. He is quite precise with the Machine Pistol however, and on the harder difficulty can take you down quickly if you're not careful. [→☐ 2]

Lieutenant
More of a cosmetic variation than anything else, the Lieutenant is similar to the Striker, but has more chance of wielding the Shotgun. Be wary of them in packs, as getting preoccupied with other Machine Pistol toting Thugs can allow the Lieutenant to move into the optimum range for the Shotgun, where his good accuracy can make you pay dearly for your lapse in concentration.

MCB Thug

	Minimum Body Shots				Minimum Headshots			
Weapon	Lowlife	Show Off	Striker	Lieutenant	Lowlife	Show Off	Striker	Lieutenant
Revolver	1	1	1	1	1	1	1	1
10mm Pistol	2	2	2	2	1	1	1	1
Machine Pistol	3	3	4	4	1	1	1	1
Combat Rifle	2	2	3	3	1	1	1	1
Heavy Rifle	2	2	3	3	1	1	1	1
Tactical Shotgun	1	1	1	1	1	1	1	1
Sniper Rifle	1	1	1	1	1	1	1	1
Crossbow	1	1	1	1	1	1	1	1
Tranq Gun (sec)	2	2	2	2	1	1	1	1
Rocket Launcher	1	1	1	1	1	1	1	1
Plasma Rifle	1	1	1	1	1	1	1	1
Laser Rifle	1	1	1	1	1	1	1	1
Stun Gun	1	1	1	1	1	1	1	1
Frag Grenade	1	1	1	1	1	1	1	1
Gas Grenade (sec)	1	1	2	2	1	1	1	1

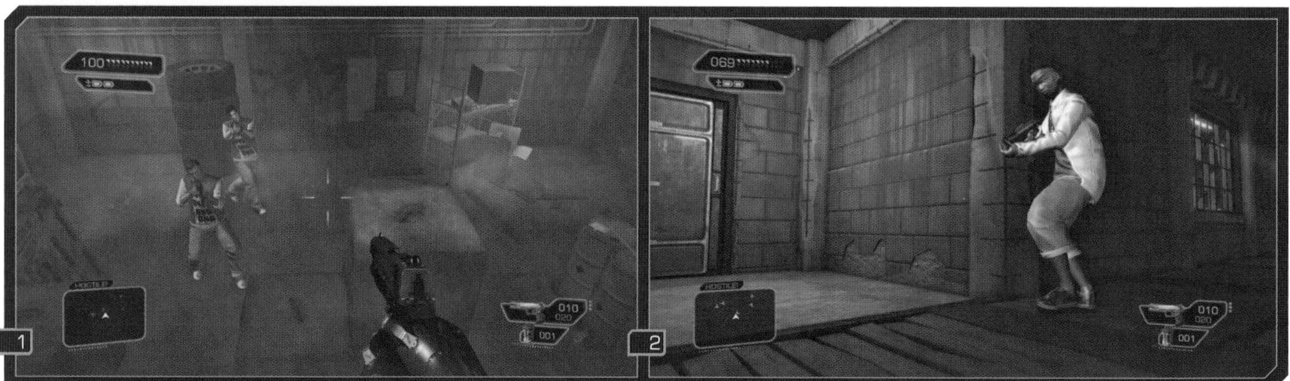

CRAZIES

Versions: None

The Crazies in Panchaea offer a unique threat. Their disrupted Augmentations have caused them to lose their mental faculties, including the ability to wield weapons. Essentially this means that Crazies will charge you haphazardly and take you down with close range melee attacks. You can still get around them stealthily, and probably should, because while they go down quickly, you will encounter them in such vast numbers that they can overwhelm you quickly.

Class	Crazy Worker	Crazy Security Guard	Crazy Spec Op
Health	30	50	80
Armor	None	Bullet Proof Vest, Helmet	Bullet Proof Vest
Possible Primary Weapons	Melee	Melee	Melee
Backup Weapon	Melee	Melee	Melee
Usable Grenades	None	None	None
Augmentation	None	None	None

Crazy Worker

Crazy Worker
The basic Crazy Worker has very little health and will go down very quickly. Be careful if you are spotted by him though, as the commotion he causes will attract other nearby Crazies, and their plentiful numbers could cause problems. Be ready to use your Typhoon Augmentation if they do surround you and you need a quick escape.

Crazy Security Guard
The Crazy Security Guard shares the same base stats as the Medium Security Guard, so he is still fairly easy to take down. However, his helmet can cause problems, somewhat negating the potency of your headshots. Try to spot him in a crowd of Crazies and take him out first, and don't hesitate to use a grenade or two to help thin out the crowd. [→☐ 3]

Crazy Spec Op
The most resilient of this archetype, the Crazy variation of the Spec Ops soldier can take quite a bit of punishment to the body. However, unlike the Medium Crazy, he does not have a helmet, so he is vulnerable to headshots. Don't panic and allow yourself to get overwhelmed. Since Crazies will always rush you as soon as possible, the rules of the Combat Area do not apply to them. As a result, you may find yourself in unfamiliar positions as the enemy attacks you from your blind spot while you are distracted. To compensate for this, try to create a choke point that you can concentrate your fire on, and keep your back to a wall or corner to ensure you aren't attacked from a blind area. [→☐ 4]

Crazy Security Guard

	Minimum Body Shots			Minimum Headshots		
Weapon	Crazy Worker	Crazy Security Guard	Crazy Spec Op	Crazy Worker	Crazy Security Guard	Crazy Spec Op
Revolver	1	2	3	1	1	1
10mm Pistol	2	5	7	1	2	1
Machine Pistol	4	8	12	1	3	1
Combat Rifle	3	7	10	1	2	1
Heavy Rifle	3	5	8	1	2	1
Tactical Shotgun	1	1	2	1	1	1
Sniper Rifle	1	1	2	1	1	1
Crossbow	1	1	2	1	1	1
Tranq Gun (sec)	2	4	6	1	1	1
Rocket Launcher	1	1	1	1	1	1
Plasma Rifle	1	2	3	1	1	1
Laser Rifle	1	1	2	1	1	1
Stun Gun	1	1	1	1	1	1
Frag Grenade	1	1	1	1	1	1
Gas Grenade (sec)	2	3	4	1	1	1

SPEC OPS

Versions: Belltower, Harvesters

The Spec Ops are a powerful and versatile set of enemies. The weakest class is still a formidable opponent, and they tend to patrol in squads and can quickly corner and overwhelm you. They pack an impressive array of weaponry also, so you won't last long against them without cover. Every class also has some armor, making headshots (when there isn't a helmet to contend with) an absolute must. With the Soldier as the bread and butter infantry, the Ogre as the tank, the Shifter as long range support and the Sneaker to catch you unawares at close range, the Spec Ops enemies are deadly at any range and in any situation.

Ogre

Class	Soldier	Ogre	Shifter	Sneaker
Health	80	180	70	90
Armor	Bullet Proof Vest	Full Body Armor	Bullet Proof Vest	Bullet Proof Vest, Helmet
Possible Primary Weapons	Combat Rifle, Shotgun, Revolver	Heavy Rifle	Sniper Rifle	Machine Pistol
Backup Weapon	Pistol	Combat Rifle	Pistol	Pistol
Usable Grenades	Concussion, Frag, Gas, EMP	Concussion, Frag, Gas, EMP	None	Concussion, Frag, Gas, EMP
Augmentation	None	Dermal Armor, Typhoon	Cloaking	Cloaking

Soldier

The Soldier is the most common form of the Spec Ops archetype. He is fairly well armed, and is usually equipped with one of the two common ballistic weapons, and rarely with the Revolver. He also is equipped with the full gamut of grenade types, so be careful about staying in one position too long against a group of Spec Ops soldiers, as the grenades will fly. For being the weakest class in the Spe Ops archetype, the Soldier has above average health and decent armor for his torso. However, this class does not come equipped with helmets, so head shots should be an absolute priority, for both stealth kills and when engaged with them in a firefight. Even a single Soldier can punish you badly out in the open, do not take them as lightly as you might the other basic classes of other archetypes. The Soldier will likely be the frontline or scout for a group of Spec Ops soldiers nearby, and is commonly used for patrolling purposes. This means he is more likely to be found on his own, but a likely sign that his allies are nearby. While he isn't a huge threat on his own, attracting the attention of a nearby patrolling Ogre or having to contend with a slippery Shifter while fighting him can spell doom. [→☐ 1]

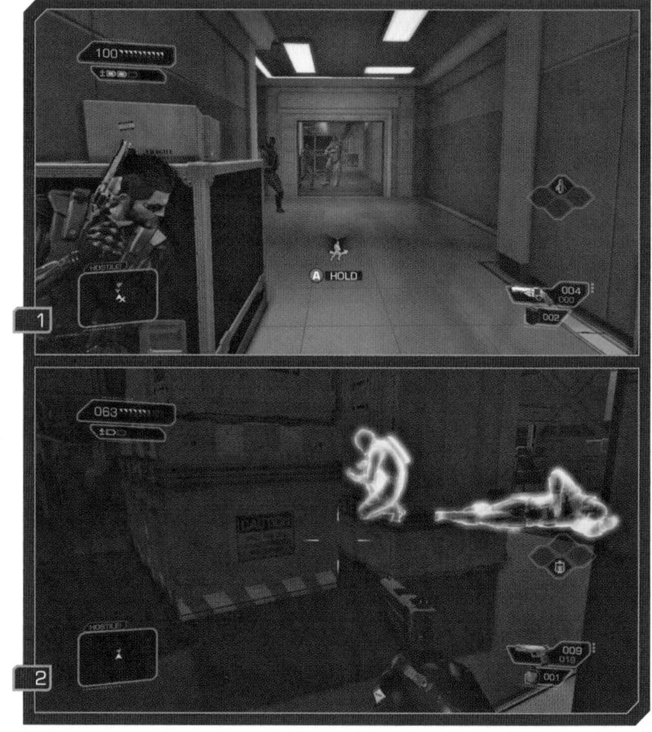

1
2

Sneaker

The Sneaker is the close range cloaked fighter in the Spec Ops corps. Thankfully he'll only ever be equipped with a Machine Pistol, but this is more than enough to be very troublesome. The Sneaker is quick and agile, and moves around often. His cloak will eventually run out and must recharge, just like yours, but if you are impatient, an EMP explosive can disrupt it and stagger him, although tossing any grenade in his general direction is a good way of dealing with him. [→☐ 2]

Shifter

The long range support for the Spec Ops, he has some basic armor to help him last a little longer, although his health is still fairly low. That bit

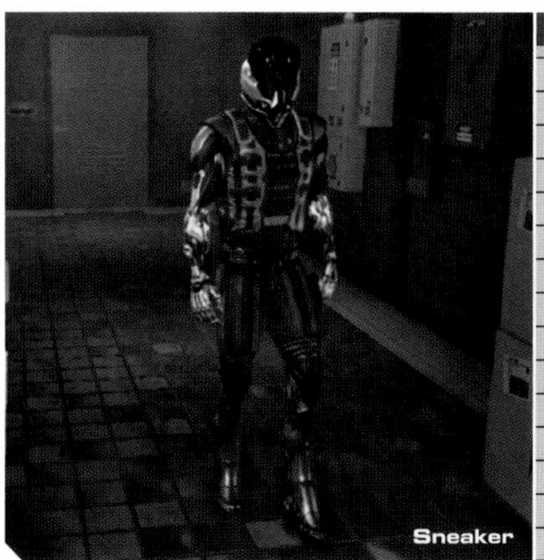
Sneaker

	Minimum Body Shots				Minimum Headshots			
Weapon	Soldier	Ogre	Shifter	Sneaker	Soldier	Ogre	Shifter	Sneaker
Revolver	3	12	2	3	1	2	1	1
10mm Pistol	7	60	5	8	1	8	1	2
Machine Pistol	12	103	8	13	1	13	1	4
Combat Rifle	10	90	7	12	1	11	1	3
Heavy Rifle	8	40	7	8	1	5	1	2
Tactical Shotgun	2	16	2	2	1	2	1	1
Sniper Rifle	2	8	2	2	1	1	1	1
Crossbow	2	12	1	2	1	2	1	1
Tranq Gun (sec)	6	12	5	6	1	2	1	2
Rocket Launcher	1	1	1	1	1	1	1	1
Plasma Rifle	3	8	3	3	1	1	1	1
Laser Rifle	2	4	2	2	1	1	1	1
Stun Gun	1	2	1	1	1	1	1	1
Frag Grenade	1	1	1	1	1	1	1	1
Gas Grenade (sec)	4	9	4	5	1	2	1	2

of extra armor and health can make all the difference though, as you don't want to be spending any more time than is necessary to take him out, especially with an Ogre bearing down on you. Add to this his cloaking ability, and it becomes imperative that you take him out before the battle begins. [→□ 3]

08_031 Ogre

The dreaded Ogre class can be your worst nightmare. As the Weapon Resistance table indicates, the Ogre's Full Body armor and Dermal Armor Augmentation make him the hardest human to take down other than a Boss. Ordinary ballistic weapons are very ineffective, so if you do fight him, bring an energy weapon with you. Realistically though, you will need alternate methods of taking him out. Stealth should be your first thought, as sneaking past him poses the least potential risk. The Ogre is a plodding sentry and easy to slip past. A silent Takedown will cost you only one bar of energy, a bargain for such a behemoth. However, if you are unfortunately caught in a firefight with a pissed off Ogre, things get a lot trickier. [→□ 4]

Although he is slow moving, you can't exploit the Ogre's weakness to melee by running in and going for a Takedown, thanks to his Typhoon Augmentation [→□ 5]. Do not make the mistake of getting close to him, no matter how dire the situation gets, as it will result in almost certain death. If you remain undetected he will not activate his Typhoon, so stealth Takedowns are still quite safe. You can also get close and use your own Typhoon before he uses his, and because you are completely invincible during the Typhoon activation animation, you are almost certain to survive. Using up a Typhoon claymore is not recommended for a single Ogre, but if the situation calls for it, don't hesitate to use it. If you can catch multiple enemies in the blast, it can still work out to be a cost effective use of the Typhoon. In terms of heavy weapons, the Grenade and Rocket Launchers can also make short work of the Ogre, but again, try to catch multiple enemies in the blast. The quickest and easiest way to deal with a hostile Ogre is with grenades and mines. A Frag can take him out in a single blast if it lands fairly near him. Gas explosives are also quite effective, and the EMP and Concussion grenades can stun him for enough time for you to either get away, or run in and go for a Takedown before he has a chance to recover and activate his Typhoon [→□ 6]. While the Stun Gun and PEPS are also quite effective at knocking him out, their use is not recommended due to how close you must get to be effective with them.

Other weapons that can stand up to the Ogre include the Plasma Rifle, which can bypass his armor and take him out quickly. Early on, a great way of fighting him is with your upgraded Revolver. The explosive rounds upgrade gives your shots a small blast radius, which if the Ogre is caught in will stagger him [→□ 7]. Once you are able to stagger him once this way, you can keep him staggered indefinitely until he dies with repeated shots. The Ogre can be staggered by all explosions in this way. You can also use the brief time he is staggered to go for a Takedown. At long range, the Ogre will use his Heavy Rifle, which he is always equipped with. The Heavy Rifle's accuracy deteriorates massively at long range, and since the Ogre moves so slowly, increasing the distance between you is easily doable. At the very limits of his range, you can even take him out with a weaker weapon, such as the Combat Rifle, as he slowly makes his way towards you. The Heavy Rifle is very powerful inside its effective range however, so don't try to fight the Ogre without cover. The Dermal Armor Augmentation is heavily recommended if you do foresee many fights with the Ogre, as is some defense against EMP and Concussion grenades. You are more likely to face the threat of grenades with the Ogre about, since you will be spending so much time in cover.

When the Ogre is part of a squad, his role is that of a sort of 'bullet sponge'. He is there to present you with a large, threatening target, taking center stage with a massive presence. His entire design is meant to exude the notion of a threat that should be dealt with immediately. However, the real danger comes in wasting all your time fighting the Ogre, while his allied Sneaker and Soldier class friends close the distance and flank you. To combat this, you should either deal with the Ogre in quick and decisive fashion, such as with a Frag Grenade, or deal with the minor enemies supporting him first, making him much easier to deal with.

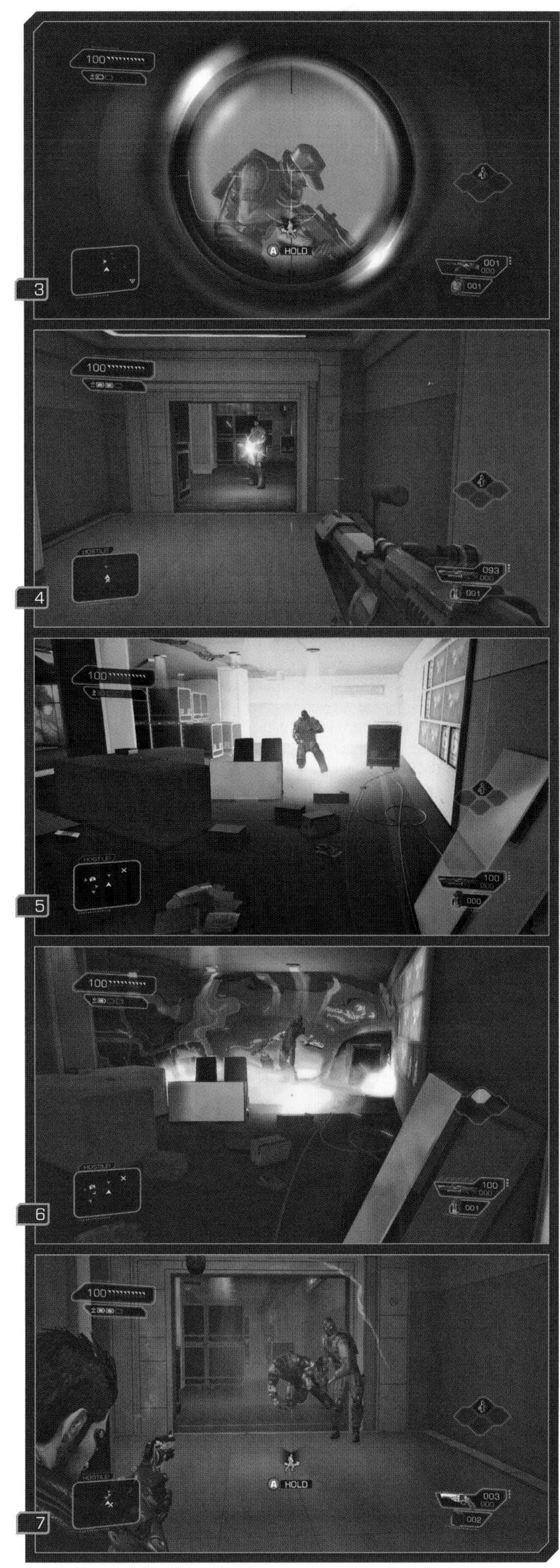

ROBOTS

Versions: Police Box Guards, Belltower Security Box Guards, Belltower Special Ops Box Guards

You will find that the robotic enemies you encounter are built to last. Very well armored and resistant to most kinds of ballistic weapons fire, they are designed to be the ultimate deterrent to a would-be enemy. Avoiding them when possible is best, but if combat does arise, remember their inherent weakness to energy based weapons and EMP explosives.

Class	Box Guard	Medium Sentry
Health	380	200
Armor	Very High	Medium
Weaponry	Dual Heavy Rifle, Rockets	Dual Combat Rifle

Box Guard

Box Guards

The ultimate weapon, the Box Guard can lay waste to anyone with its devastating firepower, which manifests in the form of Dual Heavy Rifles and a Rocket Launcher. Thankfully, they are slow and stupid, and easy to maneuver around and avoid. They are also highly susceptible to EMP explosives, and a single one can take them out. However, should you get spotted and find yourself without any EMP explosives, you still have some options. The Stun Gun and PEPS will immobilize it for a short while, giving you enough time to get to safety. Also, try to keep another enemy between you and the Box Guard [→☐ 1]. It won't shoot if there's a possibility of hitting a friendly, so use these few seconds wisely. Outside of EMP explosives, your only chance will be with the Plasma or Laser Rifle, or with the Grenade or Rocket Launchers. Spending ammo to destroy with any other weapon is not cost effective at all, and should be avoided.

Medium Sentry

The Medium Sentry is a smaller robotic enemy, not quite as potent as the Box Guard but still a deadly enemy thanks to its high health and good armor. If you can avoid raising an alarm, the Medium Sentry will not be sent out and you can avoid it altogether. It also suffers from the same weakness to EMP explosives, the Stun Gun and PEPS as the Box Guard. A well placed Frag Grenade can also deal with it quickly and efficiently. [→☐ 2]

Medium Sentry

	Min. Body Shots		Min. Headshots	
Weapon	Box Guard	Medium Sentry	Box Guard	Medium Sentry
Revolver	26	14	20	11
10mm Pistol	127	42	98	33
Machine Pistol	218	72	168	55
Combat Rifle	190	63	147	49
Heavy Rifle	169	45	130	35
Tactical Shotgun	34	12	26	9
Sniper Rifle	16	8	12	7
Crossbow	26	9	20	7
Tranq Gun (in seconds)	26	14	20	11
Rocket Launcher	2	1	2	1
Plasma Rifle	16	8	12	7
Laser Rifle	8	4	6	4
Stun Gun	4	2	3	2
Frag Grenade	2	1	2	1
Gas Grenade (seconds)	19	10	15	8

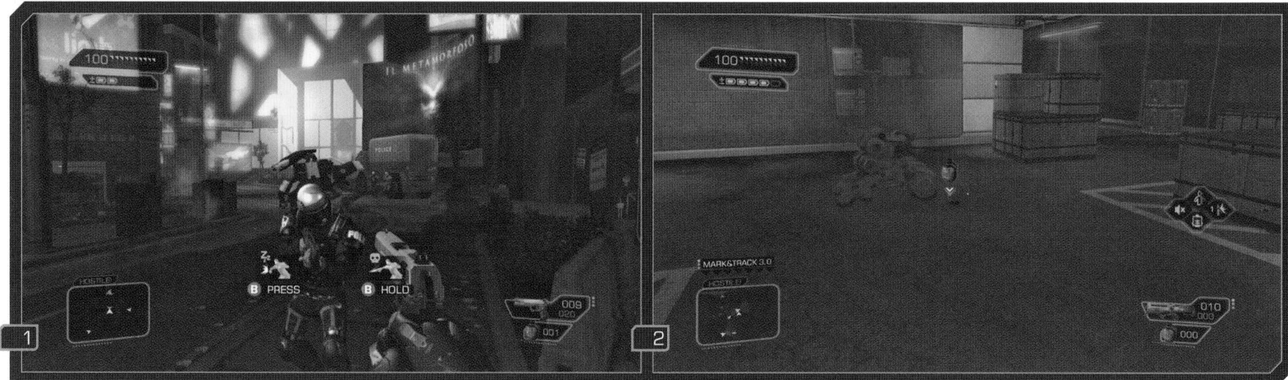

BOSSES

The deadly mercenary squad responsible for the attack on Sarif Industries makes up the majority of the Boss encounters you will experience. Each Boss will have their own unique battlefield, which will play a part in the fight. No matter your approach to the rest of the game, be it stealth or combat oriented, it is important to plan ahead for Bosses. Apportioning a significant part of your inventory for dealing with Bosses should be an utmost priority. Going into the fight with a few Frag and Gas Grenades or Mines, some Typhoon ammo, along with an explosive or energy weapon or two will go a long way to making each fight easier.

LAWRENCE BARRETT

Barrett is your basic Tank Boss, and is designed to force you to find an alternate method of taking him down instead of with conventional weapons fire. Armed with a powerful hand mounted minigun, he will move slowly, stalking you across the battlefield. It is possible to evade him long enough for him to lose sight of you, but this will cause him to throw more grenades in random locations in an attempt to flush you out. This can have the adverse effect of detonating the nearby explosive and gas canisters, which are very useful in this fight.

	Min. Body Shots	Min. Headshots
Weapon	Lawrence Barrett	
Revolver	80	32
10mm Pistol	400	160
Machine Pistol	686	275
Combat Rifle	600	240
Heavy Rifle	267	107
Tactical Shotgun	107	43
Sniper Rifle	48	20
Crossbow	80	32
Tranq Gun (sec)	80	32
Rocket Launcher	8	3
Plasma Rifle	48	20
Laser Rifle	24	10
Stun Gun	12	5
Frag Grenade	8	3
Gas Grenade (sec)	60	24

Environment

The battle will take place in a large room, which has 8 pillars near the sides. There are also various boxes, crates and low walls which you can use for cover. The whole environment is designed for you to keep something between yourself and Barrett at all times, and the layout allows you to keep moving from cover point to cover point without exposing yourself. Dotted around the room on the various crates and boxes are ammo and health pickups. At the end of the room on the right and on the left hand side near the entrance are two small side rooms, which have a weapons cache, explosives, health items and some more ammo. Be sure to visit these areas at least once during the fight [→☐ 3]. The most important aspect of this room is the various explosive and gas canisters dotted about the sides. These are integral to your success, so make sure you don't stand in a position that would allow Barrett to destroy this with his gunfire or grenades.

Attacks

Weapons Fire: This is Barrett's main form of attack. He will begin spinning the minigun attached to his arm and open fire at where he thinks you are. Occasionally he will do this while stationary, but mostly he will do it while moving towards you.

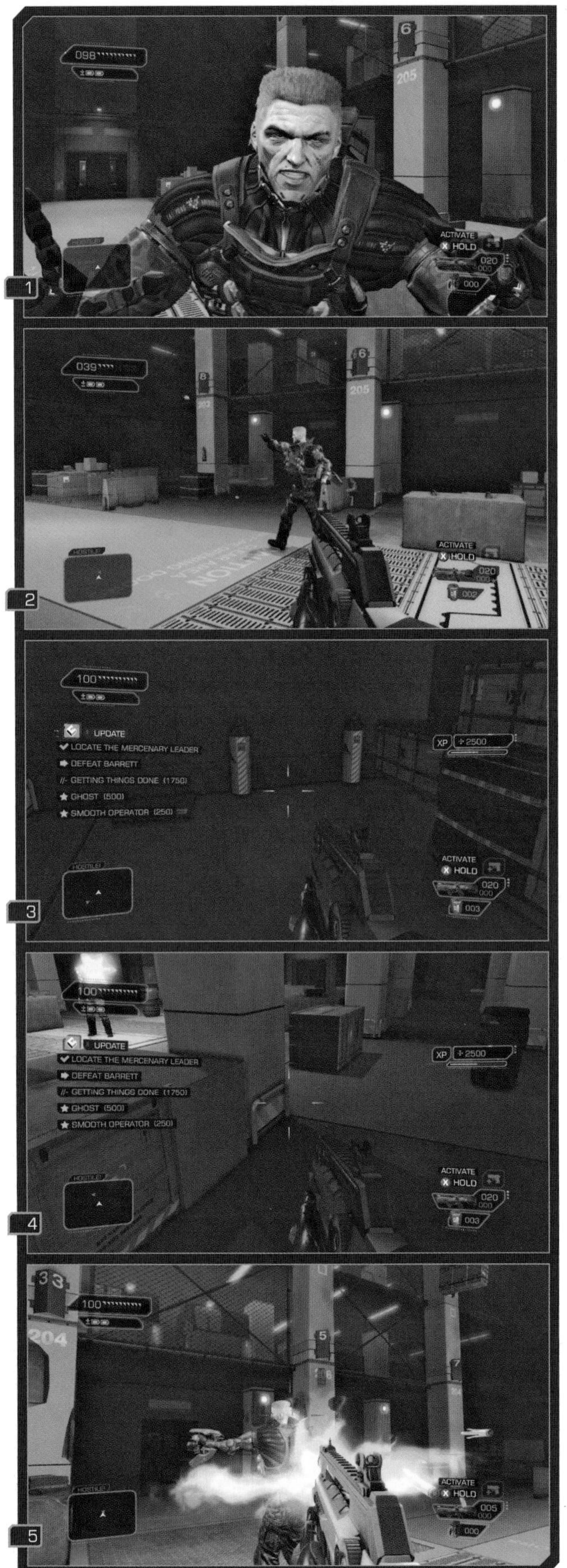

Grab and Punch: Barrett will constantly attempt to move towards where he thinks you are and close distance. His end goal is get close enough to you to execute the Grab and Punch. Once Barrett gets close to you, he will grab and punch you in an animated sequence akin to a Takedown. This is a very damaging move, so avoid it at all costs. While you are getting up, Barrett will reload his gun and get ready to fire at you again, so move away quickly as soon as you get the opportunity to do so. If you attempt to melee Barrett, he will counter with the Grab and Punch.

Grenade Toss: Barrett is also equipped with what appears to be a limitless supply of Frag Grenades. If you are staying hidden in cover for too long, Barrett will toss a grenade in your direction. There is also a chance he may throw 3 grenades at once [→□ 1]. Move quickly as soon as he does, or these grenades will finish you. Barrett won't really think about where he is when he activated this attack, so there is a good chance he can bounce the grenades of a nearby surface back onto himself.

Recommended Strategy

This strategy requires that you have at least 2 Frag Grenades with you to start the fight. It is still possible with other grenades, but will take longer. To begin, immediately throw a Frag Grenade at his feet while he prepares to fire his gun. As soon as you have thrown it, turn to your right and look in the corner of the room. There should be 2 gas canisters resting against the wall [→□ 2]. Pick one of them up, and toss it directly at Barrett. Do it quickly, while he is still stunned from the Frag Grenade, but do it accurately so the canister makes contact with him directly. If you throw it directly onto him, it will explode, stunning him again.

Now throw your second Frag Grenade at him. Just like before, turn around and grab the second gas canister from the wall and toss it at him. As soon as it explodes on him, run to the right hand side of the center of the room. There you will find a red explosive canister. It should be roughly to the right of where Barrett is currently standing [→□ 3]. Grab it and toss it at him just like you did with the gas canister, making sure to throw it directly onto him. If you have done this correctly, this final canister should spell the end for Barrett.

Alternate Strategies

There are a few other ways to fight Barrett should you feel the need. While it is a much more lengthy fight, battling from while in cover and popping out to fire at him when there is a gap in his attacks is a viable strategy. Also, if you remain hidden for long enough and move around from cover to cover without being seen by him, he will eventually lose you and begin to walk around to look for you [→□ 4]. You can use this opportunity to move around the room and collect the various items, eventually initiating the recommended strategy above when you are ready to win.

While Barrett is moving around the room, he will invariably walk close to the various canisters that are dotted around. You can use these opportunities to blow them up with gunfire to cause substantial damage to him. You can also pick up the canisters and throw them at him. His propensity to fire at you with his Minigun at every given opportunity makes this quite dangerous, since he will, as he will detonate them while you are still holding them. As such, you should stun him first or throw them after he has lost sight of you.

Barrett also responds quite poorly to grenades. Should you throw a Concussion Grenade at him, he will be stunned, and upon recovery will ALWAYS go for a triple grenade toss at your last known location. If you use a Gas Grenade, he will perform a triple grenade toss twice, giving you ample time to fire at him. And finally, should you use an EMP explosive, the heavily Augmented Barrett will be stunned for an age, and then finally be forced to perform three triple grenade tosses in sequence, allowing you to unload round after into him with no possible repercussion [→□ 5]. Use the time to get close and fire at his head with an automatic weapon, then when he is about to do the third triple grenade toss, go back into cover.

YELENA FEDOROVA

Yelena Fedorova is a deadly opponent, armed with dangerous weaponry and Augmentations. Quick and agile, she will take you out in seconds using her machine guns or Claymore Augmentation if you give her the opportunity. Her judicious use of the Claymore and Cloaking Augmentations mean she will have to recharge her energy often, which she will do while walking around the room, usually cloaked. If she spots you during this, she will fire her very powerful machine guns. She is very susceptible to electromagnetic interference, which you can create either with EMP explosives or by destroying the generators on the walls of the room.

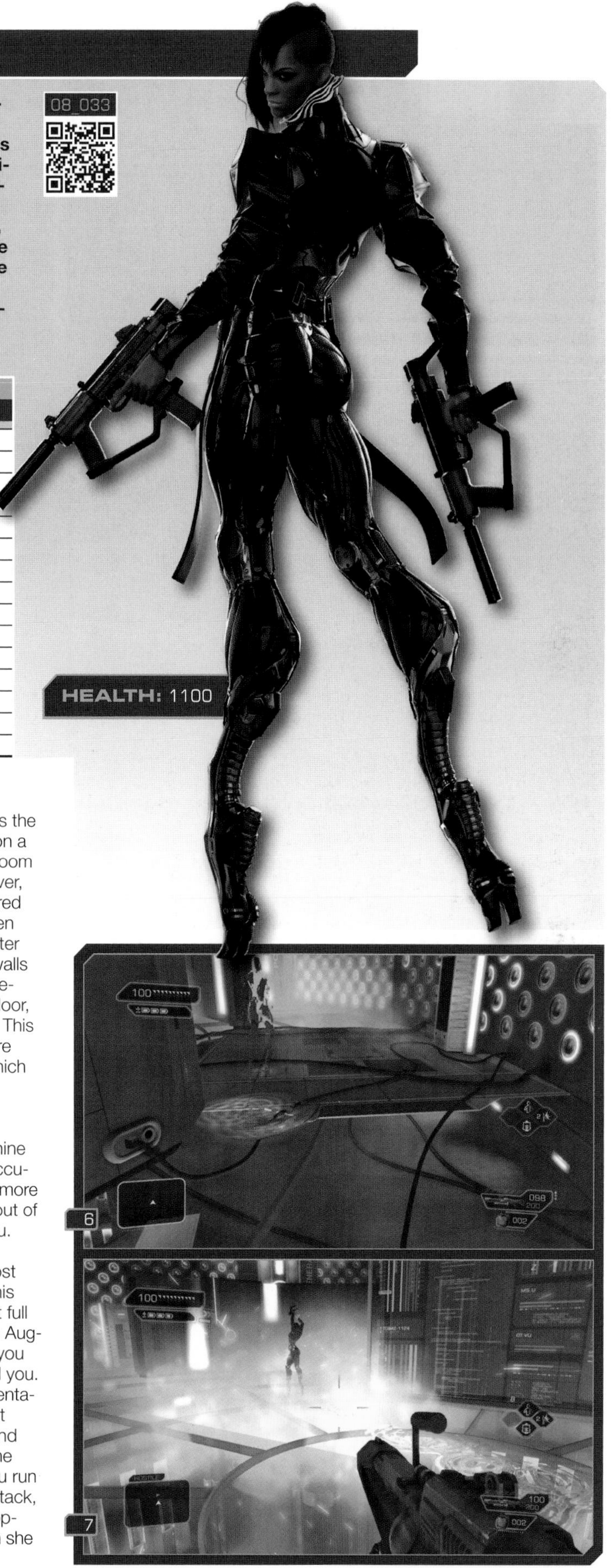

	Min. Body Shots	Min. Headshots
Weapon	Yelena Fedorova	
Revolver	40	16
10mm Pistol	200	80
Machine Pistol	343	138
Combat Rifle	300	120
Heavy Rifle	134	54
Tactical Shotgun	54	22
Sniper Rifle	24	10
Crossbow	40	16
Tranq Gun (sec)	40	16
Rocket Launcher	4	2
Plasma Rifle	24	10
Laser Rifle	12	5
Stun Gun	6	3
Frag Grenade	4	2
Gas Grenade (sec)	30	12

Environment

The environment you will battle Fedorova in is very interesting. It is the room that contains the core of Eliza Cassan, and she is present on a large screen in the middle of the room throughout the fight. The room itself is spherical, with curving walls that can be used well for cover, to hide, or to lure Fedorova into a narrow path. The floor is covered with liquid, and plays an important role throughout the fight. When she is cloaked, watching the splashes of her footsteps in the water is an easy way to spot her [→☐ 6]. Also, the generators on the walls to the left and right of the main door can be destroyed. The subsequent release of electrical energy will be conducted through the floor, damaging you and Fedorova, and disrupting her Augmentations. This can be a useful way to find her when she is cloaked too. There are also numerous lockers dotted along the walls filled with items, which should be collected at the earliest possible opportunity.

Attacks

Weapons Fire: Fedorova will stand still and fire both of her machine guns at you. This is a devastating attack, and Fedorova is very accurate. She will use this most often when she has used up her Claymore attacks and is walking around waiting for it to recharge. Staying out of her sight will ensure that she doesn't get to use this attack on you.

Claymore Dash: Fedorova's main method of attack, and the most devastating one. Whether cloaked or uncloaked, once she has this charged and has found you, she will attempt it. Dashing at you at full speed, Fedorova will slide towards you and release her Claymore Augmentation, causing a powerful explosion around her. The further you are the less damage you will take, and a direct hit can outright kill you. This is best counter-acted by releasing your own Typhoon Augmentation, timing it so by the time Fedorova reaches you, you are about to release the explosion. You can also run straight towards her, and use the sprint to pass her. Because she slides forwards before she releases the Claymore, you will be too far away from her once you run past her for the explosion to reach you. After she executes the attack, she is vulnerable as she pauses for a second [→☐ 7]. Take this opportunity to shoot her, before preparing to run past her again when she

comes in for the next attack. After three Claymore Dashes, Fedorova must recharge and will turn on her cloak and run away from you.

Counter: Fedorova will use this when you try to use a close range Takedown on her, so don't attempt one.

Recommended Strategy

As soon as the battle starts run straight towards Fedorova. She will run at you to attempt a Claymore Dash. When she does, counter attack with your own Typhoon as she comes close to you [→☐ 1]. If you don't have any Typhoon ammo or the Augmentation, run past Fedorova instead. This will take you past her Claymore Dash. As soon as you pass her, turn around and fire your most powerful weapon at her until she begins to run at you again. Do this every time she performs her Claymore Dash. When she has run out of energy, let her run away and begin searching the lockers on the walls. Find the EMP Mines, the Mine Templates and the Typhoon Ammo. Lay the EMP Mines in the side paths (remembering where you have placed them). Combine the two templates with two Frag Grenades if you have them. Wait for Fedorova to get caught in one of your EMP Mines, and then place the 2 Frag Mines next to her. If she survives, use your Typhoon the next time she uses a Claymore Dash attack against you to finish her off, or dodge the dash again and shoot her while she recovers.

Alternate Strategies

You can also use the environmental features of the room to battle Fedorova, although this is harder and riskier. Avoid her Claymore Dashes as usual, but try to lure her towards one of the generators on the walls. She will destroy it with her own Claymore. While she is stunned, take the opportunity to attack her with your most powerful weapons. [→☐ 2]

You can also play the battle stealthily, by using your Silent Movement Augmentations and Cloaking Augmentation to stay hidden. Once she has lost you and has begun looking around the arena for you, you can use hit and run tactics by finding her using the Wall Penetrating Imager Augmentation and the Mark and Track Augmentation, attacking her, then using your own cloak to get away and stay hidden.

JARON NAMIR

The aim of this battle is to keep Namir away from you at all times. He is equipped with devastating weapons that will finish you in seconds. The Plasma Rifle he wields cannot be withstood for long, and he is also loaded with almost every grenade type. He is also quite agile, able to move fairly quickly and clamber over walls to get to you faster. He also has a Cloak Augmentation, making him all the more difficult to keep track of as he moves about. He has good resistance to all grenade types, and they will only stun him very briefly at best.

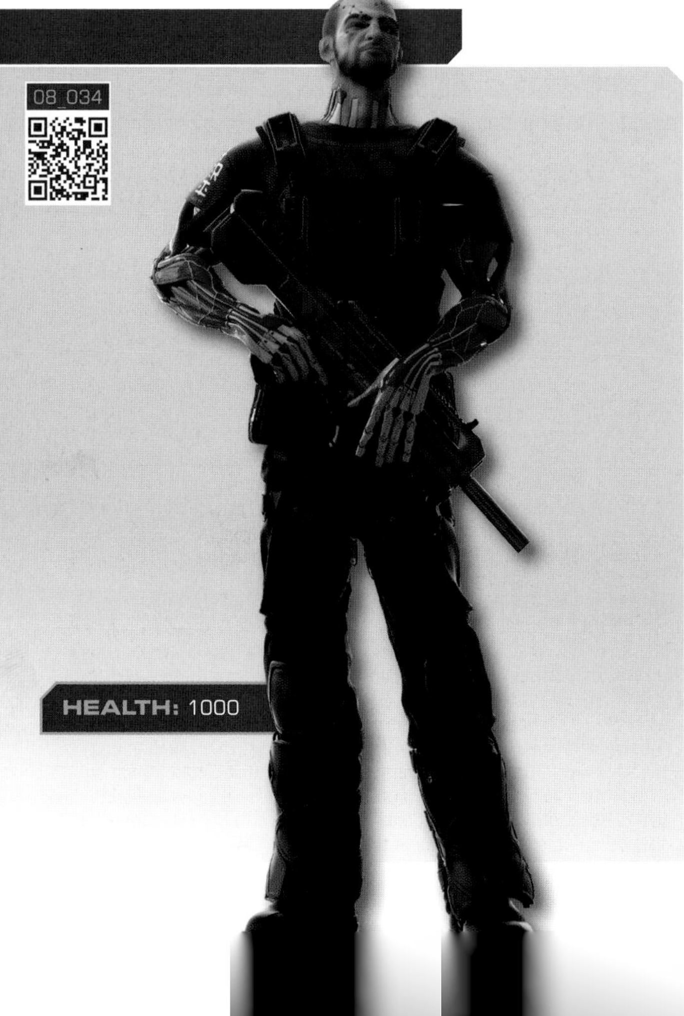

	Min. Body Shots	Min. Headshots
Weapon	Jaron Namir	
Revolver	40	16
10mm Pistol	200	80
Machine Pistol	343	138
Combat Rifle	300	120
Heavy Rifle	134	54
Tactical Shotgun	54	22
Sniper Rifle	24	10
Crossbow	40	16
Tranq Gun (in seconds)	40	16
Rocket Launcher	4	2
Plasma Rifle	24	10
Laser Rifle	12	5
Stun Gun	6	3
Frag Grenade	4	2
Gas Grenade (seconds)	30	12

Environment

The room you will battle Namir in has some unique features. There are walls near the outer edge, and a glass panel separator in the middle [→☐ 3]. This essentially creates two main sections, the outer passage and the inner area. Namir has the ability to bound over the walls to reach both areas quickly, even appearing behind you without warning. The moving statues throughout the room are standing on drawers that contain items. The glass panel in the middle can be penetrated with the Laser Rifle, which is in the drawer to the left of the entrance door. The majority of the battle will be spent using the corners of the walls as cover to keep something between you and Namir's Plasma Rifle at all times.

Attacks

Weapons Fire: Namir will fire his Plasma Rifle at you in bursts of 2 – 5 shots, before briefly pausing to fire another burst. After the second burst he will reload or wait longer before firing another 2 burst set. It only takes a few direct hits from the Plasma Rifle to get killed. Thankfully the weapon has poor accuracy, and the further you are from Namir the easier it is to avoid getting hit.

Grenade Toss: Namir will jump into the air, and throw three grenades at you at once; a Frag, EMP and Gas Grenade. Needless to say, if you are anywhere near the vicinity you will be loading your game from the last save very soon.

Counter: Much like Fedorova, Namir has a counterattack that he uses if you attempt a Takedown on him.

Recommended Strategy

As soon as the battle begins, toss a grenade at Namir's feet. It doesn't matter which grenade it is, but a Gas Grenade would be preferable. Turn around and walk around the glass and through the gap in the walls to the right, towards the entrance door. Walk down the outer passageway towards Namir and go into cover at the corner, looking down the passageway. Namir will soon appear. VERY briefly pop out to shoot at him with a powerful single shot weapon (preferably the Revolver) and go back into cover. Namir will either return fire or throw some grenades. If he returns fire, keep firing back at him in-between his bursts, being very careful not to get hit by his powerful plasma shots [→☐ 4]. When he eventually throws his grenades at you, immediately exit cover, turn around and run down the outer passageway as fast as you can, until you are around the corner. The aim is to make sure you are at the opposite end of a corridor to Namir at all times. As soon as you are, go into cover on this corner just like before, and wait for Namir to come round the corner again. When he does, fire at him as before.

When you fire at him this time, one of two things will happen. Either he will do the same thing as before, and exchange fire with you or throw some grenades, or he will stay in the corner. If he throws the grenades, just do the same thing again and run down the passageway, waiting by the corner after you pass it. He will come round the corner at the opposite end of the corridor and you can try again. If he stays in the corner, he will be stuck here, sporadically firing at you. You can now pick him off at your leisure, popping out to fire between bursts.

Alternate Strategies

If you have 3 rounds of Typhoon Ammo and a level 2 Typhoon Augmentation, this battle is short and sweet. Simply throw a grenade at him at the very start of the battle, preferably of the gas variety, and then run up and use the Typhoon 3 times [→☐ 5].

You can also fight a bit more pro-actively, by taking advantage of Namir's tendency to jump over things. Namir's game plan is to cut off the arena and close you down, climbing over walls while cloaked to attack you, preferably from behind. You must be aware of where he is at all times so you can maintain your distance. You can punish his penchant for climbing by ambushing him as he lands. Stand at one end of the glass divider in the center of the room, and wait to see which side of the glass Namir is on. When you see him, walk to the opposite side of the glass, and make sure he can see you. When he does, he will jump over the glass to get to you. Use this opportunity to

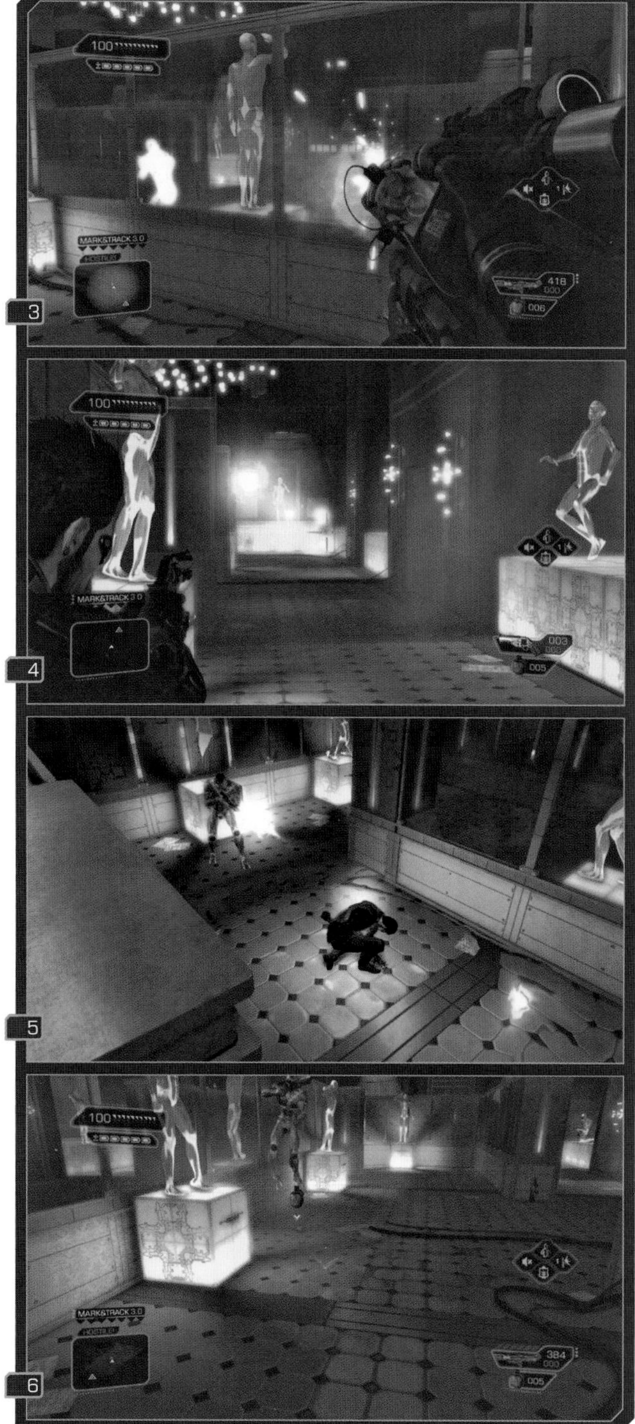

shoot him as he lands or throw a grenade, and then run to the other side before he can shoot you [→☐ 6].

He will jump over again, and so on. This is even more effective if you can shoot him though the glass with the Laser Rifle, which conveniently can be found in this very room. Be careful that he doesn't choose to walk around the glass divider instead of jumping over it. If he does, run to the opposite end of the divider and stay in cover at the end, waiting to see which side he chooses. Once you see which side he is on, run around to the other side of the glass and attempt to goad him into jumping over the divider.

THE HYRON PROJECT

The Hyron Project Boss battle is more a sequence of events and smaller obstacles to be dealt with rather than a single entity. The Hyron Project is a hive mind made up of separate consciousnesses, and as a result each of these must be deactivated in order to get to the core. These Hyron Drones are protected by automated defense systems and sophisticated security systems that are tough to hack.

08_035

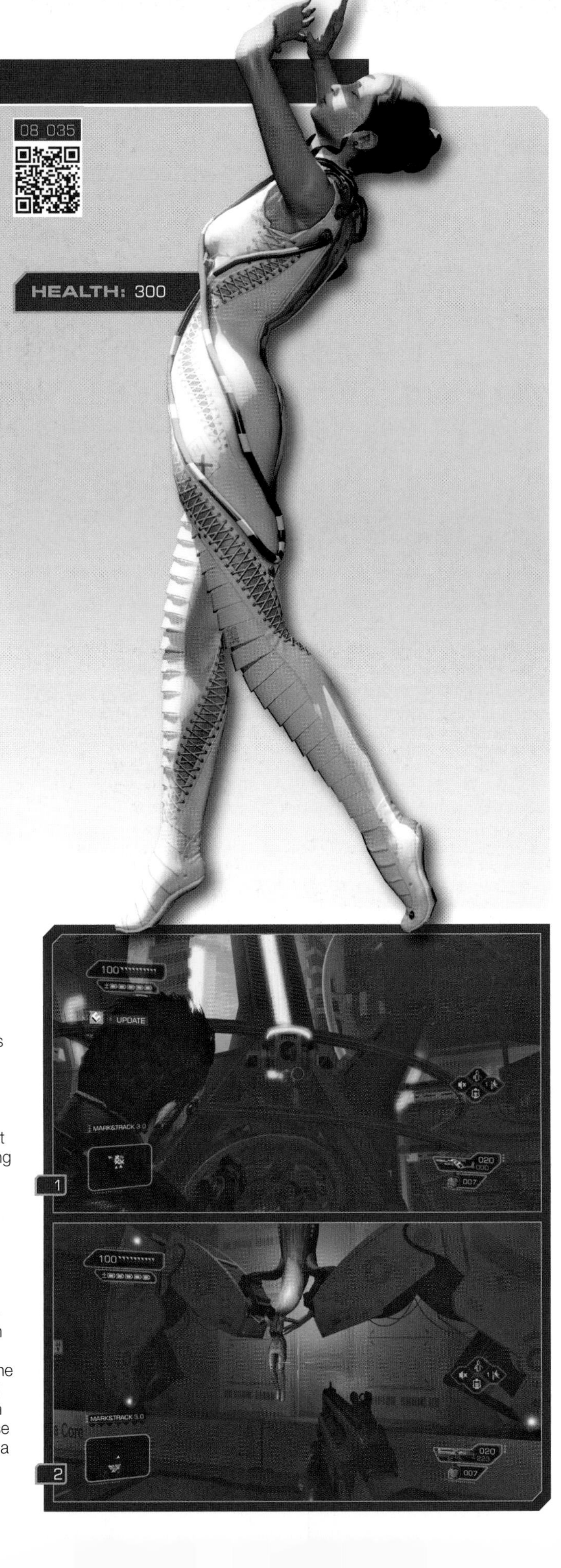

HEALTH: 300

Weapon	Min. Body Shots	Min. Headshots
	The Hyron Project	
Revolver	40	16
10mm Pistol	200	80
Machine Pistol	343	138
Combat Rifle	300	120
Heavy Rifle	134	54
Tactical Shotgun	54	22
Sniper Rifle	24	10
Crossbow	40	16
Tranq Gun (sec)	40	16
Rocket Launcher	4	2
Plasma Rifle	24	10
Laser Rifle	12	5
Stun Gun	6	3
Frag Grenade	4	2
Gas Grenade (sec)	30	12

Environment

The room you are in is dominated by the central structure that contains three Hyron Drones, who must be deactivated in order for you to get to the brain. Rotating along the top of this structure are three Turrets [→□ 1]. Next to each alcove that contains the drones is a switch that will activate a purge, which gives you a brief moment to kill the drone. There is also a hackable panel to the side of the alcove facing Zhao. Once hacked it allows you to directly deactivate each drone. Off to the side is Zhao as the Hyron Project, behind a glass panel [→□ 2]. At the top level of the room near the sides are three more hackable panels. If hacked, they lower the alcoves from which the drones emerge, allowing you to take them out safely from a distance. There are also doors at the lower level of the room that release Medium Sentries and Crazies. The bots are released after all three drones have been deactivated, and the Crazies are released after two drones are deactivated.

Attacks

The Hyron Project does not attack you in the conventional sense, but rather uses automated defense systems to stop you from deactivating the drones. Initially there are three rotating Turrets above the central structure. After two drones are deactivated, Crazies are released to slow you down. After the third drone is deactivated, you will have to deal with a Medium Sentry. Also, different sections of the floor will periodically be electrified. [→□ 3]

Recommended Strategy

The fastest and easiest way to defeat the Hyron Project is to take advantage of a unique property of the Laser Rifle: its ability to pierce thin walls and obstacles. Since Zhao is behind a sheet of glass, the Laser Rifle can penetrate this easily to kill her without having to deactivate the drones. Simply move down to a slightly lower level of the room, and go into cover behind one of the low walls. Once there, take aim with the Laser Rifle at Zhao through the glass over to the right [→□ 4]. Use the scope if necessary. Watch out for the Turrets in front of you. After a sustained burst, you will have defeated the Hyron Project.

1

2

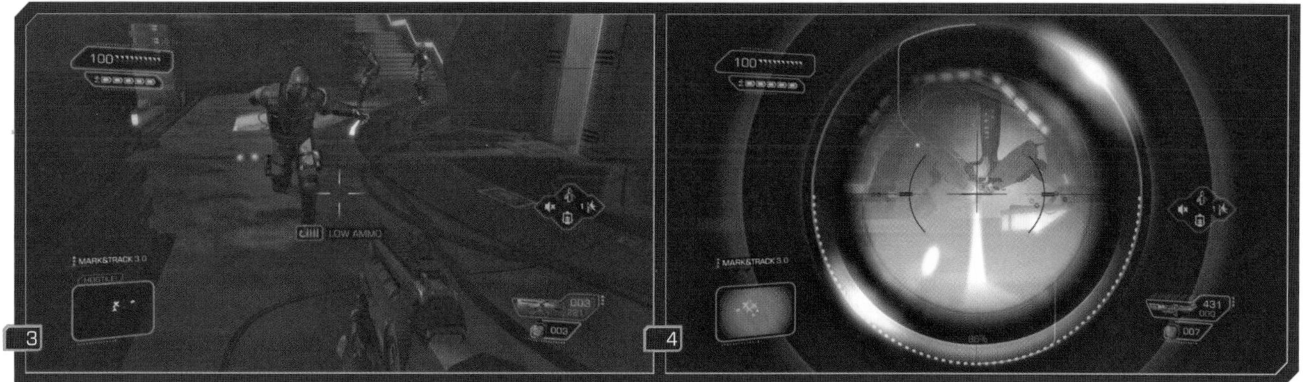

Alternate Strategies

Should you find yourself without the Laser Rifle, you will have to tackle the Hyron Project the normal way. You have a few choices when you begin. You can choose to go along the sides of the room to get to the hackable panels, hack them and expose the drones before taking them out from a distance [→☐ 5]. If you do this, you will most likely need the Cloaking Augmentation; otherwise you will be shot at by the Turrets as you are hacking. Alternatively, you can first take out the Turrets from cover near the entrance. They are resilient but at this point you should have more than enough ammo. Once they are down you can go down to the lower area and manually purge and deactivate each drone.

After the second drone, you will have to deal with some Crazies. Use your grenades or Typhoon to defeat them quickly, as you will not need them for anything else. Once you have deactivated the third drone, Medium Sentries will be released. Use EMP explosives to take them out quickly. The floor will also become electrified periodically, which is powerful enough to kill you instantly unless you have the EMP Shielding Augmentation. Stand on the side of a staircase or large crate to avoid it [→☐ 6]. Once the cracks have appeared in the glass in front of Zhao, break it by firing at it and finish her off.

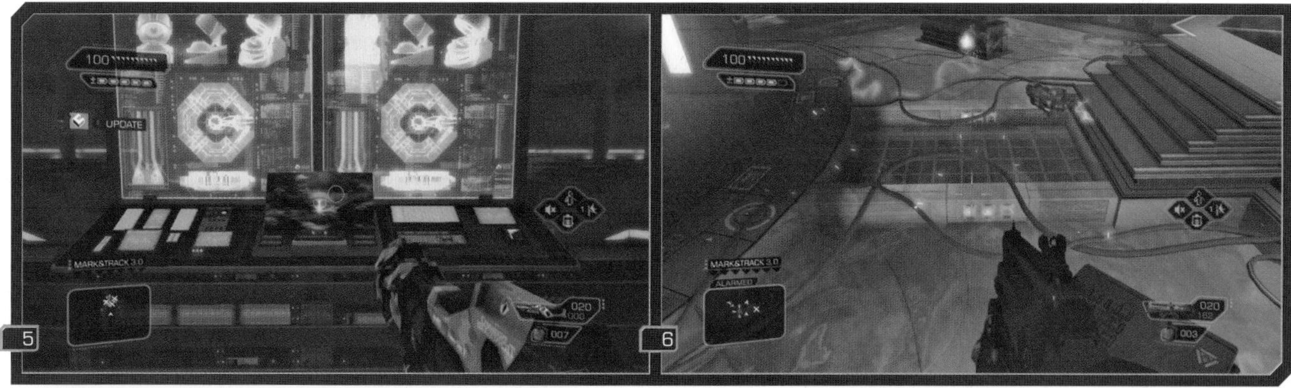

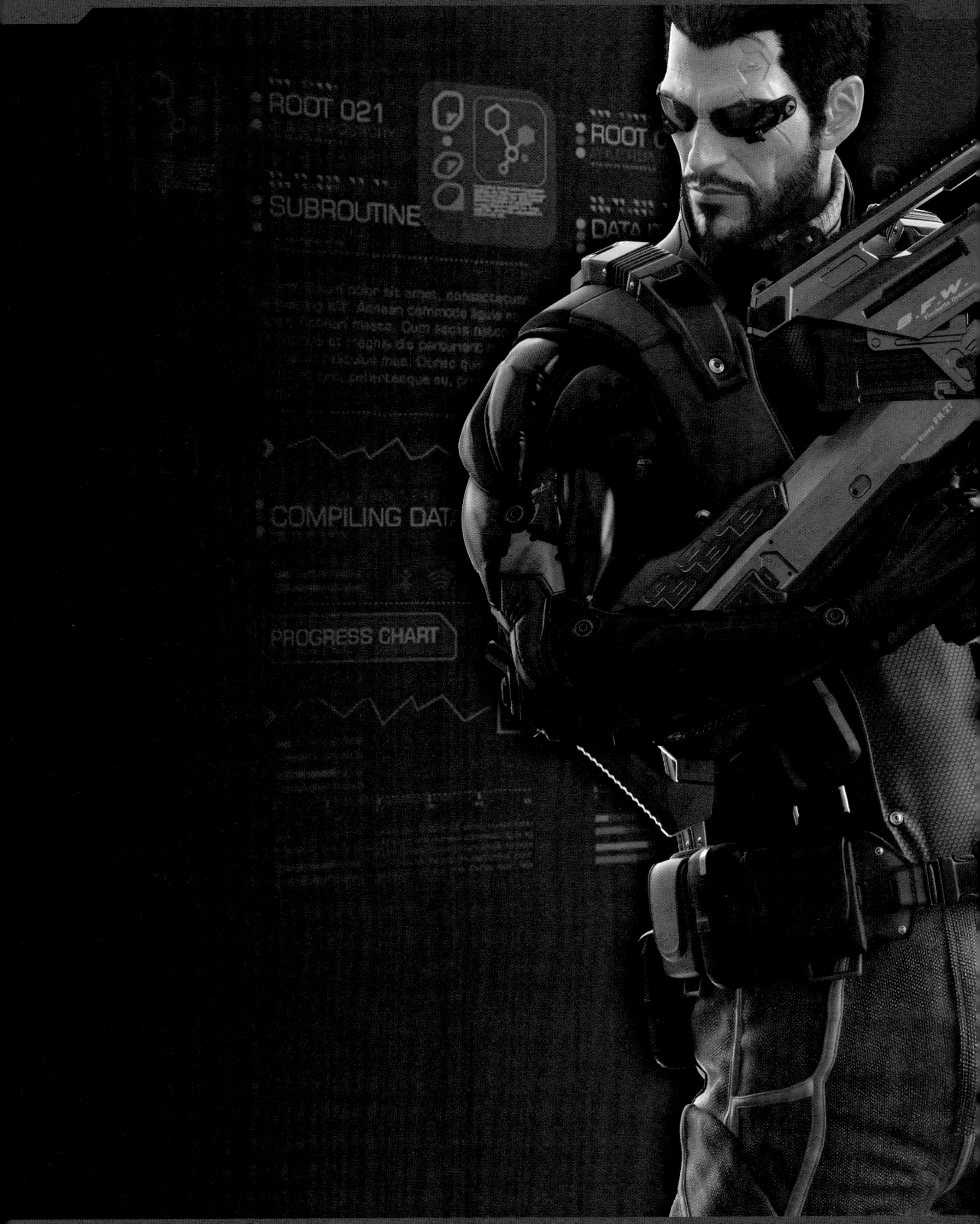
ROOT 021
SUBROUTINE
PROGRESS CHART

CH05 Walkthrough

The Walkthrough Chapter will take you through the entire game using a unique route system. Each route provides a different way through the area, allowing you to choose your own path. The routes chosen are usually of a specific type: pure Stealth, Stealth Combat, and Combat. Pure Stealth means not alerting anyone to your presence, while Stealth Combat will usually provide you with the most total XP.

ABOUT THIS CHAPTER

THE ROUTE SYSTEM

Since the game offers so many possible approaches to each situation, this walkthrough is separated into Routes that detail the primary ways of tackling each section. Some routes use pure stealth and some combat, while others use a mixture in order to maximise potential XP gain. When you reach the start of each sub-section you can also check how the various routes play out and then mix and match them to create your own ideal approach.

NOTE ON THE ROUTES:

Route 1: Stealth
Get through the game without firing a shot and not engaging a single enemy.

Route 2: Stealth Combat
Avoid all out combat, but take a path that allows you to silently take out the enemy, thus netting some extra XP which leads to faster upgrades. This route will not track down every enemy, but the path will lead you through the most viable and profitable route, whilst also remaining undetected.

Route 3: Combat
Go in guns blazing and have some fun. Kill everyone that comes running, but again, do not track down every single enemy.

CONVERSATIONS

Deus Ex: Human Revolution features complex conversations with characters that can affect the way their stories play out. You'll be able to choose your responses from a lit of three possibilities, but you'll never be sure which one will lead to best results, because the system is slightly random in nature. For this reason we've provided a path through each conversation that will be sure you come out on top, as shown here, but the exact result can still vary. There are also many minor conversations you can engage in with characters that allow you to choose your responses, but do not actually affect anything in the game or story. Many of these will be pointed out during the walkthrough, or in the Optional Exploration sections.

CONVERSATION FLOW
ZEKE SANDERS
PERSONALITY TYPE: NONE

Conversation Round	Response to Make
Round 1	Empathize
Round 2	Empathize
Round 3	Reason

TIP BOXES

There are 3 different types of tip boxes used in the walkthrough to ensure you won't miss anything important along the way. These are broken down as follows:

Achievement/Trophy
These will point out anything you need to know in order to unlock an Achievement/Trophy in the current area. The Extras chapter includes a dedicated Completion Guide that covers all Achievements/Trophies in full detail, but these boxes will serve as quick reminders.

Tip
The general Tip box is used to point out useful hints and tips that can save you time or sometimes provide you with an alternate solution or tactic for the current area being covered.

Side Quests
Deus Ex: Human Revolution is filled with optional Side Quests, and the Side Quests chapter has a separate walkthrough for each of them. When you begin each of these quests is up to you, however, so these boxes will let you know when one becomes available.

AREA MAPS

Whenever the walkthrough begins to cover a brand new area you'll be presented with all of the color maps for that area spread across multiple pages. These maps will include all of the items and terminals that can be found in the area, and as such will be a valuable reference when playing through the section they appear in.

EXAMPLE PAGE

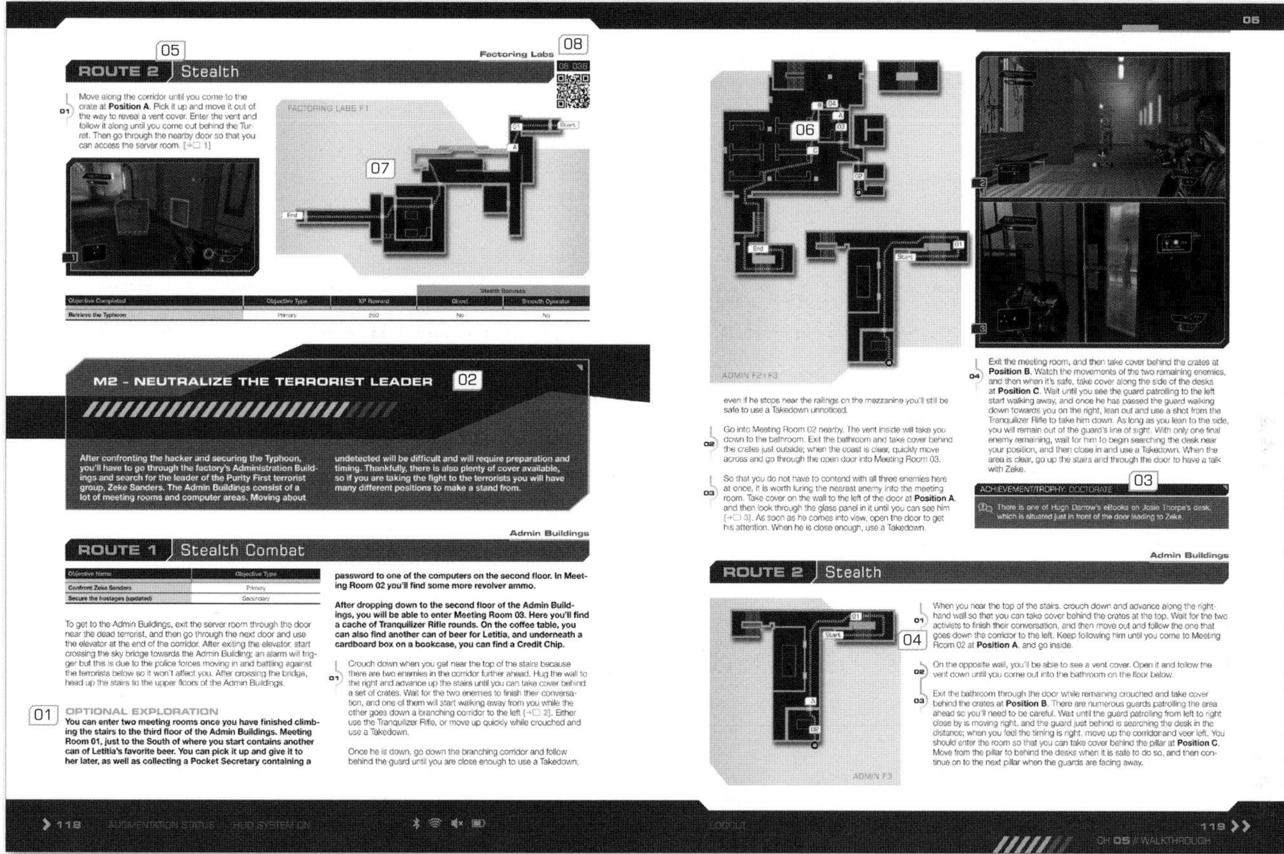

05

Factoring Labs

08

ROUTE 2 Stealth

08 036

01 Move along the corridor until you come to the crate at **Position A**. Pick it up and move it out of the way to reveal a vent cover. Enter the vent and follow it along until you come out behind the Turret. Then go through the nearby door so that you can access the server room. [→▢ 1]

Objective Completed	Objective Type	XP Reward	Stealth Bonuses: Ghost	Stealth Bonuses: Smooth Operator
Retrieve the Typhoon	Primary	250	No	No

M2 - NEUTRALIZE THE TERRORIST LEADER 02

After confronting the hacker and securing the Typhoon, you'll have to go through the factory's Administration Buildings and search for the leader of the Purity First terrorist group, Zeke Sanders. The Admin Buildings consist of a lot of meeting rooms and computer areas. Moving about undetected will be difficult and will require preparation and timing. Thankfully, there is also plenty of cover available, so if you are taking the fight to the terrorists you will have many different positions to make a stand from.

Admin Buildings

ROUTE 1 Stealth Combat

Objective Name	Objective Type
Confront Zeke Sanders	Primary
Secure the hostages (updated)	Secondary

To get to the Admin Buildings, exit the server room through the door near the dead terrorist, and then go through the next door and use the elevator at the end of the corridor. After exiting the elevator, start crossing the sky bridge towards the Admin Building; an alarm will trigger but this is due to the police forces moving in and battling against the terrorists below so it won't affect you. After crossing the bridge, head up the stairs to the upper floors of the Admin Buildings.

01 OPTIONAL EXPLORATION

You can enter two meeting rooms once you have finished climbing the stairs to the third floor of the Admin Buildings. Meeting Room 01, just to the South of where you start contains another can of Letitia's favorite beer. You can pick it up and give it to her later, as well as collecting a Pocket Secretary containing a password to one of the computers on the second floor. In Meeting Room 02 you'll find some more revolver ammo.

After dropping down to the second floor of the Admin Buildings, you will be able to enter Meeting Room 03. Here you'll find a cache of Tranquilizer Rifle rounds. On the coffee table, you can also find another can of beer for Letitia, and underneath a cardboard box on a bookcase, you can find a Credit Chip.

01 Crouch down when you get near the top of the stairs because there are two enemies in the corridor further ahead. Hug the wall to the right and advance up the stairs until you can take cover behind a set of crates. Wait for the two enemies to finish their conversation, and one of them will start walking away from you while the other goes down a branching corridor to the left [→▢ 2]. Either use the Tranquilizer Rifle, or move up quickly while crouched and use a Takedown.

Once he is down, go down the branching corridor and follow behind the guard until you are close enough to use a Takedown; even if he stops near the railings on the mezzanine you'll still be safe to use a Takedown unnoticed.

02 Go into Meeting Room 02 nearby. The vent inside will take you down to the bathroom. Exit the bathroom and take cover behind the crates just outside; when the coast is clear, quickly move across and go through the open door into Meeting Room 03.

03 So that you do not have to contend with all three enemies here at once, it is worth luring the nearest enemy into the meeting room. Take cover on the wall to the left of the door at **Position A**, and then look through the glass panel in it until you can see him [→▢ 3]. As soon as he comes into view, open the door to get his attention. When he is close enough, use a Takedown.

04 Exit the meeting room, and then take cover behind the crates at **Position B**. Watch the movements of the two remaining enemies, and then when it's safe, take cover along the side of the desks at **Position C**. Wait until you see the guard patrolling to the left start walking away, and once he has passed the guard walking down towards you on the right, lean out and use a shot from the Tranquilizer Rifle to take him down. As long as you lean to the side, you will remain out of the guard's line of sight. With only one final enemy remaining, wait for him to begin searching the desk near your position, and then close in and use a Takedown. When the area is clear, go up the stairs and through the door to have a talk with Zeke.

03

ACHIEVEMENT/TROPHY: DOCTORATE

There is one of Hugh Darrow's eBooks on Josie Thorpe's desk, which is situated just in front of the door leading to Zeke.

Admin Buildings

ROUTE 2 Stealth

04

01 When you near the top of the stairs, crouch down and advance along the right-hand wall so that you can take cover behind the crates at the top. Wait for the two activists to finish their conversation, and then move out and follow the one that goes down the corridor to the left. Keep following him until you come to Meeting Room 02 at **Position A**, and go inside.

02 On the opposite wall, you'll be able to see a vent cover. Open it and follow the vent down until you come out into the bathroom on the floor below.

03 Exit the bathroom through the door while remaining crouched and take cover behind the crates at **Position B**. There are numerous guards patrolling the area ahead so you'll need to be careful. Wait until the guard patrolling from left to right close by is moving right, and the guard just behind is searching the desk in the distance; when you feel the timing is right, move up the corridor and veer left. You should enter the room so that you can take cover behind the pillar at **Position C**. Move from the pillar to behind the desks when it is safe to do so, and then continue on to the next pillar when the guards are facing away.

118 AUGMENTATION STATUS HUD SYSTEM ON

LOGOUT 119 CH 05 // WALKTHROUGH

Here we'll go through an example double page spread from the walkthrough to briefly illustrate the function of each of the elements within it.

01 Optional Exploration

The Optional Exploration section appears at the start of each new area, and details all of the most important hidden areas, codes or items that may be found in nearby areas. These areas may not be part of the mission's required route, so you should check this section before proceeding if you want to make sure you don't miss anything.

02 Mission Boxes

These appear whenever a new main mission begins within the game. They describe the mission's objective and tables are provided showing the full details of the mission, such as objective names and types.

03 Tip Boxes

Tip Boxes can be found throughout the walkthrough, and come in three types, each of which is described on the previous page.

04 Text Points

The walkthrough text is split into numbered points to make it easier to follow. These points are linked to the route maps found on the same page, so you can quickly see the area of the game the text begins at.

05 Routes

These headers denote the start of a new route. The routes within each area are numbered and labeled as Stealth, Stealth Combat or Combat. The name of the area the route takes place within is also provided in these headers.

06 Position Markers

These letters denote points on the route maps that make it very easy to describe a specific position accurately. In the text these positions are bolded to make them stand out, so any time you come to one of these you should check the map to see where the position is.

07 Route Maps

In addition to the text points and position markers, the route maps also feature complete route lines, which let you see the entire route at a glance. You'll also find cameras and ladders marked on these maps to make navigation easier. Note that each map only covers the specific route it's connected to, and following routes in the same area will have their own separate maps. Each map is labeled with its name and floor number.

08 Video Codes

Video codes are placed at some of the toughest or more complicated parts of the game. If you want to see exactly how our strategies are applied in these sections you can type the video code into the Future Press website to instantly access the video.

SARIF INDUSTRIES – INTRODUCTION

This is the opening of the game, and there's not much to do here. As such, there is only a single route, and it's pretty straightforward. After speaking with Megan, the game will take over, making the route automatic.

01 You start off in Megan's office. You'll only be in control in the opening room, but while you're here, you can unlock an Achievement/Trophy. Since this is the only time this one will be available to unlock, it's a good idea to go ahead and do it now.

When you're ready to progress with the game, go speak with Megan. When you do, the trip to the elevator is automatic, so sit back and relax as you watch things unfold.

ACHIEVEMENT/TROPHY: OLD SCHOOL GAMER

Investigate the following six items in Megan's office to unlock this one: eBook on couch - Newspaper on desk - Picture on desk - Book "Being More" on filing cabinet - Toy Car on filing cabinet - Read all emails on PC.

//-CH 05 WALKTHROUGH

INVESTIGATE THE DISTURBANCE

This part of the game serves as a Tutorial for basic movement and combat. As you progress through the areas, you'll receive Tutorial pop-up notifications. When you see one, press and hold the In-Game Menu button to play the Tutorial.

01 Go to Sarif's elevator and access the security terminal. You need to enter the access code: 0451. After you have entered the code, get on the elevator and press the button to get moving. [→☐ 1]

02 Get off the elevator and move down the hall. You'll soon come to a blast door that is partially closed. You'll need to crouch to get under it. Click the Left Stick to Crouch and then move forward under the blast door.

03 Continue down the hall until you come to a blast door that is blocking your path. On the other side, you'll see Barrett attack two scientists. Go left into the room there to find two crates stacked on top of each other. The top crate is blocking a vent. [→☐ 2]

Approach the crate and press the Interact button to grab the crate. Move it out of the way and then jump on top of the remaining crate. Face the vent and press the Interact button to open it. Now, move forward through the air duct to the next vent cover. Press the Interact button to open that vent and get out of the air duct.

Tip **When you are holding an object, you can press the Fire button to throw it.**

04 Continue down the hall to the door on your left. Open it and immediately go to the right side of the room. Move quickly down the right side of the room and crouch down at the last lab station. Move around the lab station to the stairs ahead and take cover at the planter on the right side. Hold your position here.

A pair of guards will soon enter the room and come down the stairs [→☐ 3]. Stay in cover and wait for the guard nearest you to move away. Once he does, remain crouched and move up the stairs to the door, which leads to the next area.

1

2

Tip **If you wish to engage the guards here, take cover at the last lab station instead of going to the planter. From that cover point, you can safely take out the guards.**

05 Move up the hall and you'll see some low boxes blocking your path. All you need do here is jump over the boxes and you are free to continue.

06 Further up the hall you'll come to another door on your left. Before you reach the door, crouch and move slowly to the door. By staying crouched, you'll ensure the guards don't see you through the glass.

There are three guards inside the room ahead that you'll need to contend with. Take cover at the left of the door and open it. From your cover point, peek out to the right and watch the guards. Once they finish their conversation and move away from you, shoot the green gas canister located to the right of them. This will knock them out. [→☐ 4]

07 As they are choking on the gas, stay crouched, move to the far right side of the room and take cover as you wait for the gas to clear. When the gas has dissipated, hug the right wall and move to the door at the far side of the room.

Tip **You can stay in cover at the door and engage all three guards if you like. If you knock out the first two with the gas canister, then you'll only have to face the third in combat.**

08 Make your way to the Chemistry Lab. You'll see Fedorova attack and kill Sarif Security guards. You can't stop this, nor can you engage Fedorova, so push forward to the locked door ahead.

Wait and a scientist will open the door. As soon as he does, run left and jump over the railing where it meets the wall. Once you are on the floor below, take cover in the left-hand corner of the lab station nearest you. Stay in cover and wait for the guards to enter the room.

Hold your position, and one of the guards will get very near you and then move right into the lab station you are hiding behind. He will take position there, so wait for him to turn and leave [→☐ 5]. When he does, make your way to the door ahead and on your left. Be sure to stay crouched as you move so that you avoid detection.

Tip **If you wish to engage the guards here, it's best to stay up top and take cover at the plates on the railing. From there, you can peek out and pick off the guards below in relative safety. Your first shot should be at the gas canisters. These can take out three of the four guards in one go, if you shoot the canisters right when the guards get near.**

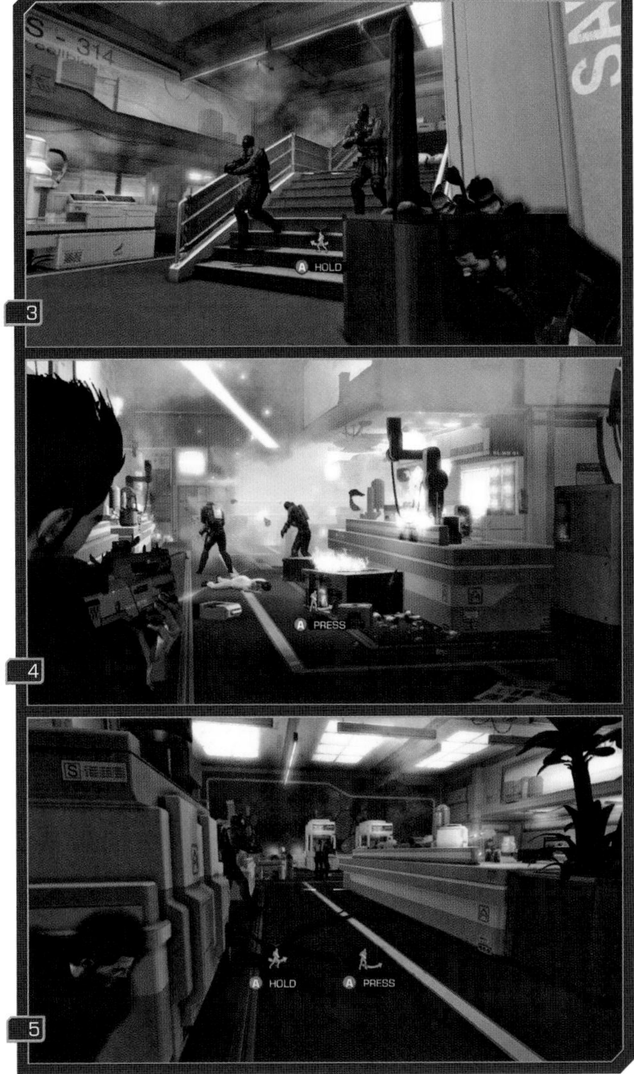

SARIF HEADQUARTERS

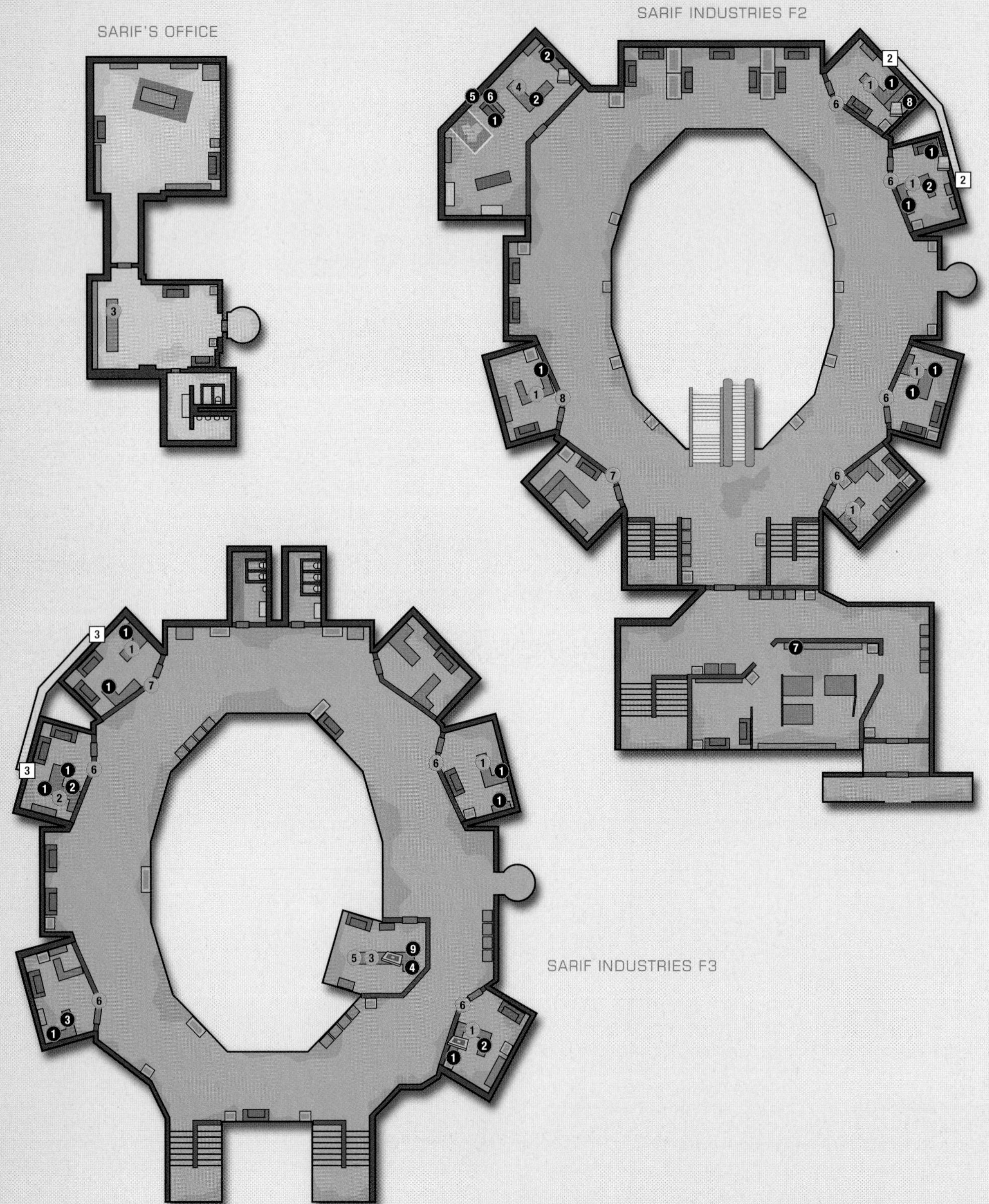

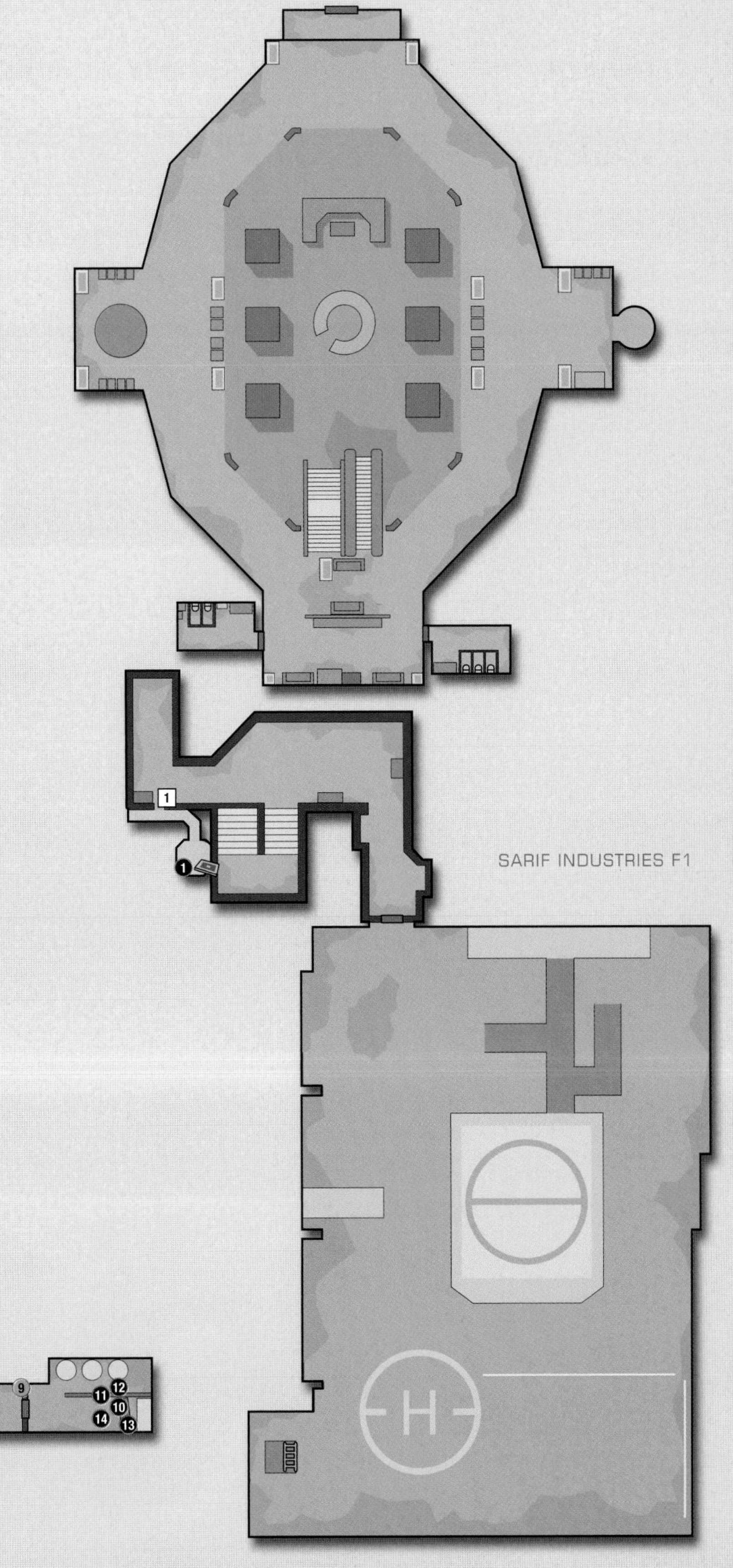

1. Credit Chip
2. Cyberboost ProEnergy Bar
3. CyberBoost ProEnergy Pack
4. Pain Killers
5. Nuke Virus Software
6. Stop Virus Software
7. Beer
8. Whiskey
9. Wine
10. Combat Rifle Ammo
11. Revolver Ammo
12. Stun Gun Dart
13. Tranquilizer Rifle Dart
14. Ammo Capacity Upgrade

- Pocket Secretary
- eBook
- [1] Vent 1
- [2] Vent 2
- [3] Vent 3

1. Computer - Unlocked
2. Computer - Level 2
3. Computer - Level 3
4. Computer - Level 5
5. Security Terminal - Unlocked
6. Security Panels - Level 2
7. Security Panels - Level 3
8. Security Panels - Level 4
9. Security Panels - Level 5

M1 - BACK IN THE SADDLE

Six months have passed since the attack on the Sarif Laboratories. Adam Jensen was severely injured in the attack, but thanks to modern technology, he pulled through better than ever thanks to augmentations or Augs. There has been another attack on Sarif Industries, this time by the anti-augmentation group Purity First. Purity First has stormed Sarif Manufacturing and taken hostages. Although it's rather soon, David Sarif has called Jensen back from sick leave to deal with the problem. While in Sarif HQ, the route is pretty straightforward.

Objective Name	Objective Type
Meet with Pritchard in the Tech Lab	Primary
Go to the Helipad	Primary

OPTIONAL EXPLORATION

Before moving on and completing the missions in Sarif HQ, there are a few areas worth exploring if you're so inclined; in particular the employee offices. When exploring the offices, make sure to use the PCs to read the emails. This gives you more info on the story and will occasionally provide new passwords and codes to other areas.

- Go to Jensen's office and read his emails for Office codes and story info.
- Go to Office 23
- Go to Office 32 (the password for the PC is on a sticky note on the desk)
- Go to Office 34 (get there via the vent and air duct in Office 32)

Warning **Be careful with your exploration at this point. If you take longer than 15 minutes before going to the Helipad, the Side Quest of rescuing the Hostages in Sarif Manufacturing will close and be lost forever.**

01 When you're ready, it's time to meet with Pritchard to get your retinal augmentations adjusted. Pritchard's office is located in the northwest corner of Floor 2. Go there and talk to Pritchard to get this done. [→☐ 1]

When you are talking to Pritchard, you can trigger extra dialogue from him that will tell you more of the story if you wish. Your choices here do not affect any part of gameplay, but will give you more backgound. Best Choices: Confront, Confront.

Tip **Before speaking with Pritchard, enter the women's bathroom on the third floor for a bit of extra dialogue with Pritchard.**

ACHIEVEMENT/TROPHY: DOCTORATE

There is a Hugh Darrow eBook in Pritchard's office on the table just to the right of him.

02 When you are finished talking with Pritchard, your next objective is to meet with Malik so that she can fly you to Sarif Manufacturing. When you're ready, make your way out to the Helipad and talk to Malik to get going. As you are talking to her, you can either Reassure or Challenge Malik here. The choice is yours and does not affect gameplay. [→☐ 2]

OPTIONAL EXPLORATION

Before reaching Helipad, go right once you reach the Cafeteria area. You'll find some stairs that lead down to the next level. At the bottom of the stairs, go left to find a vent near a soda machine. Open the vent and explore the air ducts...

Objective Completed	Objective Type	XP Reward	Stealth Bonuses: Ghost	Stealth Bonuses: Smooth Operator
Meet with Pritchard in the Tech Lab	Primary	150	No	No
Go to the Helipad	Primary	150	No	No

SARIF MANUFACTURING PLANT

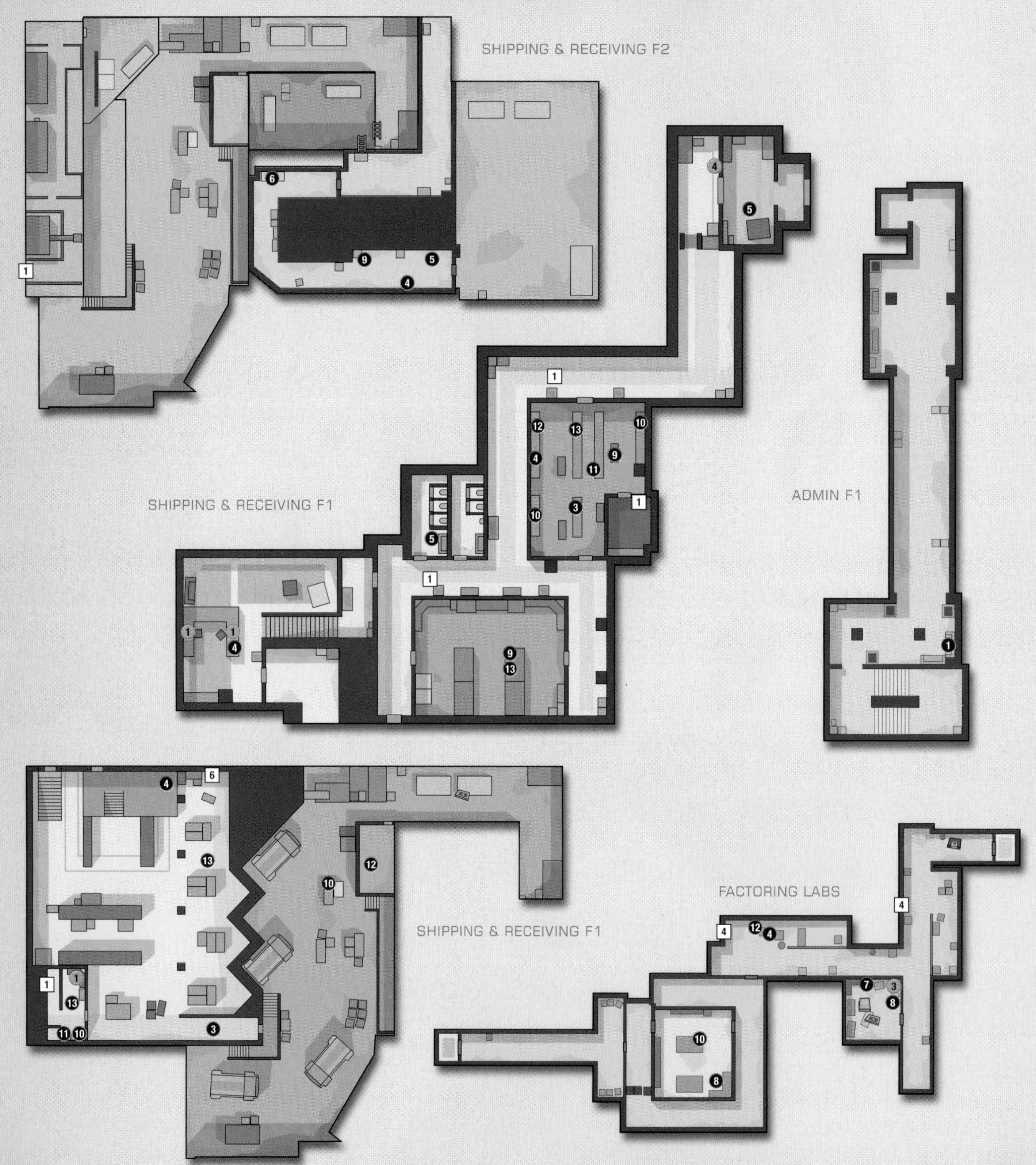

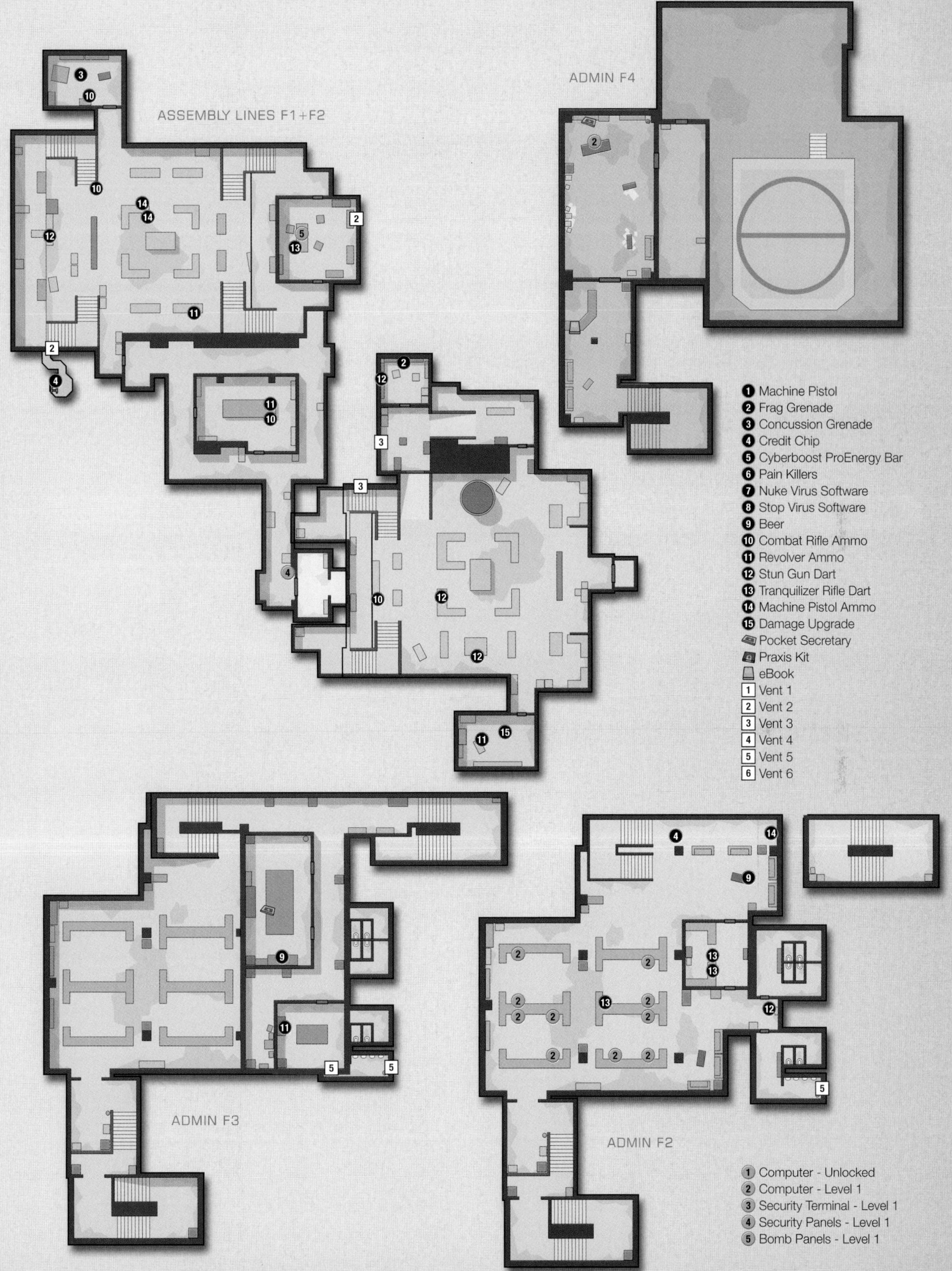
ASSEMBLY LINES F1+F2
ADMIN F4
ADMIN F3
ADMIN F2
1 Machine Pistol
2 Frag Grenade
3 Concussion Grenade
4 Credit Chip
5 Cyberboost ProEnergy Bar
6 Pain Killers
7 Nuke Virus Software
8 Stop Virus Software
9 Beer
10 Combat Rifle Ammo
11 Revolver Ammo
12 Stun Gun Dart
13 Tranquilizer Rifle Dart
14 Machine Pistol Ammo
15 Damage Upgrade
Pocket Secretary
Praxis Kit
eBook
1 Vent 1
2 Vent 2
3 Vent 3
4 Vent 4
5 Vent 5
6 Vent 6
1 Computer - Unlocked
2 Computer - Level 1
3 Security Terminal - Level 1
4 Security Panels - Level 1
5 Bomb Panels - Level 1

M1 - SECURING SARIF'S MANUFACTURING PLANT

Purity First Activists have assaulted one of Sarif's Manufacturing Plants and have taken over the building. To make matters worse, a small group of hostages has been taken and is located somewhere inside. There are two main routes that you can use to enter the building, and both of them can be approached with either stealth or combat game play. For those players focusing on combat, the Revolver should be the weapon of choice here for the extra damage it packs. Stealth players are better off with the Tranquilizer Rifle so that they can take advantage of its range.

Going through the yard is the more difficult choice since you will have to navigate past a number of enemies. If you go up to the rooftops, however, you will be relatively unopposed. Inside the building there is a network of rooms you will have to navigate through, all guarded by activists, and you will need to constantly evaluate the risks and rewards of either engaging the enemies, or sneaking past them.

Objective Name	Objective Type
Enter the Manufacturing Plant	Primary
Secure the hostages	Secondary

After exiting the chopper, head through the door and down the corridor that the S.W.A.T. team is using as a staging area. After emerging on the other side, descend the ladder just to the left of the door, and then take the next ladder nearby down to the ground.

Shipping and Receiving

ROUTE 1 Stealth

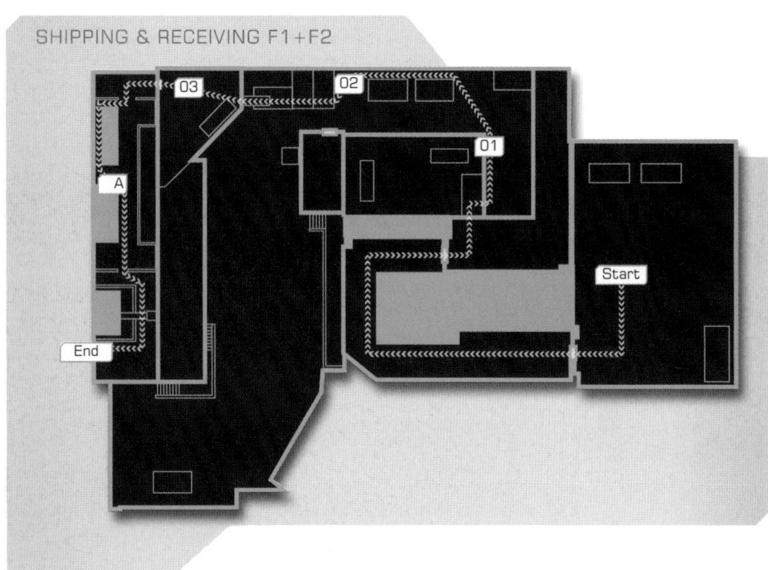

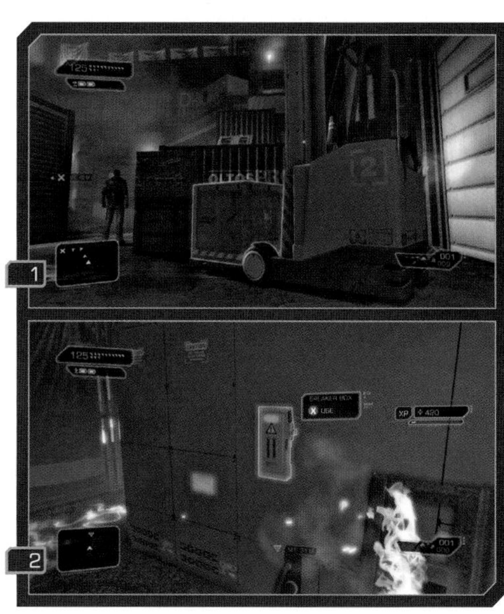

01 Move along the wall and then take cover as you near the corner, because the first enemy is just around the corner. Wait for the guard to begin moving away, and then move quietly behind him, taking cover behind the AC units near him. You can then follow them along to the end, making sure to watch the guard's movements, as he will check between the gaps in the AC units.

02 To continue, you'll need to find a way to jump up onto the boxes near the end of the AC units, and then onto the container behind them [→□ 1]. This requires making use of a crate that you can find sitting on a forklift truck nearby. Keep crouching so the guard doesn't hear you, pick the crate up and gently put it down near the other boxes and then use a crouch jump to land on top of it.

Keep jumping up the boxes until you are on the container, and then follow the path up to the next container and up the planks to the rooftop.

03 Use the ladder and the end of the lower roof to reach a higher rooftop and then go into the fenced off area you find at the top. The main path across this area has been electrified so you will need to find another way round. Just to the right of the entrance you will find a crate. Move this out of the way to reveal a crawlspace. At the end of the crawlspace you will come to an opening where you'll find a breaker box at **Position A** to switch off the current [→□ 2]. Once it is safe, continue along the path until you come to the vent at the end, providing access to the warehouse.

ROUTE 2 Stealth Combat

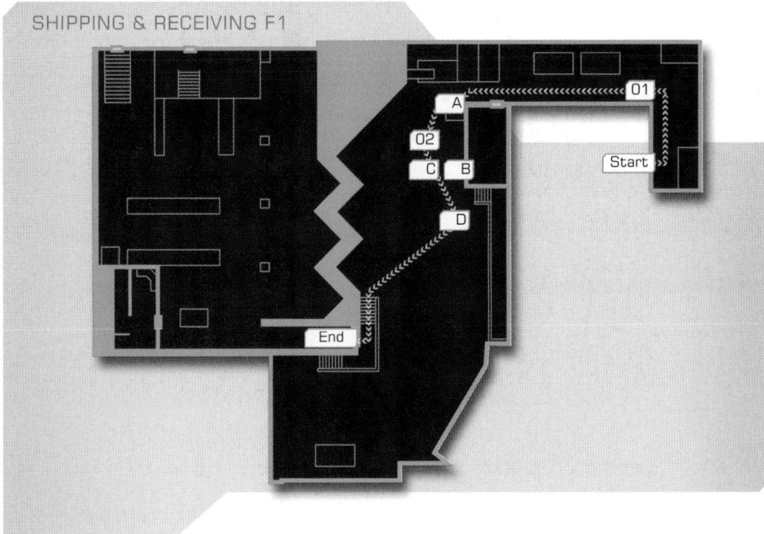

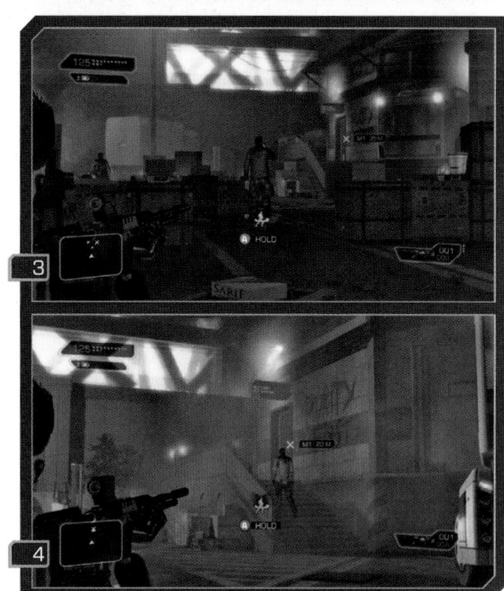

01 Before the guard moves away, crouch and move up behind him so that you can incapacitate him with a Takedown. Once he's been taken care of, stay crouched and take cover behind the crates at **Position A**. From this position, you'll be able to see the three remaining guards in the area: one is stationary just ahead of you, another is patrolling near the door you need to get to and the third takes a long route around the yard. The guard closest should be your first target, so wait for the guard nearest the door to walk away (and the guard on the long patrol to be far away) before taking him out with the Tranquilizer Rifle. [→☐ 3]

02 Quickly move up and drag the unconscious guard's body behind the crates at **Position B**, and then take cover behind the crates at **Position C**. Wait at this position for the guard on the long patrol to come back around, and then when the guard by the door is facing away, either take him out with the Tranquilizer Rifle or a Takedown. Make sure to hide his body behind the nearby crates and then take cover at **Position D**. Here you'll be able to line up an easy shot on the final guard as he is walking away again. Then you can freely enter the warehouse. [→☐ 4]

ROUTE 3 Combat

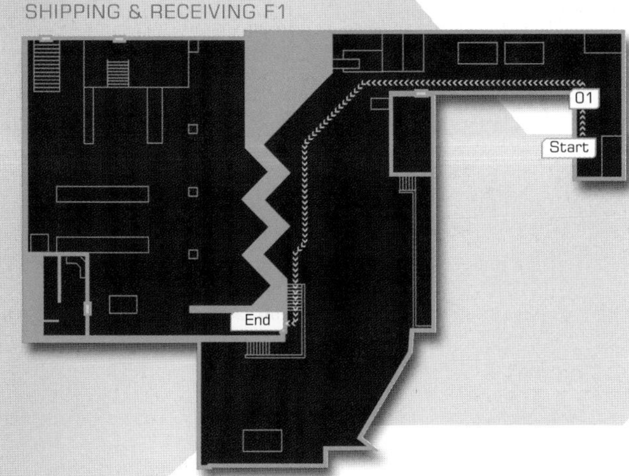

01 The Revolver is the preferred gun for this area because of its ability to take out these enemies with only a single shot, but the same tactics can easily be applied using the Combat Rifle. Lean out from the corner of the wall and take out the first guard while his back is turned. The sound of the shot will alert the other three guards in the yard and they will all come running to investigate. Maintain your position, but get back behind cover so they do not see you as they approach.

As each enemy comes into range, pop out quickly and take him out before getting back behind cover; repeat this process until all of the guards have been dealt with [→☐ 5]. If you are running low on ammo, you can scavenge a 10mm Pistol from one of the bodies, along with some ammo for it and then move up to the door and enter the warehouse.

Objective Completed	Objective Type	XP Reward	Stealth Bonuses	
			Ghost	Smooth Operator
Enter the Manufacturing Plant	Primary	200	Yes	No

ROUTE 1 Stealth

OPTIONAL EXPLORATION

There aren't too many areas to explore in Sarif Manufacturing. The ones that are available tend to hold valuable supplies, which you will no doubt be in need of this early on. After you have made it past the loading docks, the locker room to the North of the first floor is well worth going to. It has ammunition for all starting weapons types, along with other useful items such as Credit Chips and a Concussion Grenade.

01 Drop down when you come to the end of the vent, but stay on top of the boxes you land on. From these boxes, jump across to the metal beam nearby, and then jump across the large light fixtures to reach the other side of the warehouse.

02 Start walking towards the vent at the other end of the area. Next, pick up the nearby crate and place it beneath the vent so that you can jump up and enter it [→□ 1]. Turn right at the fork in the vent and then drop down into the maintenance closet at the end. You'll emerge in the locker room, which should be empty. As long as you remain quiet, you should be able to cross the locker room and exit the door on the other side. Then hack the terminal to get to the assembly lines.

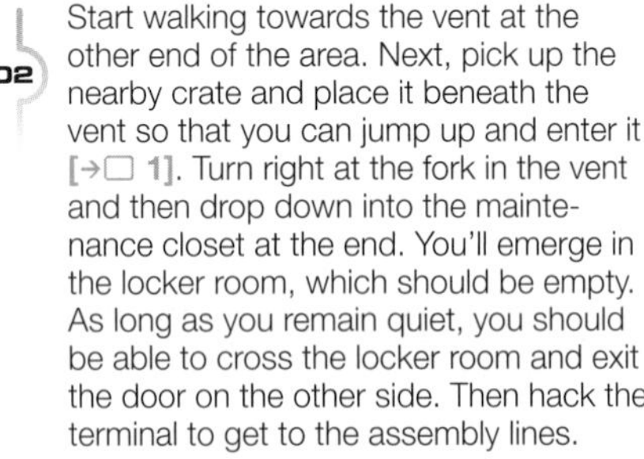

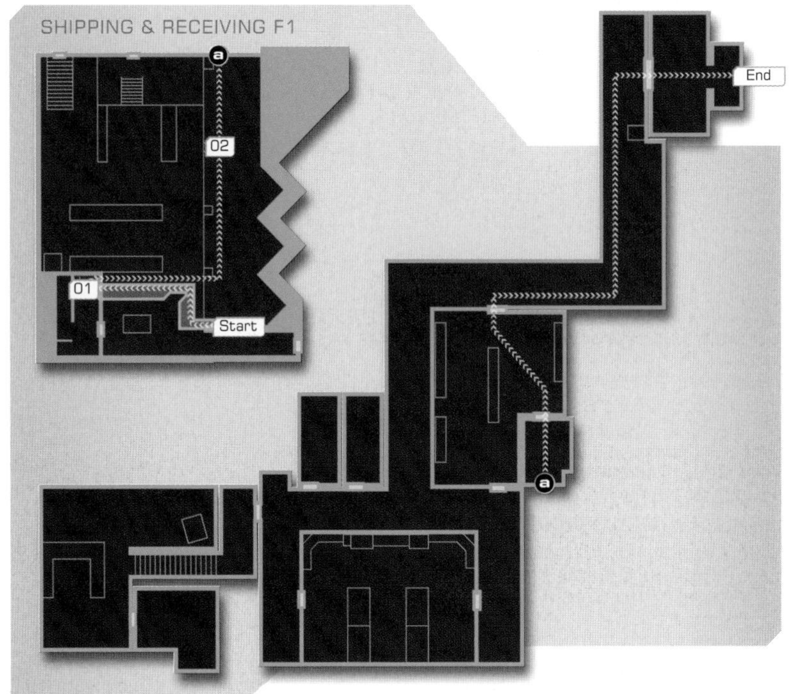

Shipping and Receiving - Warehouse

ROUTE 2 Stealth Combat

01 Drop out of the vent onto the boxes, and then drop down again, taking the ladder to the office below. Once in the office, look at your radar and identify the enemy patrolling back and forth along a short route in the main warehouse. Wait for him to be as close to you as possible and then pick up and throw one of the small cardboard boxes against the office door. The sound should cause him to come over and investigate; take cover to the left of the door and use a Takedown when he enters the office.

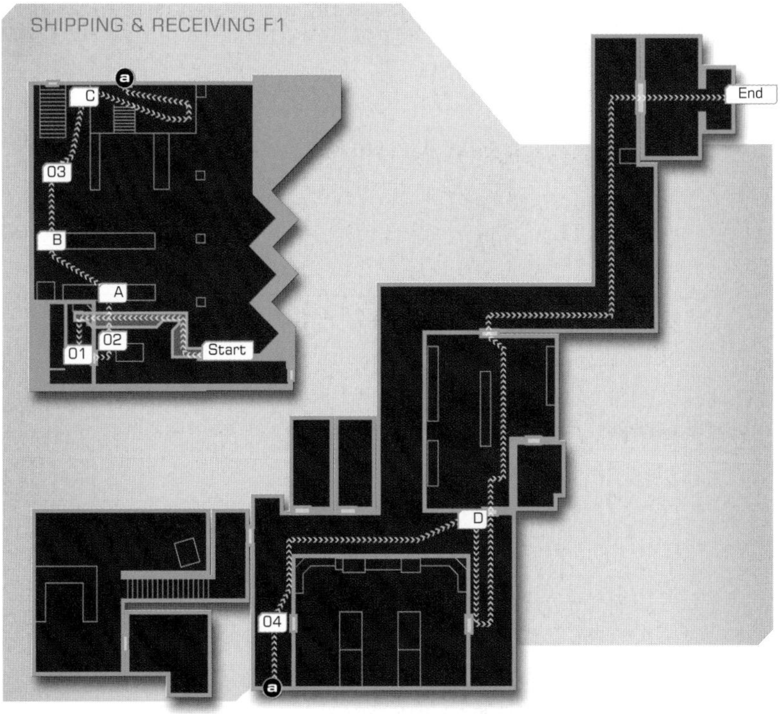

02 Move out of the office and then take cover by the shelving unit at **Position A**. Peek out use the Tranquilizer Rifle to incapacitate the guard in the next aisle, or move in for a Takedown. Next, take cover behind the crates at **Position B**. From here, you will be able to see two enemies: one searching through a crate and another patrolling the area. Wait for the patrolling guard to go round the corner opposite your position and then use a shot from the Tranquilizer gun to take him out [→☐ 2]. Move around the crates and then fire another shot to take out the next guard.

03 Move along the crates, going from cover to cover, until you are past the shelving unit where you took out the patrolling guard. Then jump up the crates at **Position C** to reach a raised area. Crouch down again and move across to the other side of this area so that you can see the final enemy through the railings, and use the Tranquilizer Rifle to take him out.

04 Enter the door on the raised area and advance along the corridor, taking cover at the end of the wall. If you wait for the three guards ahead to finish their conversation, they will split up and go on separate patrols. Two of the enemies will drop out of sight quickly, with one going into the locker room and the other into the cafeteria. The final enemy will eventually turn around and start walking up a long corridor; while he is walking away, move up quietly and use a Takedown. [→☐ 3]

Next, move up to **Position D**, and when the enemy inside is walking away from you, take him out. Move up the corridor opposite the locker room until you can see into the cafeteria; the guard inside should be looking out of the window so you can easily take him out. Once the final enemy in the area is down you're free to explore or head to the assembly lines.

3

Shipping and Receiving - Warehouse

ROUTE 3 Combat

01 Pick up the Concussion Grenade from the top of the crate as you enter the door and then take cover at the end of the wall just past the broken window. There are five guards in this warehouse area, the first of which is right in front of you. The remaining guards are deeper in the warehouse, but still close enough that they will hear the sound of your first gunshot. They will come running, so you will need to be ready.

Lean out and take out the first guard and then drop back into cover while you wait for the other enemies to close in [→☐ 4]. Once you see two or three of them group together, throw the Concussion Grenade to knock them over. Then lean out and take them out easily before they recover. The final guard normally takes cover in the shelves near the office opposite your position, so you should move up to the crates at **Position A** and take him out.

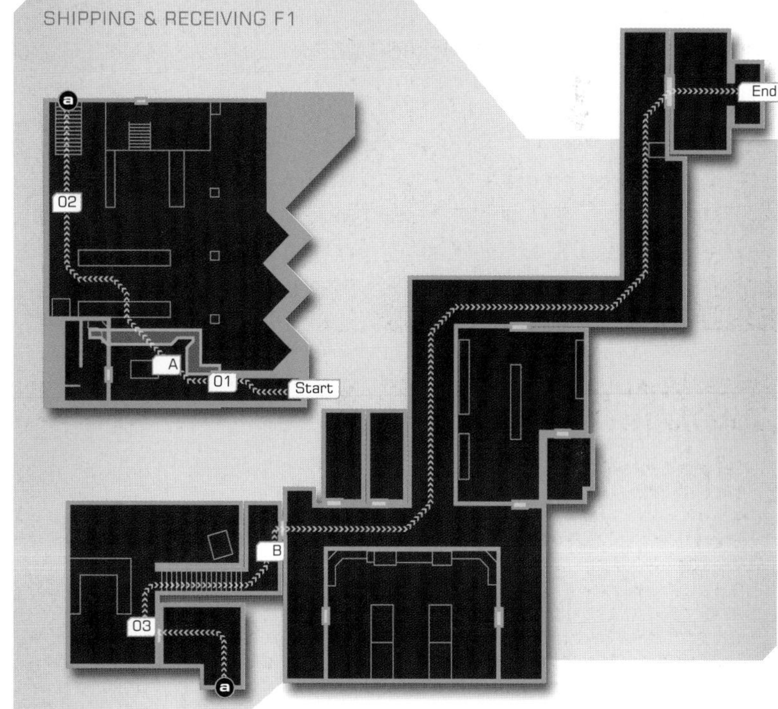

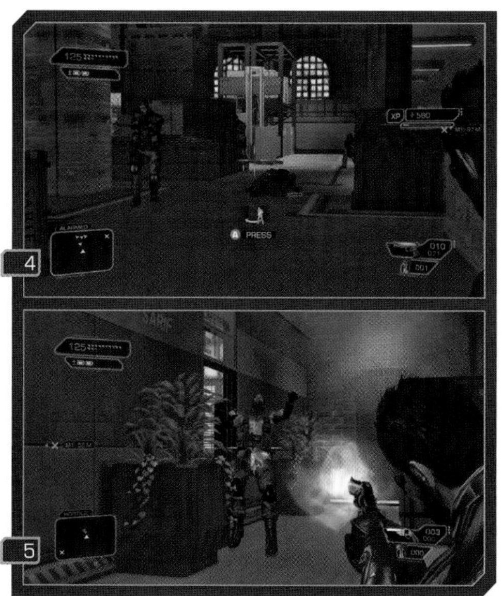
4
5

02 When all of the enemies have been eliminated, scavenge any ammo you can and then move up to the stairs leading down to the lobby. There are two more guards who will probably be alerted in the lobby, so be careful as you approach the door. Crouch down as you move through the door and take cover behind the crates immediately to the right once you are on the other side. The two enemies in this area will often move up and down the stairs as they are searching for you, so wait for them to come into view before taking them out.

03 After getting rid of the two enemies in the lobby, go up the stairs to the floor above and then take cover by the doorway at **Position B**, because there will be another group of guards searching the corridors just ahead. Using the wall for cover, pick off the enemies one at a time as they try to close in on your position; if one of them gets too close, use a Takedown on them and then get back into cover [→☐ 5]. There are only three enemies to deal with, so once you have taken them out, move along the corridors so that you can hack the terminal and get into the assembly lines.

ROUTE 1 Stealth

08_036

OPTIONAL EXPLORATION

Shortly after you pass through Assembly Ln.1, you can enter a meeting room directly South of it that contains a small ammo cache.

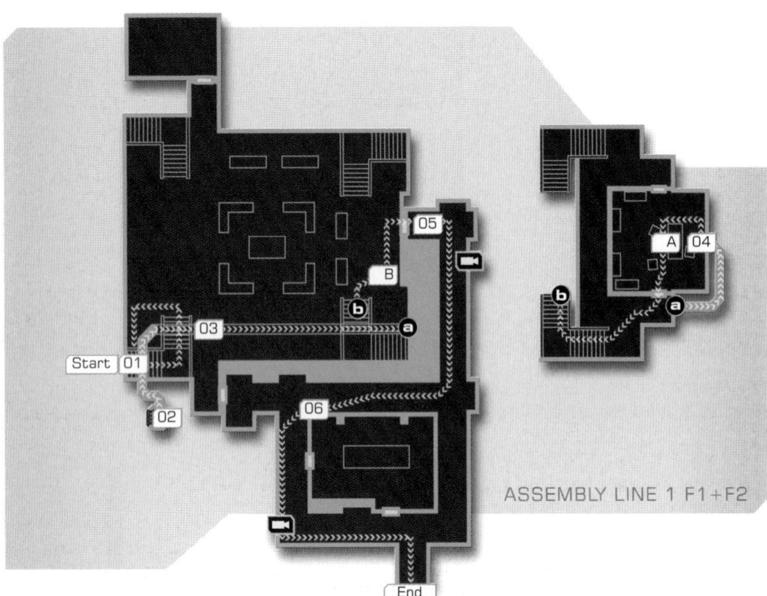

01 Initially three of the four guards are having a conversation near the middle; the fourth guard is patrolling from side to side in the room, and he should be your main focus. If you move quickly, it will be much easier, because once the enemies have finished their conversation they will split up, making moving down the stairs more difficult. Quickly head to the right and take cover near the top of the stairs so that you can watch the patrolling guard; when he is walking away, descend the stairs while crouched and hide underneath them.

02 Under the stairs you will find a vent cover hidden behind a metal crate; move the crate quietly and then go into the vent [→☐ 1]. You'll exit the vent in a large vertical shaft. Take the ladder up to the next level and go inside the vent at the top.

03 Follow this vent until you reach the end, and then move out onto the beam above the room. Quietly move along the beam so that the enemies below do not hear you and then enter the vent on the other side.

04 Follow the vent along until you enter the room containing the hostages. If you wish to rescue them and complete the Secondary Objective, you can hack the bomb at **Position A** to disarm it; there is no timer ticking down on it at this point, because you used the vents to enter the room. If you rescue the hostages, make sure to talk to Greg Thorpe. He is sitting in the chair closest to the bomb and he will give you an updated objective to rescue his wife. The door to the Server Room is directly underneath the room you are in, so you'll have to venture back into the main room. As you look back to the main room, exit through the left-hand door of the hostage room while remaining crouched. One of the guards will be patrolling up and down the area just in front of the stairs, with another around the central area; watch their movements and then go down when they are walking away. Use the generator at **Position B** for cover, and when it's safe go through the door.

05 In this area, there's both a guard and security camera to contend with, so your movements will have to be quick and quiet to get past. The guard patrols up and down the long corridor, always checking down the branching corridor to the right along the way. Wait for the guard to start walking away and the camera to pan away from you, and then while crouched, move out and hug the left side of the wall beneath the camera's field of vision. After he has checked down the corridor to the right, move down quickly while he continues along his route. [→☐ 2]

06 Take cover by the end of the wall, because there is another security camera around the corner. The large containers will shield you from the patrolling guard's vision so there's no rush here. Wait for the camera to face toward the next corridor, and then move up quickly while hugging the wall on the right so that you can get beneath its field of vision. Wait for it to pan to where you were previously, and then move along the corridor and take the path to the right, which leads to the door you'll need to hack to get into the next assembly line.

ROUTE 2 Stealth Combat

01 Wait for the three guards to finish having their conversations so that they move into their normal patrols and positions. Now simply watch and make a note of each guard's patrol route. You can take them out one at a time easily, but you'll want to time your shots so that the remaining guards aren't alerted by the bodies. Just remember when using the Tranquilizer Rifle, that you'll need to aim slightly above the enemies since the dart will dip a little.

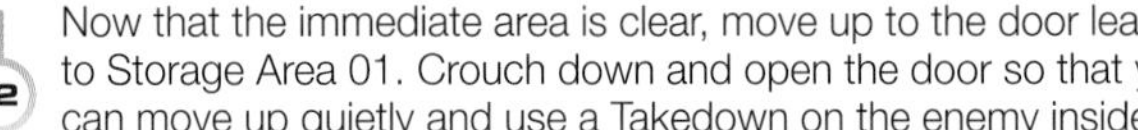

02 Now that the immediate area is clear, move up to the door leading to Storage Area 01. Crouch down and open the door so that you can move up quietly and use a Takedown on the enemy inside.

03 Now you can choose to save the hostages at **Position A**, or continue on towards the server room. If you choose to rescue the hostages, make sure to search the bodies of the enemies you took out, because one of them has a Pocket Secretary with the

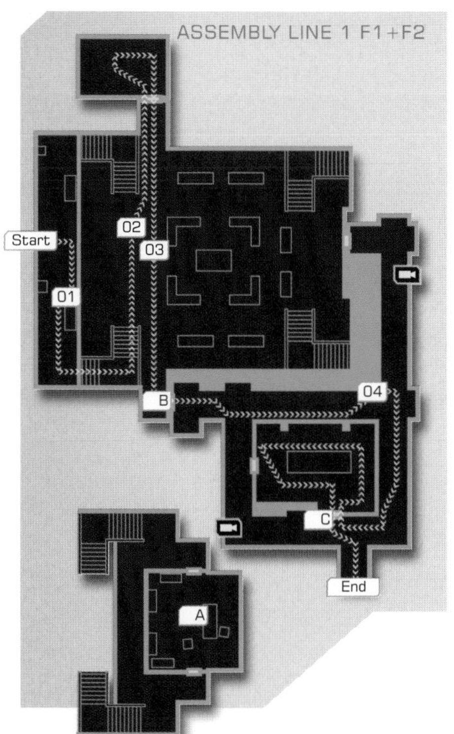

code to disarm the bomb. Next, head over to the door at **Position B** and enter the corridor. Take cover along the wall on the right here and move along to the edge so that you can see the camera around the corner. Wait for it to be facing away, and then move past it and continue along the corridor and take cover behind the large container.

Wait here for the guard patrolling the corridor ahead to be moving down to the right, and then quietly move up behind him and use a Takedown [→☐ 3]. The camera at the other end of this corridor will be pointing away from you, so quickly drag the body back into the corridor you started in, so that it is out of its view.

04 Take cover along the left of this corridor, watching the camera to the left; when it is facing away, move down to the right again and take cover behind the large container at the end. Watch the movement of the next camera, and when it's facing away, move up to **Position C** next to the meeting room door.

Open the door and wait for the enemies inside to finish talking. They'll then move into positions on opposite sides of the room with their backs to you. Now you can either use Takedowns, the Tranquilizer Rifle, or a combination of both. After they have both been incapacitated, go back out through the door you entered by and take cover behind the container on the right; when the camera is facing away, cross the corridor so that you can hack the door leading to the next assembly line.

ROUTE 3 Open Combat

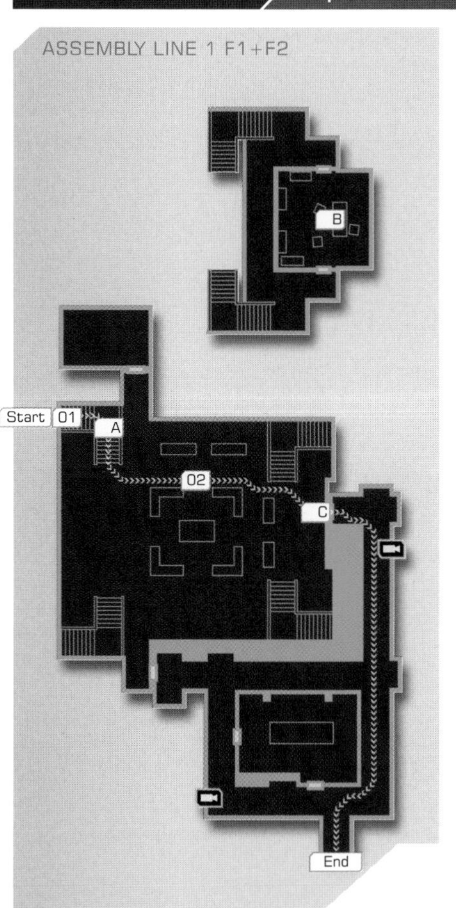

01 When you enter the room, crouch down and start moving down the stairs on the left side of the balcony. When you reach the mid-point at **Position A**, you should be able to line up an easy headshot on the guard patrolling nearby, while the paneling provides both cover and hides you from the other enemies [→☐ 4]. As they could not see you when you fired the shot, they will move out to investigate and you can normally pick them off one at a time with headshots as they come into view. The enemy who is normally in the storage room nearby will also come out, so make sure you have killed them all before you exit from cover.

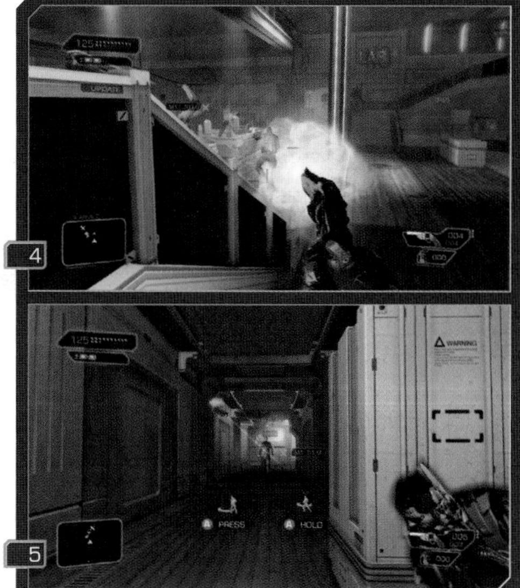

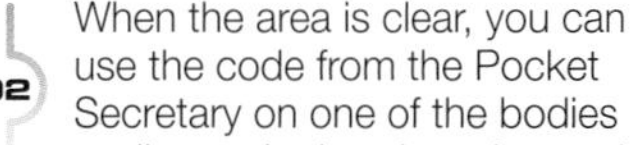

02 When the area is clear, you can use the code from the Pocket Secretary on one of the bodies to disarm the bomb and save the hostages at **Position B** if you wish, or continue towards the server room. Go through the door at **Position C** and then take cover behind the large container. The enemies in this part of the area should still be unaware of the combat that took place in the room, because of the loud sirens so they will not be alerted. Wait for the enemy patrolling along the long corridor to come into view and then line up a headshot and take him out when he comes to a stop. [→☐ 5]

Let the body be spotted by the camera, or shoot the camera to destroy it so that one of the enemies in the meeting room comes to investigate; take him out as soon as he comes into range. The second enemy will then come out to investigate so you will be able to do the same to him. With the area now completely clear of enemies, you can precede easily to the next assembly line.

Objective Completed	Objective Type	XP Reward	Stealth Bonuses: Ghost	Stealth Bonuses: Smooth Operator
Secure the Hostages	Secondary	500	No	No

ROUTE 1 Stealth Combat

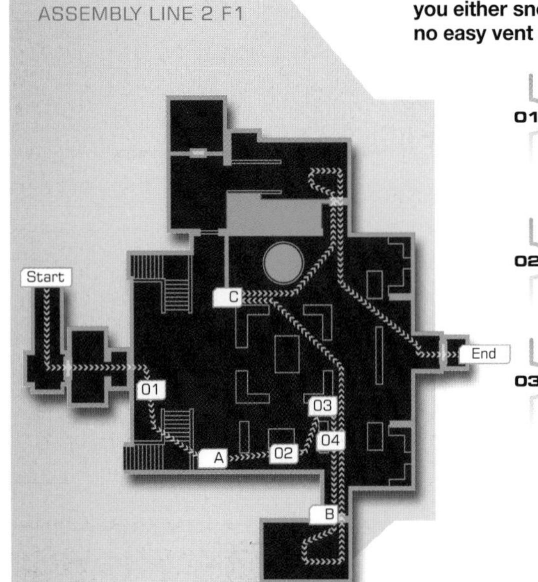

OPTIONAL EXPLORATION

There are two storage rooms that you can access from Assembly Ln.2: one to the North and one to the South. Storage Room No.2 to the North contains some Stun Gun ammunition, along with a Frag Grenade, and can be accessed via a vent hidden behind some crates to the north of where you enter. Alternatively, you can use the door from the main floor if you either sneak or take out the Purity First members. Storage Room No.3 to the South has no easy vent access, contains some Revolver rounds and a Damage Upgrade kit.

01 Crouch down as soon as you enter the room so that you can move quietly, and while the guards are talking, move around to the right under the stairs and take cover behind the generator at **Position A**. Wait until the guards have finished talking, and then when it is safe to do so, move across and hide behind the nearby workbench, and go from cover to cover to the next one.

02 Wait until you see the guard in the middle start moving away from inspecting the workbench on the left, and the closest guard finish inspecting the workbench in front of you and move right. This is the point when you should lean out to the right and use the Tranquilizer Rifle to incapacitate the closest enemy.

03 Quickly move up towards the right side of the group of workbenches and drag the downed enemy close to them so that he's not spotted by the enemy in the middle. Move along to the end of the workbench to the right. The enemy in the middle should be searching the central workbench and the far enemy will be coming to the end of his route, opposite your position.

Wait for him to stop and then use another shot from the Tranquilizer Rifle to take him down. The enemy in the middle will walk away and not see this, and the first enemy is safely tucked in so he also won't react. Wait for him to pass by your position and then move up behind and use a Takedown.

1

04 There are two more enemies you can take out now if you wish: one in Storage Room 03, and one just outside Storage Room 02. Start by going towards Storage Room 03 at **Position B** and crouch down once you have opened the door; the enemy inside is busy so you can easily move up behind him and use a Takedown. The guard near Storage Room 02 is patrolling up and down the area in between the door leading to the storage room, and the room itself. If you were to just open the door he could be standing right there, which could make things difficult.

A better option is to move up to **Position C** and look through the window, so you know when he is at this end of his patrol and far away from the door. As soon as you see him through the window, move quickly through the door and take cover behind the generator. All you have to do is wait for him to walk past you and then use a Takedown [→☐ 1]. After taking out the final enemy, gather any items you want and head to the elevator to continue.

Assembly Line 2

ROUTE 2 Stealth

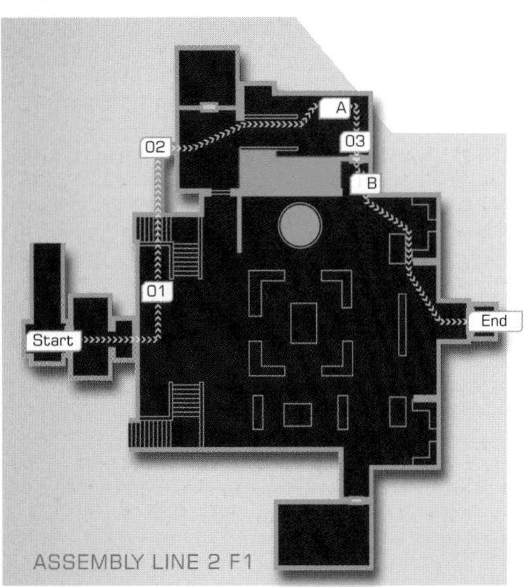

01 Crouch down straight away and start heading left once you enter the lab. When you reach the set of three crates near the stairs, move them out of the way. A vent cover will be revealed, and you can now enter the vent.

02 Before you open the cover at the end of the vent, look through it to spot the enemy patrolling just outside. Wait for him to start walking away, and then open the cover and move up behind him. When you get to the top of the ramp, go through the gap on the left and take cover behind the crates at **Position A**. Wait for the guard to start walking away again and then go through the door.

03 As soon as you are through the door, quickly get behind the crates on the left at **Position B** so that you are out of sight. Watch the guard's patrols and wait for the one closest to start walking up to the right, and the one in the middle to finish searching the central workbench. When you see this happen, exit cover and move through the workbenches to the right so that you can head straight for the elevator. Quickly press the button and get inside before any of the guards start making their way back.

ROUTE 3 Open Combat

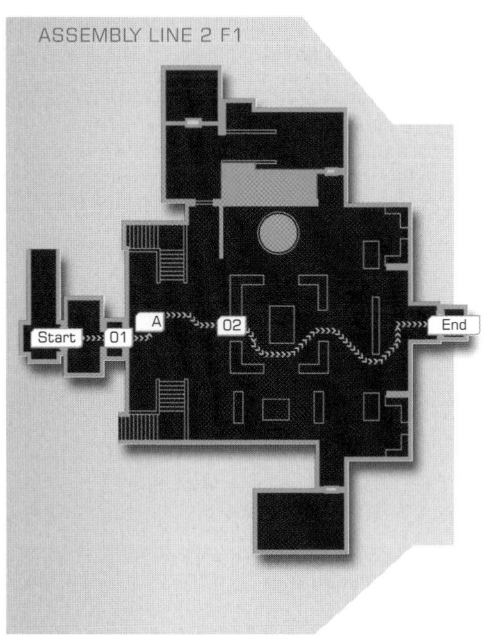

01 There are five enemies to take out in this room, and the most important thing you need to be careful of is that one of them does not flank you once the fighting begins. Crouch down and take cover behind the left hand crate at **Position A**. From here, you can easily line up a headshot on one of the enemies just ahead, and then quickly take out the next one while he turns around. [→☐ 2]

The enemy near the middle will always take cover behind one of the workbenches on the right; wait for him to pop his head up and start firing so that you can line up an easy shot. The guard running in from the right takes up a position behind one of the workbenches along the right of the room, but the guard coming in from the left is not so predictable. Wait and see where he takes cover and then deal with him first, before taking out the final enemy on the right.

02 Make sure to collect any supplies, including taking a trip into both storage rooms to acquire the Frag Grenade and Damage Upgrade kit, which you should use on your preferred weapon. When you are ready, go towards the elevator at the back of the room and take it down to the next area.

ROUTE 1 Stealth

OPTIONAL EXPLORATION

After taking the elevator down to the Server Room corridors, you will be able to enter a small security room to the South. In this room, you will find a number of useful items, along with one of Hugh Darrow's eBooks hidden underneath a cardboard box that is sitting on top of some gray crates.

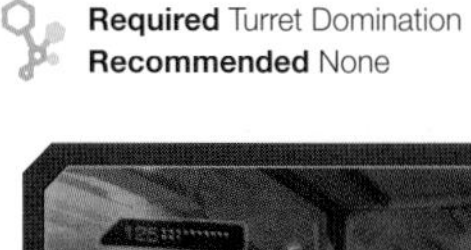

Required Turret Domination
Recommended None

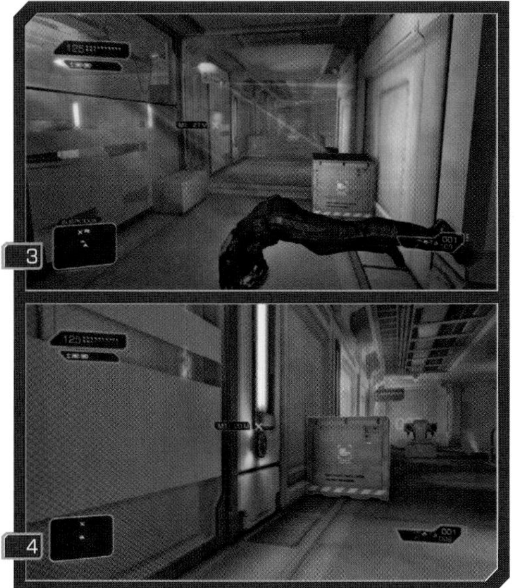

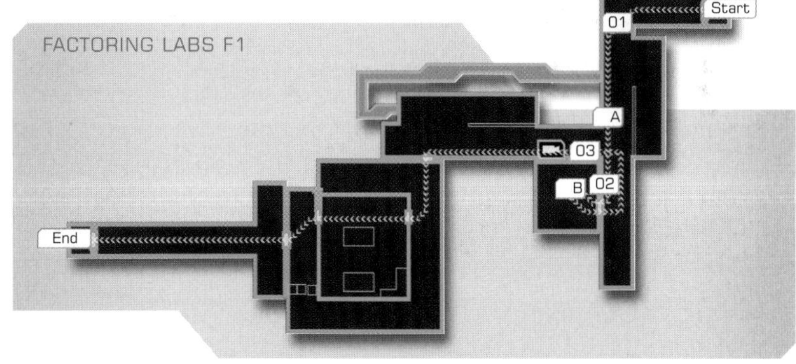

01 Move up along the corridor and take cover when you come to **Position A**. In the corridor ahead there is a camera along with a Turret at the other end; wait for the camera to pan in the opposite direction and then move from cover to cover to cross the area quickly before the Turret can identify you. [→☐ 3]

02 Go into the small room at **Position B**, in which you'll find a Security Hub. You can either hack your way into the Hub, or pick up the Pocket Secretary here, as it contains the password for it. Using the Praxis Point you got from the Kit at the start of this area, unlock the Turret Domination Augmentation from within your Capture software. Now while you are in the Hub you will be able to disable both the camera and the Turret.

03 Exit the room and slowly start making your way up the corridor, because there is a Concussion Mine on the left wall [→☐ 4]. Stay crouched and keep advancing until you can disable it, and then continue through the door at the end to the server room.

ROUTE 2 Stealth

01 Move along the corridor until you come to the crate at **Position A**. Pick it up and move it out of the way to reveal a vent cover. Enter the vent and follow it along until you come out behind the Turret. Then go through the nearby door so that you can access the server room. [→☐ 1]

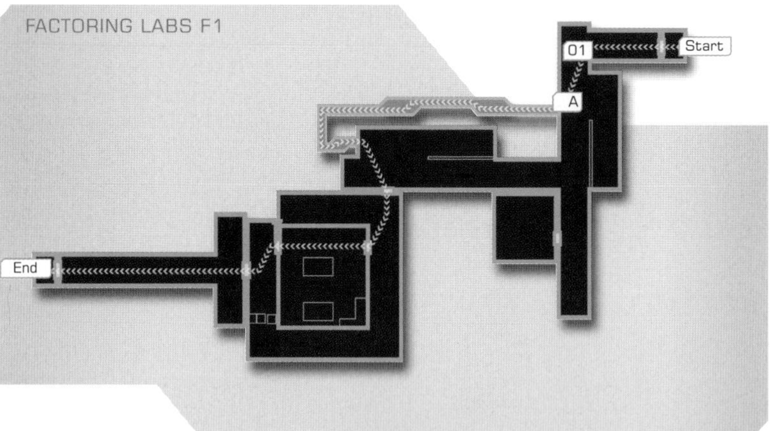

Objective Completed	Objective Type	XP Reward	Stealth Bonuses	
			Ghost	Smooth Operator
Retrieve the Typhoon	Primary	250	No	No

M2 - NEUTRALIZE THE TERRORIST LEADER

After confronting the hacker and securing the Typhoon, you'll have to go through the factory's Administration Buildings and search for the leader of the Purity First terrorist group, Zeke Sanders. The Admin Buildings consist of a lot of meeting rooms and computer areas. Moving about undetected will be difficult and will require preparation and timing. Thankfully, there is also plenty of cover available, so if you are taking the fight to the terrorists you will have many different positions to make a stand from.

ROUTE 1 Stealth Combat

Objective Name	Objective Type
Confront Zeke Sanders	Primary
Secure the hostages (updated)	Secondary

To get to the Admin Buildings, exit the server room through the door near the dead terrorist, and then go through the next door and use the elevator at the end of the corridor. After exiting the elevator, start crossing the sky bridge towards the Admin Building; an alarm will trigger but this is due to the police forces moving in and battling against the terrorists below so it won't affect you. After crossing the bridge, head up the stairs to the upper floors of the Admin Buildings.

OPTIONAL EXPLORATION

You can enter two meeting rooms once you have finished climbing the stairs to the third floor of the Admin Buildings. Meeting Room 01, just to the South of where you start contains another can of Letitia's favorite beer. You can pick it up and give it to her later, as well as collecting a Pocket Secretary containing a password to one of the computers on the second floor. In Meeting Room 02 you'll find some more revolver ammo.

After dropping down to the second floor of the Admin Buildings, you will be able to enter Meeting Room 03. Here you'll find a cache of Tranquilizer Rifle rounds. On the coffee table, you can also find another can of beer for Letitia, and underneath a cardboard box on a bookcase, you can find a Credit Chip.

01 Crouch down when you get near the top of the stairs because there are two enemies in the corridor further ahead. Hug the wall to the right and advance up the stairs until you can take cover behind a set of crates. Wait for the two enemies to finish their conversation, and one of them will start walking away from you while the other goes down a branching corridor to the left [→☐ 2]. Either use the Tranquilizer Rifle, or move up quickly while crouched and use a Takedown.

Once he is down, go down the branching corridor and follow behind the guard until you are close enough to use a Takedown;

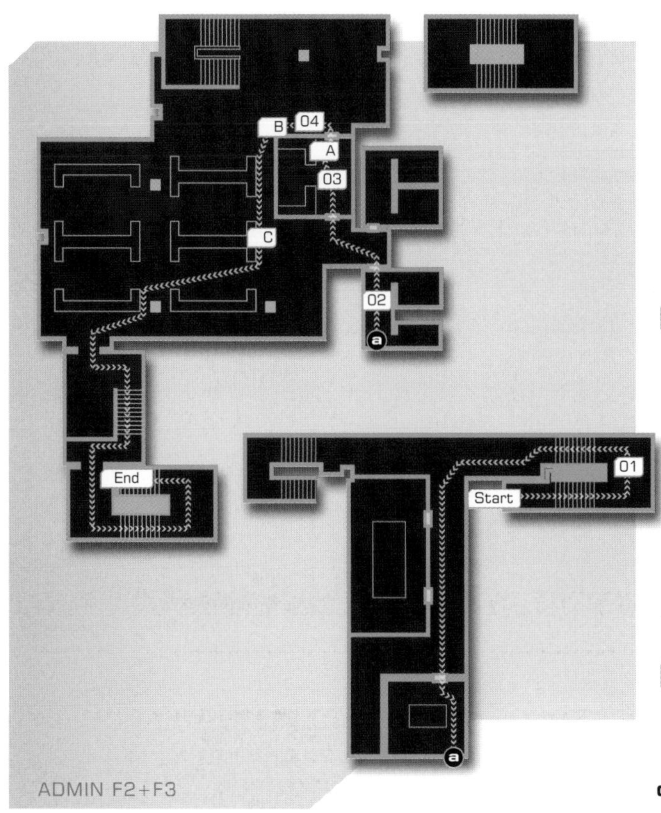

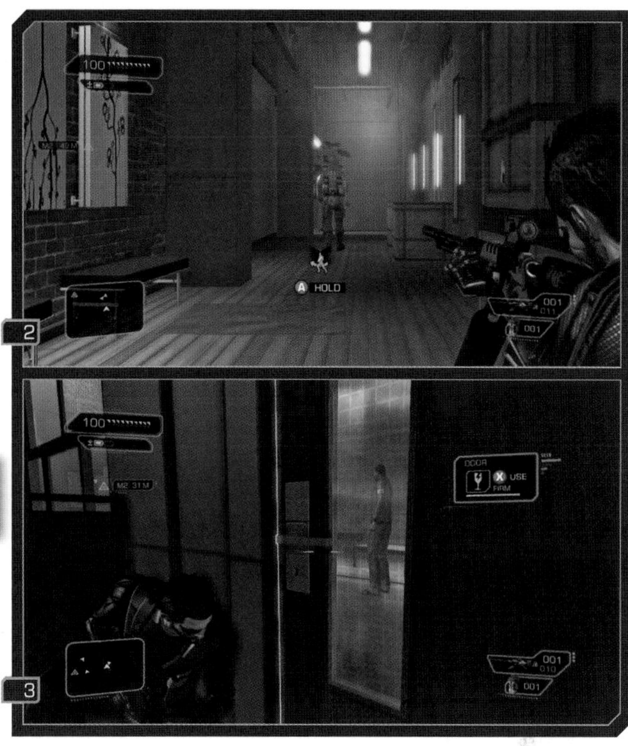

even if he stops near the railings on the mezzanine you'll still be safe to use a Takedown unnoticed.

02 Go into Meeting Room 02 nearby. The vent inside will take you down to the bathroom. Exit the bathroom and take cover behind the crates just outside; when the coast is clear, quickly move across and go through the open door into Meeting Room 03.

03 So that you do not have to contend with all three enemies here at once, it is worth luring the nearest enemy into the meeting room. Take cover on the wall to the left of the door at **Position A**, and then look through the glass panel in it until you can see him [→☐ 3]. As soon as he comes into view, open the door to get his attention. When he is close enough, use a Takedown.

04 Exit the meeting room, and then take cover behind the crates at **Position B**. Watch the movements of the two remaining enemies, and then when it's safe, take cover along the side of the desks at **Position C**. Wait until you see the guard patrolling to the left start walking away, and once he has passed the guard walking down towards you on the right, lean out and use a shot from the Tranquilizer Rifle to take him down. As long as you lean to the side, you will remain out of the guard's line of sight. With only one final enemy remaining, wait for him to begin searching the desk near your position, and then close in and use a Takedown. When the area is clear, go up the stairs and through the door to have a talk with Zeke.

ACHIEVEMENT/TROPHY: DOCTORATE

There is one of Hugh Darrow's eBooks on Josie Thorpe's desk, which is situated just in front of the door leading to Zeke.

ROUTE 2 Stealth

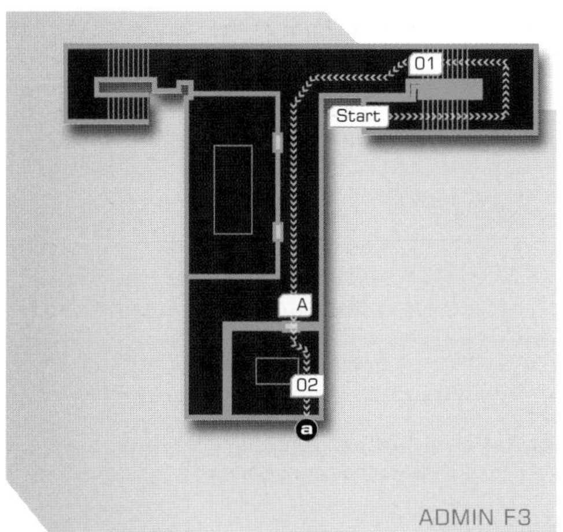

01 When you near the top of the stairs, crouch down and advance along the right-hand wall so that you can take cover behind the crates at the top. Wait for the two activists to finish their conversation, and then move out and follow the one that goes down the corridor to the left. Keep following him until you come to Meeting Room 02 at **Position A**, and go inside.

02 On the opposite wall, you'll be able to see a vent cover. Open it and follow the vent down until you come out into the bathroom on the floor below.

03 Exit the bathroom through the door while remaining crouched and take cover behind the crates at **Position B**. There are numerous guards patrolling the area ahead so you'll need to be careful. Wait until the guard patrolling from left to right close by is moving right, and the guard just behind is searching the desk in the distance; when you feel the timing is right, move up the corridor and veer left. You should enter the room so that you can take cover behind the pillar at **Position C**. Move from the pillar to behind the desks when it is safe to do so, and then continue on to the next pillar when the guards are facing away.

The guard up on the mezzanine never leaves his post so he will catch a glimpse of you as you move from the desk to the second pillar [→☐ 1]. He will not fully detect you, however, but you will need to continue quickly before he can come down to investigate. Watch the radar to see when the nearby guards are looking away, and then move up to the second set of desks. After another quick check, break cover and move into the stairwell and get behind the wall so that you are out of sight. Continue all the way up the stairs and go through the door at the top to confront the terrorist leader.

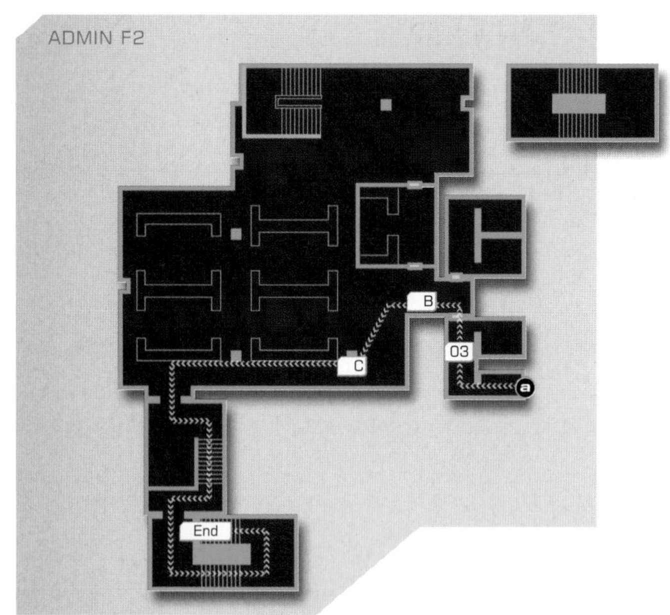

ROUTE 3 Combat

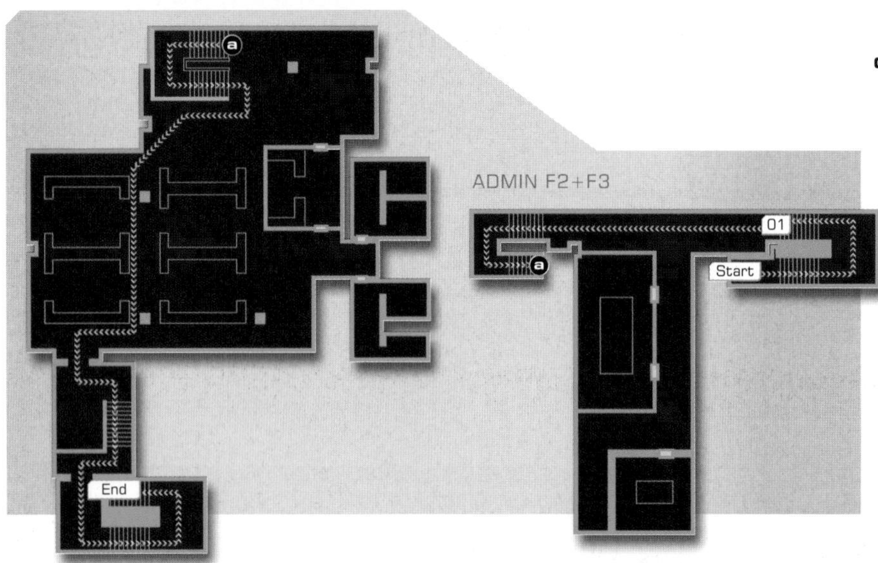

01 Fighting your way through this area is relatively straightforward thanks to the natural bottleneck created by the long corridor at the top of the stairs. Take cover behind the crates at the top of the stairs as usual, and then headshot one of the guards while they are still talking. The other guard next to him will be startled by the action, and as long as you are fairly quick, you can take him out before he can draw his weapon.

The remaining three enemies will then start to make their way up the stairs at the end of the corridor, so all you have to do is take them out one at a time as they come into view. Once everyone has been killed, you are free to explore. When you are ready, head up the stairs and make your way towards Zeke.

CONFRONTING ZEKE SANDERS

Objective Name	Objective Type
Confront Zeke Sanders	Primary
Secure the hostages (updated)	Secondary

As soon as you enter the office at the top of the stairs you will enter into a dialogue with Zeke Sanders, so make sure you have made any preparations necessary before entering. At the outset of the confrontation, you will be presented with three choices. Which you choose will decide how things proceed:

Option 1: Fight Zeke

If you choose to fight Zeke, he will attempt to execute Josie Thorpe before engaging you. During the time, it takes him to draw his weapon and aim you will have a very small window in which to kill him before he kills Josie. Your best option in this situation is to either go for a quick headshot with the Pistol, or use the Revolver and go for an easy body shot, either one will put him down for good. If you are even a fraction slow, however, Zeke will kill Josie and you will be unable to complete the secondary objective for Greg [→☐ 2]. Killing Zeke will also mean that he will be unable to return later in the game, denying you some valuable intelligence.

Option 2: Let Zeke go

If you choose to let Zeke go, he will take Josie with him and use her as a human shield against the police outside so that he can make his escape. Josie will die in the ensuing gunfight, meaning you will fail the secondary objective [→☐ 3]. Zeke, however, will remain alive so you will be able to meet up with him again later.

Option 3: Try to free Josie

If you choose to try to free Josie, you will enter into a conversation with Zeke. If you finish the conversation with a positive outcome, Zeke will let Josie go and escape the police [→☐ 4]. This means that you can both complete the secondary objective, and meet up with Zeke later, while also getting the large Silver Tongue XP bonus for an extra 1000XP.

If you fail the conversation, Zeke will escape with Josie and she will end up being killed in the crossfire with the police, failing the secondary objective. There are many different options and paths you can take through the conversation, all causing Zeke to react differently. The options listed below will guide you through each round and ensure that you finish the conversation with a positive rating.

CONVERSATION FLOW

ZEKE SANDERS

PERSONALITY TYPE: NONE

Conversation Round	Response to Make
Round 1	Empathize
Round 2	Empathize
Round 3	Reason

ACHIEVEMENT/TROPHY: UNFORESEEN CONSEQUENCES

If you are successful in your conversation with Zeke, you will unlock this Achievement/Trophy as soon as the conversation finishes.

Objective Completed	Objective Type	XP Reward	Stealth Bonuses: Ghost	Stealth Bonuses: Smooth Operator
Confront Zeke Sanders	Primary	1750*	500	No
Rescue Josie Thorpe	Secondary	750	No	No
Secure the hostages (updated)	Secondary	250	No	No

*1000 for Silver Tongue and winning the conversation play.

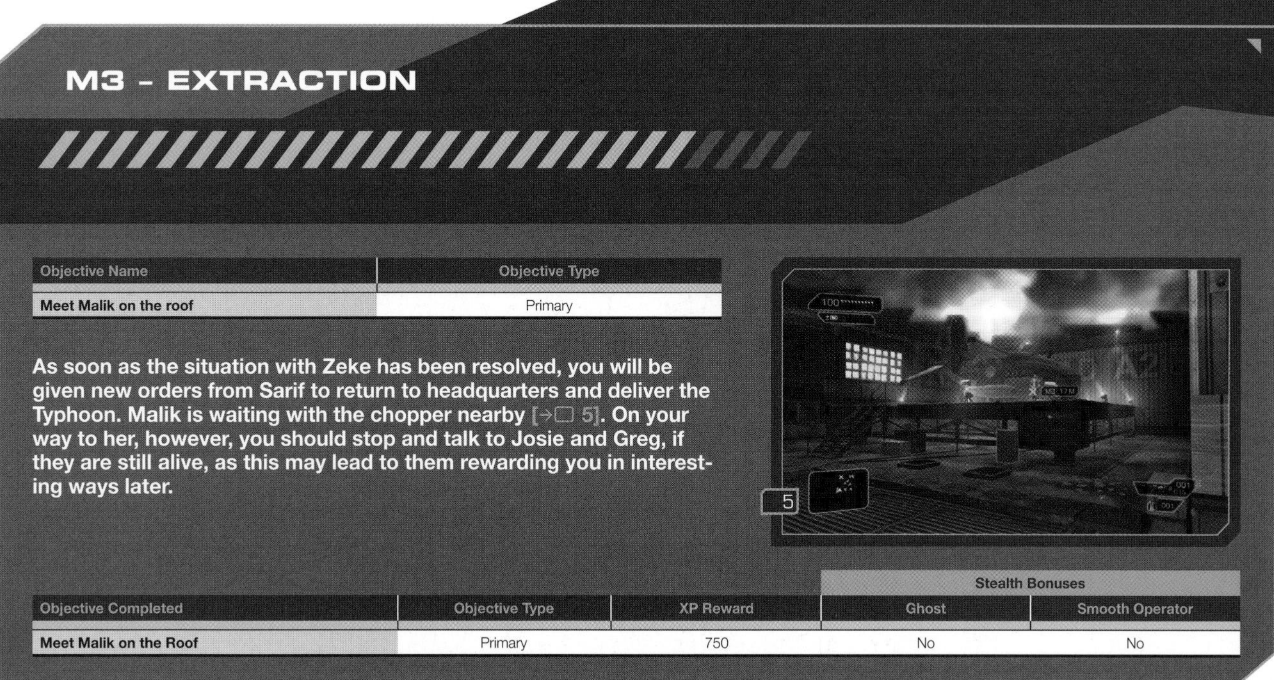

M3 - EXTRACTION

Objective Name	Objective Type
Meet Malik on the roof	Primary

As soon as the situation with Zeke has been resolved, you will be given new orders from Sarif to return to headquarters and deliver the Typhoon. Malik is waiting with the chopper nearby [→☐ 5]. On your way to her, however, you should stop and talk to Josie and Greg, if they are still alive, as this may lead to them rewarding you in interesting ways later.

Objective Completed	Objective Type	XP Reward	Stealth Bonuses: Ghost	Stealth Bonuses: Smooth Operator
Meet Malik on the Roof	Primary	750	No	No

M4 - TYING UP LOOSE ENDS

After securing Sarif Manufacturing and the Typhoon, Jensen heads back to Sarif HQ. The first order of business is to give the Typhoon to Pritchard, and then have a debriefing with David Sarif.

Objective Name	Objective Type
Give the Typhoon to Pritchard	Primary
Meet Sarif in the Penthouse	Primary

OPTIONAL EXPLORATION

Inside Sarif HQ

- **Go to Jensen's Office and read new emails for a new SQ and office codes.**
- **Go to Office 31 (find a Pocket Secretary with a code)**
- **Go to Office 27 (use vent and air ducts to get to Office 25)**
- **Go to Office 25 (by using the vents in Office 27)**

ACHIEVEMENT/TROPHY: DOCTORATE

You'll find one of Hugh Darrow's eBooks in Office 25 and Office 27.

01 After leaving Sarif Manufacturing, Malik brings Jensen back to HQ. Once the scenes are over, talk to Malik. He will tell you a bit more about the story. Your conversation choices won't affect the gameplay at all, so feel free to express yourself as you see fit.

02 After speaking with Malik, head to Pritchard's office and talk with him. Pritchard's office is located on the second floor, but if you want some specific directions, feel free to talk to the receptionist on the first floor [→☐ 1]. She's more than willing to point out the key offices in Sarif HQ.

03 After you're done talking to Pritchard, it's time to meet the Boss for a debriefing. When you're ready, take the elevator up to the Penthouse and meet with Sarif. Before going into David's office, feel free to stop and speak with his personal assistant, Athene. [→☐ 2]

04 When you're finished talking with Sarif, it's time to leave HQ and venture out into the streets of Detroit. Before leaving HQ, you may want to stop by Jensen's office for an optional Side Quest [→☐ 3]. When you're ready to leave, go to the first floor and exit the building via the main entrance.

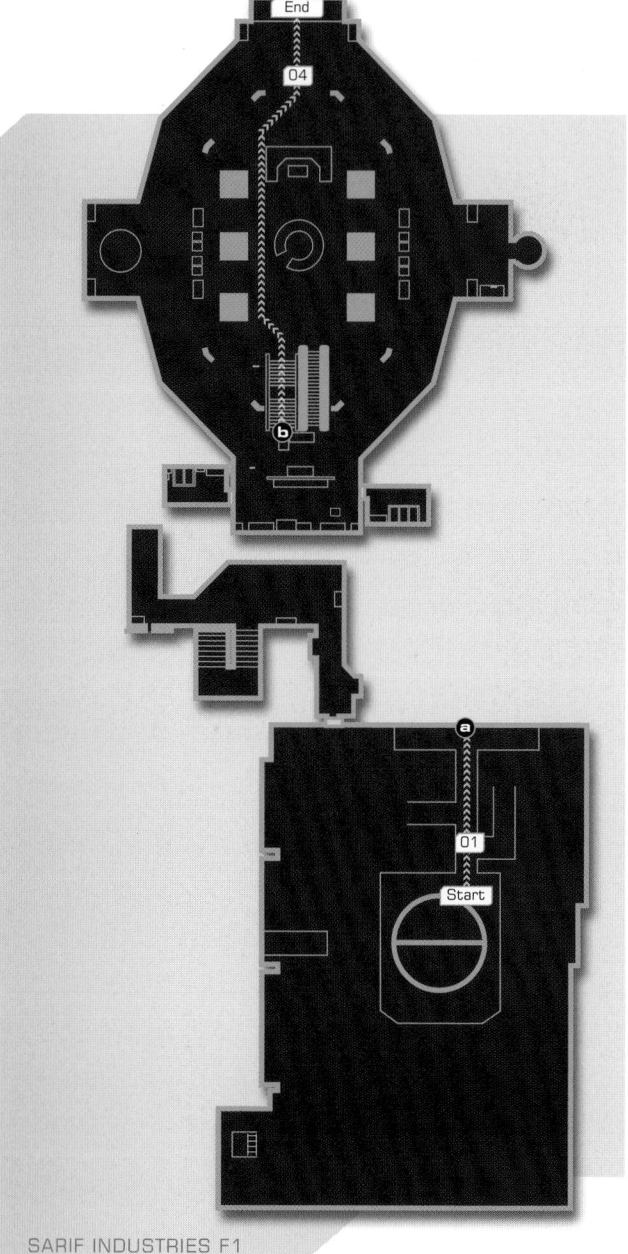

SARIF INDUSTRIES F1

SIDE QUEST

Reading Jensen's emails will open the One Good Turn Deserves Another Side Quest.

- Once you are done talking to David, the Lesser Evil Side Quest will open as you exit the elevator.
- When you leave Sarif HQ and enter Detroit, the Motherly Ties Side Quest will open.
- Upon exiting Sarif HQ, make your way to a small alley northwest of the Police Station on Grand River Road (Gd. River Rd.) directly across from the main entrance DRB territory. There you'll find Detective Jenny Alexander working undercover. Talk to her to open the Cloak & Daggers side quest.

ACHIEVEMENT/TROPHY: DOCTORATE

You'll find one of Hugh Darrow's eBooks in Thorpe's apartment.

			Stealth Bonuses	
Objective Completed	Objective Type	XP Reward	Ghost	Smooth Operator
Give the Typhoon to Pritchard	Primary	1000	No	No

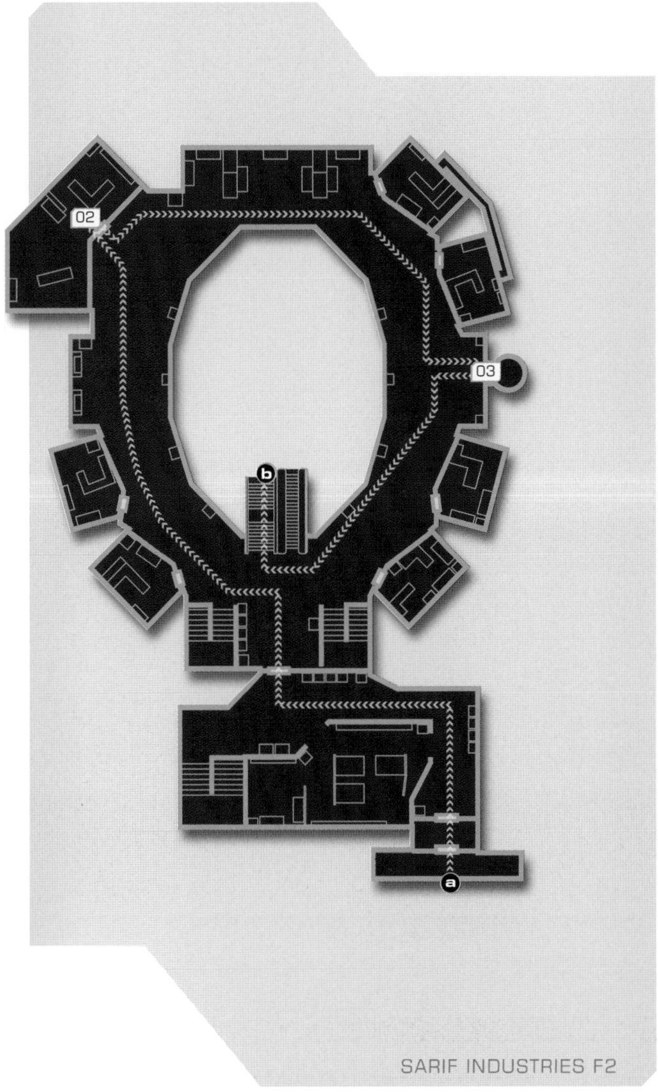
02
03
b
a
SARIF INDUSTRIES F2

SARIF INDUSTRIES
1
2
3

DETROIT CITY STREETS

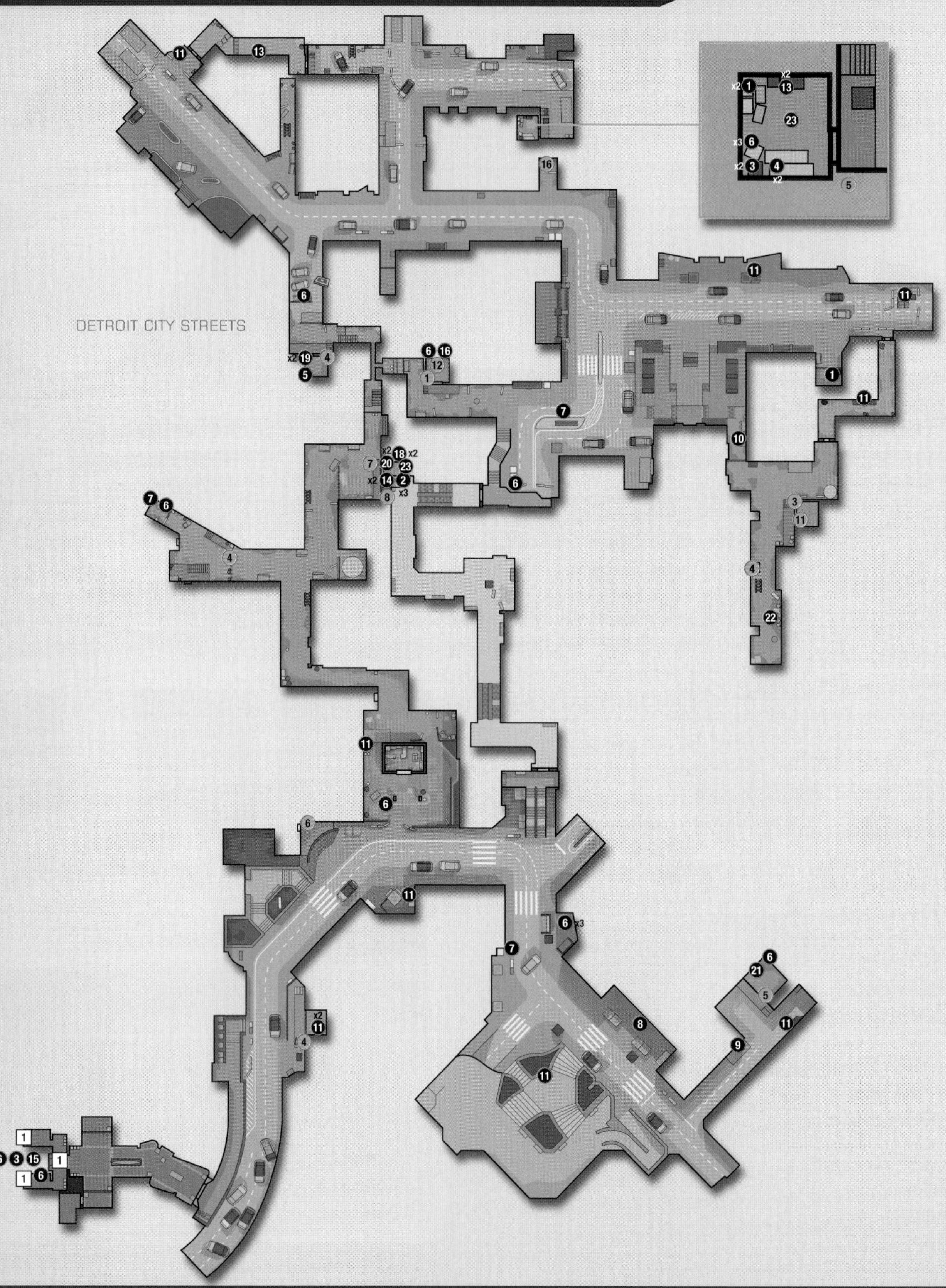

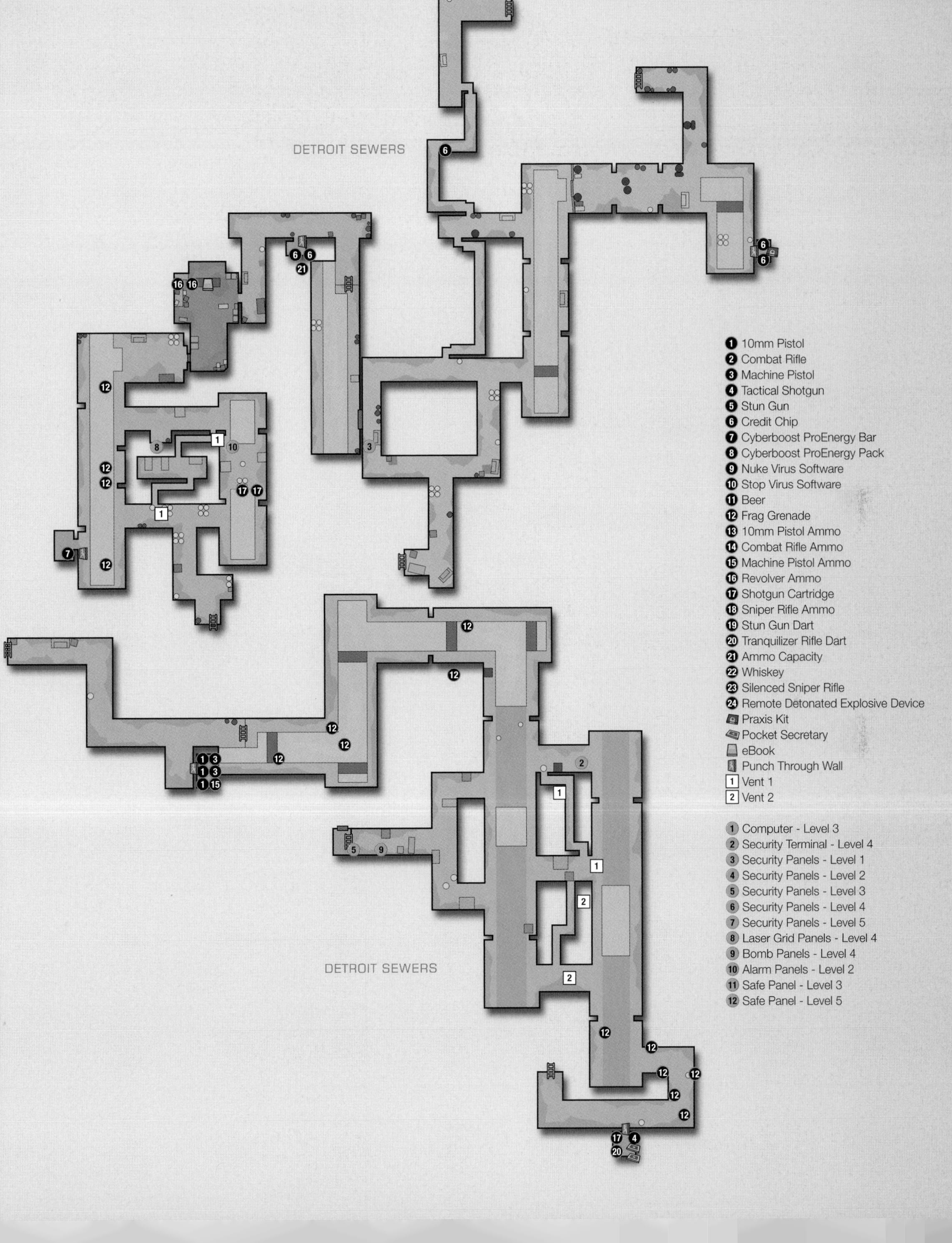
DETROIT SEWERS
DETROIT SEWERS
1 10mm Pistol
2 Combat Rifle
3 Machine Pistol
4 Tactical Shotgun
5 Stun Gun
6 Credit Chip
7 Cyberboost ProEnergy Bar
8 Cyberboost ProEnergy Pack
9 Nuke Virus Software
10 Stop Virus Software
11 Beer
12 Frag Grenade
13 10mm Pistol Ammo
14 Combat Rifle Ammo
15 Machine Pistol Ammo
16 Revolver Ammo
17 Shotgun Cartridge
18 Sniper Rifle Ammo
19 Stun Gun Dart
20 Tranquilizer Rifle Dart
21 Ammo Capacity
22 Whiskey
23 Silenced Sniper Rifle
24 Remote Detonated Explosive Device
Praxis Kit
Pocket Secretary
eBook
Punch Through Wall
1 Vent 1
2 Vent 2
1 Computer - Level 3
2 Security Terminal - Level 4
3 Security Panels - Level 1
4 Security Panels - Level 2
5 Security Panels - Level 3
6 Security Panels - Level 4
7 Security Panels - Level 5
8 Laser Grid Panels - Level 4
9 Bomb Panels - Level 4
10 Alarm Panels - Level 2
11 Safe Panel - Level 3
12 Safe Panel - Level 5

DETROIT CITY INTERIORS

- ❶ 10mm Pistol
- ❷ Combat Rifle
- ❸ Tactical Shotgun
- ❹ Concussion Grenade
- ❺ Credit Chip
- ❻ Cyberboost ProEnergy Bar
- ❼ CyberBoost ProEnergy Pack
- ❽ CyberBoost ProEnergy Jar
- ❾ Pain Killers
- ❿ Beer
- ⓫ 10mm Pistol Ammo
- ⓬ Combat Rifle Ammo
- ⓭ Stun Gun Dart
- ⓮ Tranquilizer Rifle Dart
- ⓯ Nuke Virus Software
- ⓰ Stop Virus Software
- ⓱ Armor Piercing
- ⓲ Automatic Unlocking Device
- Pocket Secretary
- eBook
- Punch Through Wall
- 1 Vent 1

- ① Computer - Unlocked
- ② Computer - Level 1
- ③ Computer - Level 2
- ④ Security Panels - Level 2
- ⑤ Security Panels - Level 3
- ⑥ Safe Panel - Level 1
- ⑦ Safe Panel - Level 3
- ⑧ Safe Panel - Level 4

APARTMENT 1 F3
APARTMENT 1 F2
APARTMENT 1 F1

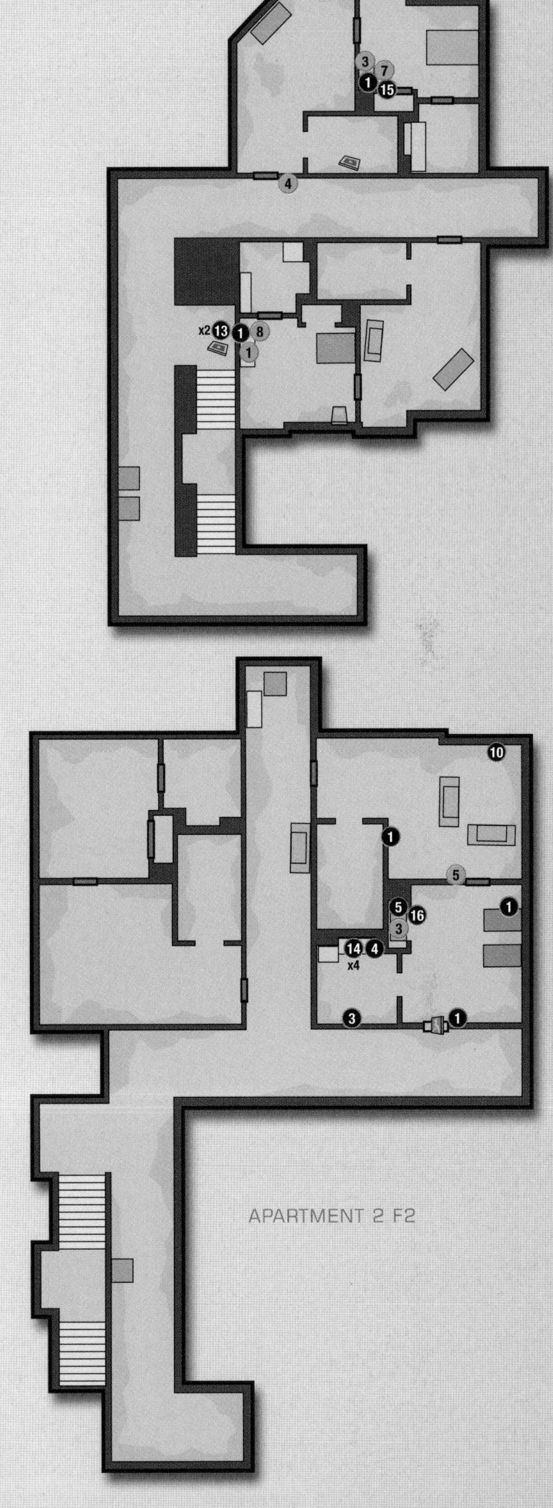
APARTMENT 2 F1
APARTMENT 2 F2

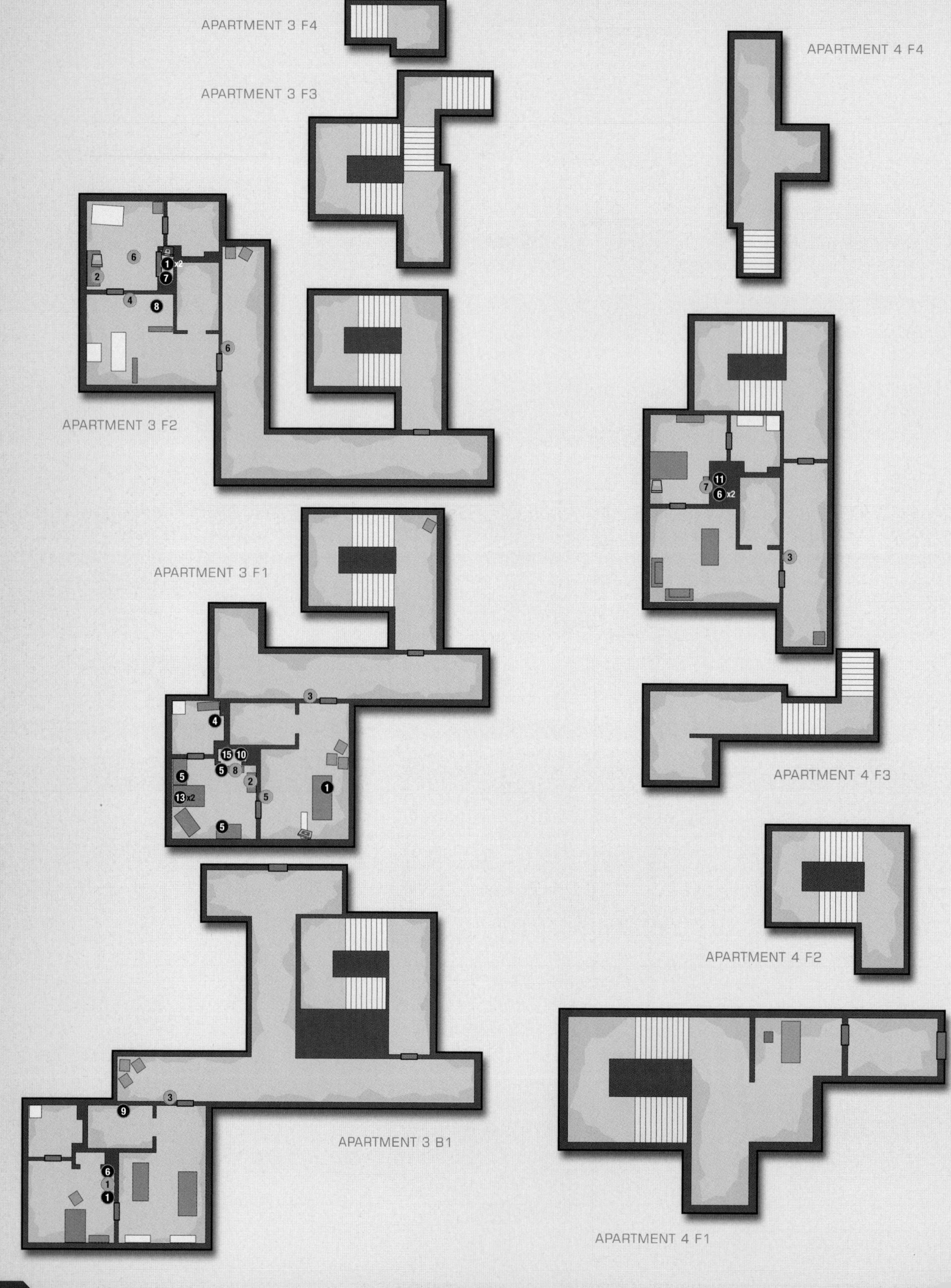

APARTMENT 3 F4
APARTMENT 3 F3
APARTMENT 4 F4
APARTMENT 3 F2
APARTMENT 3 F1
APARTMENT 4 F3
APARTMENT 4 F2
APARTMENT 3 B1
APARTMENT 4 F1

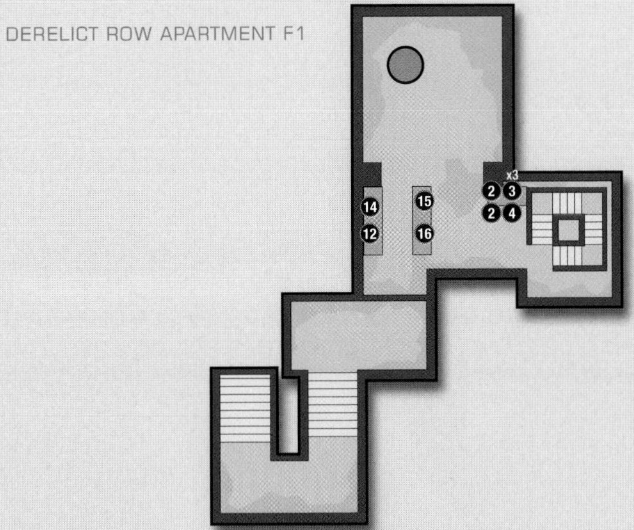

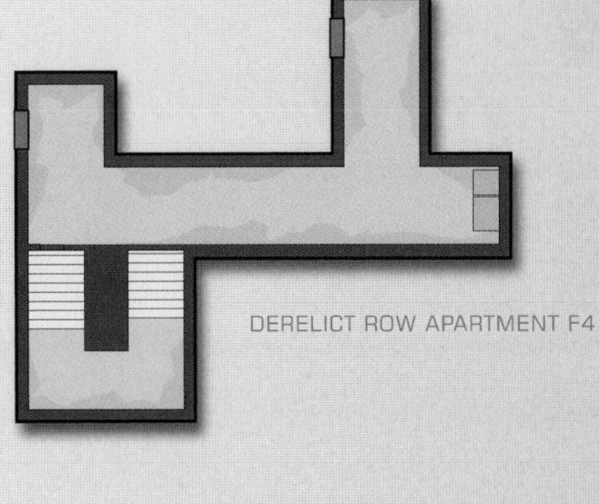

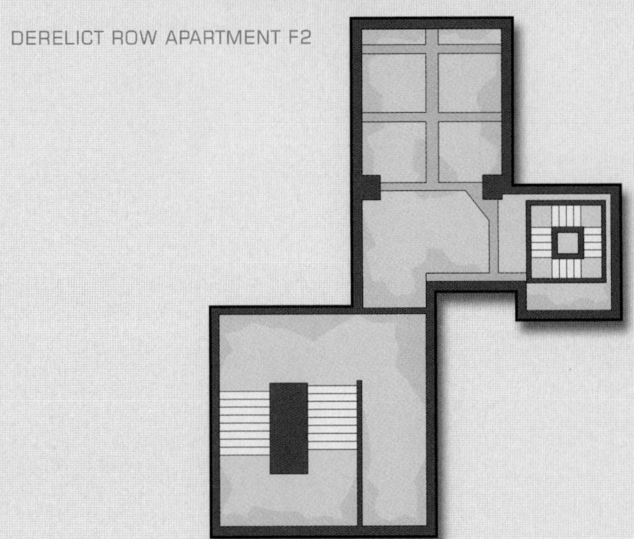

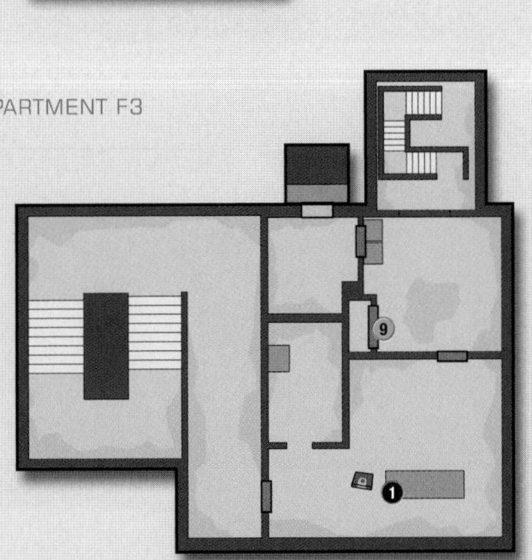

- ❶ 10mm Pistol
- ❷ Combat Rifle
- ❸ Revolver
- ❹ Tactical Shotgun
- ❺ Frag Mine
- ❻ Credit Chip
- ❼ CyberBoost ProEnergy Pack
- ❽ Pain Killers
- ❾ HypoStim
- ❿ Nuke Virus Software
- ⓫ Stop Virus Software
- ⓬ Combat Rifle Ammo
- ⓭ Crossbow Arrow
- ⓮ Revolver Ammo
- ⓯ Shotgun Cartridge
- ⓰ Sniper Rifle Ammo
- Praxis Kit
- Pocket Secretary
- eBook

- ① Computer - Unlocked
- ② Computer - Level 1
- ③ Security Panels - Level 1
- ④ Security Panels - Level 2
- ⑤ Security Panels - Level 4
- ⑥ Security Panels - Level 5
- ⑦ Safe Panel - Level 2
- ⑧ Safe Panel - Level 3
- ⑨ Safe Panel - Level 4

M6 - VISITING THE L.I.M.B. CLINIC

Doctor Marcovic is responsible for Adam Jensen's ongoing treatment and rehabilitation. Sarif has asked Jensen to go in for a checkup, but Sarif also has a little surprise for Jensen in the form of a Praxis Kit.

Objective Name	Objective Type
Meet with Doctor Marcovic	Primary

OPTIONAL EXPLORATION

On the Streets of Detroit

• A Gift For Letitia

When you exit Sarif HQ, go down the first set of stairs and make your way to the central trash bin there. Search it to find a Mahara Jan Hot Devil Ale; this is Letitia's favorite beer. Now head down the street toward the Central Station. Before you reach the station, look left to see Letitia digging around in a trash bin.

You'll want to give her four beers. If you don't have four, go left down the street to the first trash bin to find another. Continue down the street to find a storage unit on the left. It is a Level 2 Hack, and inside you'll find two beers. Once you have four beers, talk to Letitia and give them to her and you'll receive a Pocket Secretary with the codes to a Level 5 Hack storage unit at Earl's Court just South of the most northern Downtown Apartment building. You can also pay Letitia credits for information if you wish. Please refer to the Extras Chapter for a full list of the information she has to offer.

• Getting A Sniper Rifle

When you leave Sarif HQ, turn left to the stairs. As you move down the stairs, look left at the rock garden there. Search that area to find a Pocket Secretary with an access code. Now go to the LIMB Clinic, but don't enter it. Instead, look right to find a ladder. Climb the ladder to find a Level 4 Hack door.

The code you just found will open it. Go through the building to a window. If you don't have the Icarus augmentation, jump onto the window ledge and then slowly ease out to fall onto the air conditioning unit directly below you. From the AC Unit, drop to the roof. Investigate the vent ahead to find a Sniper Rifle. If you don't want to keep it, you can sell it at the Weapon Dealer's shop located directly below.

• Finding the Surgical Chop Shop

Go to the Police Department but do not go in. Instead, go left to find a small alley on your right. There is a fence made of sheet metal ahead. You'll need the Jump Enhancement augmentation for this. Get on the ledge to the right, then sprint and jump over the sheet metal fence. On the other side, you'll find a dead body. Search the body to find a Pocket Secretary for a Level 5 Hack door in the most western Downtown Apartment building. It's on Brooklyn Court. The room is on the second floor.

Enter the apartment and hack the bedroom door (Level 2). Next, hack the PC (Level 2) and read the emails for the codes to the Level 5 Hack gate in that room. Open it to get a Praxis Kit, a CyberBoost ProEnergy Pack, and 10mm Ammo. There is also a Hugh Darrow eBook next to the PC.

Note **If you don't have the Pocket Secretary Codes, or Level 5 Hack abilities, you can always use gun fire and frag grenades to destroy this Level 5 door and get inside that way!**

01 Go to the LIMB Clinic located west of Sarif HQ. When you enter the clinic, a scene will trigger. Once the scene is over, you'll be speaking with Dr. Marcovic [→□ 1]. Besides reassuring you that you're in great health, Marcovic tells you that Sarif has given you 5000 credits to buy Praxis Kits. There are two kits available, so buy them both if you have the requisite 10000 credits on you. If you don't have enough credits, don't worry; you can come back later when you have the full amount.

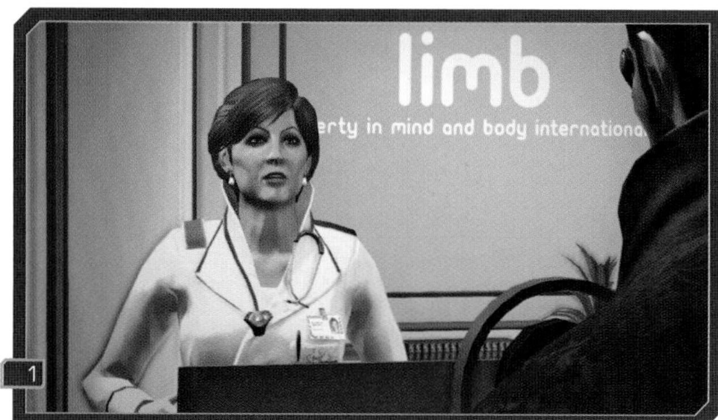

1

ACHIEVEMENT/TROPHY: DOCTORATE

You'll find one of Hugh Darrow's eBooks in the Surgical Chop Shop.

Objective Completed	Objective Type	XP Reward	Stealth Bonuses: Ghost	Stealth Bonuses: Smooth Operator
Meet with Doctor Marcovic	Primary	1000	No	No

DETROIT CENTRAL POLICE STATION

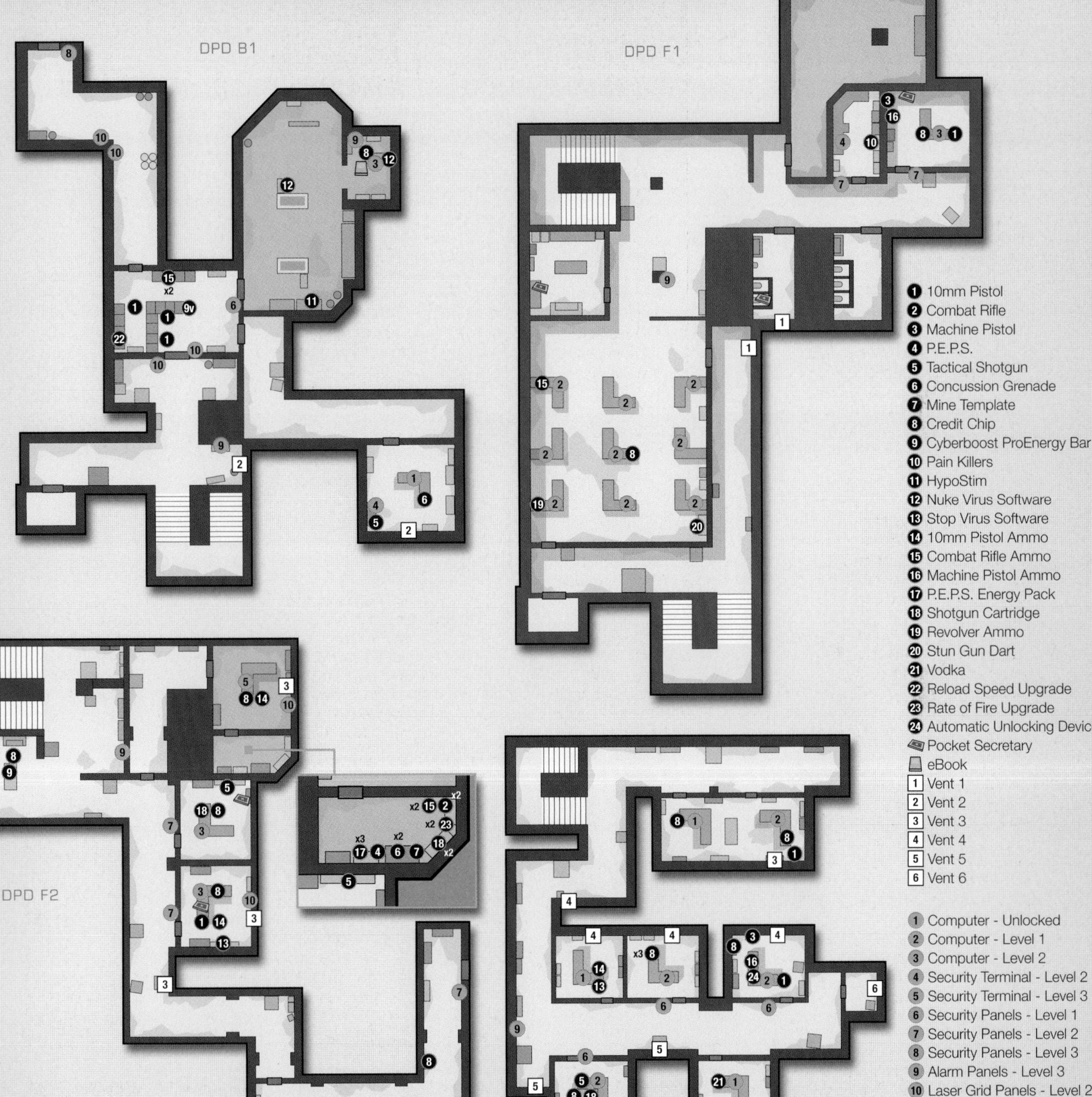
DPD B1
DPD F1
DPD F2
DPD F3
1 10mm Pistol
2 Combat Rifle
3 Machine Pistol
4 P.E.P.S.
5 Tactical Shotgun
6 Concussion Grenade
7 Mine Template
8 Credit Chip
9 Cyberboost ProEnergy Bar
10 Pain Killers
11 HypoStim
12 Nuke Virus Software
13 Stop Virus Software
14 10mm Pistol Ammo
15 Combat Rifle Ammo
16 Machine Pistol Ammo
17 P.E.P.S. Energy Pack
18 Shotgun Cartridge
19 Revolver Ammo
20 Stun Gun Dart
21 Vodka
22 Reload Speed Upgrade
23 Rate of Fire Upgrade
24 Automatic Unlocking Device
Pocket Secretary
eBook
1 Vent 1
2 Vent 2
3 Vent 3
4 Vent 4
5 Vent 5
6 Vent 6
1 Computer - Unlocked
2 Computer - Level 1
3 Computer - Level 2
4 Security Terminal - Level 2
5 Security Terminal - Level 3
6 Security Panels - Level 1
7 Security Panels - Level 2
8 Security Panels - Level 3
9 Alarm Panels - Level 3
10 Laser Grid Panels - Level 2

M5 - INVESTIGATING THE SUICIDE TERRORIST

There are four different ways to access the police station, some of which are much easier than others. Your primary choice here is between going in through the front door by convincing Wayne Hass to let you pass, or taking one of the less obvious entrances. These involve sneaking inside and will require you to remain undetected whilst inside the station unless you want to fight the entire Detroit Police force. If you choose to engage the Police, the Pistol or the Combat Rifle should be your weapon of choice, purely for the ammo you can acquire within the station to keep you going. Taking the Wayne Hass option will allow you to move around freely inside the station, but you'll still not be tolerated to stand around for too long and will need to be stealthy if you want to hack door panels. Because there is no benefit in terms of XP from taking out the Police Officers in the station, a Stealth Combat approach is not recommended.

Objective Name	Objective Type
Retrieve the dead terrorist neural hub	Primary

After your meeting with Sarif back at HQ, head back down the elevator and exit the building onto the streets. The Central Station can be seen directly ahead of the Sarif HQ building and going through there is the quickest way to reach the Police Station. If fail to convince Wayne to let you into the station, or simply prefer to use an alternate route, your mission will begin on the streets just outside the Police Station. The other ways into the Police Station are all found in a small alley that runs along the side of the building. Reaching this alley, however, is not as straight forward as it may appear.

Detroit City Streets

ROUTE 1 Stealth

Required None
Recommended EMP Shielding, Jump Enhancement, Hacking: Capture 2

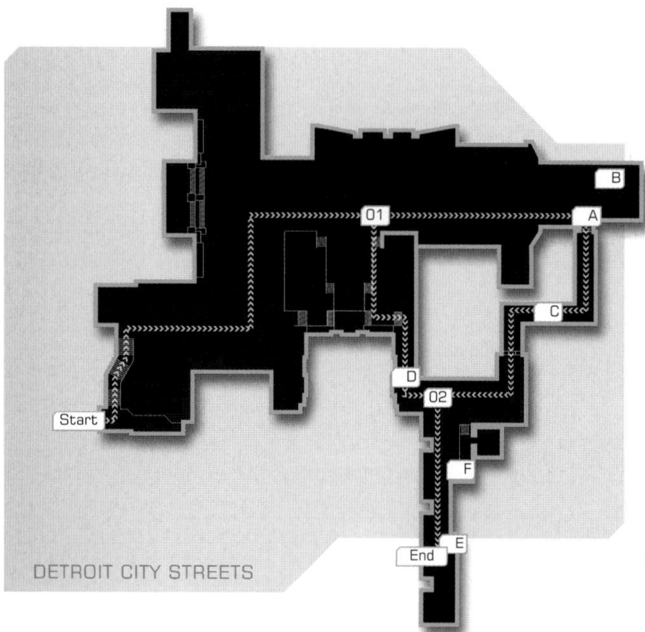

01 The most direct route to the back alley is through a narrow corridor to the north of it at **Position A**. The floor of this corridor has been electrified, however, due to a broken power line and prolonged contact would be fatal. If you have acquired the EMP Shielding Augmentation you can simply run along the corridor. You will not receive any damage from the current and will reach the alley easily.

It is still possible to make it through the corridor without this Augmentation, but it does take a bit more time and patience. Just inside the door to the corridor there is a crate, and outside behind some construction material at **Position B** you can find another one; you will require both of them to venture into the corridor safely. Place one of the crates on the ground just ahead of the electrified floor, and then jump onto it with the second crate in hand. Now if you drop this crate ahead of the first one you can walk onto it and extend your bridge. [→☐ 1]

Keep repeating this process until you are near the middle of the corridor where you will find a small patch of non-electrified floor; jump down into the clearing, and then pull the level on the breaker box at **Position C** to stop the current. Once the lever is pulled, the entire corridor will be rendered safe and you can travel along it as normal. This process may take a little while, but opening up this corridor will save time in the long run because the alley is home to objectives for multiple Side Quests.

If you have the Jump Enhancement Augmentation then you can take advantage of another way to reach the alley. Just to the side of the Police Station's main entrance at **Position D** there is a small opening that is blocked off by a tall fence. With the Jump Enhancement you can easily jump straight over this fence to directly access the alley.

02 You will need to scale the fire escape at **Position E** in the alley to get to the alternative points of entry for the Police Station. Unfortunately the ladder does not quite come down far enough. You will need to pick up one of the crates at **Position F**, and then place it below the ladder so that you can jump up [→☐ 2]. There are two possible entrances available once you are on the fire escape: a locked door on the second floor, and a vent on the third floor. To get through the door you will need to have Capture 2 software, or use the code if you have it. The vent has no such restrictions, so if you do not have the necessary Augmentations, select this route instead.

SIDE QUEST

If you are in the middle of the Motherly Ties Side Quest, you can access the storage unit. This is one of the objectives for that mission while you are in the alley.

ROUTE 2 Going Underground (Stealth)

Required None
Recommended Punch Through Walls, Hacking: Capture 3

01 Another way of reaching the alley, and thus the side entrances to the Police Station is to make use of the sewers below the city; this route is especially useful if you do not have many of the exploration Augmentations. Exit the Central Station as usual, and then turn left at the bottom of the stairs and use the manhole at **Position A** to get into the sewers.

02 On the whole you can safely move through the sewers without any trouble, but there are a couple of things to be mindful of. The water in half of the sewers has been electrified due to a broken power line falling into it, so be careful not to drop into it by accident. There are also a small group of Punks that have taken up residence in the middle of the sewers and they do not take kindly to people loitering in their turf [→☐ 3]. As long as you move through the area quickly and do not stop in front of them for too long they will leave you alone. You could also take them out and while they do not yield any XP, you can get some extra credits from them.

You have two main exits that you can choose from in the sewers: the first is a door at **Position B** that leads directly to the basement in the Police Station, and the second is another manhole at **Position C** that will take you up to the alley next to the Police Station. The basement access offers the quickest means to completing your objective, but also gives the least scope for exploration.

To get through the door you will either need to hack the terminal if you have Capture 3 software, or if you have the Punch Through Walls Augmentation, you can break through the weak wall at **Position D**. In this small alcove you will find a Pocket Secretary that has the code for the door, along with a few other useful items [→☐ 4]. If you do not have the Punch Through Walls Augmentation, then you are still able to access the alcove by breaking the wall using conventional firearms.

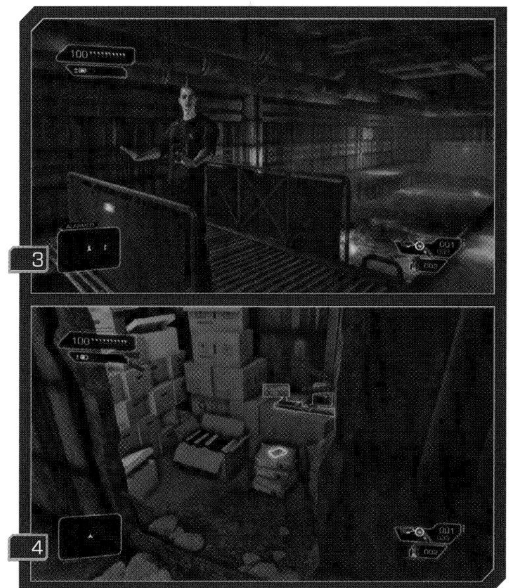

ROUTE 1 A Conversation with Wayne Haas (Stealth)

01 When you enter the station you'll see Wayne behind the reception desk ahead. To get further inside you'll need to convince him that letting you in is the right thing to do, which means having a conversation with him. Wayne has many different possible responses to each one of yours so it can be difficult to predict how he will act when you start the conversation. [→☐ 1].

The responses outlined here will normally lead you through the conversation with a positive outcome, but just in case it is recommended that you save your game beforehand. If you have the CASIE Augmentation, however, you will have the option to make use of the pheromones during the second round of the conversation. Wayne is a predominantly Omega type personality, so choosing to pressure him is the correct response.

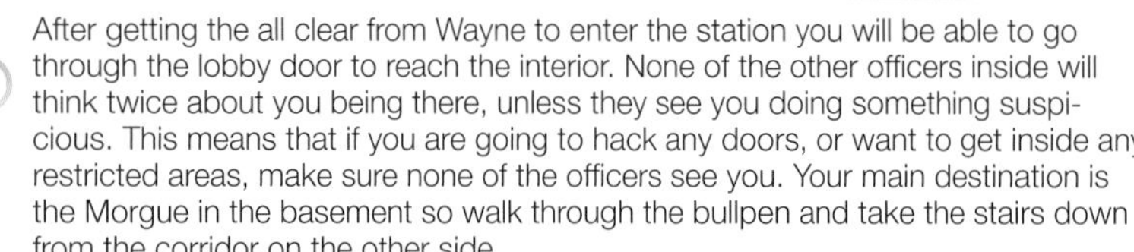

Conversation Round	Response to Make
Round 1	Absolve
Round 2	Plead
Round 3	Absolve
Round 4	Plead

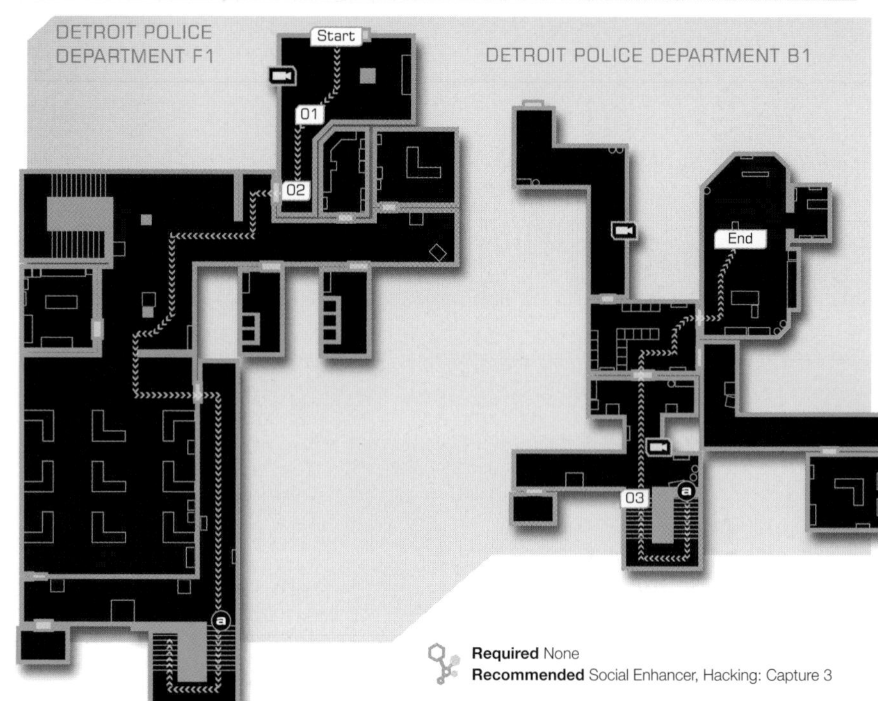

Required None
Recommended Social Enhancer, Hacking: Capture 3

02 After getting the all clear from Wayne to enter the station you will be able to go through the lobby door to reach the interior. None of the other officers inside will think twice about you being there, unless they see you doing something suspicious. This means that if you are going to hack any doors, or want to get inside any restricted areas, make sure none of the officers see you. Your main destination is the Morgue in the basement so walk through the bullpen and take the stairs down from the corridor on the other side.

OPTIONAL EXPLORATION

There are a lot of Credit Chips and other items that can be found by searching the many desk drawers within the Police Station. Since you can roam freely, there is no reason not to take advantage. Most of the offices on the second and third floors will also give you a small XP reward upon entering them, so they are also worth checking out.

The biggest single cache of items is found in the Armory on the second floor, but since the door leading to the items is extremely secure, you will either need the password or advanced hacking skills. The password can be found in the office near the lobby entrance, and you only need Capture 2 software to access it. There is an officer guarding the Armory so you can either walk in quickly and use a Takedown on him, or wait for him to leave the area on his patrol route. If you use a Takedown on him, make sure to drag the body out of the doorway so that the security camera doesn't see it.

ACHIEVEMENT/TROPHY

Desk Job Convincing Wayne to let you into the Police Station will not only net you the Silver Tongue XP bonus, but you will also unlock The Desk Job Achievement/Trophy for your skilful conversational ability.

Doctorate If you look over on the coroner's desk you will find another of Hugh Darrow's eBooks that you need to collect for the Doctorate Achievement/Trophy.

SIDE QUEST

As soon as you enter the Police Station Lobby you will be able to see Chet Wagner, an important witness for the Motherly Ties Side Quest. While you could talk to him at this point, you are much better off going to his office on the third floor to gather more information first.

Now that you have free access to almost the entire Police Station, you can easily investigate Captain Penn's office on the second floor and Detective Wagner's office on the third floor for the Motherly Ties Side Quest.

03 Once you reach the basement, you can walk straight past the officer and the camera to enter the locker room. From there take the door on the left to enter the Morgue. Walk up to the coroner who is standing near the body of the dead terrorist to initiate a short conversation, after which you will be able to take the neural hub from the body [→☐ 2]. Now that you have what you came for, leave the police station and head back out onto the city streets.

ROUTE 2 Sewer Entrance (Stealth)

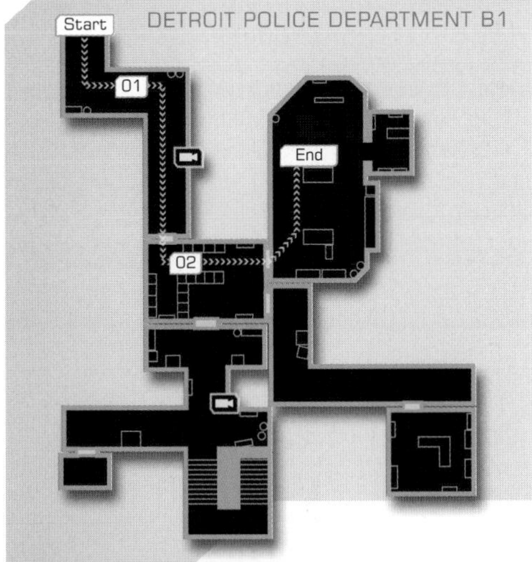

Required None
Recommended Cloaking System, Hacking: Capture 2

01 After rounding the first corner from the sewer entrance you will be able to see a security laser field, along with the dedicated terminal that controls it. There is also a security camera just behind the laser field, so be careful not to move out too far. If you have high enough Capture software you should be able to easily hack the terminal to disable the lasers. Alternatively if you have the Cloaking System you can activate it briefly and walk through them. If you have neither of these systems you can still make it past the lasers stealthily, because the bottom beam is malfunctioning slightly.

The beam will flash on and off twice quickly, and then turn off for a few seconds; use this time to crouch down and move under the remaining beams safely. Once you are past the lasers, remain crouched so that you move under the cameras field of vision [→□ 3]. Wait for the camera to pan back towards the entrance, and then move quickly and take cover to the left of the next door. The locker room on the other side of this door is part of the patrol route for one of the officers in the basement, so make sure to check your radar to ensure the area is clear before advancing.

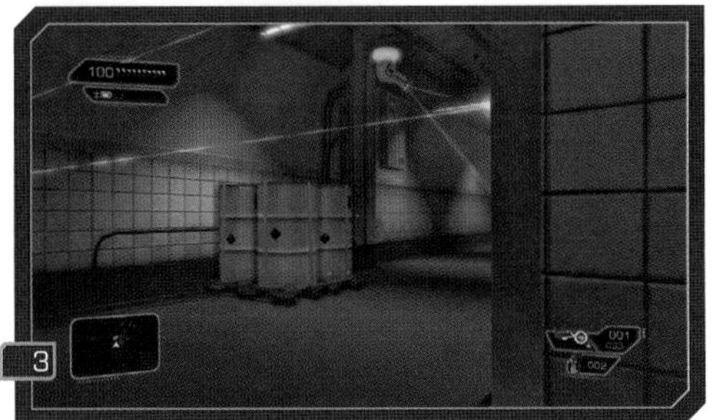

02 Before the officer can make his way back into the locker room, quickly move up to the dedicated terminal to the right of the Morgue door and hack it. It only has a security rating of one, so is easily hackable by anyone. Alternatively if you do not mind incapacitating the police officer, you can wait for him to come back into the locker room and incapacitate him to get the Pocket Secretary containing the access code from him.

Once you have unlocked the Morgue door, go inside and retrieve the Neural Hub. Then go back to the Morgue entrance and take cover next to the door; make sure the patrolling officer is not in the locker room and then go towards the sewer entrance and leave the same way you came in.

Detroit Police Station

ROUTE 3 Fire Escape Door (Stealth)

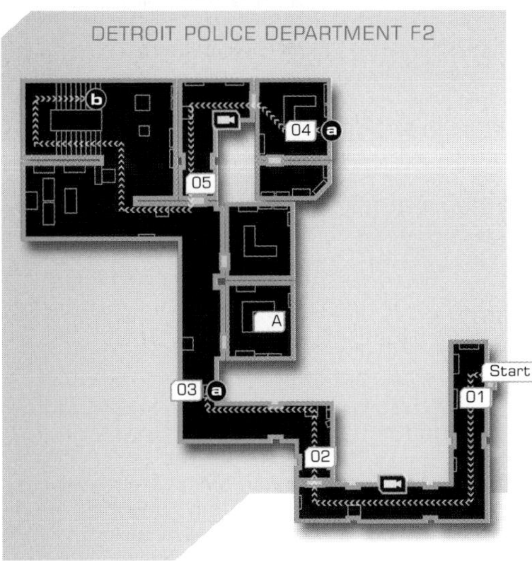

Required Hacking: Capture 2
Recommended Cloaking System, Additional Energy Cells, Hacking: Capture 3

01 Once you are inside the Police Station, walk along the corridor until you come to the first corner and then take cover before rounding it because there is a security camera on the other side [→□ 4]. Wait until the camera is starting to move back towards your position, and then crouch down and walk under its field of vision and go through the door at the end of the hallway.

02 Keep crouched and move forward until you come to the second corner of this hallway and then once again take cover. There is a police officer patrolling this area and stepping out without checking first can easily get you spotted. While you are taking cover by the wall, you will notice that there is a vent just ahead of your position; wait for the officer to start walking away and then quickly round the corner and enter the vent.

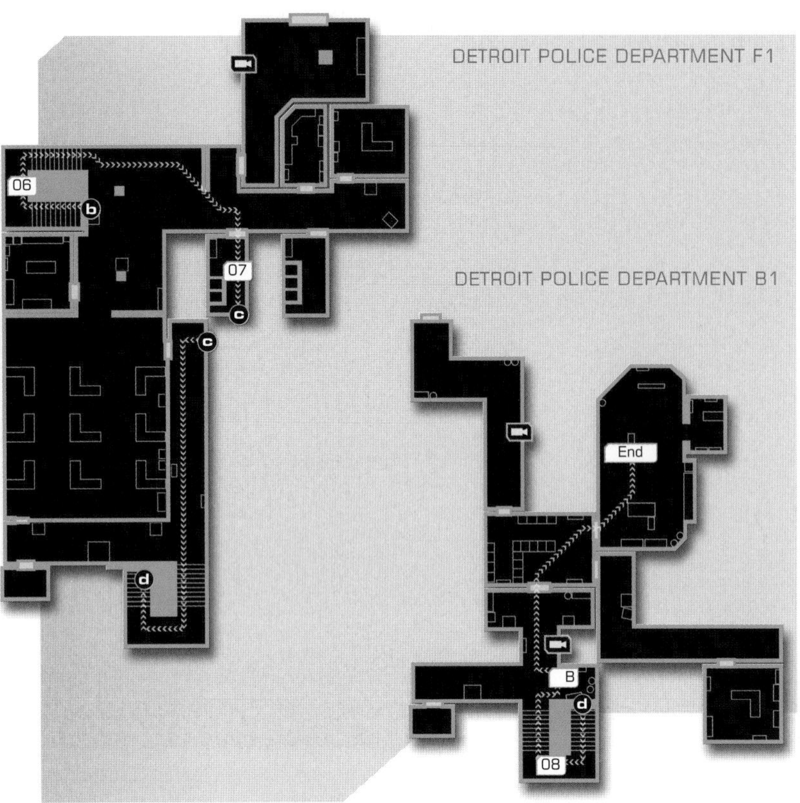

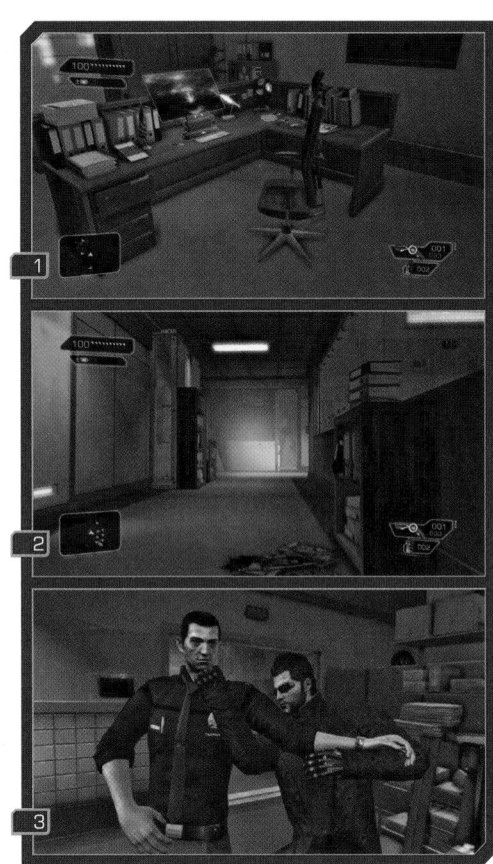

03 This vent will take you all the way down to the Armory, but a security laser field is blocking your path half way along it. If you have the Cloaking System you can use it to move safely past the lasers. If you do not have the Cloaking System, just before you reach the lasers you will find another vent cover that you can go through in order to reach Captain Penn's office at **Position A**. On the back wall of the office you will find a dedicated terminal that you can hack in order to deactivate the lasers, and on his desk you can also find a Pocket Secretary that has the code for the Morgue door [→☐ 1]. When you are done, head back into the vent and follow it along to reach the Armory.

SIDE QUEST

If you have the Motherly Ties Side Quest active, make sure you hack into Captain Penn's computer, while you are in his office. You will retrieve some vital information.

04 Once you are in the Armory room if you have the password, or a high enough Capture level you can access the secure area and loot it of its contents before you continue. While you are in the security hub, you can also disable the security cameras connected to it. When you are ready, take cover beside the door and then open it so that you can see the camera in the hallway on the other side, if it has not been disabled. Wait for it to start panning towards your position, and then keep crouched and move past it and around the corner.

05 Take cover beside the next door that you come to, and use the glass panel in it to watch the movements of the patrolling officer on the other side. Once he is at the end of the hallway with his back to you, open the door and move out to the right while crouched. You will be faced with two stationary police officers with their backs to you directly in front of you. You can sneak past them normally when crouched, but it can be safer to activate the Cloaking System if you have it. Keep going forward and then take the stairs down to the first floor when you come to them.

06 Take cover on the wall when you reach the half-way point of the stairs because there is another officer patrolling the area just below on the first floor. Wait for him to turn around and start walking away, and then begin to descend the stairs while staying in cover. About half way along his route the officer will turn around, so make sure you stay in cover until this has happened, and then press the Jump Button to dive across to the pillar in the middle of the room. Continue across the room quickly and then go into the men's bathroom on the right when you come to it.

07 Open the vent cover in the bathroom and go through the short vent into the hallway on the other side. This hallway runs along the side of the bullpen where a large number of officers are working; as long as you remain crouched and stick close to partial wall on the right, you can safely move along it towards the stairs leading down to the basement at the end. [→☐ 2]

08 Once you are in the basement, you will be forced to incapacitate at least one police officer, unless you have the Cloaking System. Take cover near the bottom of the stairs, and then when the officer at the bottom moves away slightly, crouch down to move quietly and take cover by the wall at **Position B**. The officer will stand near this position for a while and then start to walk towards the locker room; wait until he has checked behind him and then move up quietly behind him.

The security laser field in front of the locker room will disengage as the officer gets close to it, so stick close behind him and follow him through the door when it opens. If you have the Cloaking System you can activate it at this time and move around the officer and take cover behind the lockers to the left until he is gone. If you do not have the Cloak then you will need to use a Takedown on the officer to incapacitate him while his back is towards you. [→☐ 3]

When the coast is clear, either use the code or hack the terminal to gain access to the Morgue so that you can reclaim the Neural Hub. To get out of the Police Station either retrace your steps back, or exit via the sewer entrance door if you have the code or high enough Capture software.

ROUTE 4 | Fire Escape Vent (Combat)

DETROIT POLICE DEPARTMENT F3

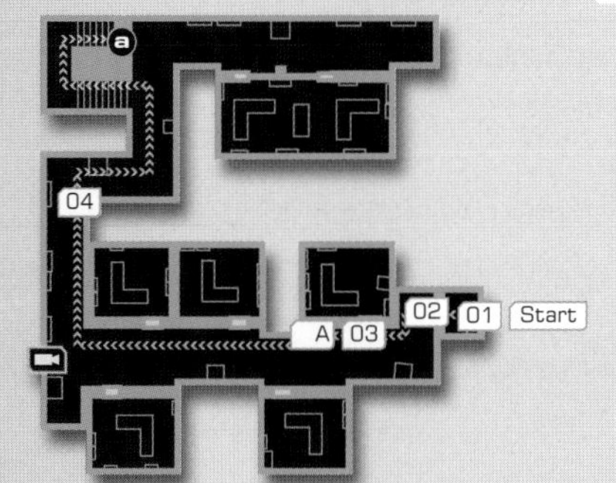

DETROIT POLICE DEPARTMENT F2

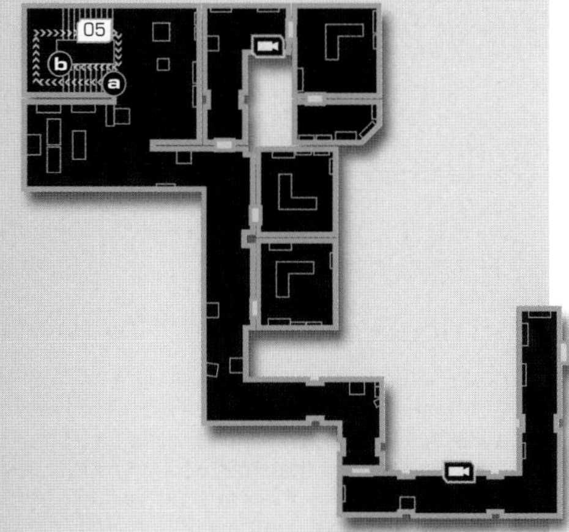

DETROIT POLICE DEPARTMENT F1

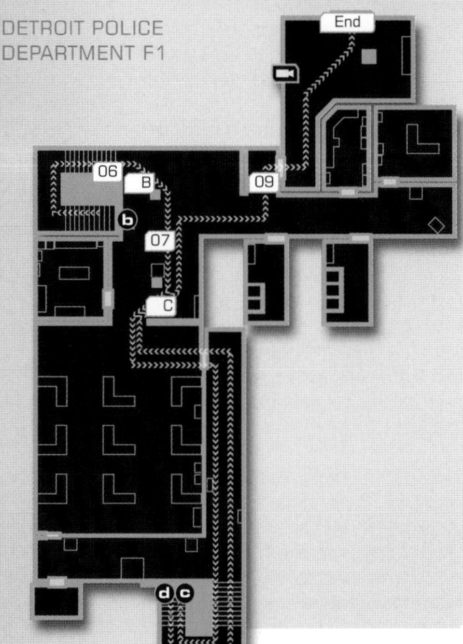

Required None
Recommended Dermal Plating, Cloaking System, Recoil Reduction

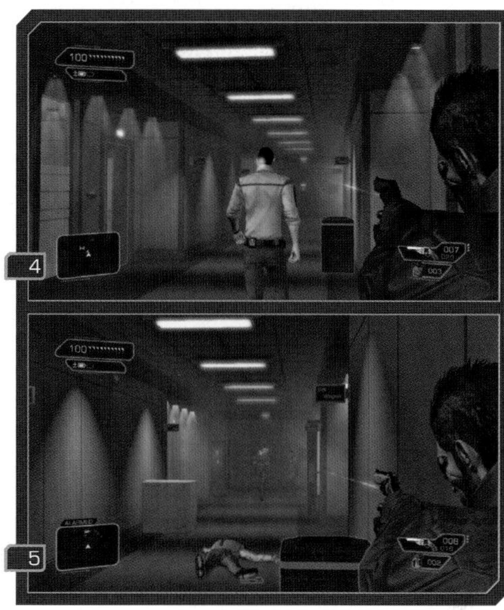

01 After entering from the vent outside you will find yourself in a tall shaft with a ladder directly in front of you that you should take down. Enter the next vent at the bottom of the ladder and then follow it along to come out into a maintenance closet.

02 Exit the closet and then quickly take cover behind the wall directly in front of you because there will be a police officer patrolling the area just ahead. The officer is usually walking away from you, allowing you to lean out from behind cover safely and take him out [→□ 4]. The sound of the gun shot will alert the whole building to your presence, but most of the police have been trained to stick to their assigned areas so only the ones in the immediate vicinity will start closing in on your position.

The first two you will have to contend with are very close by in Detective Murphy's office on the left of the corridor, and they will come out as soon as they hear the gun shot. Try to take them out quickly, one at a time, as they exit the office, because a third officer will soon start running in from the far end of the corridor.

If the two officers make it out of the office they will take up defensive positions on either side of the corridor; wait for them to pop out and start firing so that you can get a clear shot on each of them. The officer moving up from the far end will usually try to close the distance quickly, so try to take him out from a distance. If any of the officers start to close in on your position, simply blind-fire in their direction around the corner to make them retreat.

03 The area should be clear at this time, but it won't be for long, because two Riot Cops will be closing in rapidly. They are much tougher than the Desk Cops you were just dealing with. The Riot Cops will be coming in from the far end of the corridor, so quickly move up a bit and take cover behind the wall at **Position A** to get a better shot. Try to go for headshots when they come around the corner, because it will take a lot of shots to the body to bring them down [→□ 5]. Once you have taken care of the two Riot Cops, this half of the third floor will remain clear. This means you can freely explore if you wish before continuing.

Tip **The first officer you killed has a Pocket Secretary on him that contains the codes for every office on the third floor. Getting these codes and looting the offices can net you some very useful supplies.**

SIDE QUEST

While you are on the third floor you can go into Chet Wagner's office and hack his computer to get some incriminating evidence on him. Because of all the shooting, however, he will be hostile and you won't be able to talk to him when you first go down into the lobby. If you leave the police station and then come back in, the alert status will have passed and you can talk to him again to complete the objective.

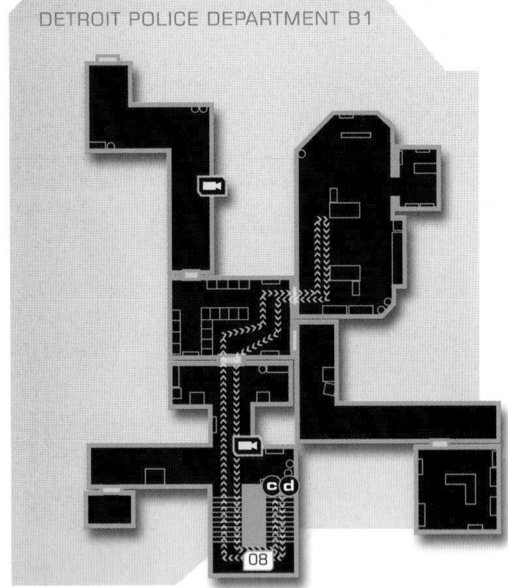

04 Continue down the corridor when you are ready and then take cover by the wall at this point. There is usually another Desk Cop in the area just ahead, so peek around the corner to try and spot his location. If you can see him you should take him out, if not move up to the next corner and look from there. Taking this officer down will alert two others that were in the interrogation room and they will come running to investigate; wait for them to start rounding the corner and then take them out one at a time [→☐ 1]. They were the final two officers on the third floor, so it's time to head down to the second floor.

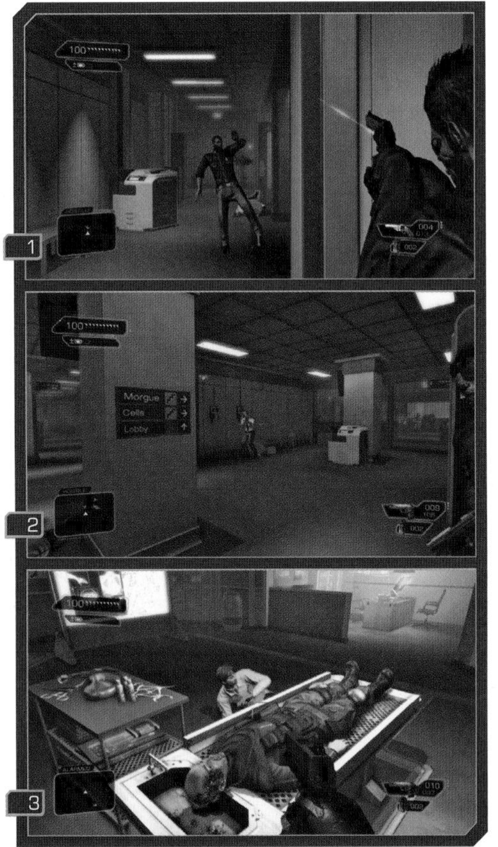

05 Take cover behind the wall as you descend the stairs because there are likely to be a large number of police officers congregated along the mezzanine, and many of them are Riot Cops. Depending on where your shots were fired on the third floor, however, they may sometimes move into the area near the armor; if this is the case fire a shot to draw them out. The Riot Cops will tend to throw grenades if you spend too long behind cover, so try to keep them engaged as much as possible. If they do get a grenade off, retreat back up the stairs to safety and then come back down when it has cleared.

Most of the officers will try to take cover around a low partition wall opposite your position on the stairs, so just keep lining up your shots from behind cover, leaning out to take them out one at a time. All of the officers on this floor will come to the area around the mezzanine, so there's no need to go looking for any others. You should then descend to the first floor.

OPTIONAL EXPLORATION

If you have high enough Capture software, or know the password, it can be worth going into the Armory at this time to re-supply, just make sure to crouch when you move around so that the officers below can't get a clean shot.

06 The officers in the first floor bullpen will still be actively searching for you, but you cannot get a clear line of sight on them from a position by the stairs. Move up and take cover behind the vending machine at **Position B** just past the stairs to get a better view of the area. All of the officers on this floor are Desk Cops with pistols, and for the most part they will all try to take cover behind the many desks in the bullpen. The main exception to this is your old friend Wayne Haas who will normally come running in from his desk by lobby once the shooting starts. Make sure to keep an eye on your radar so that you can spot him running in and take him down before he becomes a problem. [→☐ 2]

Because of the sheer number of officers in this area at the start it is best to stick to one cover position rather than trying to move around a lot, and since none of the Desk Cops have grenades they won't be able to flush you out. If you have the Cloaking System, this is the perfect time to make use of it so that you can lean out safely and line up your shots easier. The Concussion Grenades from the Armory can also be extremely useful for disorientating groups of officers in the bullpen for easy shots.

07 When you have taken out most of the officers, move up using the pillar for protection and take cover behind the wall at **Position C**. From here you should have a better view of the area and can take down the last few remaining officers with greater ease. Once the area is clear, cross the bullpen and take the stairs down to the basement.

08 When you get near the bottom of the stairs, take cover behind the wall so that you can look down to the room below and see if a patrolling officer is there. If he is in plain sight you can take him out straight away, otherwise you should wait for him to return from the locker room and then engage him. Once you fire your first shot, the two officers from the holding cells will come running to investigate, so try and take them out as they come through the locker room door.

Since you are not worried about setting off any more alarms, once all three officers have been killed, walk through the lasers and open the door to the locker room. Either hack, or use the code from the Pocket Secretary found on the body of one of the officers in this area to gain access to the Morgue. There will be no cutscene this time, because the coroner is usually cowering on the floor from the sound of the gunshots, so simply take the Neural Hub and exit the Morgue. [→☐ 3]

09 Head back up the stairs and towards the lobby so that you can leave the Police Station, but before you go through the lobby door, take cover behind the wall next to it. One final officer is usually stationed out in the lobby so open the door and take him out from behind cover, and then exit the building. Be careful if you leave the building through the lobby, however, because if you did not clear the streets of Police beforehand, they will all be waiting outside and will fire on you as soon as you leave. You can use one of the other exits to leave unnoticed, however, and the police outside should be none the wiser.

			Stealth Bonuses	
Objective Completed	Objective Type	XP Reward	Ghost	Smooth Operator
Retrieve the dead terrorist's Neural Hub	Primary	1750	Yes	Yes

M6 - NO PLACE LIKE HOME

Objective Name	Objective Type
Use my home computer to analyze the hub	Primary

After securing the Neural Hub, Sarif wants you to return to your apartment building, rather than bringing the device into Sarif HQ. The apartment is in the Chiron Building, which is on Grand River Road near DRB territory. Use the elevator in the lobby to reach the floor with your apartment on, and the door to it is the first one on the right. Enter the bedroom to the rear of the apartment and then access your computer to trigger a cutscene, during which the Neural Hub will be analyzed. [→☐ 4]

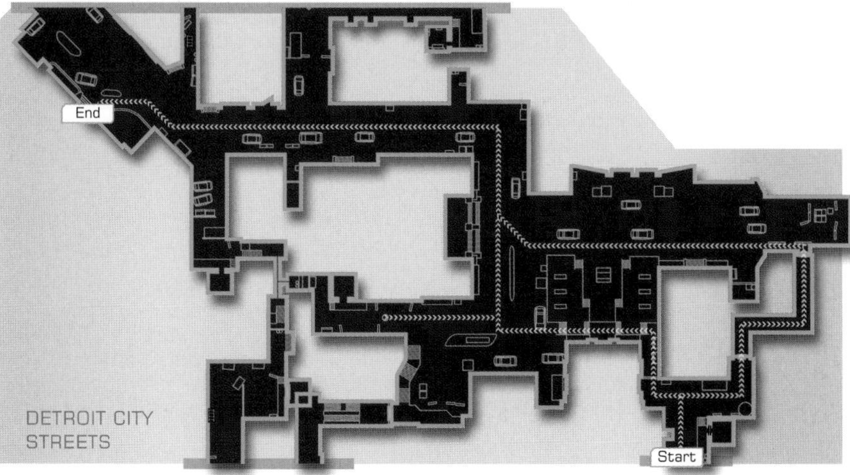

SIDE QUEST

On the way to the Chiron Building you can accept the Cloak & Dagger Side Quest by speaking to Jenny Alexander who is leaning against a wall opposite the entrance to the DRB stronghold Plum Terrace. Also, once you enter the lobby of the Chiron Building you will find Mrs. Reed waiting there so you can complete the Motherly Ties Side Quest if you have all of the information.

ACHIEVEMENT/TROPHY: DOCTORATE

On the nightstand next to the bed in your apartment is another eBook written by Hugh Darrow.

OPTIONAL EXPLORATION

There are a lot of useful items to be found in your apartment, including two Combat Rifles, but the biggest haul comes from a small hidden area behind the TV. To access the secret stash you will need to get the code from your personal computer and then input it on the dedicated terminal near the kitchen. Inside the stash you will find some ammo and Credits, along with a very useful Armor-Piercing System Upgrade for the Pistol.

			Stealth Bonuses	
Objective Completed	Objective Type	XP Reward	Ghost	Smooth Operator
Use your home computer to analyze the Hub	Primary	1000	No	No

M7 - STOPPING THE TRANSMISSION

Objective Name	Objective Type
Locate and shut down Antenna in Derelict Row	Primary

Pritchard has detected a mysterious signal emanating from an antenna in DRB territory. The signal is keeping a backdoor into Sarif's network open. Sarif needs you to shut it down. There are multiple ways to reach the antenna. The fastest and easiest route is the Stealth route, which will take you through the sewers. The Stealth Combat route will take you through heart of DRB territory, and while it takes a bit longer, it grants you more XP for upgrades. The Combat route is a guns blazing approach that is satisfying, albeit dangerous, but it nets you the least XP.

Note If you shut down the antenna during the Cloak & Daggers Side Quest, then all you need do at this point is make it to the Helipad near the Antenna for extraction.

DERELICT ROW

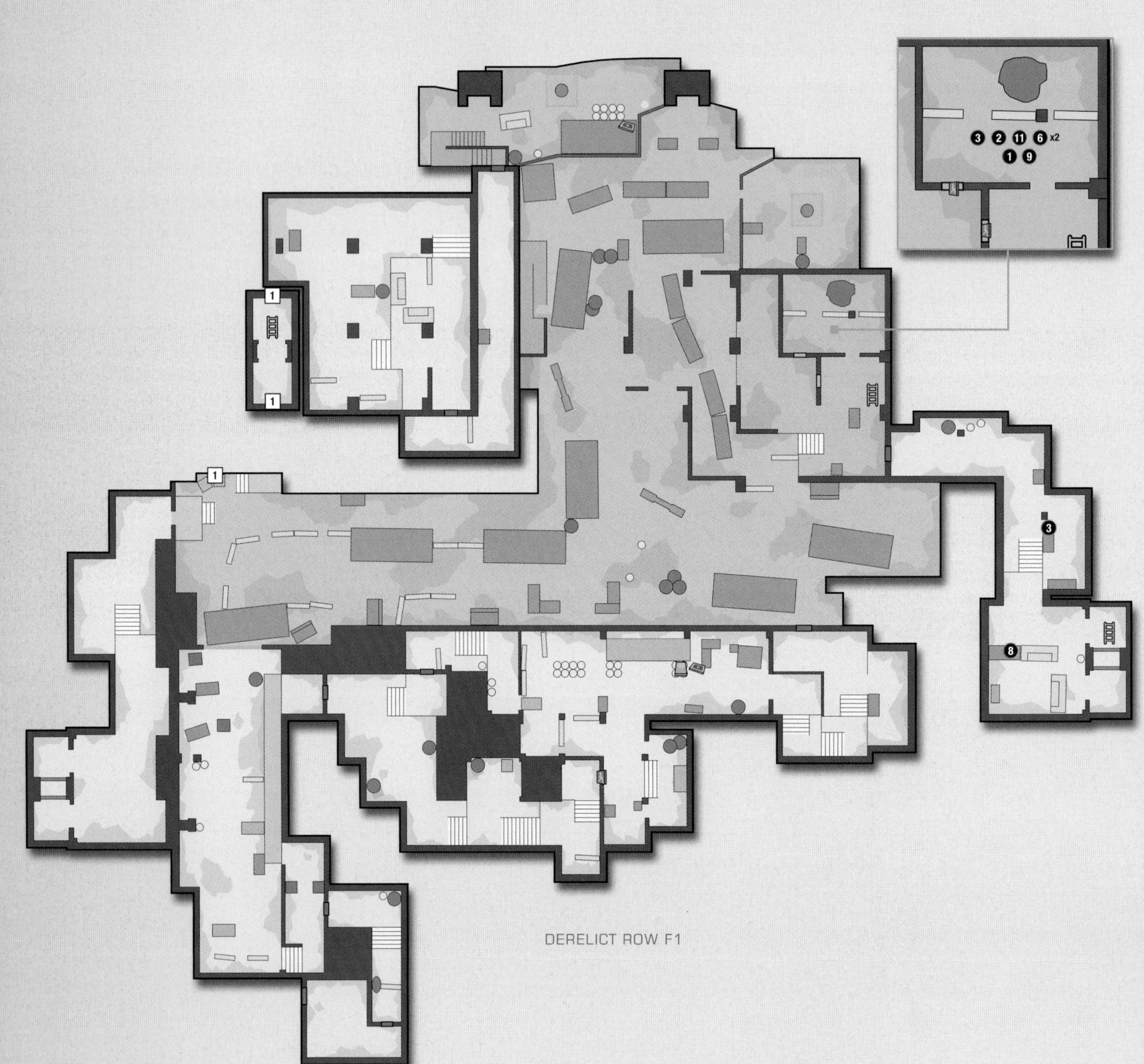

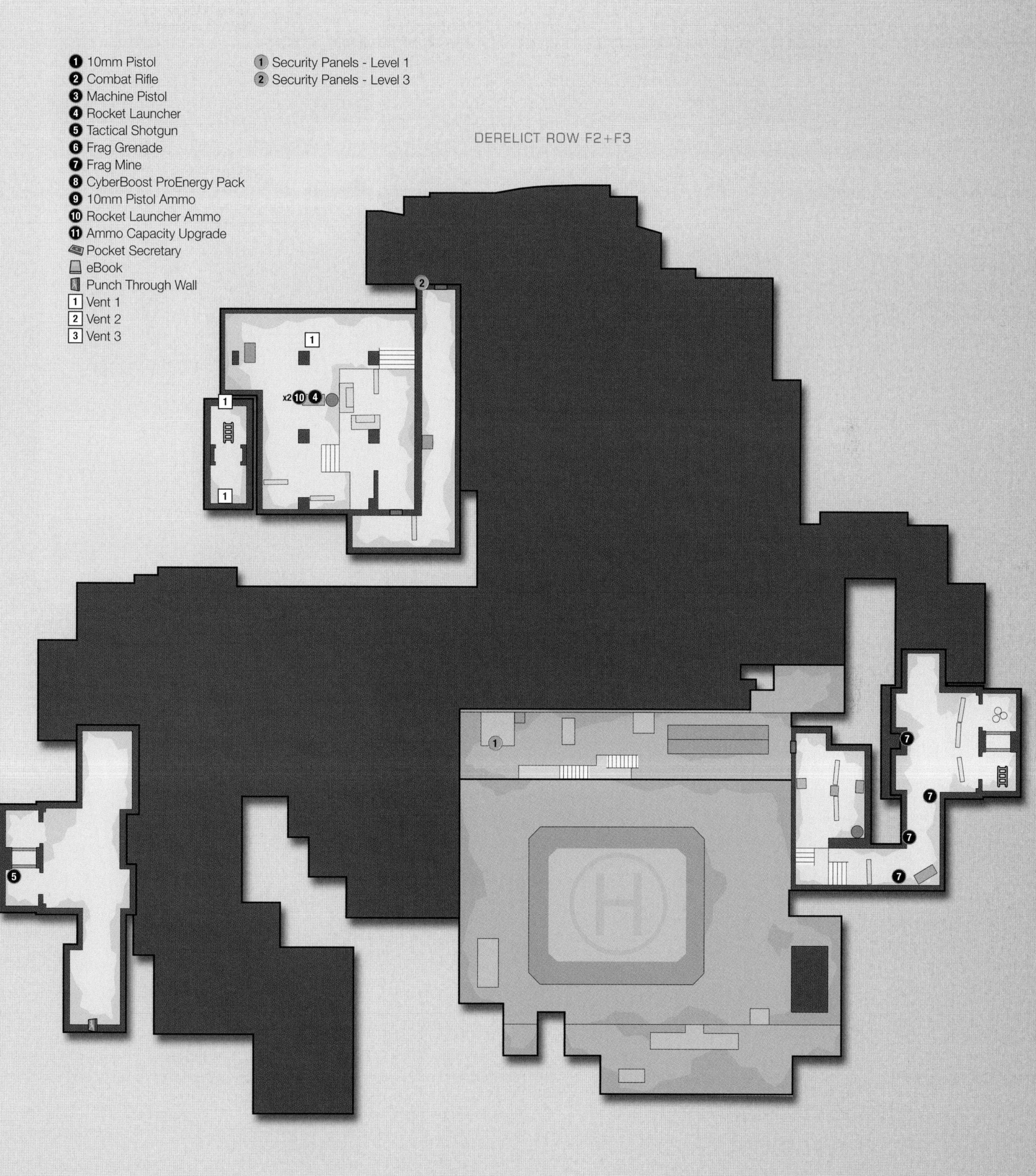

1 10mm Pistol
2 Combat Rifle
3 Machine Pistol
4 Rocket Launcher
5 Tactical Shotgun
6 Frag Grenade
7 Frag Mine
8 CyberBoost ProEnergy Pack
9 10mm Pistol Ammo
10 Rocket Launcher Ammo
11 Ammo Capacity Upgrade
Pocket Secretary
eBook
Punch Through Wall
1 Vent 1
2 Vent 2
3 Vent 3
1 Security Panels - Level 1
2 Security Panels - Level 3
DERELICT ROW F2+F3
x2

ROUTE 1 | Stealth

Required None
Recommended Icarus Landing System, Cloaking System

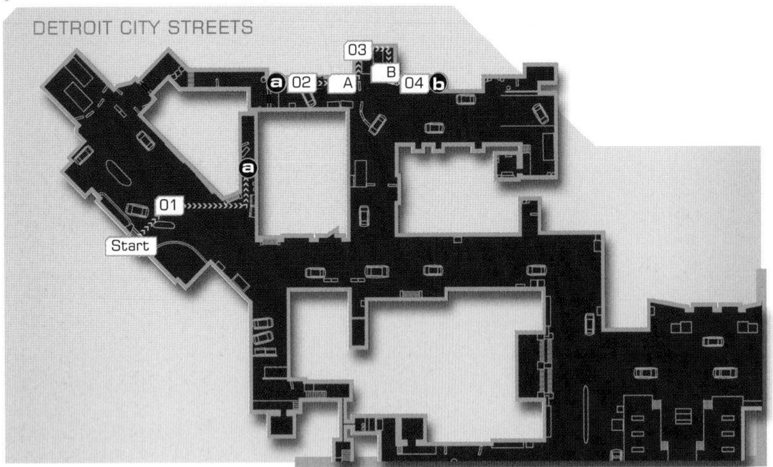

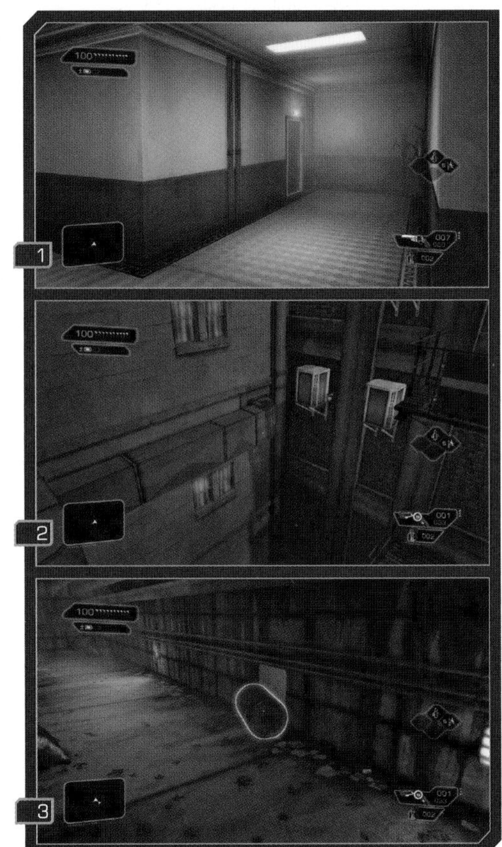

01 Start by going to the small alley across the street from the Chiron Building (the building that Jensen's apartment is located in). There you'll find a fire escape ladder that you can use to get into the building. Once inside, move through the building to the exit. [→□ 1]

02 When you exit the building, you'll be on a small rooftop area. You'll need to drop down from the roof to the alley below. If you have the Icarus augmentation, then all you need do is jump down. Without the Icarus augmentation, this fall will kill you, but there is another way.

At the edge of the building, go left to get onto an external air duct. Follow that duct to the back wall and then go right. On the wall ahead, you'll see two AC Units attached to the wall [→□ 2]. Jump on the first one, and from there, jump to the second one. After you are on the second AC Unit, it's a simple jump to make it to the fire escape. You can then use this to safely reach the ground below.

Once you are on the ground, hug the left wall and move forward. You'll come to a small area with stairs at **Position A**. Use the plates on the railing there for cover as you move forward.

OPTIONAL EXPLORATION

On the very top level of the fire escape here, you can find a Reload Speed Upgrade for one of your weapons. You'll need the Jump augmentation to get up there. If you have that augmentation, get on the highest level of the fire escape you can reach normally. There you'll see a large hole in the wall. Look left from the hole and you'll see an AC Unit attached to the wall. Jump onto that AC Unit. Then turn and jump back onto the top level of the fire escape and claim your upgrade.

03 From your cover point at the railing, go left around the large storage bin. At the back, you'll find some stairs that lead up to a door. Go up the stairs, but ignore the door. Instead go right to the corner of the building at **Position B**.

04 Stay crouched and move left around the building to the manhole cover. If you are spotted, ignore the Baller and make a beeline for the manhole cover. Once you reach it, open it and get on the ladder to climb down to the sewers below.

05 Start by going left through the sewers until you come to a small vent at the base of the wall at **Position C**. Move the barrel that is blocking the vent and then go inside and through maintenance tunnel to reach the next area ahead. [→□ 3]

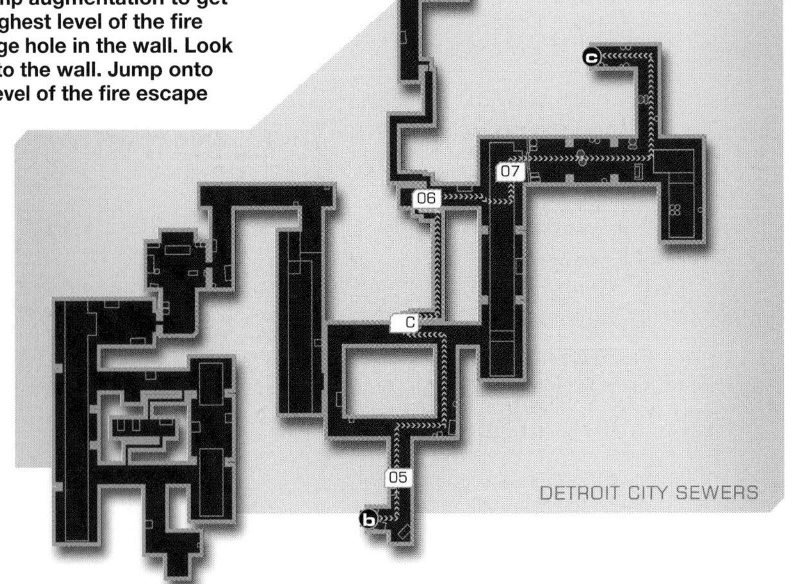

06 Take cover at the tires once you exit the maintenance tunnel. There is a Baller on patrol ahead, so watch him. He'll get close to your position and then move away. Once he goes, follow him whilst crouched to the bridge ahead. At the bridge, go right and drop into the water and then get under the bridge. Take cover by the wall ahead, and move while in cover with the Baller as he goes to the left. When you reach the next bridge, go under it to remain undetected.

07 Once you are under the bridge, move forward past a series of other bridges. You'll pass under three more Ballers, but they won't see you as long as you don't make any noise (such as firing a weapon). Once you reach the last bridge, remain crouched and jump up on the left side. Now move through the hallway ahead to the ladder that will take you out of the sewer.

OPTIONAL EXPLORATION

To the right, you can find a breakable wall. If you punch through it, you'll find a Praxis Kit and some credits. Be warned though, punching through the wall will alert the Ballers here and they will come running to engage you.

08 Once you exit the sewers, look left and slightly behind you. There you'll see a pair of barrels in front of a small opening in the base of the wall. Move the barrels and then go through the opening. Ahead you'll see a large hole in the floor. Remain crouched, and then jump up through the hole to the room above.

09 There is a Baller positioned ahead and to the right on the other side of the breakable wall. Ignore him, but be quiet so that you don't alert him. Stay crouched and go under the boards of the blocked doorway ahead. Once past that boarded up door, move ahead to the door on your left to enter the building.

10 Inside the building stay crouched, move down the hall to take cover at the corner of the wall. Hold your position in cover and wait. Soon a Baller will take up position in a corner to your left. Once he is there, move past him into the nextroom. [→☐ 4]

11 Ignore the two Ballers that are on the couches here. They're preoccupied with the television, so stay crouched and go left to the elevator shaft. Get into the shaft and then use the ladders to reach the area above.

12 There are four fragmentation mines in this hallway, so you'll need to be careful. Move very slowly towards each mine to avoid detonating them; if you move too fast, they will detonate. It helps to be crouching when moving so that you can control your speed better. Once you are close to a mine, press the Interact button to deactivate the mine. [→☐ 5]

13 Once you are past the mines, continue moving quietly through the area towards the door at the end. Go through the door, and then stick close to the wall on the left once you are through it so that you can sneak behind the two Ballers leaning against the railings. The antenna you need to hack is located on the opposite side of the rooftop at **Position D**.

Once you have hacked the antenna, immediately move up the stairs on your right to reach the helipad. If one of the Ballers sees you and goes into alert, simply take cover at **Position E** near the Helipad and wait for Mailk to arrive for the Extraction.

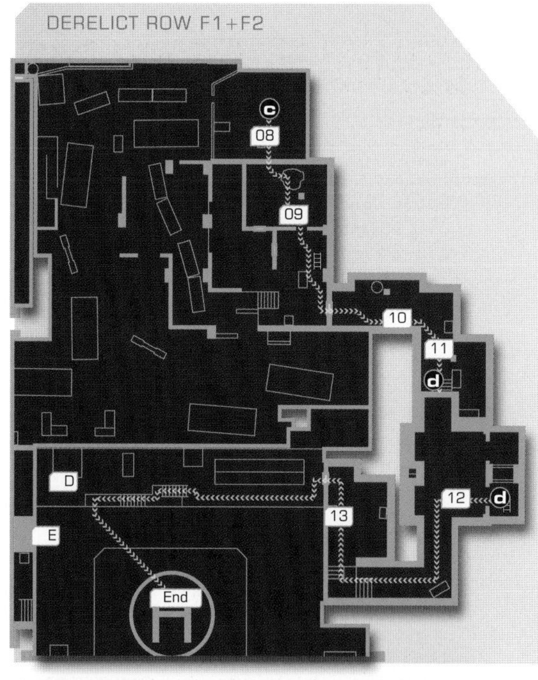

4
5

08_037

ROUTE 2 Stealth Combat

Required Move/Throw Heavy Objects
Recommended Cloaking System
Recommended Tranquilizer Rifle

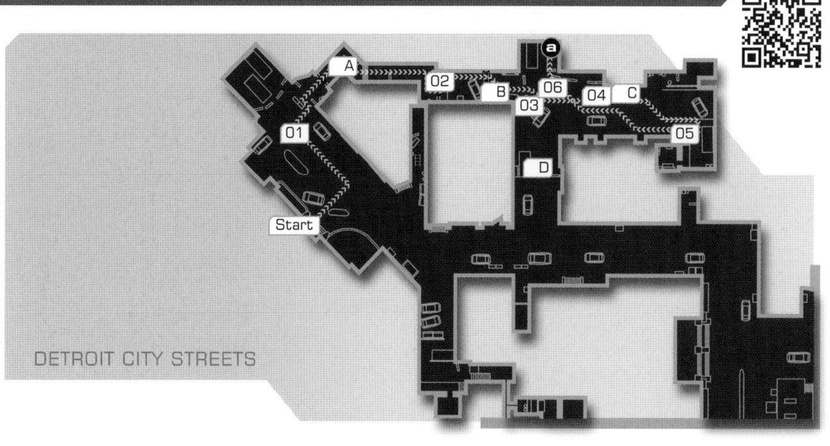

01 Go left from the Chiron building to find a door on your right. Enter that area and move the large crate on the right at **Position A**. Now take cover behind the middle crate. From cover, step out and move close to the stairs ahead to get the attention of one of the Ballers.

When he sees you, immediately move back to cover and wait. Once he gets close to investigate, quickly move over to him and incapacitate him with a Takedown. The remaining Baller will be distracted with painting graffiti, so shoot him with the Tranquilizer Rifle or sneak up on him for a Takedown. Now move forward to the door ahead.

02 Once you exit the previous area, move forward just far enough for one of the two Ballers ahead to see you and come to investigate. Once he does, move back to the wrecked car behind you and take cover. Stay in cover and wait for the Baller to get close. Incapacitate him with a Takedown once he is close enough.

With the first Baller down, move around the car and go right. Enter the concrete tubes ahead at **Position B**. Move forward in the tubes so that you can see the Baller resting on the concrete barricade ahead. Take him out with a headshot from the Tranquilizer Rifle.

Now back up and exit the tubes. Look across the yard and to the left to see another Baller resting at a car at **Position C**. Shoot him with the Tranquilizer Rifle to put him to sleep. It's a long shot, but completely possible. If you miss the first time, don't worry as he'll just move around in that general area and won't spot you, so try your shot again.

03 Move right and take cover at the junked car. There is a Baller at the head of the street at **Position D**. From your cover point at the junked car, take aim with the Tranquilizer Rifle and shoot him in the head for a fast take down. [→☐ 1]

04 There are two more Ballers to the East at the end of the street. Move to the left side of the street and take cover at the junked car at this point. Watch the two Ballers ahead, and one will move off to the right. Wait for him to do so, then move forward.

05 Stay crouched and move to the Baller that has his back to you. Immediately use a Takedown. Once he is down, switch to the Tranquilizer Rifle and shoot the remaining Baller in the back [→☐ 2]. Do this quickly, and you'll have no problems taking out both Ballers with ease.

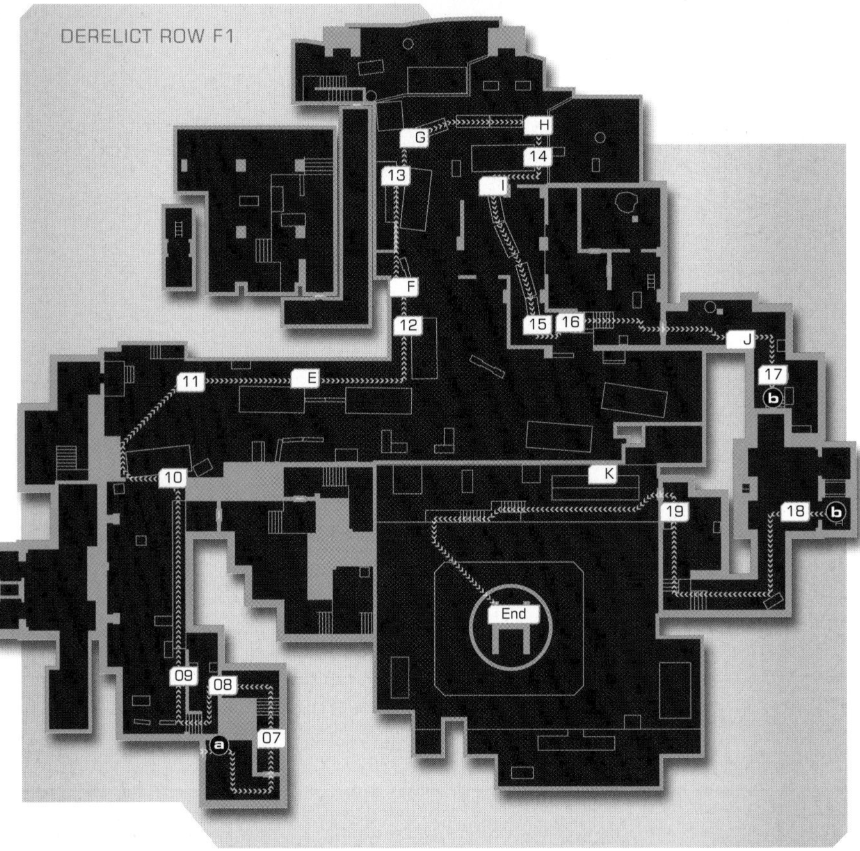

OPTIONAL EXPLORATION

There is a storage unit just past the last Baller at Position D. It is a Level 3 Hack, but the Baller you took out at Point 03 has a Pocket Secretary with the code. Inside you'll find two Weapon Cabinets (one is hidden behind a large crate) and a pair of lockers. Search them all to find Machine Pistols, Shotguns, and 10mm Ammo. You'll also find some credits on the cart located at the rear wall.

06 Backtrack to the large trash bin near where you entered this area. To the right of that bin is a door that will grant you entry into the building and thus into DRB territory. When you're ready, use that door.

07 Once in the building, move up the stairs and take cover at the corner of the wall. Peek out to the left and you'll see a Baller at the railing ahead. Move up behind him whilst crouched and use a Takedown. Now drag the body back to the door so it's not seen by anyone.

08 There is a green barrel in the hallway. Grab it and throw it at the railing where the Baller was positioned [→☐ 3]. Make sure to throw it low at the railing so that it doesn't bounce over the railing. You want the barrel to stay on this side so that the Baller that comes to investigate will be close. Once you throw the barrel, take cover at the left side of the door. Wait for the Baller to arrive, and once he relaxes and begins to move off, go after him for a Takedown.

09 Move down the stairs and stay to the right. Ahead is an opening that leads under the raised floor. Enter that crawlspace and move up to the last Baller. There is an opening on the left that will let you ease out and get into position for a Takedown. The Baller is preoccupied and won't notice you, so take him out at your leisure.

10 Go through the opening in the bent storage door and go left to get behind the large trash bin. Peek out and locate the Baller that is patrolling back and forth from East to West. When he is heading East and his back is to you, move to the first concrete barricade and take cover. Wait for the Baller to come back, and as soon as he turns around, go after him for a Takedown. Now hide the body behind the trash bin.

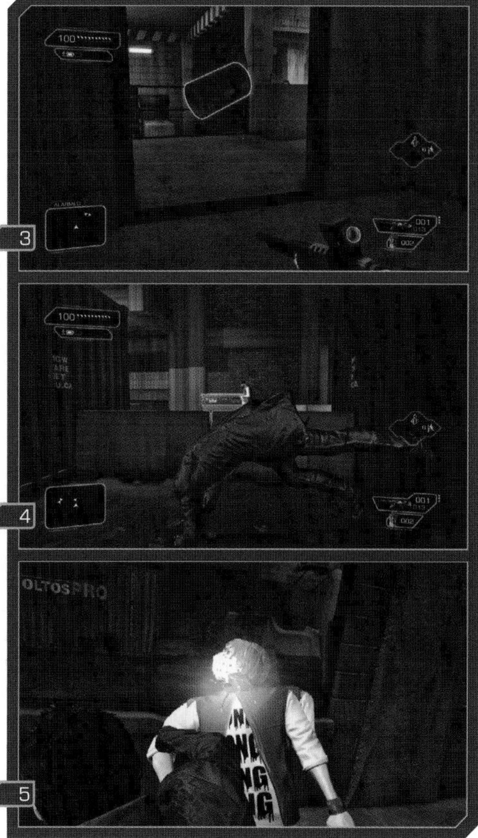

OPTIONAL EXPLORATION

Due North of the trash bin is a large crate. Move it to expose a vent. Enter the air ducts to reach an elevator shaft. If you don't have the jump augmentation, then place one of the small crates here next to the large crate. This creates a bit of a staircase, so jump from box to box to reach the next level above you.

Move the crate to expose the ladder and then climb up to the next level. There you'll find a vent you can use to reach the next room. As you move through the air ducts, you'll come to some vents in the ducts that allow you to see down into the room. Watch the two Ballers in the room and wait for them to stop talking and disperse. When they move away, move ahead to the exit vent and drop down into the room. Once you do, immediately take cover at the column on your left.

Watch the Ballers, and when they begin to walk away, follow them whilst crouched and take cover at the last column ahead. Hold your position here, and one Baller will sit on the couch while the other goes out of the door. Wait for the patrolling Baller to come back into the room and sit on the couch. Continue waiting, and he will soon get back up and go outside the room. When he does, follow him whilst crouched and take him out with a Takedown. Now take the last Baller on the couch out with a headshot using the Tranquilizer Rifle.

Pick up the Rocket Launcher in this room if you want it. Exit the room and move down the hall to a door. Go outside to the small area below. There is a Pocket Secretary in the storage bin, and a manhole cover that leads to an alternate route into the sewers. If you investigate the sewers, you'll see a red valve on the far wall, use it to turn off the gas in the maintenance tunnel on the left, and then you can go in the tunnel to find some credits. To get back into the DRB yard, use the barrels next to the storage bin as stairs to get on top of the bin and then jump the fence. Alternatively, you can use the broken window in the hallway to get on the fire escape and then drop down into the yard that way.

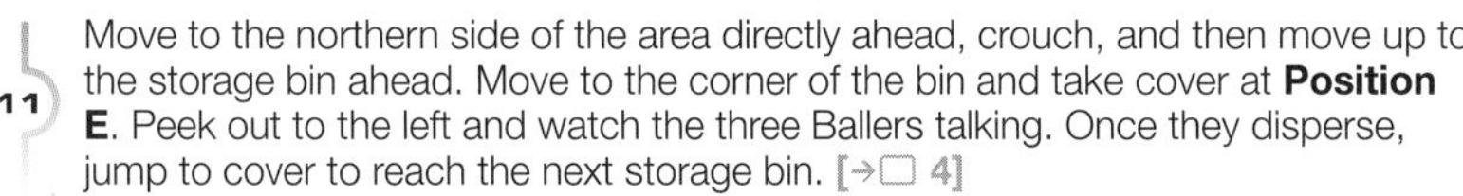

11 Move to the northern side of the area directly ahead, crouch, and then move up to the storage bin ahead. Move to the corner of the bin and take cover at **Position E**. Peek out to the left and watch the three Ballers talking. Once they disperse, jump to cover to reach the next storage bin. [→□ 4]

12 Continue forward and then left and take cover at the corner of the storage bin here. Peek out to the left and you'll see two other Ballers talking. Wait for them to disperse and then jump to cover to reach the next cover point ahead at **Position F**.

13 Take cover at the corner of the next storage bin and then peek out to the left and watch the Baller. When he moves away from you so that his back is to you, enter the concrete tubes ahead and slightly to the left at **Position G**. Move through the tubes to the far side, and when the Baller is before you, ease out of the tube and incapacitate him with a Takedown at **Position H**.

14 Move around the storage bin and take cover at the back of it. Peek out to the left and watch for a Baller to come and take up position directly ahead. Wait for him to leave and go left. Once he does, move forward and go left to enter the concrete tubes there at **Position I**.

15 At the end of the concrete tubes, do not exit yet. Instead stay just inside the tube until a Baller comes in from the left. He'll come down and take position at the window to the right. When he does, ease out while crouched and use a Takedown. [→□ 5]

16 Now go left and up the stairs to the door. Use the door to enter the building. Once you are inside, move up to the corner of the wall and take cover at **Position J**. Wait for a Baller to come in and take up position to the left in a corner. Once he does, get behind him and eliminate him with a Takedown.

17 Go to the top of the stairs and stop. There are two Ballers in the room ahead. Shoot the Baller on the left in the arm with the Tranquilizer Rifle. Make sure you shoot him in the body! You're counting on the delay it takes for him to fall unconscious.

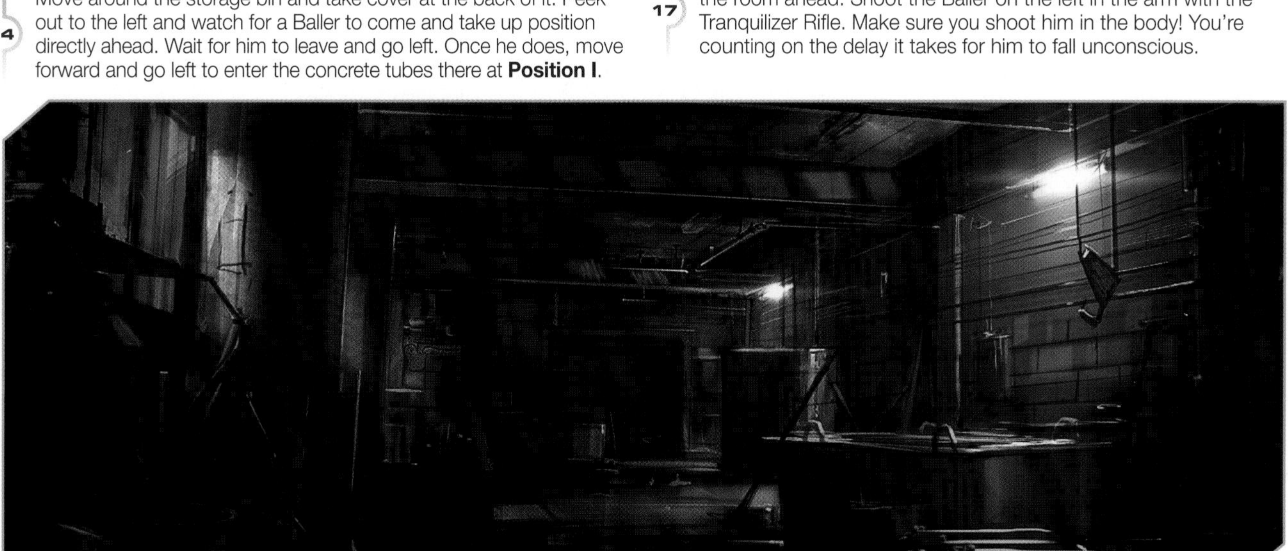

As soon as you shoot him crouch and move forward, and by the time you reach the first couch, the Baller will fall unconscious. Once he does the other Baller will get up and try to revive him. Quickly jump over the couch to get behind the second Baller for a Takedown. Now go left to the elevator shaft and use the ladders to reach the floor above.

18 Be careful of the 4 fragmentation mines here. Move very slowly whilst crouched toward a mine to avoid detonating it. Once you are close to a mine, press the Interact button to deactivate it.

19 Move to the door ahead and take cover on the left. Watch the Ballers ahead as they talk. Once they are done one of the Ballers will come over and take up position just inside the door. He'll be looking straight ahead and won't see you, so incapacitate him with a Takedown. Once he is down, immediately shoot the second Baller at **Position K** with the Tranquilizer Rifle. Alternatively, use a Cyber-Boost ProEnergy Bar to replenish your energy, and then sneak up behind the second Baller for a Takedown. You're then free to hack the antenna in peace.

ROUTE 3 Combat

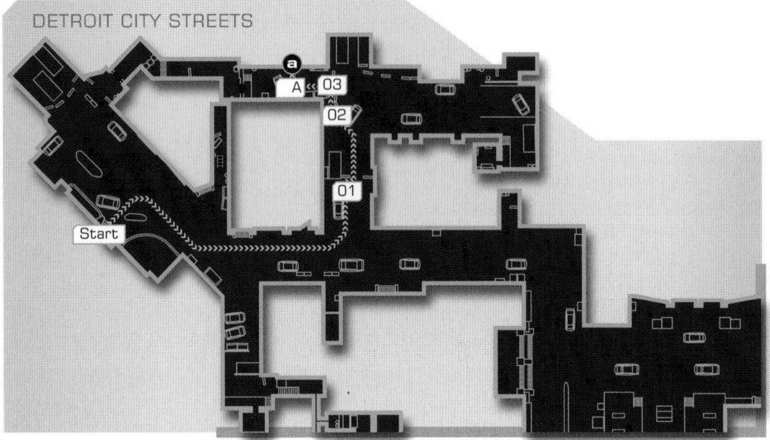

Required Punch Through Walls, Icarus Landing System
Recommended None

Recommended Combat Rifle, Revolver, 10 MM Pistol (Silenced)*, Frag Grenade
*You can buy a Silencer from Seurat.

01 Go to the main entrance of DRB Territory. There are three Ballers directly ahead. Move up to the concrete barrier, and headshot the Baller on the right at the newspaper stand. Now run quickly to the Baller in the middle of the street for a Takedown. Next, take cover at the wrecked car on the left. There is a Baller on the opposite side of the car. Take him out from your cover point.

02 Move left past the car and take cover at the concrete barrier. The remaining two Ballers in the area will converge on your position. Stay in cover at the concrete barrier, and pick them off. [→□ 1]

03 Go to the fire escape at **Position A** and climb up to the area above. You'll find a breakable wall, so punch through it thus killing the Baller on the other side [→□ 2]. Immediately take cover to the left of the hole and pick off the remaining Baller in front of you. Go to the elevator shaft ahead to the left and drop down to the next area.

04 Approach the door in front of you and open it. Then immediately take cover to the right of the door. Wait for the patrolling Baller ahead to get close and headshot him with the silenced 10mm Pistol. Since the pistol is silenced, no one will be alerted to the kill.

05 After taking out the first Baller with a headshot, move to the storage bin ahead and take cover at the right. Peek out and toss a frag between the three Ballers in view to kill them all in one go [→□ 3]. The explosion is going to alert all the other Ballers, so get ready.

06 Immediately go to the left of the storage bin and take cover at the corner of the building. A Baller will soon come running to your position, so eliminate him with a Takedown. Once he is down, move back to cover at the corner of the building and hold your position. From here, you can easily headshot the next Baller that comes running..

07 Now move forward and take cover at the end of the storage bin here. Peek out to the left to find the last Baller. Once you have his position, go for a headshot to make an easy kill. If you miss the headshot, go for repeated body shots. If he rushes you, retreat a bit and let him come to you. You can then use a Takedown or some quick shots from your weapon.

08 Run across the yard and enter the building. Take cover at the corner of the wall and wait for the Baller ahead to take up position in the corner of the room. When he does, use a Takedown. Once he is down, immediately move back to cover at the corner of the wall and pick off the next two Ballers [→□ 4]. Once they are dead, use the ladders in the elevator shaft to reach the area above.

09 Shoot the frag mines to detonate them. Now take cover at the corner of the wall and peek out to the left and pick off the two Ballers.

Alternatively, disable the mines and keep them. Crouch and move to the door ahead and plant a mine directly on the wall to the left of the door. Back up slowly and plant another mine on the concrete block to your left. Make sure to plant it on the back so that it won't trigger when the first mine blows. Now backtrack to the stairs and take cover. The Ballers will soon take care of themselves thanks to those mines.

Note **If you choose to use the mines, then you may have to fire a non-silenced weapon if you didn't get close enough to the door to trigger the Ballers outside to begin talking. If they don't disperse and come into the room on their own in a few seconds, fire a round or two from a non-silenced weapon to get their attention and then let the mines do the rest.** [→□ 5]

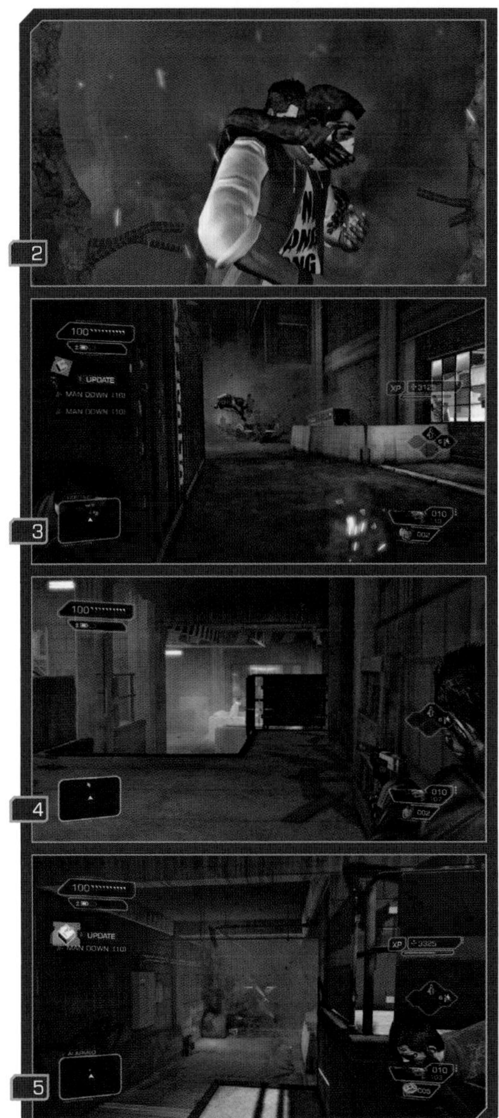

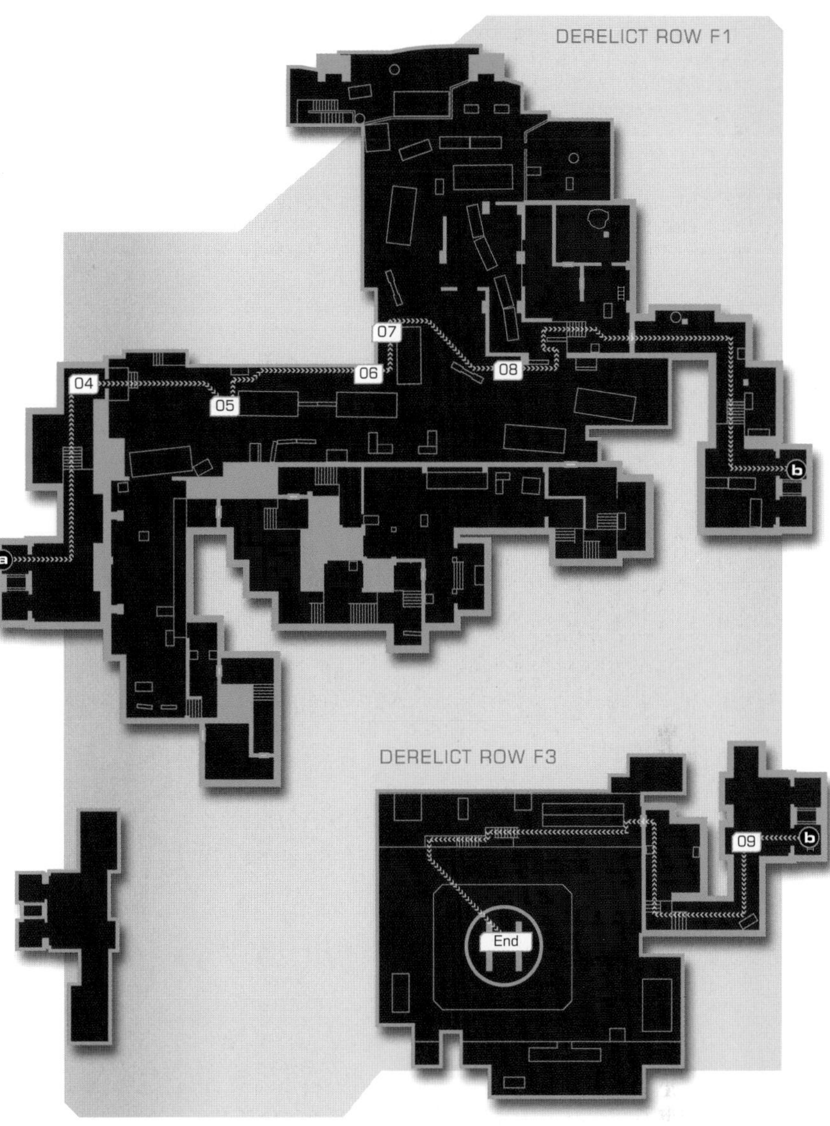

Objective Completed	Objective Type	XP Reward	Stealth Bonuses	
			Ghost	Smooth Operator
Locate and shut down Antenna in Derelict Row	Primary	2500	Yes	No

M8 - EXTRACTION

Objective Name	Objective Type
Go to the Helipad in Derelict Row	Primary

After you have hacked the Antenna, it will be time to leave Detroit and follow your next clue. From the Antenna, look back to the doorway that you used to reach this area. On your right you'll see a staircase. When the Ballers ahead aren't looking, move up those stairs to the Helipad where Malik will extract you.

Objective Completed	Objective Type	XP Reward	Stealth Bonuses	
			Ghost	Smooth Operator
Go to the Helipad in Derelict Row	Primary	1000	No	No

FEMA CAMP

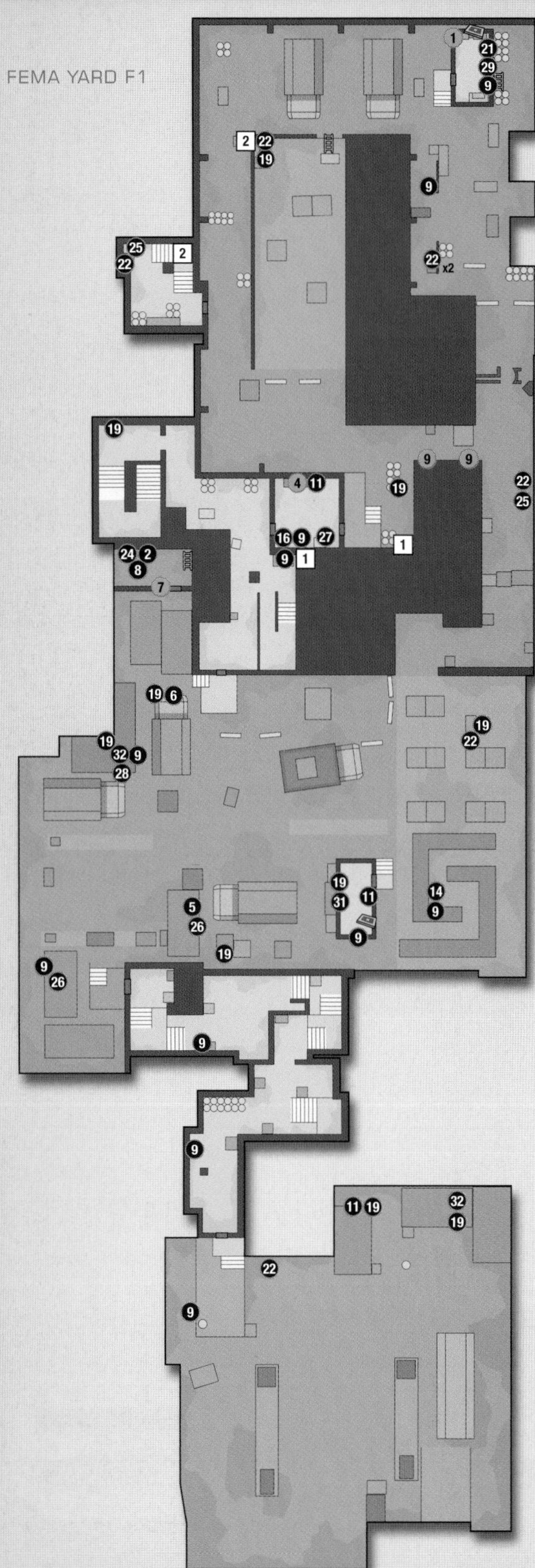

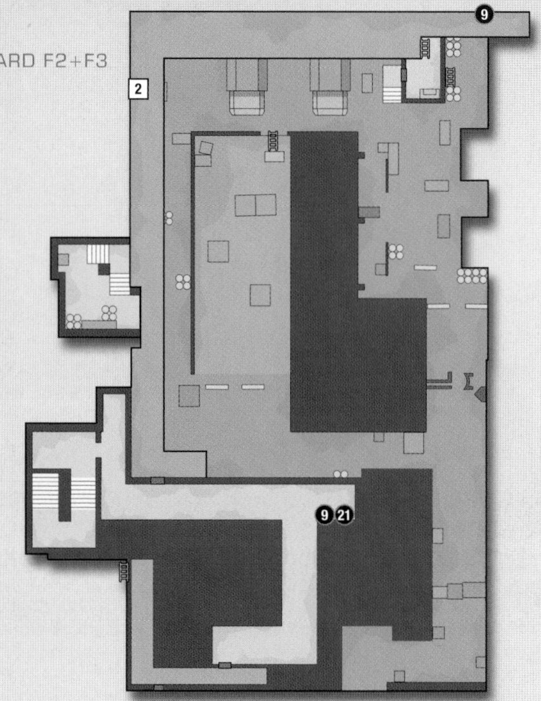

1. 10mm Pistol
2. Rocket Launcher
3. Tactical Shotgun
4. Machine Pistol
5. Stun Gun
6. Concussion Grenade
7. EMP Grenade
8. Frag Grenade
9. Credit Chip
10. Mine Template
11. Cyberboost ProEnergy Bar
12. CyberBoost ProEnergy Pack
13. CyberBoost ProEnergy Jar
14. Pain Killers
15. HypoStim
16. Nuke Virus Software
17. Stop Virus Software
18. 10mm Pistol Ammo
19. Combat Rifle Ammo
20. Machine Pistol Ammo
21. P.E.P.S. Energy Pack
22. Revolver Ammo
23. Rocket Launcher Ammo
24. Shotgun Cartridge
25. Sniper Rifle Ammo
26. Stun Gun Dart
27. Tranquilizer Rifle Dart
28. Typhoon Ammo
29. Ammo Capacity Upgrade
30. Reload Speed Upgrade
31. Laser Targeting
32. Automatic Unlocking Device

- Pocket Secretary
- eBook
- 1 Vent 1
- 2 Vent 2
- 3 Vent 3
- 4 Vent 4
- 5 Vent 5
- 6 Vent 6

1. Computer - Level 2
2. Computer - Level 3
3. Security Terminal - Level 2
4. Security Terminal - Level 3
5. Security Panels - Level 1
6. Security Panels - Level 2
7. Security Panels - Level 3
8. Alarm Panels - Level 2
9. Laser Grid Panels - Level 2

FEMA INTERIOR B1

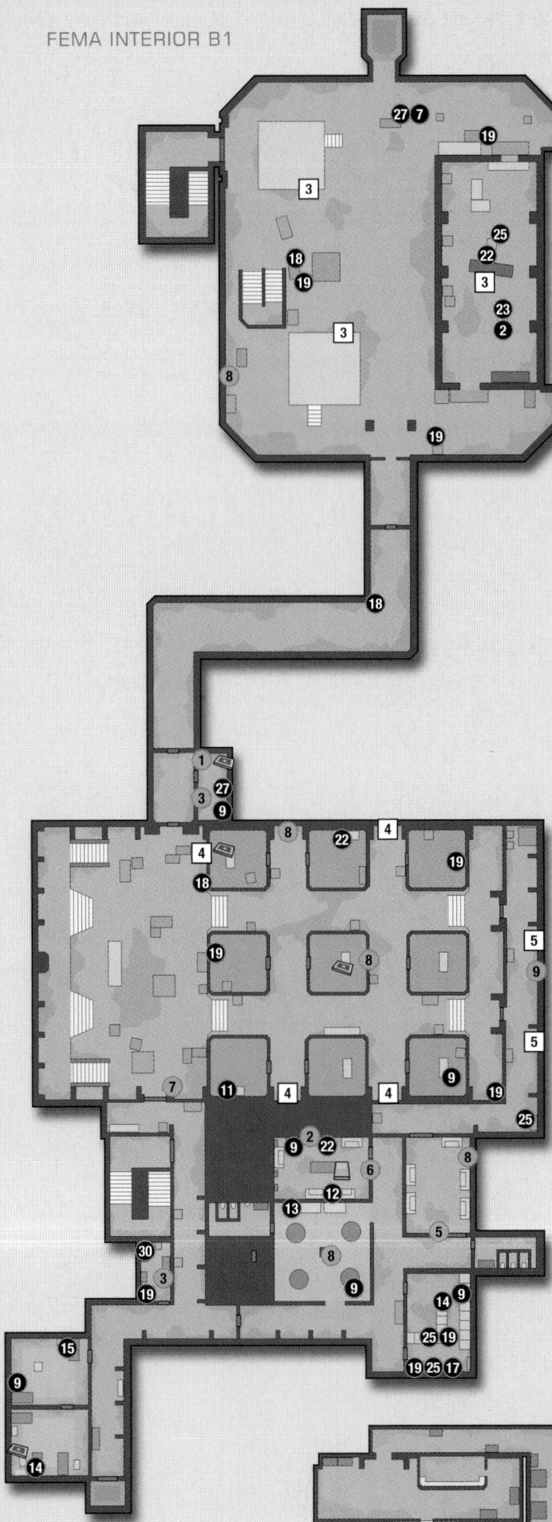

FEMA INTERIOR B3

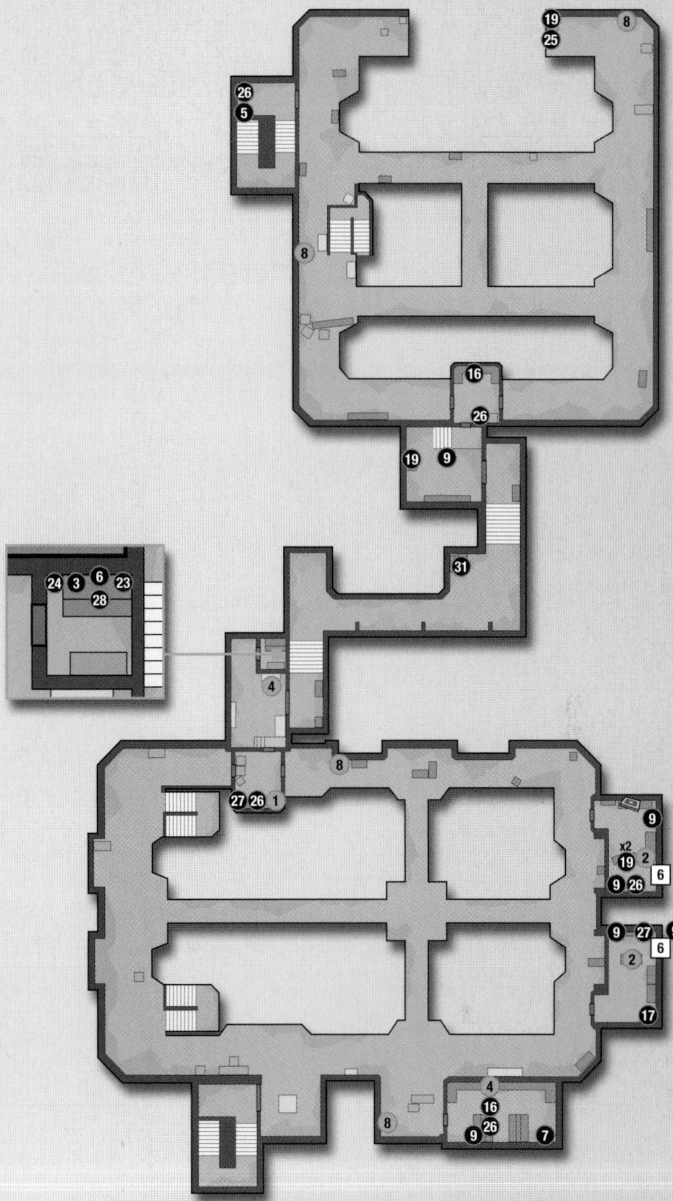

FEMA INTERIOR B5

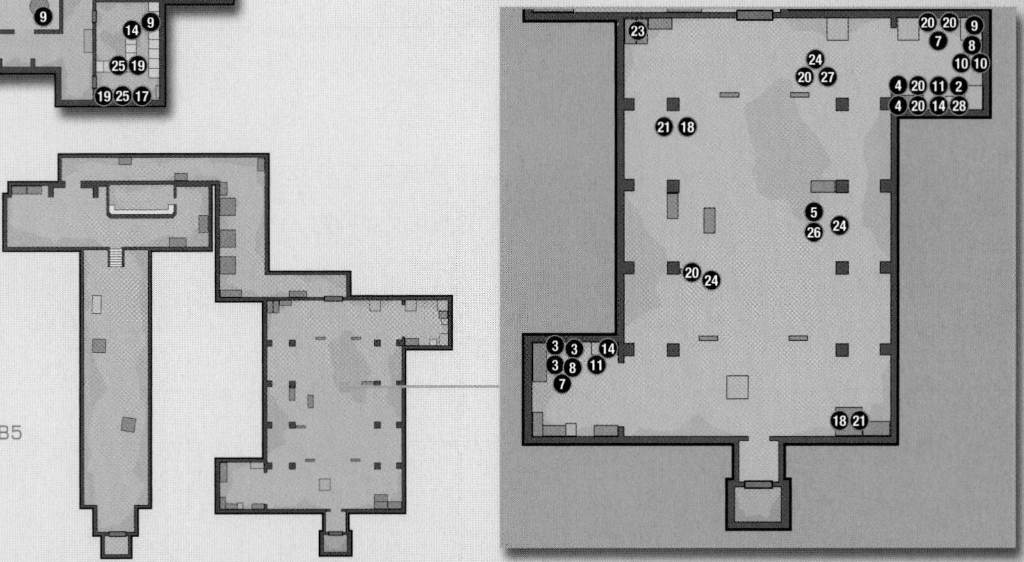

M9 - THE TRANSMISSION
M10 - FOLLOWING THE CLUES IN HIGHLAND PARK

Objective Name	Objective Type
Investigate the area	Primary

Now you'll have to find a way inside the FEMA camp to investigate the possibility that FEMA is somehow working with the terrorists that attacked Sarif HQ. There is a MCB Gang Leader here that you can talk to for more story information as well as ammo and a weapon upgrade for the Tranquilizer Rifle. When you are ready, go through the door on the left-hand side of the building in the northwest. Once inside, move forward to trigger a cutscene.

			Stealth Bonuses	
Objective Completed	Objective Type	XP Reward	Ghost	Smooth Operator
Investigate the Area	Primary	1000	No	No

Objective Name	Objective Type
Infiltrate the Mercenary Compound	Primary

OPTIONAL EXPLORATION

If you have the Jump Augmentation, you can leap from the storage bin to the broken fire escape to find revolver ammo.

Tip **If you let Zeke go at Sarif Manufacturing and completed the Voices From The Dark SQ, then you have the code for all gates and doors in this area, as well as the password for all Security HUBs.**

Outside The Factory

ROUTE 1 Stealth

Required Hacking: Capture 3
Recommended Cloaking System

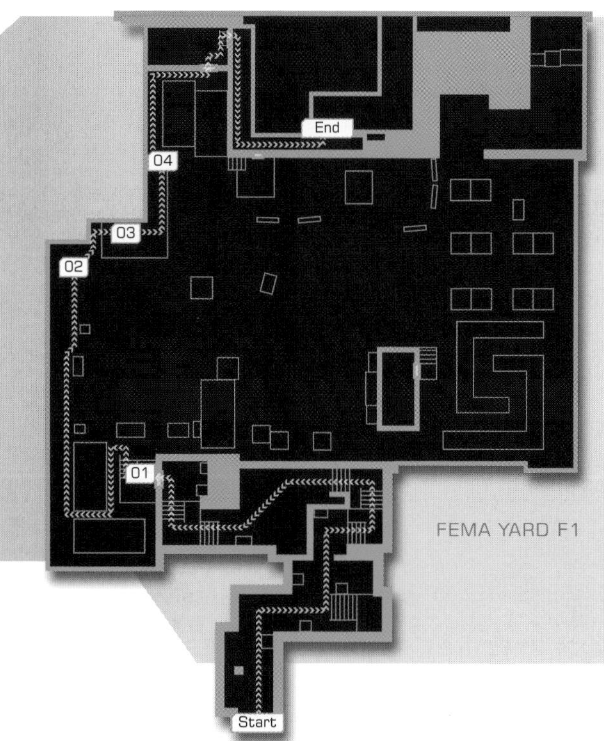

01 Go out the door, and go left around storage bins and then forward to take cover at the edge of container. From your cover point, jump to next cover point at the boom gate. Wait for the guards to disperse, then jump from cover to cover to move forward.

02 Take cover at the truck and wait for the guard to get near. When he moves away, move the large crate that is located ahead and to your left. Then go into the area before you and take cover at the large box.

03 Watch the guard from your cover point, and when he moves to the left, move forward and take cover at the low wall ahead. Stay in cover and move left to the opening. Be careful not to come out of cover, or this guard will see you.

04 There is a guard directly across from you at the door. Wait for him to come down the stairs and move right. Once he does, go left and around the storage bins. There you'll find a gate with a Level 3 Hack [→□ 1]. Hack the gate and then use the ladder to reach the area above. Once there, go around to the door and enter the building.

Tip **If you have the Jump Augmentation, you can leap onto the storage bin and jump over the gate. Be careful as the guards can see you if you try it, so make sure no one is looking before you do this.**

ROUTE 2 Stealth Combat

01 After the cutscene, shoot out the middle window with the Tranquilizer Rifle. Wait for the guard below to move behind the truck, then go for a headshot with the Tranquilizer Rifle. Once he is down, jump through the window to the ground below.

02 Hide the body behind the boxes here, then go right to find some crates blocking your path. After moving the crate on the right, go left past the building. Make sure you stay crouched as you move forward so that you don't alert the guard ahead to your presence.

03 Move forward and then right to take cover behind the large dormant Box Guards here. Wait for guard ahead to take position to the right of your position near the back of the area. Once he is in position, sneak up behind him for a Takedown.

04 Stay close to the building so that it is on your right, and move forward. Take cover at the yellow forklift, and then move to the stack of boxes just ahead at **Position A**. Take cover again and peek out to the left. Watch the guard, and he will soon take position just ahead of you. Wait for him to move to the right and then go around the boxes to sneak up behind the guard for a Takedown. Once he is down, hide his body behind the northern side of the boxes.

05 Now, take cover on the northern side of the boxes and move to the left edge. Peek out to the left, and watch for the patrolling guard to take up position directly ahead. Wait for him to face right and smoke a cigarette. When he does, back up from the boxes just far enough so that you are out of his line of sight, but can still see the forklift behind him [→☐ 2]. Shoot the forklift with the Tranquilizer Rifle. The guard will turn to investigate it, when he does, take cover at the boxes once more, then lean out to the left and shoot the guard with the Tranquilizer Rifle.

06 From the boxes, move west to the truck ahead and take cover at the tire on the left. From this cover point, watch the guard. When he moves west and is behind the truck ahead, lean out and shoot him with the Tranquilizer Rifle. Now move right and around to the front of the truck.

07 To the right of the truck is a stack of boxes and a ramp that leads up to the scaffolding above. Use that to get on the scaffolding [→☐ 3]. Go left on the scaffolding and drop down to the ground below.

08 You'll be behind a truck, and there is one final guard on the opposite side. Move to the front of the truck and then lean out to the left. Shoot the blue electrical box ahead with the Tranquilizer Rifle. The guard will go there to investigate, and when he does, lean out and shoot him with the Tranquilizer Rifle.

09 That takes care of all the guards in the yard leaving you free to explore if you so wish. There are some items worth grabbing, and pillaging the fallen bodies for ammo is always a good idea. When you are ready, go through the door at **Position B** and enter the building.

OPTIONAL EXPLORATION

With all the guards down, you're free to explore the area. In the small building in the center of the area, you'll find a Laser Targeting System for one of your weapons, as well as some ammo and credits.

Just past that building, there is a maze of electrical utility boxes and the ground inside the maze is electrified. Grab a crate from the area at the rear of the small building. Place the crate near the right-hand electrical box. Jump up on the crate, then onto the electrical box. Move forward to the breaker box and shut off the power. Now drop down and explore the maze to find ammo and credits.

Recommended Tranquilizer Rifle

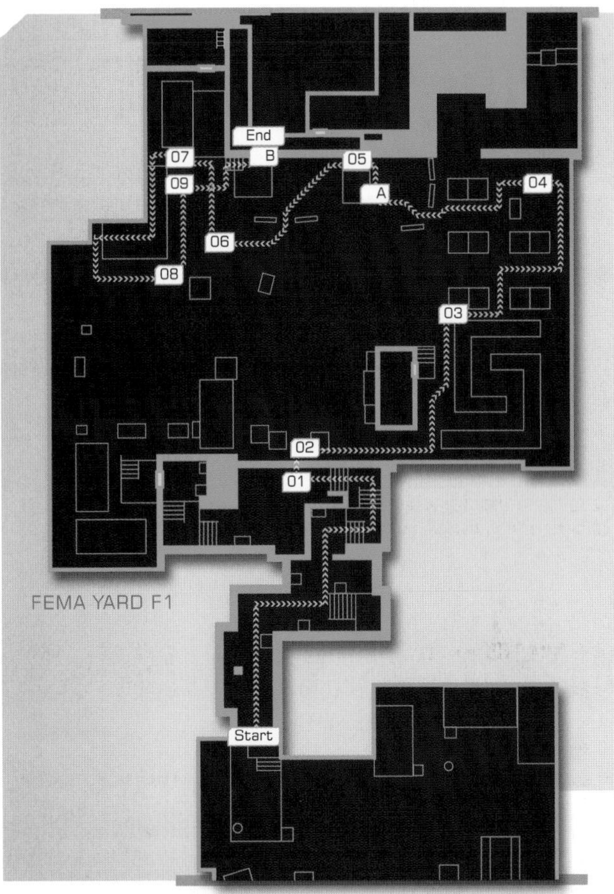

ROUTE 3 Combat

01 After the cutscene, you can shoot through the glass in the building to get a headshot on the guard outside, if you have a silenced weapon. If you miss the headshot as you fire through the glass, move right of the window and take cover at the wall there. Now, wait for the guard to move off to the left. Once he does, ease back to the window and go for the headshot. If you don't have a silenced weapon, then it's not worth alerting all the guards yet with live fire, so move on to the door.

02 If you have a frag, use it on the two guards talking ahead [→☐ 1]. Time it right, and you can get the patrolling guard there as well. Duck back into the building and take cover on the right side of the door. Stay there and pick off the guards as they come. If the guards stop rushing your position, then move outside to the railing and take cover there to finish the last few of them off.

03 Once all the guards in the area are dead, move to the northeast to find a small pathway that will take you inside the factory. Just ahead at **Position A**, there are a few crates that are in the way. Simply move the topmost crates and then jump over the remaining crate in order to move ahead.

Required None
Recommended Dermal Plating

Recommended 10mm Pistol (Silenced), Combat Rifle, Revolver, Frag Grenade

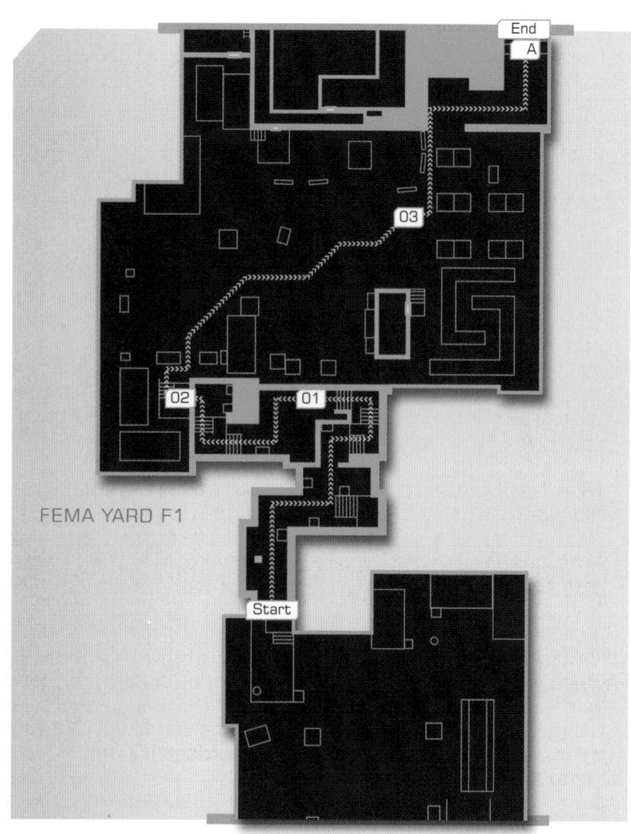

ROUTE 1 Stealth

01 Move through the building and make your way to the door located to the left of the large row of windows. Crouch down and open the door. Move down the left-hand side of the catwalk to a vent on your left. Open the vent and enter the air ducts. Once inside, make your way down to the lowest level.

02 Exit the air ducts and take cover at the box ahead. When the camera is facing the other way, move forward whilst crouched and take the elevator [→☐ 2]. At this point, you're free and clear, so enjoy the long ride down into the bowels of the facility.

Required None
Recommended Cloaking System

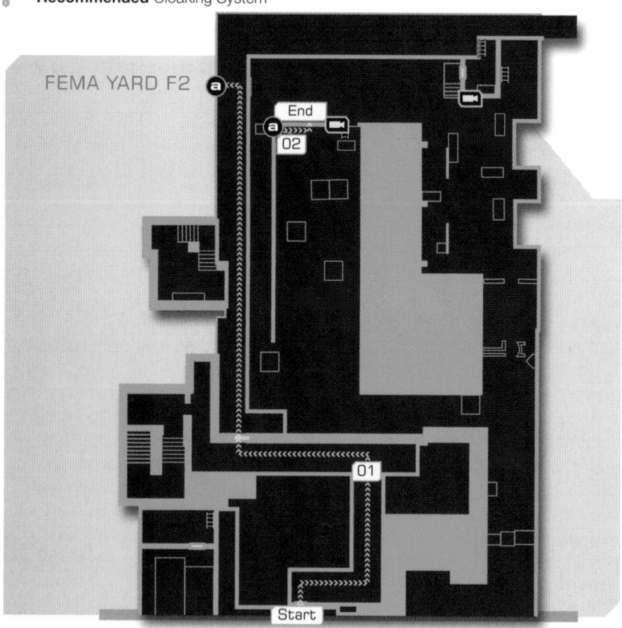

Inside The Factory

ROUTE 2 Stealth Combat

Required Hacking: Capture 3
Recommended Cloaking System
Recommended Tranquilizer Rifle

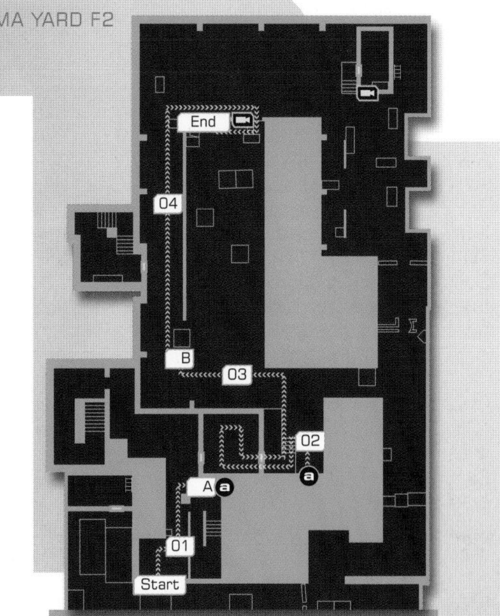

01 Begin by entering the building via the lower door near the truck parked there. Once you are inside, go forward a bit and look right to see a vent at **Position A**. Open it and enter the air ducts. Once you are inside, progress forward through the air ducts to the next area.

02 Exit the air ducts and take cover behind the barrels on your left. Wait for guard to take up a position directly ahead of you. When he does, sneak up behind him and take him out from behind with a Takedown. Then enter the control room that he came from and hack the Security Hub to turn off the cameras.

03 Leave the control room the same way you came in, and then move towards the west side of the area and take cover behind the boxes at **Position B**. Watch the guard that is on patrol here, and when he moves away from you, follow him whilst crouched and use a Takedown when close enough. [→☐ 3]

Once that guard is down, use the Tranquilizer Rifle to shoot the Sniper on the catwalk above you to the north. It's a long shot, but entirely possible. If you miss at first, just try again until you get him.

04 Move North and take cover at the low wall there. Peek out to the left and watch the guard. He'll soon come near you and then move off. Once his back is turned, sneak up behind him for a Takedown. When he is down, go forward to the break in the wall on the right and use the ladder to reach the area below. Down there you'll find the elevator that leads to the next area.

OPTIONAL EXPLORATION

Continue West and take cover at the boxes ahead. Wait for the guard to take up position near you, then ease out for a Takedown. Now move to the western side of the small control booth that is here. Crouch and then jump up on the barrels outside the window. Open the window and then headshot the guard inside with the Tranquilizer Rifle. Inside you'll find an Ammo Capacity Upgrade for one of your weapons.

3

Inside The Factory

ROUTE 3 Combat

Required None
Recommended Dermal Plating
Recommended 10mm Pistol, Combat Rifle, Revolver, Frag Grenade

01 Move forward and go left to find a laser grid. Walk through the grid to trigger the alarm, then backtrack to the boxes in the hallway and take cover behind them. Hold position here and pick off the guards as they come running. If you have a frag, it's a great time to use it, as the guards tend to bunch up here. [→☐ 4]

4

02 Now that you have killed everyone in the area, you are free to explore if you wish. When you're done, go down the ramp in the central portion of this area to reach the elevator. Use it to reach the lower portion of the facility.

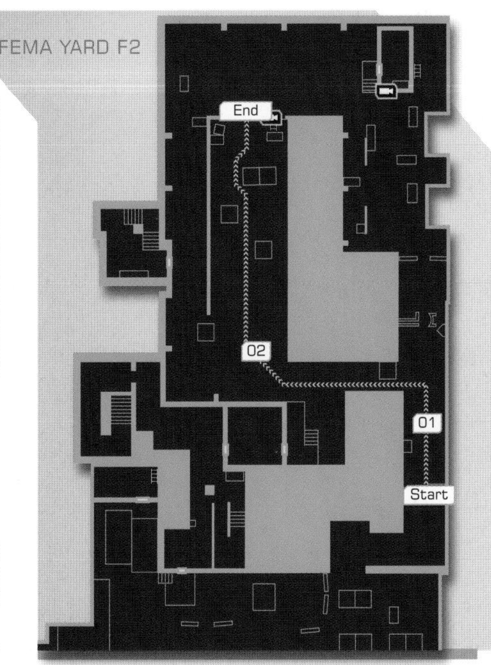

			Stealth Bonuses	
Objective Completed	**Objective Type**	**XP Reward**	**Ghost**	**Smooth Operator**
Infiltrate the Mercenary Compound	Primary	2500	Yes	Yes

ROUTE 1 Stealth

01 When then elevator opens, immediately move to the left to a doorway blocked by pipes. Once you see the pipes, turn around and look behind you to find some small crates at **Position A**. Move one of those crates to the pipes. Now, jump onto that crate and jump over the pipes to enter the room ahead. [→☐ 1]

02 Once in, waste no time and move to cover ahead. Then move from cover to cover to the far end of the room at **Position B**. Be mindful of the Box Guard and guards outside and only move when they aren't looking towards you.

03 Move out of this small area and take cover at the box directly ahead. From there, move ahead and take cover at a column ahead and wait. Watch the guards and Box Guard until they all have their back to you. Go through the door on your left.

04 Move ahead to the boxes and take cover. Watch the two guards talk and wait for them to disperse. Then wait for the single guard to get close to you. When he turns and walks away, follow him whilst crouched. At the end of his patrol move right and take cover behind the stack of iron pipes. Wait here for the guard to move off, and then move left and down the hall.

05 Go to the control booth ahead on the left-hand side. Inside, you'll find a Security Hub that you should use to turn off all cameras that are attached to it. If you have the Turret Domination Augmentation, then you should Disable the Turret as well.

06 When you are done in the control booth, go through the door to the next room. Take cover immediately you pass through the door by the boxes ahead. To your left is a vent covered by a box [→☐ 2]. Quickly move that box, so that you can open the vent and enter the air ducts.

07 Once you are in the air ducts, move forward and take the first left that you come to at **Position C**. After that left, keep going forward and then take the first right at **Position D**. Then continue onward and you'll soon come to an opening in the floor at **Position E**.

08 Quickly jump out of the vent and go right to the door at **Position F**. Once you are past the door and in the hallway, go right again to find another door at the end of the hall.

09 Walking through this door will trigger a confrontation with a pair of FEMA officials. If you let Zeke go and did his Side Quest, then you have the codes for this part and all you need do is Bluff once during the conversation. [→☐ 3]

If you didn't get the codes from Zeke, then this conversation play is a bit more advanced. To win this conversation gameplay, you'll have to make three correct choices, which are: Bluff, Bluff and Intimidate. Pick those three choices and they'll let you pass. Now go to the door and enter the code (7984) to gain access to the next area.

10 In the next room, exit through the door in the southwest. There is a camera ahead, but it has limited movement and can't turn far enough to see you, so just walk past it. Keep going down the hall to find an elevator that will take you down to the next area. A boss battle awaits you there, so prepare yourself accordingly.

Objective Name	Objective Type
Locate the Mercenary Leader	Primary

Required None
Recommended Cloaking System, Turret Domination

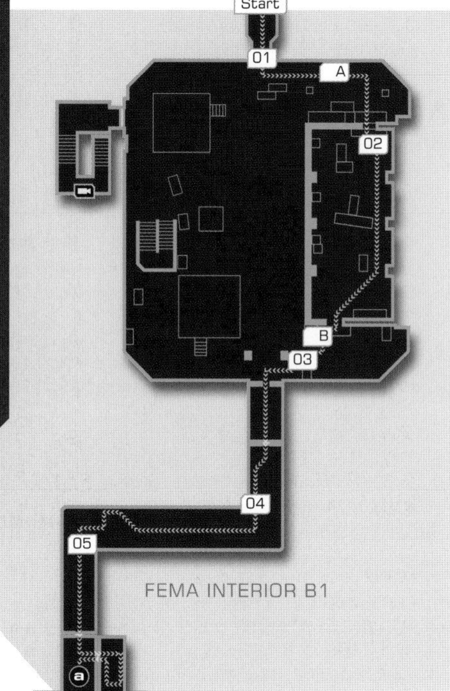

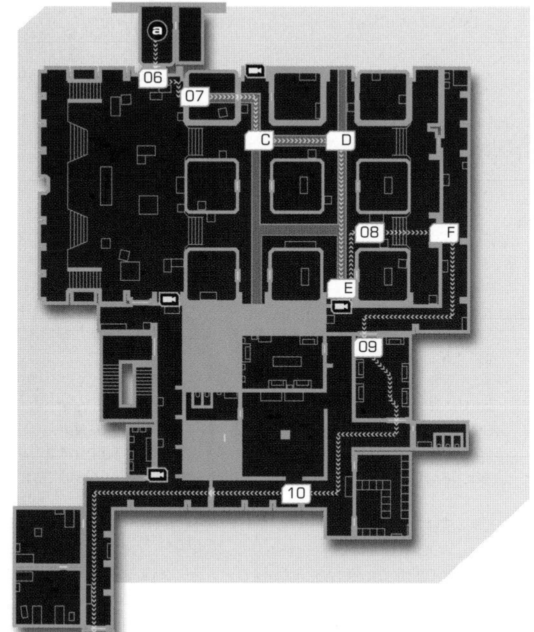

ACHIEVEMENT/TROPHY: DOCTORATE

There is a Hugh Darrow eBook in the locked office in this area.

ROUTE 2 Stealth Combat

Required Move/Throw Heavy Objects, Hacking: Capture 3
Recommended Cloaking System
Recommended Tranquilizer Rifle

01 Exit the elevator crouching and move forward to take cover at boxes ahead. Wait till the Box Guard and guards are looking away, then go right and get under the platform. Move the box covering the vent and go inside the air ducts.

02 Take the ducts to the next area ahead that is under the next platform. Take cover at the low wall to your right and watch the rear most guard. Once he gets close to you, he'll move left and away from your position. When he does, jump out from your position and follow him for a Takedown. Make sure to position his body behind the platform ahead so the Box Guard patrolling to the right doesn't see him [→☐ 4]. When you're done, move back to your previous position.

Now move to the southern side of this area. Take cover in the left-hand corner and watch your radar. When the last guard is facing right and the Box Guard is facing to the rear, move out and go through the door ahead.

03 Take cover at the boxes and wait for the guards to disperse. Let the patrolling guard get close to you and then move away. When his back is to you, move up behind him for a Takedown, then use the ladder here to climb up to the floor above.

04 Make your way forward to a room with a Security Hub. Hack the HUB to disable the camera and open the security door. Once open, you can go into the ammo room to grab the ammo there if you like.

05 From the Security Hub, enter the Control Room crouching. Go left through the door and take cover at the railing plates. Watch the sniper. You don't want to engage him right now. Instead, move forward to the East when he isn't looking. [→☐ 5]

06 Enter the first office on the left at the rear of the area. There is a vent in the southeast corner of this office that you can use to reach the next office to the South. By going through the air ducts to reach the next office, you'll easily bypass the camera outside and avoid detection.

07 Exit the air ducts to enter the eastern most office. Explore the area if you like, and when you're ready, exit the office and take cover at the railing to your left. Watch the guard ahead, and once he begins walking to the left toward Control Room A, move up behind him whilst crouched for a Takedown.

08 With the guard down, you're free to enter the Control Room. Go through the door and you'll find a Security Hub. If you don't have the codes from Zeke Sanders, then you'll need to hack this HUB, and it's a Level 3 Hack. The only thing connected to this HUB are two cameras, so access the HUB and turn them off, which will make your stealth movements a bit easier.

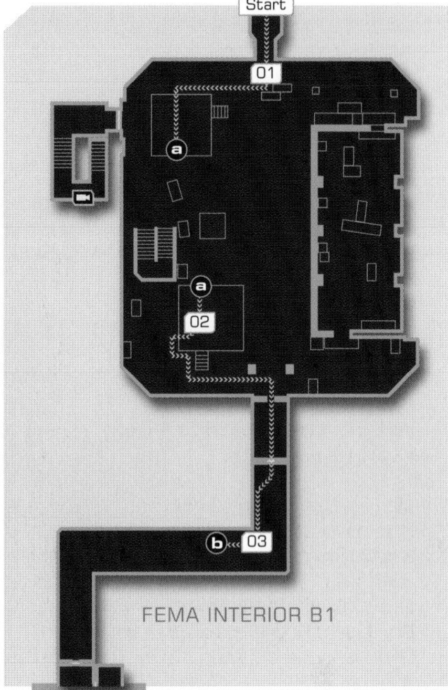

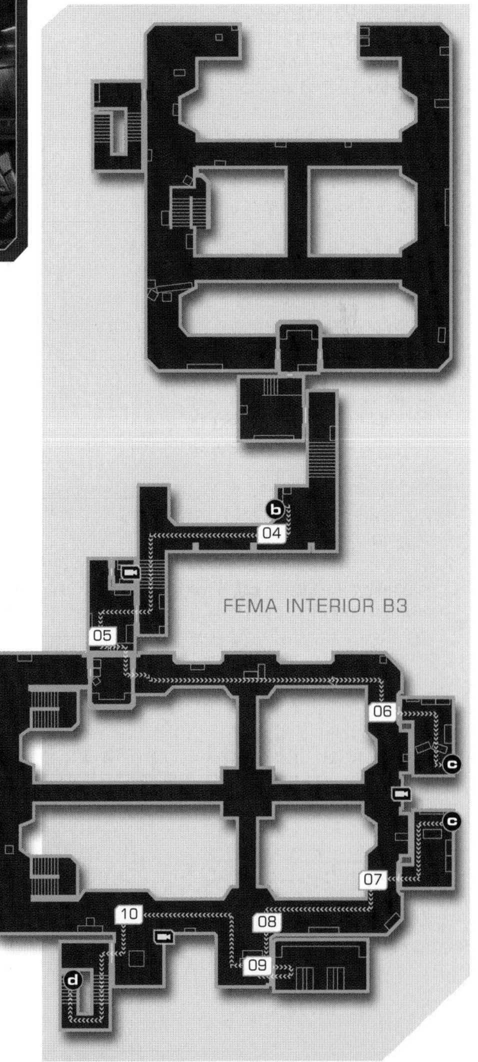

09 Exit the Control Room and take cover at the boxes ahead. Peek out to the right and wait for the Sniper to take position directly ahead of you with his back facing you. When he does this, shoot him with the Tranquilizer Rifle.

10 Once the Sniper is down, go left (West) to the boxes ahead and take cover. Wait for the guard to get close and then move away. Once he turns and walks away, follow him and take him out with aTakedown. Now go through the door to your left to reach the area below.

11 Move down the stairs to the double doors. Once through go right immediately and take cover behind the boxes there. Watch the camera ahead and when it turns away from you, move forward and under it, to avoid detection [→☐ 1]. Now go right to the elevator to the lowest level.

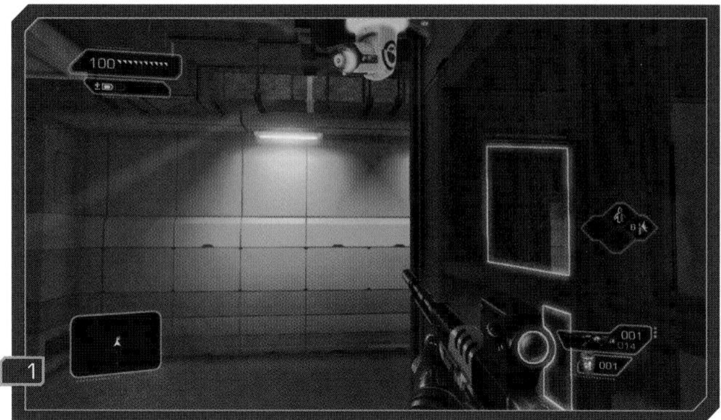
1

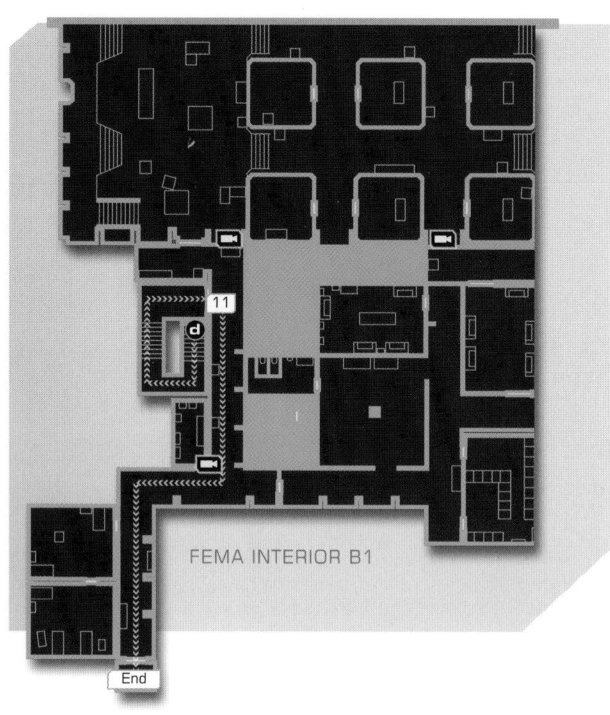

ROUTE 3 Combat

Required None
Recommended Dermal Plating, Hacking: Capture 3 Hacking: Turret Domination

Recommended Combat Rifle, Revolver, 10mm Pistol, EMP Grenade

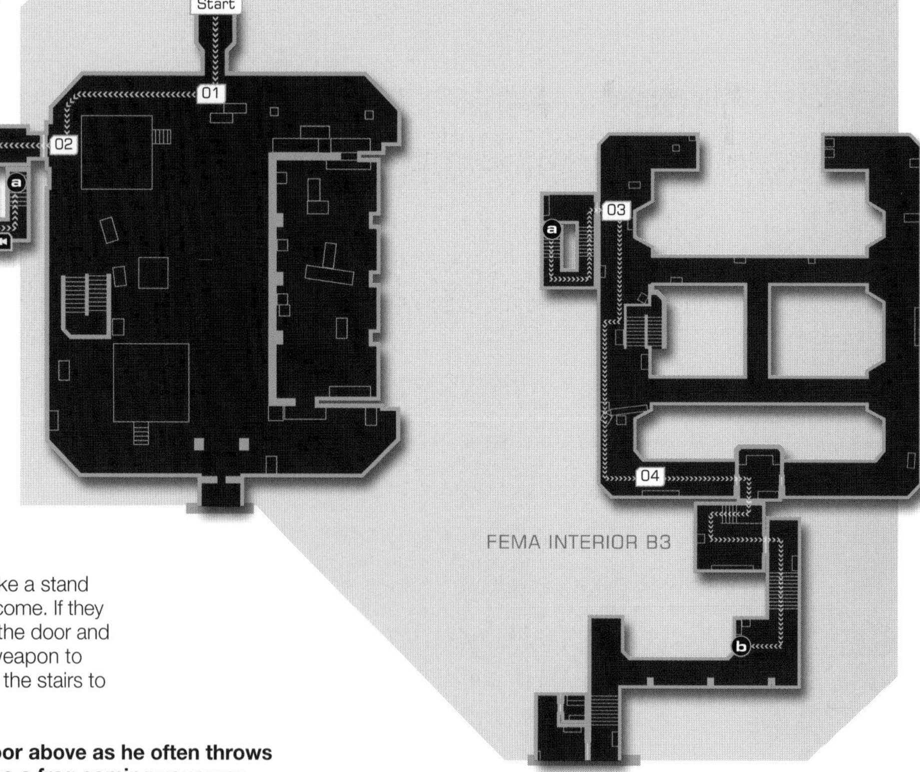

Tip **This can be a difficult area, especially on Hard mode. From cover, use the onscreen reticule to line up your shot, then peek out with a laser-equipped weapon and go for a headshot.**

01 As soon as you get off the elevator, throw an EMP at the Box Guard, then switch to frags if you have them, and toss one at the two guards ahead. There is an EMP on the box ahead if you don't have one.

02 Now run right and through the door. Make a stand at the door and pick off any guards that come. If they don't come running on their own, open the door and fire a few rounds from a non-silenced weapon to attract their attention. Once clear, go up the stairs to the floor above.

Warning **Be wary of the guard on the floor above as he often throws frag grenades at your location. If you see a frag coming your way, retreat through the door to avoid damage.**

03 Move out and take cover behind the box. Use the railing plates for cover, and line up headshots on all the guards. If the guards calm down and go off alert while you're in cover, then Takedowns are possible.

04 Go to the southern part of this area and enter the Control Booth. Push forward to a skylight type area and look down. Headshot the patrolling guard in this area and then drop down to the floor below. [→□ 2]

05 Move forward to the control booth on the left with the Security Hub. If you have the Turret Domination Hack Augmentation, use it to turn the turret in the next room on the enemy [→□ 3]. Otherwise, take cover at the door, and then peek out when they stop firing to return fire. When all the guards are dead, target the turret.

06 Now that the room is clear, feel free to take a little time to explore and pillage the bodies of the fallen for items and ammo. When you are ready to carry on, go to the door at the south end of the room. This door is a Level 3 Hack, so hack it and move forward.

07 Once you are past that door, you'll see a camera ahead, but since this is the Combat route, you've little concern for it, so move past it and to the right. Continue onward down the hall to the elevator.

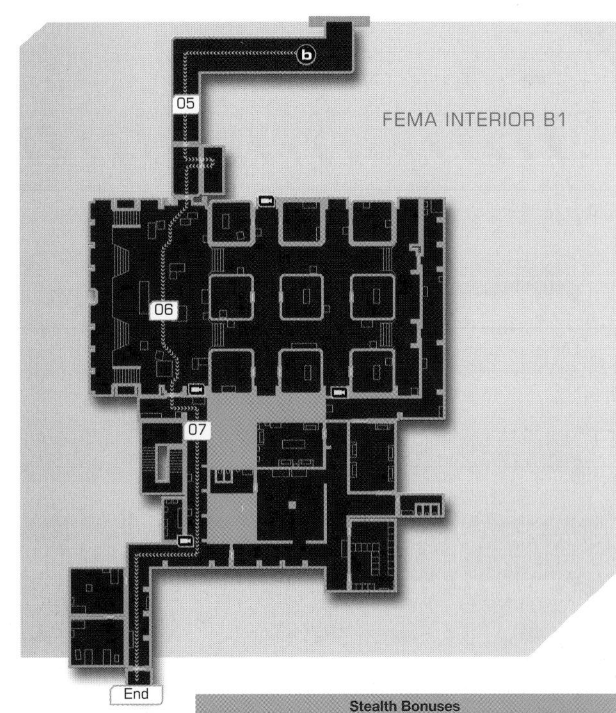

			Stealth Bonuses	
Objective Completed	**Objective Type**	**XP Reward**	**Ghost**	**Smooth Operator**
Locate the Mercenary Leader	Primary	1750	Yes	Yes

BOSS FIGHT LAWRENCE BARRETT

Required None
Recommended Typhoon
Recommended Combat Rifle, Revolver, 10mm Pistol, Frag Grenade

Now you will face the first Boss of the game. We'll give you a few tips here to get you started. For full strategies on how to take down this formidable Boss in a variety of ways, please refer to the Opponents Chapter.

- Throw the gas and explosive canisters at Barrett for easy damage.
- Stun Barrett with Frag, EMP, or Gas grenades and then move off to another location.
- Barrett tracks your last known location, so use cover and move often to keep him moving to locations that you've already left. This allows you to not only get away safely, but to also get behind him for your own attacks.
- Use Typhoon if you have it. [→□ 4]

			Stealth Bonuses	
Objective Completed	**Objective Type**	**XP Reward**	**Ghost**	**Smooth Operator**
Locate the Mercenary Leader	Primary	2500	No	No

M10 - FOLLOW THE CLUES IN HIGHLAND PARK

Objective Name	Objective Type
Meet Malik at our original landing site	Primary

Once Barrett is dead, use the elevator at the south end of the room. Once the elevator stops, step out and you'll see a door directly ahead of you. Go through that door and you'll be in familiar territory. Malik is dead ahead waiting to extract you. If there's anything you'd like to explore before leaving, now is the time to do it. When you're ready, go to the chopper and talk to Malik.

			Stealth Bonuses	
Objective Completed	Objective Type	XP Reward	Ghost	Smooth Operator
Meet Malik at our original landing site	Primary	1000	No	No

M11 - WHISPERS OF CONSPIRACY

Objective Name	Objective Type
Meet Sarif in the Penthouse	Primary
Meet Pritchard in my office	Primary

Objective Name	Objective Type
Confront Sarif about the security leak	Secondary
Meet Malik at the Helipad	Primary

OPTIONAL EXPLORATION

Inside Sarif HQ

- Search Jensen's office for email, but avoid Pritchard for now
- Search Office 30 (you'll get the code from Jensen's email)

At this point, you should have Hack Level 3 or higher, so you can get into all of the offices if you like. In particular, hack Office 33 that belongs to Tim Carella. Read Tim's email, and you'll get the code for Malik's office, # 22.

Now go to Malik's office and read her emails to get the code to the Helipad Storage Unit, a Level 5 Hack. With that code in your possession, go out to the Helipad and then go to the southwest corner to find a hole in the ground that leads down to a locked door. Use the code and inside you'll find lots of ammo and an Ammo Capacity Upgrade for one of your weapons.

You can also explore the vent in the southwest portion of Floor 1. It's located in the lower area near the Helipad. Look for a soda machine down there, and you'll find this vent. If you explored it before, this time it will have new items - P.E.P.S and Tranquilizer Rifle ammo.

You can also hack Pritchard's PC and read his emails after he has given you his secondary objective for this area. However, it's a Level 5 Hack.

SARIF HQ

Required None
Recommended Social Enhancer, Hacking: Capture 5

01 When you're ready, ignore Pritchard and go to the penthouse. When you step off the elevator, you'll meet William Taggart. Speak with him to learn more of the story. Your conversation choices don't affect gameplay here, so act as you wish. Once you're done with Taggart, you can speak to Isaias Sandoval, Taggart's aide. Speaking with Sandoval gives you a few conversation options, and as with Taggart, the choices you make won't affect gameplay. [→☐ 1]

Tip **If you don't exhaust every conversation option, then Sandoval and Taggart will show up in the Cafeteria area when you're done with Sarif. You can go to them there for any dialogue you skipped in the initial meeting.**

1

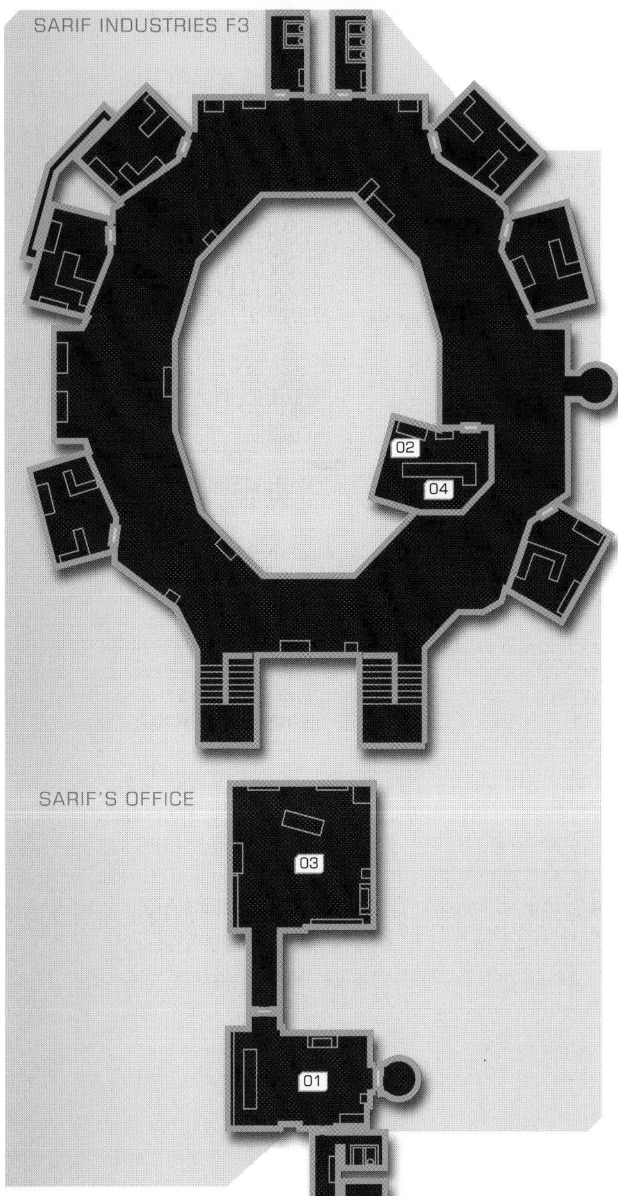

When you're ready, go see Sarif and he'll give you your next mission. Once you've finished talking to Sarif, head back down to Jensen's office. You can see Pritchard first if you like. It only changes the order in which you get your conversations for Sarif.

02 After speaking with Sarif, speak to Pritchard in Jensen's office. Pritchard has found a back door into Sarif Industries' network security, and he believes David Sarif is responsible. As much as it pains him, Pritchard wants you to investigate it for him, so head back to Sarif's office and engage him in a conversation gameplay. [→☐ 2]

03 Make your way back to the elevator and use it to reach the Penthouse. Taggart and Sandoval will be gone this time, so go straight to Sarif and speak with him.

CONVERSATION FLOW
DAVID SARIF
PERSONALITY TYPE: ALPHA

Conversation Round	Response to Make
Round 1	Refocus
Round 2	Defend
Round 3	Refocus
Round 4	Defend

ACHIEVEMENT/TROPHY: YES BOSS

You'll unlock this one when you win the conversation gameplay with Sarif.

04 Now that you're done with Sarif, head back to Jensen's office. Pritchard won't be there, so you'll need to read all of the new emails Sarif sent to Jensen's PC. The emails reveal some interesting tidbits about Jensen himself. After you have read them all, Pritchard will show up just outside Jensen's office, so go out there to talk to him.

SIDE QUEST

Reading the emails on Jensen's computer is important. It will trigger an additional scene with Pritchard, and will subsequently open up the Acquaintances Forgotten Side Quest later on.

05 When you've finished talking to Sarif and Pritchard, it's time to move on. You can explore Sarif HQ before leaving if you choose. When you're ready, make your way down to the Helipad and speak with Malik and she'll take you to China. [→☐ 3]

			Stealth Bonuses	
Objective Completed	Objective Type	XP Reward	Ghost	Smooth Operator
Meet Sarif in the Penthouse	Primary	1000	No	No
Meet Pritchard in my office	Primary	1000	No	No
Confront Sarif about the security leak	Secondary	2000*	No	No
Meet Malik at the Helipad	Primary	1000	No	No

*1000 from the Silver Tongue Bonus

HENGSHA CITY STREETS

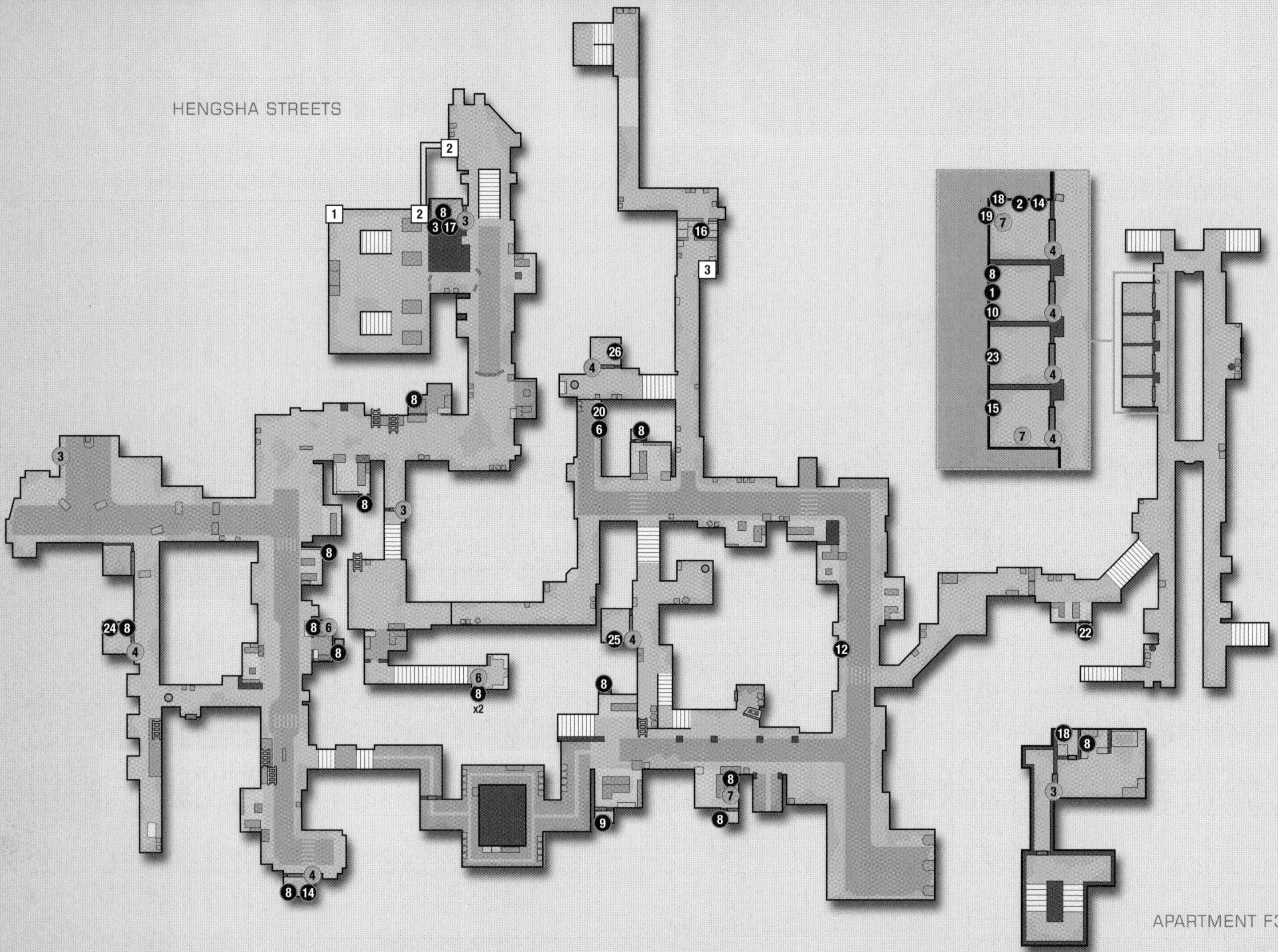

HENGSHA STREETS

APARTMENT F3

APARTMENT F2

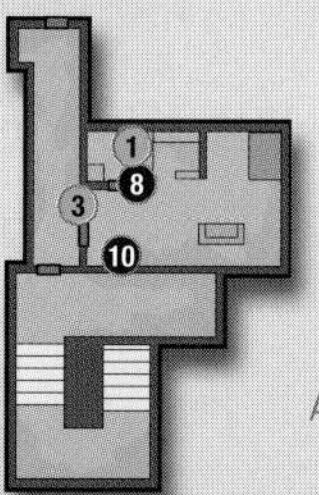

APARTMENT F1

- 1 10mm Pistol
- 2 Combat Rifle
- 3 P.E.P.S.
- 4 Revolver
- 5 Tactical Shotgun
- 6 Stun Gun
- 7 Tranquilizer Rifle
- 8 Credit Chip
- 9 Cyberboost ProEnergy Bar
- 10 Nuke Virus Software
- 11 Beer
- 12 Spirits
- 13 10mm Pistol Ammo
- 14 Combat Rifle Ammo
- 15 Crossbow Arrow
- 16 Machine Pistol Ammo
- 17 P.E.P.S. Energy Pack
- 18 Revolver Ammo
- 19 Shotgun Cartridge
- 20 Stun Gun Dart
- 21 Sniper Rifle Ammo
- 22 Tranquilizer Rifle Dart
- 23 Typhoon Ammo
- 24 Ammo Capacity Upgrade
- 25 Reload Speed Upgrade
- 26 Target Leading
- 27 Burst Round
- Pocket Secretary
- eBook
- Punch Through Wall
- 1 Vent 1
- 2 Vent 2
- 3 Vent 3
- 1 Computer - Unlocked
- 2 Computer - Level 2
- 3 Security Panels - Level 1
- 4 Security Panels - Level 2
- 5 Security Panels - Level 3
- 6 Safe Panel - Level 1
- 7 Safe Panel - Level 2

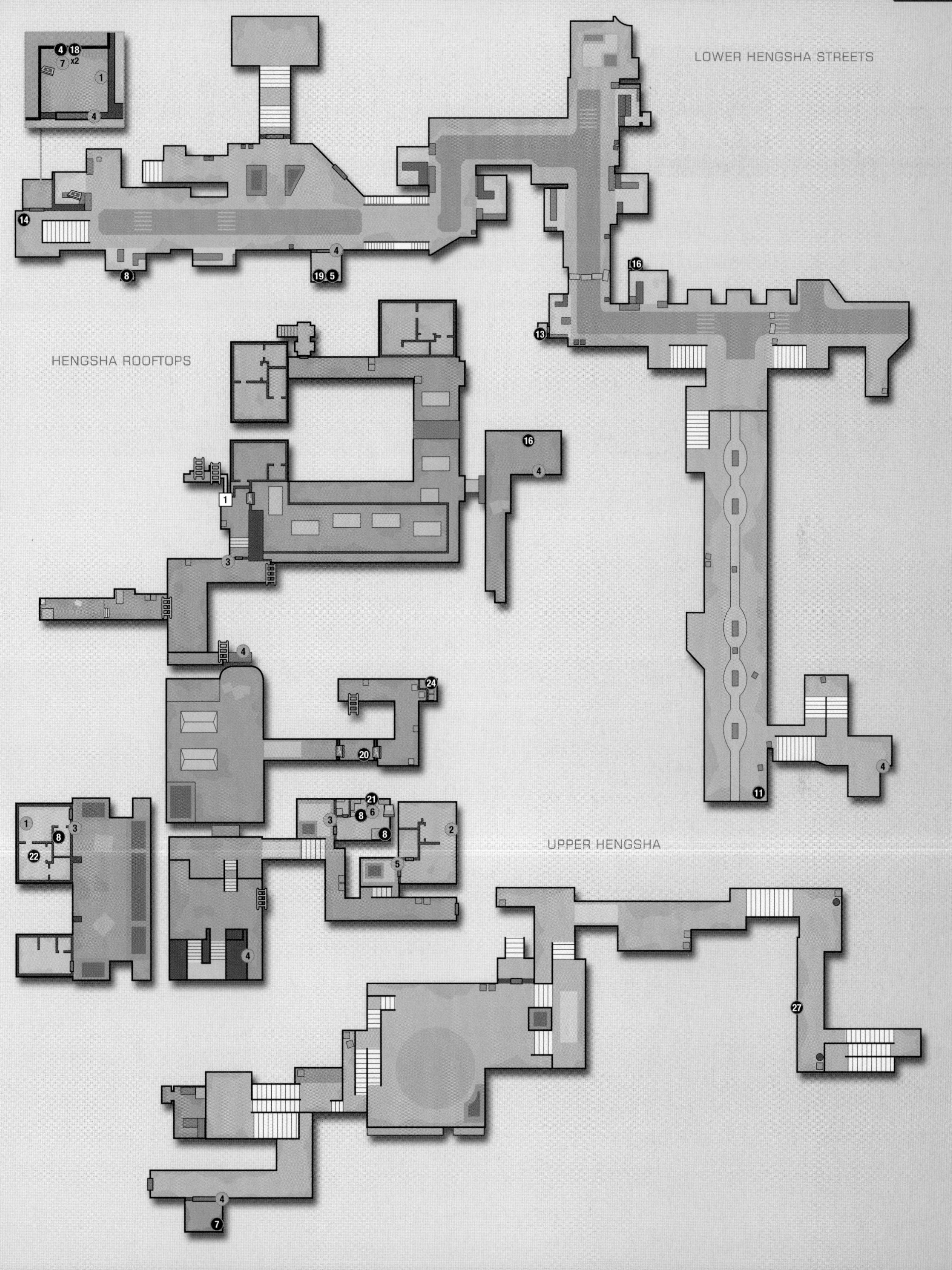
LOWER HENGSHA STREETS
HENGSHA ROOFTOPS
UPPER HENGSHA

HENGSHA CITY INTERIOR

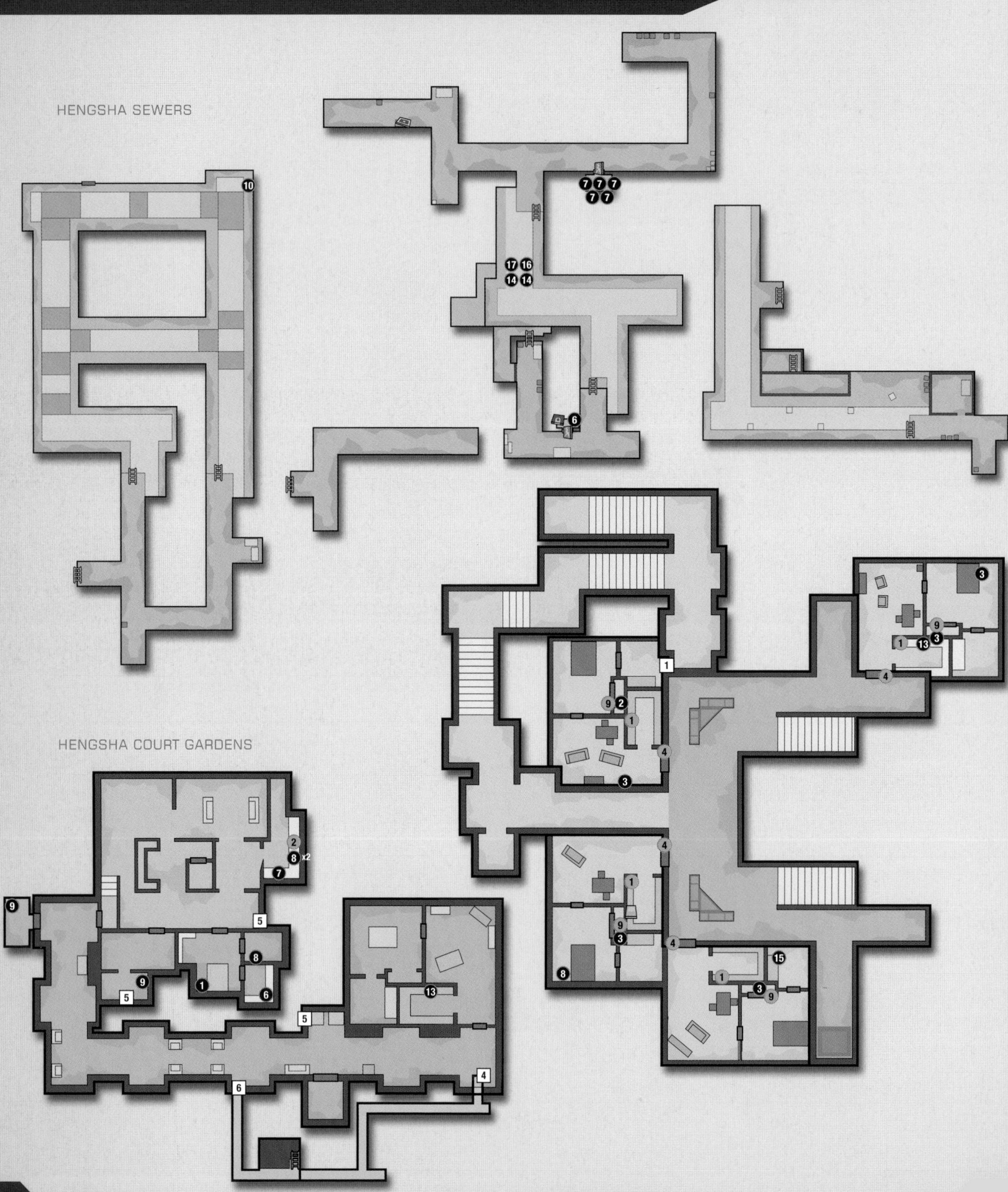

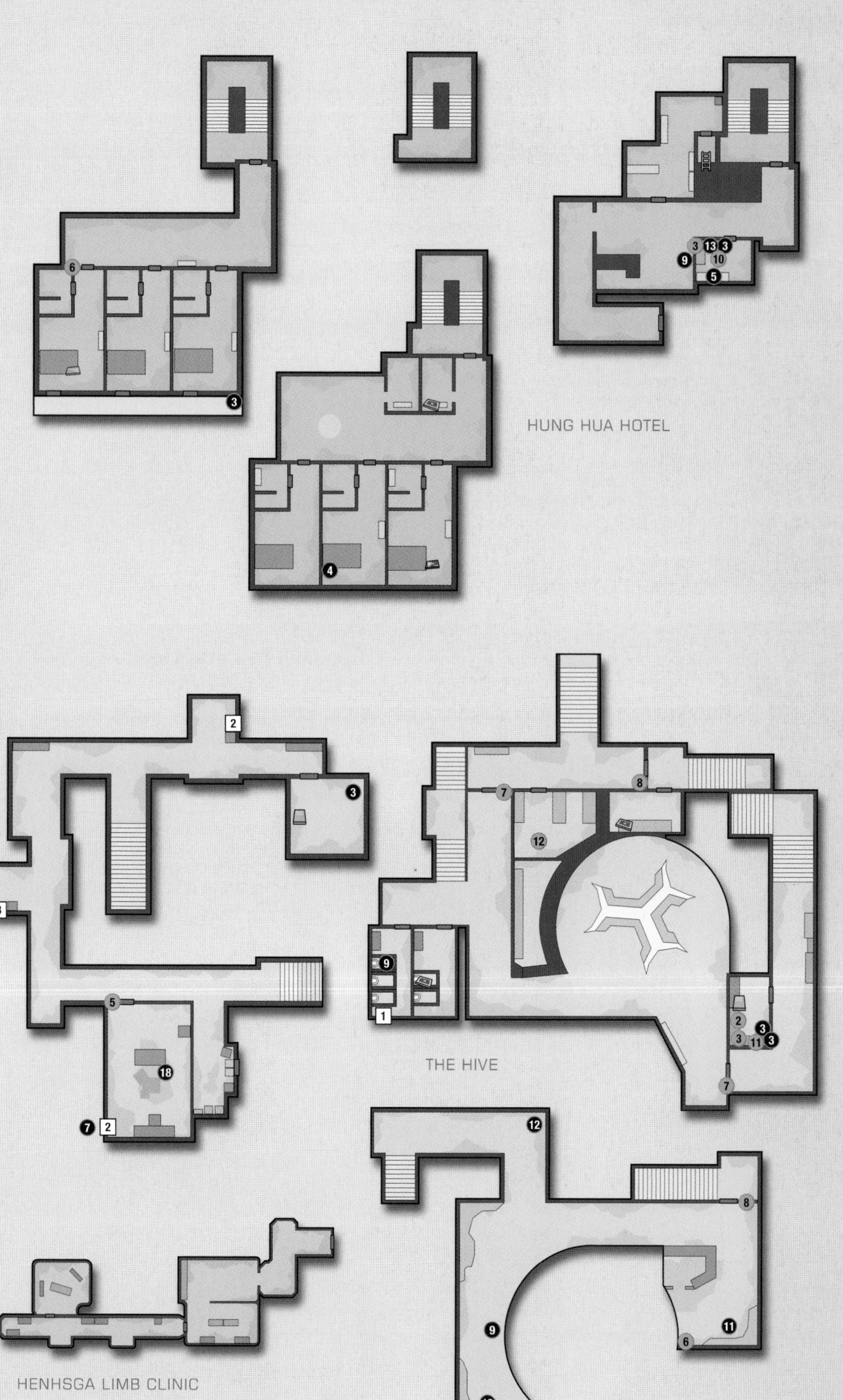

- 1 10mm Pistol
- 2 Machine Pistol
- 3 Credit Chip
- 4 Cyberboost ProEnergy Bar
- 5 CyberBoost ProEnergy Pack
- 6 Pain Killers
- 7 Nuke Virus Software
- 8 Stop Virus Software
- 9 Beer
- 10 Spirits
- 11 Vodka
- 12 Wine
- 13 10mm Pistol Ammo
- 14 Machine Pistol Ammo
- 15 Revolver Ammo
- 16 Stun Gun Dart
- 17 Mine Template
- 18 Rate of Fire Upgrade
- TYM Smart Card
- Hive Membership Card
- Praxis Kit
- Pocket Secretary
- eBook
- Punch Through Wall
- 1 Vent 1
- 2 Vent 2
- 3 Vent 3
- 4 Vent 4
- 5 Vent 5
- 6 Vent 6

- 1 Computer - Unlocked
- 2 Computer - Level 1
- 3 Security Terminal - Level 2
- 4 Security Panels - Level 1
- 5 Security Panels - Level 2
- 6 Security Panels - Level 3
- 7 Security Panels - Level 4
- 8 Security Panels - Level 5
- 9 Safe Panel - Level 1
- 10 Safe Panel - Level 2
- 11 Safe Panel - Level 3

M1 - HUNTING THE HACKER

OPTIONAL EXPLORATION

As soon as you are off the chopper and free to move, it's a good idea to go into the Hung Hua Hotel to get the TYM Smart Card on the fourth floor. You'll need it for Van Bruggen later, so save some time and get it now.

The Smart Card is located in the third room on the right, but the door is locked. There is a guard inside who can see you if you come in through the front door. Instead, go into the first or second room and use the door at the back to reach the balcony. Now go right across the balconies to reach the last room. Crouch and ease into the room and you'll see the Smart Card on the table at the foot of the bed. Once you have it, backtrack the way you came.

Also, while in the hotel, go to the third floor and get the Hive Membership Card. It is located in the first room on the left after you enter the third floor area. Go into that room and look on the small table at the foot of the bed to find the card.

Objective Name	Objective Type
Investigate the Penthouse Apartment	Primary

You can also visit the weapon dealer Lin Fu Ren located on the first floor of the Hung Hua Hotel.

Once you are on the streets, make sure to go to the LIMB Clinic and get the two Praxis Kits that are available there.

On the streets of Hengsha you'll see many vendor shops. Most shops have a door at the rear that leads to a small storage area. If you enter those areas, you'll gain some exploration XP as well as finding Credits and other items.

SIDE QUEST

You can find Mei in the first room on the left on the fourth floor of the Hung Hua Hotel. Talk to her to trigger the Rotten Business Side Quest.

Hengsha Court Gardens

ROUTE 1 Stealth

Required Move/Throw Heavy Objects
Recommended Icarus Landing System, Cloaking System

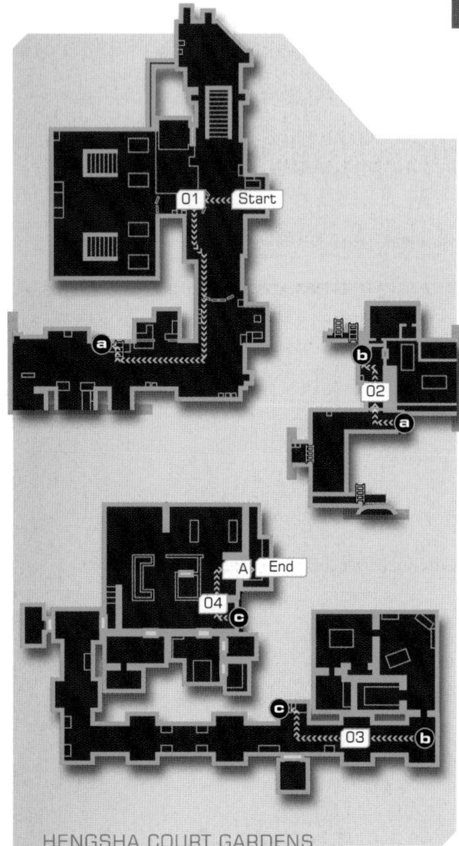

ACHIEVEMENT/TROPHY: DOCTORATE

There is a Hugh Darrow eBook in the apartment on the second floor of the Downtown Apartment complex in the southern area of the Youzhao District.

01 Approach the Penthouse Building's main entrance, and you'll be denied entry [→☐ 1]. Now go left to the south and move around the corner. You're on Pandeng Rd, and just ahead is a ladder on the right that you can use to reach the area above. After climbing the second ladder above you, go left and jump onto the AC units to make your way west to a final ladder that will take you to the rooftop.

02 Just ahead and on the right is a locked door. It is a Level 1 Hack that's easy enough to get past. Hack the door and go inside to the small area beyond the door. There is a breakable wall on your right, but do not punch through it, as it will alert the guards that are patrolling the rooftop on the other side. Instead, use the vent on the left to enter the air ducts.

You'll emerge in an elevator shaft. Use the ladder in front of you to reach the next level. As soon as you climb up to the next level, the elevator below will begin moving up. If you're quick, then you can jump over the railing and land on top of the elevator. This gives you an easy ride to the topmost level of the shaft, where a vent is located.

If you don't jump on the elevator, then use the ladders to climb up two levels. From there, go right to some boxes and climb on top of them. From there, turn around and jump to the next level where another ladder is located. Climb that ladder to the level above.

1

On the next level, there is a vent that you can use to get into the building. Alternatively, you'll find a crate here that you can use to jump on top of the elevator and reach the topmost level and the vent there. Both vents get you inside the building to the same hallway, so the choice is yours.

OPTIONAL EXPLORATION

If you jump down to the bottom of the elevator shaft, you'll find a Praxis Kit. It's a long fall, so the Icarus Aug is required to survive it. Alternatively, you can use the series of ladders to facilitate your descent and return to the top.

03 Once you are in the Penthouse hallway, locate the two soda machines in the middle of the hall. Move the one on the left to expose the vent there. Enter the air ducts and take the first right to reach Van Bruggen's apartment.

04 From the vent, you're just left of the PC, which is your objective. Move out of the air ducts whilst crouching and go right. At **Position A**, you'll see a large hole in the wall. Jump through the hole and hack Van Bruggen's PC. Then read all of his emails to complete your objective. Retrace your steps to exit the building.

ROUTE 2 Stealth Combat

Required Move/Throw Heavy Objects
Recommended Cloaking System

Recommended Tranquilizer Rifle

01 Head to the Penthouse Building's main entrance, then go left and around the corner. You'll be on Pandeng Rd, and just ahead you'll see a ladder. Once you've climbed the second ladder above you, go left and jump onto the AC units to make your way west to a final ladder, leading to your rooftop destination.

02 Once you are on the roof, go right and take cover at the large AC units ahead. There is a guard patrolling this area you'll want to take out. Move to your right from cover to cover. As soon as you are past the guard, move around the AC units and then get behind him for a Takedown. [→☐ 2]

03 Crouch and move across the roof toward the next guard. Once you are close, keep the large crate between you and the guard so he doesn't see you. Take cover at the large crate and watch the guard. He'll take up position near another large crate directly ahead at **Position A**. Wait, and once he begins moving away from you, move up behind him whilst crouching for a Takedown.

After the guard is down, use the door at **Position B** to enter the building. Make your way down the stairs in the building to the elevator. Use the elevator to reach the Penthouse.

04 Exit the elevator and approach the vending machines that are directly ahead. Move the vending machine on the left to expose the vent. Do not use the vent yet, instead, move up the hallway to the left and take cover at **Position C**. Just around the corner you'll see two guards having a conversation, and one's route will take him into the Penthouse where your objective is located, causing problems later on. Move back along the hallway slightly and take cover in the small alcove at **Position D**; once the guard has moved past you, sneak up behind him for a Takedown. Enter the vent you exposed earlier and follow it to come out into a small storage closet, from which you can enter the bedroom.

Tip **For some additional XP, sneak around the corner at Position C and use another Takedown on the guard leaning against the wall.**

This guard is problematic in that his patrol takes him all the way to the end of the hall just past you, and then he'll return and enter the Penthouse. This means he could catch you in the Penthouse as you're trying to complete your objectives, so it far better to take him out now.Hold your position in cover and watch the oncoming guard. As he passes by you, get behind him for a Takedown. Now, use the vent you exposed earlier to enter the air ducts and make your way to the very end of the ducts where you can enter the bedroom.

05 Once you are in the bedroom, take cover on the right side of the door leading out to the rest of the apartment. In the room ahead there are three guards that you will have to take care of before searching the area. One of them is patrolling a route between the far side of the room and the central area; wait for him to start walking away, then open the door and use the Stun Gun to incapacitate him.

06 After you knock out the first guard, move up and take cover behind the kitchen unit. The second guard always remains stationary looking out of the window just ahead, and the third patrols a small area in front of the window to the right. Wait for the third guard to be looking out of the window, and then use the Stun Gun on the second one. Wait for the third guard to start walking away from you and them move up for a Takedown. When the area is clear, interact with the soft toy at **Position E** to open up a secret passage to the hacker's office. Follow the passage and hack into his PC at **Position F** to read the emails and complete the objective. Once you have finished in the area, retrace your steps to the exit [→☐ 3].

Hengsha Court Gardens

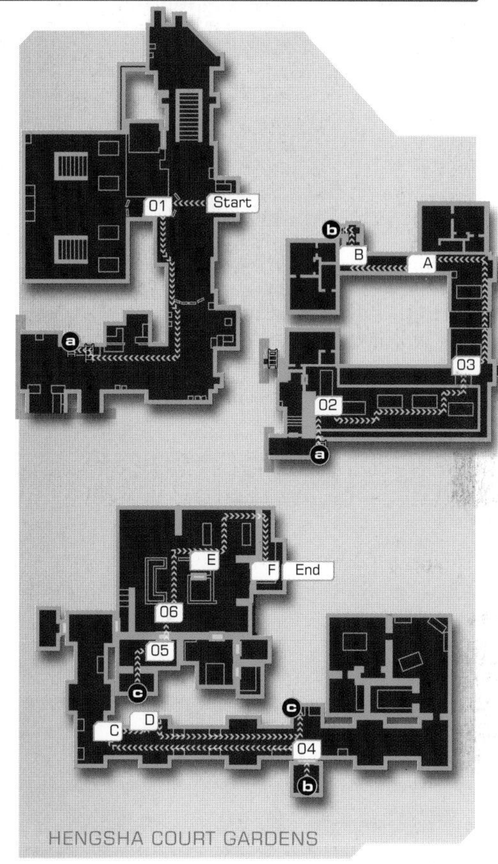

ROUTE 3 Combat

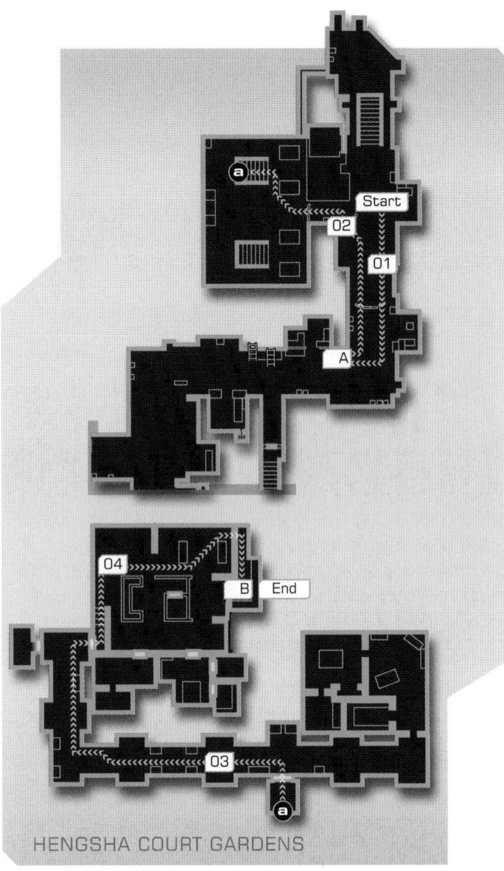

Required None
Recommended Dermal Plating, Reflex Booster

Recommended Combat Rifle, 10mm Pistol (Silenced), Frag Grenade

01 From the main entrance, go left and take cover at the edge of the building at **Position A**. Peek out and headshot the guard there, preferably with a silenced weapon. Wait for the next guard to come investigate, and headshot him. There will be at least two more guards, so hold your position and use cover to safely take out the guards.

02 Once all the guards in the street are down, take cover at the main entrance and headshot all the guards as they crowd around the opening. If you have a frag then toss it into the crowd as they bunch up ahead. When all of the guards are dead, head up the stairs through the front entrance and take the elevator up to the Penthouse floor.

ACHIEVEMENT/TROPHY: DOCTORATE

You'll find one of Hugh Darrow's eBooks in the apartment on the left of the main entrance to Van Bruggen's building.

03 Exit the elevator and go left down the hall. Take cover at the edge of the wall and peek out to see the two guards around the corner; before one of them can walk away, throw a Frag Grenade to take them both out [→☐ 1]. Immediately throw a Frag Grenade to take all three of them out. If you don't have a Frag, then engage them with gunfire.
Now hold position here and the other two guards in the Penthouse will come running. Pick them both off from your cover point, and then you're free to enter the apartment.

04 Locate the toy doll in the center of the room and investigate it to open a secret door in the northeast corner of the room that leads to Van Bruggen's secret office. Enter his office and hack his PC at **Position B**. When you've accessed his PC, read all of his emails to complete your objective. Now simply backtrack across your entrance route to leave the building.

Objective Completed	Objective Type	XP Reward	Stealth Bonuses	
			Ghost	Smooth Operator
Investigate the Penthouse Apartment	Primary	2500	Yes	No

ROUTE 1 Stealth

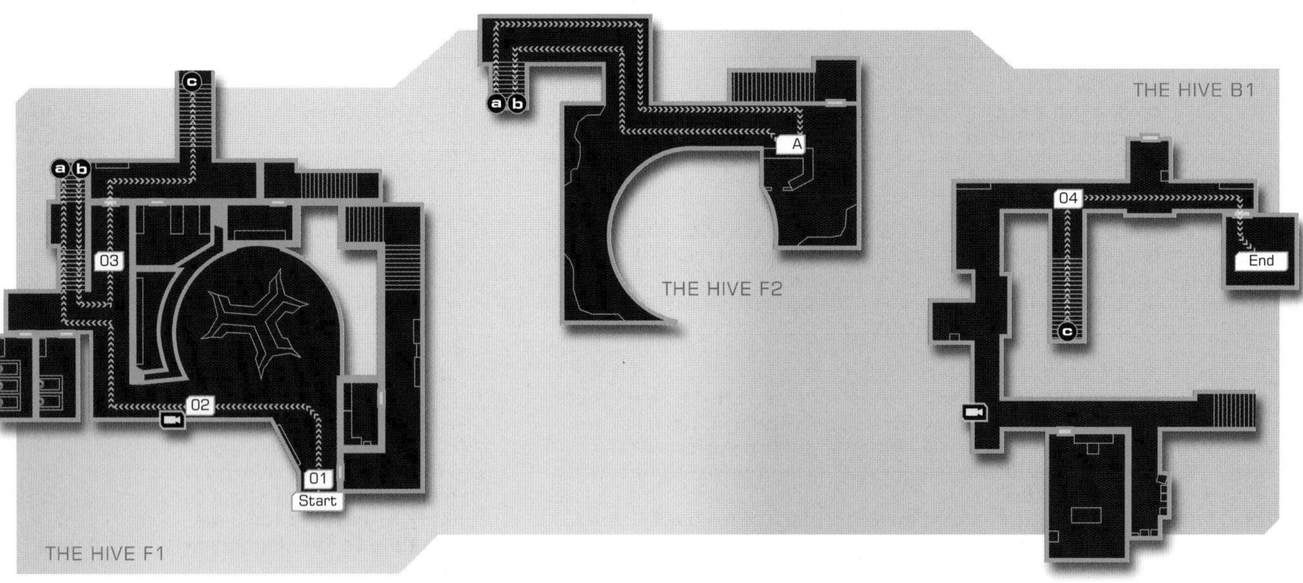

Objective Name	Objective Type
Get inside the Hive Nightclub	Primary
Find and speak with Tong Si Hung	Primary
Meet Tong in his office*	Primary

* This objective only opens if you win the conversation gameplay with Tong

Required None
Recommended Social Enhancer

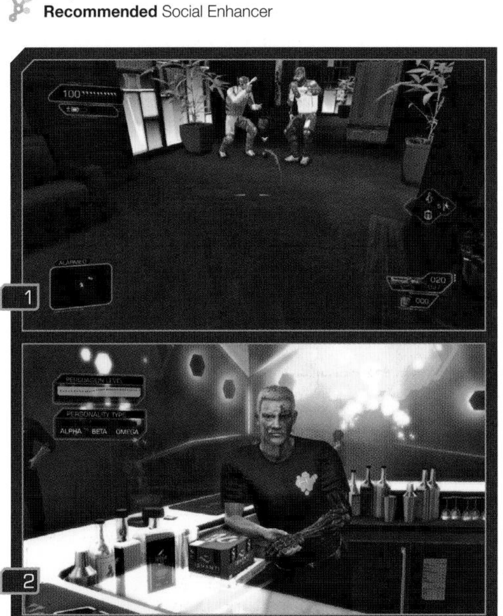

01 You can find a Hive Membership card in a room on the third floor of the Hung Hua Hotel. This card lets you get past the Bouncer at the front door. If you don't have the card, then you'll have to cough up some Credits to take this route.

02 When you are inside the Hive, go forward and then left to the stairs in the north-west. Make your way up to the next level and approach the "Manager" behind the bar at **Position A** to trigger a conversation gameplay sequence [→□ 2]

CONVERSATION FLOW
TONG SI HUNG
PERSONALITY TYPE: ALPHA

Conversation Round	Response to Make
Round 1	Pinpoint
Round 2	Advise
Round 3	Pinpoint

ACHIEVEMENT/TROPHY: DARKER SHADES

Win the conversation gameplay with Tong and you'll unlock this Achievement/ Trophy.

03 When you've finished talking to Tong, make your way to the basement access door. Just inside that door, on the same level, you'll find a door to your right, a door dead ahead, and some stairs to your left. The path is to your left and down the stairs. The door ahead is a Level 5 Hack. The door on the right leads to a closet that has nothing more than a bottle of wine inside. Take the stairs on your left down to the next level when you're ready.

04 At the base of the stairs, go right and you'll find a red door on your right at the end of the hall. There is also a vent on your left, but ignore it. It leads to a duct vent that overlooks Tong's office and only comes into play if you didn't win the Tong conversation. When you're ready, enter Tong's office and speak with him. [→□ 3]

ACHIEVEMENT/TROPHY: DOCTORATE

You'll find one of Hugh Darrow's eBooks on a table on the right-hand side of Tong's office.

The Hive Nightclub

ROUTE 2 Stealth Combat

Required Punch Through Walls
Recommended Social Enhancer, Cloaking System

Recommended Tranquilizer Rifle

01 Start off by traveling to the Kuaigan District and go to the Hung Hua Hotel. On the first floor of the Hotel, enter the Weapon Dealer's room and move past him to the right where you'll find an entrance to the sewers. Go through the door and drop down into the sewers below.

02 Follow the sewers to reach the Hive entrance. Before you get to the entrance, you'll encounter a large cloud of poisonous gas. You can't make it through this without the Rebreather augmentation. Fortunately, on your right you'll find a breakable wall you can punch through at **Position A**. Once you are through the wall, use the valve there to turn off the gas, and then you can proceed to the Hive entrance at **Position B**.

OPTIONAL EXPLORATION

- **As soon as you enter the sewers and are at the base of the ladder from the hotel, look right at the ground to find a vent that leads to a Maintenance tunnel. Follow that tunnel to the next area where you'll find an exit to the Kuaigan District as well as a breakable wall. Punch through the wall to find ammo and a mine template.**
- **As soon as you enter the sewers and are at the base of the ladder from the hotel, go forward and left and you'll find a breakable wall on your left. Punch through it to find a Praxis Kit and some Pain Killers.**

03 When you exit the sewers, move forward and take cover at the corner of the wall. Peek out to the right and you'll see a camera. Watch it, and when it begins panning to your right, rush forward and get underneath it to avoid detection. Now that you're under the camera, you're safe and can go left and up the hall with no worries since the camera doesn't pan far enough in that direction to spot you.

OPTIONAL EXPLORATION

Just past the camera is a small alcove on your left. There you'll find a vent that you can use to access some air ducts. Follow the ducts forward and you'll find a Nuke Virus in the ducts. When you exit the ducts, you'll be in a room with a dead body. Apparently, he angered Tong. Also in that room is a Rate Of Fire Upgrade for one of your weapons.

04 Take cover at the corner of the wall and peek out to the left to see a guard patrolling the hallway. Watch his Patrol route, and he'll move to **Position C**. That is as close as he will get to you on his normal route. Once he turns away from this position, crouch and move up behind him for a Takedown.

Now go use the vent at **Position D** to gain a vantage point over Tong's office. A cutscene will trigger, and you'll eavesdrop and gain all the information you need [→☐ 1]. Now all you need do is backtrack along the way you came to get out of here.

ACHIEVEMENT/TROPHY: DOCTORATE

From the sewer exit, go right instead of left. Continue up the stairs and you'll find an unlocked door on your right that leads to the Bartender's office. Crouch down before entering the office so that you aren't seen through the windows. On the desk to the right of the PC you'll find one of Hugh Darrow's eBooks.

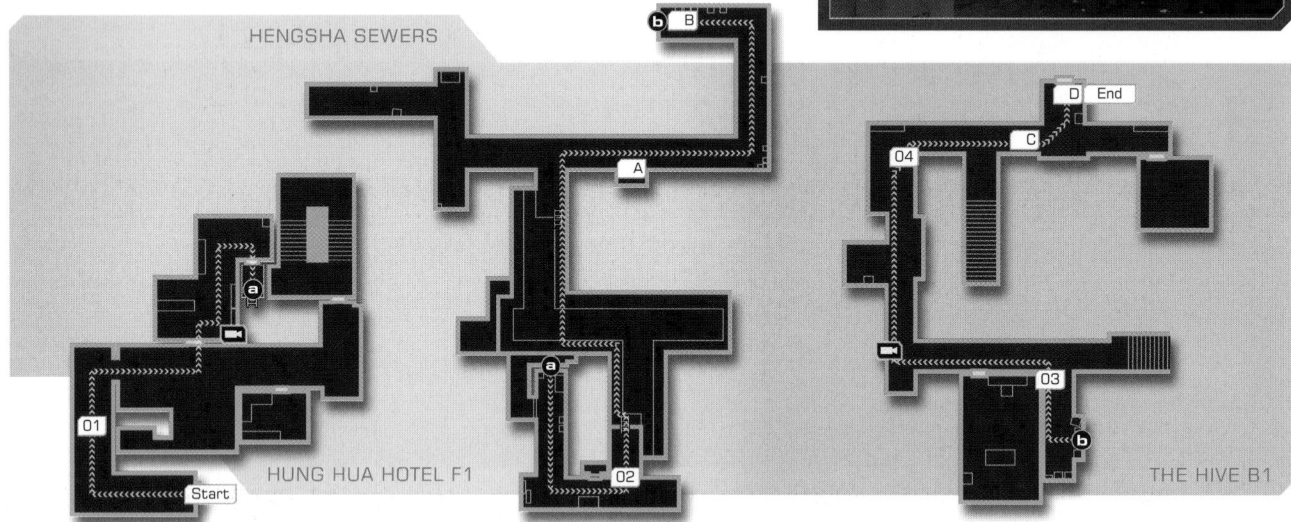

The Hive Nightclub

ROUTE 3 Combat

Required None
Recommended Dermal Plating, Typhoon

Recommended 10mm Pistol (Silenced), Combat Rifle, Revolver, Frag Grenade

01 Approach the Hive's main entrance. From there, go left and into the alley ahead on the right. Make your way to a large dumpster at **Position A**. Move the box on top of the dumpster to expose the vent. Jump on top of the dumpster and use the vent to get inside the Hive. [→☐ 2]

02 When you exit the vent, you'll find yourself in the women's bathroom. While this might disturb Pritchard even more, it's just a brief stop on your path. Leave the bathroom and go right to **Position B** in the men's bathroom and look in the first stall on the right to find a Pocket Secretary, which has the code for the basement door.

03 You're not looking to start a firefight just yet. The guards in the Hive are numerous, so you'll want to pick your position before starting the fireworks. Exit the men's bathroom and move ahead and slightly to the right to find a locked door. The PS you just found in the bathroom has the code for this door. Use it to go through the door, and then head left down the stairs to the next area.

04 At the bottom of the stairs, take cover at the corner of the wall and peek out to your left. There is a guard patrolling this hallway here. Wait for him to move away from you, then lean out and shoot him in the head with a non-silenced weapon. The sound of the gunfire will set off the alarm and cause the rest of the guards to come running. You've no time to waste, so head left to the next position.

05 Go left and up the hall and then left again. Just ahead is a small alcove on your right where you'll want to make your stand. Take cover here and then peek out to the right. Pick off the first one or two guards that come running. When they all bunch up ahead, toss a Frag amongst them to thin the crowd. Stay in cover and pick off the remaining guards.

Tip **Shoot at camera in this area to ensure the guards know where to find you.**

06 When all the guards are dead, make your way back to the basement door and take cover at the left side at **Position C**. Peek out and look for any remaining guards. If none are visible, then fire a non-silenced weapon to get their attention. Hold your position and pick off the last of the Hive's guards. There are five to contend with here, so make sure you get them all before moving on.

07 Now that all the guards in the Hive are dead, all you need do is track down Tong. Head back down into the basement. At the bottom of the stairs, go right and just ahead on your left you'll see a vent. Open it and enter the air ducts to get a view of Tong's office. A cutscene will be triggered, where you eavesdrop on Tong's conversation, thus gaining the intel you need. Now, with no one left to get in your way, all you need do is exit the Hive any way you wish.

SIDE QUEST

After dealing with Tong, talk to the Bartender Bobby Bao on the first floor and choose the Operation option to trigger the Bar Tab Side Quest.

			Stealth Bonuses	
Objective Completed	Objective Type	XP Reward	Ghost	Smooth Operator
Get inside the Hive Nightclub	Primary	250	Yes	No
Find and speak with Tong Si Hung	Primary	1750*1	Yes*2	No
Meet Tong in his office	Primary	1000*3	No	No

*1 1000 from the Silver Tongue Bonus
*2 You only get this if you don't talk to Tong and use the vent to eavesdrop instead.
*3 This objective only opens if you win the conversation gameplay with Tong.

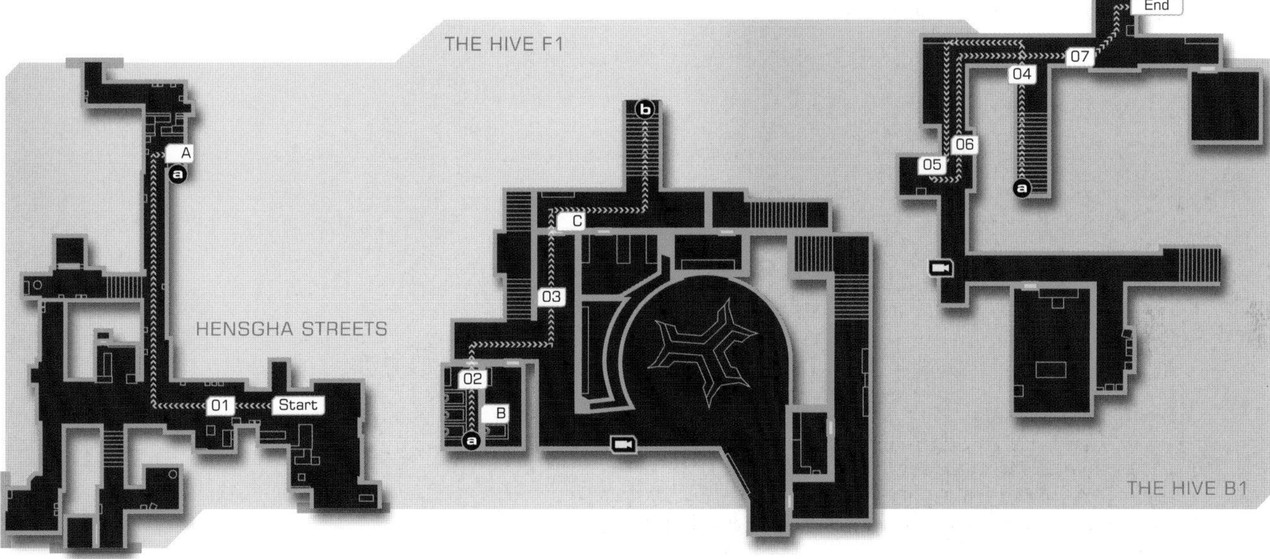

GO TO ALICE GARDEN PODS

Objective Name	Objective Type
Meet Van Bruggen in the Alice Garden Pods	Primary

Make your way over to Alice Garden Pods in the Kuaigan District. It's located in the northeast of Level 2 of the city streets. Once you reach the area, go through the large double doors to enter Alice Garden Pods.

OPTIONAL EXPLORATION

Directly west of the entrance to Alice Garden Pods on the opposite side of the catwalks, you'll find four locked storage units. These are all Level 2 Hacks, but you only need to hack one of them, since the codes for the other three are painted on the wall.

Face the units, and then start with the one on the far left. On the wall to the left of the security terminal you'll see many numbers painted all over. Look to the lower left, and there you'll see a long string of numbers. The first four of these numbers are underlined; these four digits are the security code for this unit.

Check the next two units, and again look to the left of the security terminal to find a string of numbers with four digits underlined, thus indicating the code. The last unit on the right doesn't have a code displayed here, so you'll have to hack it.

Shuighou Plaza Storage Units		
Unit 1	1381	Crossbow ammo, Safe with 328 Credits
Unit 2	1339	Typhoon ammo
Unit 3	1379	Nuke Virus, 10mm pistol, 105 Credits
Unit 4	7845*	Combat Rifle , Combat Rifle ammo, Safe with Revolver and Shotgun ammo

*From a Pocket Secretary

ALICE GARDEN PODS

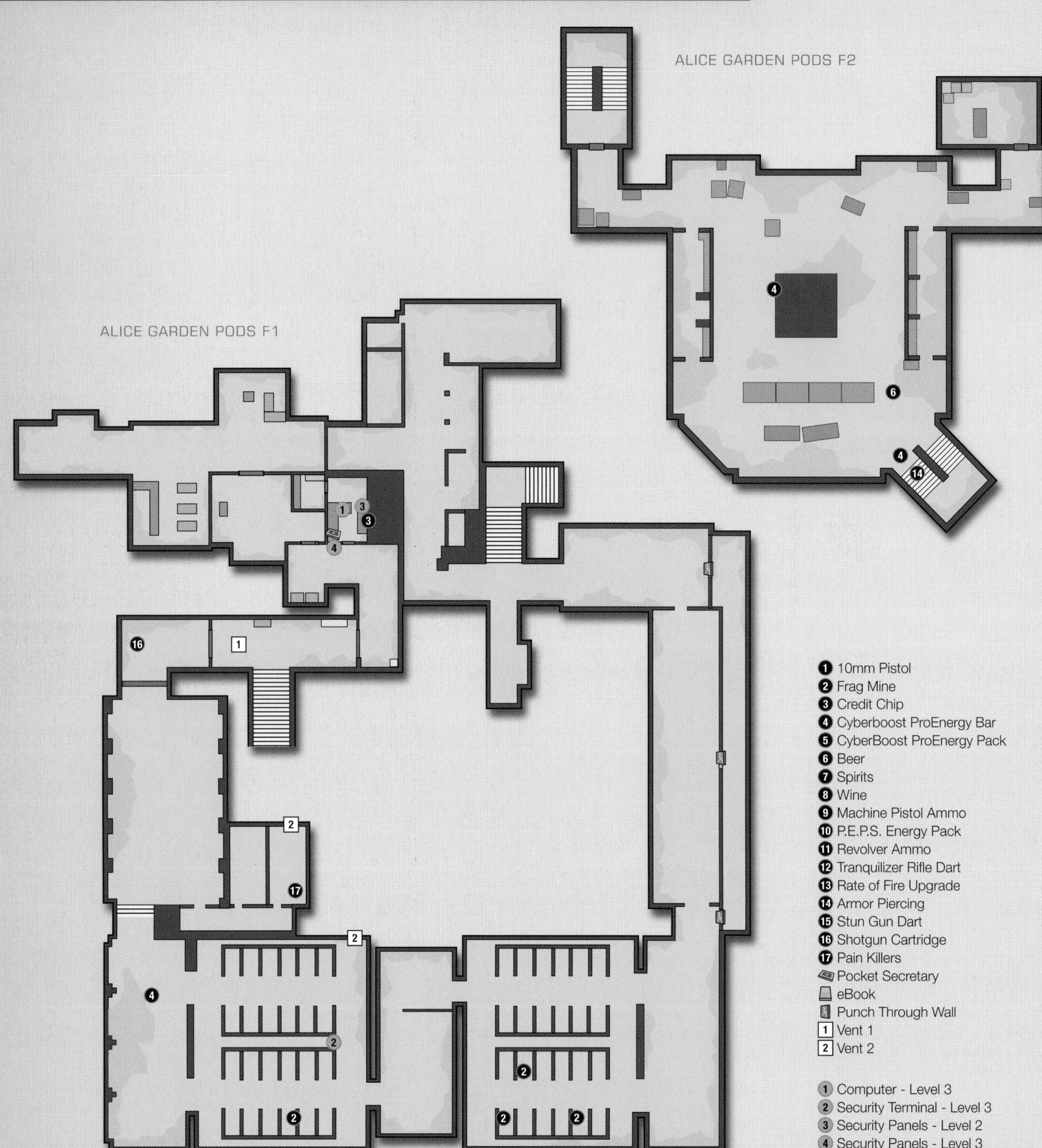

ALICE GARDEN PODS F2
ALICE GARDEN PODS F1
1 10mm Pistol
2 Frag Mine
3 Credit Chip
4 Cyberboost ProEnergy Bar
5 CyberBoost ProEnergy Pack
6 Beer
7 Spirits
8 Wine
9 Machine Pistol Ammo
10 P.E.P.S. Energy Pack
11 Revolver Ammo
12 Tranquilizer Rifle Dart
13 Rate of Fire Upgrade
14 Armor Piercing
15 Stun Gun Dart
16 Shotgun Cartridge
17 Pain Killers
Pocket Secretary
eBook
Punch Through Wall
1 Vent 1
2 Vent 2
1 Computer - Level 3
2 Security Terminal - Level 3
3 Security Panels - Level 2
4 Security Panels - Level 3

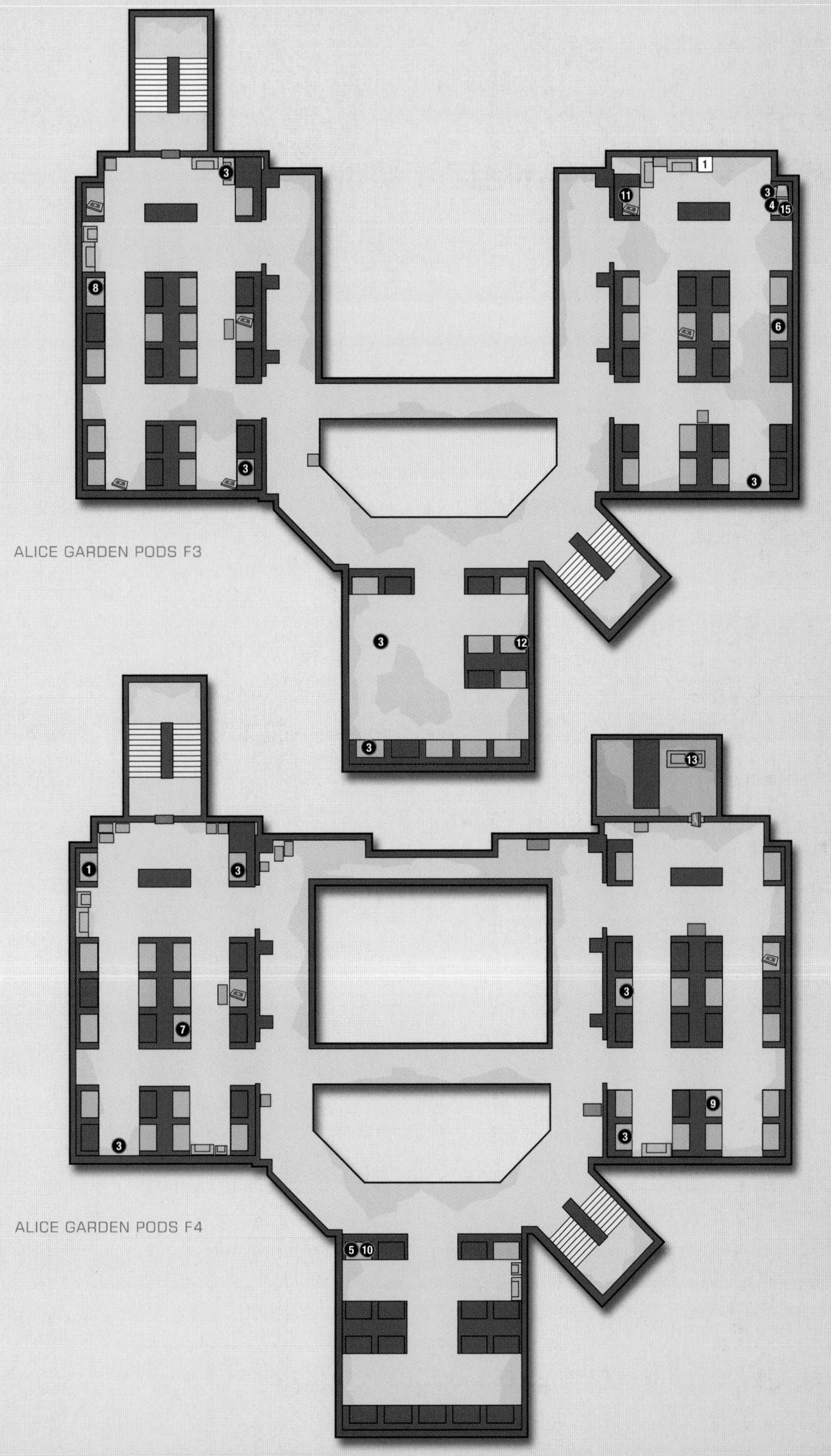

ALICE GARDEN PODS F3
ALICE GARDEN PODS F4

M2 - GAINING ACCESS TO TAI YONG MEDICAL

When you're ready, make your way to Level 3 and go to the Pod section to the south. This area contains the Pods in the 300 range, and you'll find Van Bruggen in Pod # 301 in the southwest corner. Van Bruggen will ask you for a TYM Employee Card, and if you don't have one, you'll have to go back to Hung Hua Hotel and check the room on the right to find one on the small table at the foot of the bed. If you already picked that up earlier, then the scene will progress to the next part. [→☐ 1]

Once the scenes are over, Belltower Guards will ambush Alice Garden Pods looking for Van Bruggen. At this point you have the option of giving Van Bruggen a weapon. Doing so is not required, but it will net you a considerable amount of Credits later in the game if you do. The choice is yours.

1

Objective Name	Objective Type
Steal an Employee Card from a TYM employee	Primary
Bring the Employee Card to Van Bruggen	Primary
Escape the Alice Garden Pods Ambush	Primary

Tip **Before talking to Van Bruggen, you can find a Machine Pistol in Pod #429, or a 10mm Pistol in Pod #543 that you can give to Van Bruggen later. If you are trying to keep both of those weapons for yourself, then you can go to the Weapon Dealer on Level 2 and buy a weapon that you're willing to part with.**

OPTIONAL EXPLORATION

Floor 1

Just past the Reception area, you'll find a locked door that leads to the Manager's Office. It's a Level 3 Hack, but you can find the code on a Pocket Secretary in Pod # 243. Inside the office you'll find a Pocket Secretary under the left side of the desk that has the password to the PC. Also there is a safe with a Level 3 Hack, and inside you'll find 1015 Credits.

Floor 2

You can find the Weapon Dealer Peng Xin Hao in a storage closet in the northeast. You should definitely buy the Exploding Rounds Package for the Revolver! Also, a Gas Grenade is a good purchase for the Stealth Combat route.

You can find an Armor-Piercing System for the 10mm Pistol under the stairs in the southeast. If you already have this upgrade, then sell it for 750 Credits to the Weapon Dealer.

Third Floor

- 009 - Items for Shanghai Justice SQ
- 017 - Tranquilizer Rifle ammo
- 025 - Story eBook

- 101 - Revolver ammo, Story Pocket Secretary
- 119 - Story Pocket Secretary
- 139 - Beer
- 143 - Darrow eBook, 99 Credits, Stun Gun Darts, Energy Bar

- 205 - Story Pocket Secretary
- 211 - 95 Credits
- 241 - Wine
- 243 - Pocket Secretary with code to office

Fourth Floor

- 301 - Van Bruggen
- 333 - P.E.P.S ammo, Energy pack

- 405 - 95 Credits
- 411 - 96 Credits
- 425 - Story eBook
- 429 - Machine Pistol
- 441 - Story Pocket Secretary

- 501 - 103 Credits
- 505 - Story Pocket Secretary
- 517 - Spirits (alcohol, +10 HP)
- 543 - 10mm Pistol

In the Pod Area for the pods in the 400 range, punch through the breakable wall to the north to find a Rate of Fire Upgrade for one of your weapons.

ACHIEVEMENT/TROPHY: DOCTORATE

There is a Hugh Darrow eBook in Pod #143 on Level 3.

SIDE QUEST

Malik's Shanghai Justice Side Quest will open once you enter the second floor of Alice Garden Pods.

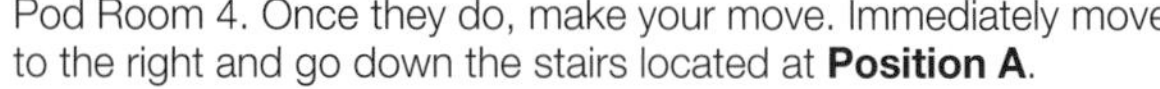

ROUTE 1 Stealth

Required Punch Through Walls
Recommended Cloaking System, Jump Enhancement, Move/Throw Heavy Objects

01 Move to the doorway of the Pod room and take cover at the box located at the right side of the door. Peek out and watch the guards to your right. Wait for the guards to disperse and enter the Pod Room 4. Once they do, make your move. Immediately move to the right and go down the stairs located at **Position A**.

02 Take cover at the bottom of the stairs on the right side. From your cover point, peek out and look to the right. Watch the two guards ahead and wait for them to enter Pod Room 1. When they do,

move forward and take cover at the right side of the Pod Room door at **Position B**. Once there, watch the guards in the room, and when they aren't looking, jump to cover across the doorway and move forward to the end of the area. [→□ 2]

03 Take cover at the right side of the door and watch the guards in the Pod Room. They will soon come and investigate the area directly ahead. Wait for them both to move off to the left. When they do, watch your radar, and when the guard closest to you (the lower radar icon) is looking up or down and not in your direction, move ahead to the vent located at **Position C**.

Use the vent to enter the air ducts. Move all the way to the end where you'll find an exit vent. Do not stop as you move through the vent, especially once you come to the vented areas that look over the Food Court. If you pause there, the guards could very well see you. Once you reach the exit vent, open it and drop out of the air ducts.

04 Once out of the vent, go west to the Locker Room doors. Take cover at the left side of the door and then open it. Make sure the guard ahead is off to the left, and then move forward and take cover at **Position D**. From your cover position watch for the guard to appear ahead. Once he appears and then moves back to the right, move from cover to cover to reach **Position E**.

05 From your cover point, look ahead; there is a camera on the wall, and a guard on patrol. Wait for the guard to go to the camera and look around. As soon as he turns and heads back to the left, move forward and right to the door at **Position F**. The camera is stationary and only looks left, so as long as you stay to the right, you'll remain undetected. [→□ 3]

06 Once you are through the door, go left and enter the women's bathroom. There is a crate against the northern wall concealing a vent. Move it out of the way and then use the vent to enter the air ducts and reach the next area.

07 There are two guards and a Turret ahead. Wait for the guards to move to the right and take up position. When they do, open the vent and move left to the shower room entrance located at **Position G**. There is a Security Hub here, but if you try to hack it, the guards will see you, so just ignore it.

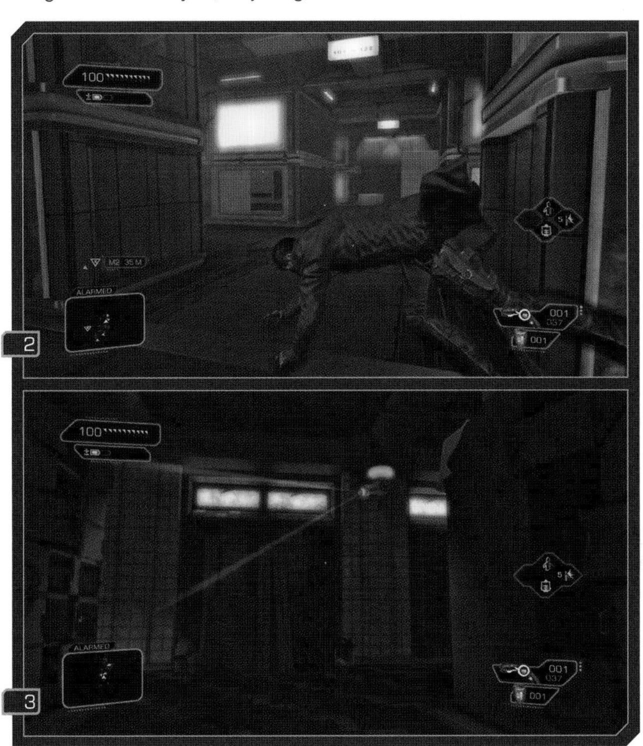

ALICE GARDEN PODS F4

Start 01 A a
02 B 03 C b

ALICE GARDEN PODS F3

L End K 13 J 12 11 H
04 b D E 05 F 06 c

ALICE GARDEN PODS F1

07 c G 08 09 10 I

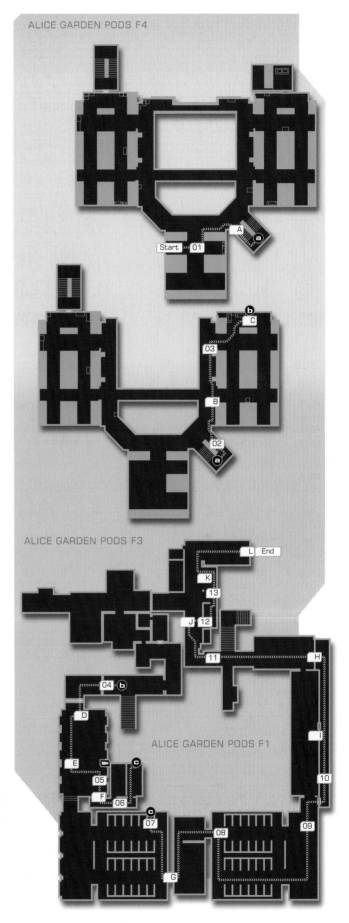

08 Move forward to make your way to the showers. The floor here is electrified on the left side of the room, and booby-trapped with Frag Mines on the right. If you have the Jump Aug, stay on the left and move forward by jumping over the low shower walls. Otherwise, go right and move very slowly up to each mine so that you can deactivate it. In all, there are three mines you'll need to deactivate if you choose to go up the right-hand side of the room.

09 Once you are past the showers, enter the next room and move north to the door. However, don't walk through the door. Instead, look right to find a breakable wall. Punch through it and enter the area behind the walls and go left.

10 You'll see two more breakable walls, one in the middle, and one at the end. Wait for your energy to replenish, and then go to the breakable wall at the end of the area at **Position H** and punch through that wall. The noise from breaking the wall will draw the guards, so immediately move back to the left where the other breakable wall is at **Position I**.
Wait until your energy replenishes, then punch through this last wall. The noise will draw the guards to this location, so quickly exit through the hole you made at **Position H** and move due West to the next area. [→□ 1]

11 Take cover at the corner of the wall and look down the hallway to see two guards. One guard will move off to the left, and the Heavy will move toward you. When the Heavy is close, wait for him to move away from you, then go forward and take cover at the box located at **Position J**.

12 The Heavy will move off to the North and take up a position looking off to the right. Wait for the second guard to move down and get close to the Heavy. When he does, move to your right through the raised door and take cover in that area.

13 Hold your position and wait for the guards to come back on patrol. Watch your radar and once the Heavy takes up position off to your left and the other guard is in the small alcove to the West. Move to your right and head North to the opening at the far end of this area located at **Position K**. Waste no time once you reach the end; keep moving quickly out and to your right to find the exit door at **Position L**. Go through the door, and you're done.

Alice Garden Pods

ROUTE 2 Stealth Combat

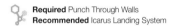

Required Punch Through Walls
Recommended Icarus Landing System

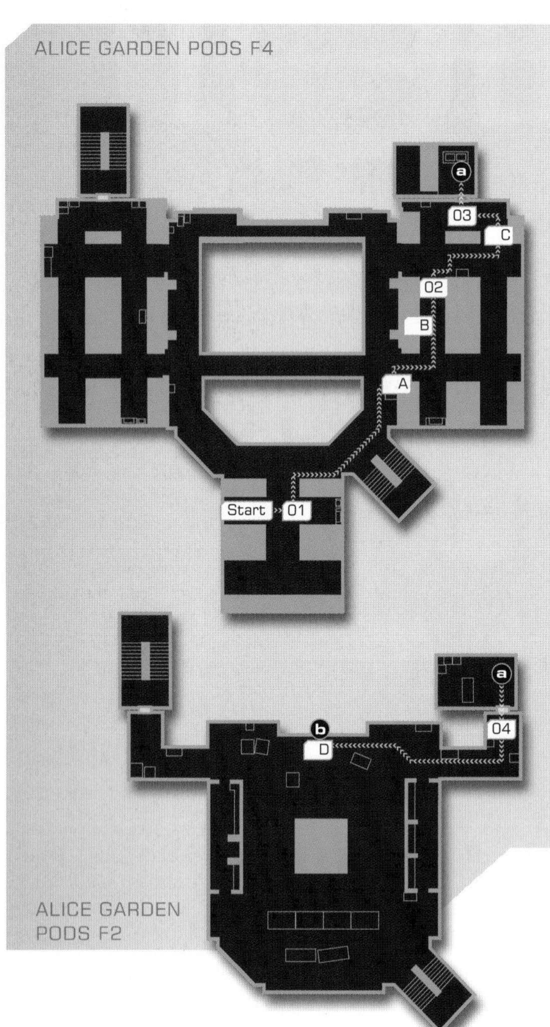

01 When finished with Van Bruggen, move to the doorway and wait for the guards to left and right to enter their respective pod rooms. Now go right and past the stairs to Pod Room 4 and take cover at the right side of the door at **Position A**. Hold your position and wait for the guard nearest you to move off to the left. As he does, move inside and go left. If you're quick, you can easily use a Takedown as he investigates Pod #405 at **Position B**.

02 Move north and then go right to take cover at the vending machine there. Hold your position here and let your energy replenish. Wait, and soon the last guard in this room will move to the left to investigate Pod #443 at **Position C**. Once he does, move up behind him for a Takedown. [→□ 2]

03 When you have taken down the last guard, go north to find a breakable wall. Punch through it and move forward. There is a drop to your left that will let your reach the floor below, but it is a long fall. If you have the Icarus Aug, then just drop down. Otherwise, use the vents, scaffolding, and table to drop down in small steps so that you take no damage.

04 Move forward and take cover at the box. Look out into the Food Court, and you'll see three guards. When all three of them head to the left towards the far end of the room, move forward and to your right to the stairwell located at **Position D**. Go down the stairs and then to the left to reach the Locker Rooms.

Tip **If desired, you can take out the three guards in the Food Court. Stay at the bottom of the stairs and take cover at the left side. Wait here, and soon Narhari Kahn will move close enough to the stairs for you to see him from your position. He will have his back to you, so ease up the stairs, making sure that you are mindful of the Heavies on the left and right. Get behind Kahn and take him out with a Takedown. Once he is down, immediately drag his body back down the stairs and hide it off to the left.**

Now go back to your cover point to the left of the stairs and wait. Watch your radar, and when the guard on the right gets close and then moves away, make your way up the stairs and go left and take cover in the food vendor stand there. Stay crouching and move south inside the vendor stands to the end and take cover. The Heavy will take position to the left. When he moves away, go after him for a Takedown, and then hide his body in the vendor stands.

Watch for the last heavy to appear east of your position in the western vendors' stands. When he turns around and goes back to the left, move up and take position at the row of soda machines ahead. Wait for the heavy to come back and then move off again. When he does, follow him for a Takedown.

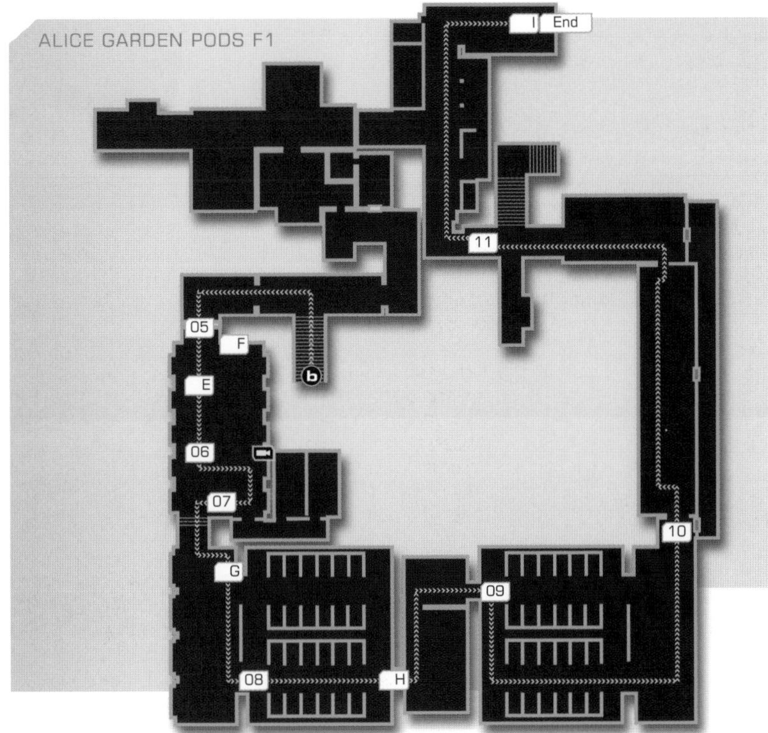

05 Once you are through the Locker Room door, take cover at the first row of lockers at **Position E**. The patrolling guard here will stop just ahead on the right side. Lean out to the left and fire a Tranquilizer Rifle dart at the wall at **Position F**, just to the left of the lockers. [→☐ 3]
Make sure you hit the wall there so that the guard is behind the row of lockers where you're taking cover out of view of the camera. The guard will go to investigate where the Tranquilizer Rifle dart hit, and when he does, get behind him for a Takedown.

06 When the guard is down, stay on the western side of the locker room and move to the end and go left past the camera. The camera only faces left, so stay to its right and you'll get by undetected.

07 Ignore the door on the left and go through the open doorway on the right instead. Stay crouching and make your way to the left of the next doorway at **Position G** and take cover. Watch the guards ahead, and when both are looking away from you, jump to cover across the doorway. The Turret ahead will get a brief look at you, but it will not be able to lock on, so ignore it.

08 Remain crouched and go into the shower area on the right. There is a Frag Mine ahead, so approach it very slowly and deactivate it. The guards in this room are off to the left. They won't be able to see you past the showers that are between you and them, so stay crouching and you'll remain undetected. When you're done with the Frag Mine, move to the end of the showers to **Position H**.

Tip **If you want to take out the two guards here, some creative distraction will do the trick. There is a trash can next to the Security Hub located to the left of Position H. Grab the trash can, and throw it at the wall to the right of the exit door ahead. Now take cover in the left-hand shower stall and wait for the guards to come and investigate.**

One guard will get very close and go right to the trash can, the other will stay back a little. Watch your radar, and you'll soon see the second guard walk off. Now watch the remaining guard near you. When he begins to move off to the left, get behind him for a Takedown. Hide his body in the middle room to the east so that the next guard won't see him.

To get the remaining guard, simply repeat the procedure of throwing the trash can at the wall and waiting for him to come and investigate. Once he begins to walk off, follow him for a Takedown.

09 Move forward to make your way to the showers. The floor here is electrified on the left side of the room and booby-trapped with Frag Mines on the right. If you have the Jump Aug, stay on the left and move forward by jumping over the low shower walls. Otherwise, go right and move very slowly towards each mine, so that you can deactivate it. There are three mines in all that you'll need to deactivate, if you choose to go up the right side of the room.

10 Crouch down in front of the Laundry Room doors, enter the Laundry Room and take cover behind the laundry cart ahead. Wait, and a guard will come up on your left. Watch him, and as soon as he turns his back to you, ease out and take him down with a Takedown [→☐ 4]. Now take cover at the washing machines just past the laundry cart and look right to see a guard that has taken up position just ahead. Wait, and he will soon move up close to you and on your right. Stay in cover, and once the guard turns his back, ease out for a Takedown.

11 Move through the Laundry Room and go left. Keep going and take cover at the corner of the wall at the next hallway. Ahead you will see two guards, a Heavy and a regular guard. The regular guard will go into a small alcove on the left, and the Heavy will move toward you and stop halfway up the hallway.
When the Heavy turns around and begins moving away from you, lean out and shoot him in the back with the Tranquilizer Rifle. Make sure you hit him in the body as you are counting on the delay of a body shot so that the Heavy is able to get back down the hall before passing out. The second guard will come out just as the Heavy falls at the far end.

When the remaining guard notices his comrade is down, he will rush over and try to revive him. As soon as you see the remaining guard going to the Heavy, quickly sprint to his location and use a Takedown [→☐ 1]. Now go through the exit located at **Position I** to finish this.

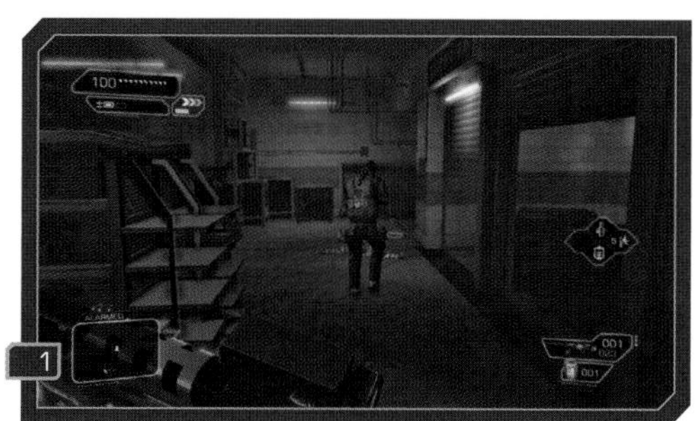
1

ROUTE 3 Combat

Required Reflex Booster
Recommended Dermal Plating, Typhoon

Recommended Combat Rifle, Revolver (w/ Exploding Rounds), Frag Grenade

01 When you're ready exit the Pod Room you are in. Sprint to the right to the 400s Pod Room and use a Takedown on one guard. If you're fast, you can get a Double Takedown. Otherwise, take cover and then shoot the other guard.

02 Enter Pod Room 4 and go left. Exit through the doorway and then take cover at the plating on the railing ahead. Hold your position here and then target the guards directly opposite you. When you have taken them out, begin targeting the guards on the catwalk below you.
Stay on this level. Move as needed so as to target the enemies below from your cover point at the railing. Once all guards on your level and Level 3 below are dead, only the three guards in the Food Court will remain. When only those three are left, make your way down to the second floor using the fire escape stairs located in Pod Room 5.

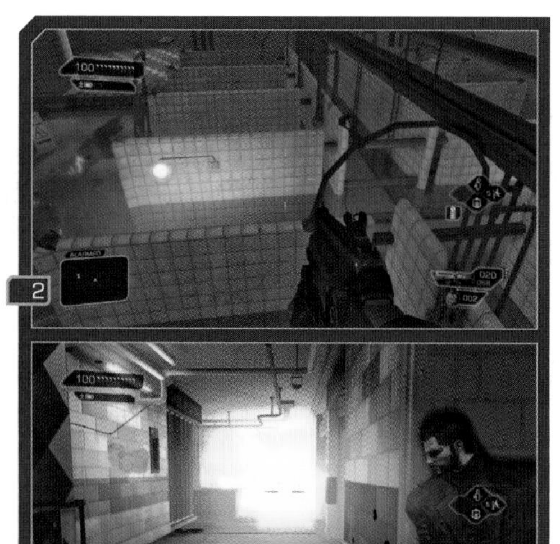
2
3

03 When you come out of the fire escape stairwell, immediately take cover at the corner of the wall ahead. Peek out to the right and watch for the guards. When you see one, go for a headshot. Now hold your position here, and pick off the remaining guards. When they are all dead, make your way to the stairs located at **Position A**.

04 Go through the Locker Room and go left to take cover at the end of the row of lockers. Look left, and shoot the guard with an un-silenced weapon, once his back is to you. Hold your position here and pick off the next two guards as they come running. If you lose sight of one of the two guards, keep an eye on your radar as he may be trying to circle around and shoot you in the back.

05 Exit the Locker Room and go through the doorway on the right. Move to the next room and take cover on the left-hand side of the door. From your cover point, you can easily lean out to shoot the Turret in the next room. To avoid damage, peek out for one or two shots, then fall back into cover. Keep doing this until the Turret has been destroyed. To make this even easier, use a Frag or EMP Grenade on the Turret.

06 Move forward to make your way to the showers. Here, on the left side of the room, the floor is electrified and, on the right, booby-trapped with Frag Mines. If you have the Jump Aug, stay on the left and move forward by jumping over the low shower walls [→☐ 2]. Otherwise, go right and approach each mine very slowly so that you can deactivate it. There are three mines in total that you'll need to deactivate, if you decide to go up the right-hand side of the room.

07 Push forward and go into the Laundry Room. As soon as you pass through the Laundry Room doors, take cover behind the laundry cart ahead. Peek out left, and unload on the two guards ahead. The Combat Rifle's high rate of fire makes this very easy, and the Revolver's Explosive rounds are also an excellent choice.

08 Go through the Laundry Room and then move left. Go down the hallway and take cover at the corner of the wall at the end of the hall where it turns to the right. The gunfire in the Laundry Room area will usually have the guards on alert here. If you have a Frag Grenade, then lean out from cover and toss it between the two guards in the hallway ahead [→☐ 3]. If you don't have a Frag, just hold your position at the corner and then lean out for headshots to take out both guards. When they are both dead, move forward to **Position B** to find the exit door.

			Stealth Bonuses	
Objective Completed	Objective Type	XP Reward	Ghost	Smooth Operator
Meet Van Bruggen in the Alice Garden Pods	Primary	1000	No	No
Steal an Employee Card from a TYM employee	Primary	1000	No	No
Bring the Employee Card to Van Bruggen	Primary	1000	No	No
Escape the Alice Garden pods Ambush	Primary	1000	Yes	No

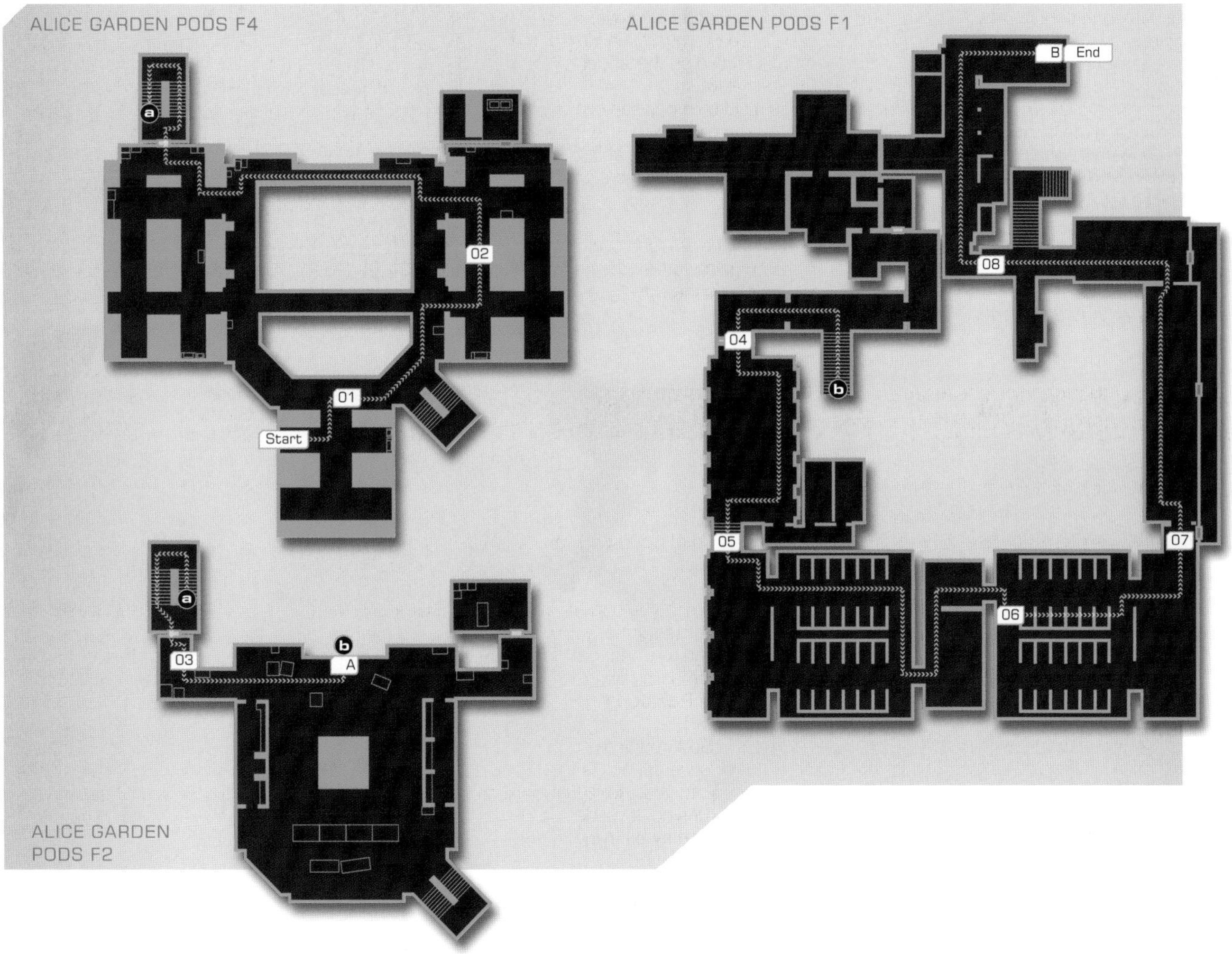

ALICE GARDEN PODS F4

ALICE GARDEN PODS F1

ALICE GARDEN PODS F2

Start 01 02 03 04 05 06 07 08 A B End

TAI YONG MEDICAL EMPLOYEE SHUTTLE

Objective Name	Objective Type
Go to TYM via the Employee Shuttle	Primary

Now that you've made it out of Alice Garden Pods alive, it's time to press on with your mission. Van Bruggen encoded your TYM Employee Card with your biometrics so that you can use the shuttle to reach TYM. Make your way to the Shuttle Station located to the left of the LIMB Clinic in the Kuaigan District. Enter the station and then go to the shuttle to board it. [→☐ 4]

			Stealth Bonuses	
Objective Completed	Objective Type	XP Reward	Ghost	Smooth Operator
Go to TYM via the Employee Shuttle	Primary	1000	No	No

TAI YONG MEDICAL

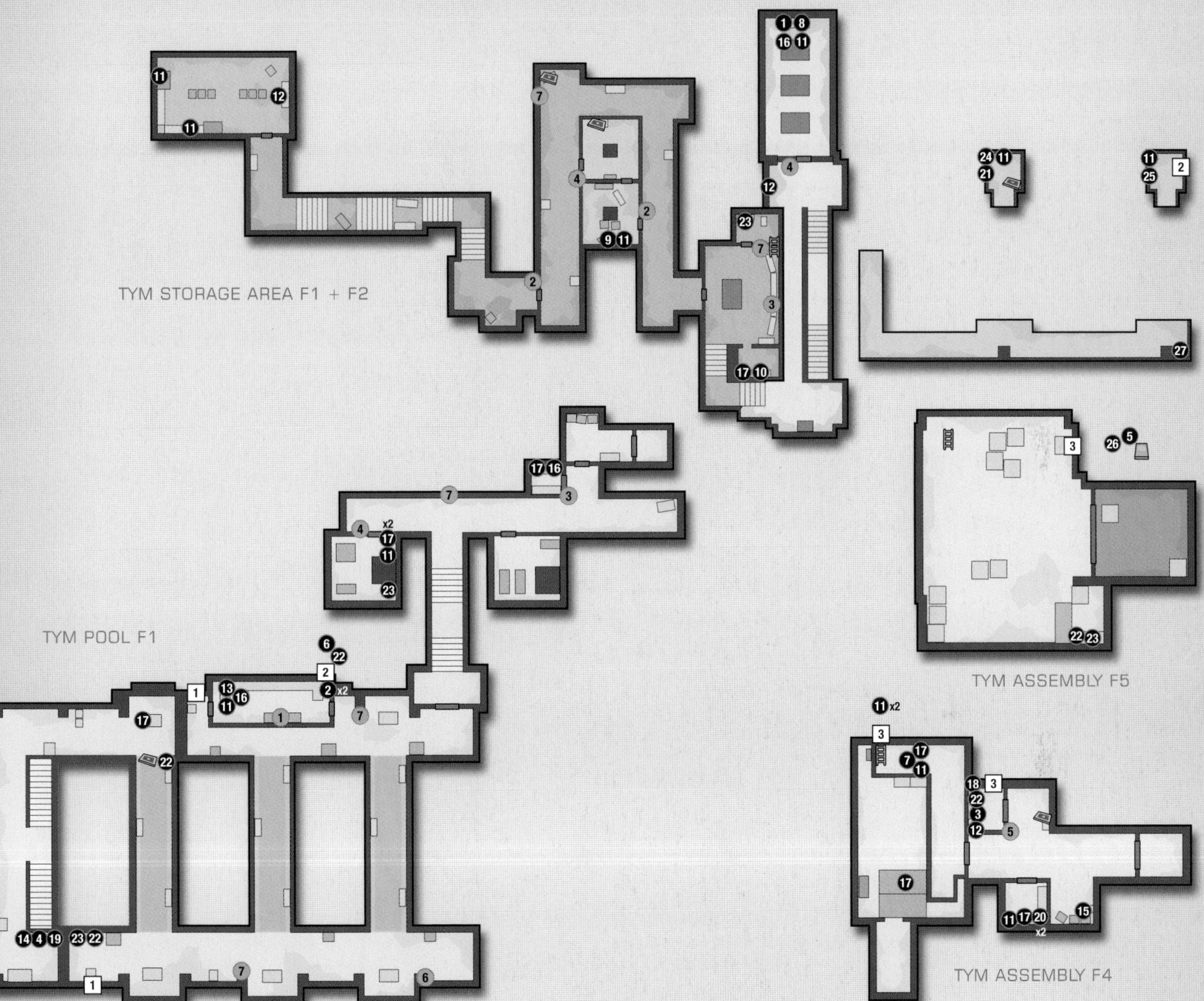

1. 10mm Pistol
2. Combat Rifle
3. P.E.P.S.
4. Revolver
5. Tranquilizer Rifle
6. Stun Gun
7. Concussion Grenade
8. EMP Grenade
9. Gas Grenade
10. Mine Template
11. Credit Chip
12. Cyberboost ProEnergy Bar
13. CyberBoost ProEnergy Pack
14. Nuke Virus Software
15. Stop Virus Software
16. 10mm Pistol Ammo
17. Machine Pistol Ammo
18. P.E.P.S. Energy Pack
19. Revolver Ammo
20. Shotgun Cartridge
21. Sniper Rifle Ammo
22. Stun Gun Dart
23. Tranquilizer Rifle Dart
24. Crossbow Arrow
25. Ammo Capacity Upgrade
26. Reload Speed Upgrade
27. Silenced Sniper Rifle

- Praxis Kit
- Pocket Secretary
- eBook
- Punch Through Wall
- 1 Vent 1
- 2 Vent 2
- 3 Vent 3

1. Security Terminal - Level 2
2. Security Panels - Level 1
3. Security Panels - Level 2
4. Security Panels - Level 3
5. Security Panels - Level 4
6. Laser Grid Panels - Level 2
7. Alarm Panels - Level 3

TAI YONG MEDICAL F1

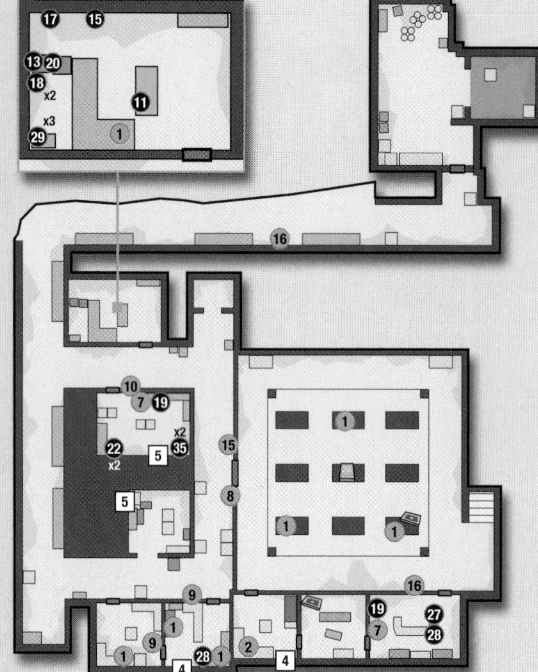

TAI YONG MEDICAL F2

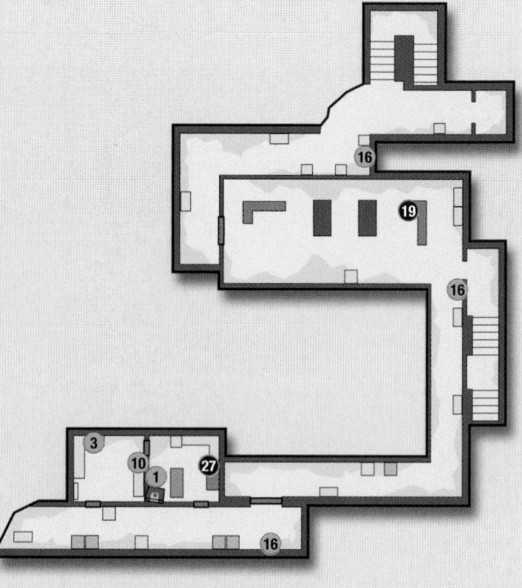

TAI YONG MEDICAL F3

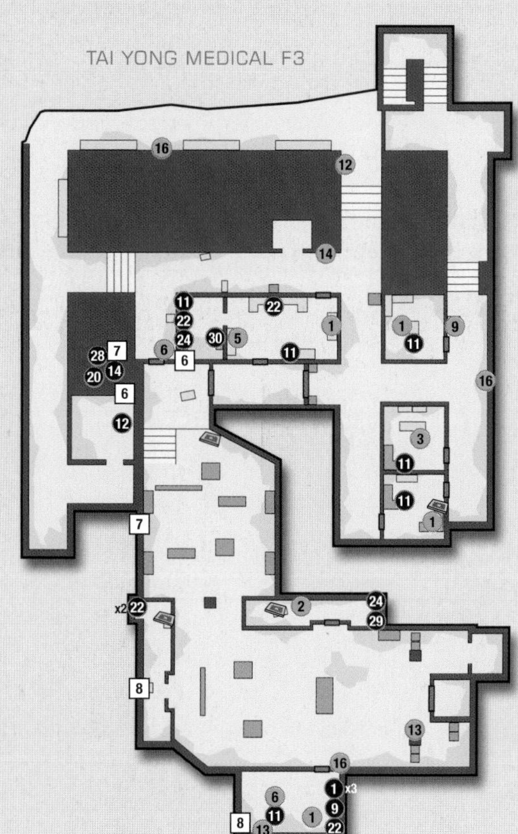

- 1 Combat Rifle
- 2 Heavy Rifle
- 3 Machine Pistol
- 4 P.E.P.S.
- 5 Revolver
- 6 Rocket Launcher
- 7 Frag Grenade
- 8 EMP Grenade
- 9 Gas Grenade
- 10 Mine Template
- 11 Credit Chip
- 12 Cyberboost ProEnergy Bar
- 13 CyberBoost ProEnergy Pack
- 14 CyberBoost ProEnergy Jar
- 15 Pain Killers
- 16 HypoStim
- 17 Nuke Virus Software
- 18 Beer
- 19 Combat Rifle Ammo
- 20 Crossbow Arrow
- 21 Heavy Rifle Ammo
- 22 Machine Pistol Ammo
- 23 P.E.P.S. Energy Pack
- 24 Revolver Ammo
- 25 Rocket Launcher Ammo
- 26 Shotgun Cartridge
- 27 Stun Gun Dart
- 28 Tranquilizer Rifle Dart
- 29 Typhoon Ammo
- 30 10mm Pistol Ammo

- Praxis Kit
- Pocket Secretary
- eBook
- Punch Through Wall
- 4 Vent 4
- 5 Vent 5
- 6 Vent 6
- 7 Vent 7
- 8 Vent 8
- 9 Vent 9
- 10 Vent 10

- 1 Computer - Unlocked
- 2 Computer - Level 2
- 3 Computer - Level 3
- 4 Computer - Level 4
- 5 Security Terminal - Level 1
- 6 Security Terminal - Level 2
- 7 Security Terminal - Level 3
- 8 Security Panels - Level 1
- 9 Security Panels - Level 2
- 10 Security Panels - Level 3
- 11 Security Panels - Level 4
- 12 Laser Grid Panels - Level 1
- 13 Laser Grid Panels - Level 2
- 14 Laser Grid Panels - Level 3
- 15 Alarm Panels - Level 1
- 16 Alarm Panels - Level 3
- 17 Safe Panel - Level 5

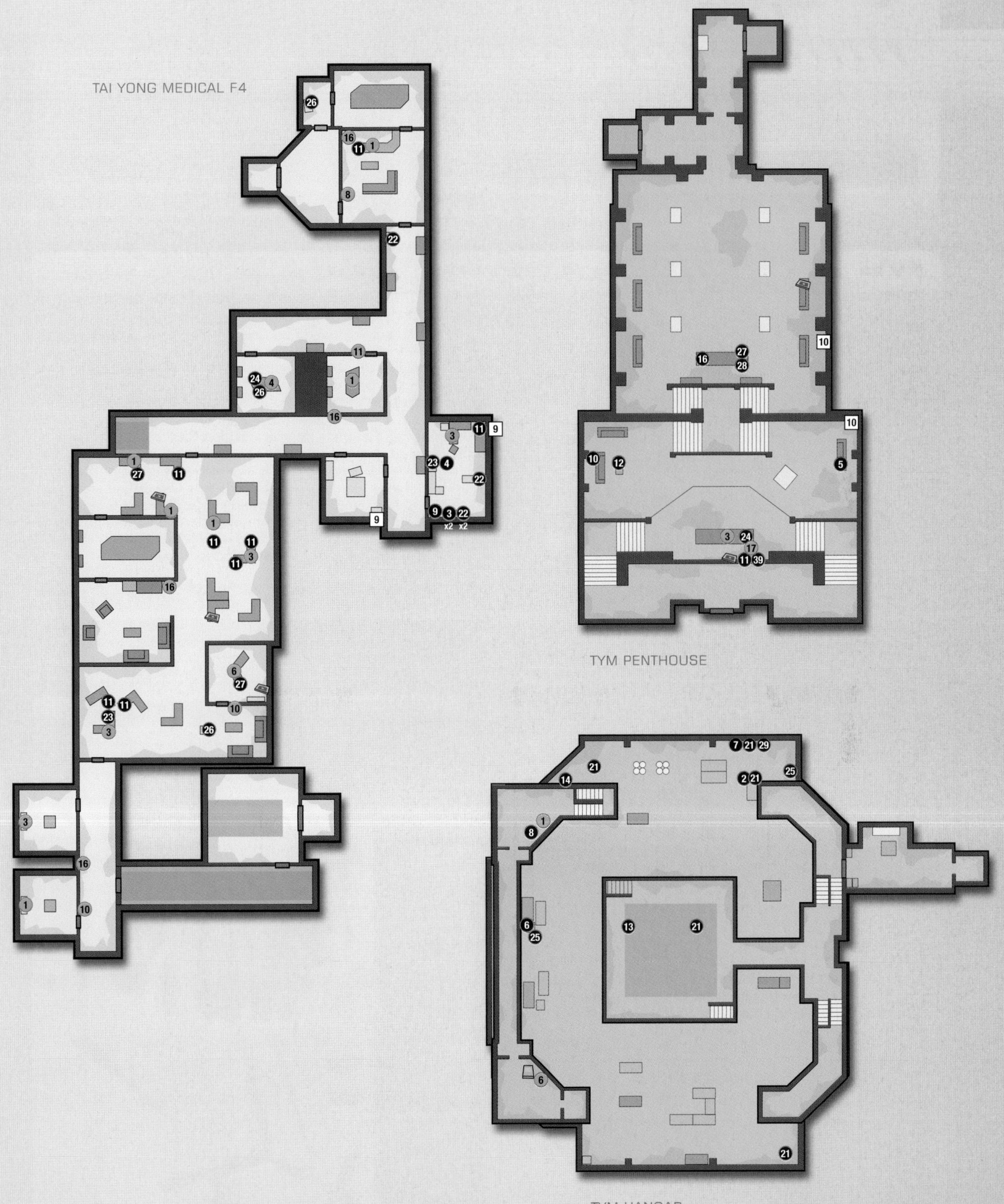
TAI YONG MEDICAL F4
TYM PENTHOUSE
TYM HANGAR

M1 - SEARCHING FOR PROOF

Objective Name	Objective Type
Enter TYM's tower by passing through the Pangu	Primary
Rescue a TYM employee	Secondary

TYM AUGMENTATION STORAGE AREA

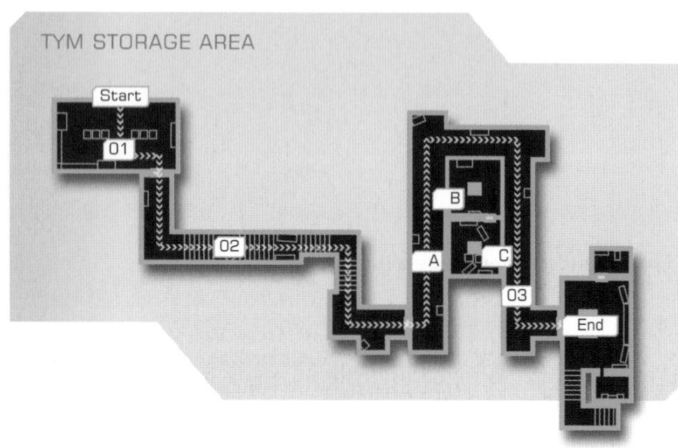

01 When you get off the TYM Employee Shuttle, you'll be in the TYM Shuttle Station. There are some lockers here you can search for items and a credit chip under the vending machine in the northwest. When you're ready, go through the Emergency Service door to reach the next area.

02 Proceed through the service hallways to reach a locked door. It's a Level 1 Hack, so it won't present much of a problem. Once you are past the door, move to **Position A** to trigger a cutscene and a secondary objective of saving a TYM employee.

OPTIONAL EXPLORATION

To save the employee and complete the Secondary Objective, there is a door at Position B that is a Level 3 Hack. It's a tough Hack and you'll probably need to use Worms and Nukes to get past it. Once you have managed that, use the valve in the next room to turn off the gas.

Alternatively, there is a door at Position C that is only a Level 1 Hack and so is much easier to hack, but that door leads to the gas-filled room. If you have the Rebreather Aug, enter the room and turn the gas off. Then make your way over to the employee and talk to him. To reach the employee, you'll need to move two small crates and then crouch to get under the wreckage blocking your path. Talking to the employee will give you an easy way past the guard that is located in the next room.

03 Continue forward to the control booth of the Cryo-Sterilization Pool. When you go through the door and enter the room, a cutscene will trigger, and you'll face a choice with the guard in the room. If you saved Lee earlier for the Secondary Objective, then mentioning Lee is the best option. [→☐ 1]

Security Guard Choices

Choice	Outcome
Intimidate	Sounds alarm and you fight.
Bluff	He goes on patrol down the stairs, so take him out.
Bribe	He takes credits and leaves, same as employee option.
Mention Lee	He goes away leaving you free to explore.

Inside Tai Yong Medical

ROUTE 1 Stealth

Required Icarus Landing System, Cloaking System
Recommended Jump Enhancement, Move/Throw Heavy Objects

OPTIONAL EXPLORATION

Before moving the catwalk, use its current position to reach a room at Position A with Credits, ammo, and a Pocket Secretary with the Pump Room code. Once you've visited that room, backtrack to the Control Room and move the catwalk. Note: You have to hack the Security Keypad first to open the doors of the catwalk.

01 In the control booth, go to the Security Keypad on the east side of the room. It's a Level 2 Hack, so hack it to enable the catwalk positioning controls. After you've hacked the terminal, press the red button to move the catwalk. Then go left out of the door and use the ladder at **Position B** to get on the catwalk above you.

02 Follow the catwalk around to a room with a vent and some lockers you can explore. You'll find an Ammo Capacity Upgrade for one of your weapons and some Credits in the locker on the left. When you're ready, open the vent and enter the air ducts to reach a large vertical air tunnel There is no ladder here and the fall will kill you, so the Icarus Landing System is required [→☐ 2]. When you reach the bottom, go through the air duct to the next vent.

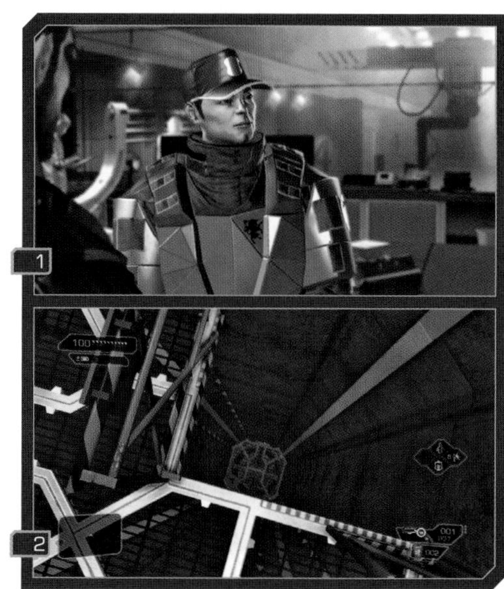

03 Open the vent, and ease out into the room ahead. Stay crouched and move through the door on the left. Once you are out of the door, hug the left wall and move forward under the camera to the door at **Position C**. Go through the door to reach the stairwell there.

04 Move slowly up the stairs just far enough to see the guard. Wait for him to move right and stop. Move up to the corner of the wall and take cover at **Position D**. Watch the guard, and when he walks away down the hall, follow him. When you reach the door on the left at the far end of the hall, the guard will turn left to the door. Stay to the right and ease past him and take cover at the electrical unit located at **Position E**. Hold your position here, and wait for the guard to go back down the hallway. Then go to the door and use it to enter the room ahead. Once through the door, you will find an elevator at **Position F** that you can use to reach the next area.

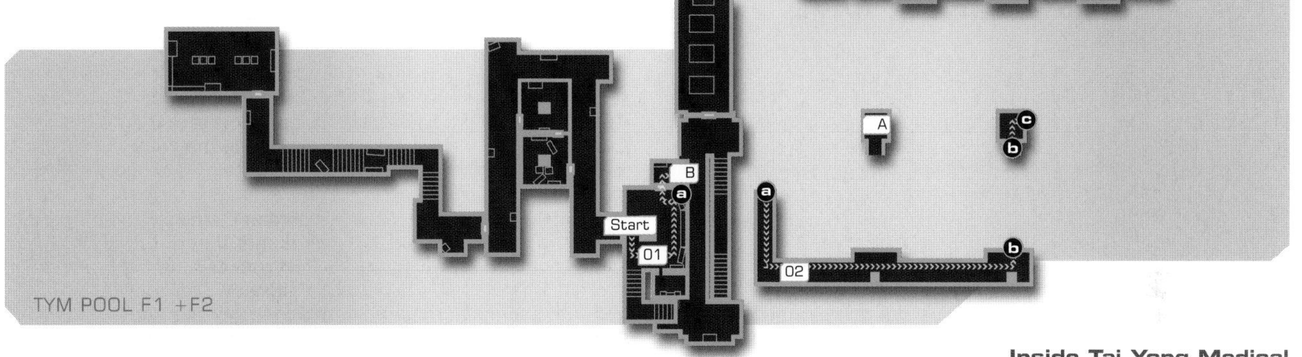

ROUTE 2 Stealth Combat

Required Move/Throw Heavy Objects, Reflex Booster, Hacking: Capture 2
Recommended Icarus Landing System, Cloaking System

Recommended Tranquilizer Rifle

01 Start by exiting the control booth and use a Takedown on the Security Guard for some extra XP. He will be there if you mentioned Lee during the earlier confrontation. When he is down, drag the body a little way along the hall so the scientists in the control booth don't see the body through the glass door. Now go back into the control booth and go right down the stairs at **Position A**. Then make your way down to the bottom floor.

02 Go forward to the northern end of the area and look right. Ahead is a camera. Watch it, and when it is facing to the left, sprint forward and get under it so that it can't see you. Stay under the camera and watch its motion. When it is facing to the right, move forward whilst crouched and take cover at the equipment located at **Position B**.

03 There is another camera just ahead on the southern wall. Watch its movements, and when it is facing to your right, move forward while crouching and get under it. Now, watch the camera again, and when it pans back to the north, go left to the west and get behind the large crate at **Position C**. Move the crate a bit, and you'll expose a vent [→☐ 3]. Open it and move into the air ducts. As you move through the air ducts to the exit, you'll come across a cardboard box with a Pocket Secretary in it. It's worth grabbing that Pocket Secretary as it has codes for doors later on in the level.

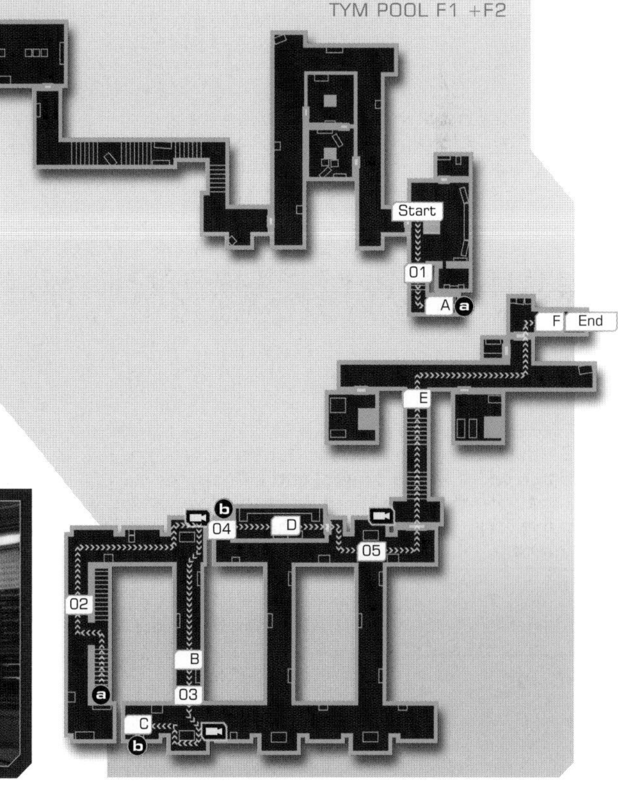

04 There is a door to your left and two guards inside the room ahead. Open the door, then move forward whilst crouched and stay to the right. Once you are close enough to the guards, perform a Double Takedown to dispatch them both. Now take cover at **Position D** and look south to see a guard on patrol. Shoot him with the Tranquilizer Rifle. With that done, hack the Security Hub here and turn off all the cameras. It's a Level 2 Hack, which shouldn't give you too much trouble.

05 Exit the control booth via the eastern door and move ahead to the door on your left. Ease up the stairs ahead slowly so that you can just about see the guard patrolling the corridor at the top. Once he starts moving to the right, quietly ascend the stairs and take cover at **Position E**.
When the guard moves off and passes the first door on the right he will have his back to you, so move up behind him for a Takedown. Now go forward to the elevator at **Position F** and use it to reach the next area.

Inside Tai Yong Medical

ROUTE 3 Combat

Required Reflex Booster
Recommended Dermal Plating, Typhoon

Recommended Combat Rifle, Revolver (w/ Exploding Rounds), 10mm Pistol (Silenced), Frag Grenade

01 Follow the Security Guard out of the control booth and kill him with a Takedown or a silenced weapon. Now go back into the control booth and go right down the stairs located at **Position A** and make your way to the bottom floor.

02 Go north and then take a right. There is a camera ahead that you should get under. Once you are there, shoot the camera to set off the alarm, and then take cover at the equipment box here. Lean out to the right and watch the bridge ahead. It won't be long before the guards will come running, so hold your position here and pick them all off. [→☐ 1]
There are also two Medium Sentrys in the area, so don't leave this position until they have shown up and you've destroyed them both. When all of them are dead, make your way over to the elevator at **Position B**. There are no more guards in the area to offer you any resistance, so it's a simple walk to reach the elevator.

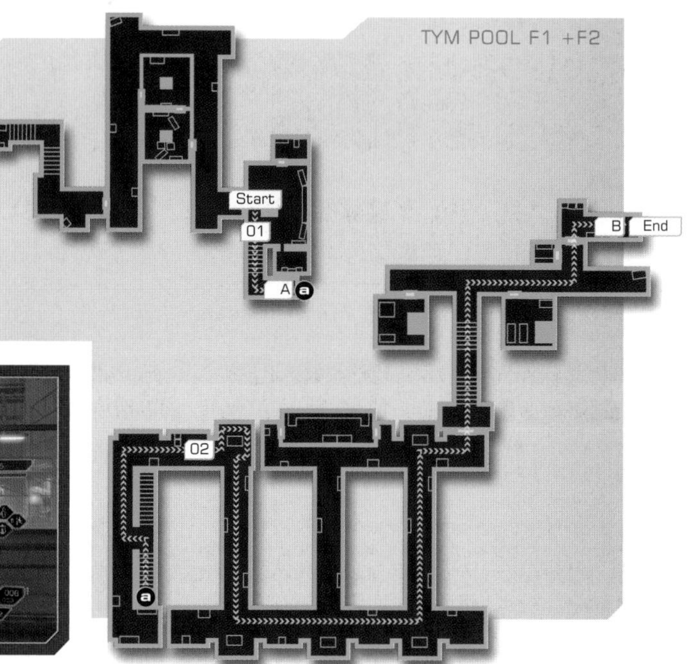

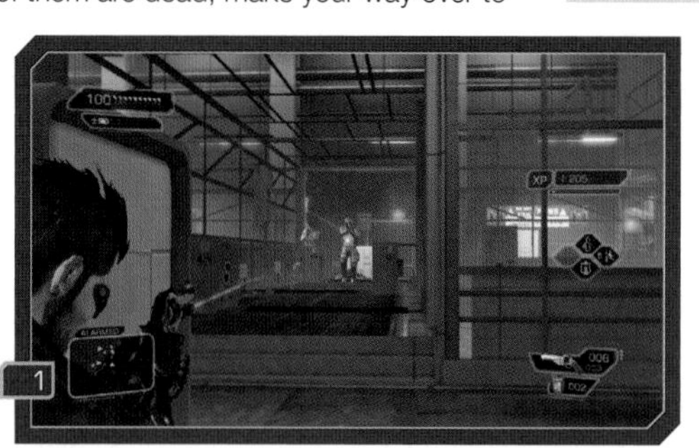
1

TYM Assembly Lines

REACHING THE MAINTENANCE ELEVATOR

Recommended Icarus Landing System, Jump Enhancement

01 When you get off the elevator, you'll see an electrified floor in the room ahead. The cut-off switch for the electricity is in the locked cage to your right, but it is a Level 4 Hack to get in. However, there is another way. Move into the next room, making sure you stay clear of the electricity, and go right to **Position A**.
There you'll find a vent. Open it and enter the air ducts. Move forward and take your first right to find another vent that will let you into the locked cage. Flip the switch to turn off the electricity, and then exit the cage and go to the next room.

Tip **To the right of the vent are some tall crates. Jump over them to enter the small area behind. There you'll find a pair of lockers. Inside the one on the left is a Concussion Grenade that will come in handy later.**

02 On the southern side of this room is a storage area with some crates, shelving and other equipment. You need to jump up onto the shelving and then jump to the catwalk on the eastern side of the room. If you have the Jump Enhancement augmentation, then this is pretty easy [→☐ 2]. Without it, you'll need to use the small crates in the area to help you make the jump to the shelves above. Once you are on the catwalk above, go to **Position B** and use the ladder there.

03 The elevator you need to use is directly ahead to the east. It's a simple matter to use it to reach the next area. However, before you do, we strongly suggest you do the Optional Exploration in this area as it will make this mission a bit easier in the areas ahead.

2

Note **The Stealth route assumes that you are going to do this Optional Exploration and will get the Employee Access Card that is here.**

OPTIONAL EXPLORATION

Go to Position C and grab the large crate there. Move that crate to the left-hand side of the room and place it at Position D just below the vent. If you don't have the Jump Aug, you'll need to get the small crate from the room at Position C and place it near the large crate in order to jump on top of it. If you have the Jump augmentation, then jump up onto the large crate and open the vent.

Go through the air ducts and drop down the large vertical air tunnel. The fall is long and will kill you unless you have the Icarus Landing System. When you reach the bottom, investigate the dead body to find an Access Card that you will need later in this mission. You'll also find some Credits, a Darrow eBook, a Tranquilizer Rifle, a Pocket Secretary and Reload Speed Upgrade for one of your weapons.

When you're ready, use the vent on the eastern wall to get into the air ducts. Use the air ducts to reach the previous area, and then follow your earlier route to get back to the elevator at Point 03.

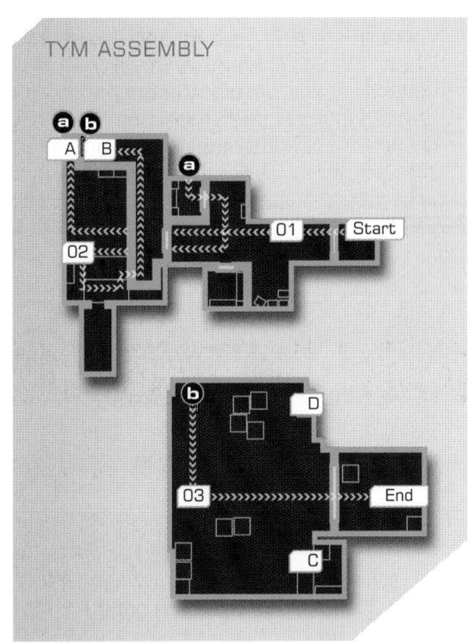

ACHIEVEMENT/TROPHY: DOCTORATE

If you do the Optional Exploration in this area, you'll find one of Hugh Darrow's eBooks.

Objective Completed	Objective Type	XP Reward	Stealth Bonuses: Ghost	Stealth Bonuses: Smooth Operator
Enter TYM's tower by passing through the Pangu	Primary	1750	Yes	Yes
Rescue a TYM employee	Secondary	750	No	No

Tai Yong Medical Laboratories

ROUTE 1 Stealth

Required Icarus Landing System, Cloaking System
Recommended Jump Enhancement, Move/Throw Heavy Objects, Social Enhancer

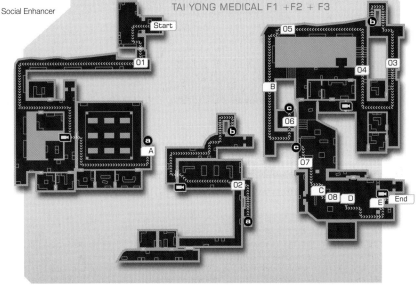

TAI YONG MEDICAL F1 +F2 + F3

01 After you exit the elevator, go left through the door and then head right down the walkway. Take the first left, ignore the two guards there and you will come to a guarded door. You should have done the Optional Exploration earlier in this section and have the Employee Access Card. This allows you to pass by the guard easily.
If you don't have the card, then please refer to the Stealth Combat Route for this area to learn how to obtain it. Alternatively, you could backtrack to the previous area and do the Optional Exploration. Once you are past the guarded door, move through the labs to the stairs on the eastern side of the room at **Position A**. Take the stairs up to the next level.

02 Move forward through this room to the door on the western side of the room. Go through the door and head to the right. Press onward, and you'll soon come to some stairs on the left. Use the stairs to reach the next level above you.

3

03 Go through the hallways and take a right just past the stairs. Approach the guard that is positioned under the camera for a cutscene. If you have the Social Enhancer (CASIE Aug), then you can use Pheromones to get some additional information from this guard. He is a Beta Personality type.

04 Go to the laser grid at the bottom of the stairs to the north. Once there, wait for the guards to disperse. After they are gone, hack the laser grid. It's a Level 1 Hack so it won't present too much of a problem. There is a lone guard patrolling this immediate area, so wait for him to come back. When he moves away on patrol, crouch down and follow him. [→☐ 3]
Stay close, and as he turns right to go to the railing, move left next to the planter to avoid detection, then ease past him. If you have problems getting past this guard, then activate your Cloak at the last minute to get past him easily.

05 Once past the first guard, take cover at the planter here, and peek out to the right. Watch the Heavy that is patrolling in the distance. He will move to **Position B** and stop. He'll be facing your direction, so wait until he turns around and moves away. Then move forward whilst crouched. Be aware of the door to the left as you press forward. If the guard patrolling that area is facing in your direction, then activate Cloak to get past the door.
Press onward and catch up with the Heavy ahead. When you reach him, go left into the hallway there and then take another left to reach a small storage room.

06 In the storage room, move the two crates at the northern wall to expose a breakable wall. Watch your radar and wait for the heavy to move off. Once he is out of earshot, punch through the wall and then use the ladder inside to reach the upper platform [→☐ 1]. On that platform is a vent. Open it and use the air ducts to gain access to the Data Core room.

07 You'll exit the vent and be in the Data Core room on top of some equipment. Look about the room before dropping down, and you'll see a very complex laser grid security system. Start by moving right and dropping off the boxes you are on. Move forward while crouching to get under the lasers just ahead.
When you're ready, activate Cloak and move to the equipment array just ahead at **Position C** and take cover there. Stay in cover so as to avoid detection by the guards in the Security Room to the south. Hold your position here and wait for your energy to replenish.

08 When you have sufficient energy, activate Cloak and move ahead and to the right to take position behind the equipment array at **Position D**. Look to the east to see two small crates. Move the crate on the right and then press forward to the elevator at **Position E**. As you move to the elevator, be mindful of the camera located just above it. It has a limited scan radius, so as long as you stay a bit to the right, you can get under the camera and push the elevator button. Use the elevator to reach the next area.

ROUTE 2 | Stealth Combat

Required Hacking: Capture 3, Reflex Booster, Cloaking System
Recommended Jump Enhancement

Recommended Tranquilizer Rifle, Stun Gun

01 Move through the area and make your way to where the two guards are talking just outside the Security Room. Get close to them, and use a Double Takedown to take them both down. Now that you've taken care of them, turn around and go left up the walkway.

02 Make your way to this storage room. Once you are inside, look left to the northwest corner and you'll see a vent covered by two small boxes [→☐ 2]. Move those boxes and enter the vent. Follow the air ducts around to the Security Room.

03 In the Security Room you'll find an Employee Access Card. If you didn't get the one during the Optional Exploration in the previous area, then you need this one. Grab the card and then hack the Security Hub if you wish. It's a Level 3 Hack, and it's a bit tough, so you'll need to use Stops and Nukes to get past it. Once you access it, turn off the camera.

04 Make your way to the guarded door that leads to the lab. You should have an Employee Access Card at this point, so you'll get past the guard easily. If you hacked the Security Hub in the Security Room and turned off the camera here, then go ahead and take out this guard with a Takedown for some extra XP. Now go through the door and through the lab to **Position A** and take the stairs up to the next level.

ACHIEVEMENT/TROPHY: DOCTORATE

You'll find one of Hugh Darrow's eBooks on a box under the Lab Station in the middle of the room.

05 There are a couple of guards ahead, but since you haven't set off an alarm, they won't bother you. Move through the areas ahead and make your way to the stairs that lead up to the next level.

06 Proceed through the hallways. Take a right just past the stairs and approach the guard positioned under the camera for a cut scene. If you have the Social Enhancer, you are able to use Pheromones to get additional information from this guard. His Personality type is Beta.

07 Go to the first laser grid on the left. Wait for the guard patrolling this area to come to your position. Watch, and he'll soon turn around and move off. Once he does, crouch down, activate Cloak, and move through the laser grid. [→☐ 3].
Keep following the guard and incapacitate him with a Takedown or the Stun Gun. When he is down, search him to find a Pocket Secretary with the codes to the Data Core room door.

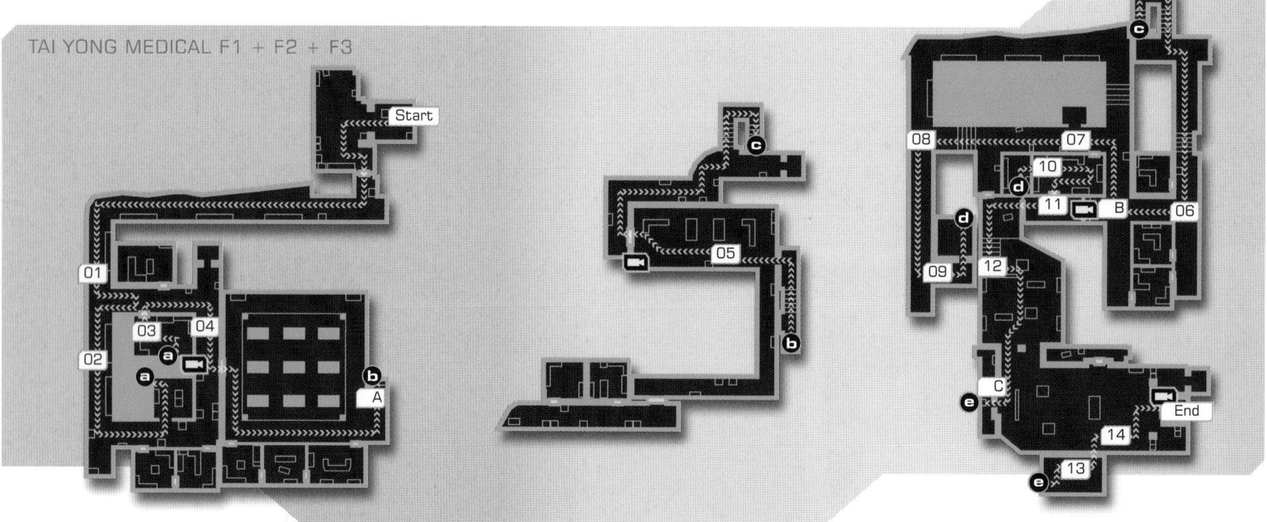

08 Just up the hall and on the left is the locked door to the Data Core room. You can use the code you just got from the Pocket Secretary to open the door now if you wish, but there is some more XP to be had if you desire. Make your way to the western end of the hall you're in and take cover at the left corner. Look out to the right and you'll see a Heavy. Let him get close and take up position near you. When he moves off and has his back to you, sneak up behind him for a Takedown.

09 Move to the southwest and enter the Storage Room there. On the right, you'll see a vent high up on the wall. Jump up on the crates under the vent so that you can reach it. Enter the air ducts and make your way to the other side.

10 Exit the vent and stay crouching. Approach the two guards in the next room and take them both out with a Double Takedown. Once they are down, you'll want to access the Security Hub. It's an easy Level 1 Hack, but you can find the password for it in an email on the PC in this room. Access the Security Hub and turn off all the cameras and open the locked door.

11 Go out of the door to the left of the Security Hub. Now crouch down and sneak up on the guard at **Position B**. Eliminate him with a Takedown. Next, backtrack down the hall and enter the Data Core room.

12 Position yourself behind the glass panel located at the foot of the stairs. When you're ready, activate Cloak and then sprint across the room and to the right. Up ahead is a small area on the right. There is another glass panel in front of that area's doorway, so once you get inside, you'll be safe from detection. [→☐ 4].
You can reach **Position C** with one energy cell if you have all the Longevity Upgrades for your Cloaking System Aug. Once you get to **Position C**, move the small crate there to expose the vent. Use the vent to enter the air ducts.

13 Open the vent and ease out into the room ahead. Stay crouched and stick close to the right-hand wall as you approach the guard directly ahead. When you are close enough, perform a Takedown. Now sit still and let your energy replenish, or use an Energy Bar. When you're ready, stay crouching and approach the remaining two guards. Get directly behind them and then stand up. They are preoccupied and won't see you, but because one is sitting down, you can't perform a Double Takedown.

Position yourself just behind and to the side of the standing guard, and then use a shot from the Stun Gun to incapacitate the one sitting down. As soon as you have fired your shot, perform a Takedown on the standing guard before he can turn around to take them both out without getting detected. [→☐ 5]

Note **Alternatively, a well placed Gas Grenade can also take out all three guards simultaneously. The weapons locker in this room has a Gas Grenade inside it, so you will get one back straight away even if you do use one.**

Now go back to the first guard you took down and hack the Security Hub on his desk to disable the camera outside. Then hack the Security Keypad on the wall to turn off all the laser security system.

14 Exit the Security Room and make your way to the elevator. Before boarding the elevator, there is a small room on the north side of the room that you can explore if you wish. When you're ready, use the elevator to reach the next area.

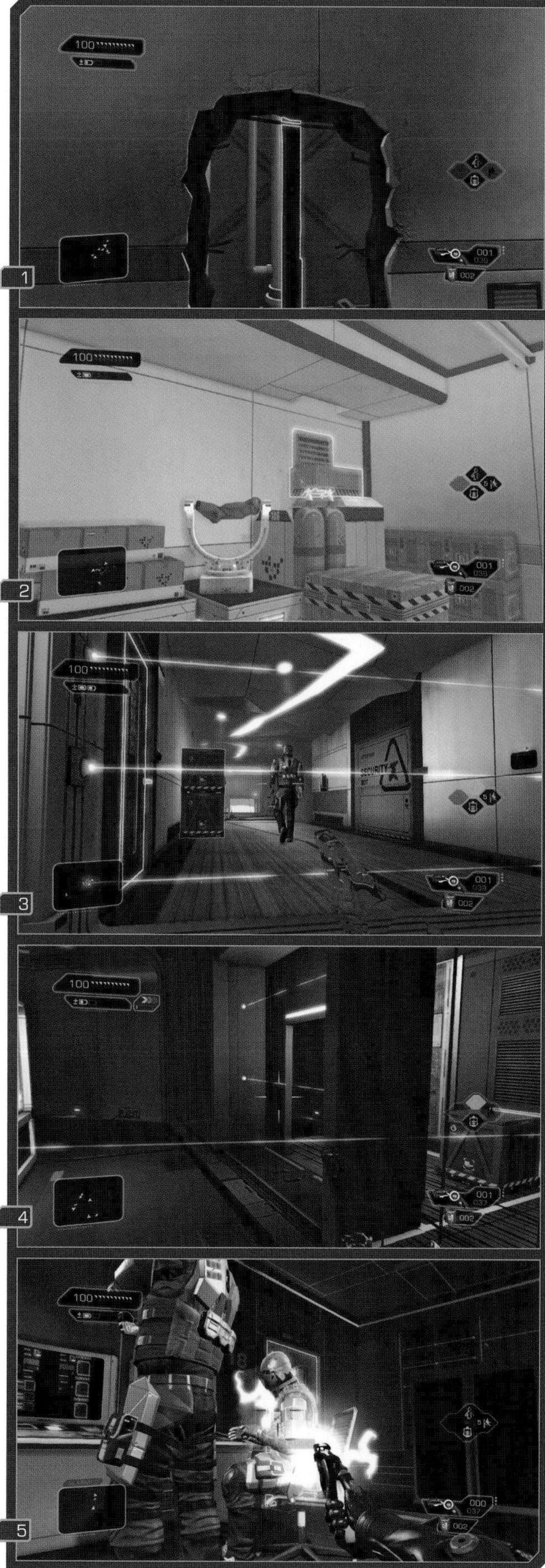

ROUTE 3 Combat

Required Reflex Booster
Recommended Dermal Plating, Typhoon

Recommended Combat Rifle, Revolver (w/ Exploding Rounds), 10mm Pistol (Silenced), Frag Grenade

01 Move through the area and make your way to where the two guards are talking just outside the Security Room. Get close to them, and use a Double Takedown to take them both down. Now back up and take cover at the corner at **Position A** and then pick off the next guard and the Medium Sentry as they come up the hallway.

02 Go to the lab door and hack it to gain entry to the lab. It's a Level 1 hack, which shouldn't present you with any problems. Now enter the lab and take cover at the first low barrier directly ahead. Peek out to the right and pick off the guards as they come running.

03 Make your way up the stairs to the area above. Take cover to the left of the door and pick off the Medium Sentry and any guards that come. When the Bot has been destroyed, make your way to the stairs at **Position B** and go up to the next level. [→☐ 1]

04 Due to the gunfire in the previous area, there will often be guards near the stairs, so approach them carefully, and if any guards appear, take cover at the corners of the wall and pick them off. When it's clear, make your way to **Position C** and take cover at the corner. There is a Medium Sentry in the area, so wait for it to show up and then destroy it.

05 Go to the Security Booth ahead. Shoot out the window and then take cover immediately below the window. From your cover point, pick off the guards inside the Security Room. Once they are dead, jump inside and hack the Security Hub in the Security Room to open the door to the Data Core Room.

06 Make your way into the Data Core room and walk through the lasers to trigger the alarm. Immediately take cover at the equipment box at this point [→☐ 2]. Lean out to the right, wait for the guards to appear and then pick them off. There is also a Medium Sentry to contend with, so hold your position here and destroy it. Once that is done, go to the elevator at **Position D**.

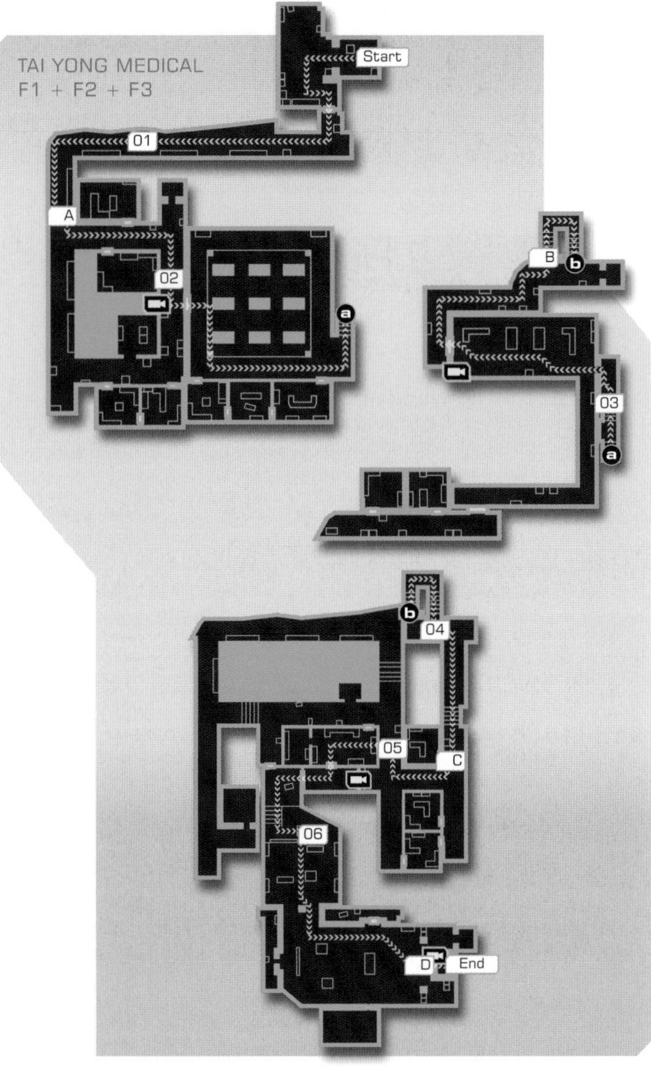

Objective Completed	Objective Type	XP Reward	Stealth Bonuses	
			Ghost	Smooth Operator
Find and view Van Bruggen's recording	Primary	2500	Yes	Yes

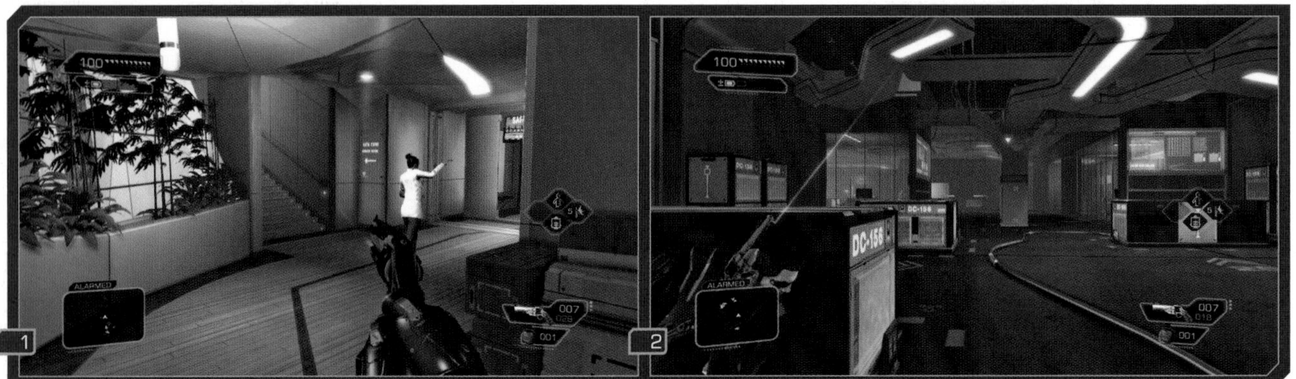
1
2

Objective Name	Objective Type
Confront Zhao in the Penthouse	Primary

Tai Yong Medical Penthouse

ROUTE 1 Stealth

Required Cloaking System
Recommended None

01 After you exit the elevator, a cutscene will trigger. When it is over, go left through the door. In this hallway you'll face four laser systems that you must get past in order to access the door at the far end of the hall. Simply activate Cloak and sprint past them all to the door.

02 When you are past the door protected by the lasers, go right to another door. Move forward and to the right to take position at the corner of the cubicle wall. Look right and watch the guards. There are two in this room. One is a regular guard at the far end of the room, and the other a Heavy on the other side of the wall where you're taking cover.
Wait for the Heavy nearest you to move out into the open and head north and away from you. Once he does, hug the left wall, move forward and duck into the area the Heavy just came from. Then make your way to the Conference Room door at **Position A**.

03 Move through the conference room and out of the opposite door and immediately take cover at the first desk on your right. The Heavy will soon take up position just ahead of you and will be looking your way [→☐ 3]. Hold your position, and once he moves off, activate Cloak and move through the door that is just ahead on the left at **Position B**. Once you get through the door, close it behind you before Cloak runs out.

04 After you're through the door, stay there until your energy replenishes, as you'll need Cloak again soon. When you're ready, move forward and hug the right-hand wall until you reach the next hallway ahead. You'll be directly under a fire extinguisher. Now activate Cloak and move to the left to the far end of the hall. Once you reach the door, take cover at the left side at **Position C**.

05 Once your energy has replenished, open the door and then activate Cloak. Sprint across the room to the door just ahead which is located under the camera. Go through that door and then head left to find another door that will let you into a small area with a breakable wall at **Position D**. [→☐ 4]

06 Punch through the wall and then go to the elevator just ahead and on your right. The camera in the other room has a limited range over which it can pan, and even though there are windows between these two rooms, the camera cannot see you in here due to its limited range, so use the elevator at your leisure.

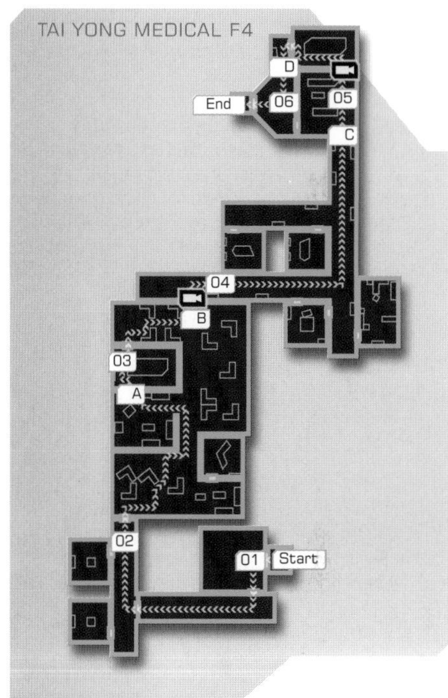

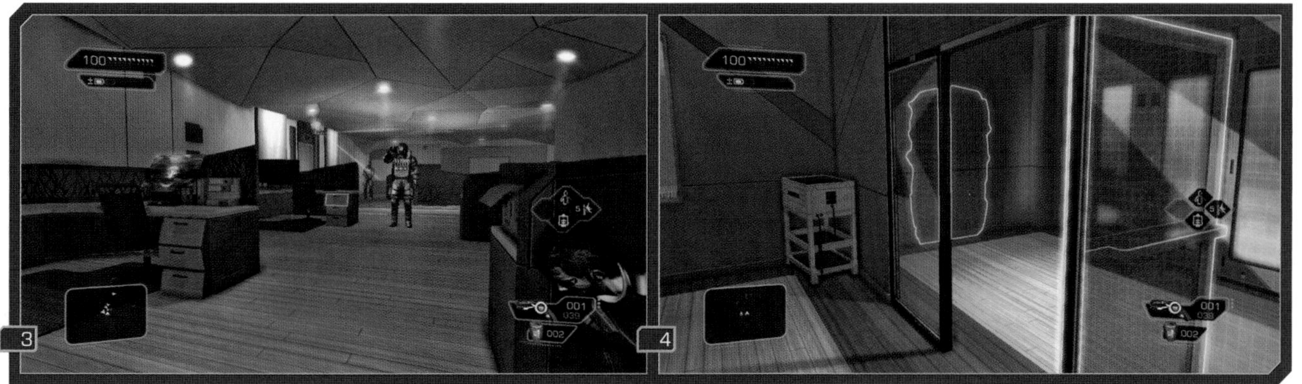

ROUTE 2 Stealth Combat

Required Move/Throw Heavy Objects, Cloaking System, Reflex Booster
Recommended None

Recommended Tranquilizer Rifle

01 Once you exit the elevator, a cutscene will trigger. After this, go left through the door. You'll face four laser systems here that you must get past in order to access the door at the far end of the hall. Simply activate Cloak and sprint past them all to the door.

02 When you are past the door protected by the lasers, go right to another door. Enter the room ahead and immediately go right to find a locked office. Hack the door to get in (Level 3 Hack) and then hack the Security Hub inside (Level 2 Hack). Once you gain access to the Hub, turn off the camera.

03 Exit the office and take cover at the corner of the wall. Watch the Heavy on patrol. When he begins walking north and away from you, sneak up on him whilst crouched and use a Takedown. Do this quickly, and you'll be able to down him at **Position A** [→☐ 1]. Now hold your position here, and watch the remaining guard. Wait for him to take up position in the north just right of the camera and then shoot him in the head with the Tranquilizer Rifle.

04 When you're ready, go through the door to the north and then head right up the hallway and into the last room on the right. In this room you will find a large crate that you will need to move in order to expose the vent there. Open it and enter the air ducts.v

05 Exit the air ducts and drop down into the Security Room. Ahead are two guards, so approach them whilst crouched. Once you are close enough, take them both out with a double Takedown. After clearing the area, head back out into the main corridor and take cover next to the door at the far end. [→☐ 2]

06 When your energy is replenished, open the door and activate Cloak. Then sprint across the room to the door that is located under the camera just ahead. Go through that door and then head left. You'll find another door that will let you into a small area with a breakable wall at **Position B**.

07 After punching through the wall, go to the elevator just ahead of you on your right. The camera in the other room has only a limited range over which it can pan. Though there are windows between the two rooms, the camera cannot see you here due to its limited range, so you're free to use the elevator.

ROUTE 3 Combat

Required Reflex Booster, Punch Through Walls
Recommended Dermal Plating, Typhoon, Cloaking System

Recommended Combat Rifle, Revolver (w/ Exploding Rounds), 10mm Pistol (Silenced), Frag Grenade

01 After you exit the elevator, a cutscene will trigger. Once it's over, go left through the door to a hallway where there are four laser systems. You must get past them in order to access the door at the far end of the hall. Just activate Cloak and sprint past them all to the door.

Tip **By avoiding the lasers here, you'll have avoided tripping the alarm. This makes the upcoming fight a bit easier.**

02 Run into the room here and take cover at the cubicle wall. Then lean out to the right and pick off the two guards here. Hold your position, and soon a Medium Sentry will open the door at the far end of the room and come in. Destroy the Medium Sentry and then move forward.

03 As soon as you go through the door, take cover at the display case to your left. Hold your position here, and lean out to the right to pick off the three guards in this area [→☐ 3]. Once they are all

down, make your way to the door at **Position A** and hack the door there (Level 1 Hack). Then go forward to the elevator in front of you.

When you exit the elevator, move ahead and go right through the large open room. At the northern end of the room you'll find some stairs that lead up to Zhao's office area. Past that are more stairs that lead up to a door, which takes you to Zhao's personal quarters. [→☐ 4]

4

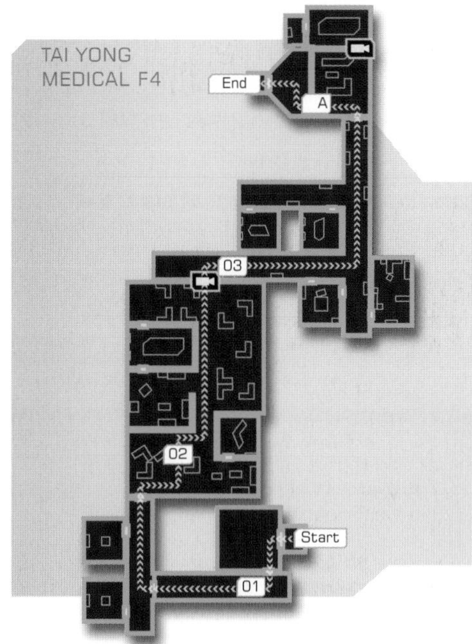

Objective Completed	Objective Type	XP Reward	Stealth Bonuses	
			Ghost	Smooth Operator
Confront Zhao in the Penthouse	Primary	750	Yes	Yes

MAKE YOUR ESCAPE

Objective Name	Objective Type
Go to the chopper and extract	Primary

Escaping The Penthouse

ROUTE 1 Stealth

Required Cloaking System, Hacking: Capture 2, Hacking: Robot Domination, **Recommended** Energy Level Upgrade (energy cells)

01 You're going to need two full energy cells here, so use a CyberBoost ProEnergy Bar before entering Zhao's room. After the cutscene, go right and down the stairs and then jump over the railing to reach the floor. Make your way forward to the arched opening on the right near the TV. Take cover at the wall to the right of the arched opening. Look out into the room ahead and watch the guards. Wait for them to disperse, then crouch down and go to the vent at **Position A**.

Tip **It is important to wait and watch the guards until they disperse. It won't take long and the time allows the guards to get into a regular patrol pattern, that you'll be able to bypass later. If you move any faster, they will change their patterns.**

02 Move to the exit vent and press the Interact button to open it. Activate Cloak right after you have pressed the button. Do this quickly and smoothly, and you'll be Cloaked just as the vent opens. No one will see you. Now move to the right past all the couches. Remain crouched as you make your way forward, or the guards will hear you. Move to the door at **Position B** and then you should stand up and sprint to the elevator at **Position C** [→☐ 5]. Now use the elevator to exit the area.

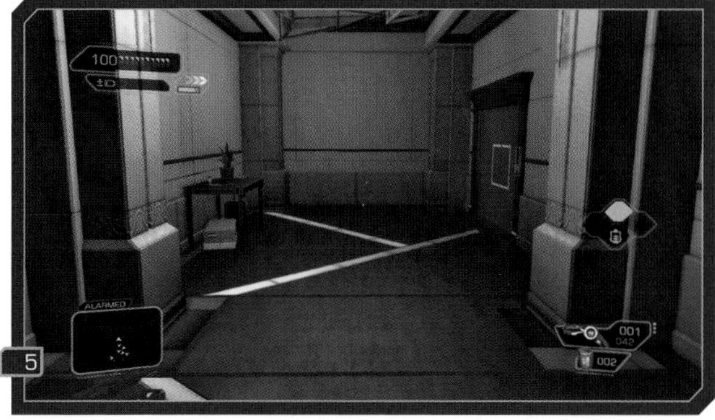
5

03 Go through the door ahead and then go right. Move to the railing and jump over it to reach the ground below. There are two Box Guards in the area that are going to activate when you enter the room, so move quickly and jump the railing before they can activate.

04 Move to the right behind the boxes and sprint forward to the barrels here [→☐ 1]. Take cover at the barrels and wait for the Box Guards to move off to the left. Once they are over at the eastern side of the room, make your way to the stairs at **Position D** and use them to reach the control booth above.

05 The switch to open the hangar bay doors is here, but it has been deactivated due to the Box Guards on the floor below, so you'll have to shut them down to reactivate the switch. Before moving on, go ahead and grab the EMP Grenade in the desk drawer. It will come in handy later. When you're ready, go out via the southern door and make your way across the catwalk to the booth ahead.

06 There is a Security Hub in this room. As it's only a Level 2 Hack it shouldn't present you with much trouble. Once you hack it, disable the Box Guards using the Robots option on the left of the screen of the Security Hub. The Robot Domination augmentation is required for this. Once the Box Guards are disabled, go back to the previous control booth at Point 05 and press the button to open the hangar bay door. When Malik arrives, make your way to the chopper and leave this area.

Tip **After you have disabled the Box Guards, you can go down and destroy them for some very easy XP. An EMP Grenade is ideal for this. You'll get 250 XP for each Box Gaurd you destroy. As easy as taking candy from a baby.**

ACHIEVEMENT/TROPHY: DOCTORATE

You'll find one of Hugh Darrow's eBooks on the desk near the one with the Security Hub on it.

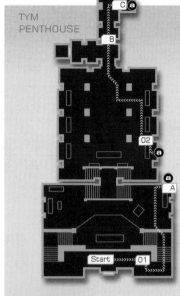

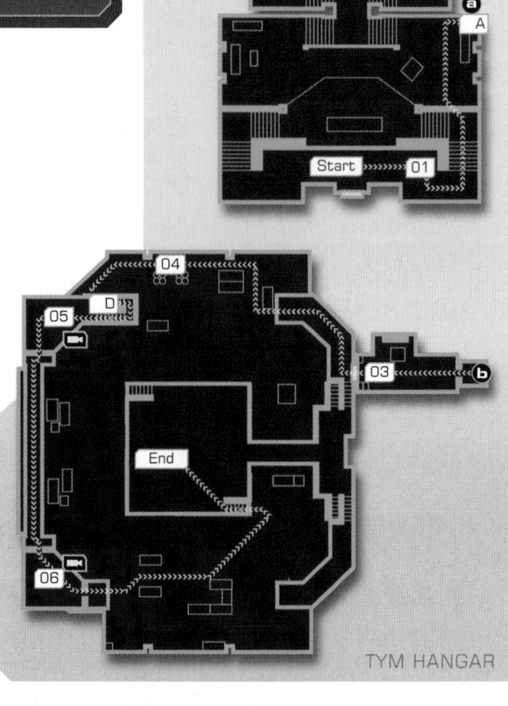

Escaping The Penthouse

08_039

ROUTE 2 Stealth Combat

Required Cloaking System, Hacking: Robot Domination, Jump Enhancement
Recommended Hacking: Capture 2

Recommended Tranquilizer Rifle, Concussion Grenade, Gas Grenade (2x), EMP Grenade, 10mm Pistol (Silenced)

01 After the cutscene, jump the railing and run forward to the stairs. Crouch and move down the stairs and take cover at the banister on the level below. Watch the guards ahead, and then wait for the last guard near the elevator to come running out to join the group. Once he is there, activate Cloak and stand up.

Start by throwing a Concussion Grenade into the center of the group. Immediately switch to Gas Grenades, and then throw one near the front of the pack and one near the rear. When you have thrown them both, crouch down and take cover at the banister once more. Do this correctly and all the guards will fall unconscious. Being Cloaked, no one will have seen you, and you'll still get the Ghost XP Bonus. [→☐ 2]

Before leaving, search all the fallen bodies for items. In particular, you will find a Pocket Secretary with the password to the Security Hub in the next area. When you're ready, go to the elevator located at **Position A**.

02 Go through the doors ahead and immediately head to the left. Move all the way forward to the far area and take cover at the railing at **Position B**. Since the alarm has already been triggered by Zhao, go ahead and shoot out the camera directly ahead at **Position C** with a silenced weapon. If you don't have a silenced weapon, then ignore the camera. Hold your position here and watch the Box Guard on the floor. When it gets to the midway point of the Helipad, it will turn and look to the west and away from you. Quickly lean out from cover and toss an EMP Grenade to destroy it.

03 The other Box Guard will be moving up on the right, so to be sure you aren't seen, activate Cloak and then jump over the railing. While Cloaked, run to the shelving ahead at **Position D**. There are three levels of shelving here that you can use as stepping stones to get into the control booth ahead [→☐ 3]. Jump onto the lowest shelving, then move ahead and jump onto the second highest shelf. Now turn right and jump onto the third shelf. From the third shelf you can reach the control booth.

04 Enter the control booth and access the Security Hub. You should have the password from the Pocket Secretary you pilfered from the guard in the previous area. If not, then it's only a Level 2 Hack. When you have accessed the hub, turn to disable the Robots. With that done, make your way to the control booth at **Position E** and press the button to open the hangar bay doors. When Malik arrives, board the chopper to leave this area.

2
3

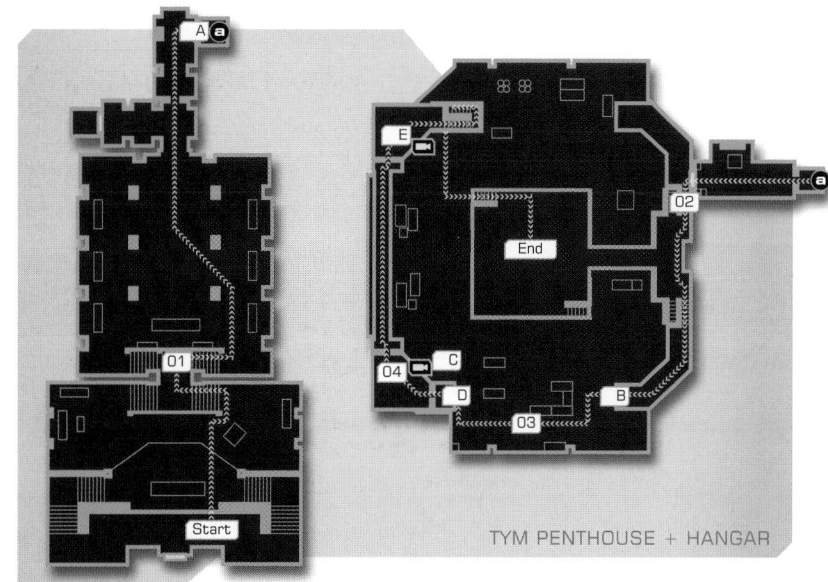

ROUTE 3 | Combat

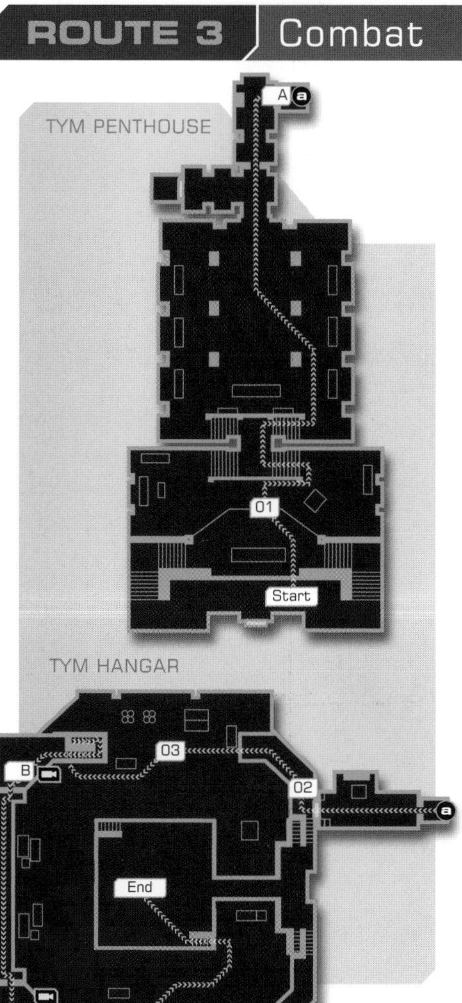

Recommended Revolver (w/ Explosive Rounds), Combat Rifle, Concussion Grenade, Frag Grenade, EMP Grenade

01 After the cutscene, jump over the railing and run forward to the stairs and take cover at the wall. Wait for the last guard at the elevator to come running in and join the rest of the guards. Once he does, toss a Concussion Grenade into the middle of the pack of guards. Now switch to Frag Grenades and toss one of those as well. The blast will kill most of the guards, and the survivors will still be stunned from the Concussion Grenade. [→☐ 4] Hold your cover position here, and pick off the remaining guards using your Revolver. When you have dispatched them all, search the fallen bodies for items. Then go to the elevator located at **Position A**.

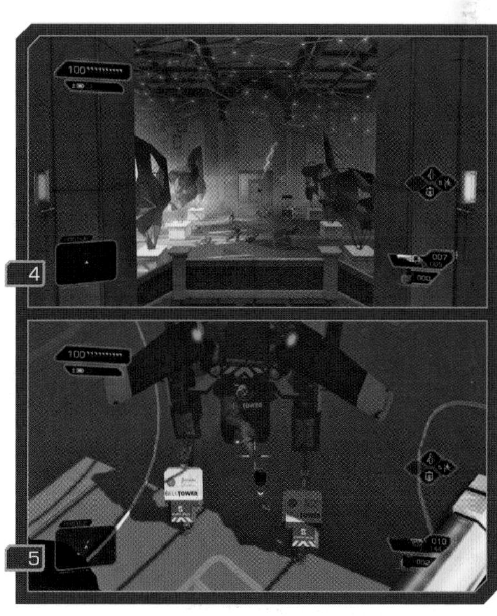
4
5

02 Go through the doors and then move to the right. Take position at the railing and wait for the Box Guard ahead to become active. Let it move towards you a bit, and then toss a Frag at it. Once you have thrown the grenade, switch to the Revolver and finish the Box Guard off from your cover point.

03 Jump the railing and sprint to the stairs ahead and make your way to the control booth above at **Position B**. Check the desk drawer to find an EMP Grenade. After collecting the EMP Grenade, go through the door on the right to reach the catwalk. Move halfway down the catwalk and then take cover at the plating on the railing. Locate the second Box Guard below you, and toss the EMP at it for an easy victory [→☐ 5]. Now that both Box Guards are down, go back to **Position B** and press the button to open the hangar bay doors. When Malik arrives, board the chopper to leave this area.

			Stealth Bonuses	
Objective Completed	Objective Type	XP Reward	Ghost	Smooth Operator
Escape and get to the hangar	Primary	2500	Yes	Yes

PICUS

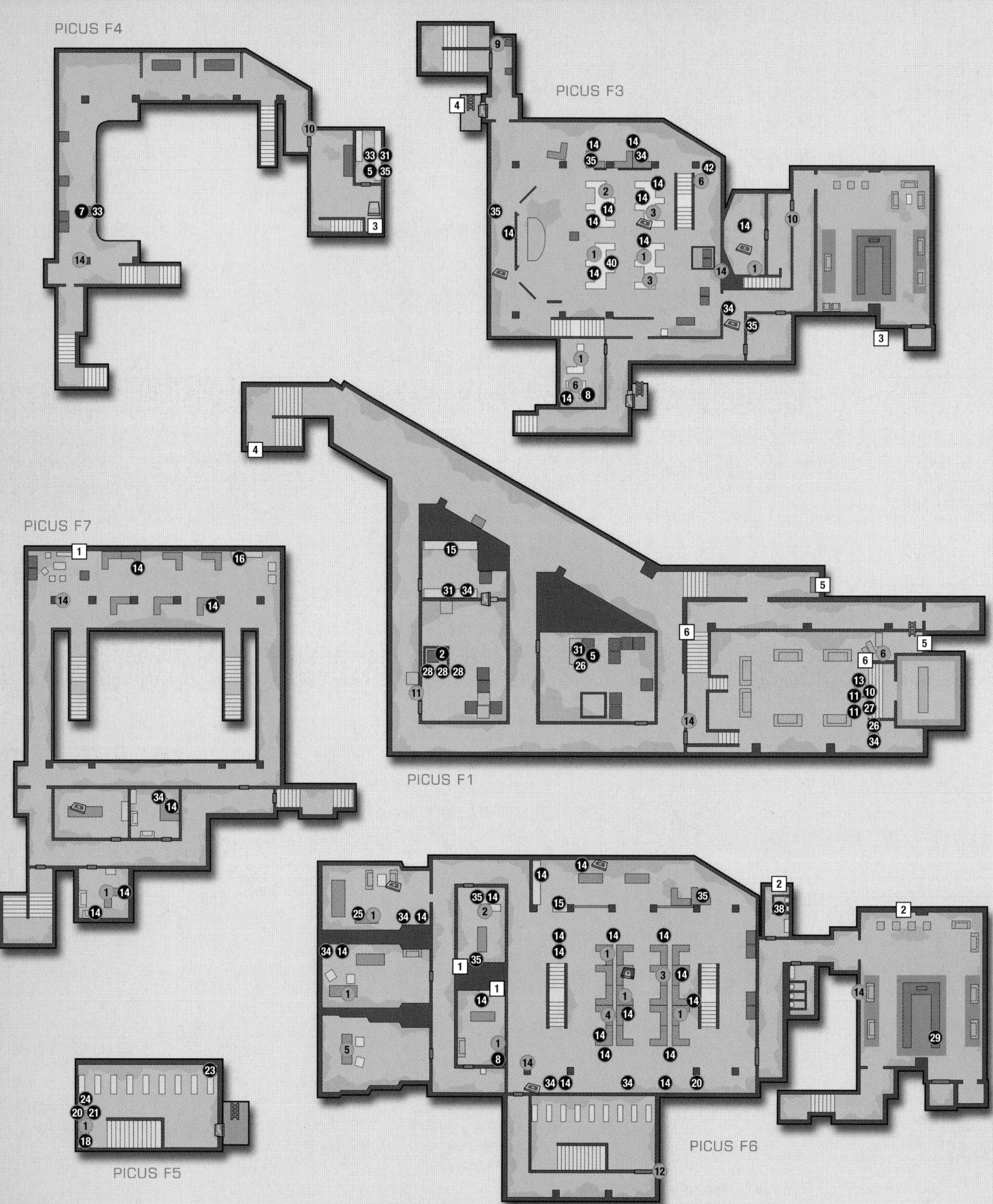

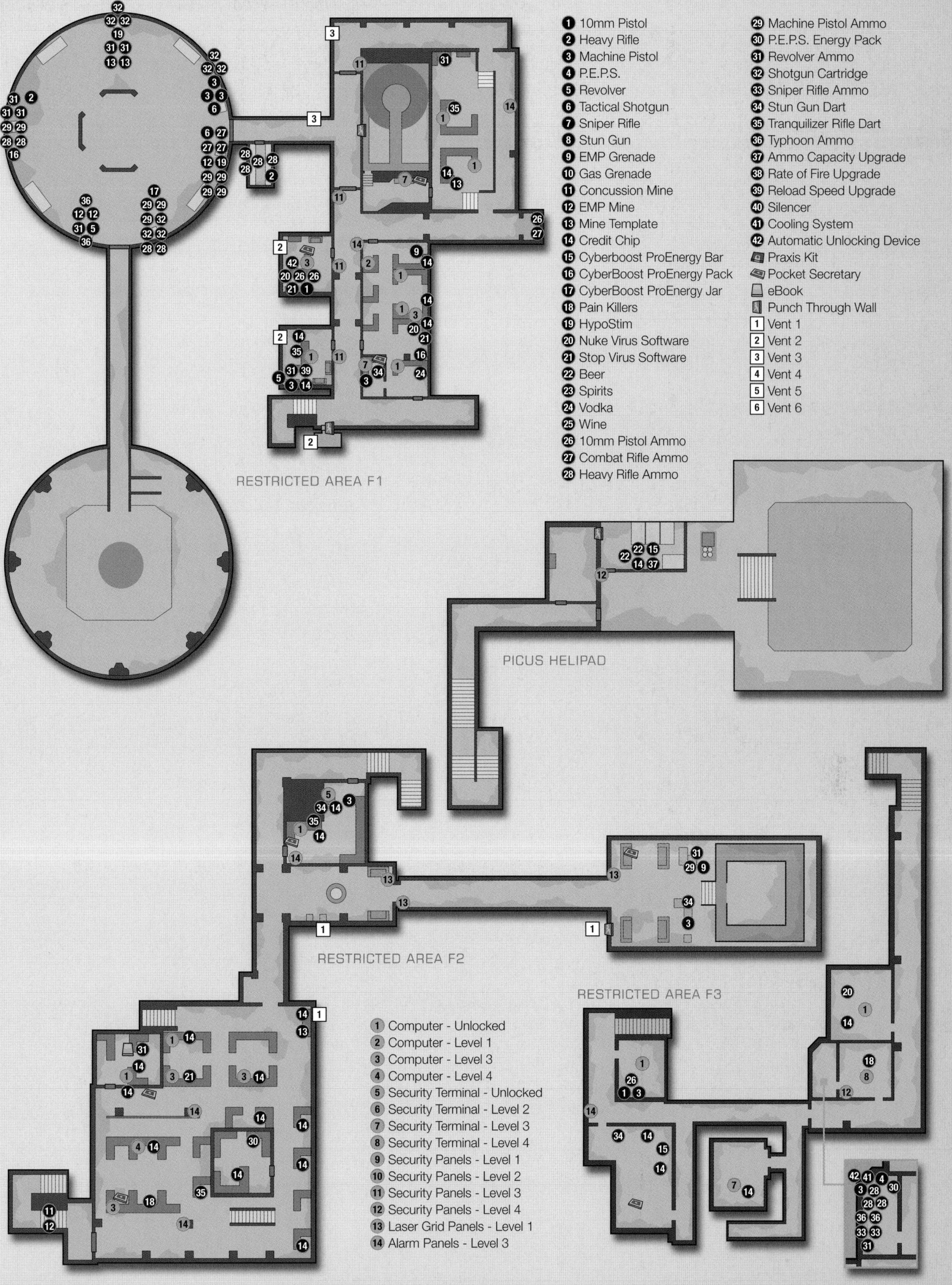
RESTRICTED AREA F1
PICUS HELIPAD
RESTRICTED AREA F2
RESTRICTED AREA F3
1 10mm Pistol
2 Heavy Rifle
3 Machine Pistol
4 P.E.P.S.
5 Revolver
6 Tactical Shotgun
7 Sniper Rifle
8 Stun Gun
9 EMP Grenade
10 Gas Grenade
11 Concussion Mine
12 EMP Mine
13 Mine Template
14 Credit Chip
15 Cyberboost ProEnergy Bar
16 CyberBoost ProEnergy Pack
17 CyberBoost ProEnergy Jar
18 Pain Killers
19 HypoStim
20 Nuke Virus Software
21 Stop Virus Software
22 Beer
23 Spirits
24 Vodka
25 Wine
26 10mm Pistol Ammo
27 Combat Rifle Ammo
28 Heavy Rifle Ammo
29 Machine Pistol Ammo
30 P.E.P.S. Energy Pack
31 Revolver Ammo
32 Shotgun Cartridge
33 Sniper Rifle Ammo
34 Stun Gun Dart
35 Tranquilizer Rifle Dart
36 Typhoon Ammo
37 Ammo Capacity Upgrade
38 Rate of Fire Upgrade
39 Reload Speed Upgrade
40 Silencer
41 Cooling System
42 Automatic Unlocking Device
Praxis Kit
Pocket Secretary
eBook
Punch Through Wall
1 Vent 1
2 Vent 2
3 Vent 3
4 Vent 4
5 Vent 5
6 Vent 6
1 Computer - Unlocked
2 Computer - Level 1
3 Computer - Level 3
4 Computer - Level 4
5 Security Terminal - Unlocked
6 Security Terminal - Level 2
7 Security Terminal - Level 3
8 Security Terminal - Level 4
9 Security Panels - Level 1
10 Security Panels - Level 2
11 Security Panels - Level 3
12 Security Panels - Level 4
13 Laser Grid Panels - Level 1
14 Alarm Panels - Level 3

M1 - CONFRONTING ELIZA CASSAN

Objective Name	Objective Type
Go to Room 404	Primary

OPTIONAL EXPLORATION

As you get off the Helipad, you'll see a locked cage area on the right. You can jump over the fence if you have the Jump Enhancer, or go into the room ahead and punch through the wall to get in. If you choose to jump over, first get onto the electrical boxes against the wall on the eastern side of the caged area, and then you can easily make the jump. Otherwise, it's a Level 4 Hack to get in. There is an Ammo Capacity Upgrade in the caged area.

ENTERING PICUS

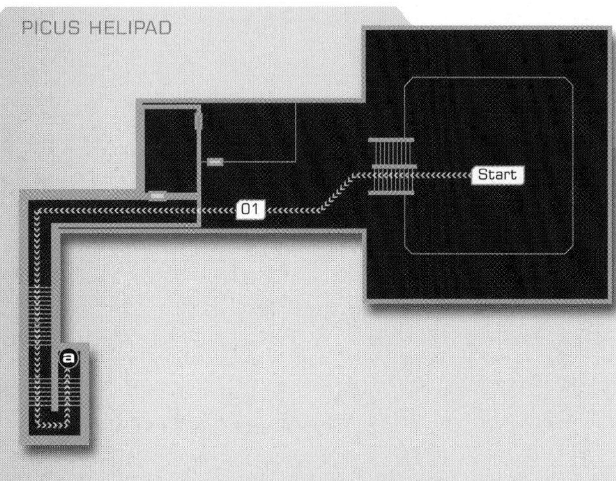

01 Once you are off the chopper and on the Helipad, move forward and go through the door ahead. You'll come to a series of stairs, so follow them all down to the floor below. The building is currently deserted, so you're free to move about as you wish for now.

02 Again, since the building is deserted, this is straightforward. All you need to do is move down the hall and go downstairs to reach the floor below. Before going down, there is a work area to the north that you can explore to find some Credits and a CyberBoost ProEnergy Pack.

03 When you're ready to move on, go to the hallway at **Position A**, and then follow the hallway to reach Room 404, which is ahead and on your right at **Position B**.

OPTIONAL EXPLORATION

Check all the drawers of all the desks for Credits and other items. In particular, there is a Praxis Kit in the desk at Position C.

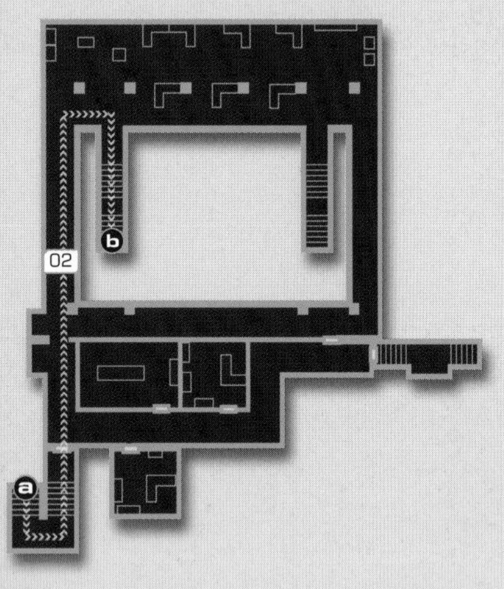

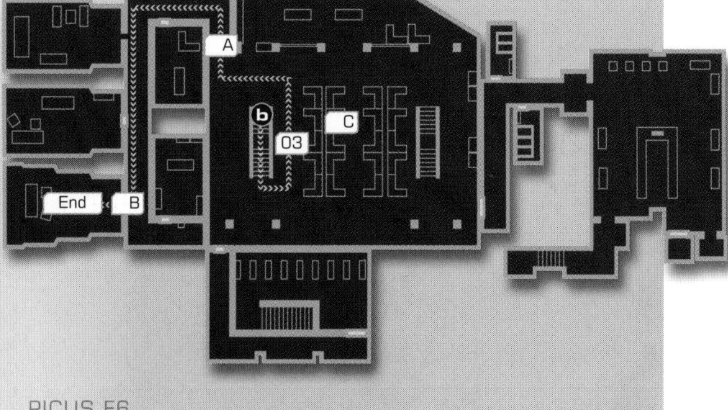

Objective Completed	Objective Type	XP Reward	Stealth Bonuses: Ghost	Stealth Bonuses: Smooth Operator
Go to Room 404	Primary	250	No	No

SLIPPING PAST THE AMBUSH

Objective Name	Objective Type
Escape the ambush by reaching a lower floor	Primary

ROUTE 1 Stealth

Required Cloaking System, Icarus Landing System
Recommended None

01 Before leaving Eliza's office, use the Security Hub on her desk to turn off the cameras. This Hub isn't password-protected, so it's an easy matter to turn off the cameras. When you're ready, go to the office across the hall at **Position A**. There you'll see a vent in the northeast corner. Jump onto the cabinets beneath the vent. Now enter the air ducts. Ignore the left path and instead go straight ahead.

02 Before exiting the vent, use an energy bar so that you have two full energy cells. Now open the vent and then activate Cloak. Stay crouching and move ahead, and to the right, and across the catwalk there. When you reach **Position B** you'll have 3/4 of a cell left, so stand up and sprint while still Cloaked and enter the hallway at **Position C** ahead [→□ 1] Once there, continue down the hall to the stairs at **Position D** and use them to reach the next level below.

03 When you reach the bottom of the stairs, crouch and hug the left-hand wall. Move forward and around the corner to the left, and then take cover at the left side of the door. Stay here and wait for your energy to replenish. Once you have a full cell, activate Cloak and enter the room. Immediately move right to **Position E** where you'll find an open elevator shaft. Enter the shaft and then fall to the bottom. [→□ 2]

At the bottom of the shaft, use the air duct there to reach a ladder. Climb up the ladder and then enter the next level and another air duct, which you should go through to reach the next area.

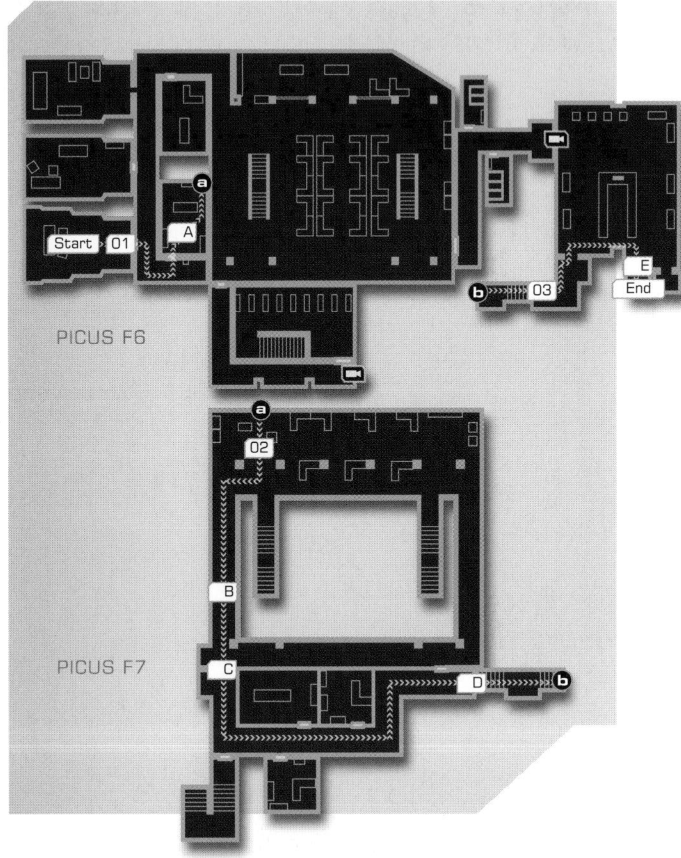

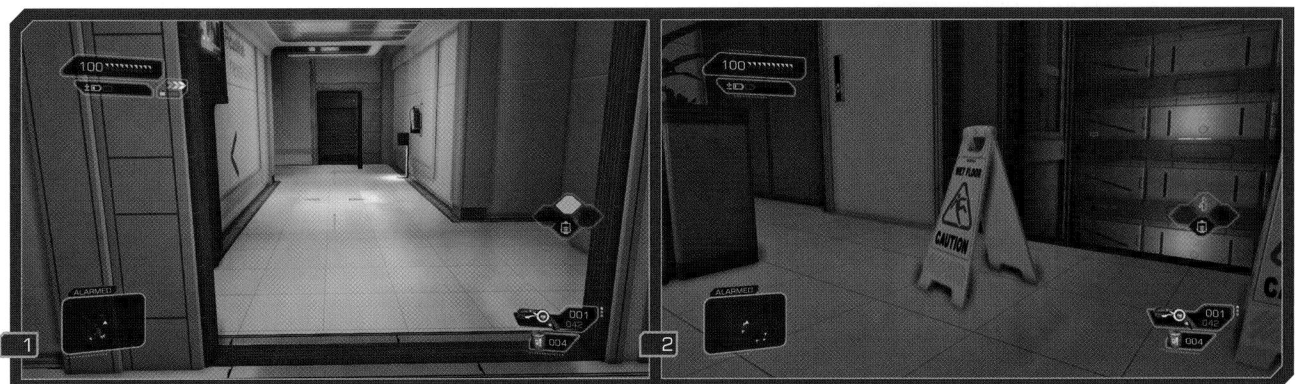

ROUTE 2 Stealth Combat

Required Cloaking System
Recommended Reflex Booster

Recommended Tranquilizer Rifle

01 Before leaving Eliza's office, turn off the cameras by using the Security Hub on her desk. The Hub isn't password-protected, making it easy to turn off the cameras. When you're ready, go to the office across the hall at **Position A**. In this office you'll see a vent in the northeast corner. Jump onto the cabinets beneath the vent and enter the air ducts. Ignore the left path; go straight ahead instead.

02 Wait in the air ducts until the guards ahead disperse. Once they do, exit the ducts and go right and take cover at the right side of the planter directly ahead [→□ 1]. Now watch the guard closest to you on the left, and when he turns his back to you, move right to the catwalk and follow the guard who is moving to the room to the south. Make sure you stay crouching so that the catwalk railing hides you.

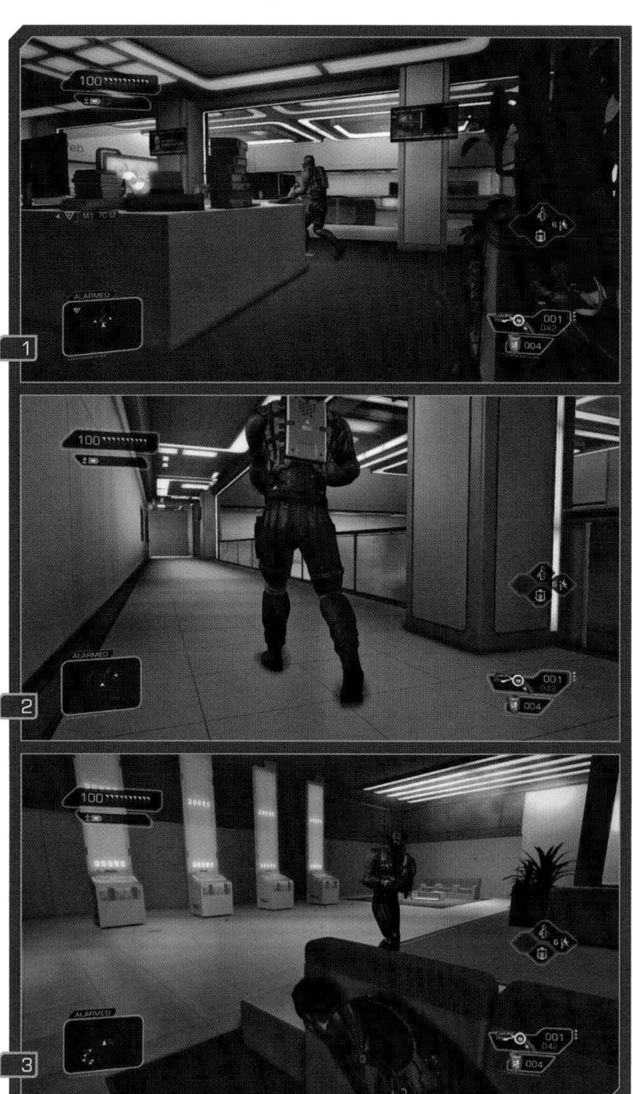

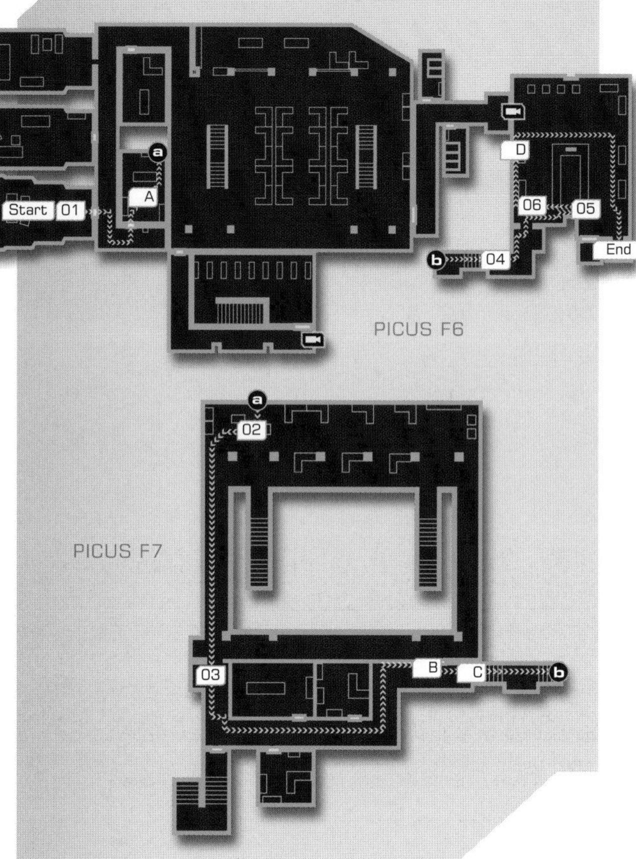

03 Enter the hallway ahead and take cover at the corner. Watch the guard in the hall and once he moves away from you, sneak up behind him for a Takedown. Now move to the door at **Position B** and take cover at the left side. Wait for a guard to show up, and when he moves back to the left, sneak up behind him for another Takedown [→□ 2]. After taking him down, return to the hallway and take the stairs at **Position C** down to the next level.

04 When you reach the bottom of the stairs, crouch and hug the left-hand wall. Move forward and around the corner to the left, and then take cover at the left side of the door. Watch the guards inside, and when they meet and begin to talk in the northeast portion of the room, enter the room and go right.

05 Take cover at the counter here and wait for the guards to disperse. One will go off to the left. The other will get close to your position. When he has his back to you, sneak out for a Takedown. After downing him, hide his body behind the counters you were taking cover.

06 Watch the remaining guard, and when he is on the left side of the room, move to the couches and then take cover at **Position D** at the end of the couch [→□ 3]. Watch the last guard, who will get close to you. When he turns with his back to you, move up behind him for a Takedown. When he is down, use the elevator southeast corner of the room to reach the next area.

OPTIONAL EXPLORATION

Enter the men's bathroom just outside the western exit of this room to find a Rate of Fire Upgrade for one of your weapons.

ROUTE 3 Combat

Required None
Recommended Dermal Plating

Recommended Revolver (w/ Explosive Rounds), Combat Rifle, 10mm Pistol (Silenced), Frag Grenade

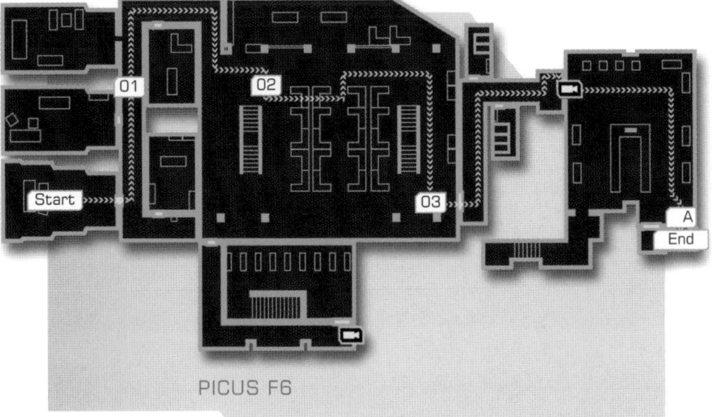

01 Leave Eliza's office and go left and around to the main work area. Take cover at the planter ahead and peek out. Toss a Frag at the three guards ahead. Hold position here and go for headshots as the guards come running in. There are two guards on the floor above you, and occasionally one will go round to your right and target you. If so, take cover at the copy machines here and head-shot him.

02 Move right and jump over the cubicle wall. Take cover at the right side of the cubicle you've just jumped over. Peek out from cover and target the guards on the floor above you and take them out.

03 Move to the door at the southeast corner and make your way to the elevator room. Do not enter yet, but instead take cover at the left side of the door. Locate the guard inside and then go for a headshot to put him down. Once he is dead, take the elevator at **Position A** down to the next floor.

			Stealth Bonuses	
Objective Completed	Objective Type	XP Reward	Ghost	Smooth Operator
Escape the ambush by reaching a lower floor	Primary	2400	Yes	Yes

ROUTE 1 Stealth

Objective Name	Objective Type
Get to the Funicular	Primary

Required Cloaking System
Recommended None

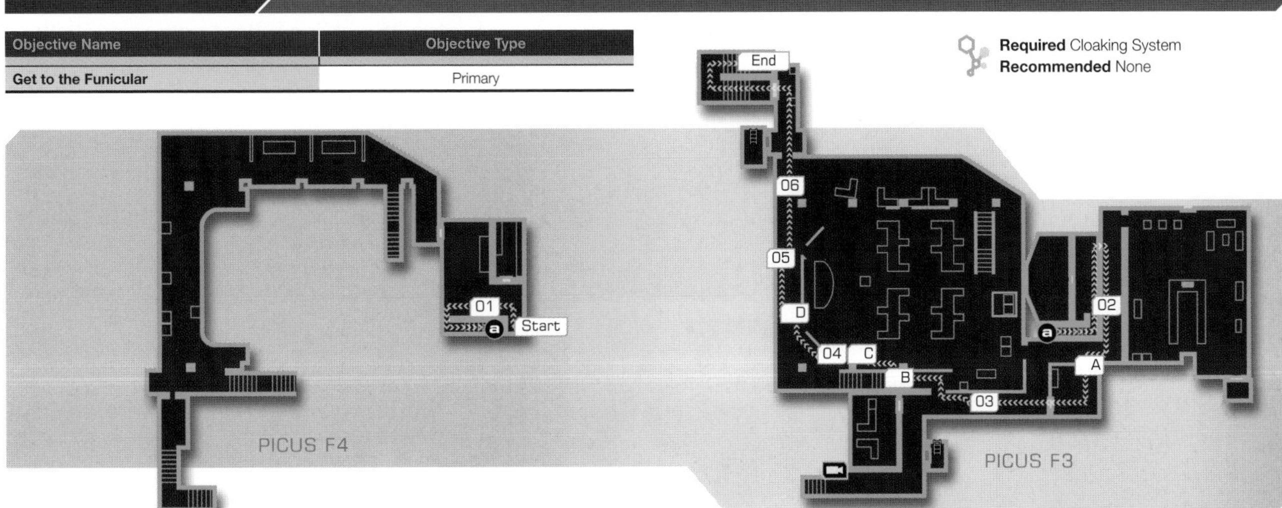

01 When you exit the vent, you'll be in a small Control Room. There is a large window ahead that enables you to survey the area below if you wish. When you're ready, take the stairs at the southern part of the room down to the next level.

ACHIEVEMENT/TROPHY: DOCTORATE

There is a Hugh Darrow eBook beneath the large TV on the southern wall where the exit vent is located.

02 Go through the door in the northeast corner of the room and then take a right and move forward in the hallway. To avoid being seen, go through the Storage Room at **Position A** and exit via the door in the southwest corner. On exiting the Storage Room, crouch and move forward to the open door that is ahead and on the right.

03 Take cover at the right side of the door and look into the room ahead. Watch the guard on patrol directly ahead in the middle of the room. When his back is to you, crouch and move to the stairs to the left and stop at **Position B** just left of the luggage on the other side of the railing [→☐ 4]. Now activate Cloak and jump over the railing. Stay crouching and move left to take cover behind the wall at **Position C**.

04 Take cover on the left side of the wall and look up to your right; when no one is looking, move from cover to to cross the gap. Do the same for the next gap and then take cover behind the boxes at **Position D**. [→☐ 1]. When he walks to the right and takes up position there, he'll be looking to the right and won't see you, so move forward whilst crouching to the next point.

05 Take cover here and look out to the left. Wait for the heavy to come back and take a position just ahead of you. Once the heavy turns and heads back to the right, activate the Cloak again and move forward while crouched to the hallway ahead.

06 The door at the end of the hallway is your goal, but it is locked. It's a Level 1 Hack that is easy to get past, so move to it and hack it. Don't worry about the heavy on patrol you've just passed. He'll never look into the hall, which means he'll never see you, so hack the door at your leisure. Once through the door, use the stairs to reach the next area below.

Tip **Move down the stairs while crouching because there are two guards at the base of the stairs on the next floor.**

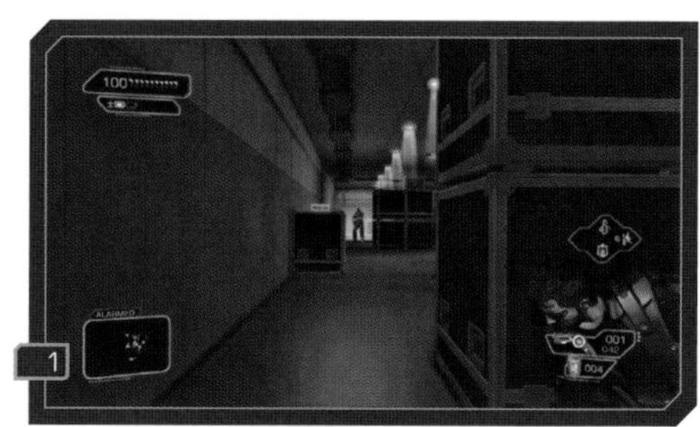
1

Path to the Funicular

ROUTE 2 Stealth Combat

Required Cloaking System
Recommended Reflex Booster

Recommended Tranquilizer Rifle

01 Exit the elevator and make your way forward to the first doorway in the hallway ahead. Hack this door (Level 2 Hack) and then enter the room. Use the stairs to the left to reach the floor above you.

02 Go to the door in the northwest corner of this room and open it. Crouch and move forward, then take cover at the corner of the railing ahead. Peek out to the right, where you'll see a guard on patrol. Wait for him to start moving away and then shoot him in the back with the Tranquilizer Rifle. [→☐ 2]

03 Move forward and take cover at the Picus display ahead and on your left. Stay behind cover here and watch the guard patrolling the area around the corner. When he is moving away from you, close in and use a Takedown to incapacitate him.

Note **While you are up on this level, always be crouching so that the guards below you don't hear you.**

04 Move to the railing here and then activate Cloak. Jump over the scaffolding ahead. Move straight ahead and drop to the floor, making sure you don't touch the guard patrolling this area [→☐ 3]. Once you are on the floor, immediately move west and take cover behind the boxes there.

05 Peek out to the left and watch the Heavy here. When he moves to the right and is facing right, get behind him for a Takedown. Now quickly hide his body behind the boxes where you were taking cover so that the other guards don't see it. To make sure the other guards don't see you do this, keep an eye on your radar. Only go after the Heavy, when the other guards are on the southern side of the room.

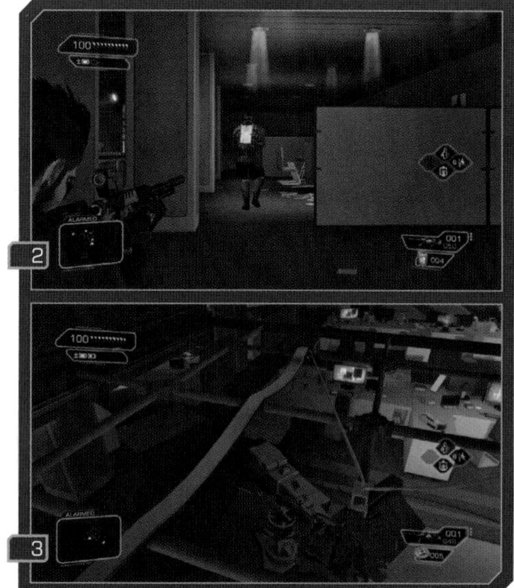
2

3

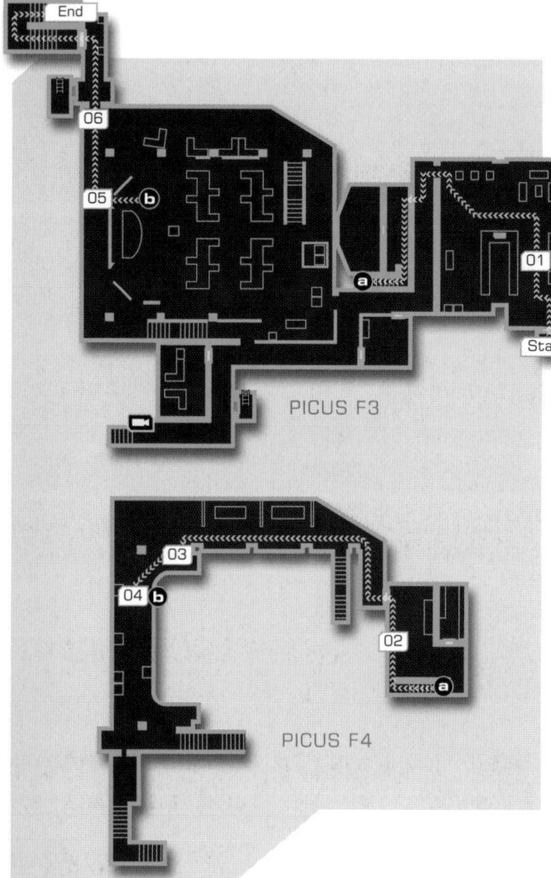

06 Once you've dealt with the heavy, go to the hallway ahead and approach the locked door on your left. It's a Level 1 Hack, which won't present much of a problem. When you have it open, crouch down, move forward and then down the stairs to the next level below.

ROUTE 3 Combat

Required Hacking: Capture 2
Recommended None

Recommended Revolver (w/ Explosive Rounds), Combat Rifle, 10mm Pistol (Silenced), Frag Grenade

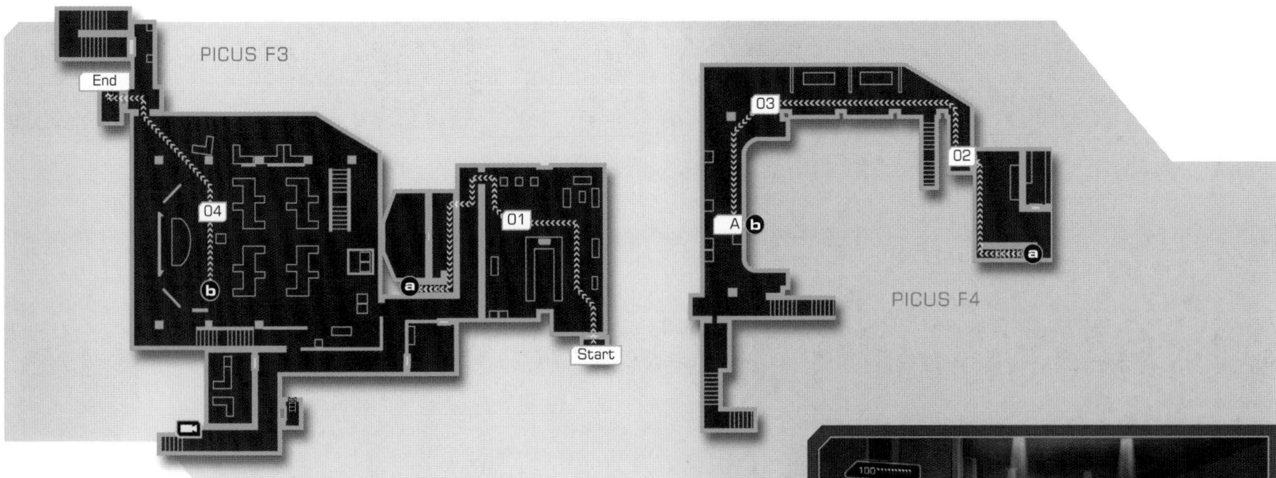

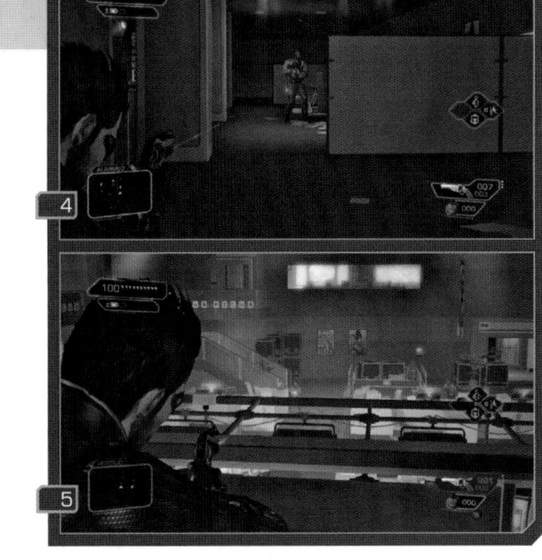

01 From the elevator, go left and into the hallway to find a locked door. Hack the door (Level 2 Hack) and then move inside. You can explore the area here if you like, but your main goal is to take the stairs to the left up to the next floor.

02 Exit via the door of this room. Take cover at the column at the end of the railing. Wait for the guard to get close, then lean out to get his attention [→☐ 4]. Move back into cover. Wait for the guard to get close to investigate. When he does, eliminate him with a Takedown.

03 Run straight ahead to the far end of the room and take cover at the column there. Hold your position and pick off the guards as they come for you. All but two will come, so once you've killed the first wave, move forward to the railing at **Position A** at the southern end of the area. From there, peek over the railing and line up your shots to kill the last of the guards down below [→☐ 5]. There is also a Turret down there that you should destroy. Now jump down to the floor below.

04 Go into the hallway where the exit door is located. To the left of the door is a breakable wall. Punch through it to find a ladder. Take that down to the level below and then use the vent there to reach the next area.

			Stealth Bonuses	
Objective Completed	Objective Type	XP Reward	Ghost	Smooth Operator
Escape the ambush by reaching a lower floor	Primary	2500	Yes	Yes

ROUTE 1 Stealth

Objective Name	Objective Type
Summon the Funicular	Primary

Required Cloaking System, Move/Throw Heavy Objects
Recommended Reflex Booster

01 Don't move too far past the base of the stairs, as there are two guards ahead. Let them finish talking and then move off and down the hallway. Be patient, because one of the guards turns around and looks behind him. He can spot you if you move too soon, so let them get all the way down the hall.

Tip **If they don't move off quickly enough for your taste, then sneak up behind them for a Double Takedown.**

02 Once the guards reach the end of the hall, crouch down and follow them. When you reach the split in the hallway, go left down the stairs, making sure you stay crouching. Once down the stairs, go to the door ahead on your right.

03 Take cover at the right side of the door and peek in. There are two guards in the room in front of you. Watch their patrols, and when they aren't looking, jump to cover to get past the door. Now move to **Position A** and move the soda machine to expose a vent. Use the air ducts to reach the next area.

04 When you come out of the vent, be careful to move straight ahead and take cover at the column. From cover, peek out to the left and watch for the guard who will show up there shortly. When the guard moves away from your area, watch the radar and wait until both guards are at the back of the room so that they won't hear your next move.

05 Activate Cloak and then jump over the railing to the left, push the button to call the Funicular, then jump over the railing next to the button. Once over the railing, take cover behind the box there [→☐ 1]. Look to your right and you'll see a small tunnel that leads under the stairs. Go inside the opening and wait for the funicular to arrive.

Tip **It takes two and a half minutes for the Funicular to arrive, so be patient.**

Once the Funicular is there, the room will be packed with guards. Activate Cloak and move out to the left. Jump over the railing, get inside the Funicular, and go right to where the button is. Push the button, and you're done. [→☐ 2]

ROUTE 2 Stealth Combat

Required Cloaking System
Recommended Reflex Booster

Recommended Tranquilizer Rifle, Gas Mines

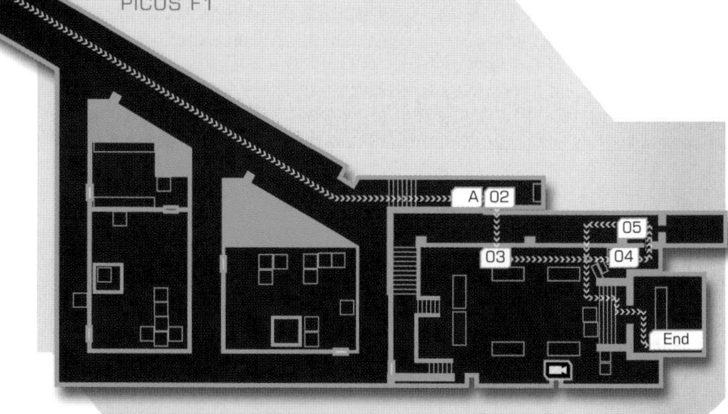

01 From the base of the stairs, stay crouching and move forward toward the two guards ahead. Get close and then perform a double Takedown to dispatch them both. Now move through the halls ahead to the door located at **Position A**.

02 Take cover to the right of the door so that you can get a clean view of the two guards in the room ahead. During their patrol route they will both come quite close to the door and will turn their backs for a short time; use this opportunity to fire a shot from the Tranquilizer Rifle into the nearest one [→☐ 3]. The other guard will rush in to try and revive his fallen comrade, allowing you to land an easy shot on him with the Tranquilizer Rifle. Alternatively, if you want to close in, you can activate the Cloak so the Turret does not see you, and then move up and use a Takedown on the final enemy. This does require two Energy Cells, however, so make sure you have enough energy before you leave cover.

03 Use the couches for cover, and move to the northern side of the room. Stay crouching, and continue using the couches for cover so

that the Turret and cameras do not see you, and make your way to the northeast corner of the room.

04 Hack the Security Hub here. Even though it's only a Level 2 Hack, it is a bit tricky. Don't hesitate to use Stops and Nuke to get through this one. Once you have access, turn off the camera and disable the Turret. Now press the button on the right side of the funicular door to call it. Having done that, go back to the ladder behind the Security Hub and climb up to the next level.

05 Take cover at the column here and wait. A guard will eventually come up and get near your position. Look over the railing and then move away [→☐ 4]. As soon as he has his back to you, get behind him for a Takedown. Hold your position and wait for the funicular to arrive. When it does, activate Cloak and jump over the railing, then sprint into the Funicular. Once inside, use the button on the right side of the cabin to get it moving.

ROUTE 3 Combat

08_040

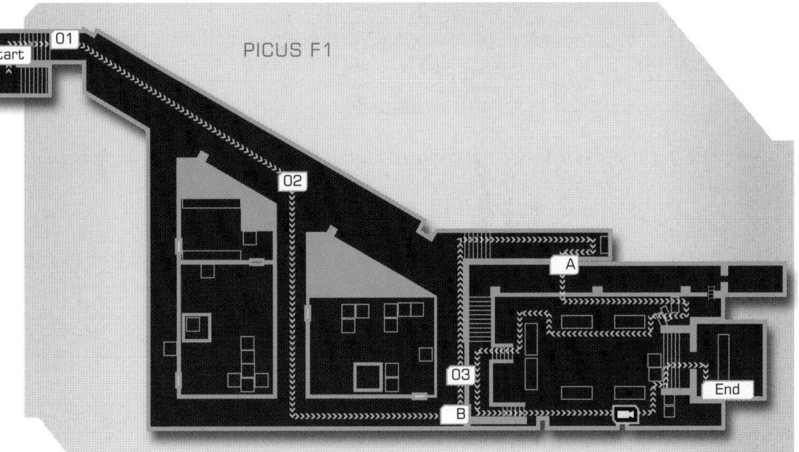
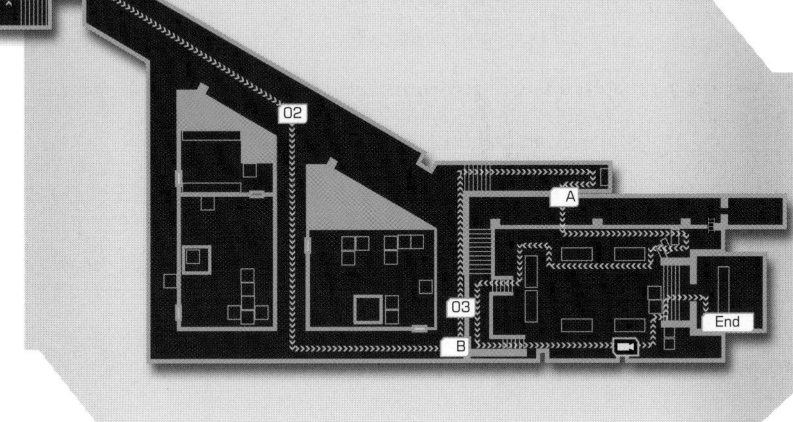

Required Hacking: Capture 3
Recommended None

Recommended Revolver (w/ Explosive Rounds), Combat Rifle, 10mm Pistol (Silenced), Frag Grenade

01 Move down the stairs while crouching and slowly approach the two guards located at the base of the stairs. Get close to them, and then take them both out at once with a Double Takedown. Search the bodies if you like and then move on.

02 Go to the western door of the Funicular Room. Open it, take cover on the left and peek in. Headshot the guard on the right side of the room and then wait for the remaining guard to come for you. Hold your position and pick him off.

03 If you wish, you can lay a rather nasty trap for the guards who will be ambushing you soon. To do this, go to the northern door, grab the soda machine and throw it down the hall so that it lands horizontal and flat. Now position it in front of the northern door and **Position A**. In the Funicular Room are a small and a large crate. Position the small one next to the soda machine to fill the gap of the northern door. [→☐ 5]

Hack the Security Hub and turn the Turret on the enemies. Position the Turret just outside the western door at **Position B**. Now grab the large crate you see in the room and position it across the inside of the western door. [→☐ 6]

This blocks both doors and keeps the guards out. Now go out and carefully lay any mines you have in the hall. Frags are good near the northern door, while Concussion mines are good near the western door, so that the guards get stunned and the Turret has more time to work on them. With the trap set, call the Funicular and then take cover at the crates near its doors. [→☐ 7]

If you don't want to set this trap, then destroy the Turret in the room. After doing this, push the call button for the Funicular and then take cover behind the crate on the southern side of the Funicular staircase. Hold your position here and pick off any guards who come in. Once the Funicular arrives use it to reach the next area.

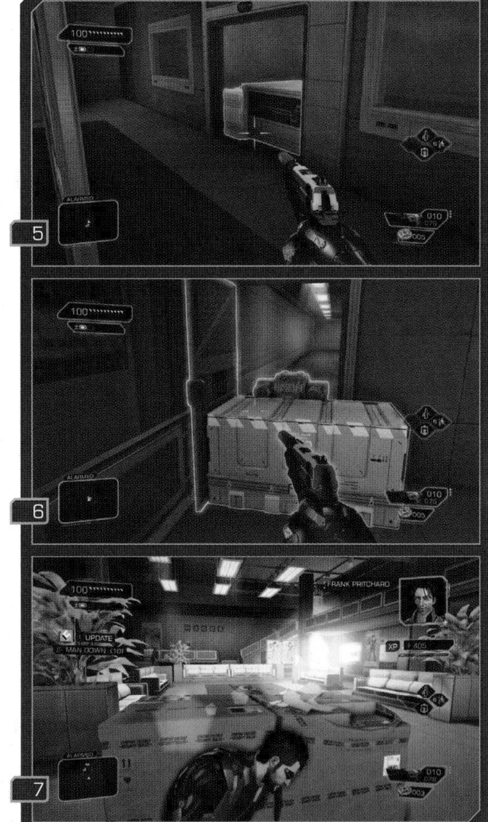

Objective Completed	Objective Type	XP Reward	Stealth Bonuses	
			Ghost	Smooth Operator
Summon the Funicular	Primary	250	Yes	Yes
Wait for the Funicular	Primary	2500	Yes	Yes
Use the Funicular to reach the sub-basement	Primary	250	No	No

ROUTE 1 Stealth

Objective Name	Objective Type
Get inside room 802-11	Primary

Required Cloaking System, Move/Throw Heavy Objects
Recommended None

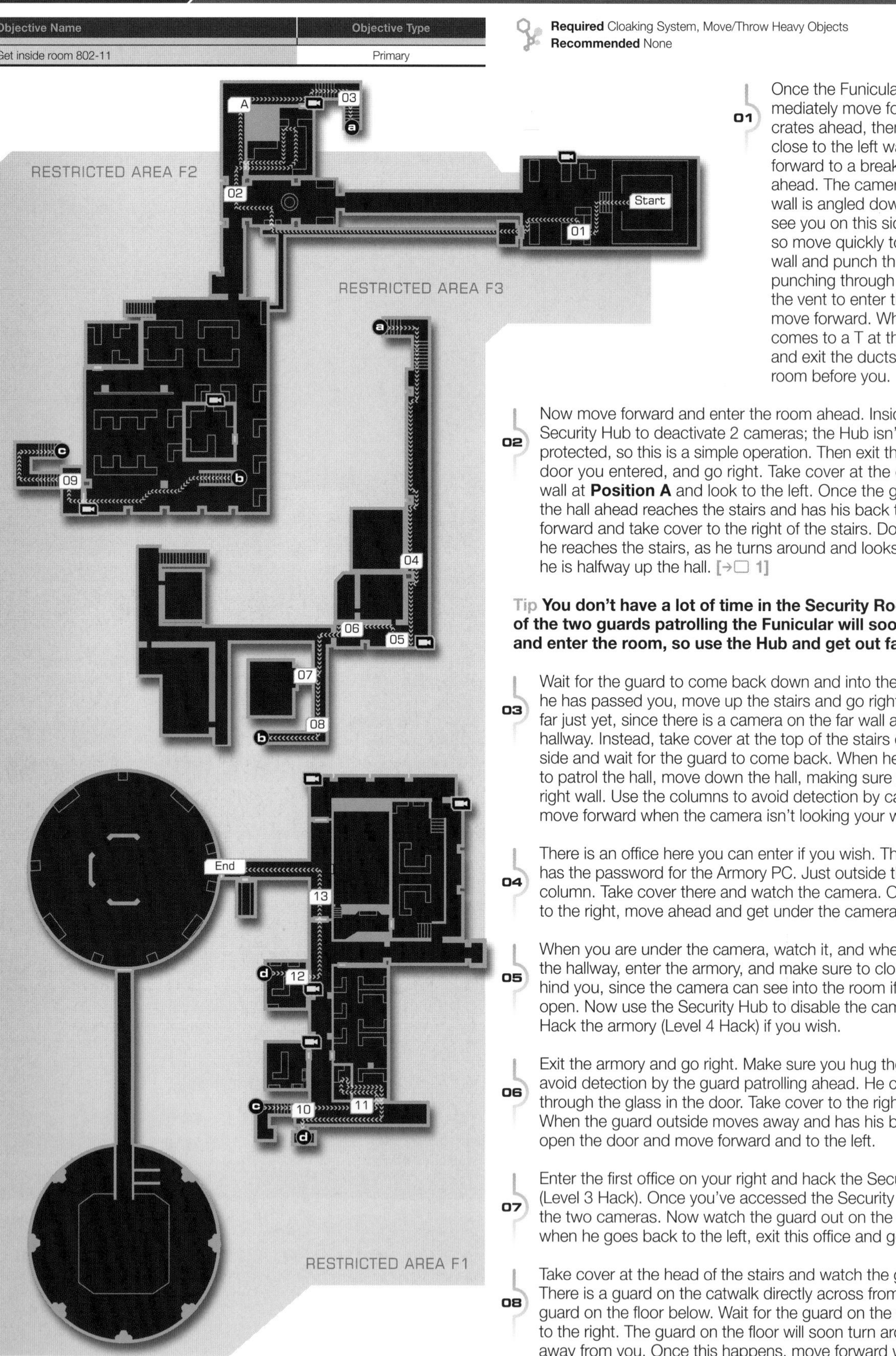

01 Once the Funicular stops, immediately move forward to the crates ahead, then go left. Stay close to the left wall and move forward to a breakable wall ahead. The camera on the right wall is angled down and can't see you on this side of the room, so move quickly to the cracked wall and punch through it. After punching through the wall, use the vent to enter the air ducts to move forward. When the duct comes to a T at the end, go right and exit the ducts to enter the room before you.

02 Now move forward and enter the room ahead. Inside, use the Security Hub to deactivate 2 cameras; the Hub isn't password protected, so this is a simple operation. Then exit the room via the door you entered, and go right. Take cover at the corner of the wall at **Position A** and look to the left. Once the guard patrolling the hall ahead reaches the stairs and has his back to you, move forward and take cover to the right of the stairs. Don't move until he reaches the stairs, as he turns around and looks back when he is halfway up the hall. [→☐ 1]

Tip **You don't have a lot of time in the Security Room, as one of the two guards patrolling the Funicular will soon come back and enter the room, so use the Hub and get out fast.**

03 Wait for the guard to come back down and into the hallway. Once he has passed you, move up the stairs and go right. Don't go too far just yet, since there is a camera on the far wall at the end of the hallway. Instead, take cover at the top of the stairs on the left-hand side and wait for the guard to come back. When he leaves again to patrol the hall, move down the hall, making sure you hug the right wall. Use the columns to avoid detection by camera, and only move forward when the camera isn't looking your way.

04 There is an office here you can enter if you wish. The PC inside has the password for the Armory PC. Just outside this office is a column. Take cover there and watch the camera. Once it looks to the right, move ahead and get under the camera.

05 When you are under the camera, watch it, and when it looks down the hallway, enter the armory, and make sure to close the door behind you, since the camera can see into the room if the door is left open. Now use the Security Hub to disable the camera outside. Hack the armory (Level 4 Hack) if you wish.

06 Exit the armory and go right. Make sure you hug the right wall to avoid detection by the guard patrolling ahead. He can see you through the glass in the door. Take cover to the right of the door. When the guard outside moves away and has his back to you, open the door and move forward and to the left.

07 Enter the first office on your right and hack the Security Hub here (Level 3 Hack). Once you've accessed the Security Hub, disable the two cameras. Now watch the guard out on the catwalk, and when he goes back to the left, exit this office and go right.

08 Take cover at the head of the stairs and watch the guards ahead. There is a guard on the catwalk directly across from you and a guard on the floor below. Wait for the guard on the catwalk to go to the right. The guard on the floor will soon turn around and walk away from you. Once this happens, move forward whilst crouched and go through the door at the far end of the room.

09 Be careful and move slowly through the door, since the stairs ahead are booby-trapped with a Concussive Mine and an EMP Mine. Move slowly to each one and disable it, and then continue down the stairs to the floor below.

10 At the base of the stairs, take cover and peek out to the right to a Heavy on patrol. Watch him. When he turns to go up the hall, jump to cover to reach the opposite wall quickly, thus avoiding detection by the camera further up the hall. [→☐ 2]

11 Move inside the room here and hack the Security Hub (Level 3 Hack). Disable the two cameras. Now backtrack to the stairs and look left to find a breakable wall. Wait for the Heavy to make his way to the opposite end of the hall, then punch through the wall. Punching through the wall will alter the Heavy's patrol path when he sees the hole. This is very beneficial for the upcoming hack you'll need to do in order to progress.

12 When you have punched through the wall, use the vent inside and move forward in the air ducts to the very end. Exit the ducts to enter the office here. Now open the door ahead and look right to see the heavy go into the office area, thus clearing the hall for you. Go to the door and hack it (Level 3 Hack).

13 Once you are past the door, move up the hall and go left to the large doors of the room Data Storage 802-11. Beyond those doors is a Boss Fight, so prepare yourself.

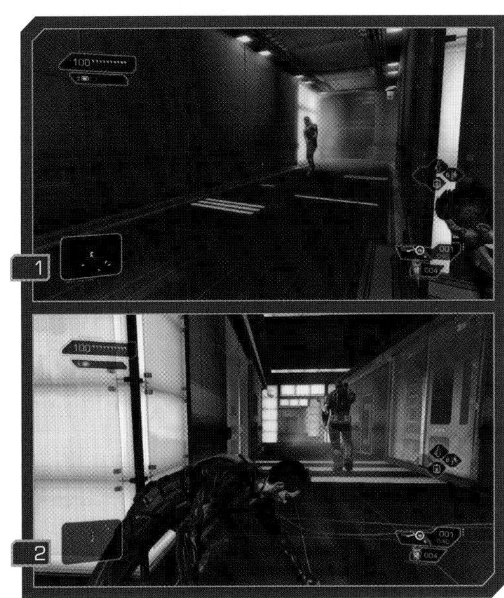

Path to the Broadcast Room

ROUTE 2 Stealth Combat

Required Cloaking System, Punch Through Walls
Recommended Reflex Booster

Recommended Tranquilizer Rifle, Gas Mines

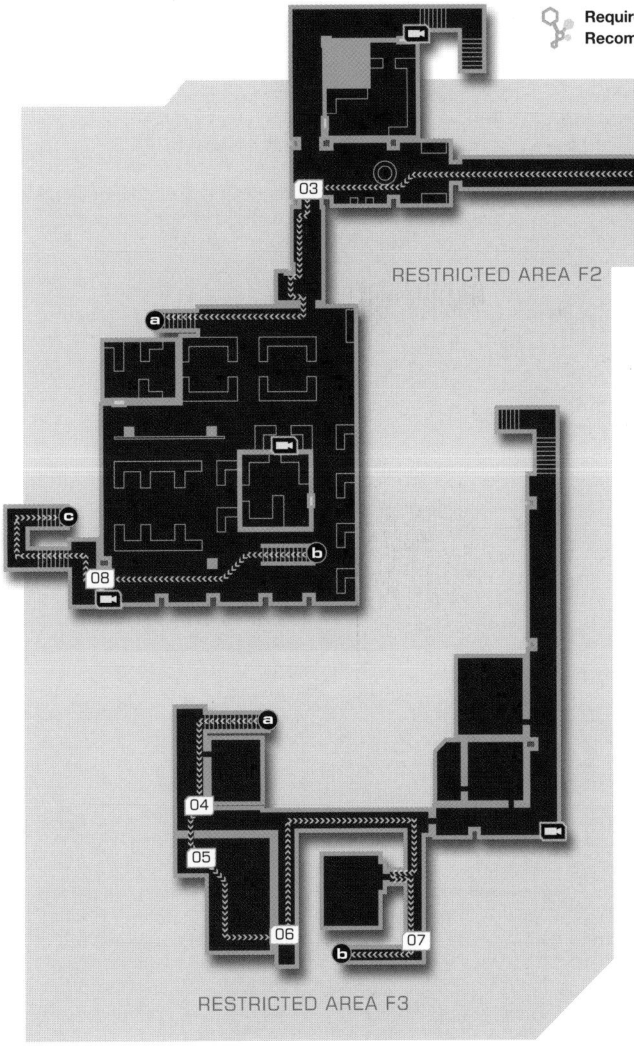

RESTRICTED AREA F2

RESTRICTED AREA F3

01 When the ride is over, move forward into the room to trigger the auto-save. Now head back and around the Funicular. The back of the Funicular is low enough so you can climb on top of the Funicular and then crouch. Stay there and watch the hallway ahead. Soon, two guards will come walking up the hallway. Use the Tranquilizer Rifle to shoot the guard on the left, as he is lagging behind. After the reload, shoot the remaining guard. [→☐ 3]

02 Hug the right wall of the room and move forward under the camera. Once you are there, activate Cloak and then quickly move through the laser grid ahead. When you're past the laser grid, deactivate Cloak to save energy. At the end of this hallway is another laser grid you'll need to use Cloak to get past.

03 Go left and approach the door here. As you get close, make sure you hug the right wall and then take cover at the right side of the door. Look through the glass in the door and watch the guard on the catwalk ahead. When he moves off to the right, open the door and activate Cloak. Move into the room and immediately go right and up the stairs to the next area.

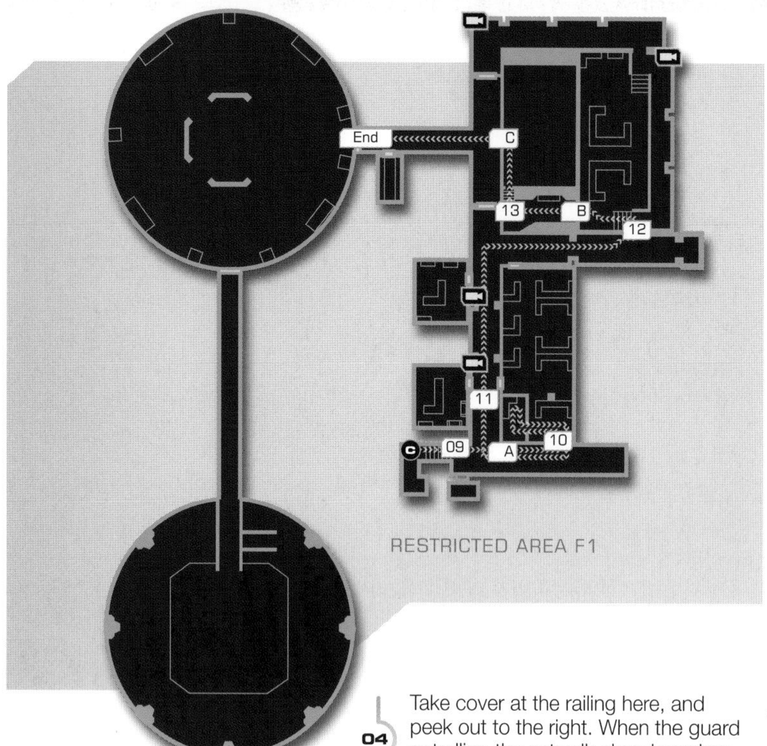

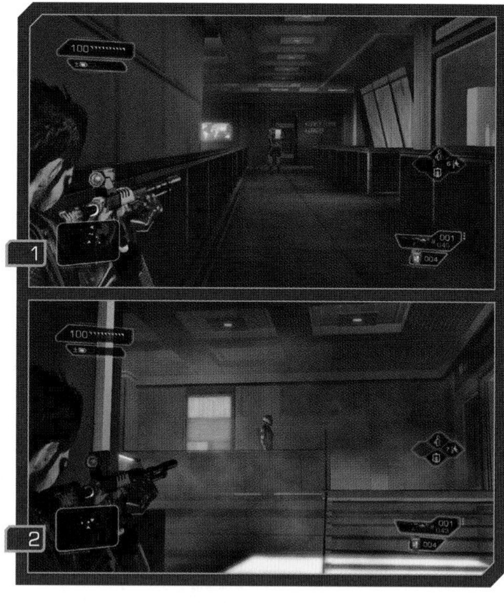

04 Take cover at the railing here, and peek out to the right. When the guard patrolling the catwalk ahead reaches the far end to the east, lean out and shoot him in the back with the Tranquilizer Rifle to take him out. At that end of the catwalk, the other guard there will never see him. [→☐ 1]

05 Go through the door on your right and head left. Keep the wall and filing cabinets to your left and move forward to the door ahead. Take cover at the left side and wait for the guard to move into position before you. When his back is to you, move out for a Takedown.

06 Stay crouching as you move, to make sure the guard below doesn't hear you. Now move to the Security Room and hack the Security Hub (Level 3 Hack) and turn the two cameras off. Once the cameras are out of action exit the room and go to the right.

07 Take cover at the right side of the railing and watch the guard below. Wait for him to get as close as his patrol takes him, and when he turns and goes back the other way, move whilst crouching to get behind him for a Takedown.

08 Go through the door here to reach the stairs, but proceed slowly and with caution. There are two mines ahead that you'll have to ease past. It's best to approach each one slowly and deactivate it. Once you've done so, move on to the next floor below.

09 As you reach the base of the stairs, take cover and peek out to the right to a Heavy on patrol. Watch him. As he turns to go up the hall, jump to cover and reach the opposite wall quickly, avoiding detection by the camera further up the hall.

10 Move inside the room here and hack the Security Hub (Level 3 Hack). Disable the two cameras. Now backtrack to the corner of the wall at **Position A**. Watch the Heavy here and wait for him to get close. Once he turns and moves away, get behind him for a Takedown.

11 Go up the hall and the turn right to reach the door ahead. Take cover at the left side of the door and watch the guards inside. When both of them are at the far end of the room with their backs to you, move into the room and go left to the door ahead.

12 Inside this room is a Security Hub that you can hack (Level 3 Hack). Do so, and then turn off the two cameras attached to it. With the cameras down, go back to the door you just came through and take cover at **Position B**. Look out to the right, and wait for the guard furthest away from you to take position directly ahead. When he does, shoot him with the Tranquilizer Rifle. [→☐ 2]

13 When he is down, watch the final guard. He'll get close to the other guard's position and will then turn and head back to the left. When he does, move out whilst crouched and use a Takedown. Now return to the previous room and go to **Position C** to find a breakable wall. Punch through it, and the room Data Storage 802-11 is directly ahead.

Path to the Broadcast Room

ROUTE 3 Combat

Required None
Recommended Typhoon

Recommended Revolver (w/ Explosive Rounds), Combat Rifle, 10mm Pistol (Silenced), Frag Grenade

01 When you get out of the Funicular, start by shooting out the camera. This will make the guards come running. Take cover at the right side of the doorway. If you have the shotgun, equip it. Wait for the guards to get close, then peek out and blast them. Three guards will come, so wait for them all before moving forward. Hold your position here and wait for the Medium Sentry to come. When it does, peek out from cover and destroy it. [→☐ 3]

02 Now that the first wave is dead, go to the door of Operating Area 03, which is ahead and to the left. Take cover at the right side of the door and then open it. Peek in and headshot the guards. The guards tend to rush the door here. If they do, jump out and use Typhoon, if you have it.

If the Medium Sentry didn't come out earlier then it will be in this room, and eventually it will come for you. When you see it, retreat back down the hall to the office. From there, use an EMP to take out the Meduim Sentry. If you don't have an EMP, stay evasive, and whittle away the Sentry's health with gunfire until it's dead. With the Sentry gone, return to the door and pick off any remaining guards.

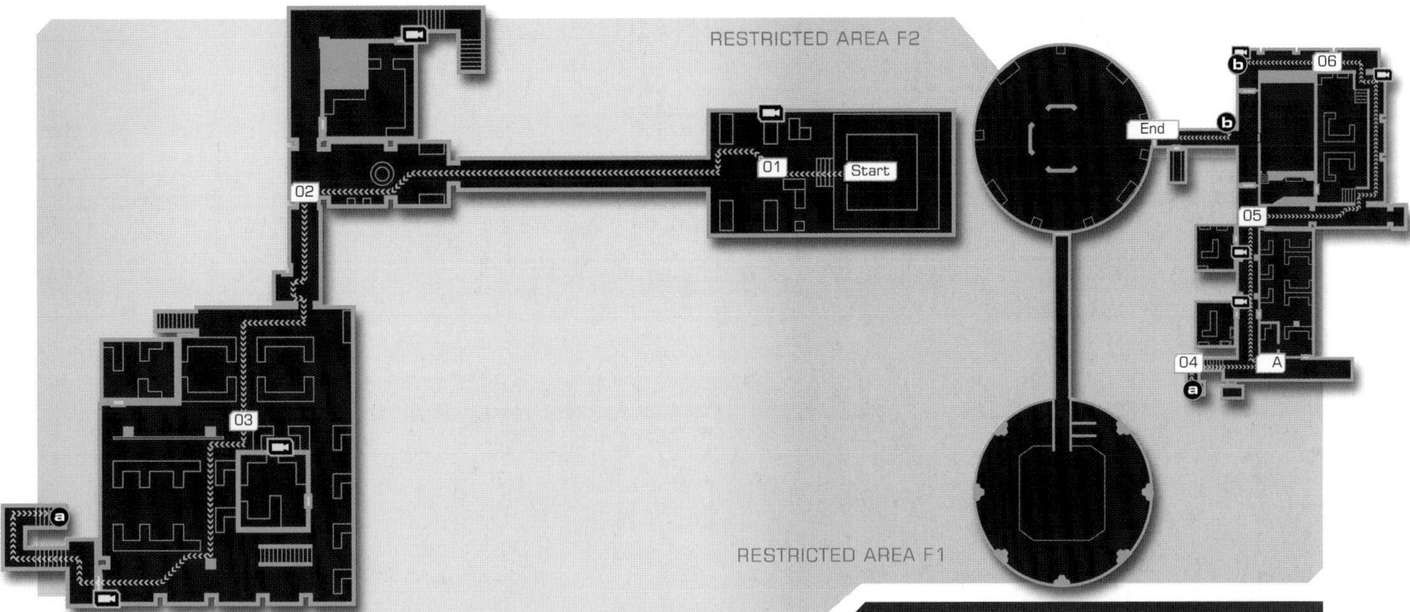

03 Now that you've cleared the area of the enemy, you are free to explore if you wish. When you are ready, go to the exit in the southwest. Once you are through the doors, drop to a crouch and move slowly ahead so that you can see the mines. Shoot them both to dispose of them.

04 Take cover at the corner of the wall just before the last section of the stairs. Now peek out to the left and you'll see a Medium Sentry just ahead. Lay into the beast with constant gunfire to destroy it. Now move down to **Position A** and take cover at the corner of the wall. Peek out to see the heavy and hit him once with heavy gunfire to stun him. Once he drops to his knees, run to him for a Takedown. [→☐ 4]

05 Move to the doorway here and then peek out and locate the guards in the room and then target them with your gunfire. The guards in here are Sneakers, so you'll often have to lean out to draw their fire in order to find them. Once they are both dead, exit the room via the door to the north.

06 Ignore the camera here and make your way to the vent. Open the vent and then enter the air ducts. Follow the ducts to the next vent and then move out into the hallway. The room Data Storage 802-11 is to your left. There is a Boss Fight waiting for you in there, so prepare yourself. When you're ready, go through the door.

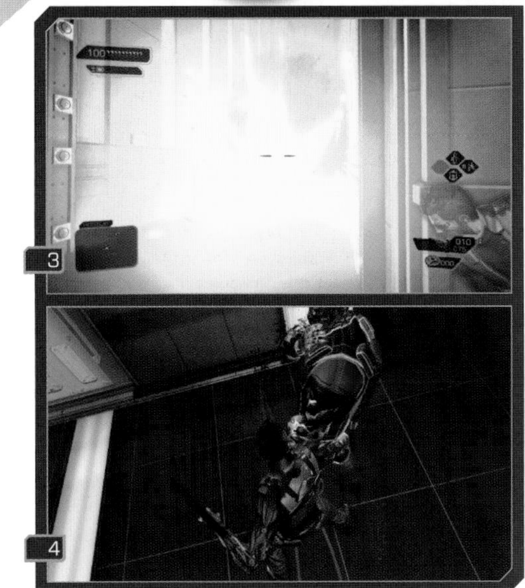
3
4

Objective Completed	Objective Type	XP Reward	Stealth Bonuses	
			Ghost	Smooth Operator
Get inside room 802-11	Primary	1750	Yes	Yes

BOSS FIGHT YELENA FEDOROVA

Required None
Recommended Typhoon

Recommended Combat Rifle, Revolver, 10mm Pistol, Frag Grenade

Here you face the second Boss of the game. We'll give you a few tips here to get you started. If you prefer a full strategy on how to take down this formidable Boss, please refer to the Opponents Chapter of this guide.

- The power generators on the wall can be destroyed in order to deliver electricity to the floor, but it can also hurt you unless you have the EMP Shielding Augmentation.
- The Stun Gun and P.E.P.S rifle do a remarkable job of stunning Fedorova and stopping her from unleashing her Typhoon.
- Use mines to booby-trap her path to you.
- Use Typhoon if you have it.

ACHIEVEMENT/TROPHY: THE MANTIS

You'll unlock this one once you have defeated Yelena Fedorova.

Objective Completed	Objective Type	XP Reward	Stealth Bonuses	
			Ghost	Smooth Operator
Defeat the Mercenary Leader	Primary	2500	No	No

TAKE US HOME

Objective Name	Objective Type
Go to the Chopper and extract	Primary

Once you're done with Fedorova, check all the lockers in the area for a wealth of ammunition and items. Also, don't forget to check the body of Fedorova herself for some Credits and Typhoon ammo. When you're ready, go through the southern door to the Helipad and board the chopper for extraction.

Objective Completed	Objective Type	XP Reward	Stealth Bonuses: Ghost	Stealth Bonuses: Smooth Operator
Go to the chopper and extract	Secondary	750	No	No

M1 - CONFRONTING SARIF

Objective Name	Objective Type
Meet Sarif in my apartment	Primary

OPTIONAL EXPLORATION

Once you get off the chopper, go to the northwest corner of the area to find a breakable wall. Punch through it, grab the crate inside and place it beneath the vent to access the air ducts. You'll find 615 Credits in the ducts. In the main room of this area is a pair of lockers. Inside them, you'll find a CyberBoost ProEnergy Bar, and on top of the lockers is an Ammo Capacity Upgrade for one of your weapons.

Once you exit the chopper, leave the Helipad and head to the southeast corner of the area to enter the building. Inside, make your way to the elevator and use it to reach the floor Jensen's apartment is on. Enter Jensen's apartment to confront Sarif.

Objective Completed	Objective Type	XP Reward	Stealth Bonuses: Ghost	Stealth Bonuses: Smooth Operator
Meet Sarif in my apartment	Primary	750	No	No

M2 - FINDING ISAIAS SANDOVAL

Objective Name	Objective Type
Investigate Convention Center for Sandoval's location	Primary

OPTIONAL EXPLORATION

- **Visit both Weapon Dealers for new items, particularly weapon upgrade kits.**
- **Go to the LIMB Clinic for Praxis Kits; they have respawned since your last visit.**

SIDE QUEST

Once you exit the Chiron building and begin moving up the street, Pritchard will contact you with some information. This will open the Acquaintances Forgotten Side Quest.

When the meeting with Sarif is over, exit Jensen's building and get down to the Detroit streets. If you got into the Police Station via Wayne Hass, he'll be in the lobby waiting for you. [→☐ 1]. You'll be given a choice during the meeting with Wayne. Choose Absolve for a good ending, otherwise you'll fight him. When you're ready, go to the Convention Center in the southwest corner of Detroit.

1

DETROIT CONVENTION CENTER

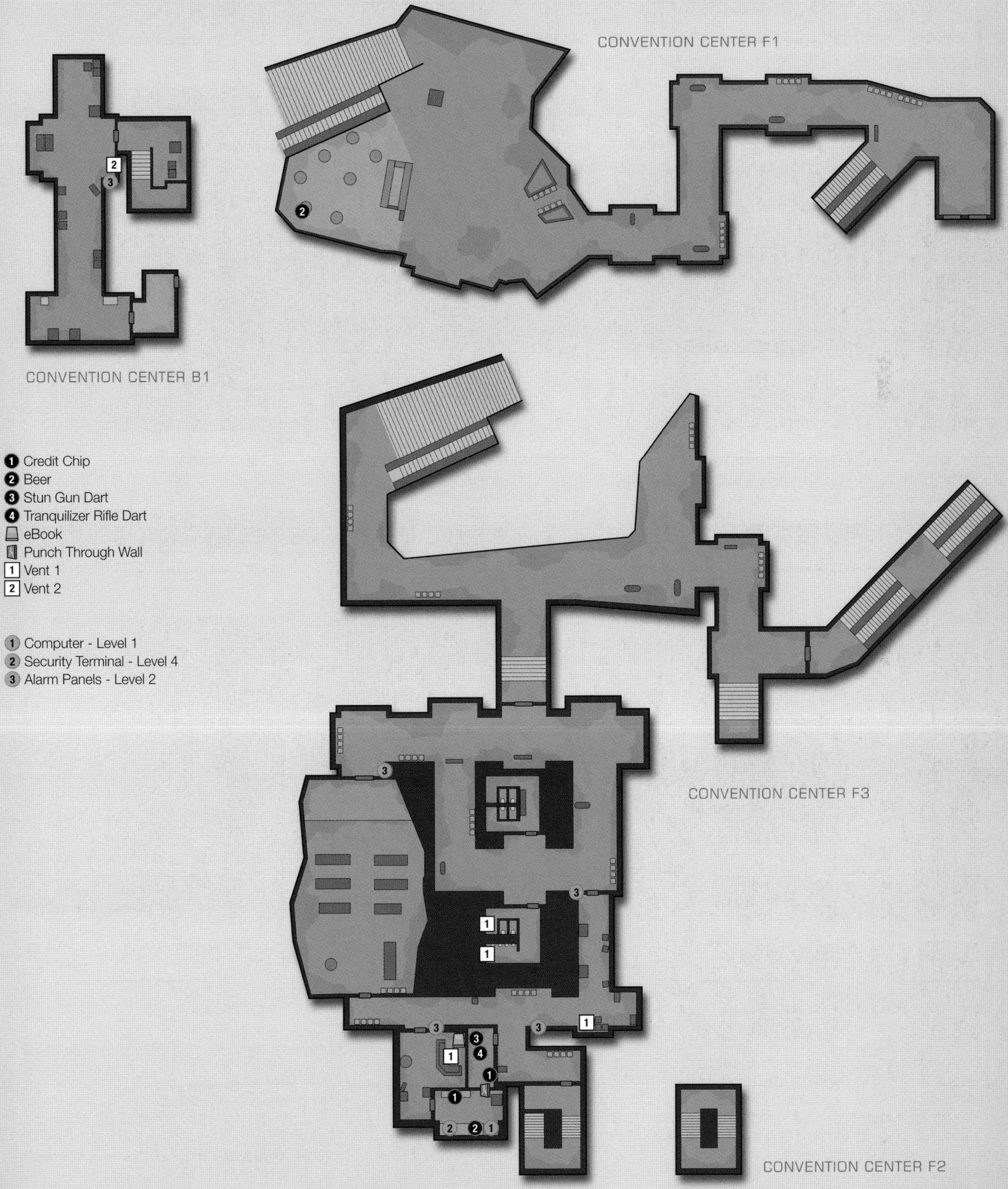

CONVENTION CENTER F1

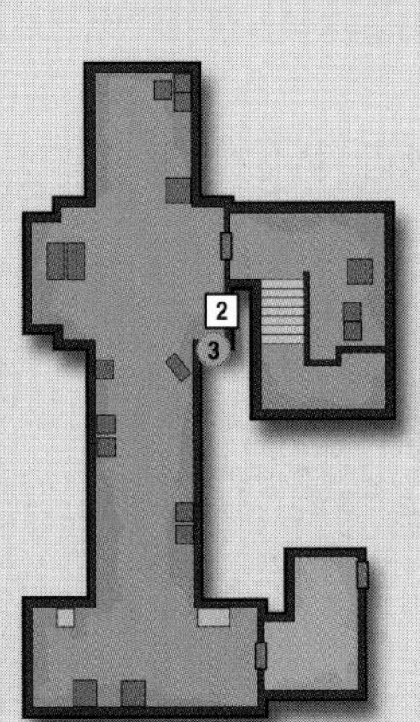

CONVENTION CENTER B1

- 1 Credit Chip
- 2 Beer
- 3 Stun Gun Dart
- 4 Tranquilizer Rifle Dart
- eBook
- Punch Through Wall
- 1 Vent 1
- 2 Vent 2

- 1 Computer - Level 1
- 2 Security Terminal - Level 4
- 3 Alarm Panels - Level 2

CONVENTION CENTER F3

CONVENTION CENTER F2

ROUTE 1 | Stealth

Required None
Recommended Social Enhancer

01 Once you are inside the Convention Center, go right through the double doors. Now, proceed forward to find some stairs on your left. Use these to reach the third floor above.

02 From the stairs, head right and make your way to the Meeting Hall ahead. When you are in the Meeting Hall, go right to Room 2005 and confront Taggart. Once you do, you will trigger a conversation gameplay. [→□ 1]

1

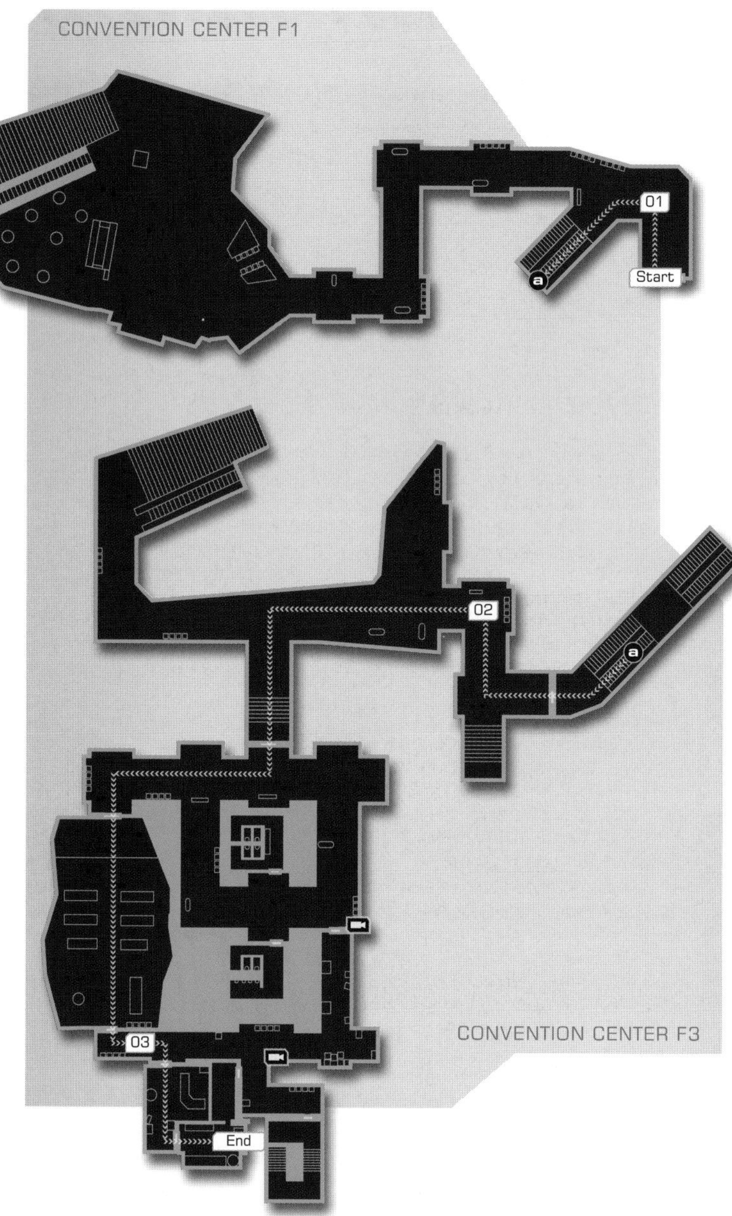

CONVERSATION FLOW
WILLIAM TAGGART
PERSONALITY TYPE: ALPHA

Conversation Round	Response to Make
Round 1	Confront
Round 2	Confront
Round 3	Confront
Round 4	Confront

03 After you have won the conversation gameplay with Taggart, exit the room through the newly opened door at the rear. Go through it and turn left. Take the first door on your right and then enter Taggart's private room and speak with him. After talking with Taggart, exit the Convention Center the way you came in.

SIDE QUEST: DOCTORATE

Once you enter Taggart's Waiting Room, look left to find one of Hugh Darrow's eBooks lying on a table in the corner.

Inside The Detroit Convention Center

ROUTE 2 | Stealth Combat

Required Move/Throw Heavy Objects, Punch Through Walls, Hacking: Capture 4
Recommended None

Recommended Tranquilizer Rifle

Tip **You don't get any XP for taking out the Bodyguards here, so only incapacitate the ones that are in your way.**

01 Once you are inside the Convention Center, go right through the double doors. Now, proceed forward to find some stairs on your left. Go up them to the third floor above.

02 After entering the Meeting Hall, turn left, go around the corner and talk to the guard that is standing under the cameras next to the Backstage Door. Once you get close to him, he'll tell you that you shouldn't be there. Triggering this event changes this guard's patrol habits, which becomes important shortly.

Now go to your right and enter the men's bathroom at **Position A**. Once inside, wait 30 seconds, and the guard that has a position under the camera at the Backstage Door will come into the bathroom and use one of the urinals. When he does, get behind him and use a Takedown. [→□ 2]. Once he is down, you can search him and find a Pocket Secretary with the code to the Backstage Door.

At this point in time
and then move on

02 Sprint to the southw
above. There are th
use energy bars to
then run to each of

03 Once those three a
F to reach the level

Use an energy bar
Takedown. After yo
sniper on the secon

Finally, if anyone is
then run to them fo
in time and Malik w
south at **Position I**

ROUTE

Required Reflex Booster
Recommended Cloaking
System

01 This is a tough fight
energy. For weapon
Rounds for the regu
and jump up on the
forward making sur

02 Run forward to the
Now approach the
A Box Guard will sh
directly ahead, and

03 Drop down and turn
run to the chopper
Now look back acro
him and you're don
few Credits, ammo,
to the south to exit

OPTIONAL EX

**If you have the Derma
water and not be hurt
under construction. T
Shielding Aug, you ca
a hidden area contain**

04 Once the elevator ri
and turn right. In the
portion of this small
find a set of double
leads out to streets
Once you go throug
you won't be able to
to this area. This me
want to explore the
tion Site, you need t
When you're ready,
the doors.

Objective Completed

Escape the Construction Site

Tip **You can use the vents here to access Taggart's room at this point, but getting out will be a little more difficult. There are many guards patrolling the hallways in the next area.**

Now go back to the Backstage Door, and you'll find that it is already open. Make sure none of the guards can see you and then go through the Backstage Door ensuring you shut it behind you to conceal your upcoming activities.

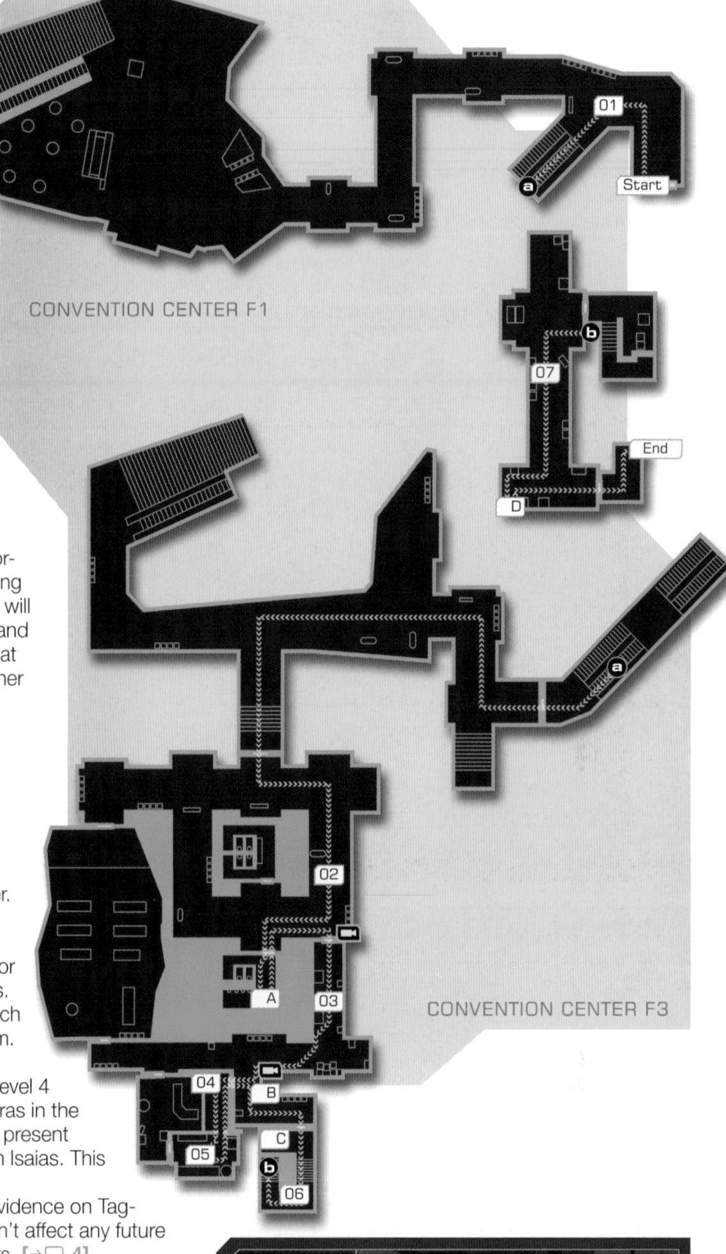

03 Once you are through the Backstage Door, take cover at the corner of the wall and look to your right. There are two guards talking near a camera. Wait for them to disperse and the blonde guard will go down the hall to the left. Once he does, watch the camera, and when it is facing away from you, move to the corner of the wall at **Position B**; make sure to move whilst crouching so that the other guard in the hallway doesn't notice you.
From your cover point at **Position B**, watch the blonde guard, and when his back is to you, sneak up behind him for a Takedown. Now hide the body at the top in the stairwell behind the door at **Position C**.

04 Go into the small storage room here. Once inside, take cover at the right side of the door and peek out. Now shoot the wall directly ahead with the Tranquilizer Rifle and then return to cover. This will attract the nearby guard, and when he is close, sneak up behind him for a Takedown. [→☐ 3]
With that done, go back into the storage room and shut the door behind you. At the rear of the room you'll see some large crates. Move them out of the way, and you'll find a breakable wall. Punch through the wall and you'll gain access to Taggart's private room.

05 In Taggart's room you'll find a Security Hub that you can hack (Level 4 Hack) if you wish. If you do hack the Hub, disable the two cameras in the area. Next, hack Taggart's PC. It's a Level 1 Hack that shouldn't present you with any problems. Once you are in, read the first email from Isaias. This email will give you Isaias' location.
Once you're done, Sarif will contact you and ask you to plant evidence on Taggart's PC. You can decline if you like, but by accepting, you won't affect any future gameplay, and you will gain an extra 750 XP. The choice is yours. [→☐ 4]

06 Go back through the Storage Room and turn right to the stairs where you hid the bodies earlier. Move whilst crouching, but waste no time as there is a new guard patrolling the hallway now. If you move quickly, you can get to the stairs before he walks by your position. Otherwise, wait for him to reach the eastern end of the hall, and then go to the stairs.
When you reach the stairs, stay crouched and move down the stairs just far enough to trigger the two guards to begin talking. As soon as you hear them, backtrack to the top of the stairs and take cover at the railing. Wait, and one of the guards will take up position just below you on the first landing below. Hold your position, and he'll soon begin to walk off, once he does, sneak up behind him for a Takedown. Now move down the stairs to where the guards where talking to find a vent. Open it and then enter the air ducts.

07 Go through the ductwork and exit through the next vent. As soon as you come out of the ducts, go left and make sure to stay on top of the external ducts. There is a guard below, but if you stay up top on the ducts, then you'll be able to move past him easily. Move forward to the southwest corner of this area and then drop down behind the crates on the floor below. Take cover behind the crates at **Position D** so that you can see back up the hallway you just passed over. When the patrolling guard is facing the other way, move up to the door opposite your position and exit the Convention Center.

ROUT

Required Cloakin
Recommended H

Tip **If you take t later. Also, if sh**

01 Run right and there, take co and join the fr

02 Now that the to the end. Go you're done h

03 Once the elev tion of this sm Hengsha. Onc this area. This do it now. Wh

ROUT

Required Cloakin
Recommended

01 You're going t use this route plenty of Cybe & Packs. You energy upgrad all five energy

At the start, g Stay to the rig an opening at **Position A**. G move up to th incapacitate h

Once he is do gas grenade a Heavy directly guard in the a

Now activate right to **Positi** on the Heavy tive, and go to use a Takedo

HARVESTER TERRITORY

1 Laser Rifle
2 Credit Chip
3 Cyberboost ProEnergy Bar
4 Pain Killers
5 Beer
6 Spirits
7 10mm Pistol Ammo
8 Combat Rifle Ammo
9 Heavy Rifle Ammo
10 Laser Rifle Battery
11 Machine Pistol Ammo
12 Sniper Rifle Ammo
13 Stun Gun Dart
14 Tranquilizer Rifle Dart
15 Typhoon Ammo
16 Damage Upgrade
17 Ammo Capacity Upgrade
18 Cooling System
19 Automatic Unlocking Device
20 Remote Detonated Explosive Device
Pocket Secretary
eBook
Punch Through Wall
1 Vent 1

1 Computer - Unlocked
2 Computer - Level 1
3 Computer - Level 3
4 Security Terminal - Level 3
5 Security Panels - Level 3
6 Security Panels - Level 4
7 Safe Panel - Level 5

LOCATING THE GPL

OPTIONAL EXPLORATION

- Go to the LIMB Clinic for two more Praxis Kits, they have respawned since you were last here.
- At LIMB, you have the option of completing the Secondary Objective of getting new Biochip. We strongly suggest you do not do this as it makes the Namir Boss Fight later in the game much harder.
- Visit the new weapon dealer, Peng Xin Hao. You'll find him in the most southern tip of Youzhao district.
- Go to Hung Hua Hotel for an NPC confrontation and to visit the Weapon Dealer there.

Objective Name	Objective Type
Find Vasili Sevchenko's GPL Device	Primary
Get a new Biochip at the L.I.M.B Clinic	Secondary

SIDE QUEST: TALION A.D.

In the LIMB Clinic, you can talk to Doctor Wing to trigger this Side Quest. Dr. Wing is located just to the left of the main counter.

SIDE QUEST: A MATTER OF DISCRETION

As soon as you enter the Youzhao District, Hugh Darrow will contact you and make this Side Quest available.

Harvester Sewers

ROUTE 1 Stealth

08_042

Required Cloaking System
Recommended Smart Vision

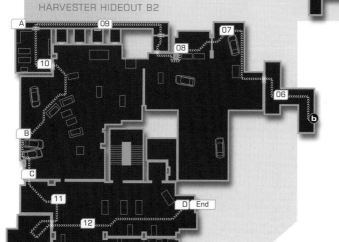

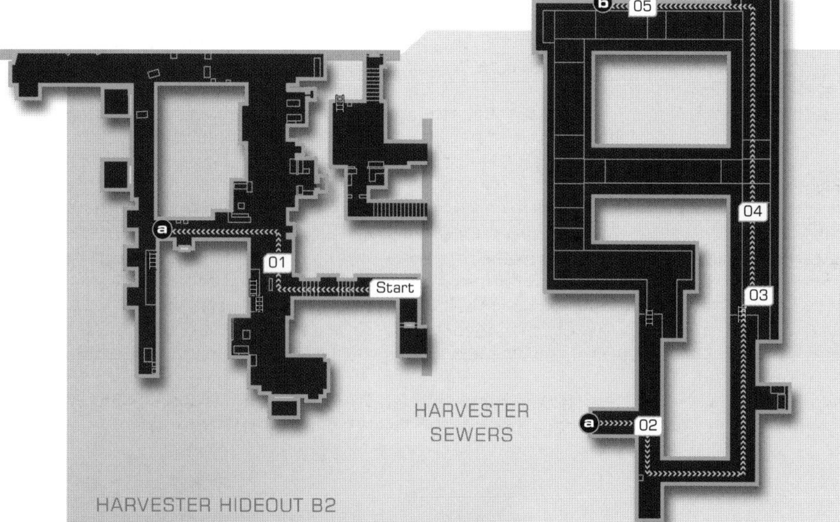

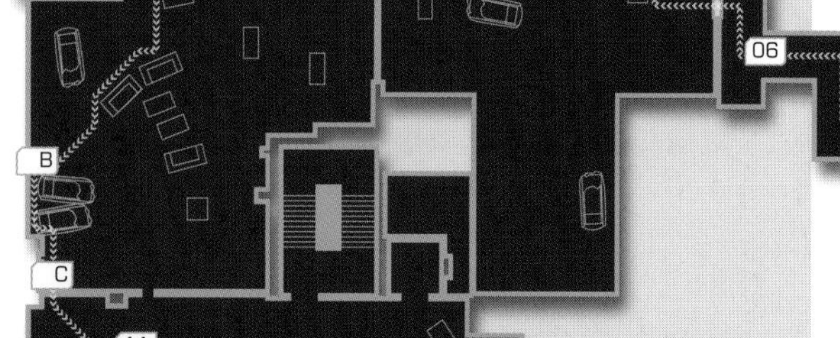

01 Just south of the main Harvester entrance, and behind the Downtown Apartments, you'll find a manhole cover. Make your way there and then open the manhole cover to enter the sewers.

02 Enter the sewers and go right. Follow the sewers around to the ladder. Climb down the ladder to drop down to the next level. Be careful here as there are guards on patrol directly ahead.

03 Get into the water, crouch down, and move ahead as the first guard before you moves off to the left. There is another guard further up looking your way, so move slowly forward making sure to keep the concrete divider on the bridge between you and his line of sight.

04 The second guard will turn and walk away from you. Move forward as he does and follow him but be sure to remain crouching and in the water. You'll come to a left-hand turn at a large bridge. Move to the edge of that bridge and look ahead. You'll see the door to the Harvester Hideout ahead and on the right.

05 When you're ready, activate cloak and move forward to the door that is just ahead and on the right. Stay crouching to minimize noise as you move forward. You can reach the door with only one energy cell, so waste no time getting to the door and going through it. [→☐ 1]

06 From the sewers, crouch and peek through the slots in the bottom of the door here. There are two guards ahead. The one on the couch doesn't move. Wait for the guard on the left to move away on patrol, when he does, open the door and move to cover at the wrecked car on the right.

07 From the car, move forward to the large box in the alcove ahead. Be quick, and you can do this before the patrolling guard moves. Take cover at the box, and watch the patrolling guard. Wait for him to go to the car ahead and take position so that he is facing away from you. Once he does, make your move. [→☐ 2]

08 Move right and hug the wall and you'll come to a door. Open it and enter the bathroom. Close the door behind you to muffle any noise! There is a breakable wall here, so punch through it.

09 Enter the area behind the wall and go left to the second breakable wall. Be careful here. If you are going for the Pacifist Achievement and don't want to kill anyone, then you can't just punch through the wall when the Harvester is near as this will kill him.

Instead, go to **Position A** and take cover at the fence there. Now use Smart Vision to see when the Harvester has taken up position at the breakable wall. Once he has, shoot the wall with the Revolver and its explosive rounds to break the wall. Alternatively you can use a Frag Grenade or a Frag Mine to break the wall as well – the Typhoon will even work for this.

Once the wall explodes, the concussive force of the explosion will knock out the Harvester, but he'll still be alive and well – just asleep. Since the door in this room is closed, no one will have heard the noise, so you're safe. [→☐ 3]

Note **If the explosion of the wall doesn't knock out the Harvester, you'll have to move in fast for a Takedown or use the Stun Gun.**

Tip **It's best to skip the middle breakable wall as the noise attracts the guards and changes their positions. You can come back to this cell later after meeting Tong to get the Damage Upgrade that is there.**

Tip **If you didn't save Malik at the construction site, you'll find her body on the table in this room. This is a bit disturbing...**

ACHIEVEMENT/TROPHY: DOCTORATE

In this room you'll find one of Hugh Darrow's eBooks on the computer desk located in the northwest corner of the room.

10 Take cover at the door of this room, and open it. If one of the patrolling Harvesters gets suspicious, hold your position in cover and you'll be fine. Now, activate Cloak and move forward to take cover at the concrete block ahead. The Harvester to watch is the Heavy on patrol in the middle of the room. [→☐ 4]

When the Heavy is looking the other way, move from cover to cover until you reach the wrecked car at **Position B** and then take cover behind that car.

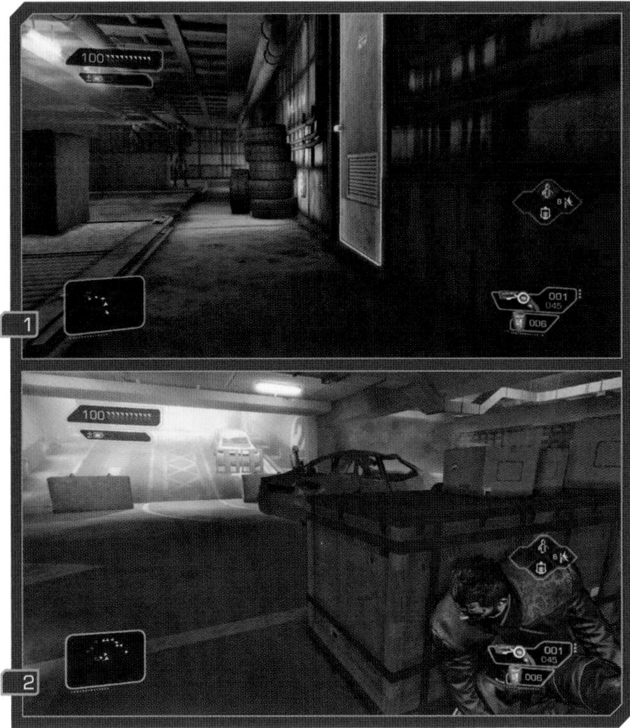

Watch the Heavy, and when it's clear, move from cover to cover to the far wall. Once there, move the box at **Position C** to expose the small opening in the bottom of the wall.

11 It's a clear shot here and no one will see you as long as you stay-crouching. When you're ready, go through the opening to find the door to the Harvester Leader's room just ahead and on the right.

12 Once the meeting with Harvester Leader is over, you're free to go. Before leaving the office, look around to find some credits, Spirits, and a Laser Rifle. The Laser Rifle takes up a lot of inventory space, but it is very effective against the End Boss and will make that fight easier if you choose to carry it with you. When you are ready, exit this area and enter the sewers via the door on the east side of the area at **Position D**.

Tip **After the meeting with Tong, you are free to explore the Harvester Hideout if you wish. No one will stop you.**

ROUTE 2 Stealth Combat

Required Icarus Landing System, Reflex Booster, Cloaking System
Recommended None

01 Just northeast of the Harvester Hideout's main entrance you'll find a ladder that will get you up onto the rooftops of the building here. Go there and use the ladders and scaffolding to reach the rooftops above you.

02 Once on the rooftops, go forward and then left. Make your way across the rooftops to find a vent located just above the main entrance of the Harvester Hideout. Use that vent to enter the air ducts and get inside the hideout. [→☐ 1]

03 After exiting the air ducts, you'll find yourself in an elevator shaft. Drop down to the bottom of the shaft. This is a long drop and requires the Icarus Landing System Aug to survive it. Once you reach the bottom, use the ladder to climb back up one level, and then open the door and move out to the next area.

04 After exiting the elevator shaft, turn right to find two Harvesters talking. Make sure to move whilst crouching, and they'll never see you. Take them both out with a Double Takedown. Now you are free to pilfer both bodies and to search the immediate area for items if you so choose.

05 When you're ready, head back to the east and take cover at the concrete barrier here. Look ahead and you'll see a Harvester on patrol. He goes left toward two other Harvesters and a camera, then he heads back to the right and takes up position at a truck. When he reaches his position to the left in front of the other two Harvesters, lean out from cover and shoot him in the back with the Tranquilizer Rifle.

Make sure to hit his body, as you'll be counting on the delay of the dart's drug here. Do this correctly, and the Harvester will walk to the truck on the right and then pass out shortly after reaching it. Once he passes out there, the camera and other two Harvesters will not see him. [→☐ 2]

06 Now head north and down the ramp. At first, stick close to the left-hand wall. When you reach the junked car ahead, move a bit to the right so that you can see the two Harvesters at the bottom of the ramp. Immediately shoot the closest Harvester with the Tranquilizer Rifle. The Harvester sitting in the chair is asleep, so you first concern is the patrolling Harvester.

1

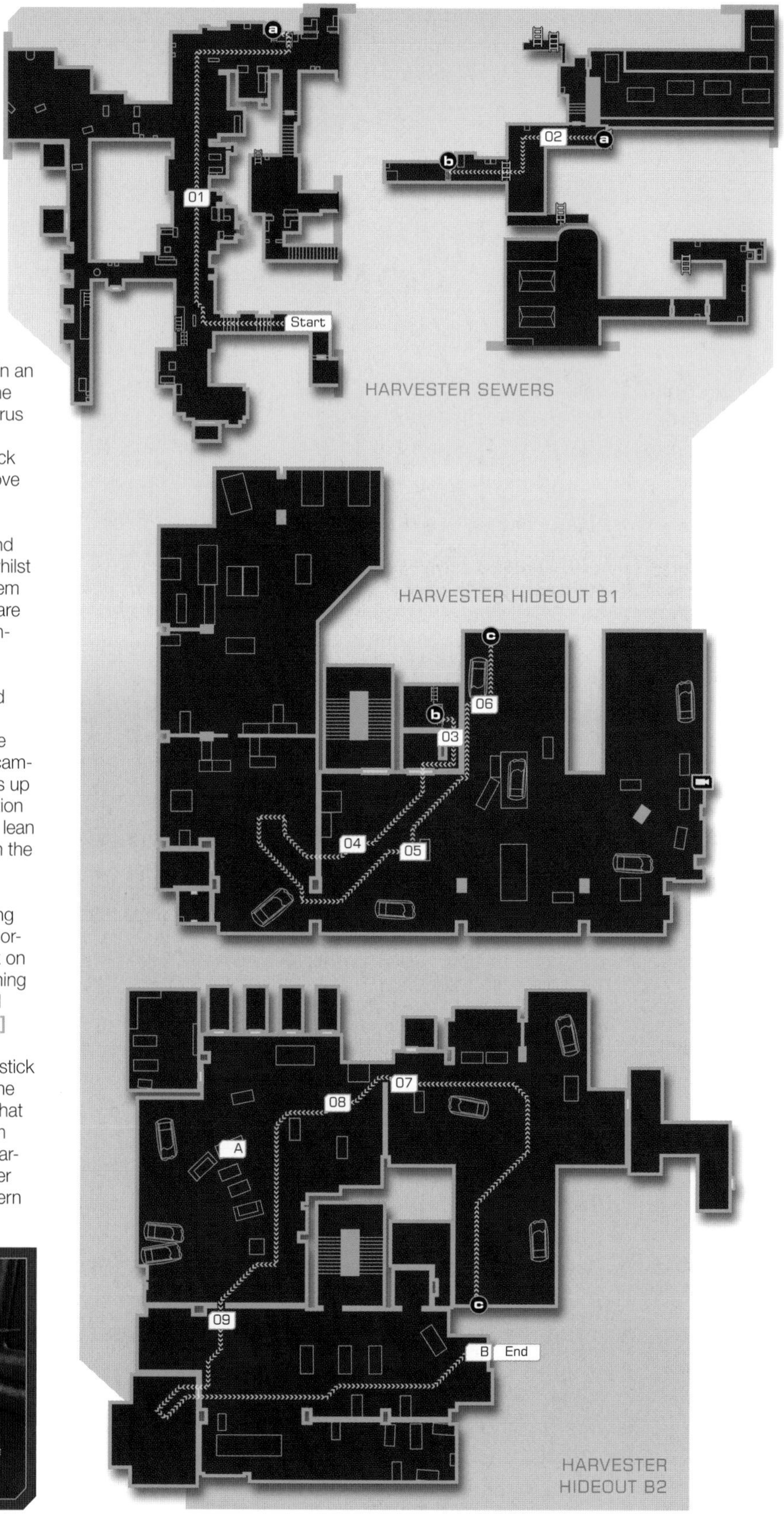

HARVESTER SEWERS

a
02
b
01
Start

HARVESTER HIDEOUT B1

c
b
06
03
04
05

HARVESTER HIDEOUT B2

07
08
A
09
c
B
End

If you're quick, you'll be able to shoot him before he moves off to the left on his patrol. If you don't make it in time, then take position at the wrecked car here. Wait for him to patrol off to the left, and then come back and take up position with his back to you at the concrete barricade.

Once that Harvester is down, stay close to the left wall and move down the ramp whilst crouching. At the bottom of the ramp, go right to the sleeping Harvester in the chair. When you are close enough, perform a Takedown.

07 After dealing with those two, head to the west and take cover here. Now lean out to the right and target the Harvester at **Position A** with the Tranquilizer Rifle. Shoot him and then wait for him to pass out. The other Harvester on the couch is asleep and will not see him pass out. Now look just left of the sleeping Harvester on the couch and you'll see a Heavy on patrol. Wait for him to go south and out of your line of sight before making your move.

08 Once the Heavy walks away, crouch and move forward to the box ahead and take cover at the right side. Watch the Heavy that is on patrol, and when he reaches his position to the southwest and is facing the western wall, lean out from cover and look due south. There is a Harvester standing at a window looking in your direction. Your position here at the box is 25 meters away, so the Harvester can't see you. Quickly shoot the Harvester in the window with the Tranquilizer Rifle and then get back into cover. [→☐ 3]

Wait, and the Heavy on patrol will come back around and face your position. Once he turns and starts to go back to the southwest, move forward whilst crouched and get behind him for a Takedown. After you've dealt with him, go to the Harvester that is sleeping on the couch and perform a Takedown on him.

09 Move to the south and go through the door to reach the next area. There are two Harvesters in the bunk area to the east sitting on beds with their backs to you. You can take them out if you wish, or simply go meet the Harvester Leader now. If you wish to take them out, it's best to shoot them in the head with the Tranquilizer Rifle. Since they are sitting on the bed, you can't perform a Takedown on them. [→☐ 4]

However, they'll never turn around, so you can get close and then take your time to go for a headshot to get the extra Marksman XP. When you are ready, go through the door and meet with the Harvester Leader. When you're done there, exit this area and enter the sewers via the door on the east side of the area at **Position B**.

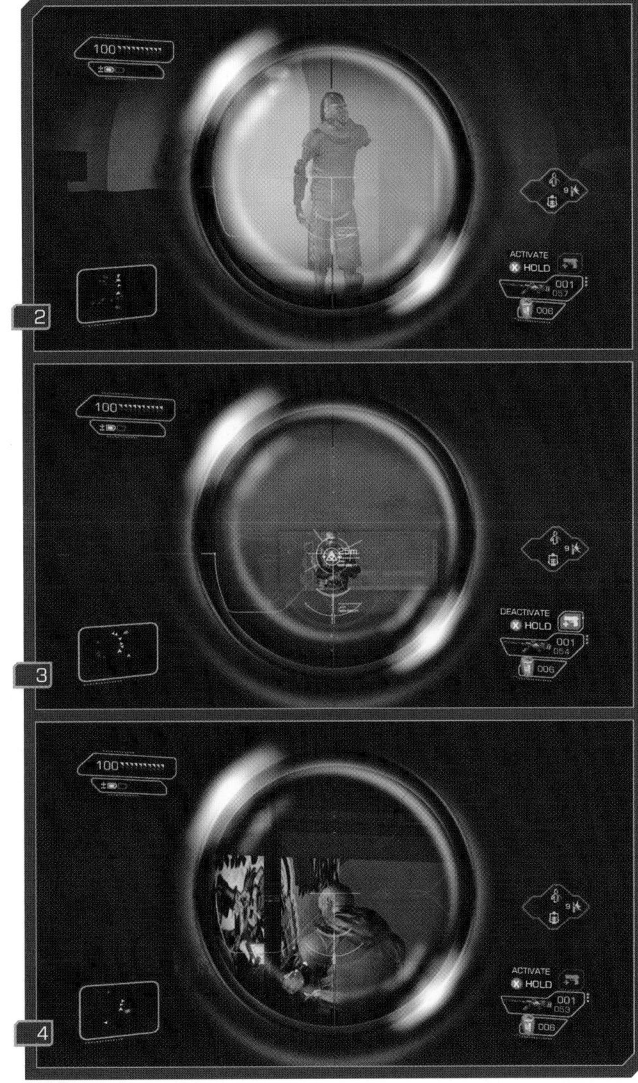

ROUTE 3 Combat

Required Reflex Booster, Punch Through Walls
Recommended Dermal Plating, Smart Vision, Hacking: Capture 4

Recommended Revolver (w/ Explosive Rounds), 10mm Pistol (Silenced), Frag Grenade, Gas Grenade, EMP Grenade

01 Enter the alley south of the Harvester Hideout main entrance via the small alley just north of the Downtown Apartments. At the southern end of the alley you'll find a ladder. Climb up it to the area above you. Ignore the second ladder here and instead move north on the sheet metal to **Position A**.

Equip the Revolver and Frag Grenades, and then look down to the north to see a Harvester on guard. Headshot the guard with the Revolver so that the sound lures in the other Harvesters from the area ahead. Because of your position it will be extremely difficult for them to pinpoint your location as they move in to investigate.

Once all the Harvesters are grouped together at the end of the alley, toss a Gas Grenade into the middle of the pack. The wide area dispersal of the gas will take them all out. If you prefer, you could use a Frag Grenade instead. Proper timing of tossing it will usually kill all but one or two Harvesters. [→☐ 1]

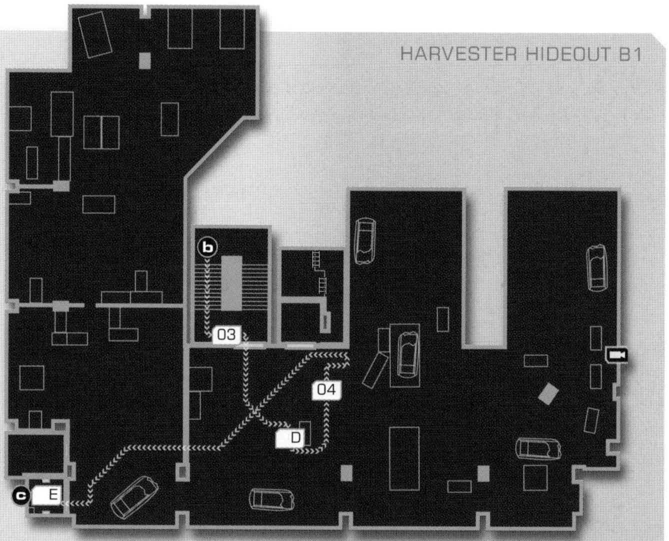

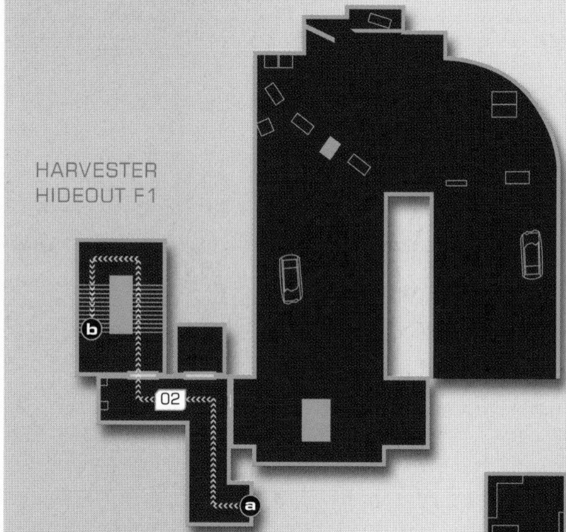

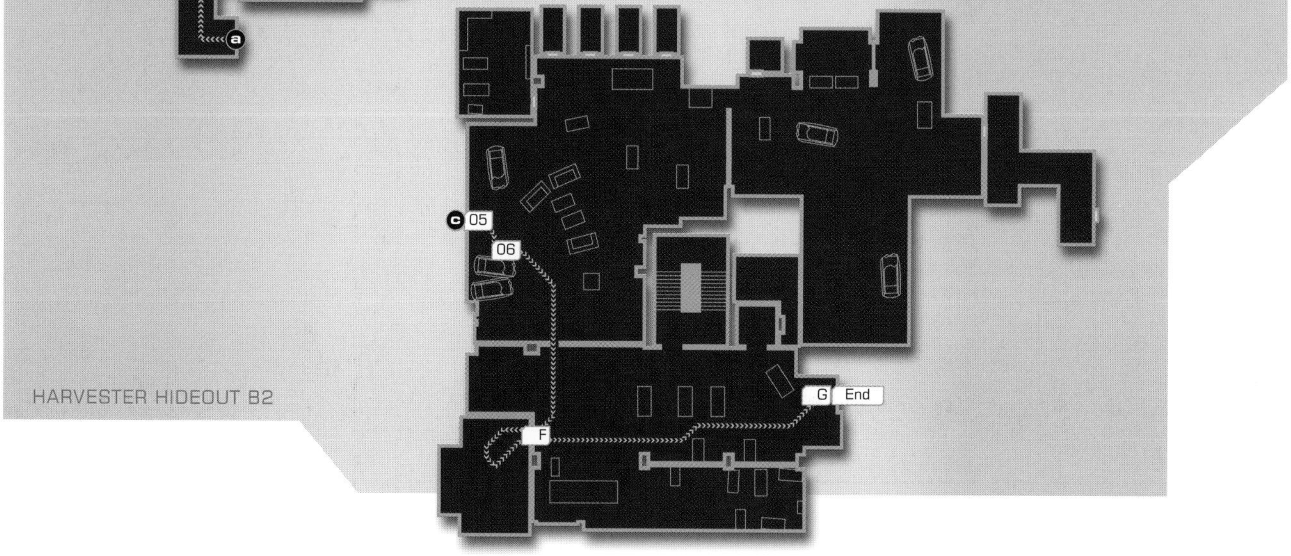

HARVESTER SEWERS

HARVESTER HIDEOUT B1

HARVESTER HIDEOUT F1

HARVESTER HIDEOUT B2

Once you toss the Frag, back straight up to the south and fall to the ground below, then immediately go left and take cover at the Alcove at **Position B**. Hold you position here and pick off the remaining Harvesters with headshots, and toss another Frag if you have it. Be warned though, one of the Harvesters here throws a Frag Grenade, so if you see one being tossed your way, turn and run back up the alley to escape the blast.

Now go to **Position C** and hack the door (Level 1 Hack) to get inside the Harvester Hideout.

02 There is a Level 4 hackable glass door here. Either hack it open, or simply blast it with the Revolver or a Frag Grenade to destroy it. Once you have the door open, proceed forward and down the stairs to the next level.

03 Here you'll find a Level 3 hackable glass door. Again, either hack it to get it open, or just blast it with the Revolver or a Frag Grenade to destroy it. Once you have the door open, immediately take cover at the right side of the door and then lean out and kill the Harvester that is ahead and on your right. Sticking to cover, begin picking off the Harvesters that come running. [→□ 2]

Once you have most of them down, there will be a Heavy off to the left that won't come close enough for you to shoot him. Watch him on the radar or with Smart Vision, and when he is moving, quickly sprint forward and take cover at **Position D**. From there, pick off the Heavy.

There are still two more Harvesters ahead and off to the left on the ramp. It's hard to pick them off from this position as they rarely get close, so stay in cover and wait from them to revert from a Hostile to Alarmed state. Once they do, they will move away from your position. [→□ 3]

04 Move to the corner of the wall here and take cover. Lean out to the right, and you'll see the other two Harvesters ahead. Stick to this cover point and pick them both off. Once they are down, turn around and go to the southwest corner of the area at **Position E**. Go through the door there to find a breakable wall. Punch through the wall, and then go right up the tunnel and use the ladder halfway along it to descend to the floor below.

05 There is a breakable wall here and on the other side is a Harvester. Punch through the wall to instantly kill the Harvester, and then take cover at the left side of the hole you just made. There are three more Harvesters in the room ahead to deal with, so hold your position and pick them off.

06 Move forward while crouched to take cover at the rear of the wrecked car here. Lean out to the left, and you can see into the room ahead. There are three more Harvesters in that room that you'll need to take out [→□ 4]. Hold your position here, and pick them off. Once you have done so, move forward and go through the door at **Position F** to meet with the Harvester Leader. When you're done there, exit this area and enter the sewers via the door on the east side of the area at **Position G**.

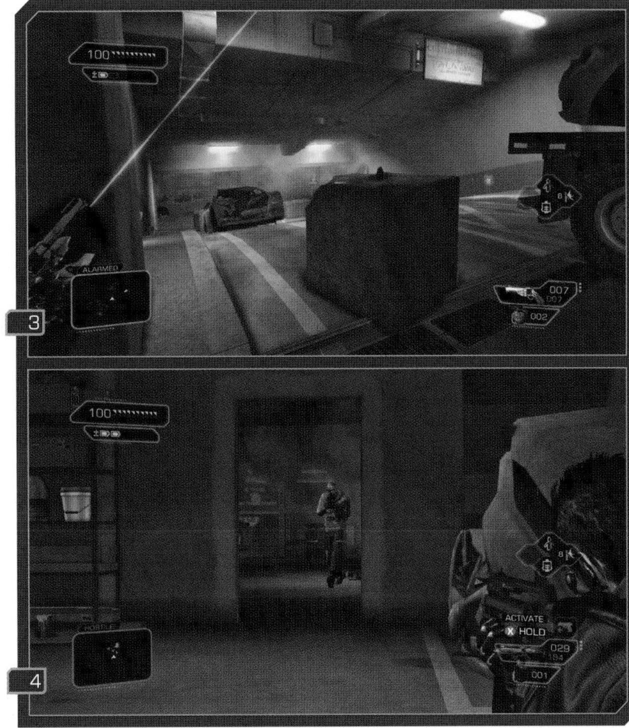

Objective Completed	Objective Type	XP Reward	Stealth Bonuses	
			Ghost	Smooth Operator
Find Vasili Sevchenko's GPL Device	Primary	1000	No	No
Get a new Biochip at the L.I.M.B Clinic	Secondary	250	No	No

HENGSHA SEA PORT

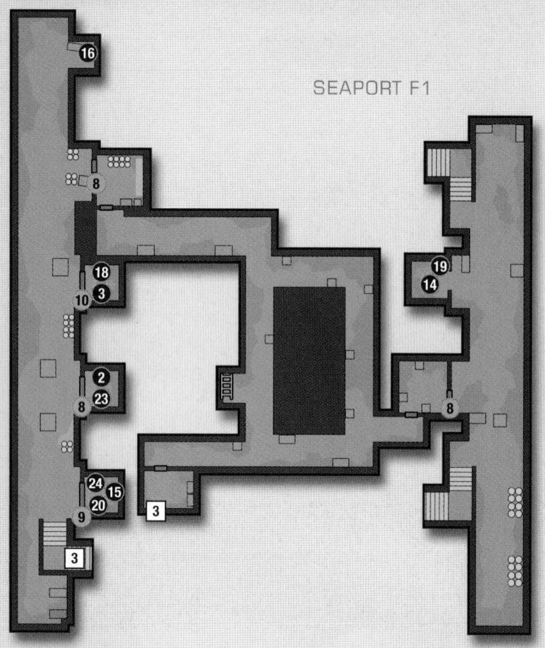

1 Crossbow
2 P.E.P.S.
3 Rocket Launcher
4 Stun Gun
5 Tranquilizer Rifle
6 Concussion Grenade
7 Credit Chip
8 CCyberboost ProEnergy Bar
9 CyberBoost ProEnergy Jar
10 HypoStim
11 Nuke Virus Software
12 Stop Virus Software
13 10mm Pistol Ammo
14 Combat Rifle Ammo
15 Crossbow Arrow
16 Heavy Rifle Ammo
17 P.E.P.S. Energy Pack
18 Rocket Launcher Ammo
19 Shotgun Cartridge
20 Sniper Rifle Ammo
21 Stun Gun Dart
22 Tranquilizer Rifle Dart
23 Damage Upgrade
24 Rate of Fire Upgrade
25 Reload Speed Upgrade
26 Target Leading
27 Automatic Unlocking Device
28 Grenade Launcher Ammunition
Pocket Secretary
Punch Through Wall
1 Vent 1
2 Vent 2
3 Vent 3

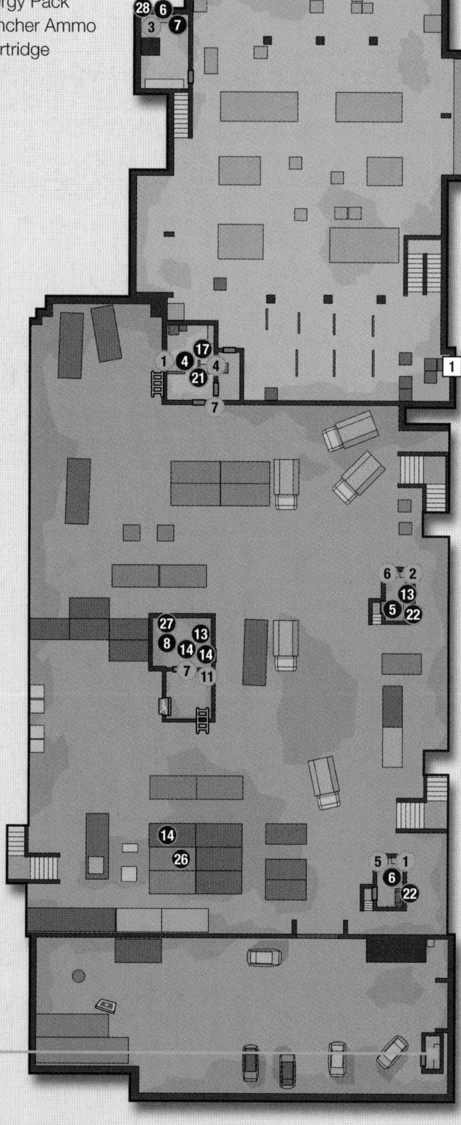

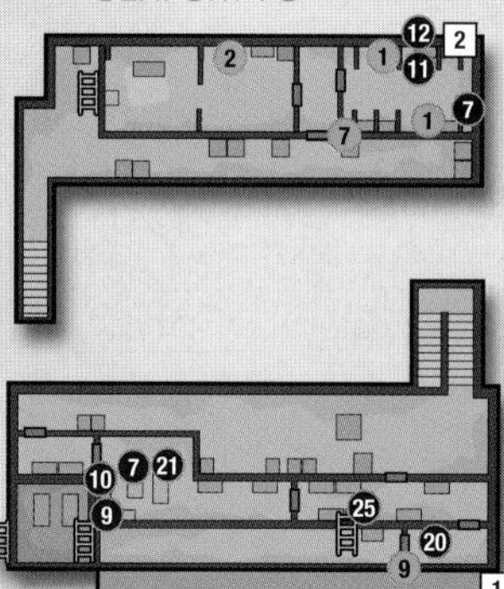

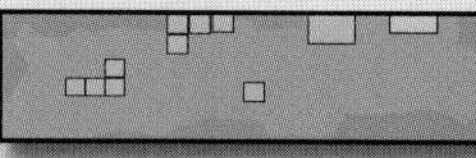

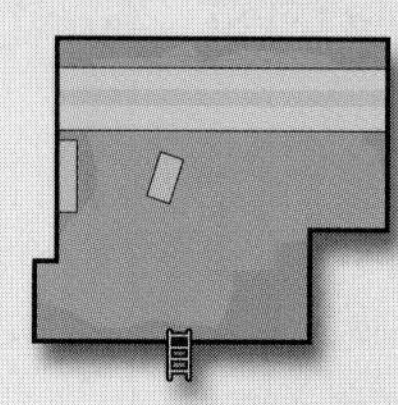

1 Computer - Level 2
2 Computer - Level 3
3 Security Terminal - Level 1
4 Security Terminal - Level 2
5 Security Terminal - Level 3
6 Security Terminal - Level 4
7 Security Panels - Level 1
8 Security Panels - Level 2
9 Security Panels - Level 3
10 Security Panels - Level 4
11 Alarm Panels - Level 2

SEAPORT SEWERS

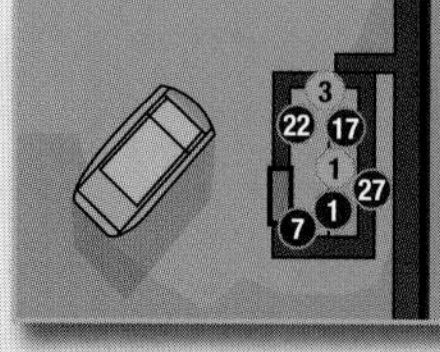

M4 - STOWING AWAY

Objective Name	Objective Type
Get inside Belltower's Port	Primary
Retrieve Tong's Package from the Shed	Primary
Place the C4 on Administrator Wang's Desk	Primary

01 After you enter the sewers, move forward and then left, to where the Weapon Dealer Lu Pin Rong is located. Deal with him if you like, and then look to the right to find an opening in the wall that leads to a maintenance tunnel. When you're ready, go through the tunnel and to the ladder at **Position A** to exit the sewers.

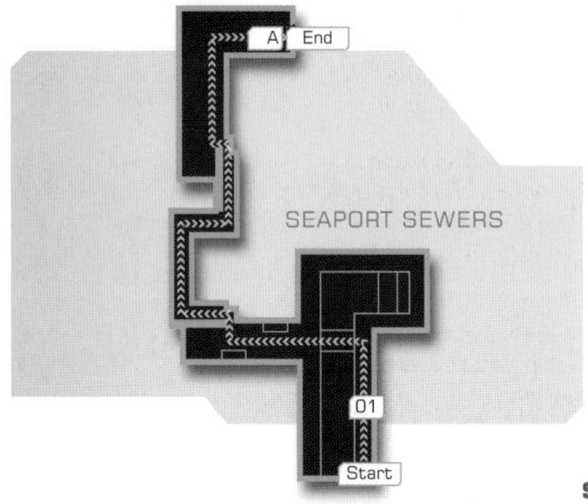

Sea Port

ROUTE 1 Stealth

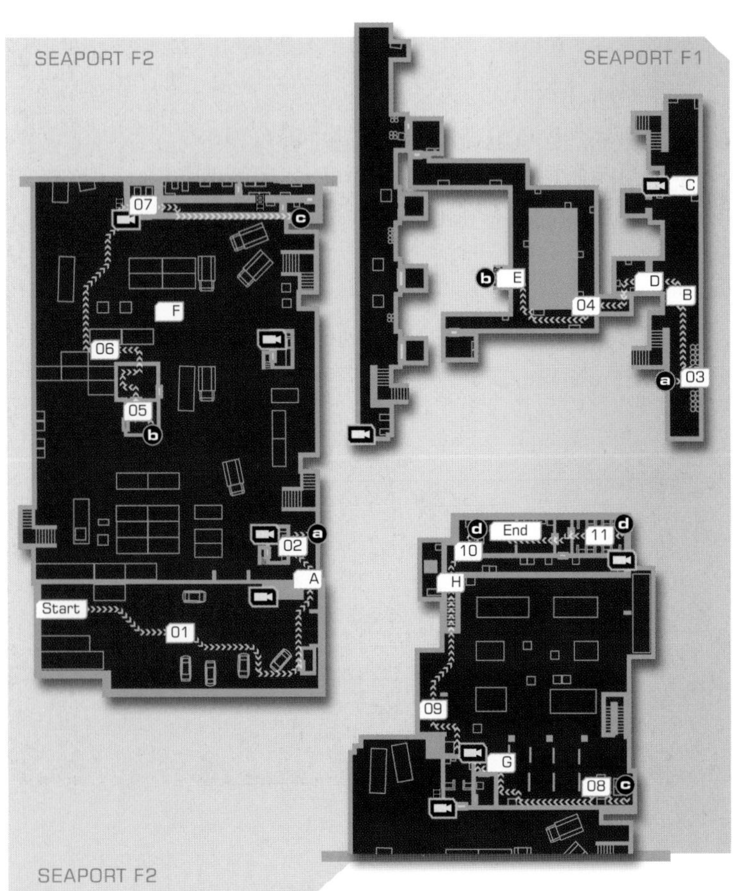

Required Rebreather, Cloaking System, Hacking: Capture 2, Hacking: Robot Domination, Move/Throw Heavy Objects
Recommended Smart Vision

01 Make your way to the control booth ahead and enter it. Inside you'll find a Security Hub that you'll need to hack (Hacking: Capture 1). Once you gain access, disable the camera and the Robots, but do not open the door, as that will alert the guards to your presence. With that done, exit the booth and go right to **Position A**. Move the large crate there to expose the opening in the fence.

02 Go through the opening in the fence and take cover at the building ahead. When you're ready, turn away from the building and face East. Ahead is a railing, go over to it and jump over it to reach the area below.

03 There is a Heavy on patrol ahead, so take cover at the barrels here and watch his route. Wait until he reaches **Position B**, which is the closest he'll get to your location. When he gets there, he'll turn around with his back to you. At this point crouch to take cover at the large box just to the right of **Position B**. Hold your position and wait for the Heavy to move away. Once he reaches **Position C** and his back is to you, move to **Position D** and hack the door (Level 2 Hack). [→□ 1]

You have to be fast here, so you don't have much time to waste on normal hacking. Use at least two Nuke Viruses on the first two nodes to speed things up, and then you can hack the last three nodes normally. If you have more than two Nukes, don't hesitate to use them to get past this. Once you have hacked it, open the door, move inside and then close the door behind you.

04 Go through the next door and enter the maintenance halls ahead. Go left and make your way to this point and take cover at the corner of the wall. Once you get close to the corner, crouch as you move to the cover point. There is a Medium Sentry on patrol in the hallway, which is filled with gas, meaning you must have the Rebreather Augmentation here. [→☐ 2]

From cover, look right to watch the Sentry's route. It will get very close to you, but don't panic. Hold your position in cover and it will not see you. Once it moves away, follow behind it while crouched, and then use the ladder on the left at **Position E** to reach the shed above.

05 Search the locker in the shed to retrieve Tong's package. Once you have it, crouch and open the door. There is a guard in the room ahead, but he is asleep. Move to the window behind the sleeping guard whilst crouching. Open it and jump out, and then go left to take cover at the corner of the storage container.

06 Stay crouching at the edge of the container and peek out to the left to see a guard patrolling. Once he goes to the right past your container, ease around the container and watch the guard. Wait for him to go as far forward as his patrol takes him, which is at **Position F**.

Once he stops, make your move. Activate Cloak and move forward to the ladder under the camera. With the guard so far away on patrol, he won't hear you walking regularly, and you can sprint when you get close to the camera. At the ladder, climb up to the first level above and take cover at the plating on the railing there. [→☐ 3]

07 Tip **It's a good idea to save here since this part is a bit tricky and you may be spotted if you move at the wrong time. With a save here, you can reload and try again.**

Wait in cover for your energy to replenish. Hold your position and wait for the Sniper above to get close to the top of the ladder. You'll know he's there when you see the laser from his sniper rifle, or you can use Smart Vision to track him. Once he moves away from the ladder and heads east down the walkway he's on, climb up the ladder to the walkway above.

Once you are on the walkway, crouch and watch the Sniper. As soon as he stops at the railing ahead and begins to scan the yard below, jump over the railing from your crouching position onto the ledge on the other side. [→☐ 4]

On the ledge, hug the left wall and activate Cloak before moving forward. There is a guard on patrol in the yard below with exceptional vision that can see you up here depending on where he is on his patrol route. To be safe, use Cloak to cross the ledge to the vent ahead. If you only have one cell of energy, you'll run out just before you reach the vent, but by then, you're far enough to the north that the patrolling guard below won't see you. On reaching the vent, open it and enter the air ducts.

08 Exit the vent, and take cover at the box ahead. Look to your right to see three guards grouped together and talking. Wait for them to disperse and then go left to drop down off the box. Hug the back wall to the south and move forward whilst crouching to the camera ahead at **Position G**. At the camera, continue to hug the wall and follow it around to get under the shelving ahead and take cover at the boxes there. [→☐ 5]

09 From your cover point at the box, look right and watch the guard on patrol here. He will get close and then stop so that he is facing your direction, Wait for him to turn around so that his back is to you, then move to the left and up the stairs. Take cover at the top of the stairs at **Position H**.

10 From your cover point at the top of the stairs, look left to see two guards, a Turret, and a camera. The Turret can spot you when you make your move, so activate Cloak to avoid detection and then move straight ahead to the ladder. Climb up it to the level above and make your way forward to the northwest corner of the area to find an open vent. Use it to drop down into the rooms below.

11 Now that you are inside, no one can see or hear you, so explore the offices here if you like. When you are ready, move through the offices and plant Tong's bomb on Wang's desk. With that done, a cutscene will trigger, and you're done with this area. [→☐ 6]

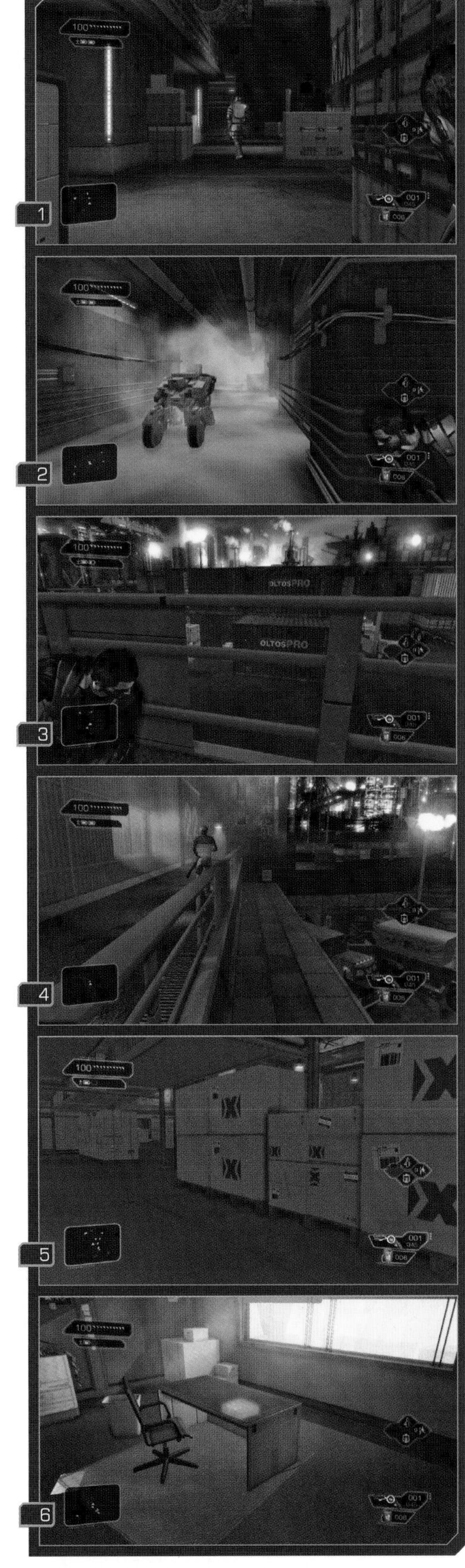
1
2
3
4
5
6

ROUTE 2 Stealth Combat

Required Jump Enhancer, Hacking: Robot Domination, Reflex Booster
Recommended Smart Vision, Hacking: Capture 4

Recommended Tranquilizer Rifle (w/ Target-Leading System)

01 Make your way to the control booth ahead and enter it. Inside you'll find a Security Hub that you'll need to hack (Hacking: Capture 1). Once you gain access, disable the camera and the robots, but do not open the door, as that will alert the guards to your presence. There is also a switch here to turn off the electricity that has electrified the top of the small food stand out in the parking lot, so use the switch to kill the power.

02 Exit the control booth and backtrack across the parking lot to the small food stand. Jump up on top of the stand, and then jump over the fence there to the storage container on the other side. Hold your position here, and watch for the guard directly ahead and below you. Once he is at **Position A**, shoot him with the Tranquilizer Rifle to knock him out.

03 Now move ahead and jump up onto the storage containers just ahead. Make your way to the top of the container stack, and then equip the Tranquilizer Rifle for some sniping. [→☐ 1]

First, shoot the Sniper at **Position B** directly ahead of you. Now look slightly to the right and wait for the guard in the yard to reach **Position C** at the barrier, and then shoot him with the Tranquilizer Rifle. Further to the right you'll see another guard; wait for him to get under the camera at **Position D**, and then take him out. Do this correctly, and he'll collapse under the camera and his body will not be seen.

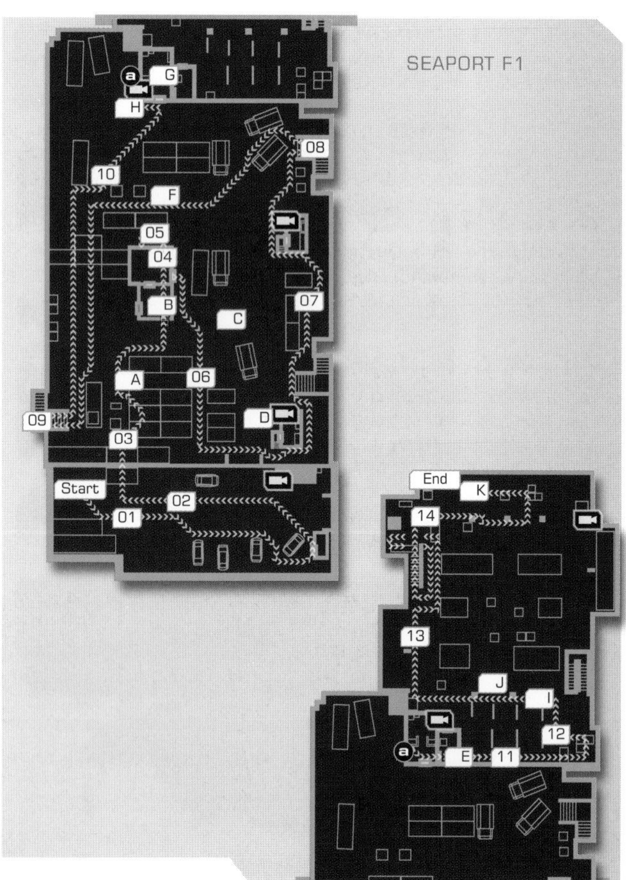

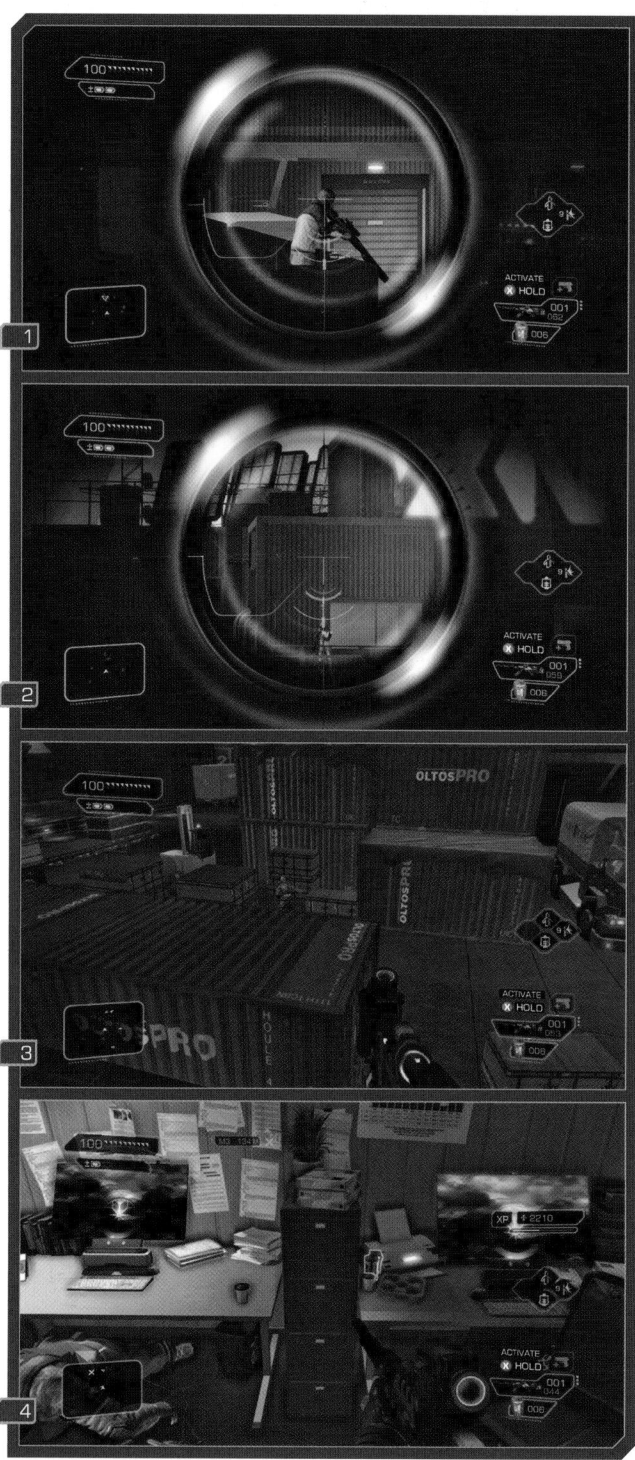

There is one more Sniper across the yard on the catwalk of the building ahead at **Position E**. This is a very long shot, but it is possible. With the Target Leading System, you can line up the shot. If you don't have the Target Leading System, then look through the scope and notice the "T" in the center of the view, and then the three curved lines below the T. [→☐ 2]

Those curved lines help align long distant shots due to the drop of the dart as it travels greater distances. To align this shot, use the very bottom tip of the reticule just below the third curved line at the bottom of the view. If you miss, it won't matter since the Sniper can't see you this far out, so try as often as you like. If this proves too difficult, then you can pick off this Sniper at the next location.

04 Move forward and climb the small building ahead where the first sniper was located. If you didn't take out the second sniper at the previous location, then shoot him now. With that done, move to the northern portion of the rooftop, look down and to the left. There is a guard on patrol here. Wait for him to reach **Position F**, where he'll take up position. Wait a bit longer, and he'll walk off to the north, as he does, shoot him in the back. Do this correctly, and he'll pass out before he's in view of the camera. [→☐ 3]

05 Drop down to the ground below and go to the window on the north side of the building you were just on. There is a window here, and inside is a sleeping guard. Open the window, and then crouch, now jump through the window and then incapacitate the sleeping guard with a Takedown. Now hack the door ahead (Level 1 Hack) and then search the locker in the next room to find Tong's package.

06 **Optional**
Make your way to the security building in the southeast corner of the area. Be careful to avoid detection by the camera mounted to the building, and move around to the southern side of the building. There you'll find a window. Open it and then shoot the guard that is sitting at the Security Hub in the head with the Tranquilizer Rifle. Now go inside and hack the Security Hub and turn off the cameras and the Turret. [→☐ 4]

07 **Optional**
Stay to the east and make your way forward to the next security booth ahead. Jump through the window on the southern side of the building and then hack the Security Hub (Level 4 Hack) and disable the cameras and robot.

08 **Optional**
Make your way to the top of the stairs here and take cover. Look out to the left, and watch the Heavy on patrol here. He will get close to your position and then move away. His back will be to you when he moves back off again, so sneak up behind him for a Takedown. There is a storage unit here you can investigate if you like.

09 **Optional**
Push forward and make your way across the yard to the stairs on the west side. Take cover at the top of the stairs and watch the Heavy on patrol here. He will get close to your position and eventually move away with his back to you. Sneak up behind him for a Takedown when he moves. [→☐ 5]

There three storage units here you can investigate if you like. They are all locked, but if you search the bodies of all the guards you have taken down in the yard, you'll find Pocket Secretaries with the codes to each.

10 Move down the center of the yard and head north to the building ahead. Go to the door at **Position G** and hack the terminal to get inside (Level 1 Hack). Once you are in, hack the Security Hub here (Level 2 Hack) and turn of the cameras. Now go back outside and use the ladder at **Position H** to reach the walkway above.

11 Move down the walkway to the door ahead. The Sniper here is unconscious due to your earlier attacks, so no worries. Hack the door here (Level 3 Hack), and then go inside the building.

12 Halfway along the first hallway you will find a Reload Speed Upgrade for one of your weapons, so make sure to grab it before continuing. Open the first door on the right, and then take cover by the railings at **Position I**. Below you on the warehouse floor you'll be able to see three guards having a conversation ,so wait for them to finish and disperse. The first guard to leave will walk almost directly below you and come to a stop at **Position J**; incapacitate him with a headshot using the Tranquilizer Rifle as soon as he stops moving. [→☐ 6]

Tip **Occasionally, there will be an additional forth guard who patrols the walkway you are on; always check the radar to see if he is there before opening the door. If he is there, just wait for him to walk to the west, and then move up behind him quietly and use a Takedown on him.**

Tip **If you have any Gas Grenades, throw one down between the three guards while they are still talking to take them all out at once.** [→☐ 7]

The second guard will then start walking across to the west side of the warehouse where he will eventually come to a stop, giving you with another easy shot using the Tranquilizer Rifle. The final guard takes a break in his patrol route just to the side of the stairs to the right, so when he does, take him down to finish them all off. Now that the middle of the warehouse is clear, move to the western side of the walkway and then jump down to the floor below.

13 Stay close to the western side of the room and move forward to the north. There is a Security Booth under the stairs ahead. Go past the stairs and take cover at the right of the Security Booth door. Wait for the guards inside to finish talking, and one of them will come out and go on patrol. Once he exits the booth, let him get a few meters past you and then sneak up on him from behind for a Takedown.

Now crouch down and go inside the security booth. Sneak up on the guard sitting in the chair and take him out with aTakedown. Once the guard is out, hack the Security Hub (Level 1 Hack) and disable the Turret and the camera. [→☐ 1]

14 Exit the Security Booth and go right to the stairs. At the top of the stairs, go right towards the guards, but make sure you stay close to the building on your left. Move forward whilst crouching as you hug the building on your left and sneak up on the two guards here. Once you are close enough, perform a Double Takedown. Search the fallen guard for a Pocket Secretary that has the code to the office door. Now open the door and go to **Position K** to plant Tong's bomb on Wang's desk. [→☐ 2]

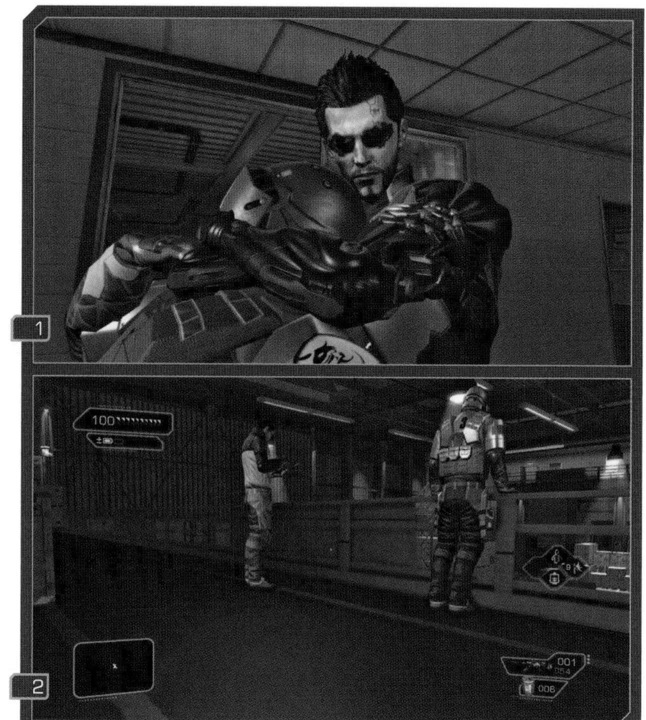

1

2

Sea Port

ROUTE 3 Combat

Required Reflex Booster, Icarus Landing System, Jump Enhancement
Recommended Dermal Plating: EMP Shielding

Recommended Revolver (W/ Explosive Rounds), 10mm Pistol (Silenced), EMP Grenade

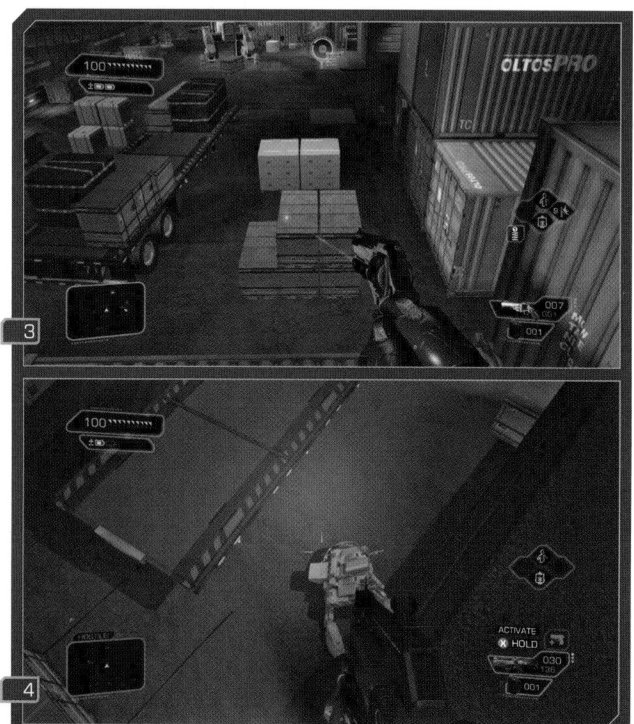

3

4

01 If you have the EMP Shielding Augmentation that protects you from electricity, jump up onto the food stand here that has an electrified roof. If you don't have that Aug, go to the control booth at the opposite side of the yard and use the switch there to turn off the electricity. Once you are on top of the roof, jump over the fence and drop into the yard. [→☐ 3]

02 Run directly ahead to the Building 2 in the center of the yard. Use the ladder here to climb up to the roof. Immediately perform a Takedown kill on the Sniper here. Take the Sniper's Rifle, and kill the Sniper on the ledge to the north. Now, take cover at the low wall of the roof and pick off all the guards in the yard. When the Medium Sentry gets close, throw an EMP grenade at it for an easy win. [→☐ 4]

Now drop down and enter the building you are on. Use the Revolver to blow the door open, and then search the locker in the next room to find Tong's package.

03 Exit the building and head north to the building there. Climb the ladder located at the corner of the building to the upper area. Move forward to the ladder on the left and climb it to reach the skylight. [→☐ 5]

Stand on the boards on the skylight and shoot out the glass window. Look down through the skylight, and pick off the guards from here – the Revolver is a good choice here. As you kill one, others will come running in. Stay here until you've killed all the guards. When that is done, drop down to the floor below and immediately take cover at the boxes.

04 A Box Guard will soon drop through the other skylight, so hit it with an EMP. Next, from your cover point, peek out to the right with the Revolver and target the Turret on the upper walkway at the back of the room. There are two guards there, and when the turret explodes, it will most likely kill one or both of them. If the guards survive, hold your position and pick them off. [→☐ 6]

05 Go to the office door and either hack it or blow it open with the Revolver or a Frag Grenade. Once you are inside the building, go left and make your way to the desk and plant the explosives. A cutscene will trigger, and you're done with this mission.

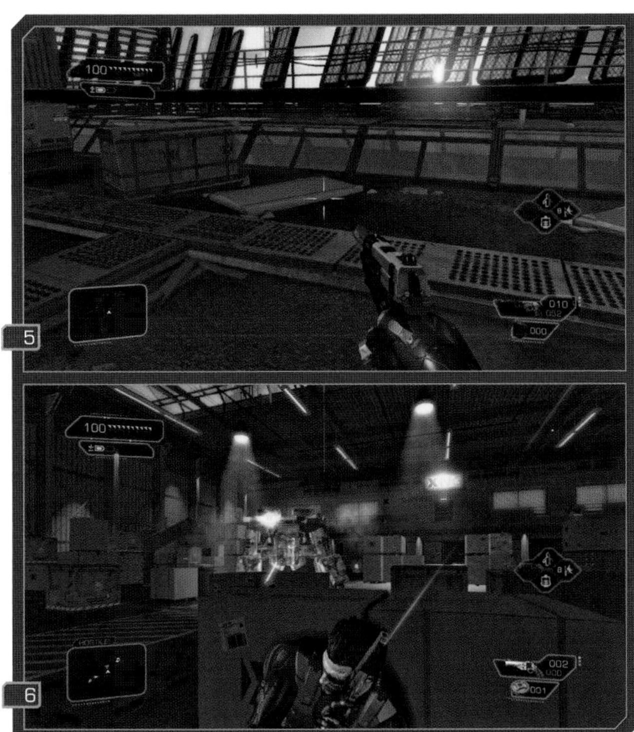

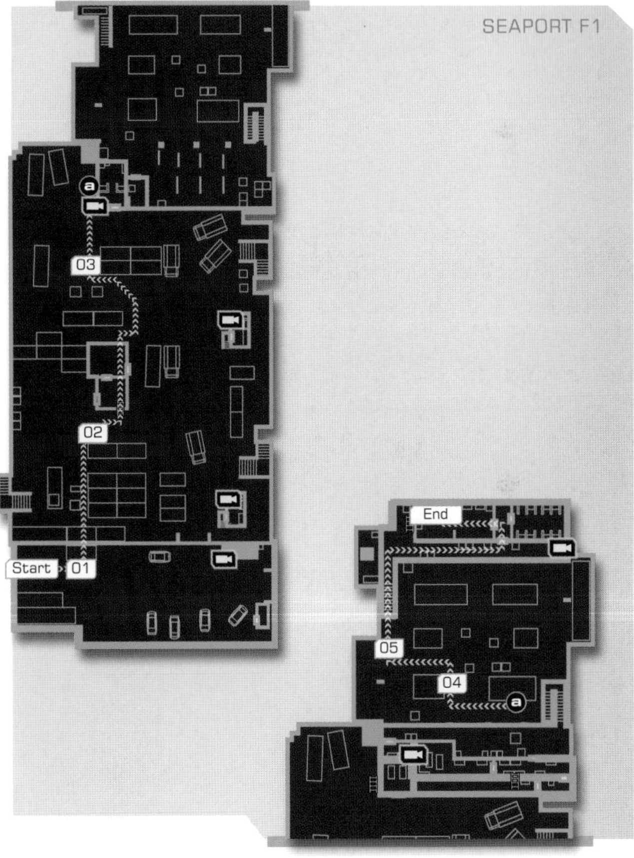

Objective Completed	Objective Type	XP Reward	Stealth Bonuses: Ghost	Stealth Bonuses: Smooth Operator
Get inside Belltower's Port	Primary	750	No	No
Retrieve Tong's Package from the Shed	Primary	1000	Yes	Yes
Place the C4 on Administrator Wang's Desk	Primary	1000	Yes	Yes

OMEGA RANCH

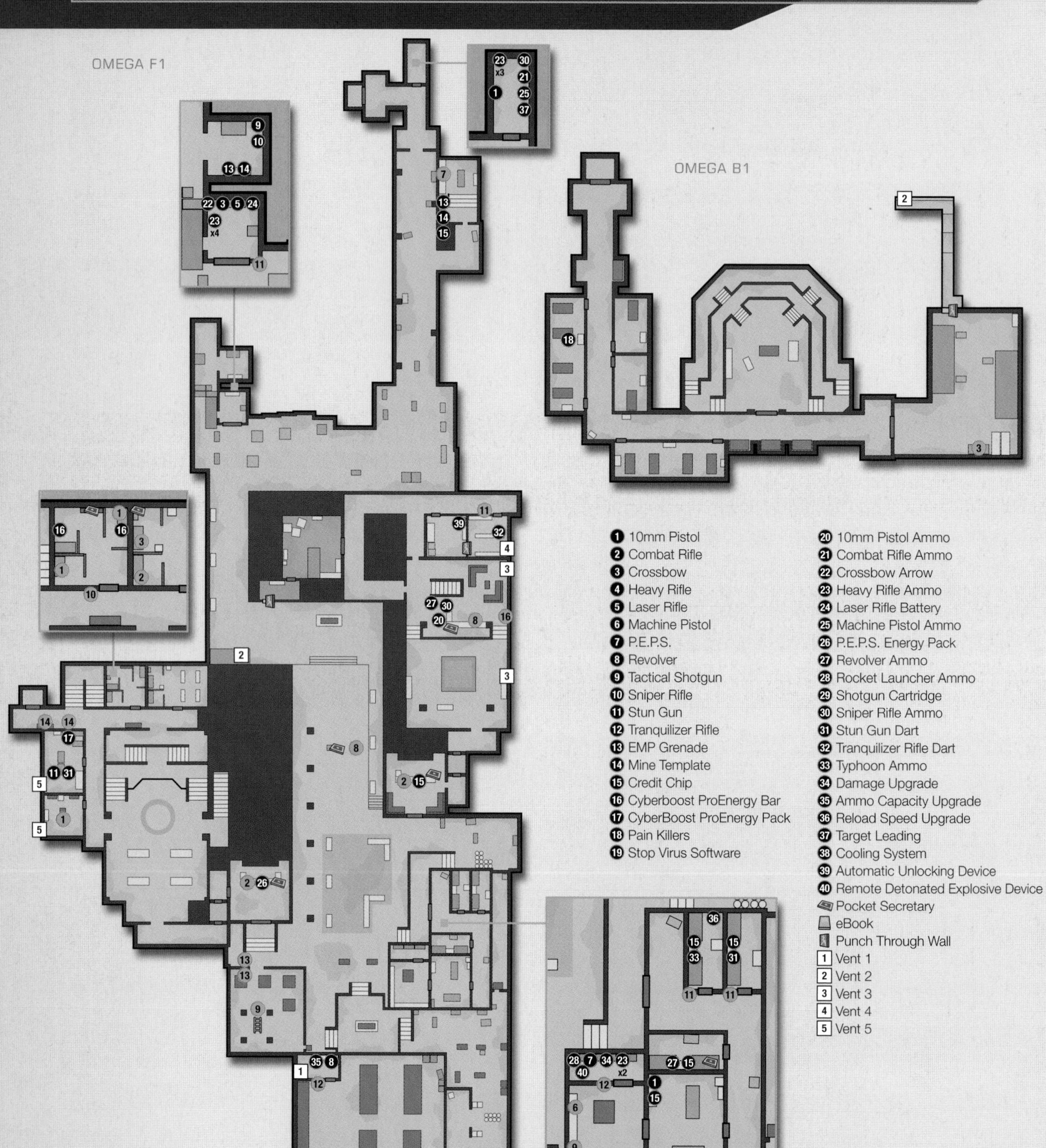
OMEGA F1
OMEGA B1
1 10mm Pistol
2 Combat Rifle
3 Crossbow
4 Heavy Rifle
5 Laser Rifle
6 Machine Pistol
7 P.E.P.S.
8 Revolver
9 Tactical Shotgun
10 Sniper Rifle
11 Stun Gun
12 Tranquilizer Rifle
13 EMP Grenade
14 Mine Template
15 Credit Chip
16 Cyberboost ProEnergy Bar
17 CyberBoost ProEnergy Pack
18 Pain Killers
19 Stop Virus Software
20 10mm Pistol Ammo
21 Combat Rifle Ammo
22 Crossbow Arrow
23 Heavy Rifle Ammo
24 Laser Rifle Battery
25 Machine Pistol Ammo
26 P.E.P.S. Energy Pack
27 Revolver Ammo
28 Rocket Launcher Ammo
29 Shotgun Cartridge
30 Sniper Rifle Ammo
31 Stun Gun Dart
32 Tranquilizer Rifle Dart
33 Typhoon Ammo
34 Damage Upgrade
35 Ammo Capacity Upgrade
36 Reload Speed Upgrade
37 Target Leading
38 Cooling System
39 Automatic Unlocking Device
40 Remote Detonated Explosive Device
Pocket Secretary
eBook
Punch Through Wall
1 Vent 1
2 Vent 2
3 Vent 3
4 Vent 4
5 Vent 5

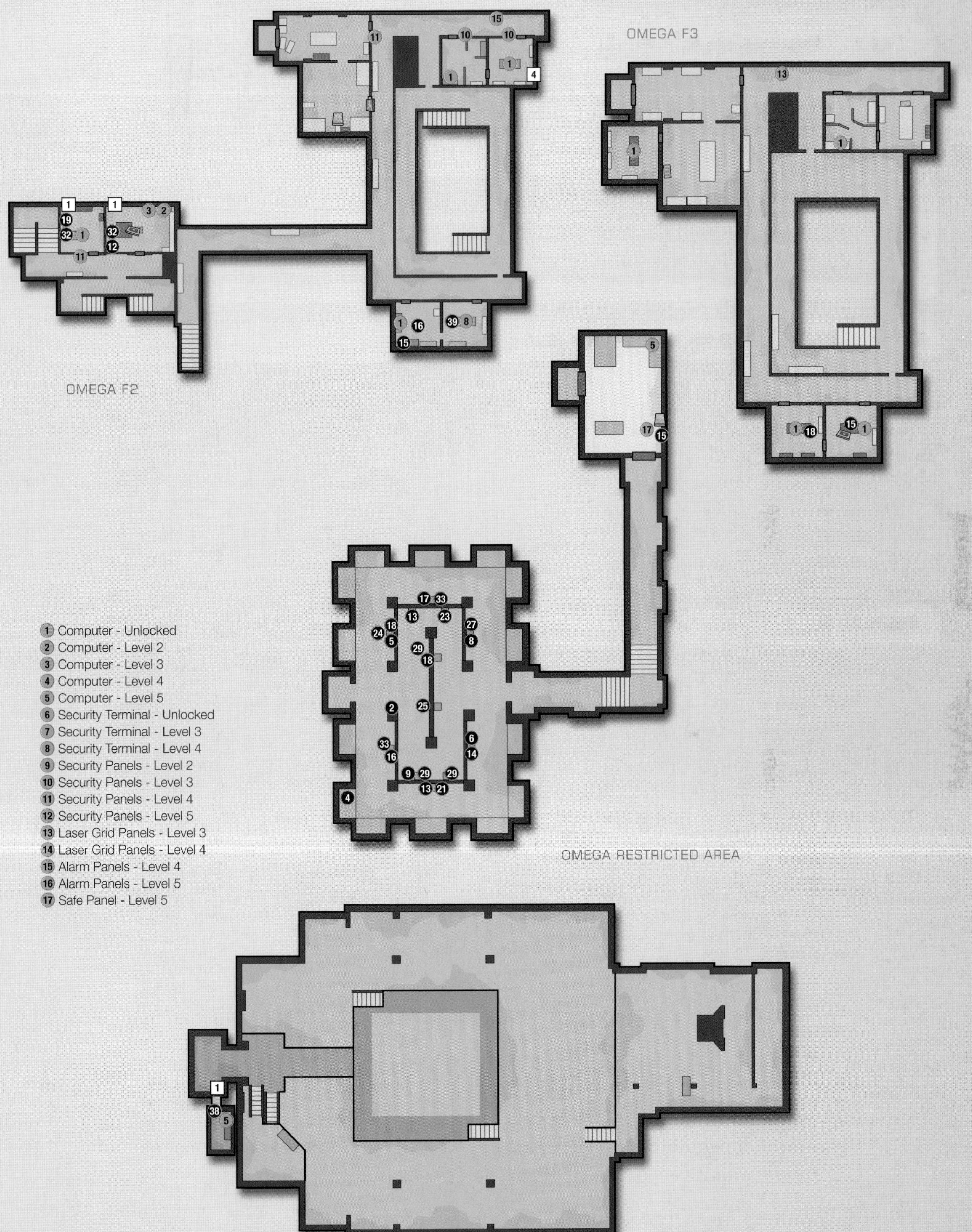
OMEGA F3
OMEGA F2
OMEGA RESTRICTED AREA
1 Computer - Unlocked
2 Computer - Level 2
3 Computer - Level 3
4 Computer - Level 4
5 Computer - Level 5
6 Security Terminal - Unlocked
7 Security Terminal - Level 3
8 Security Terminal - Level 4
9 Security Panels - Level 2
10 Security Panels - Level 3
11 Security Panels - Level 4
12 Security Panels - Level 5
13 Laser Grid Panels - Level 3
14 Laser Grid Panels - Level 4
15 Alarm Panels - Level 4
16 Alarm Panels - Level 5
17 Safe Panel - Level 5

M1 - RESCUING MEGAN AND HER TEAM

Objective Name	Objective Type
Search For Signs of Megan's Team	Primary
Disable the Signal Jammer	Secondary
Find and speak with Declan Faherty	Primary
Find and speak with Eric Koss	Primary
Find and speak with Nia Colvin	Primary
Upload a virus to the security computer and enter the restricted area.	Primary

ENTERING OMEGA RANCH

Use the door to the southeast to exit the room. However, don't just go barging out, but instead, crouch and move outside slowly. There are two guards ahead that are talking, so you'll want to keep them unaware of your presence until you have decided how to handle them.

OPTIONAL EXPLORATION

There is a Level 5 Hack door in this room. With the Jump Enhancer Aug, you can jump on the boxes in the southwest corner, then jump on the top shelf of the shelving, and then get on the roof of the locked room. There is a vent on the roof that lets you in. Inside this room you'll find an Ammo Capacity Upgrade for one of your weapons.

Inside Omega Ranch

ROUTE 1 Stealth

08_043

Required Move/Throw Heavy Objects, Rebreather Hacking: Capture 4, Punch Through Walls
Recommended None

01 Exit the room while crouched, and then take cover behind the railings directly ahead. There are two guards having a conversation on the other side, so wait for them to disperse. Follow the one moving left by going from cover to cover and then wait at the small section of the railing because the guard will look through the gap. [→☐ 1]

02 Once the guard moves on, move to the next section of railings and hold your position again. Watch the radar and wait for the guard to head to the left around the building, and then move up towards the northeast corner of the area.

03 There is a hole in the fence ahead, but a trash bin is blocking the path. Grab the bin and move forward. Don't throw the bin as it will make noise and alert the guards. Once you are past the fence, move to **Position A** and get on top of the boxes there. Next, open the window and jump through it to get inside the building. [→☐ 2]

04 Move to the door and look through the vent at the bottom. Wait for the guard patrolling the hallway to enter the dormitory ahead. Once he is inside the room, open the door and move forward to take cover at the wall at **Position B**.

05 Wait for the guard to come out of the room and go back up the hallway. When he does, follow him and stay slightly left. When he turns right to go into the next room, move left and take cover at the left side of door at **Position C**. Hold this position and wait for the guard to come out again and go back down the hall. Once he does, enter the room.

06 Move ahead and open the door. Enter the room and then close the door behind you. Use the Security Hub here (it's unlocked) to turn off the camera. Next, hack the signal jammer and turn off the signal. It's a Level 2 Hack, but not difficult.

With that done, go back to the door and wait for the patrolling guard to come back. When he returns, wait for him to exit the room. Just as he is leaving open the door and follow him.

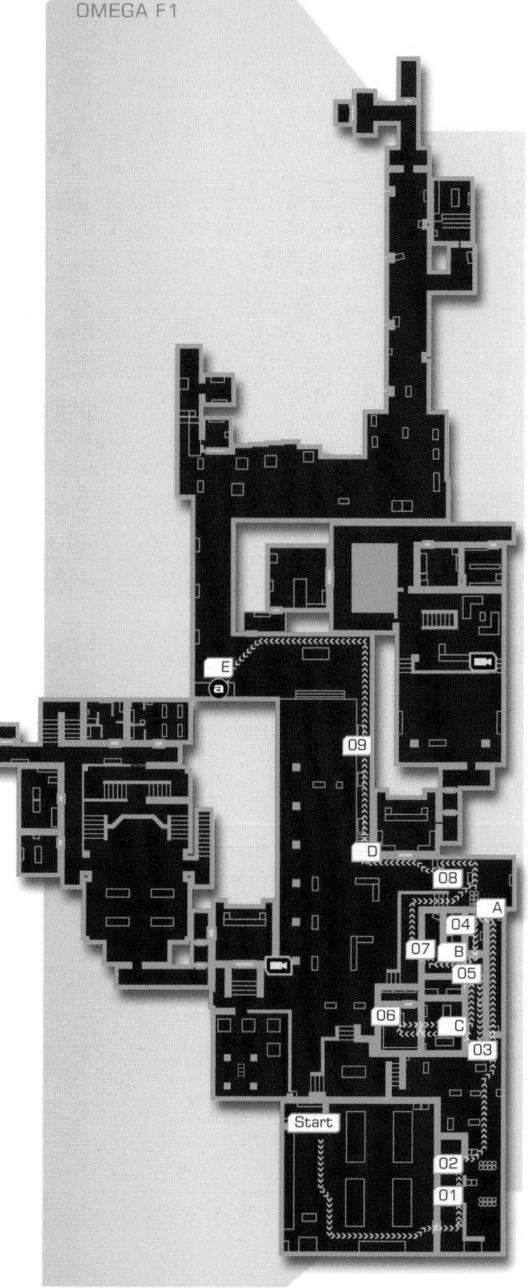

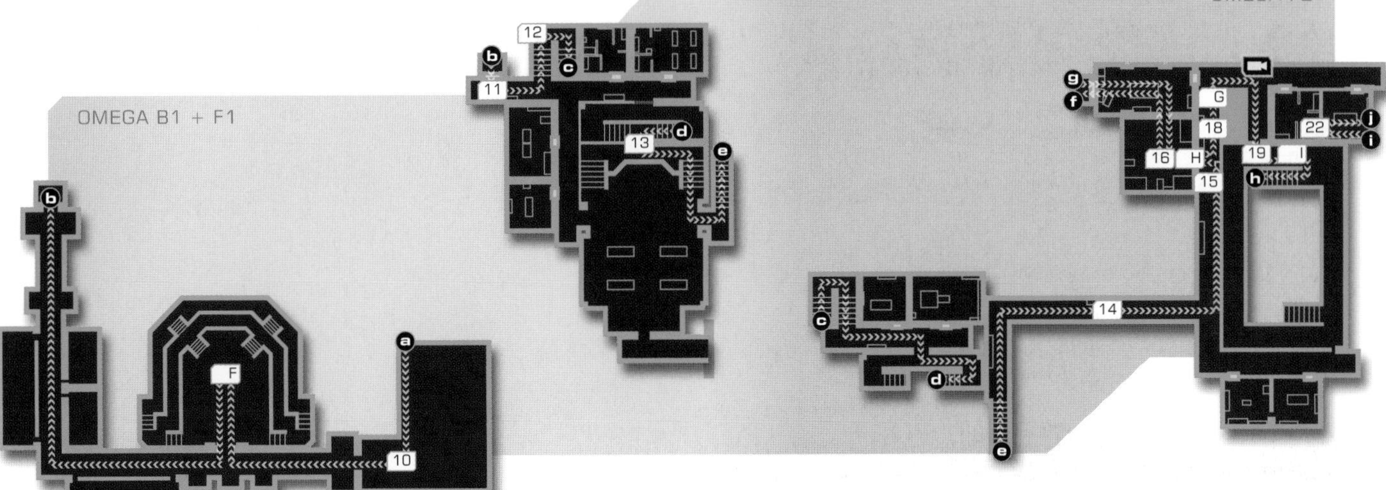

07 Move past the guard as he enters the dormitory and go to the front door of the building. Now go through the door and go right down the porch of the building. At the end of the porch, go to the bottom of the stairs and take cover behind the boxes ahead.

08 Look ahead and watch the guard that is on patrol. Once he goes left, move up to the boxes on the right. Watch the guards ahead. There is a regular guard close to you, and a Heavy in the distance. Wait for them both to go off to the left.

Now watch the radar, the smaller guard will turn around and look back once. After he's done so, move forward to the corner of the building at **Position D**. As you get close to the building, activate cloak so the Heavy ahead won't see you, then go right up the stairs to the porch there. [→☐ 3]

09 Move down the porch to the far wall ahead. Once you reach the wall, go left to find a large air conditioning unit on the left at **Position E**. Jump up onto the AC unit. There you'll find a vent. Use the vent to reach the next area.

Go through the vent and drop down into the narrow tunnel at the end. the tunnel is filled with gas, but the Rebreather Augmentation will keep you safe. At the end of the tunnel you will find a valve that you can use to turn off the gas, and a breakable wall that you should punch through to reach the next area.

10 You'll find yourself in a storage area. Move ahead to the door on the right. Go through the door and down the hall to the Surgery Auditorium and talk to Declan Faherty at **Position F**. With that done, you now need to find the other two scientists. Exit the auditorium and go right to the elevator at the end of the hall. Use it to reach the next area. [→☐ 4]

11 Get off the elevator and use the dedicated terminal on the wall on your right to deactivate the laser grid. The control panel on this side is unlocked, so no need to hack it.

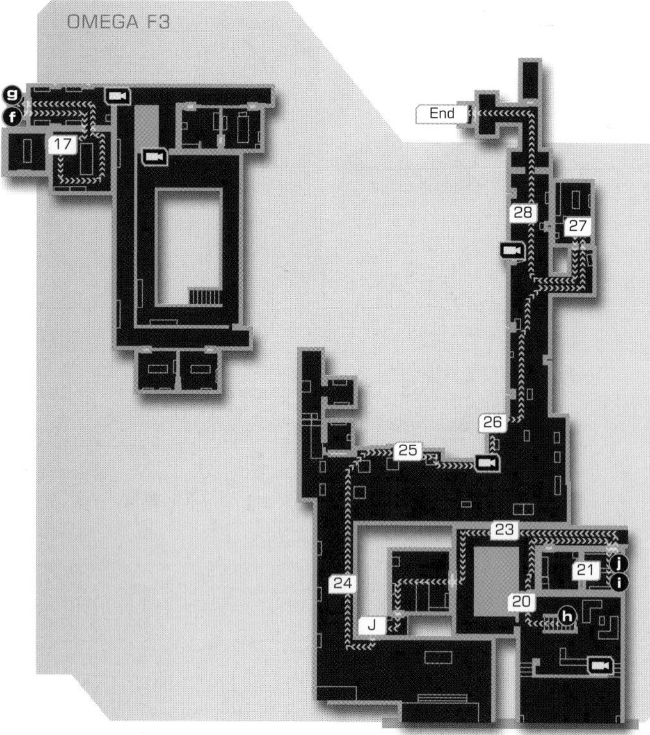

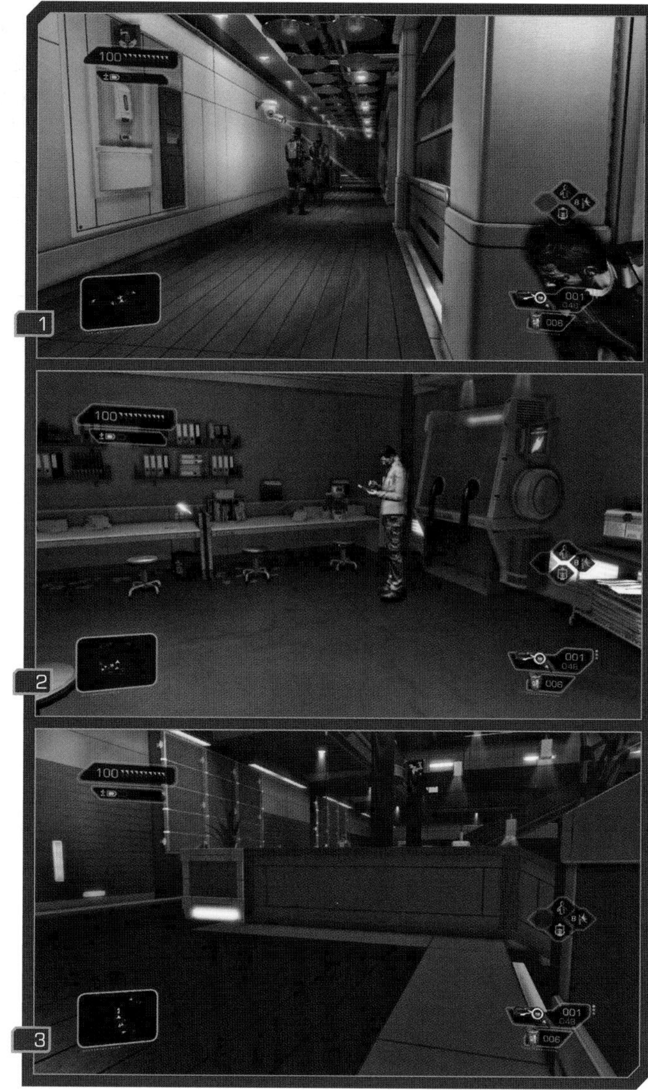

12 Go left and up the stairs to the area above. Move to the large door overlooking the lobby below. Crouch down, and go down the left-hand stairs to the final set of stairs, just before you reach the main floor.

13 Stay crouching, and when you're ready, activate Cloak and quickly move forward and left through the door on the left to the skywalk. There are two guards in the room, so make sure you stay crouching so that they do not hear your movements.

14 Move across the Skywalk to the next building. There are no guards around the skywalk area, so feel free to sprint if you wish. At the end of the skywalk, go left to the end of the hall and take cover by the corner of the wall at **Position G**. [→□ 1]

15 From your cover point, look left to see two guards talking. Let them finish, and one guard will leave the area, whilst the other will move to the end of the hall and sit in a chair. Once in the chair, he's too far away to hear you. Now backtrack down the hall to the breakable wall at **Position H** and punch through it.

16 With that done, enter the room ahead. Make your way to the elevator in the northwestern corner of the area and use it to reach the floor above. There are some large crates blocking access to the elevator, so you'll need to move them first.

17 Move forward and to your right to find another scientist. This is Eric Koss. Go and speak with him to complete your objective. Once you are done, back track to the elevator and return to the floor below. [→□ 2]

18 Take cover at the corner of the wall, and watch the guard. Wait for him to sit in the chair at the end of the hall, and then activate Cloak and walk forward (not crouching) and to the right. The guard is to far away to hear you, so move quickly, and take cover at the planter next to the railing ahead and on the left at **Position I**.

19 There is a guard patrolling the left side of the area just across from you. Wait for him to turn around and walk away from your position. Don't move just yet, as this guard will turn around shortly after he walks away, so watch and wait for him to do that. Once he has turned around and then continued with his patrol so that his back is to you, move whilst crouching forward and around the planter and then go down the stairs to the floor below. [→□ 3]

20 At the bottom of the stairs, go right and up the hallway, but stop at the corner as there is a guard in the room on the right. Take cover at the right side of the door and watch the guard in the room. When he moves to the southwest corner of the room, his back will be to you. Once he does this, move past the door and continue down the hallway.

21 The door here is a Level 4 Hack, but it isn't that bad. The Diagnostic Subroutine (red tower) is reachable on this hack, so go that route. Once you have hacked the terminal, open the door and enter the room. In the back left corner are some boxes; move them to expose the vent. Use it to reach the room above you.

22 Exit the vent, and you'll find yourself in Nia Colvin's room. She is directly ahead, so go and speak with her. She'll give you a copy of Vasili's virus that you'll need to use to disable the facility's security system. When you're ready, backtrack the way you came through the vent and back to the floor below.

23 Leave the room and go left down the hall making sure to Cloak as you pass the open door of the room ahead, since the guard is still in there and could see you. At the end of the hall, go left to find a large door numbered G-13 on your right. Go through it to enter the room ahead. At the back left-hand corner of the room is another door. Go through this to find a breakable wall at **Position J**. Punch through the wall and go outside.

15 Stay in cover at the bottom of the stairs and watch the Sneaker guard at the south end of the room. Wait for him to go to **Position F** in the southwest corner of the room, and then shoot him with the Tranquilizer Rifle. Once he falls unconscious, activate Cloak and move into the room. Take cover at the barrier ahead at **Position G**. Now watch the Heavy as you wait for your energy to replenish. He'll move to your right and stand there for a bit, and then he'll move back to the west. Once he is close to you, watch him, and as soon as he turns to go back to the west, sneak up on him for a Takedown.

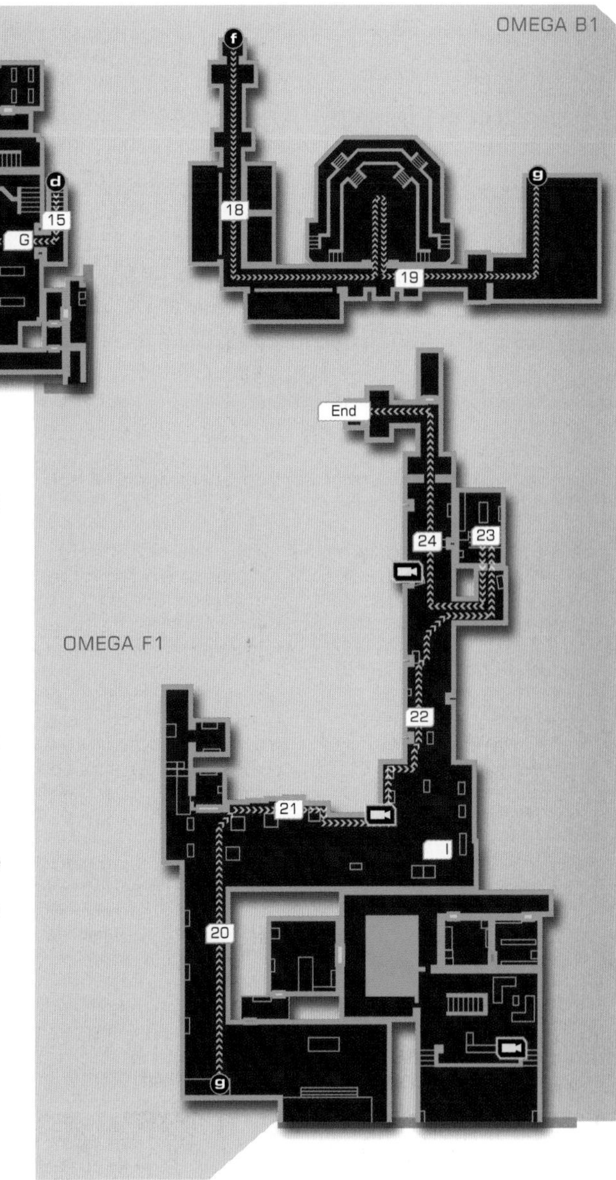

16 Take the western exit and enter the hallway there. Straight ahead is a door that leads to an office. Enter the office and check the western wall to find a copy machine. Move the machine to expose a vent. Enter the air ducts and follow them around to the next vent at **Position H**. There is a guard in this room, so don't leave just yet. Watch the guard through the vent, and when he sits in the chair and has his back to you, exit the air ducts and sneak up on the guard for a Takedown. [→☐ 4]

17 After dealing with the guard, exit the room and go left down the hall to the elevator. There is a laser grid blocking your path, so either hack it via the Terminal on the wall, or activate Cloak to get past the lasers. Now, take the elevator to the floor below.

18 Once you are off the elevator, move down the hall to the Surgical Auditorium and talk to Declan Faherty. Since he is the last scientist you talked to on this route, he will be the one to give you the data disc with Vasili's virus on it.

19 Exit the auditorium and go left to the morgue ahead. Once you are in the morgue, go to the northwest corner of the room to find a breakable wall that you need to punch through. Just past the hole you made in the wall is a valve on the right. You don't have to move forward into the room to use it. Simply look at it from your current position and you can access it without stepping forward and into the gas ahead. [→☐ 5]

After you've used the valve to turn off the gas, move forward through the maintenance tunnel. You'll need to jump up on the pipes in a few places to get through here. Your goal is an air duct at the end of the tunnel that will lead you back outside.

20 Move to the corner of the building and look left to see a Medium Sentry on patrol. Once it moves east to the far end of the yard and stops at **Position I** just out of range of the camera, ease away from the building and toss an EMP grenade at the Medium Sentry. It's a long throw, so aim high so that the arc of the thrown grenade will allow the EMP to reach the Medium Sentry. This will destroy the robot without setting off the alarm or being detected by the camera. Once the Medium Sentry is down, go across the yard to the next building and get behind the large crates.

21 Move the small crate to open the route forward. Hug the building on your left and move forward and left. There is a camera here, but if you hug the building you'll slip under it.

22 Push forward, and continue to stay close to the building. Follow the wall forward, and you'll see another camera ahead. Hug the wall and work your way up to the yellow power generator ahead and take cover there. Now look left and watch the camera, once it is looking off to the right, move forward and get under it. When under the camera, watch it and when it looks back down the hall to your right, sprint forward and go left to the room ahead. [→☐ 6]

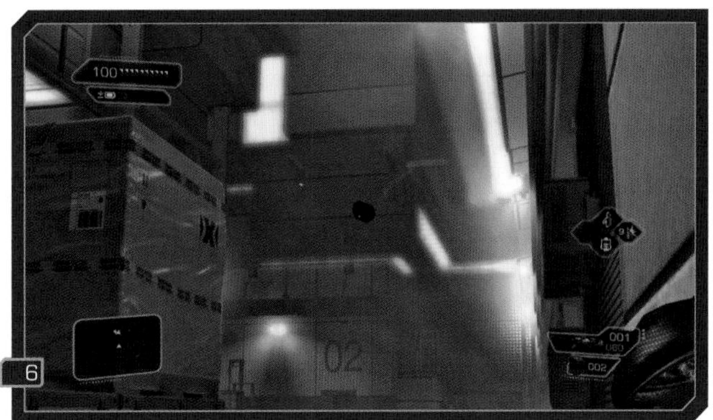

6

23 Hack the Security Hub (Level 3 Hack) inside the security booth and turn off the camera. Now use the Disk Reader to the left of the Hub to upload Vasili's virus. Now wait for the scientist to enact Jensen's plan, and then an alarm will sound. Ahead and to the right a security door will open and three guards will come running out. Hold your position and let them pass. Now access the Hub again and disable the robot.

24 When you're ready, enter the area the guards came running out of and go left. There is an elevator here that will take you to the next Boss fight of the game, so prepare yourself. When you are ready, use the elevator.

ROUTE 3 | Combat

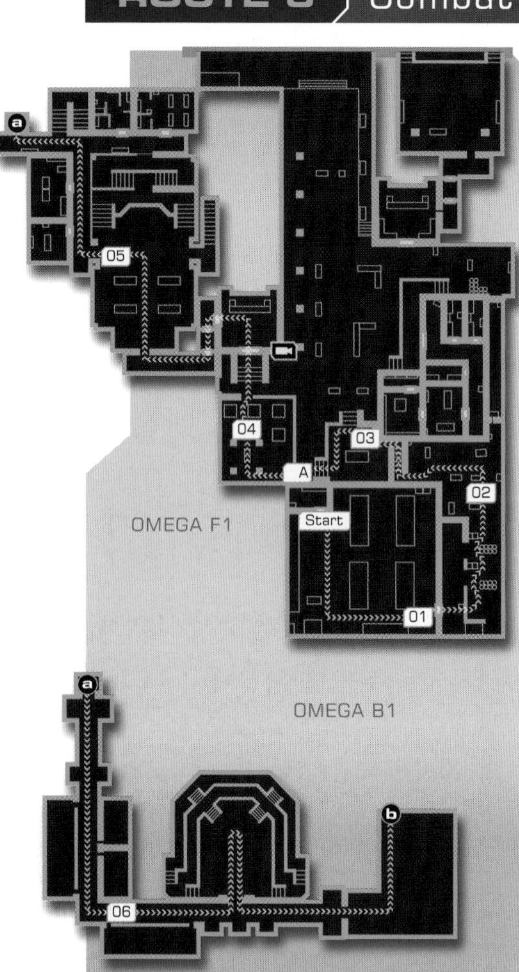

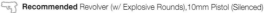

Required Reflex Booster, Hacking: Capture 2, Punch Through Walls, Typhoon, Move/Throw Heavy Objects
Recommended Cloaking System, Jump Enhancement, Rebreather, Icarus Landing System

Recommended Revolver (w/ Explosive Rounds),10mm Pistol (Silenced)

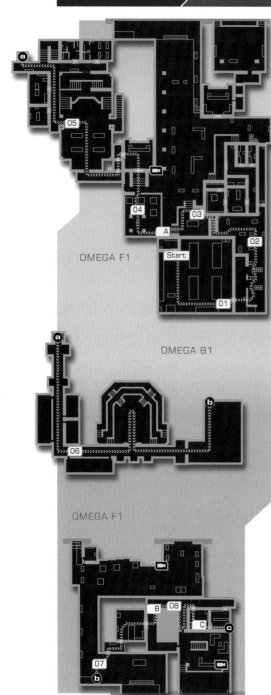

01 Exit the warehouse, and waste no time. Immediately sprint forward and jump over the railing to land amongst the two guards here. Quickly perform a Double Takedown on the two guards to take them both out before they can fire a shot. [→☐ 1]

02 Move ahead whilst crouching to the large boxes here. Look north to see a window in the building ahead. Just past that window are two guards. Shoot the window out with the silenced 10mm Pistol and then immediately toss a Frag Grenade through the window to kill both of those guards. Now take cover at the boxes and look to the right. Hold your position here and pick off the three guards that come running.

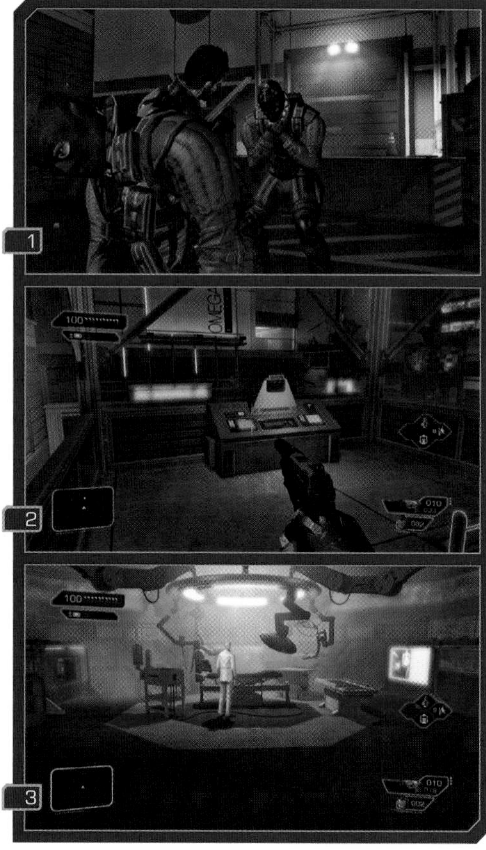

03 Go to the west and take cover at the corner of the building. Peek out to the left and take out the two Heavies that are in the yard ahead. Once they are down, continue to the west to the caged area at **Position A**. There is a hole in the fence in the southeast corner of the caged area. Move the box to expose the hole, and then crouch down and move inside the caged area. Climb the ladder here and hack the terminal to disable the jammer signal. [→☐ 2]

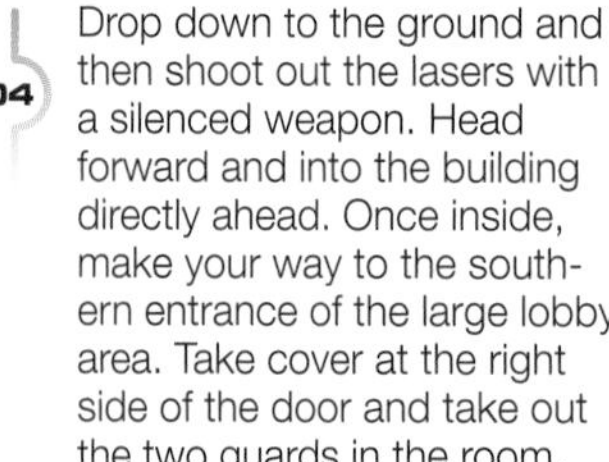

04 Drop down to the ground and then shoot out the lasers with a silenced weapon. Head forward and into the building directly ahead. Once inside, make your way to the southern entrance of the large lobby area. Take cover at the right side of the door and take out the two guards in the room.

05 Exit the room via the western door and then follow the hallways to the elevator. When you come to the laser grids, you can hack them, shoot them out with a silenced weapon, or briefly activate Cloak to get past them. Now use the elevator to reach the floor below.

06 Once you are off the elevator, move down the hall to the Surgical Auditorium and talk to Declan Faherty.

Exit the auditorium and go left to the morgue ahead. Go to the northwest corner of the morgue to find a breakable wall that you need to punch through. Just past the hole you made in the wall is a valve on the right. You don't have to move forward into the room to use it. Simply look at it from your current position and you can access it without stepping forward and into the gas ahead. [→☐ 3]

After you've turned off the gas using the valve, move forward through the maintenance tunnel. You'll need to jump up on the pipes in a few spots to get through here. Your goal is the vent at the end of this tunnel, which will lead you back outside.

07 Once you leave the vent, go directly ahead to the building in front of you. There is a breakable wall here, so punch through it to enter the building. Now make your way to the hallway and then go left to take cover at the corner of the wall at **Position B**. Wait for the guard to exit the room ahead, then shoot him with a non-silenced weapon to make enough noise so that you attract the other guards.

08 Once he is down, move to the hallway ahead and on the right. Take cover at the right side of the door and then look left and pick off the two guards that come running. After you've dispatched them. Go into the room at **Position C** and punch through the wall there. In the next room, move the boxes to expose the vent, and then use the air ducts to reach the room above you.

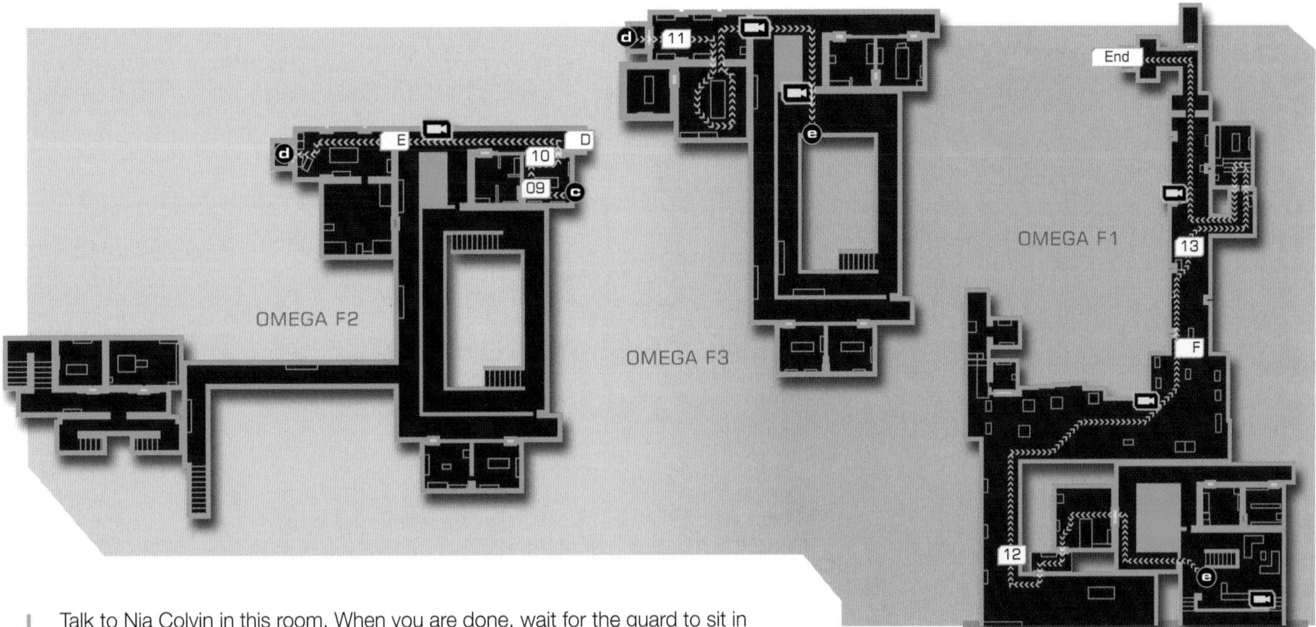

09 Talk to Nia Colvin in this room. When you are done, wait for the guard to sit in the chair outside of Nia's Room at **Position D**. Then open the door and perform a Takedown on him. Now, shoot out the camera in this hall to attract the other guards.

10 Take cover at the left side of the doorway here and wait for the guards to come running. In all, up to five will come. The first one is easy to pick off as he comes alone. Depending on the other guards patrol routes, they may all arrive at once and rush the door. Take them out fast, because if one gets too close to you, he will try to flank you. [→☐ 4]

If this happens, immediately use a Typhoon to take him down. Now hold your position and pick off the remaining guards. When the guards are all dead, continue down the hall and blow open the door at **Position E**. Enter the room and move the crates and use the elevator to reach the floor above you.

11 Exit the elevator and go forward and to the right to find Eric Koss. Talk to him to complete the objective. Since he is the last scientist you talked to on this route, he will be the one to give you the data disc with Vasili's virus on it. Once you are done, exit via the door to the east. Go to the large central area and make your way down to Level 1. If you have the Icarus Landing Augmentation, then just jump the railing to get down fast.

12 Exit the building and head north. There is a Medium Sentry in this area, so take cover at the wall, and when you see it, toss an EMP Grenade at it to destroy it. Now run forward and left and enter the tunnel. Immediately take cover at the box at **Position F**, since the cameras will have detected you and sounded the alarm.

This means a second Medium Sentry will soon enter the area from the left side of the tunnel just ahead. Wait for the Medium Sentry to show up, and then use an EMP to take it out. If you don't have an EMP, then hold your position in cover at the box and tear the Sentry to pieces with gunfire. [→☐ 5]

13 Before you enter the security booth, lay down any Frag or Gas Mines you have near the end of the tunnel, and then enter the booth and use the Disk Reader. Now when the scientists cause the distraction and the guards come running out the security door, they will trigger your Mines for an easy victory. Once the guards have been dispatched, head to the elevator on the other side of the security door and prepare for a Boss encounter. [→☐ 6]

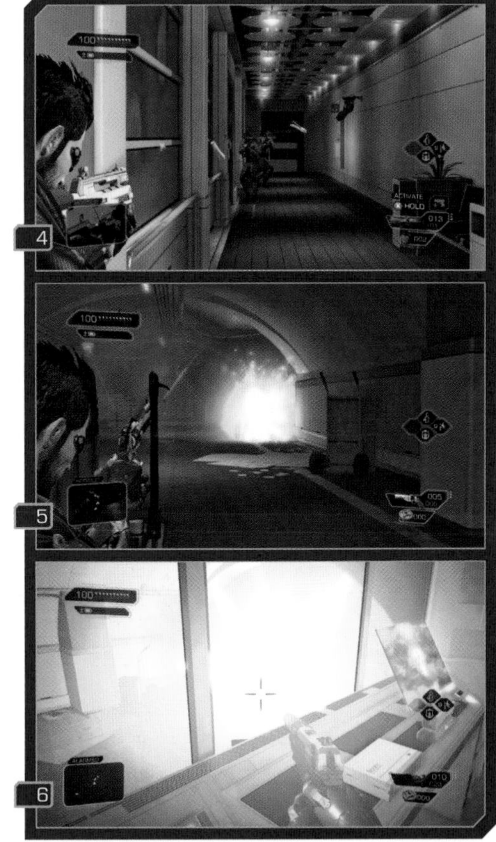

Objective Completed	Objective Type	XP Reward	Stealth Bonuses	
			Ghost	Smooth Operator
Search For Signs of Megan's Team	Primary	250	Yes	Yes
Disable the Signal Jammer	Secondary	250	Yes	Yes
Find and speak with Declan Faherty	Primary	250	No	No
Find and speak with Eric Koss	Primary	250	No	No
Find and speak with Nia Colvin	Primary	250	No	No
Upload a virus to the security computer and enter the restricted area.	Primary	750	Yes	Yes

BOSS FIGHT JARON NAMIR

Here you face the third Boss of the game. We'll give you a few tips here to get you started. For a detailed strategy on how to take down this formidable Boss, please refer to the Opponents Chapter in this guide. [→☐ 1]

- Use Typhoon if you have it.
- Don't sit still for long. Move in a clockwise fashion about the outer ring of the area, and take cover at the corners to trade fire with Namir as he follows you.
- If you have mines, plant them in his path.
- When in cover, use grenades to stun Namir and give you more time to fire on him.

ACHIEVEMENT/TROPHY: THE SNAKE

Once you defeat Jaron Namir, you'll unlock this one.

INSIDE THE RESTRICTED AREA

Objective Name	Objective Type
Find Megan Reed	Primary
Open the Hangar Roof	Primary
Use the Leo Shuttle to reach Panchaea	Primary

ACHIEVEMENT/TROPHY: HANGAR 18

Hack the PC in the secret room to unlock this one.

OMEGA RESTRICTED AREA

Start, 01, 02, A, a, End

01 After defeating Namir, exit the area via the eastern doorway and follow the hallway to Megan's room. Go through the door to trigger a cutscene. When that's over, search Megan's room if you like, then use the elevator to the west to reach the next area. [→☐ 2]

02 Exit the elevator and move forward to the control panel. Push the button there to open the hangar doors. If you saved Malik earlier in the game, she will show up and kill all of the Crazies in the room. If you didn't save her, then you'll need to sprint past the Crazies to reach the Leo Shuttle. If you stick to the middle of the room and sprint directly across the Helipad to the Leo Shuttle, you'll make it without a single Crazy attacking you. When you're ready, make your way to **Position A** and push the button there to activate the Leo Shuttle. [→☐ 3]

OPTIONAL EXPLORATION

Leave the room and turn left. Move the crate there to expose the hole in the wall. Inside you'll find a Cooling System upgrade for one of your weapons and a hackable PC unlocks the Hangar 18 Achievement/Trophy.

Objective Completed	Objective Type	XP Reward	Stealth Bonuses	
			Ghost	Smooth Operator
Find Megan Reed	Primary	250	No	No
Open the Hangar Roof	Primary	250	No	No
Use the Leo Shuttle to reach Panchaea	Primary	250	No	No

PANCHAEA

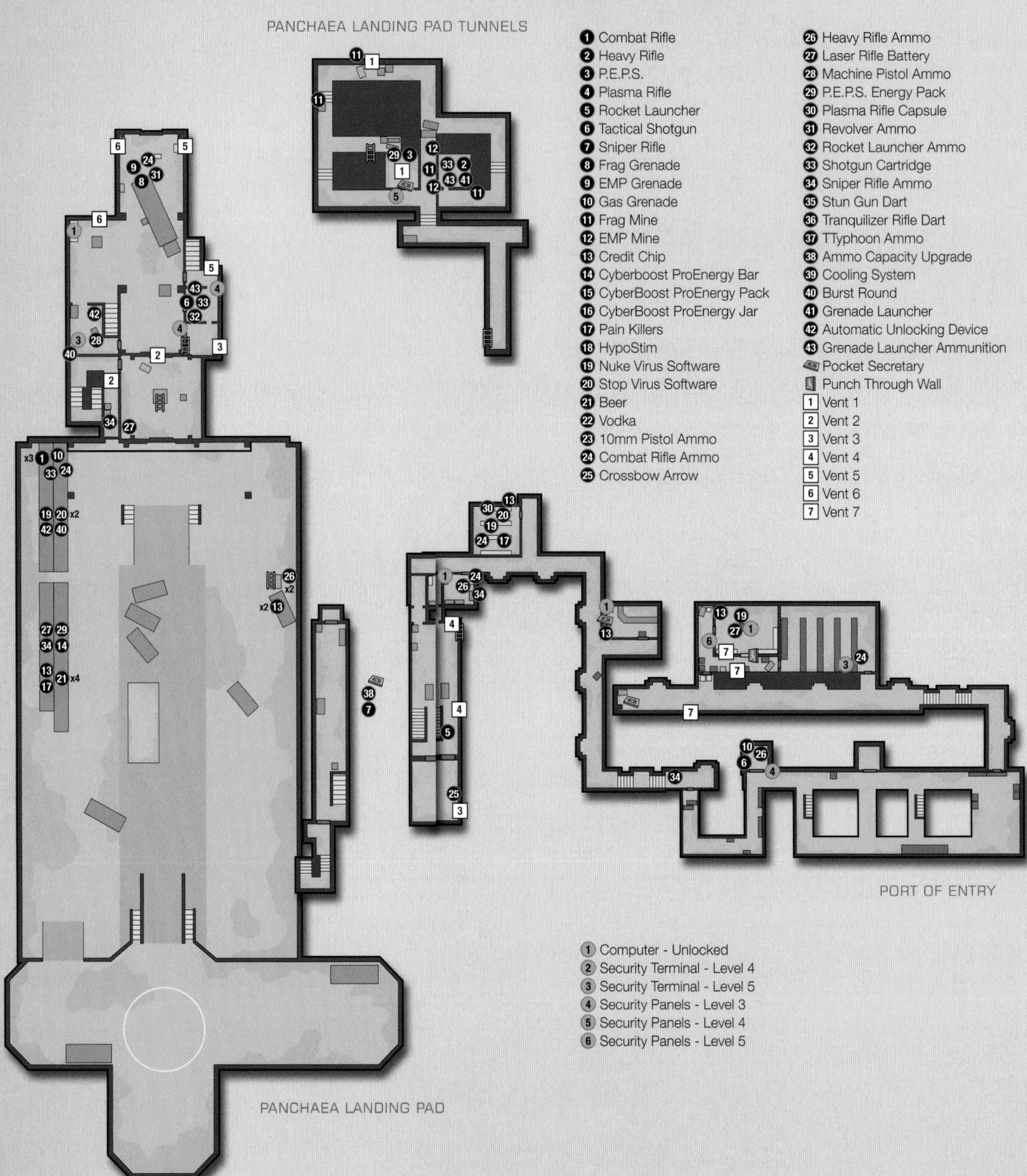

1 Combat Rifle
2 Heavy Rifle
3 P.E.P.S.
4 Plasma Rifle
5 Rocket Launcher
6 Tactical Shotgun
7 Sniper Rifle
8 Frag Grenade
9 EMP Grenade
10 Gas Grenade
11 Frag Mine
12 EMP Mine
13 Credit Chip
14 Cyberboost ProEnergy Bar
15 CyberBoost ProEnergy Pack
16 CyberBoost ProEnergy Jar
17 Pain Killers
18 HypoStim
19 Nuke Virus Software
20 Stop Virus Software
21 Beer
22 Vodka
23 10mm Pistol Ammo
24 Combat Rifle Ammo
25 Crossbow Arrow
26 Heavy Rifle Ammo
27 Laser Rifle Battery
28 Machine Pistol Ammo
29 P.E.P.S. Energy Pack
30 Plasma Rifle Capsule
31 Revolver Ammo
32 Rocket Launcher Ammo
33 Shotgun Cartridge
34 Sniper Rifle Ammo
35 Stun Gun Dart
36 Tranquilizer Rifle Dart
37 TTyphoon Ammo
38 Ammo Capacity Upgrade
39 Cooling System
40 Burst Round
41 Grenade Launcher
42 Automatic Unlocking Device
43 Grenade Launcher Ammunition
Pocket Secretary
Punch Through Wall
1 Vent 1
2 Vent 2
3 Vent 3
4 Vent 4
5 Vent 5
6 Vent 6
7 Vent 7

1 Computer - Unlocked
2 Security Terminal - Level 4
3 Security Terminal - Level 5
4 Security Panels - Level 3
5 Security Panels - Level 4
6 Security Panels - Level 5

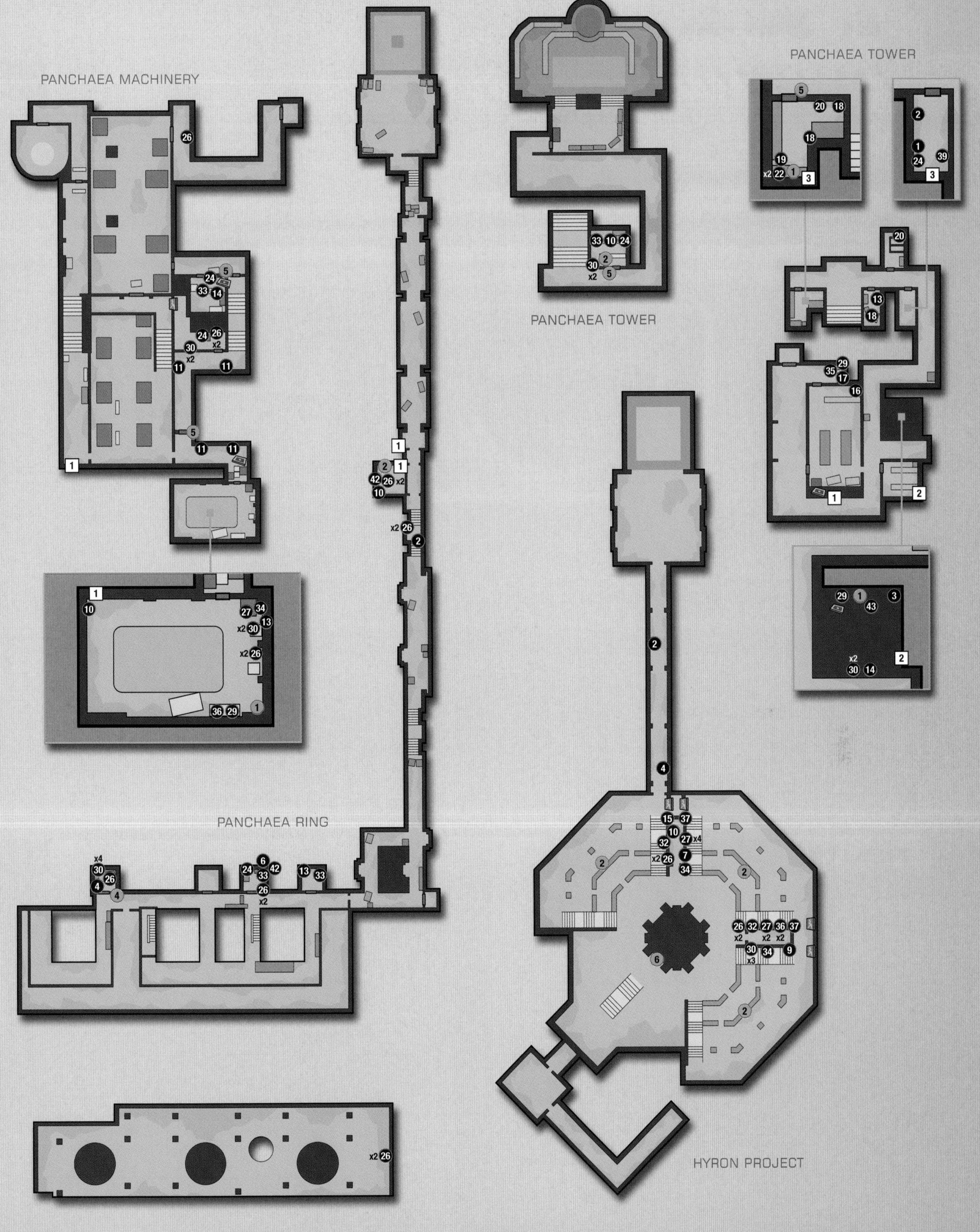
PANCHAEA MACHINERY
PANCHAEA TOWER
PANCHAEA TOWER
PANCHAEA RING
HYRON PROJECT

M1 - SHUTTING DOWN DARROW'S SIGNAL

Objective Name	Objective Type
Get inside the tower and disengage the lockdown.	Primary

Panchaea - Landing Pad

ROUTE 1

Required Jump Enhancement

01 If you have the Jump Enhancement Augmentation, there is a very quick route you can take to reach the tower. Start by moving to the far left-hand corner of the area. There is a storage container sticking out a bit that makes a perfect ledge. Jump onto it then turn to the right. There is another storage container you can reach there. Jump diagonally to the right to get on it. Now jump up on the next two containers and then move to the catwalk. Move down the catwalk to the open vent on your left at **Position A**. Go through it to the air duct ahead and use the air duct to reach the next area. [→☐ 1]

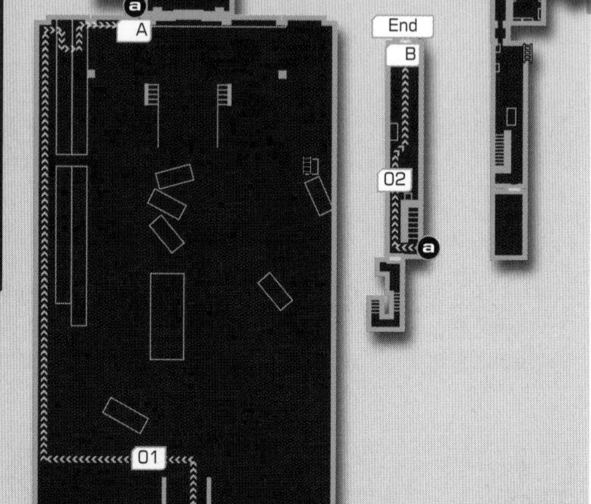

OPTIONAL EXPLORATION

Before using the elevator, explore the entire area here. Right now, there are no enemies about, so you can explore at your leisure in total safety.

02 Once you exit the air ducts, don't move too far forward or you'll fall to the ground below. Instead, carefully go left on the pipes to reach a broken window ahead. Jump through the window, then go left to fall down to the floor below. The elevator you need to use to reach the tower is directly ahead at **Position B**.

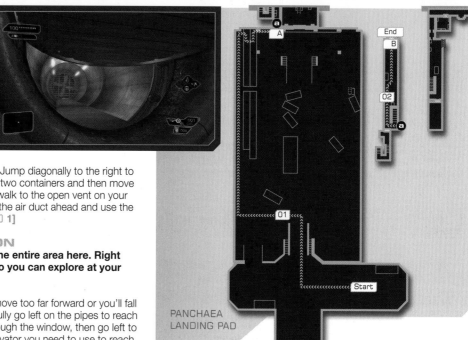

Panchaea - Landing Pad

ROUTE 2

Required None
Recommended EMP Shielding, Move/Throw Heavy Objects

01 Without the Jump Enhancement Augmentation you are required to take a slightly more scenic to the elevator. Go towards the north of the Landing Pad, and then drop down into the maintenance tunnel at **Position A**.

02 Move forward in the tunnel, and then take a left at the fork when you come to it. A short distance down the tunnel you will come to another branch on the right, but make sure not run straight down there. The entire next section of the tunnels has been flooded with electrified water. [→☐ 2]

The only way to progress is to make your way along a large pipe that is just above the water on the right side of this tunnel, but make sure to move slowly because there are two EMP Mines on the wall along the way. If you do not want to recover the Mines, simply throw one of the wooden crates from **Position B** down the tunnel to detonate them before walking along it.

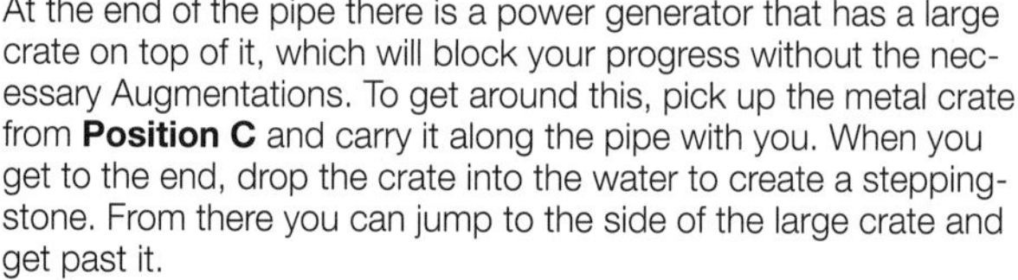

At the end of the pipe there is a power generator that has a large crate on top of it, which will block your progress without the necessary Augmentations. To get around this, pick up the metal crate from **Position C** and carry it along the pipe with you. When you get to the end, drop the crate into the water to create a stepping-stone. From there you can jump to the side of the large crate and get past it.

Tip **If you have the EMP Shielding and Move/Throw Heavy Objects Augmentations, you can make your way through this area much faster. With the EMP Shielding you can just walk safely through the electrified water without fear of injury. The Move/Lift Heavy Objects Augmentation allows you to easily move the large crate on top of the first generator and use it to create a bridge to reach the pipe on the other side.**

03 From the top of the generator, drop down and quickly jump onto the next pipe on the left to avoid taking too much damage, and then follow that pipe around the corner. The area you need to reach

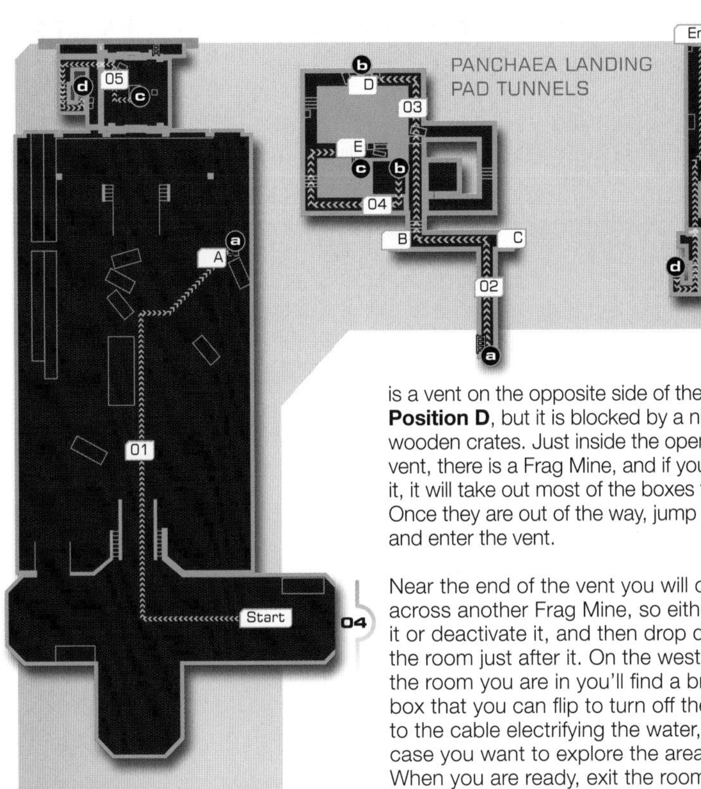

is a vent on the opposite side of the tunnel at **Position D**, but it is blocked by a number of wooden crates. Just inside the opening of the vent, there is a Frag Mine, and if you shoot it, it will take out most of the boxes for you. Once they are out of the way, jump across and enter the vent.

04 Near the end of the vent you will come across another Frag Mine, so either shoot it or deactivate it, and then drop down into the room just after it. On the west wall of the room you are in you'll find a breaker box that you can flip to turn off the power to the cable electrifying the water, just in case you want to explore the area [→☐ 3]. When you are ready, exit the room and follow the tunnel around to the right to reach a ladder at **Position E**, and then climb it to the floor above.

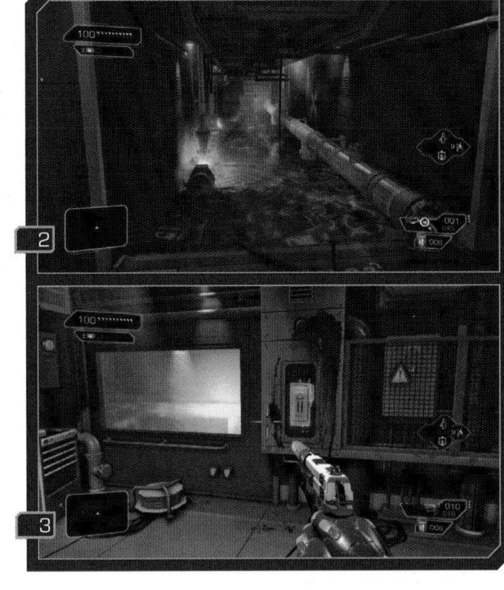

05 When you exit the tunnels you will be in a small warehouse and still have to make your way up to the elevator. Exit the room through the door in northwest, and then follow the corridor straight ahead to reach a staircase that you can use to take you to the floor with the elevator.

PANCHAEA TOWER

01 Exit the elevator and move forward through the halls. Simply follow the halls to the stairs located in the north. There are a few rooms you can explore along the way to find some items if you wish. When you're ready, take the stairs up to the next floor.

OPTIONAL EXPLORATION

Before talking with Hugh Darrow, explore the entire area here. Right now, there are no enemies about since the facility is in lockdown, so you can explore at your leisure in total safety.

Tip **In this area, the Tower Section, there are lots of dead bodies scattered about. However, none of them have anything on them, which means it's a waste time searching them.**

02 At the top of the stairs go left and then stop at the first door on your left. There is a Security Hub in this room that you can use to deactivate the Turret in the next hall. The door is a Level 4 Hack, so hack it and get inside. Once you do, go to the Security Hub on the left and hack that (Capture 4 required). After you gain access, disable the Turret. If you prefer, you can take cover at the corner of the wall and then shoot the Turret until it is destroyed.

03 Move up the hall to the Turret and go left. Just ahead and on the right is a broken window near a camera. Jump through that window to enter the television broadcast room that Hugh Darrow is in. Move forward in that room to trigger a conversation with Darrow.

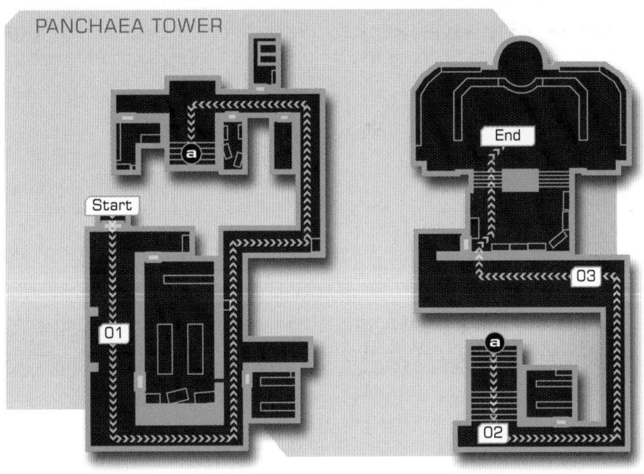

CONVERSATION FLOW
HUGH DARROW
PERSONALITY TYPE: OMEGA

Conversation Round	Response to Make
Round 1	Extrapolate
Round 2	Appeal
Round 3	Extrapolate
Round 4	Extrapolate

Objective Completed	Objective Type	XP Reward	Stealth Bonuses	
			Ghost	Smooth Operator
Get inside the tower and disengage the lockdown.	Primary	1500*	Yes	Yes

*1000 from the Silver Tongue bonus when you win the conversation gameplay

REACHING THE HYRON PROJECT

In this area you'll face Crazies. They are normal Augmented people that have been driven insane by Darrow's signal. With their hyperactive senses they can often hear and find you, when a normal enemy could not. Once alerted, they all move on you in a mad and frenzied pack. Further, taking out a Crazy does not net you any XP. As such, there is no Stealth Combat route for Panchaea.

The Stealth Route will show you how to get through the entire area without being seen, without killing anyone, and without setting off an alarm. Use this route if you are going for the Pacifist and Foxiest of the Hounds Achievements/ Trophies. If you're looking for some gun blazing fun, then follow the Combat route and kill them all!

Objective Name	Objective Type
Reach the Broadcast Center	Primary
Find and speak with Taggart	Secondary

Panchaea Interior

ROUTE 1 Stealth

08_044

Required Cloaking System, Jump Enhancement, Icarus Landing System, Hacking: Capture 4
Recommended None

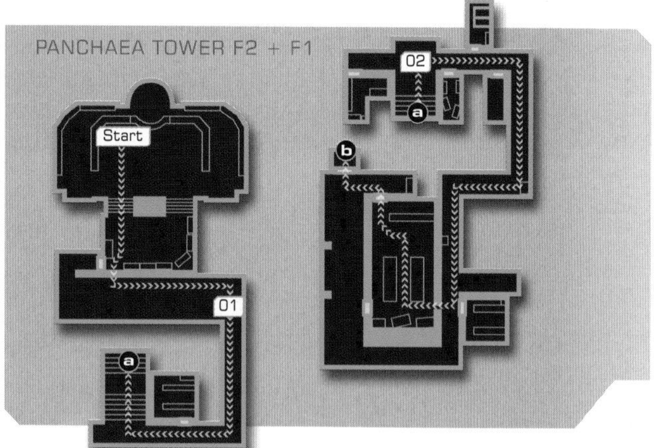

01 Once you are done with Darrow, backtrack the way you came and return to floor below. From the base of the stairs at Level 1 go right and follow the hallway. Stop and take cover before moving out into the hallway because it is now full of Crazies. From cover, peek out and watch the Heavy. Once he goes around the corner at the end of the hall, move forward whilst crouching and go right through the doorway into the kitchen. [→☐ 1]

02 Exit the kitchen via the door on the opposite side of the room to the north. Immediately take cover at the corner of the wall and look left. Watch the Crazies here. There is one in particular that will move close to your position. Keep an eye on him, and once he turns his back on you, move while crouching to the elevator and use it.

03 Off the elevator, move while crouching to the shelving and boxes in the southeast corner to the left of the door. Jump onto the pallets, and from there up onto the top shelf. Then jump onto the box on that top shelf. This will often force you to crouch, so position yourself under the opening in the ceiling above and then stand back up. Now jump into the crawl space in the ceiling.

04 Go through the broken window and then go right to get on the pipes. Use them to cross over to the far side of the room. Once there, go left to the next crawl space in the ceiling on the side of the room. Ahead, you'll find a vent that you can use to enter the air ducts and reach the floor below.

05 Exit the large vertical air shaft and go right in the air ducts to a vent. The room ahead is full of crazies, so you'll need to be careful. When you're ready, activate Cloak and then open the vent. Immediately move forward and go right through the open door. Just ahead is a broken window at **Position A** that you need to jump through to enter the next area. [→☐ 2]

06 Move forward through the halls to the LIMB Clinic. There is a soda machine blocking the door, so move it out of the way to gain access to the room. Talk to the clerk at the counter to buy Praxis Kits and other items if desired. When you're ready, continue south down the hall to the door at **Position B**.

07 As soon as you walk through the door to the outside, you'll see a large stack of black iron bars. Jump onto this stack and turn right. Carefully jump onto the scaffolding. Now go right to the building's ledge. Once you get to the ledge, jump up once more to the smaller ledge above that. Now turn right and walk to the end.

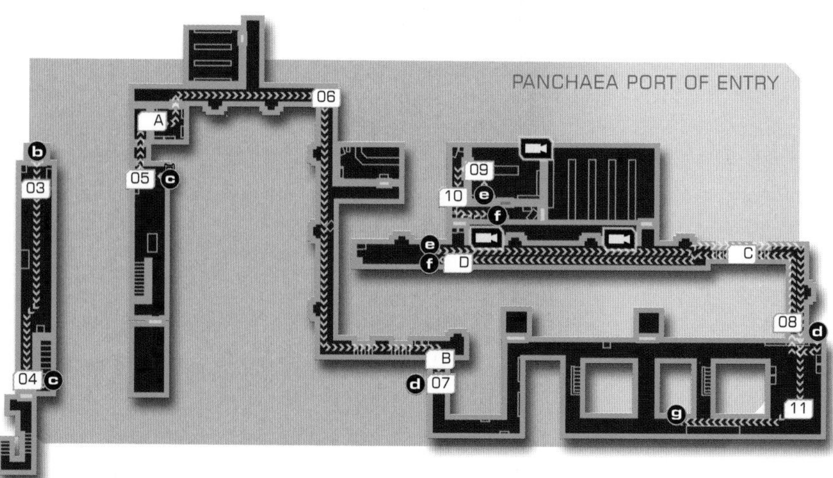

08 Drop down and crouch to get under the rubble blocking the door. Once you are in the hallway, go to the last section of stairs and stop at **Position C**. There are two cameras ahead. Watch the closest one and when it begins moving away from you, go left and drop down to where the pipes are located. Immediately take cover at the low wall, and then move forward while in cover to avoid detection. Move up to **Position D** where you'll find a vent. Open it and then enter the air ducts. [→☐ 3]

09 Follow the ducts straight ahead and ignore the right-hand branch – you'll use it later. You'll soon come to a ladder. Climb up to another vent and use it to get to Taggart's room. Approach Taggart and speak with him to complete this Secondary Objective. When you have finished talking to him once, talk to him a second time for some extra dialogue.

10 Exit the room via the door to the west, then follow the hallway around to a stack of boxes. Move the boxes to expose a vent. Open it and enter the air ducts – this is the right-hand branch of the air ducts you passed earlier. Move forward to where the ducts come to a "T" and then go left out of the vent there. Immediately take cover at the low wall and then move in cover back to the stairs to the east.

11 From here, backtrack the way you came and move back outside. For this next part, you'll need the Icarus Landing System and two full energy cells, so use an energy bar to gain the needed energy. While remaining crouched, move to the southern edge of the platform and then follow the catwalk along to the west until you come to the middle hole. Now, approach the hole and activate cloak, and then immediately jump down.

As soon as you land, go through the door to the north and make sure to close it behind you – and make sure to stay away from the door or they'll see you through the glass once cloak deactivates [→☐ 4]. The noise of your landing will Alarm the Crazies, but since you are cloaked, they cannot see you. The noise of your landing will keep the Crazies in the room investigating the noise meaning they'll ignore the fact that you open and close the door to exit the room.

12 Now move south down the hall to the room ahead. Crouch before opening the door. Once the door is open, move forward whilst crouching and jump over the stack of pipes ahead. Hug the left wall and move forward to the next set of stairs. There are Crazies in the room to your left, but if you stay crouched and hug the left wall, they'll never see you.

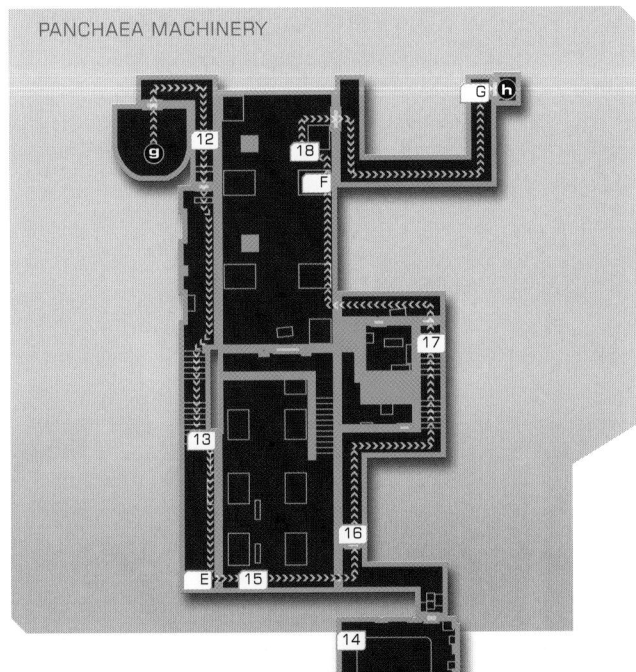

13 At the bottom of the stairs, stay crouched. Once again, there are Crazies on the left that can see you. Stay crouching and hug the left wall as you move forward to the end. Jump up onto the electrical unit on the back wall to the south and use the vent at **Position E** to enter the ducts and reach Sarif's room.

14 Drop down out of the vent and talk to David Sarif. Once you have spoken with him once, speak to him again for some extra dialogue. The door to this room is blocked by large crates and booby-trapped with mines. If you try to go that way, the explosion of the mines will draw the Crazies to the area, so it's best to backtrack the way you came.

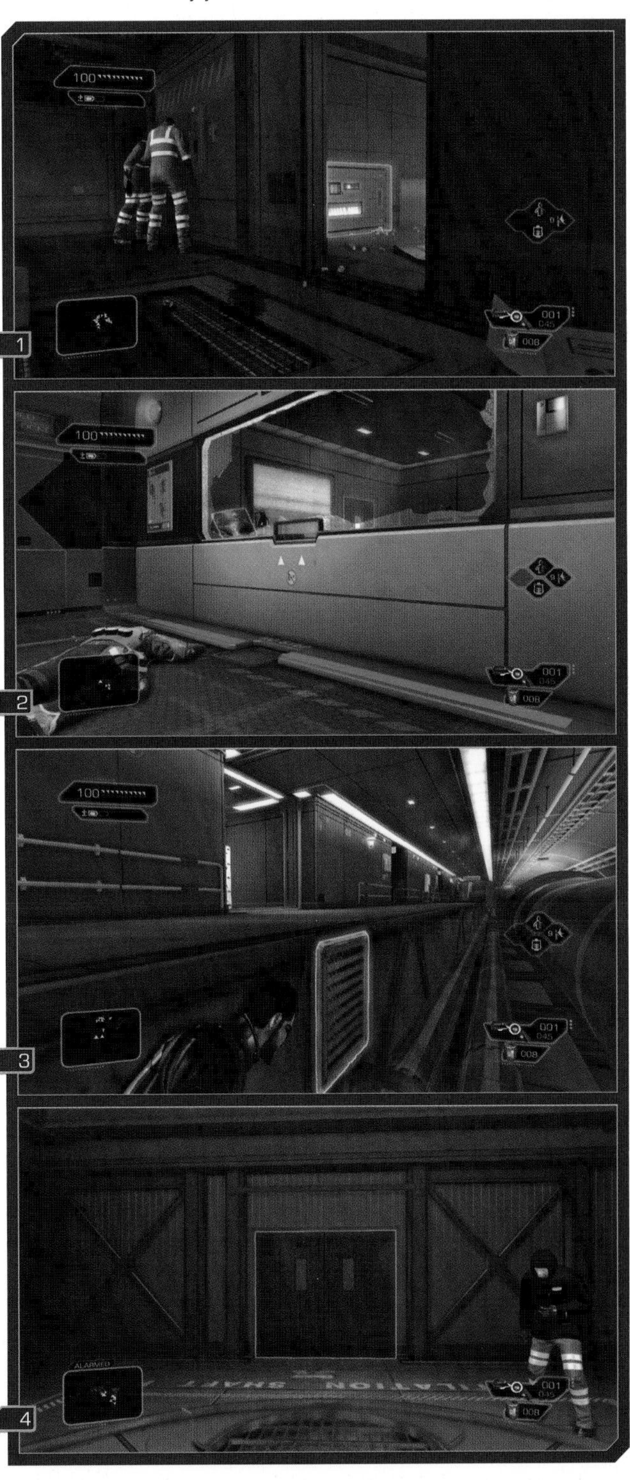

15 Go back through the vent, drop down and go right to the door of the room full of Crazies. When you're ready, activate Cloak and move straight ahead to the room across the way. If you only have one energy cell, you'll run out just before you reach the door, but that is ok since you'll be past the watchful eyes of the Crazies in the room. As you go through the door, don't go too far or you'll trigger the mines. Once through the door, immediately turn left and hack the door (Level 4 Hack).

16 Once you go through the door, do not move forward just yet. There are two mines in this hallway, the first is directly ahead, and the other is around the corner on the right. Start by moving slowly to the first mine you can see and deactivate it. Now turn and go down the next section of the hallway very slowly to deactivate the next one. Once you're done, go up the stairs to the floor above.

17 Stay crouching as you move so that the Crazies don't hear. Go up the stairs and then left to the door at the end of the hallway. Go through the door crouching, turn immediately right and stop behind the equipment. From this hiding spot behind the heavy equipment, activate Cloak and move ahead making sure to hug the right-hand wall. When you reach the next heavy piece of equipment at **Position F**, hide and let your energy replenish if you wish.

18 When you're ready, from the second hiding spot at **Position F**, activate Cloak go forward and left around the large piece of equipment that is before you. Pass the equipment and make your way to the door on the eastern wall to your right. Make sure to close the door behind you once you are through it. This next stretch of hallway is clear of Crazies, so simply follow the hallway to the elevator at **Position G** and use it to reach the next area. [→☐ 1]

19 Get off the elevator and immediately go right. Move all the way up to the closed doors and stop when you can see them. There's a rough stretch ahead with lots of crazies. It's also the last part of the game before the final Boss fight.

Now is the time to use as many energy bars as it takes to give yourself full energy. With full energy, and fully upgraded Cloak, you can easily activate Cloak here and move forward, making sure to touch no one, and reach the end unscathed. [→☐ 2]

20 If you don't have energy bars, then you'll have to do it a piece at a time. Once the doors open, activate Cloak and move ahead and to the right. Go through the break in the rail here to land on the catwalk below. Take cover and let your energy replenish.

21 Activate Cloak and hop up on the bridge and move to the right. Push forward to a break in the rail on the left. Use it to reach the catwalk below. Take cover again and let your energy replenish.

22 When ready, stick to cover and move forward to the next break in the railing. Activate Cloak and jump up to the catwalk and immediately move ahead and to the right to the next break in the railing. Drop to the catwalk, take cover and let your energy replenish. [→☐ 3]

23 This is the last stretch. While on the catwalk, move in cover to the next break in the railing. Once you reach the break, activate Cloak, go right, then move forward and duck behind the boxes ahead. Now, jump over the boxes and take the stairs to the elevator at **Position H**. When you're ready, use the elevator to reach the final Boss Fight.

ROUTE 2 | Combat

Required Reflex Booster, Typhoon, Move/Throw Heavy Objects, Jump Enhancement
Recommended Dermal Plating

Recommended Revolver (w/ Explosive Rounds), 10mm Pistol (Silenced), Frag Grenade

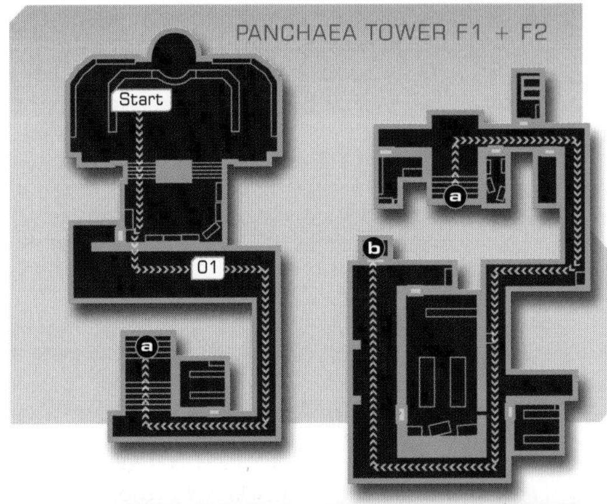

01 Once you are done with Darrow, return the way you came and go back to floor below. From the base of the stairs at Level 1 go right and follow the hallway. Stop and take cover before moving out into the hallway, because it is now full of Crazies. [→□4]

Step out into the hallway and shoot one of the Crazies with an explosive revolver round. This will draw their attention and send them running at you in a frenzy. Pick them off with the Revolver or Shotgun as they rush in. Backpedal to keep ground between you and the Crazies. If one or two get two close, immediately go for a Takedown. If several get close, then use Typhoon.

If there are any stragglers that don't come running, move up the hallway a bit to get their attention. When they are all dead, go to the elevator.

02 Get off the elevator and head to the second set of windows on your left. Use a silenced weapon to shoot out the large pane of glass. Jump through to the floor below and then immediately jump on the two stacked crates near the truck below. From there, jump onto the truck.

From the top of the truck, you can easily pick off the Crazies below and in the area to the east. Simply shoot through the glass of the eastern area to kill the Crazies in there. When they are all dead, jump down and go through the door beneath the camera. Make your way up the stairs at **Position A** to reach the next area.

Tip **Do not shoot the Box Guard or it will activate and target you!**

03 Keep going forward and jump through the broken window on the right. Once you are in that room, go out of the door and then head right. Make your way to the first hallway on your left at **Position B**. Go down that hallway and enter the locker room there. Inside is a single Crazy, so get close to him for a Takedown kill. Once he is dead, you're free to search all the lockers for items.

04 Exit the locker room and head back up the hall to the LIMB Clinic. Move the soda machine that is blocking the doorway and then talk to the clerk. There are two Praxis Kits for sale, as well as Typhoon ammo and energy and health supplements. When you're ready, make your way down the hall to the exit in the south at **Position C**.

05 Before going out, use any energy bars you have to stock up on energy. As you walk out the door, pay attention to the pile of black bars ahead of you. If something goes wrong, you can run and jump over these to retreat, as the Crazies can't get past them.

Go out onto the catwalk until you can see the first group of Crazies. Toss a Frag at the wall above the first Crazy in a yellow jacket. This should kill three or four of the crazies, and get the rest running toward you.

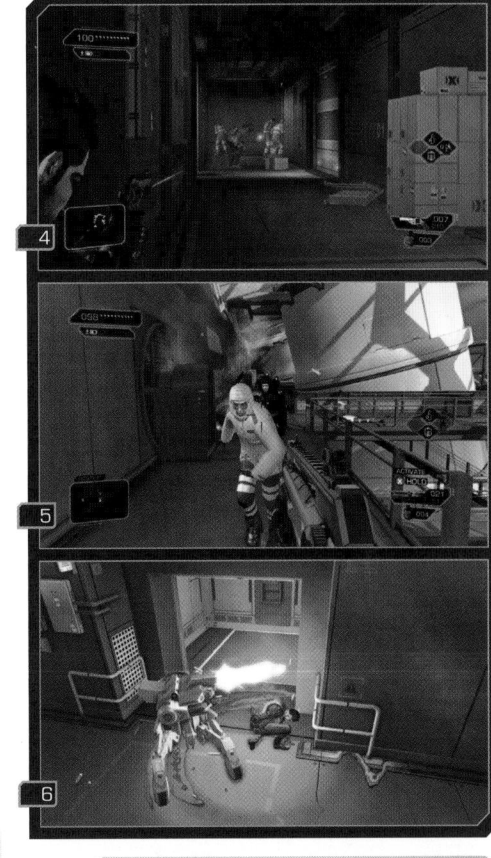

06 Run toward the encroaching horde and jump over the lead Crazies. This will put you into the middle of a large group. Now use a Typhoon. Hold your ground and pick off the next two or three that come running. Soon a large group will come up from below,. As before, run to them, jump over the lead Crazies, and then use a Typhoon. Start backing up now, and pick off any stragglers that are left. [→□ 5]

07 Move to the last door on the left that is blocked by rubble. Crouch and go under the rubble blocking the door. Now make your way forward to the stairs and go down them. Sprint past the cameras to the end of the area where a Medium Sentry will emerge at **Position D**. Once the cameras trigger the alarm, the door will begin to open. Get close to the door, and once it is open, use a Typhoon to take out the Sentry. [→□ 6]

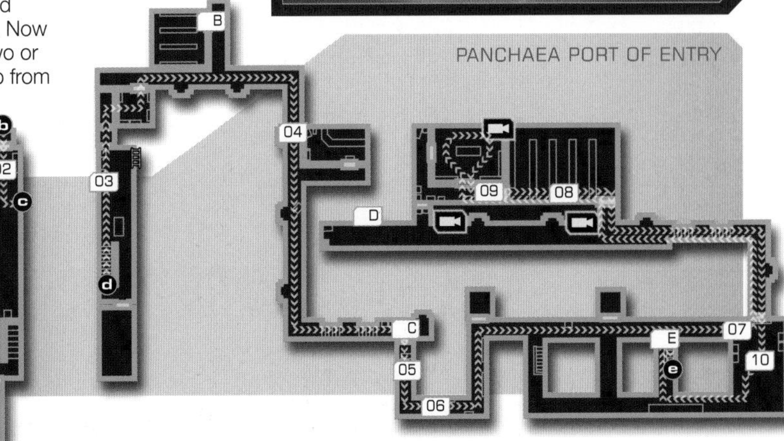

08 Now backtrack to the first door near the stairs. As you are making your way there, a Crazy or two may come running out, since they have been alerted to your presence when you destroyed the Medium Sentry. Pick off any that come running and then enter the room. As soon as you enter the room, turn left to see a bank of servers. Jump on top of the servers and then go left. Ahead are some cabling trays suspended from the ceiling. Jump on top of them and then look down at the floor below. You're safe to pick off all the Crazies at your leisure from here. [→☐ 1]

09 Once they are all dead, exit the room via the door to the southwest. There is some equipment and boxes blocking your way, so jump over the boxes to proceed. Just ahead is a breakable wall on your right. Punch through it or blow it open with the Revolver and then enter Taggart's room. Talk to Taggart twice to hear all of his dialogue, and then back track the way you came to the outside area.

10 Take the stairs at **Position E** down to the next level below. Once you get off the stairs, go right and make your way to the elevator that leads to the Machine Room where David Sarif and his people are hiding.

11 Exit the elevator and then follow the hall to a set of double doors. Enter the next room and look left. There is a large machine labeled as "B". Jump on top of it to pick off the Crazies below. There are explosive barrels in this room, so target them first to take out two or three Crazies in one go.

12 Move ahead to the Section B door. Take up position to the right of the yellow power generator that is in front of that door. If the Crazies come running singly, hold your ground here and take them out as they try to get through the door to get you. If any come close, then use a Takedown or a Typhoon blast. [→☐ 2]

If they don't come running, then walk out onto the catwalk ahead and toss Frag Grenades at them until you're out of Frags, and then pick off any stragglers.

13 Once all are dead, move down the stairs and to the door in the southeast corner of the room. Don't go through the door yet as there are Frag Mines ahead. From the safety of the doorway, shoot the mines to detonate them. Then go forward and move the two large crates that are blocking the door. Now enter the room and talk to David Sarif twice to hear everything he has to say. [→☐ 3]

14 Exit the room and go to the locked door ahead. Either hack the door (Level 4 Hack) or blow it open with the Revolver. Once you are past the door, don't go too far forward yet as there are two mines in this hallway. You could shoot and detonate them, but they will come in handy later. So move forward slowly and deactivate and take each mine. Use the stairs ahead to reach the next floor.

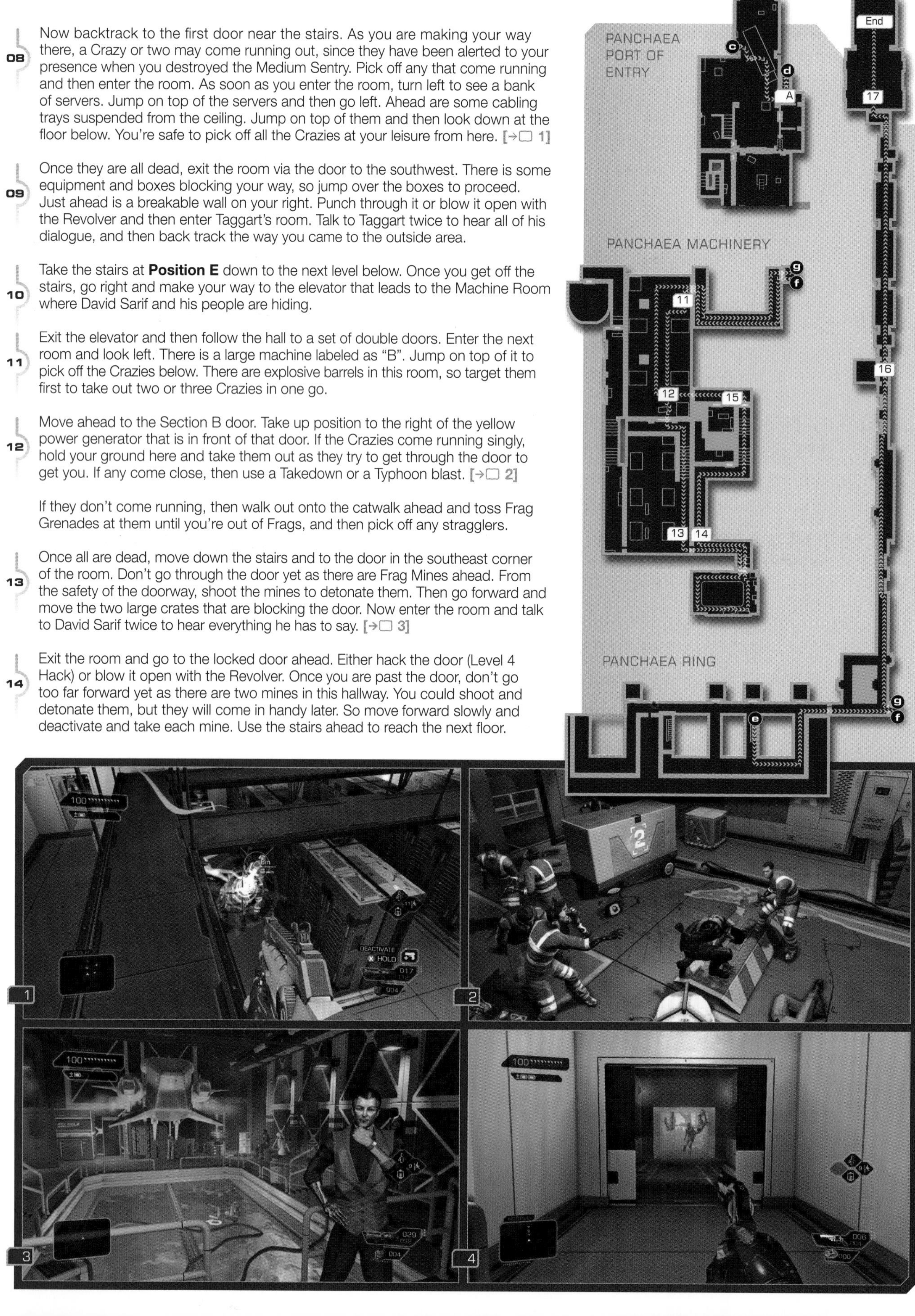

15 With all the Crazies dead, there is no threat left in the area. Explore if you wish, and when you are ready, backtrack to the elevator that you used to reach this area. Use the elevator to return to the previous area.

16 Exit the elevator and go right down the long hall. Approach the security door; if you have got the Frag Mines, drop one at the door, then back up a few meters and drop another. Return to the stairs and start shooting at the mass of Crazies ahead. They will begin to charge, so keep shooting them. As they reach the mines, begin backing up and continue to pick them off. If any get too close, use a Takedown or Typhoon. [→□ 4]

Alternatively, move toward the door ahead until it opens. Equip the Revolver and shoot the red barrel ahead. Hold your ground and use the Revolver to pick off the Crazies as they come running. Back up as needed, and if any get too close, use a Typhoon.

Tip **Go into the gas room on the left and hack the hub to turn the Turrets on the enemies for an easy win.**

17 Once you have killed all the Crazies here, Panchaea will be completely clean of enemy presences except for the last Boss below. If you wish, you can still go to every area of Panchaea, so if you'd like to explore, now is the time to do it. When you're ready, go to the elevator at the end of the hall and use it to reach the final Boss of the game. [→□ 5]

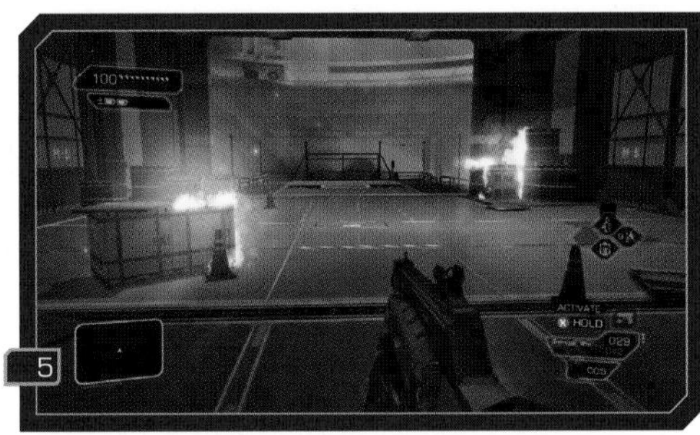
5

Objective Completed	Objective Type	XP Reward	Stealth Bonuses	
			Ghost	Smooth Operator
Reach the Broadcast Center	Primary	500	Yes	Yes
Find and speak with Taggart	Secondary	500	No	No
Find and speak with Sarif	Secondary	500	No	No

BOSS FIGHT HYRON PROJECT

6

Here you'll face the final Boss of the game. We'll give you a few tips here to get you started. For the complete strategy on how to take down this formidable Boss, please refer to the Opponents Chapter in this guide. [→□ 6]

- There is a protective shield around Zhao. To disable it, you have to disable the Tertiary Pods first.
- If you have the Laser Rifle, you can shoot Zhao immediately through the shield. Make sure to activate Cloak to avoid being hit by the Turrets.
- There is a security terminal for the Tertiary Pods on the southwest corner of the Tertiary Pod construct.
- If you won the conversation gameplay with Darrow, then use his codes on the security terminal for the Tertiary Pods to immediately disable them and then attack Zhao. If you don't have Darrow's codes, then hack the terminal (Level 5 Hack). Use all your Stops and Nukes to make it easier.
- Once the Tertiary Pods are down and the shield protecting Zhao cracks, get close to Zhao and use three Typhoons in a row.

Objective Completed	Objective Type	XP Reward	Stealth Bonuses	
			Ghost	Smooth Operator
Defeat the Hyron Project	Primary	1000	No	No

END GAME

With that done, head through the door behind Zhao to reach the main Broadcast Room. You now have a choice to make. By default, you have two options, Darrow's Message, and your own. If you found Taggart, then you have the choice of his message, and if you found Sarif, then you can choose his message. If you found and spoke with them both, then you have four options to choose from. Pick your desired path, and broadcast the message. [→□ 7]

7

Congratulations, you have beaten Deus Ex: Human Revolution!

CH06 Side Quests

Side Quests allow you to delve deeper into the game's world by exploring back stories, while letting you encounter completely new characters and story threads. Outside of the rich story offerings, Side Quests are also an excellent source of additional XP and rare items, such as Praxis Kits and Weapon Upgrades. There are also many Achievements/Trophies related to Side Quests, so completionists will not want to miss out on this Chapter.

SIDE QUESTS

Most Side Quests are opened up by specific characters approaching you and asking for assistance, or by going up and talking to the right people. This Chapter will take you through every quest the game has to offer and let you know exactly how and where they begin, and what potential rewards they may offer. Every objective within each quest is highlighted, so as you progress through them, you will always be able to keep track of exactly where you are, and where you need to go.

//-CH 06 SIDE QUESTS

DETROIT 1

S1 & S2 Lesser Evils

This first Side Quest leads directly into the next one, and is primarily used as a tutorial of sorts to let you know that additional missions can be acquired by talking to different people within the world. After handing over the experimental Typhoon to Pritchard, and meeting with Sarif in his Penthouse, after returning from the Manufacturing Plant, you will hear a message come over the building's PA system calling you to your office. Inside your office on the third floor you will find another employee, Tim Carella. He has a slight problem that he needs assistance with.

Objective Completed	Objective Type	XP Reward	Add. Reward
Go to my Office	Primary	500	–

It appears that Carella, along with another employee named Tindall were the ones behind the mysterious Neuropozyne thefts that have been going on for the last couple of months. Carella wants out of the situation, but Tindall has incriminating security footage of him and is using it to blackmail him into continuing. In order to help Carella, you will need to investigate the situation and try to recover the security footage from Tindall.

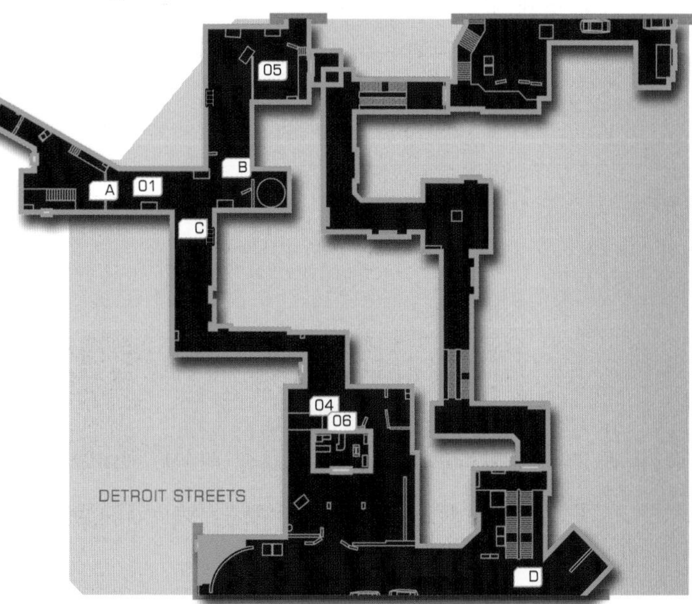

1

Required Jump Enhancement or Hacking: Capture 2

01 **» Locate Tindall's apartment building**

Carella's first clue for you is that the footage might be on Tindall's Computer, which is in his apartment located near Brooklyn Court. This apartment building is protected by a high security fence, which means you cannot access it normally and will require the use of some advanced Augmentations. The most direct path into the building is through the security gate in the fence at **Position A**; this can be hacked if you have Capture 2 software. Alternatively, if you pick up the crate from **Position B** and place it just in front of the fence, you can use the Jump Enhancement Augmentation to jump over it. From there you just need to descend the stairs and enter the apartment building.

There is another way that also requires the Jump Enhancement Augmentation and you can find it by climbing the fire escape at **Position C**. At the top of the fire escape you will see some wooden planks extending out towards the apartment building you need to reach. Run along these planks and then jump across to the adjacent rooftop and enter the building through the door on the roof [→☐ 1]. If you do not have any of the required Augmentations you will need to continue with other missions until you have enough Praxis Points to get them, or use the code for the gate if you have it.

Objective Completed	Objective Type	XP Reward	Add. Reward
Locate Tindall's apartment building	Primary	300	–

02 » Gain access to Tindall's apartment

Tindall's apartment is on the basement floor of the building and to get inside you will need to hack the access terminal on the wall outside. The terminal only has a security rating of 1 so you will not need any additional Augmentations to get inside. If you don't want to hack the door, however, you can always choose to destroy it with conventional weapons.

Objective Completed	Objective Type	XP Reward	Add. Reward
Gain access to Tindall's apartment	Primary	300	–

03 » Investigate Tindall's computer

Carella seems to think that the incriminating footage that Tindall is blackmailing him with will be on a computer in this apartment, and you can find it in the bedroom on the opposite side of the apartment. The computer is unlocked, so you can access it without hacking, but unfortunately the footage is not on the computer; Tindall has it on him. One of the emails gives you the access code for the security gate outside, if you need it, and the other concerns a meeting between Tindall and one of his clients, which will take place behind the gas station.

Objective Completed	Objective Type	XP Reward	Add. Reward
Investigate Tindall's computer	Primary	300	–

As soon as you access the second email, one of the local junkies will enter the room looking for Tindall so you can not spend too long reading it. Take cover next to the bedroom door so that you can see out into the living area where the junkie is before taking any action. If you want to incapacitate the junkie, simply run up quickly and use a Takedown on him. If you want to sneak past him, maintain your position by the door until the junkie enters the bedroom, and then quickly crouch down and move into the living area. You can then exit the apartment safely while the junkie is investigating the bedroom and head back towards the gas station.

04 » Meet with Tindall

You can find Tindall leaning up against a large container near the side of the gas station; when you are within range, initiate a conversation with him. Tindall claims he is giving away the Neuropozyne and using it to help people who cannot afford to buy it for themselves, but unfortunately, that is where his goodwill seems to end. Tindall will not give up the security footage unless you help take care of two local drug dealers who have been harassing him for undercutting their profits.

Tip **Although it is not a fully-fledged, multi-part conversation, you can still make use of the Social Enhancer Augmentation during your conversation with Tindall. During his dialogue you will still see the personality-type indicator on screen and be able to use it to see which type is dominant for him. Then, when he asks you to make a choice between accepting or declining his terms, you will have the option of using the Pheromones. Tindall is predominantly an Alpha-type personality, so if you make that choice you will convince him to hand over the security footage straight away,**

2

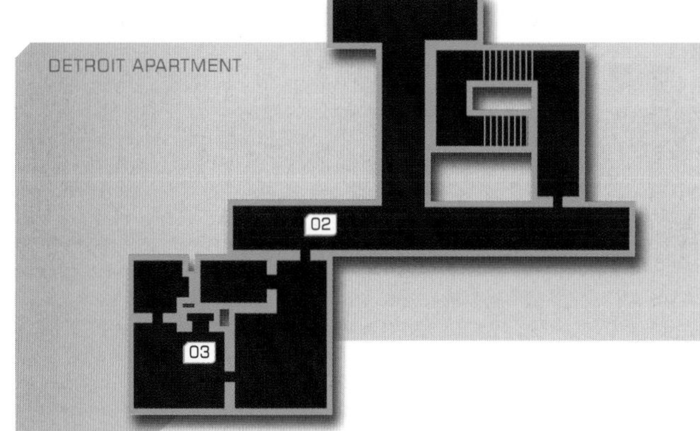

without you having to take out the two dealers. If you do not have this Augmentation at the time you first talk to Tindall, you can still choose to decline his offer and then come back later when you have the Social Enhancer. When you talk to him again at this point, you will have the option of using the Pheromones straight away, so make sure you pick the correct personality type. Using this method, however, you will miss out on the XP you would get for completing the objectives relating to the dealers.

Objective Completed	Objective Type	XP Reward	Add. Reward
Meet with Tindall	Primary	100	–

05 » Locate the two Dealers
» Neutralize the two Dealers

The two dealers can be found hanging out on the basketball court near Earl's Court. How you deal with them is entirely up to you and you can choose to kill them, or simply incapacitate them. The easiest way to take them both out is if you have the Multiple Takedown Augmentation, since that will allow you take them both out simultaneously. [→☐ 2] Outside of that, the best means is to generally use either a lethal or non-lethal weapon to incapacitate one of them from close range, and then instantly use a Takedown on the other before either of them can draw their weapon. If you do this quickly enough with non-lethal weapons you can easily avoid any of the other NPCs in the area becoming altered. If you want to make sure they do not, then you can just use the Tranquilizer Rifle on both of the drug dealers from long range.

Objective Completed	Objective Type	XP Reward	Add. Reward
Locate the two Dealers	Secondary	100	–
Neutralize the two Dealers	Secondary	750	–

06 » Return to Tindall
» Return to Carella

Once you have incapacitated both dealers, return to Tindall near the gas station to inform him of the news. No matter how you took care of the dealers, Tindall will be happy with the result and hand over the security footage to you. Afterwards you can choose to put him in contact with someone to help him continue his work, or wash your hands of it. Now that you have the footage, you can bring it back to Carella, who is waiting in front of the subway station at **Position D**. Talk to Carella about handing over the security footage. He will be so appreciative that he will even hand over a weapon mod to you; when the conversation is over the Side Quest will be completed.

ACHIEVEMENT/TROPHY TIP

Upon returning the security footage to Carella and completing the quest, you will automatically unlock the Lesser Evil Achievement/Trophy.

Objective Completed	Objective Type	XP Reward	Add. Reward
Return to Tindall	Primary	100	–
Return to Carella	Primary	1000	Laser Targeting System mod

S3 One Good Turn Deserves Another

Although this Side Quest technically begins in Sarif HQ, the pieces to set it in motion appear back in the Manufacturing Plant. To begin with, when you reach the first Assembly Lab you will need to rescue the hostages, and then talk to Greg Thorpe. During this conversation he will tell you that his wife was taken hostage and he pleads with you to try to rescue her if you can. When you finally confront Zeke Sanders and see that he has Greg's wife, Josie, with him, make sure you prevent her from being killed either in the cross-fire or by Zeke's hands.

Once Josie is safe, make sure you talk to Greg again on the way to the roof of the Manufacturing Plant where Malik is waiting with the chopper. When you get back to Sarif HQ and have delivered the Typhoon to Pritchard and debriefed Sarif, you will need to head back to your office and access your personal computer. Inside you will find an email from Greg asking that you visit his apartment so that he can thank you properly.

1

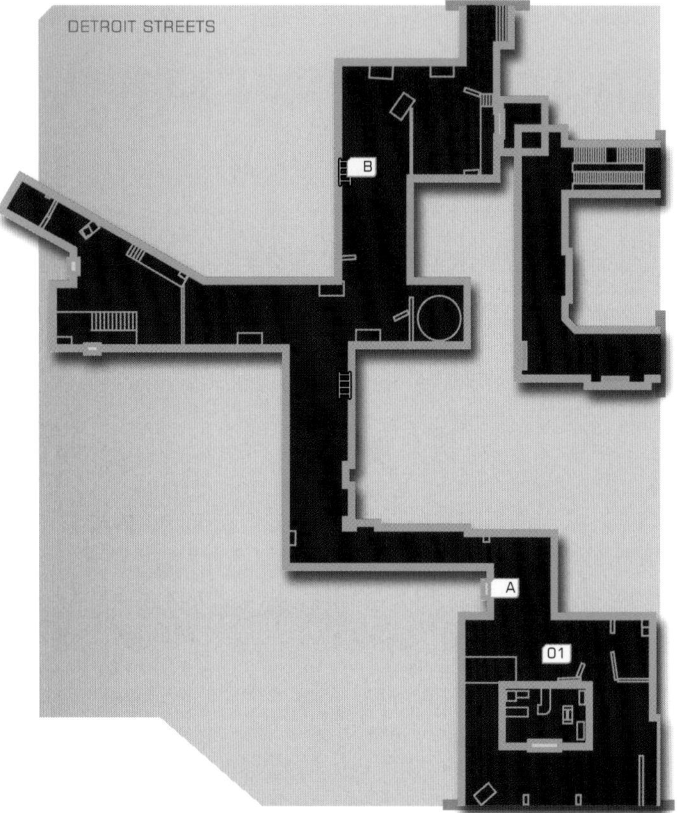

01 » **Meet with Greg Thorpe**

Exit Sarif HQ and follow the road along until you come to the gas station, and then head into the alleys that run behind it. The door for the apartment building you want is located at **Position A**, and Greg's apartment is on the third floor. The door is unlocked, so you can enter normally when you reach it and then strike up a conversation with Greg, who is sitting on the couch. To reward your heroic actions in rescuing both him and his wife, Greg informs you of a weapons' dealer he knows who goes by the name of Seurat.

Seurat is currently operating out of an apartment in a building near Earl's Court, and if you mention Greg's name to him you will be able to receive a sizable discount on his wares. There is no door that you can access to get into Seurat's building, so you will need to use the fire escape at **Position B** to climb up, and then enter through one of the windows. [→☐ 1]

ACHIEVEMENT/TROPHY TIP

On the nightstand in Greg's bedroom you can find one of Hugh Darrow's eBooks for the Doctorate Achievement/Trophy. You can also find another one of his books in the bedroom of the apartment being used by Seurat.

Tip **This apartment building is the same one you need to go to in order to speak with Detective Chase at the start of the Motherly Ties Side Quest, so you can do both at the same time.**

Objective Completed	Objective Type	XP Reward	Add. Reward
Meet with Greg Thorpe	Primary	750	Discount from weapons' dealer Seurat

S4 Motherly Ties

As you exit the Sarif HQ building, Mrs. Reed, the mother of your former girlfriend Megan, will approach you and automatically strike up a conversation. Mrs. Reed is concerned about the circumstances of her daughter's death after hearing from a police detective that the case was not handled properly. After doing all she can, Mrs. Reed feels that only you can continue the investigation and try to find out the truth behind the suspicious death of her daughter.

01 » **Locate Detective Chase's Building**

The Detective that Mrs. Reed spoke to is Detective Chase, who is working as a part-time Security Guard in an apartment building near Brooklyn Court. He wouldn't give any more details to her, but it might be worth heading there to try and see if you can convince him.

Objective Completed	Objective Type	XP Reward	Add. Reward
Locate Detective Chase's Building	Primary	100	–

02 » **Meet With Detective Chase**

Upon entering the building you will need to go through a security gate, behind which you will find Detective Chase sitting at a desk. Start a conversation with Chase, and because of your background as an ex-cop, he is far more forthcoming with information than he was with Mrs. Reed. Chase feels that he was always being hindered during Megan's case, either by those higher up in the chain of command denying lines of investigation, or other officers doing poor work. Fearing for his job security, Chase could never pursue the matter further, but he feels that Jensen is more than up to the task of following up his remaining leads.

His first suspicion is that there may be some evidence left on Captain Penn's computer in the Police Precinct regarding the orders to shut the case down prematurely. He also feels that a Detective Chet Wagner was brought onto the case specifically to tamper with evidence. Investigating him while you are in the precinct lobby where he is stationed would be a good idea. His final recommendation is that you check out the evidence that was locked up in a secure storage unit in an alley near the Police Precinct, the code to which is 4891.

Objective Completed	Objective Type	XP Reward	Add. Reward
Meet With Detective Chase	Primary	100	–

03

» Locate the DMPD Storage Unit
» Go to the Police Station Lobby
» Locate Captain Penn's Office
» Locate Officer Wagner's Office

Since all of the objectives revolve around the Police Station, head straight there from the apartment building to continue the investigation. The objectives can be handled in any order you like, but for the purpose of this guide, we will take you through the most efficient order. Go into the Police Station via the front door so that you are in the lobby. You will find Chet Wagner waiting there.

Objective Completed	Objective Type	XP Reward	Add. Reward
Go to the Police Station Lobby	Primary	100	–

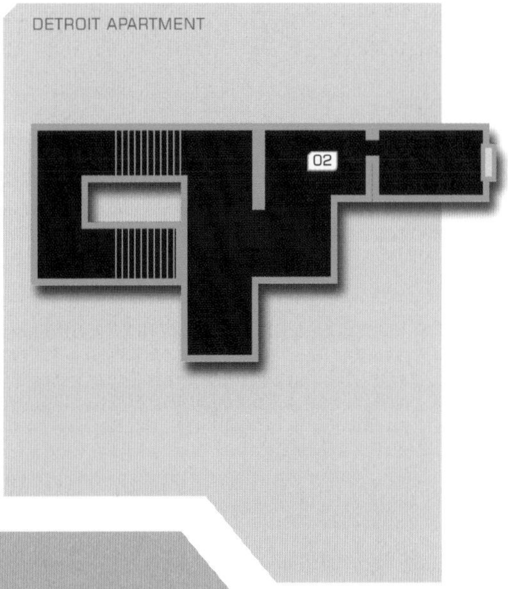

DETROIT APARTMENT

02

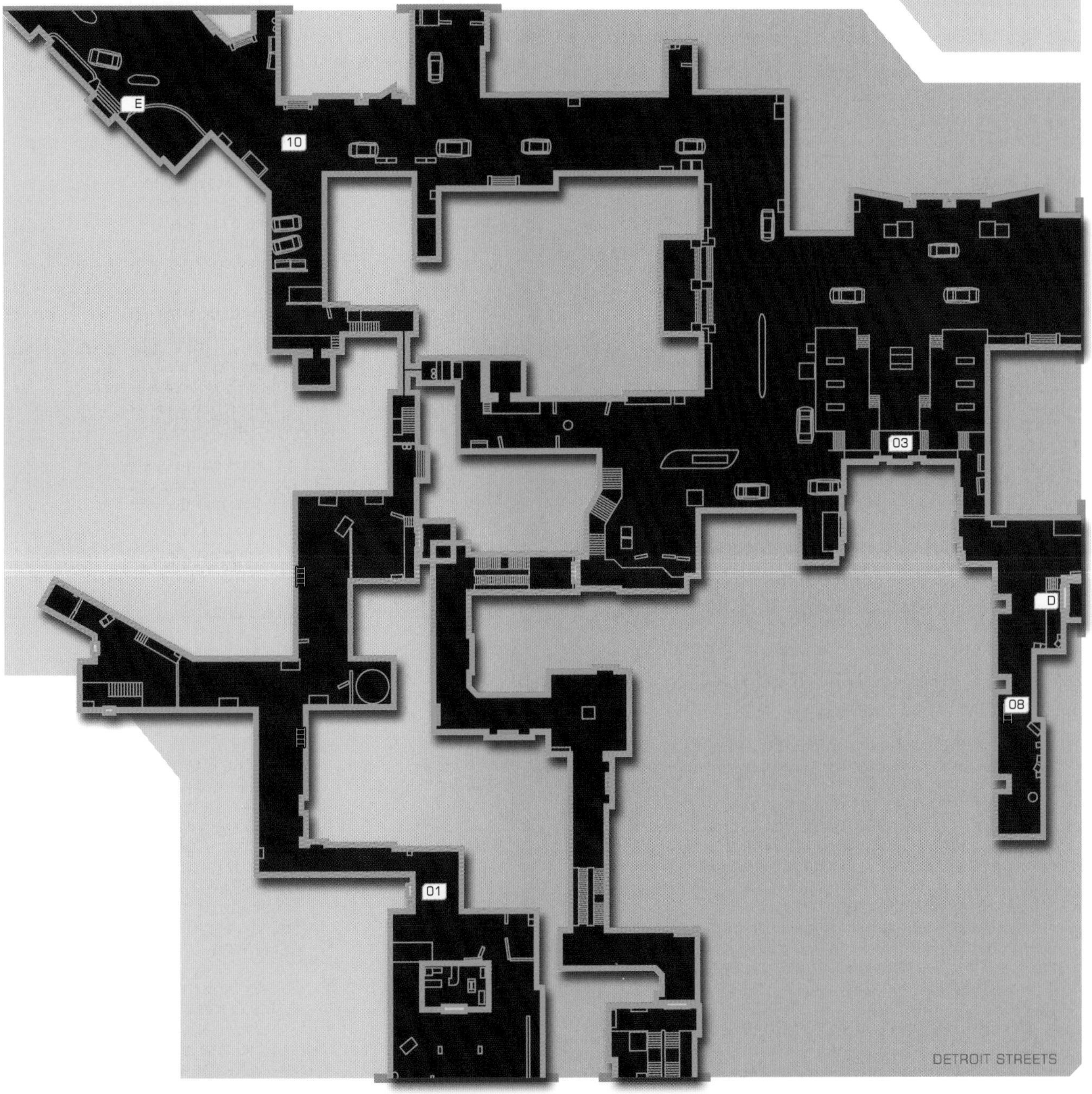

E
10
03
D
08
01

DETROIT STREETS

04 » **Locate the DMPD Storage Unit**
» **Meet with Officer Wagner**
» **Locate Captain Penn's Office**
» **Locate Officer Wagner's Office**

Walk up to Wagner and start a conversation with him, but as Chase suspected, he will not be forthcoming with any information, since you have nothing on him [→☐ 1]. In order to get anything out of him you will need to dig up some incriminating evidence by searching through his personal computer. The easiest way to continue the quest is by convincing Wayne Haas to let you into the Police Station. For additional methods of entry, please refer to Page 132 of the Walkthrough Chapter.

Tip **If you have the Social Enhancer Augmentation, you can use the Pheromones to convince Chet Wagner to tell you all he knows without getting the dirt on him from his office. Wagner is predominantly an Omega personality, so if you select that, you will be able to pressure him into giving up all he knows. Using this method, however, will cost you the XP you would have got from investigating his office.**

Objective Completed	Objective Type	XP Reward	Add. Reward
Meet with Officer Wagner	Primary	100	–

Required Hacking: Capture 2

05 » **Locate the DMPD Storage Unit**
» **Obtain Information from Officer Wagner**
» **Locate Captain Penn's Office**
» **Locate Officer Wagner's Office**

After going through the Lobby, take the stairs up to the second floor of the Precinct, and then walk along the mezzanine until you come to the vent hatch at **Position A** and enter it. Follow the vent along until you come to the first hatch, and then open it to gain access to Captain Penn's office. Once you are inside his office you can hack his personal computer, if you have Capture 2 software, and uncover some additional information about Megan's case. If you do not have the required hacking skills, you will have to forgo this line of investigation. Once you have finished with Penn's computer, exit his office the same way you entered to avoid suspicion, and then head back to the stairs and up to the third floor. [→☐ 2/3]

Objective Completed	Objective Type	XP Reward	Add. Reward
Locate Captain Penn's Office	Primary	300	–
Investigate Captain Penn's Computer	Primary	750	–

06 » **Locate the DMPD Storage Unit**
» **Obtain Information from Officer Wagner**
» **Locate Officer Wagner's Office**

Turn right when you reach the top of the stairs, and then enter the vents through the hatch at **Position B**. Follow the vents along and exit via the second hatch on the right to come out in Chet Wagner's office [→☐ 4]. There is not much to be found in the rest of his office other than some Credits in the desk drawer. The information you require is all stored on his personal computer. Thankfully, this computer only has a security rating of 1, so anyone can hack it. In the fourth email on his computer you will find some information that implicates him in taking bribes, the perfect thing to hold over him to get the information you need.

Objective Completed	Objective Type	XP Reward	Add. Reward
Locate Officer Wagner's Office	Secondary	300	–
Investigate Officer Wagner's Office	Secondary	750	–

07 » **Locate the DMPD Storage Unit**
» **Obtain Information from Officer Wagner**

If you have not used any other means to access the alley behind the police station, you will still need to get into the storage unit located there; thankfully you can do so via a vent located on this floor. Exit Wagner's office the same way you came in, and then follow the corridor along until you come to a small maintenance closet at **Position C**. Inside this room you will find another vent, which you can use to exit out into the alley. [→☐ 5]

Recommended Hacking: Capture 3

08 Descend the staircase and then head over to the storage unit at **Position D**. The unit is locked by a Level 1 terminal, but Chase gave you the code earlier (4891) so you can just use that to enter. The evidence you need to find comes in the form of four eBooks, scattered around the storage unit, and you will need to read all of them. The first two are located on the table to the left of the unit, the third is on the table to the rear, and the final one can be found on the table to the right, sitting next to the safe [→☐ 6]. When you have read all the eBooks, climb back up the fire escape and re-enter the Police Station through the vent on the roof.

Tip **If you have high enough Capture software, it is well worth hacking the safe in the storage unit. Inside it you will find another eBook containing insights into Megan's experiments, along with a bracelet that belongs to her, which also happens to be an item required for unlocking an Achievement/Trophy later on.**

Objective Completed	Objective Type	XP Reward	Add. Reward
Locate the DMPD Storage Unit	Primary	100	–
Find all Evidence Related to the Case	Primary	300	–

DETROIT POLICE DEPARTMENT F1-3

09 » Obtain Information from Officer Wagner

Head all the way back down to the precinct lobby and start another conversation with Officer Wagner. Now that you have some incriminating information about him, he will be more than happy to tell you everything he knows about Megan's case.

Objective Completed	Objective Type	XP Reward	Add. Reward
Obtain Information from Officer Wagner	Primary	300	–

10 » Return to Cassandra Reed

Now that you have exhausted all possible leads and gathered all the information, it's time to turn over your findings to Mrs. Reed. Instead of heading back to Sarif HQ, where you first spoke with her, she decided to arrange the meeting in the lobby of your apartment building, the entrance to which is on Grand River Road at **Position E**.

As soon as you are in the lobby of the building you will find Mrs. Reed standing near a pillar in the middle; start up a conversation with her and go through all the evidence [→☐ 7]. After explaining everything to Mrs. Reed she will finally be able to rest easier and the quest will be complete.

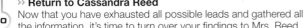

ACHIEVEMENT/TROPHY TIP

If you hacked the safe in the storage unit and acquired the Bracelet, you will be given the option of either keeping it or handing it over, once you have gone through the evidence with Mrs. Reed. If you choose to keep hold of this valuable memento, that once belonged to your girlfriend, you will unlock the Sentimental Value Achievement/Trophy. Deciding to keep it or not has no effect on the actual quest, so if you have it, there's no harm in keeping it. Once you have finished going over the final details with Mrs. Reed, you will also then unlock the Motherly Ties Achievement/Trophy.

Objective Completed	Objective Type	XP Reward	Add.Reward
Return to Cassandra Reed	Primary	1000	–

6
7

S5 Cloak & Daggers

When you exit the Police Station for the first time you will get a message over the Infolink from Pritchard telling you that a former colleague, Jenny Alexander, wants to have a meeting with you. Jenny is working undercover on Grand River Road, and you can find her leaning against a wall near some phone booths opposite Plum Terrace. Jenny is always in this location, so if you want to start this Side Quest earlier, you can approach her at any time, and do not have to wait for the message to be delivered.

Tip **If you do not to undertake this Side Quest, you may still want to incapacitate Jenny, as you will be able to take an Ammo Capacity Upgrade and 1000 Credits off her when she is down.**

Jenny needs your help on a case against a particularly elusive dirty cop named Jack O'Malley, because everything that she can accomplish through official channels has run dry. To gather enough evidence on O'Malley and wrap up her investigation, Jenny will need you to follow three main lines of investigation.

First, you will need to travel to O'Malley's apartment and see if you can find anything incriminating. Second, she received a tip that O'Malley delivered a shipment of weapons to the local DRB gang and needs you to track it down. Finally, she wants you to approach O'Malley and pose as a hitman willing to take care of a potential witness in a murder he had commissioned. As usual, these objectives can be handled in any order you wish, but we will provide the most expedient route here.

01

» **Meet with O'Malley**
» **Locate O'Malley's Apartment**
» **Go to Derelict Row**
» **Remain Undetected while in DRB Territory**

Because O'Malley has some additional objectives for you to complete, going to the meeting with him first is usually a good idea. O'Malley can be found standing in the alley next to the Police Station at **Position A**; use your preferred method of entering the alley, and then start up a conversation with him [→☐ 1]. O'Malley wants you to retrieve a weapon and use it to take out a member of the MCB who is holed up in a fourth floor apartment of a building near Earl's Court.

Killing the MCB member will instantly end Jenny's investigation, and thus this Side Quest would also come to an end. The weapon is much better used as another piece of evidence against O'Malley, so you will not need to bring it with you to the MCB hideout and can collect it later before you return to Jenny.

Tip **If you have the Social Enhancer Augmentation you can use the Pheromones to convince O'Malley to pay half of the reward money up front during your initial conversation with him. O'Malley is predominantly a Beta personality, so select that option to charm him into giving you the money.**

Objective Completed	Objective Type	XP Reward	Add. Reward
Meet With O'Malley	Primary	100	500 Credits (if you use the Social Enhancer)

02 **» Locate the MCB Gang's Hideout**
» Retrieve O'Malley's Package
» Locate O'Malley's Apartment
» Go to Derelict Row
» Remain Undetected while in DRB Territory

Now that you have spoken to O'Malley there are two objectives that you can complete around the apartment buildings, cutting down any potential backtracking. Exit the alley and then go through Central Station to reach the other side of town before going into the alley near the gas station. O'Malley's apartment is located in the same building as Tindall's from the Lesser Evil Side Quest, and you can find the door for it at **Position B**.

03 O'Malley's apartment is on the second floor of the building and to get inside it you will need to either hack your way past the Level 1 terminal, or destroy the door. Once you are inside the apartment you will need to try and find some form of evidence that will incriminate O'Malley. There is nothing of real value in the first room of the apartment, so you will need to venture into the bedroom to continue the search; unfortunately, the door leading back there is secured with a Level 4 terminal. If you have high enough Capture software you can hack the terminal, otherwise you can find a Pocket Secretary located in the bottom shelf of the white bookcase protruding from the back wall, on which you will find the code for the door. [→☐ 2]

Do not rush straight into the bedroom once the door has been opened because the ever paranoid O'Malley has booby-trapped the room with multiple Frag Mines [→☐ 3]. There are three in total around the room, so you can either crouch down and move up to each one slowly and disarm it, or get back to a safe distance and throw in a cardboard box to detonate them all. Once all the mines have been taken care of, you can enter the room to gather the evidence.

There are three pieces of evidence that you can collect in the bedroom, and while there are no bonuses for collecting them all, it will make Jenny's case a bit easier. The first piece of evidence is a package of drugs that you can find on a small table nestled between two large weapon crates to the left of the door. Secondly, there is a shipment of weapons sitting on a case on the bed that you can inspect, and finally you can hack into O'Malley's personal computer to access an incriminating email. Once you have found all three things exit the apartment building back onto the street.

Objective Completed	Objective Type	XP Reward	Add. Reward
Locate O'Malley's Apartment	Primary	300	–
Find at Least One Piece of Incriminating Evidence	Primary	300	–

Recommended Revolver/Combat Rifle (Lethal), Tranquilizer Rifle/Stun Gun (Non-Lethal)

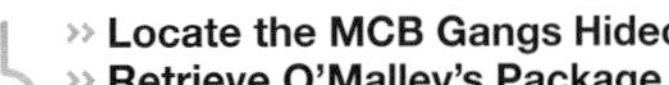

04 **» Locate the MCB Gangs Hideout**
» Retrieve O'Malley's Package
» Go to Derelict Row
» Remain Undetected while in DRB Territory

Your next destination should be the hideout being used by the MCB. You can access the building by climbing up the fire escape opposite the basketball court at **Position C**. Go up to the fourth floor of the building and then follow the corridor along and take cover behind the wall at **Position D**. Just around this corner is the MCB hideout, but your target, Double-T has brought some friends with him for protection [→☐ 4]. There are five guards in total: two out in the corridor outside the apartment, another two in the living room, and one more with Double-T, secured in the bedroom.

Objective Completed	Objective Type	XP Reward	Add. Reward
Locate the MCB Gang's Hideout	Primary	100	–

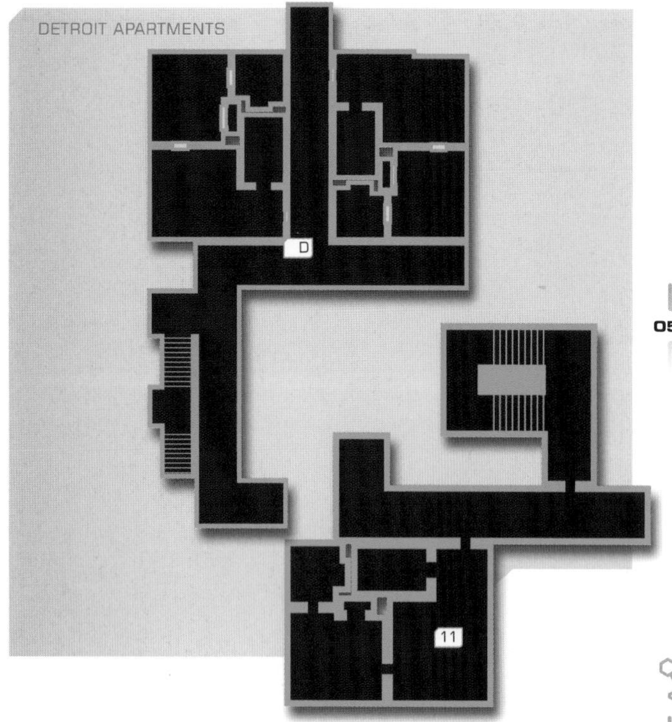

If you do not mind open combat, simply use the wall for cover and start firing on the two guards in the hallway. The rest of them will then come running out after being alerted by the sound and you can pick them off one at a time. Make sure you are careful when taking this approach, as you do not want to accidentally kill Double-T. He is wearing a bright yellow body warmer, so you can easily tell him apart from the other gang members.

Once they have all been killed just wait for him to reload and then run in for a non-lethal Takedown. Alternatively, if you have the Punch Through Walls Augmentation you can also forgo a frontal assault by continuing down the corridor slightly from **Position D**, where you will find a wall you can destroy. This wall backs directly onto the room where Double-T is hiding so you will only have to take one person out before you get to him. The noise will alert the other MCBs in the area, but they won't be able to react before you take him down.

If you are playing fully non-lethal you should use the Tranquilizer Rifle to incapacitate the two in the hallway first, and then move up and take cover by the door leading into the apartment. From here you can use the Tranquilizer Rifle to take out one of the gang members sitting on the couch, and then switch to the Stun Gun and quickly move in to take out the other. [→☐ 1]

If you were quiet when taking down the first group of enemies, Double-T and the final body guard should still be locked in the bedroom; search the body of one of the gang members in the corridor outside to find a Pocket Secretary with the code for the bedroom door. Input the code and take cover next to the door before opening it so that they do not spot you, and then incapacitate them one at a time with the Stun Gun. Once you have dealt with all of the MCB members you can loot the apartment for items, and then return down to the street.

Objective Completed	Objective Type	XP Reward	Add. Reward
Neutralize All MCB Opposition	Primary	750	–
Knock Out Double-T	Primary	100	–

05 **» Retrieve O'Malley's Package**
» Go to Derelict Row
» Remain Undetected while in DRB Territory

The next objective to tackle should be retrieving O'Malley's package, so head through the alleys after exiting the MCB hideout, and when you come out on Grand River Road, turn left. The door you want to go through is located at **Position E** near the end of the road. Once you are in the narrow corridor, go forward towards the pile of boxes and garbage bags along the back wall and retrieve the Crossbow from behind them [→☐ 2]. When you have secured the item, go back along Grand River Road towards DRB territory.

Objective Completed	Objective Type	XP Reward	Add. Reward
Retrieve O'Malley's Package	Primary	100	–

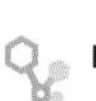

Recommended Cloaking System and Smart Vision

06 **» Go to Derelict Row**
» Remain Undetected while in DRB Territory

The final objective to complete for Jenny is to sneak into DRB territory to try and locate a shipment of weapons that can be tied back to O'Malley. Getting in and out undetected will make the wrapping-up of her investigation much easier, so for this section we will provide a stealth route here that forgoes engaging any enemies. For alternative routes through the area please refer to Page 142.

Go to the entrance to Plum Terrace, and then walk along the left-hand wall until you come to a dumpster; jump on top of the dumpster and then crouch down and move through the large section of pipe. Drop out of the end of the pipe and take cover behind the barricade before moving along it and using a short cover swap to reach the nearby car.

Continue along the car and the barricades that come after it while in cover, until you come to the end of the next set of barricades. Maintain that position until the gang member facing you turns around and walks away, at which time use short cover swaps to cross the gaps to the large container. Turn right at the end of the container and, while still crouched, move up the planks and go through the door into the building.

07 Continue along the corridor in the building until you come to the corner at **Position F** and then take cover before going any further. There is another gang member ahead with his back to you and he will not move until you start moving towards him. Crouch down and move up quietly towards him, and then follow along behind

him at a safe distance until you come to the barricade at **Position G**. Take cover behind the barricade because the enemy you are trailing will always turn around to check behind shortly after passing this point [→☐ 3]. Wait for him to continue moving away, and then head towards the small crawl space on the right of the room. Follow the crawl space all the way to the end, and then move underneath the broken shutter into the next area.

Objective Completed	Objective Type	XP Reward	Add. Reward
Go to Derelict Row	Primary	100	–

08 **›› Locate the DRB Weapon Cache**

›› Remain Undetected while in DRB Territory

Quietly jump on top of the dumpster and then wait for the gang member just up ahead to start walking away; when he does, drop down and then cross over to the other side of the area. From here you can move up safely behind the containers until you come to a large gap, at which time you should move in slightly and hug the barricades before coming back out along the next container. Keep moving quietly behind the containers again until you come to the end of them at **Position H**, and then take cover before continuing. Hold this position until the two gang members around the corner have finished their conversation, then cross the gap to the concrete barricade and carry on to the end of the next container. [→☐ 4]

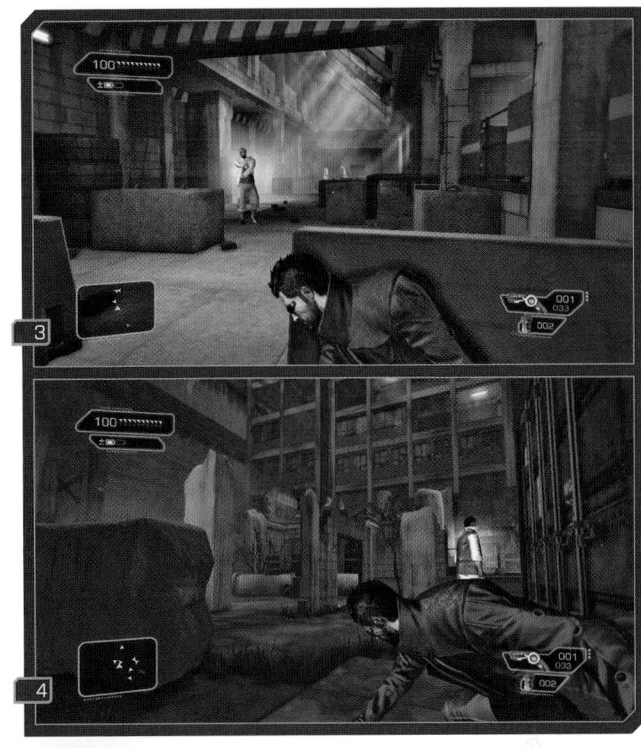

DERELICT ROW F1

09
H
08
G
F
07

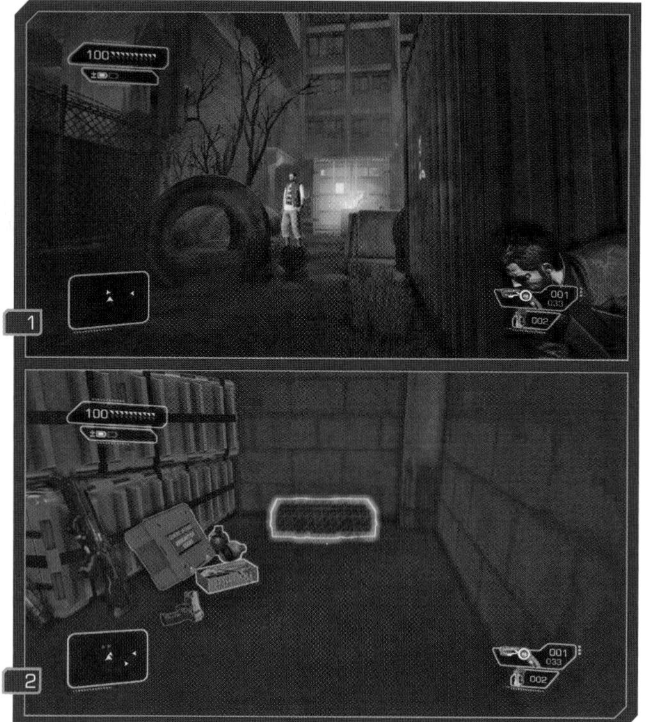

09 Wait at the end of this container for a short while because one of the gang members, who was just having a conversation, will soon move into this area and, if you move out, he will spot you. Wait for him to pass and then move forward into the small pipes and follow them along to the end. From the end of the pipes you will be able to see a small opening in the bottom of a fence directly ahead. When it is safe to do so, go through the hole and into the clearing on the other side. [→□ 1]

In this small open area you will be able to see two barrels along the side wall, and if you move one of them out of the way you will reveal an opening into another crawl space beneath the building. At the back of this area you will be able to see the weapons cache you were looking for; there are a number of useful items you can take for yourself, but the main thing you need to do for Jenny is investigate the black case lying on the floor [→□ 2]. Once you have identified it as coming from O'Malley, retrace the same route back out of DRB territory.

Objective Completed	Objective Type	XP Reward	Add. Reward
Locate the DRB Weapon Cache	Primary	750	–
Identify O'Malley's Weapon Shipment	Primary	100	–

10
» Return to Jenny
» Remain Undetected while in DRB Territory

Now that you have all of the evidence you need, it's time to go back and speak with Jenny, who should be directly ahead of you as you leave DRB territory. While you are going through all of the evidence with Jenny, you can choose to keep the Crossbow you picked up, if you wish; Jenny should have more than enough evidence without it, so keeping it will have no real effect. After you have gone over the details, Jenny will give you the choice of either letting her wrap the case up and make the arrest, or face O'Malley and make the collar yourself. If you choose to let Jenny make the arrest the quest will be over, but paying O'Malley a visit will present you with an additional opportunity. [→□ 3]

Objective Completed	Objective Type	XP Reward	Add. Reward
Return to Jenny (1)	Primary	1000	Ammo Capacity Upgrade, 1000 Credits
Remain Undetected While in DRB Territory	Secondary	750	–

11
» Go to O'Malley's Apartment

Cut through the alleys near Jenny's position and use them to quickly reach O'Malley's apartment building again. Enter his apartment on the second floor when you come to it and you'll find O'Malley standing calmly behind his desk; strike up a conversation with him to see what he has to say [→□ 4]. Being the calculated operative that he is, O'Malley respects your actions and wants to offer you a deal. If you let him go he will pay you off with a large sum of money and some goods that he will leave waiting for you in your apartment.

You can choose to either accept or decline his deal, but if you decline it he will immediately draw his weapon. The quickest way to deal with him if that happens is to close the distance and then use a Takedown on him. If you take his deal, he will simply slip away into the night. Regardless of your choice, you will have to report back to Jenny one last time to let her know what happened and complete the case for good; you can find her in the alley just outside this apartment building.

ACHIEVEMENT/TROPHY TIP

If you choose to accept O'Malley's deal and let him escape, you will unlock The Take Achievement/Trophy when you return to Jenny for the second time and complete the quest. At this time you will also unlock the Cloak & Daggers Achievement/Trophy, regardless of how you dealt with O'Malley.

Objective Completed	Obj. Type	XP Reward	Add. Reward
Go to O'Malley's Apartment	Primary	100	–
Deal With O'Malley	Primary	100 (if you take his deal) 300 (if you talk to him and decline the offer)	Bottle of Great Wall Red Chardonnay Wine and 3000 Credits (if you accept O'Malley's deal)
Return to Jenny (2)	Primary	1000	–

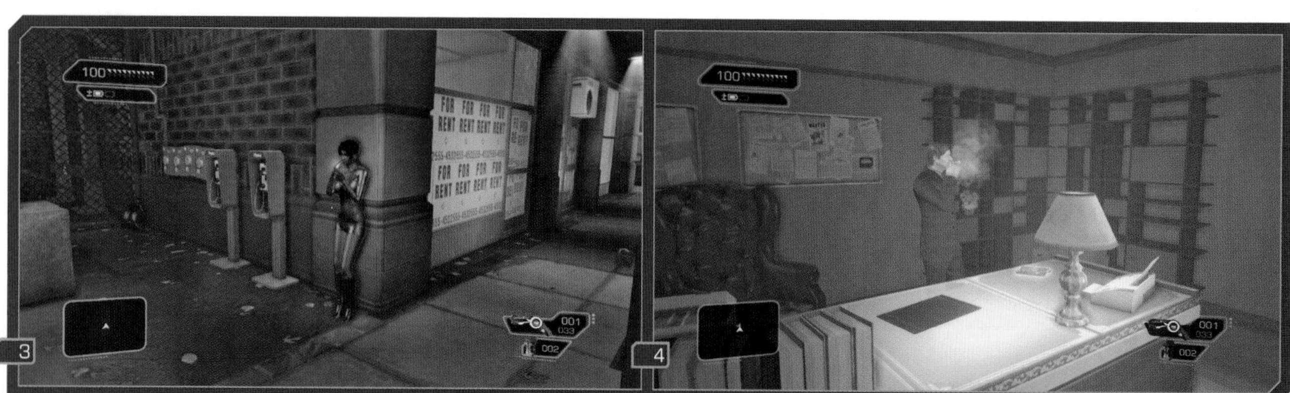

S6 Voices from the Dark

If you chose to let Zeke Sanders escape at the Manufacturing Plant at the beginning of the game, you will get a message from Pritchard shortly after retrieving the information from the Neural hub and exiting your building. He claims that the message is from an informant of yours and that he is demanding a meeting in an alley off Bagley Avenue near Sarif HQ.

» Meet the Mysterious Informant

01 Cut through the alleys near your apartment building, and then head left after you get out onto the road past the gas station. Follow the road along past the Sarif HQ building, and then head into the alley on the left, where you will find the informant at **Position A** [→☐ 5]. The informant turns out to be Zeke himself, looking to repay the debt he owes you for letting him go back in the Manufacturing Plant. It turns out that, in the wake of the double-crossing he received at the plant, Zeke decided to do some investigating on his own and managed to get hold of a Pocket Secretary containing codes and passwords. The information in the Pocket Secretary can be very useful when you are inside the FEMA Facility, and with it, Zeke feels his debt is paid.

Objective Completed	Objective Type	XP Reward	Add. Reward
Meet the Mysterious Informant	Primary	750	Pocket Secretary with FEMA Facility codes/passwords

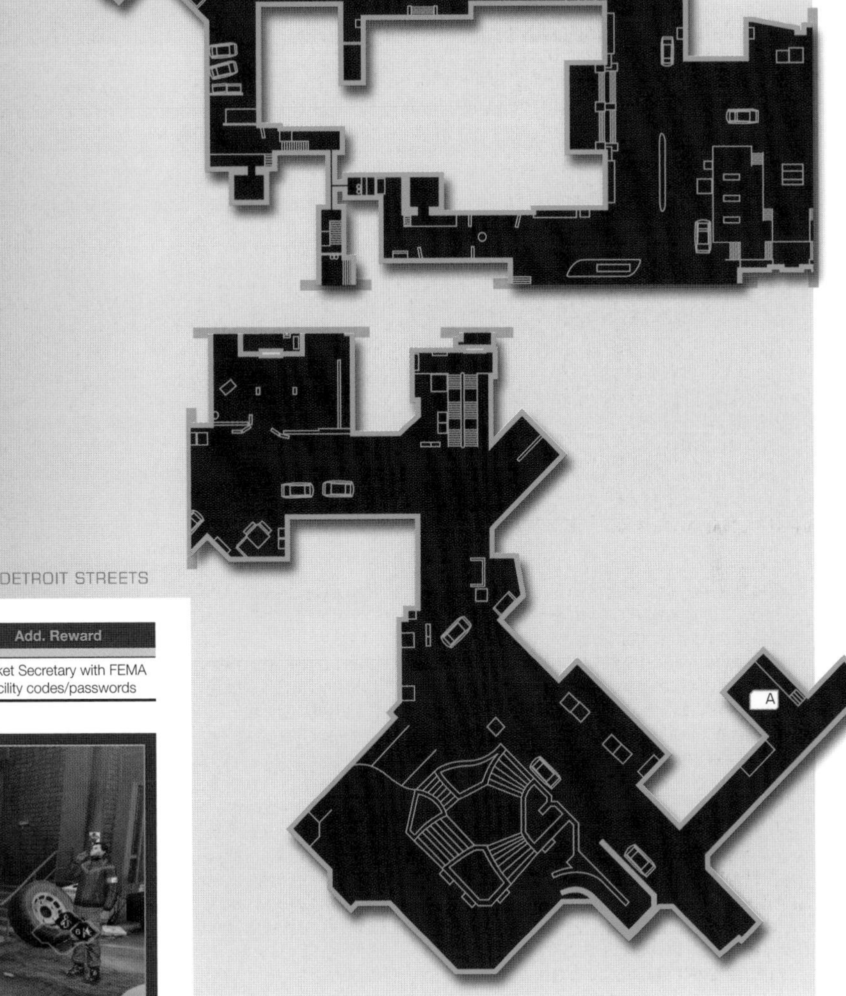

HENGSHA 1

S1 A Rotten Business

Close to where you initially land in Hengsha you will find the rooftop access door for the Hung Hua Hotel; go through the door and take the stairs to the fourth floor, and then enter the first room you come to. Inside you will find the Hotel's top working girl, Mei Suen, and her years of experience tell her that you might be the man to help her with a problem. The owners of the Hotel want the girls to become Augmented so that they can bring in more money, and while Mei might be safe from their pressure, the new girls are not so lucky.

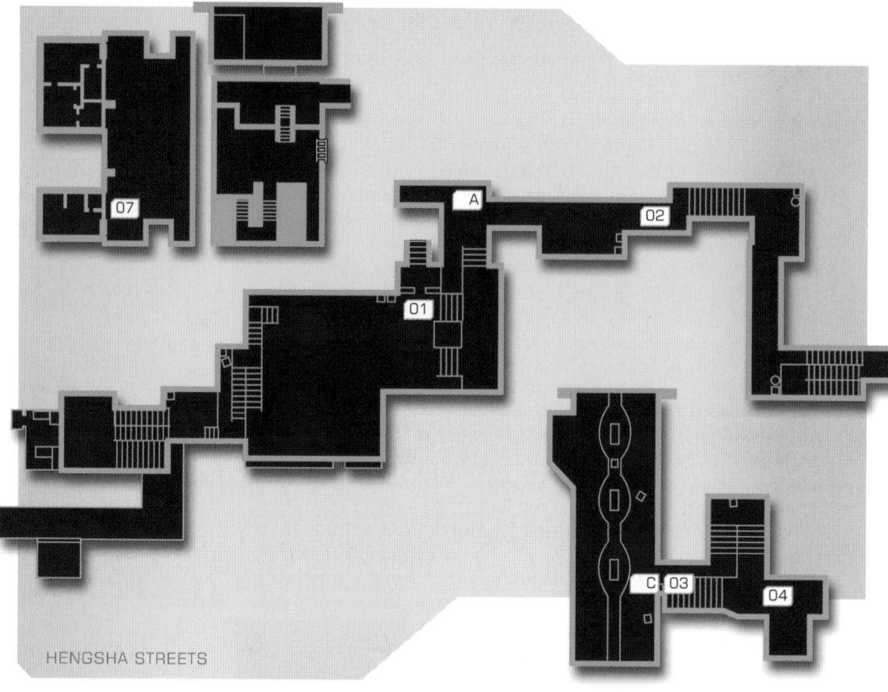

One of Mei's friends, Ning, is the latest to feel the pressure from the hotel, and while they usually backed down after she refused to become Augmented, this time things are different. Ning was taken against her will and Mei thinks she is being held somewhere until a doctor arrives to perform the procedure.

Mei is willing to pay you to find out where Ning is being held while awaiting the procedure, and then rescue her from her captors. Her only clue as to the whereabouts of Ning is that she is definitely in the Daigong district and that Ning is most likely being held by members of the local triad gang. Additionally, she feels that one of the Hotel's bouncers, a man named Chuanli, may be able to provide you with more information. If you do not want to help Mei and the other girls in the Hotel, you may still want to incapacitate her while you are there, because you can get the 3000 Credits reward money from her body; make sure you close the door to her room first, however, so that nobody sees the body.

Recommended Social Enhancer

01
» **Find Ning**
» **Speak to Chuanli**

You can find Chuanli on the roof of the Hotel, so head back up there. It is a good place to start gathering information. Leave Mei's room and go back up the stairs you came down on, and then head left across the rooftop to find Chuanli leaning against a railing at **Position A** [→□ 1]. Chuanli does not want to give any information freely regarding Ning, and to find out what he knows you will have to pay him 2000 Credits.

Alternatively, if you have the Social Enhancer Augmentation you can use the Pheromones to help you persuade him into giving over the information freely by selecting to Appease him. If you have the Credits to spare, and lack the Social Enhancer, paying him what he wants can be worth it for the amount of XP you get in return for completing the objective. If you cannot afford to pay him, however, you can still continue the search without his information.

Objective Completed	Objective Type	XP Reward	Add. Reward
Speak to Chuanli	Secondary	100	–
Convince Chuanli to Reveal Ning's Location	Secondary	300+750	–

Recommended Revolver (Lethal), Stun Gun (Non-Lethal)

02
» **Find Ning**

Ning is being held in a storage unit near the open drain on the other side of the district near the Alice Garden Pods. To get there, cross the bridge near Chuanli and then follow the series of staircases all the way down until you come out near the open drain. The alley you are looking for is on the other side of the drain, and there are two ways you can enter it. The first, and most direct route, is to take the staircase straight down into it at **Position B**, and the second is via a tunnel leading off from within the drain at **Position C**.

Objective Completed	Objective Type	XP Reward	Add. Reward
Find Ning	Primary	300	–

03 ›› **Eliminate Ning's Guards**

There are three members of the Harvesters (the local triad gang) guarding the storage unit where Ning is being held, and you have no option but to deal with them before you can save her. Because of the number of Police Officers around the top of the drain, engaging the triads from the top of the alley is a risky choice. A much better option is to go down into the drain and close in via the tunnel. Although you have to incapacitate the three Harvesters, you still have the choice of going lethal or non-lethal. Follow the tunnel along from the storm drain until you come to the stairs leading back up, and then take cover along the wall.

One of the Harvesters will usually come walking over towards the stairs, so if you are playing stealthy, wait for him to get out of the other two's line of sight before you take him out with the Stun Gun [→☐ 2]. The other two are usually outside the storage unit, so walk up the stairs and then Stun Gun one of them, and quickly use a Takedown on the final one. If you are using the Revolver, it doesn't matter too much when you take out the first Harvester, because the other two will come running in either way, and you can take them out one at a time as they come into view.

Objective Completed	Objective Type	XP Reward	Add. Reward
Eliminate Ning's Guards	Primary	750	–

04 ›› **Speak to Ning**

The storage unit where Ning has been stashed is secured by a Level 2 terminal, so you can hack it if you have high enough Capture software. Alternatively, you can search the bodies of the incapacitated Harvesters to find the one who has a Pocket Secretary on him containing the code. After making sure Ning is safe, she will tell you that she has to get out of the city and away from Chan, the man who was responsible for her kidnapping. Once she is gone, return to Mei back at the Hung Hua Hotel.

Objective Completed	Objective Type	XP Reward	Add. Reward
Speak to Ning	Primary	100	–

05 ›› **Return to Mei (1)**

When you return to Mei and inform her that Ning has been found and is safe, she will offer you another job opportunity that pays significantly more than the previous one. The man behind the kidnapping of Ning, as well as various other crimes, goes by the name of Diamond Chan, and Mei wants you to take care of him. Her main wish is that you kill him and make it look like a suicide, but through further conversation with her, you can also open up a non-lethal way to deal with him by planting drugs in his apartment and framing him for the police.

Objective Completed	Objective Type	XP Reward	Add. Reward
Return to Mei	Primary	1000	1000 Credits

06 ›› **Enter Diamond Chan's Apartment**

›› **Drop Chan off the Roof**

Diamond Chan's Apartment is in the Youzhao district, just above Yuanmeng Road. The quickest way to get to the Youzhao district is to go down the hotel stairs, exit the lobby and head right, and then go into the tunnel and go through the door at the other end. After entering the Youzhao district through the door, follow the next tunnel along until the end, and then climb up the series of ladders at **Position D**. Once you are on the rooftops, go up the stairs to the right and jump off the corrugated iron sheet onto the adjacent rooftop.

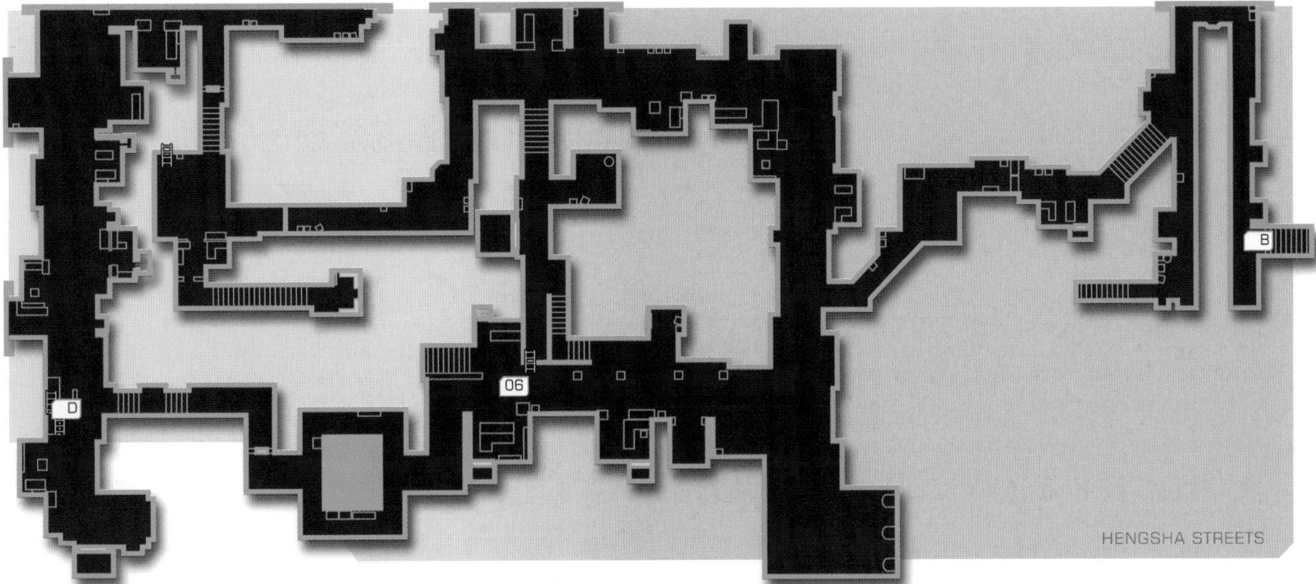

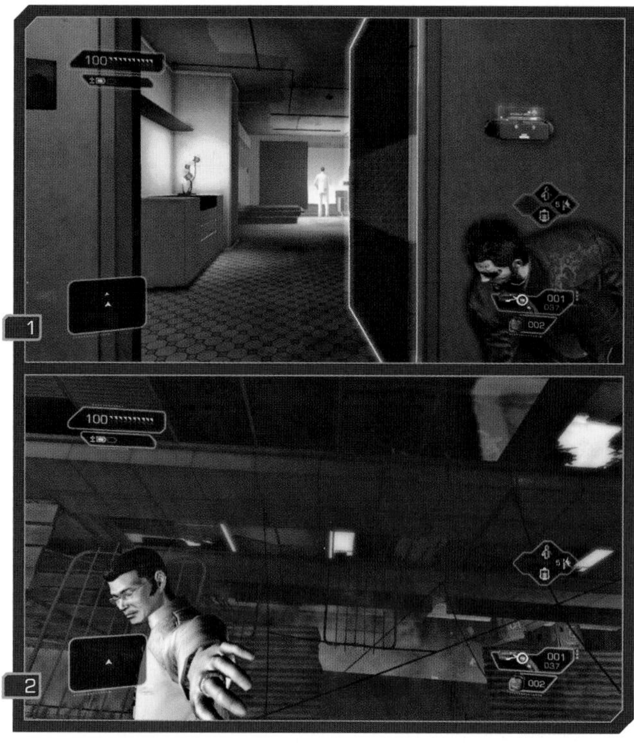

07 Chan's Apartment is located in the far left corner of this rooftop, and the door is open, so you can enter it straight away; providing you are quiet when you open the door, Chan will usually not be alerted to your presence [→☐ 1]. How you deal with Chan is entirely up to you, but some options are more beneficial to Mei than others.

You can simply decide to kill him outright straight away, but this will cause the police to know it was murder, which could cause problems for Mei and the other girls down the line. If you choose to knock him out, you must do so using hand-to-hand techniques only, so that no traces of weapons fire are found on the body.

Since you can enter his apartment undetected, you can easily crouch down and get close enough for a Takedown before Chan even knows you are there.

When he is unconscious, you then have another choice to make. If you want to avoid killing Chan, you can plant the drugs given to you by Mei on the coffee desk in his apartment so that they can be found by the police. To make it look like a suicide, drag Chan's body over to the ledge of the rooftop and then throw his body over the side so that it falls to the ground [→☐ 2]. After completing the task in whichever manner you prefer, return to Mei back at the Hung Hua Hotel.

ACHIEVEMENT/TROPHY TIP

If you choose to drop Chan off the roof and make his death look like a suicide you will also unlock The Fall Achievement/Trophy. If you want to choose a non-lethal way of dealing with Chan and still get the Achievement/Trophy, you should save your game after you render him unconscious, and then, after throwing him off the roof, you can reload and plant the drugs.

Objective Completed	Objective Type	XP Reward	Add. Reward
Enter Diamond Chan's Apartment	Primary	300	–
Knock Out Chan/Kill Chan	Primary	100/300	–
Plant the Drugs/Drop Chan off the Roof	Primary/Secondary	100/100	–

08 » Return to Mei (2)

Speak with Mei once again when you are back in the Hotel and report the news back to her about how you dealt with Chan. Regardless of how you decided to play the situation out, Mei will still be grateful for your assistance and give you the reward she promised.

ACHIEVEMENT/TROPHY TIP

As soon as you speak with Mei and complete the quest you will automatically unlock the Rotten Business Achievement/Trophy.

Objective Completed	Objective Type	XP Reward	Add. Reward
Return to Mei (2)	Primary	1000	2000 Credits

S2 Bar Tab

After finishing your conversation with the manager of the Hive club you will need to speak with the bartender, Bobby Bao, to activate this Side Quest. If your meeting with the manager did not go well, speaking to Bobby and completing the quest will be your only means of proving your worth to Tong. If your dealings with the manager were successful, however, it will simply be a lucrative business opportunity for you. Bobby wants you to track down a woman who is proving to be very elusive and get her to give you the money she owes to Tong.

The woman is a local broker named Jaya. Tong paid for her to get a very expensive Social Enhancer Augmentation to help her business, but now she is refusing to pay what she owes. Although Jaya has gone into hiding, she is still using her phone and laptop to carry on her business, which means you can track her. The triads at the club lack the hardware necessary to triangulate her signal, so your first task will be hacking into Belltower's surveillance network and using that to locate Jaya. The terminals controlling access to the network all require Hacking: Capture 2 software, so if yours is not high enough you will have to return to the quest once it is.

 **Required** Hacking: Capture 2

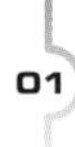

01 » Disable the First Communication Relay

The first communication relay that you need to hack into is on a roof in the Youzhao district (near Diamond Chan's apartment from the previous Side Quest), so you will need to start by heading there. Exit

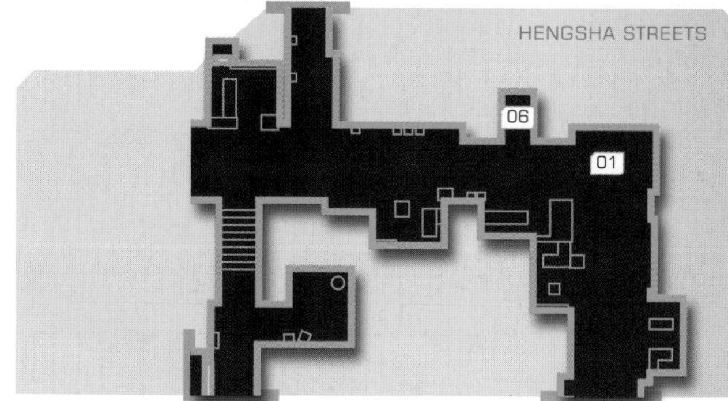

the Hive through the main door, and then turn left and follow the street around the corner and past the Hung Hua Hotel. Continue until you come to the tunnel, and then enter it and go through the door at the end to reach the Youzhao district. Exit the next tunnel and then use the series of ladders opposite the exit to reach the rooftops; the first relay can be found on a wall near the edge of the roof at **Position A** [→☐ 3]. Hack the terminal to gain control of it, and then change the setting to inactive to disable the first relay.

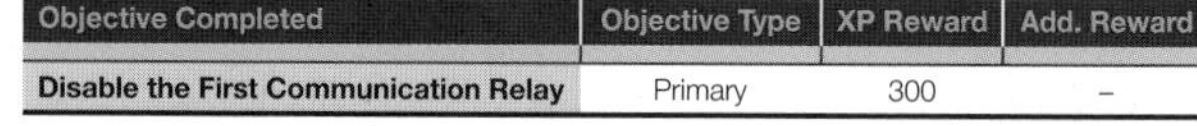

Objective Completed	Objective Type	XP Reward	Add. Reward
Disable the First Communication Relay	Primary	300	–

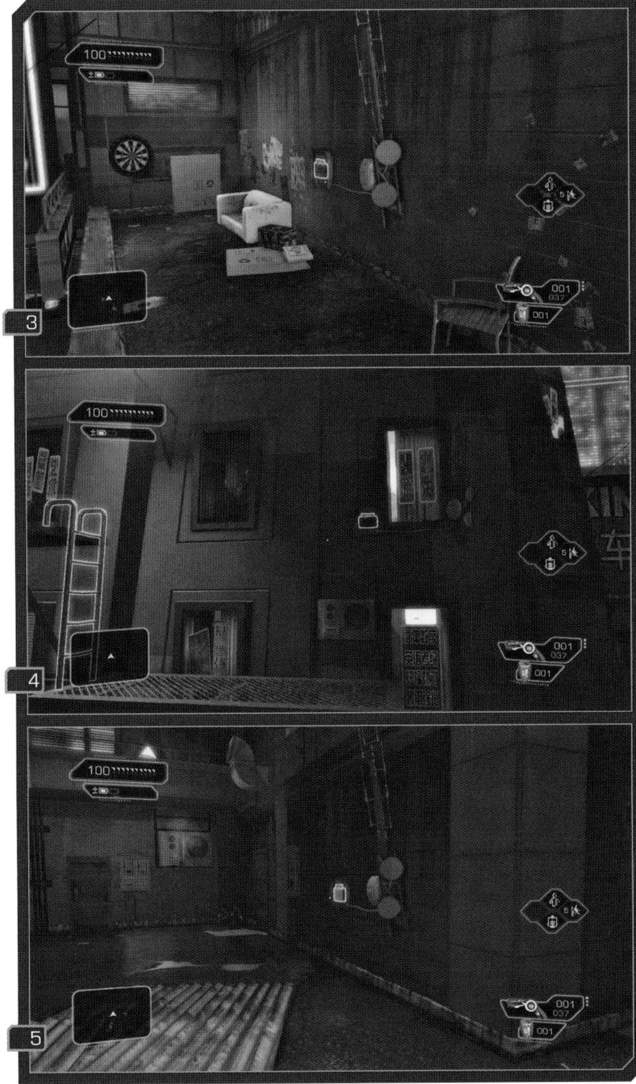

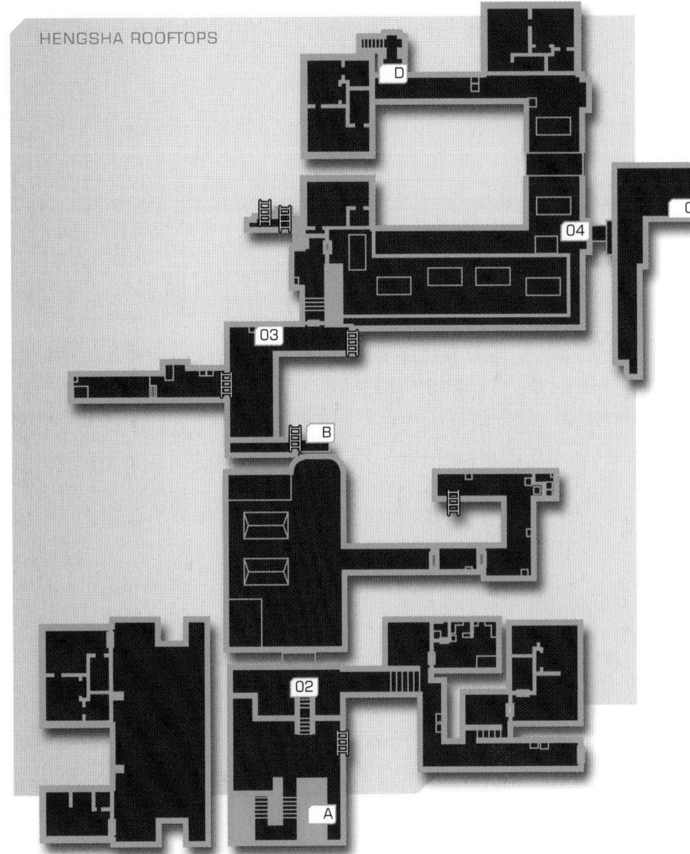

02 **» Disable the Second Communication Relay**

Turning off the first relay will reveal the location of the second one for you, and it is just a short trip across the rooftops. Go up the nearby stairs and then jump down to the adjacent rooftop; follow this roof along and jump on top of the large sign at the end. From there you will need to jump up onto a ventilation unit so that you can reach the second relay, located at **Position B** [→□ 4]. Like before, hack the terminal and set the relay to inactive to disable it to reveal the location of the third and final relay.

Objective Completed	Objective Type	XP Reward	Add. Reward
Disable the Second Communication Relay	Primary	300	–

03 **» Disable the Third Communication Relay**

Climb up the nearby ladder, and then run along the back of the billboard and jump onto the rooftop to the right when you come to it. Follow the rooftop around to the right, and then go through the small gap between the wall and the billboard on the left when you come to it. If you have already been through this area when you were investigating Van Bruggen's apartment you may have already dealt with the two guards on the rooftop. If you have not, however, then you will need to take care of them now.

The first guard is usually patrolling very close to this area, so quickly take cover behind one of the large AC units nearby; wait for him to start walking away from you and then move up behind and use a Takedown to incapacitate him. The other Belltower guard is usually on the opposite side of the roof near the entrance to the apartment building; use the AC units for cover and work your way around to him, and then use your weapon of choice to take him out once you are in range.

Now that the area is clear you can get to work on hacking the third terminal. In the mid-section of the rooftop you will find a corrugated metal sheet lying between two signs that you can use to cross over to the small rooftop where the final relay is located at **Position C** [→□ 5]. After disabling the last relay, Bobby Bao will triangulate Jaya's position and let you know that she is in an apartment within the Hengsha Court Gardens Building, which is very close by.

Objective Completed	Objective Type	XP Reward	Add. Reward
Disable the Third Communication Relay	Primary	300	–

04 **» Go to Jaya's Building**

Go back across the corrugated metal sheet to the previous rooftop, and then enter the Hengsha Court Gardens Building via the access door at **Position D**. Follow the stairs inside all the way down to the lobby area, and then take the elevator up to the penthouse. If you haven't already taken out the guards on this floor, make sure the area is clear before exiting the elevator; when it is safe to do so, follow the corridor down to the right and enter Jaya's apartment.

Objective Completed	Objective Type	XP Reward	Add. Reward
Go to Jaya's Building	Primary	100	–

05 **» Meet with Jaya**

If you demand that Jaya hands over the monthly payment when talking to her, she will tell you that you'll have to take it from her. You can then choose to incapacitate her, allowing you to take the money from her body. You can also choose to take her Augmentation Chip, if you like, and bring that back to Bobby, although he will not be too happy about losing the monthly income. If you have

the Social Enhancer you can also influence Jaya by using Alpha Pheromones during the conversation. You will then be faced with a similar choice: to take either the payment or the chip.

If you are feeling slightly more helpful and want to try and get Jaya out of her predicament, you can choose to offer her help during the conversation. This option will open up a new Secondary Objective where you will need to try and convince Bobby Bao to leave Jaya alone once and for all. Because of the extra objective, going down this path will net you much more XP than the other means of completing the quest. After you have decided how to handle the situation, return to the Hive to report back to Bobby.

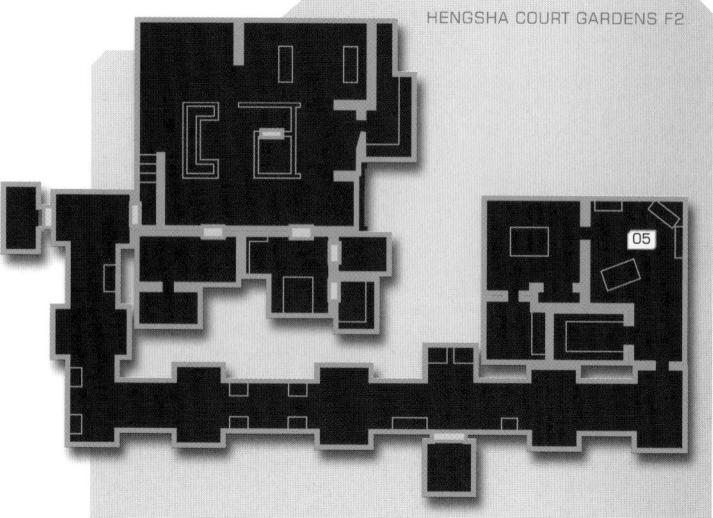

Objective Completed	Objective Type	XP Reward	Add. Reward
Meet with Jaya	Primary	100	–
Obtain the money owed to Tong (if you take the payment from Jaya)	Primary	750	–

06 **» Bring Jaya's Payment to Bobby Bao/Bring Jaya's Augmentation Chip to Bobby Bao**
» Convince Bobby Bao to Leave Jaya Alone

You'll find Bobby behind the bar in the Hive as usual, so approach him and ask him about the job once you are inside. Returning to him with Jaya's Augmentation Chip will cause a lot of problems, and cost the triads a valuable source of future income, so he will be none too happy with the results. Giving him the monthly payment will result in a much more positive outcome, and he will be grateful enough to hand over a Praxis Kit for you as a reward.

If you choose to be chivalrous and help Jaya out, you will need to select the option of trying to make a deal with Bobby. To let Jaya off the hook for her monthly payments, Bobby wants you to hand over a year's worth of payments for her, which rounds up to 5000 Credits. If you choose to pay the sum, Jaya will be free and Bobby will still be happy enough to hand over the Praxis Kit for helping him out.

Objective Completed	Objective Type	XP Reward	Add. Reward
Bring Jaya's Payment / Bring Jaya's Augmentation	Primary	1000	Praxis Kit (if you deliver the payment)
Convince Bobby Bao to Leave Jaya Alone	Secondary	1000	Praxis Kit

ACHIEVEMENT/TROPHY TIP

If you choose to pay off Jaya's debt and free her from triad oppression, you will unlock the Guardian Angel Achievement/Trophy after you have finished speaking with Bobby Bao. At this time you will also unlock the Bar Tab Achievement/Trophy, regardless of how you finished the quest.

S3 Shanghai Justice

When you first enter the Alice Garden Pods on your way to meeting the hacker, Van Bruggen, you will be approached by a rather melancholic Faridah Malik. After a brief conversation she reveals that when she used to live here she had a close friend named Evelyn, who recently died in a suspicious accident. Malik is sure that her death was no accident, and that she was murdered by her boyfriend, but her death was immediately ruled an accident and there was no real investigation.

To try and uncover the facts about what actually happened and reveal the truth about Evelyn's death, Malik wants you to help her investigate the case. A friend of Malik's has already left the police report for her to read, and he has also arranged a meeting with another contact who works at the local LIMB Clinic to try and secure her autopsy report; through these initial clues Malik hopes that new evidence will point you towards the truth. Although you could meet with Van Bruggen while you are here, it is worth completing this quest first so that you do not have to contend with suspicious Belltower troops outside.

01 **» Meet the LIMB Contact**
» Check Pod #009

To complete this investigation fully you will need to gather every available piece of evidence, so your first order of business should be to read the information that was left in pod #009. Pod #009 is on the third floor of the building, in the section near the southeast staircase, and you can find the Pocket Secretary containing the report on a shelf just above the bed [→☐ 1]. On the same shelf you will also find an eBook containing a news story about the incident that will give you more information; you will need to read both documents in order to complete the objective.

Objective Completed	Objective Type	XP Reward	Add. Reward
Check Pod #009	Secondary	100	–

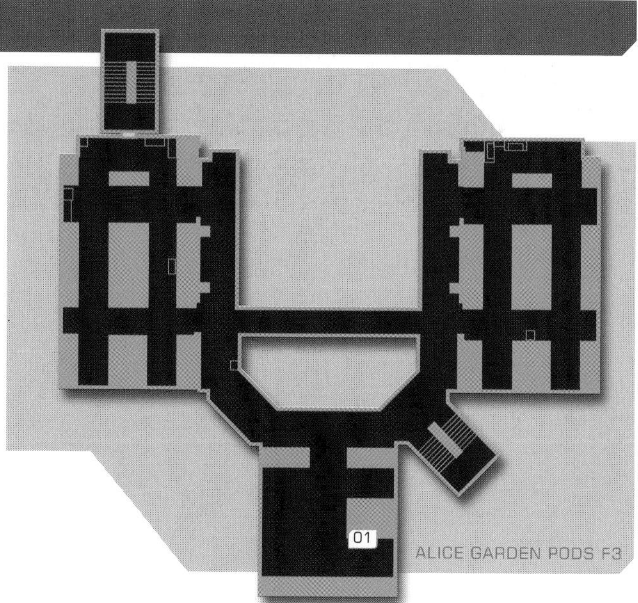

02 **» Meet the LIMB Contact**

Your next destination is the LIMB Clinic to have a meeting with Anonymous X, so leave Alice Garden Pods and make your way back out onto the streets. The path to the clinic is quite straightforward; just head right when you exit Alice Garden Pods and go down the stairs at the end of the open drain to reach the street below. Keep heading up the street away from Alice Garden Pods, and after rounding the first corner you should be able to see a sign for the LIMB Clinic. Turn left down the street indicated by the sign, and then follow that street along until you see the LIMB Clinic on the right at the top of the ramp.

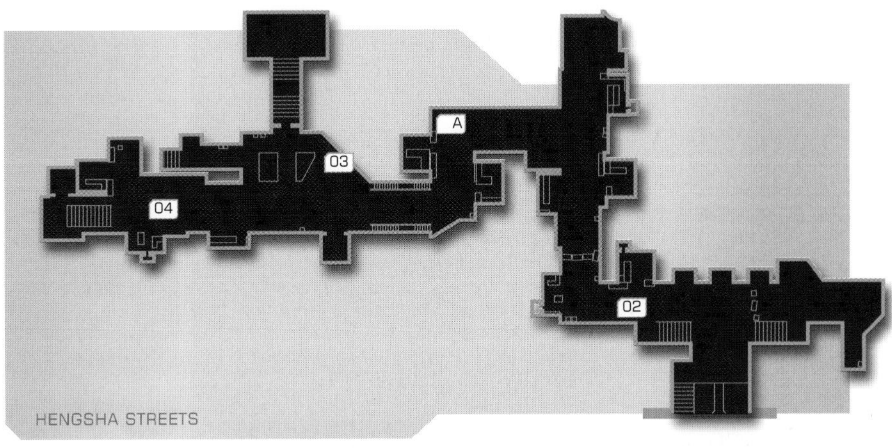

03 When you enter the LIMB Clinic, walk up and start a conversation with Anonymous X, who you'll find working out of the right window in the main lobby. The correct line he is looking for is the professional response starting with death and life; picking any of the other options will still have the same outcome; only some of the dialogue will change. After a brief conversation, Anonymous X will tell you to meet him on the street outside the clinic at **Position A**. [→☐ 2]

After a quick comment on your performance during the initial meeting, Anonymous X will hand over Evelyn's autopsy report, but apparently he was under the impression that he would be getting paid for it. Whether or not you choose to pay him the 1000 Credits he is asking for has no real impact on the game, so unless you are feeling especially generous, it is best to keep your money. The autopsy report was given to you on a Pocket Secretary and reading it will reveal a number of details that seem to contradict the official explanation of Evelyn's death.

Objective Completed	Objective Type	XP Reward	Add. Reward
Meet the LIMB Contact	Primary	100	–
Obtain Autopsy Report	Primary	100	–
Read Evelyn's Autopsy Report	Primary	100	–

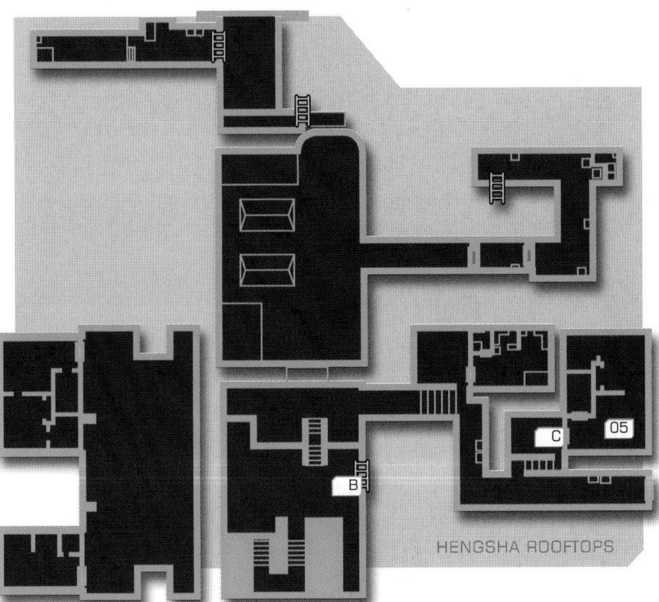

Recommended Hacking: Capture 3

» Find Lee's Apartment

04 Because of the new information you uncovered, Malik wants you to investigate the apartment of the man she suspects was involved in Evelyn's murder, her boyfriend Lee Hong. Lee's apartment is in the Youzhao district, so the quickest way to get there from here is to head up the street past the LIMB Clinic and go through the metro station at the end. Exit the metro station and follow the main street all the way around the district until you come to the series of ladders at **Position B**, and then use them to reach the rooftops.

Go up the nearby stairs and follow the path across the bridge to the right; keep going along the alley until you get to Lee's apartment at **Position C**, just before a gate leading back to the Kuaigan district [→☐ 3]. The door into Lee's apartment is secured with a Level 3 terminal, so if you cannot hack your way in you will need to destroy the door.

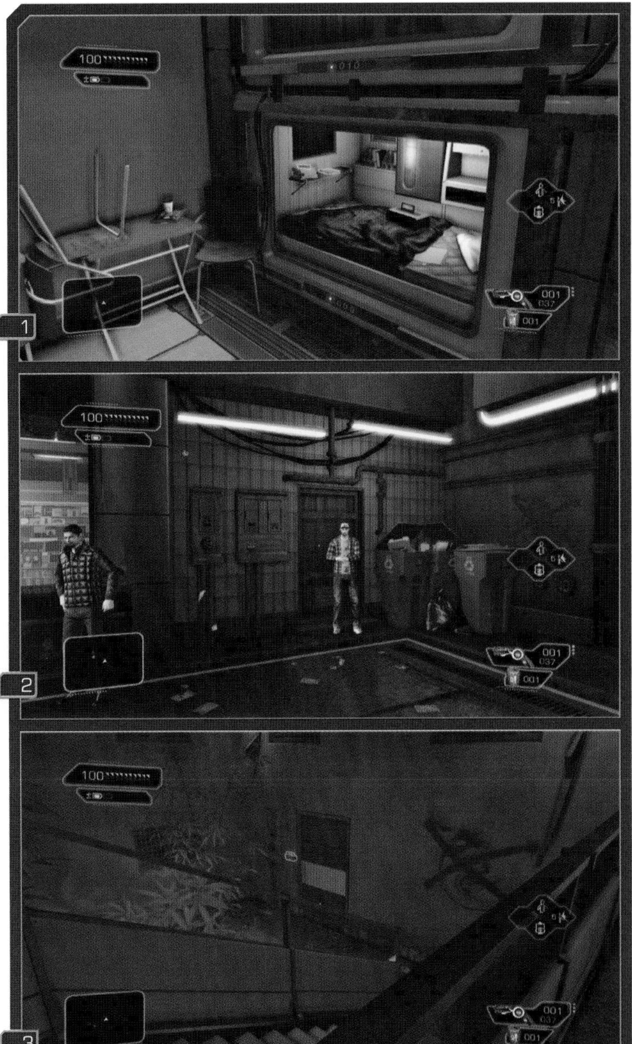

Objective Completed	Objective Type	XP Reward	Add. Reward
Find Lee's Apartment	Primary	300	–

Required Hacking: Capture 2

» Find Lee

05 Once you are inside Lee's apartment, you will first need to check every room to see if he is anywhere inside. Unfortunately, Lee is elsewhere, but this does give you an opportunity to thoroughly search the apartment for any more evidence. There are four items in the apartment that potentially contain clues and you will need

to find them all to clear the area. The first object is the answering machine on one of the dressers next to the bed, and the message it contains points you towards the Hive as a place where Lee is likely to be.

The second one is the computer on a small coffee table in the bedroom; the computer has a security rating of 2, so you will need high enough Capture software to hack into it. The first email on the computer lets you know about Lee's family ties to LIMB, and the second one gives you a potential motive, as it outlines his family cutting off his money if he didn't clean up his act. Also in the bedroom you'll find the third item you can investigate, which is an antique clock on a large dresser near the closet [→□ 1]. The clock is a good fit as a potential murder weapon and the hands on the face have stopped at the same time as Evelyn's estimated time of death.

The final item is the baseball bat leaning against the wall near the apartment's front door, but although this is also a potential murder weapon, it does not fit as well as the antique clock. Once your search is complete, go back down to the street the way you came, and then take the tunnel opposite the ladders back to the Kuaigan district so that you can return once again to the Hive.

Objective Completed	Objective Type	XP Reward	Add. Reward
Find Lee	Primary	100	–
Search Lee's Apartment	Primary	750	–

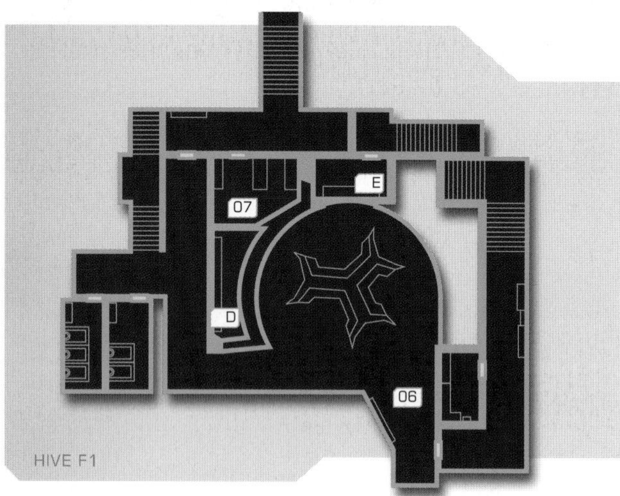

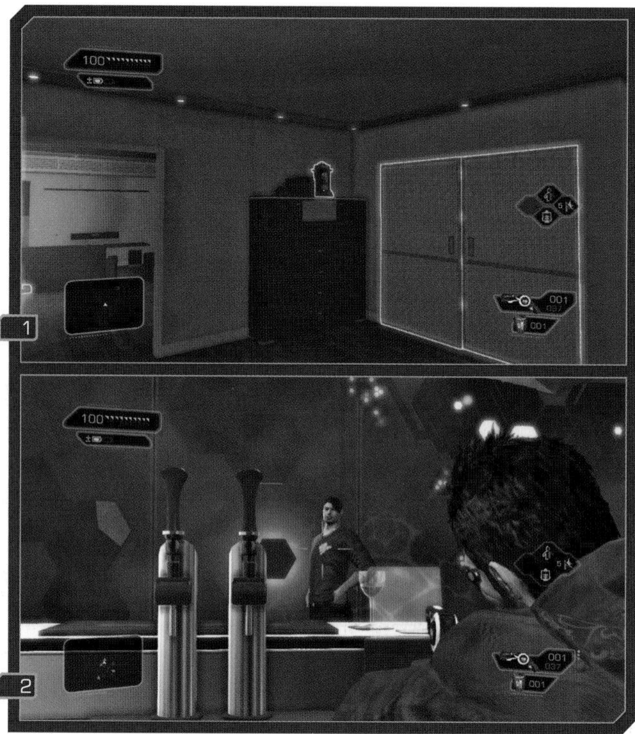

06 » **Get Inside the Hive**

When you are inside the Hive, Malik will tell you that she wants you to try and find Lee, and then, using the evidence you have uncovered, cause him to panic into confessing while she records him. Lee is sitting down in the corner of the mezzanine on the second floor of the club at **Position D**, and when you have found him you should start a conversation. Malik wants it to look like you are attempting to blackmail Lee by providing the true details behind her death.

Lee is extremely combative at first, and you will systematically have to go through the evidence you have gathered and try to convince him that you know what happened. If you give too many incorrect answers to Lee he will know that you do not have all the facts and tell you to get lost. Your only hope of salvaging the situation at that point is if you have the Social Enhancer Augmentation, since you will be able to use Alpha Pheromones to Appease him and convince him to come clean with the information.

The first piece of evidence you discuss is the police report, which you know to be highly inaccurate, and to back that up you can tell him that you know she wasn't drunk that night. After pointing out the faults in his original story, you need to start going over the details of how he killed Evelyn. The first thing to point out is the murder weapon; the antique clock from the apartment is the most likely item, and when it comes to the motive, finding out she is pregnant is right up there.

The final piece of the puzzle is the cover-up, and thanks to the emails on his computer, you know his family has strong ties to LIMB, and that they used them to bury the autopsy report. With all the facts in place, Lee will crumble and give in to your blackmail attempts while also openly confessing to the crime, which is all Malik needed. Now that you have what you came for, you can walk away from Lee and go over the situation with Malik.

ACHIEVEMENT/TROPHY TIP

If you talk about each piece of evidence correctly, you will unlock the Super Sleuth Achievement/Trophy as soon as you finish your conversation with Lee.

Objective Completed	Objective Type	XP Reward	Add. Reward
Get Inside the Hive	Primary	100	–
Find Lee Inside the Hive	Primary	100	–
Speak to Lee	Primary	100	–
Walk Away From Lee	Primary	750	–

Required Hacking: Capture 3

07 » **Disable the Hive Terminal's Security Protocols**

Before handing over the evidence to the authorities, Malik wants to get in some of her own special brand of street justice. The first step in the plan requires you hack a terminal in the Hive and disable some of their security protocols. The terminal in question is on the opposite side of this floor at **Position E**, near the lounge area where you met Tong. The terminal is in the direct line of sight of one of the club's bouncers, so if you want to hack it you will need to make use of any Nukes you have in order to get it done quickly.

If you are having trouble completing the hack in time, go through the nearby door so that you are behind the small bar, and then either incapacitate or kill the bouncer [→□ 2]. Quickly crouch down and take cover behind the bar because the other bouncers will come running to investigate; as long as you stay in cover and out of sight, however, they will return to their normal positions after a short time. Once they are gone you will be free to take your time hacking the terminal. When you have deactivated the security protocols, exit the Hive and meet Malik out front.

Objective Completed	Objective Type	XP Reward	Add. Reward
Disable the Hive Terminal's Security Protocols	Primary	100	–

» Meet Malik Outside

08 After exiting the club, head up the street to the left to meet up with Malik so that she can express her thanks by giving you a valuable Praxis Kit. The only thing left to do is find out what Malik has planned for Lee, so turn around and start walking back towards the Hive to initiate the show.

ACHIEVEMENT/TROPHY TIP

Shortly after Malik's version of justice starts to play out on the exterior monitors of the Hive, you will unlock the Shanghai Justice Achievement/Trophy for completing this quest.

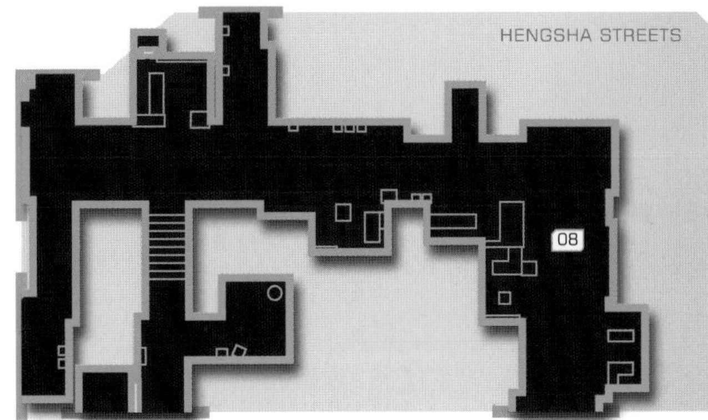

Objective Completed	Objective Type	XP Reward	Add. Reward
Meet Malik Outside	Primary	100	Praxis Kit
Face the Hive Exterior	Primary	1000	–

DETROIT 2

S1 Acquaintances Forgotten

The seeds of this Side Quest first begin after you return from the FEMA Facility and are in the Sarif HQ building. After talking to Pritchard at that time you will need to confront Sarif about some of his activities revolving around a loophole in the network security. If you successfully convince Sarif to tell you the truth about the incident, he will send some emails to the computer in Jensen's office that will reveal more about his past. Make sure you enter your office and read these emails, and then, when you leave your office, Pritchard will approach you and tell you that he's going to run a back-trace on the information to find out where it came from.

Much later in the game, when you are heading to the Convention Center to question Taggart, you will get an incoming message from Pritchard giving you some information, which includes the results of his trace. The stream originated in an apartment belonging to a Detective named Brent Radford, and speaking with him may reveal even more information about Jensen's past.

» Investigate Pritchard's Lead

01 The building you are looking for is near Earl's Court and the quickest way to get there from where you usually receive the message is to cut through the alleys near the gas station. The building is the same one as the one that Seurat the weapons' dealer operates from, so you will need to climb the ladder at **Position A** and then enter through one of the windows; the apartment you are looking for is on the fourth floor near the room where you encountered Double-T during the Cloak & Dagger quest.

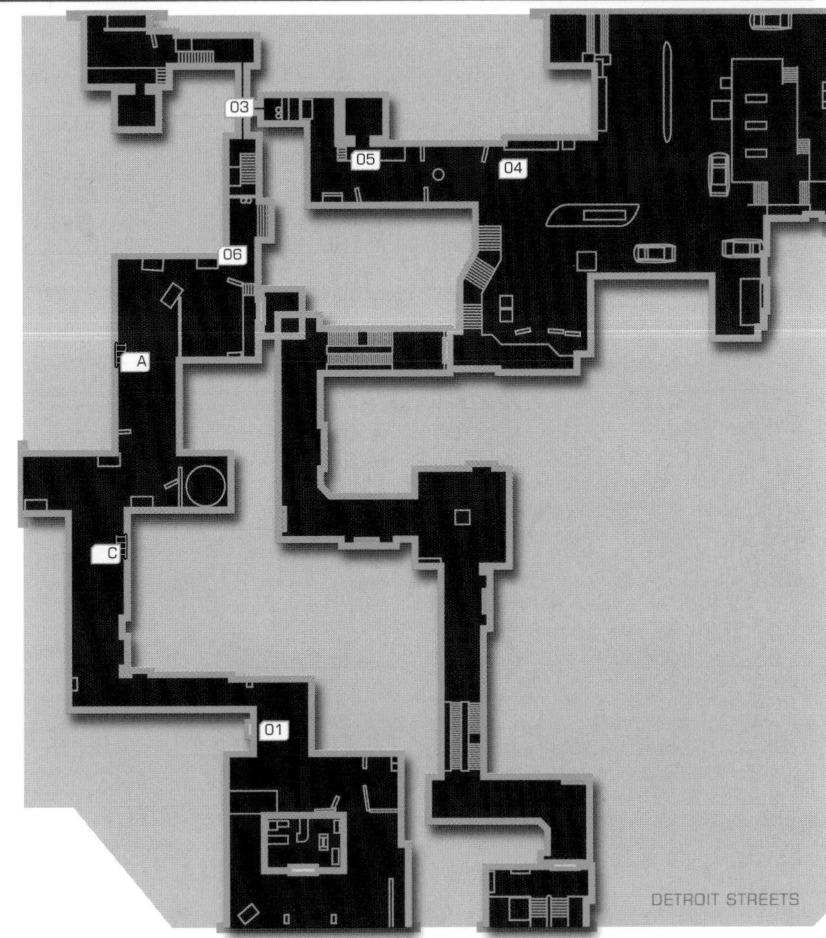

02 The first thing you'll notice upon entering the apartment is that there are obvious signs of a struggle with furniture knocked over and a blood trail leading into the back rooms. Follow the blood trail quietly towards the bedroom, because the person responsible for creating the mess is still in the apartment. You'll find the mysterious person standing over an injured man in the bathroom; his back is towards you so move up behind him and use a Takedown on him [→□ 1]. If you happen to make too much noise when initially moving through the apartment, this man will come out to investigate and won't hesitate to open fire on you.

Once you have dealt with the would-be assassin, return to the bathroom and start a conversation with the injured person, who happens to be the Detective you were looking for, Brent Radford. Brent immediately recognizes you, but refuses to answer anymore questions until you bring him some morphine to help relieve his pain. The Trauma Kit containing the morphine you need to give him is located in the bedroom closet behind a box at **Position B**; when you have it, return to Radford in the bathroom. [→□ 2]

Choose to give Radford a shot of the morphine to ease his pain and enable him to talk with you. Radford lets you know that digging up the information about Jensen's past seems to have angered some very dangerous and powerful people, and they are looking to get rid of any evidence that was uncovered. Radford kept most of his information in a secure storage unit and he is sure that is the next place they will go.

If you want to get more details about the quest out of Radford you'll need to give him another shot of the morphine, after which one of the things he reveals to you is the combination for the safe in the storage unit. Once you have all the information you require and try to leave, Radford will tell you that the only way he could survive his injuries and still live a normal life would be to become Augmented, and that's not something he could live with. Radford wants you to inject him with a lethal dose of the remaining morphine rather than be forced to live out his life any other way.

Whether you choose to administer the dose or not is up to you, but if you have the Social Enhancer you can also open up another option. If you choose to inquire about why Radford hates Augmentation so much, you will be able to use Pheromones to convince him that living with Augmentations isn't so bad; Radford is an Alpha personality, so choosing to Appease him is the correct response. After deciding how to handle Radford's fate, leave the apartment and go back down to the alley outside.

ACHIEVEMENT/TROPHY TIP

If you choose to end Radford's suffering by giving him the lethal dose of morphine, you will unlock the Kevorkian Complex Achievement/Trophy for showing your compassionate side.

Objective Completed	Objective Type	XP Reward	Add. Reward
Investigate Pritchard's Lead	Primary	100	–
Find Radford's Trauma Kit	Primary	100	–
Give Radford the Morphine Shot	Primary	100	–

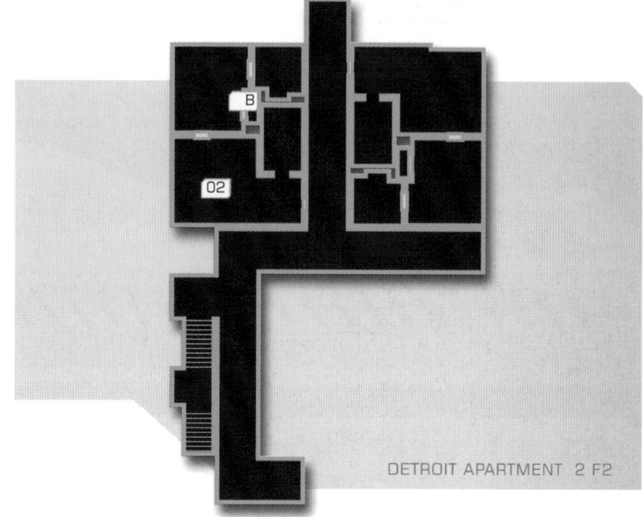

» Investigate Radford's Storage Unit (1)

03 The storage unit you need to get to is located in an alley near the Police Station. If you have the Move/Throw Heavy Objects Augmentation you can take the shortcut through the nearby maintenance tunnel by moving the dumpster out of the way [→□ 3]. If you do not have that Augmentation, you will need to exit the alleys on Grand River Road, and then take the long way around to the storage unit.

Recommended Frag Grenade/Typhoon or Revolver (Lethal), Gas Grenade or Tranquilizer Rifle/Stun Gun (Non-Lethal)

04 Crouch down and start moving quietly as soon as you are near the storage unit, because a group of men in suits is already there searching the area. In total there are four of them, three outside the storage unit and one inside. Before you can go looking around for yourself, you will have to deal with them. Your main focus in this situation should be to take all the enemies out as quickly and as quietly as possible; any sounds of gun fire or explosions will draw in a large number of police officers from the street.

If you are intent on killing the men in suits, making noise is unavoidable, so you will have to take them out quickly, and then hide until the police officers drop out of alert status. The easiest way to deal with the three enemies outside the storage unit is to use either a Frag or Gas Grenade to take them all out at once [→□ 4]. The Typhoon will also work equally well for dealing with the first three, if you can spare the ammo for it. You can then quickly run up into the storage unit and use a Takedown on the final enemy before he can react.

If you want to use conventional weapons, take cover behind one of the concrete barriers, and then, if you are using lethal tactics, use the Revolver and fire a single shot to the body on the first three. Going for body shots allows you to switch between targets much faster than lining up headshots, and since speed is key here, it's the better option. If the final enemy doesn't come out of the storage unit during the gun fire, you should close in quickly and take him out so that you can hide from the incoming police.

For non-lethal, fire a shot to the body with the Tranquilizer Rifle at the furthest of the three men you can see, and then quickly switch to the Stun Gun. Before that enemy falls unconscious, move up quietly and use the Stun Gun to take out the middle enemy, and then use a Takedown on the closest one [→☐ 5]. Now, take cover against the low wall in front of the storage unit so that the enemy inside does not see you, and once the Stun Gun is reloaded use a shot from it to incapacitate him. If done correctly you should be able to keep the noise levels down so you won't have to deal with the police.

Objective Completed	Objective Type	XP Reward	Add. Reward
Investigate Radford's Storage Unit (1)	Primary	100	–
Eliminate the Men in Black Suits	Primary	300	–

05 » **Investigate Radford's Storage Unit (2)**

When all the enemies have been eliminated, you will be free to enter the storage unit and begin your own search for evidence. There is a lot of information about Jensen's past on the computer in the storage unit, but the main thing you need to read on it is the email relating to Michelle Walthers. After reading the emails, use the code given to you by Radford (4062) to open the safe, retrieve the photos inside and then read the eBook to complete the search. [→☐ 6]

Objective Completed	Objective Type	XP Reward	Add. Reward
Investigate Radford's Storage Unit (2)	Primary	100	–

06 » **Find Michelle Walthers**

Radford had already mentioned Michelle Walthers while you were talking to him, and this additional information about her only confirms the need to talk to her. Michelle's apartment building is near Brooklyn Court, so you will need to head back through the alleys to reach it. Once you are there, you will need to climb the fire escape at **Position C** all the way up to the roof, and then enter the building from the rooftop door. Michelle's apartment is on the second floor of the building and the front door is unlocked, so you can enter normally and start a conversation with her. [→☐ 7]

Time has not been kind to Michelle and her memory is not what it once was, so you will need to tread lightly when you are trying to find out about your past. The first thing she wants is for you to hand over the photos you found in Radford's storage unit, and once you do she starts to remember some things. During the conversation you can choose to inquire further about the boy in the pictures to get some more information, but there are still a lot of holes. If you have the Social Enhancer Augmentation you can use Pheromones to help Michelle concentrate and find out some additional facts; she has a Beta personality, so charming her is the way to go.

Once she begins talking about her dinner she has told you all that she is capable of remembering for now, so it is best to leave her alone. When you try to leave, Michelle will offer to give you some money that she has been saving up for Adam; if you choose to take the money you will receive the 200 Credits, declining it will give you one final piece of information about Jensen's past. To complete the quest, leave Michelle's apartment so that she can rest.

ACHIEVEMENT/TROPHY TIP

Once you have left Michelle's apartment and have begun arranging the security detail with Pritchard, you will automatically unlock the Acquaintances Forgotten Achievement/Trophy to find out the details of Jensen's past.

Objective Completed	Objective Type	XP Reward	Add. Reward
Find Michelle Walthers	Primary	100	–
Speak to Michelle Walthers	Primary	100	–
Give Ms. Walthers the Photos	Primary	100	200 Credits
Let Ms. Walthers Rest	Primary	1000	–

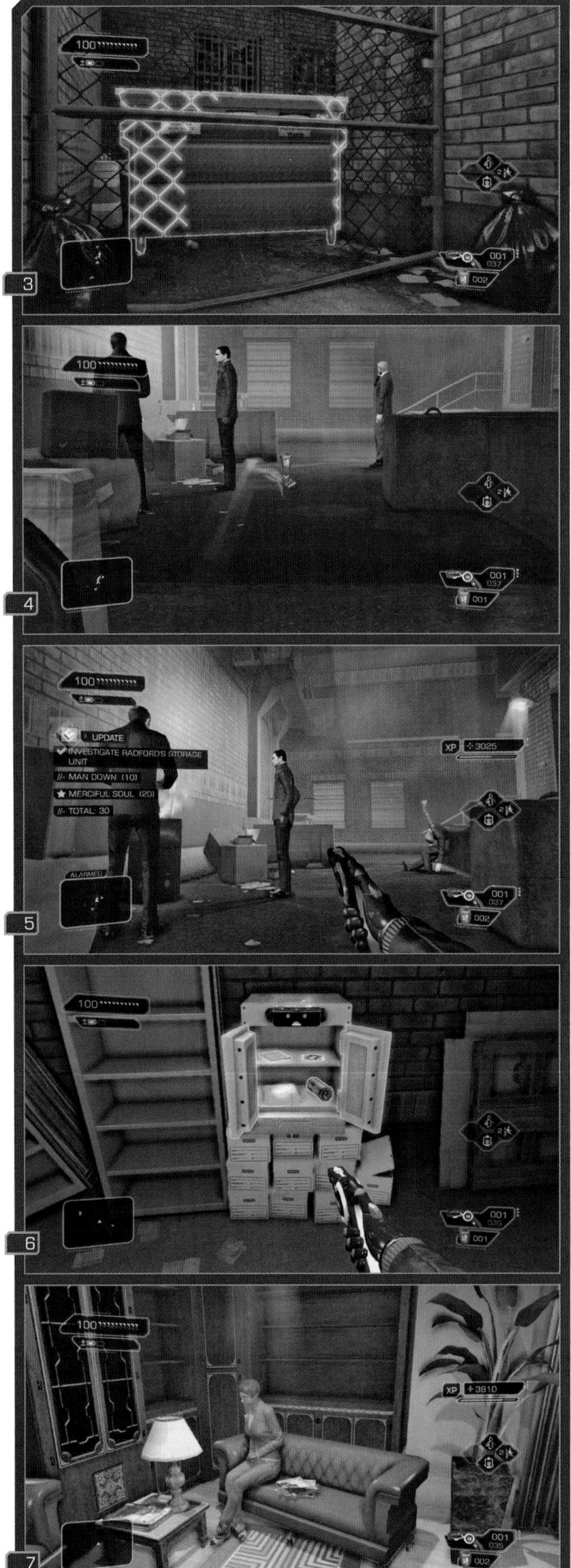

S2 Smash the State

As you are leaving the Detroit Convention Centre after finding out Sandoval's location, you will be approached by a former colleague from the police force named Nicky. Nicky has received a tip from one of his informants warning of an imminent bomb threat by a member of the MCBs, Jacob White, who has somehow managed to get hold of military-grade explosives. Unfortunately, after only briefly checking out the information, the police officials think that the informant has just given out bad information and that there is no real threat; Nicky, however, thinks otherwise.

Because Nicky is unable to get away due to the riots, he wants you to investigate potential areas that Jacob may target and see if there are any signs of a bomb. Jacob is known to have a strong hatred for the police, so the target is likely to be near the Police Station. After agreeing to take on the task for Nicky, he will attempt to try and narrow down the search area for you by pointing out some likely targets. However, because he is so agitated by the events, it is hard for him to think straight, so you will need to get him to calm down. Choosing to either Encourage or Chastise him will allow him to focus enough to reveal three potential target areas: the metro station, the alley behind the Police Station and the sewers beneath it.

If you have the Social Enhancer Augmentation you can get Nicky to focus even more by Pressuring him with Pheromones for his Omega-type personality; doing this will allow him to eliminate the metro station as a potential target area, saving you from investigating it. However, because you have to go through there anyway to get to the alley, it is worth taking one of the two normal options so that you can pick up a bit of extra XP along the way.

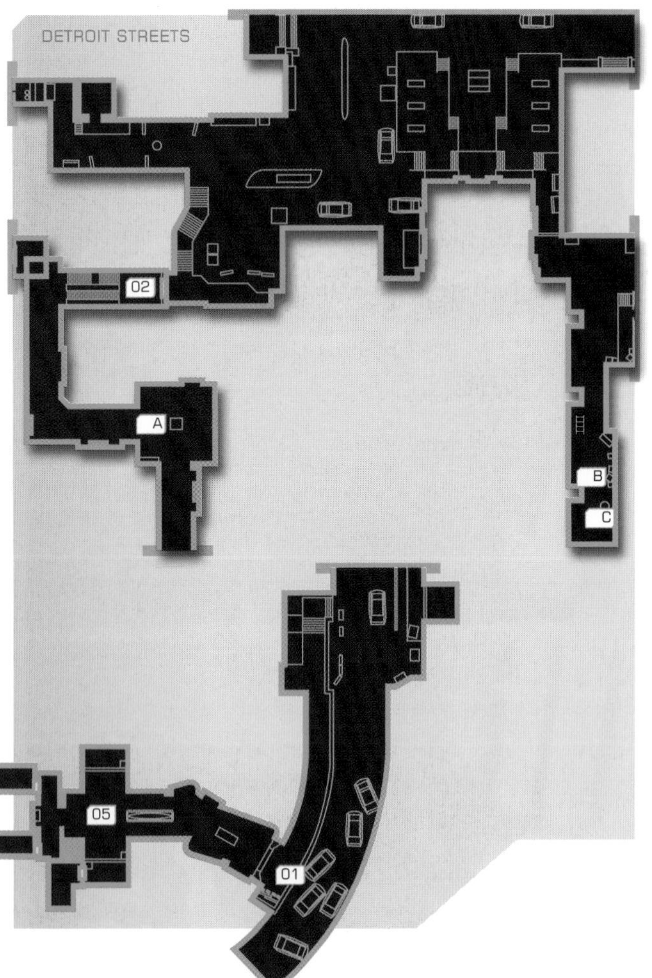

01

» Search the Metro Tunnel
» Search the Alley
» Search the Sewers

Investigating the metro station should be your first stop, since it is on the way to the other two locations, so exit the Convention Centre and follow the street along past the gas station. The stairs leading up to the metro station have been blocked off slightly, so you will need to jump over the barricade and then navigate through the bystanders to get inside. Head to **Position A** within the station where the police have arrested some local punks to ensure that the area is clear. [→□ 1]

Objective Completed	Objective Type	XP Reward	Add. Reward
Search the Metro Tunnel	Primary	100	–

Recommended EMP Shielding/Jump Enhancement

02

» Search the Alley
» Search the Sewers

The next place to clear should be the alley behind the Police Station, so continue through the metro tunnel and exit out onto the streets on the other side. The front door of the Police Station has been fully barricaded because of the riot so you will be unable to go through it to reach the alley and will have to use one of the alternate methods. The area you need to search is at **Position B** near the back of the alley.

Objective Completed	Objective Type	XP Reward	Add. Reward
Search the Alley	Primary	100	–

Recommended Hacking: Capture 4, Turret Domination

Recommended Upgraded Revolver/Frag Mines (Lethal), Tranquilizer Rifle (Non-Lethal)

03

» Search the Sewers

After clearing the alley you will have only the sewers left to check, so use the manhole nearby at **Position C** and head down there. Jacob White has been extremely busy down in the sewers and

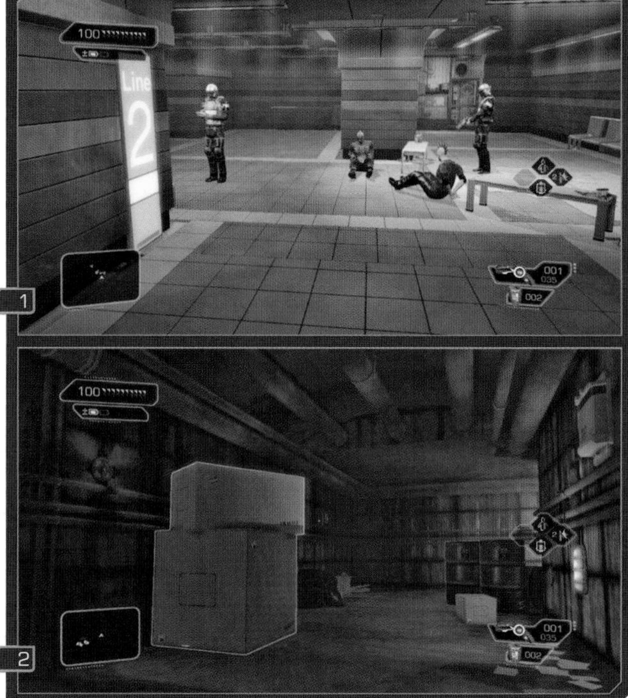

has set up numerous Frag Mines to try and deter people from looking around, which is a good sign that he is still in the area. You will need to be extremely careful when moving through this area as the mines are often placed on the back of walls where they are difficult to see until it is too late. If at any time you set one of the mines off, you will immediately alert Jacob to your presence and he will move out of his normal patrol area to come and investigate.

3

The first mine you will need to disarm is located at the bottom of the wall near **Position D**, and the next three are very close by at **Positions E**, **F** and **G** [→☐ 2]. The fifth mine is around the next corner behind some crates at **Position H**, and the final one is up high on the opposite wall at **Position I**. All these mines will come in handy for the upcoming encounter with Jacob, so pick up as many as you can along the way.

The mines are not the only things that Jacob took the time to set up. He also has a number of Turrets guarding the large sewer tunnel next to the one you are in; as long as you stay in this tunnel you will be out of their line of sight and in no danger. Continue along the tunnel you are in until you come to the Security Hub at **Position J**, and then, if you have high enough Capture software, hack your way into it. You'll need to be quick when doing this because Jacob will soon be making his way into the area from his patrol route at **Position K**, and he will be able to see you.

If you want to take Jacob out using non-lethal means you should choose to deactivate the Turrets so that they are no longer a threat. If, however, you want to take Jacob out permanently, you can choose to have them engage enemy targets so they take him out for you. If you do not have high enough Capture software to access the hub, take cover behind the nearby crate and wait for Jacob to start walking into the area.

Jacob is armed with a deadly Heavy Rifle, so make sure you take him out quickly and do not let him close in. Once he is in view, either incapacitate him with the Tranquilizer Rifle or use the explosive rounds from the Revolver to stagger him, and finish him off with one of the Frag Mines [→☐ 3]. Once Jacob is down, you can then use the remaining Frag Mines to take out the two Turrets for some extra XP.

Tip **It is worth trying to take Jacob alive, as it will lead to an extra bonus from Nicky at the end of the mission.**

Objective Completed	Objective Type	XP Reward	Add. Reward
Search the Sewers	Primary	100	–
Take out Jacob White	Primary	750	–

04

» Return to Officer Nicholas
» Disable Jacob's Bomb

Be careful as you round the corner to this point, as there is one final Turret in the area to take care of, if you did not disable the Turrets earlier. Take cover behind one of the crates and then use another Frag Mine to destroy it. The bomb Jacob was defending can be found at **Position L**, but, unlike the reports, it's more of a gas dispersal system than an explosive device. You can disarm the bomb in the same manner as the others you've encountered thus far by either hacking the terminal (if you have high enough Capture software) or destroying the gas containers on each side.

Once you've dealt with the bomb you need to return to Nicky and let him know what has transpired. Leaving the way you came is the safest option, because taking the other exit out of the sewer means navigating past more Frag Mines, but since Jacob is no longer an issue you do not have to worry if you set one of them off.

ACHIEVEMENT/TROPHY TIP

While Jacob may be a self-confessed military genius, when it comes to choosing his codes he is not quite as bright. For some inexplicable reason he decided to use a code so obvious that nobody would ever think to try it, but if you're feeling lucky, try inputting 0000. Doing this will not only disarm the bomb but you will also unlock the Lucky Guess Achievement/Trophy.

Objective Completed	Objective Type	XP Reward	Add. Reward
Disable Jacob's Bomb	Secondary	750	–

05

» Return to Officer Nicholas

You'll find Nicky in the lobby of the Convention Center where he originally approached you, so once you are back there start a conversation with him. Nicky will be overjoyed that you managed to find Jacob White, and while you were investigating for him, he also managed to convince his superior officers to send some men to help sort out the situation. As a reward for your efforts, Nicky will give you the proceeds of a deadpool the officers had going for anyone who manages to take down a cop killer; if you took Jacob down non-lethally he will also give you a handy Silencer. After informing him about the bomb and making sure it is taken care of properly your work here will be done.

ACHIEVEMENT/TROPHY TIP

As soon as you have finished talking to Nicky you will automatically unlock the Smash the State Achievement/Trophy for keeping the streets safe from an obsessed madman.

Objective Completed	Objective Type	XP Reward	Add. Reward
Return to Officer Nicholas	Primary	1000	1000 Credits, Silencer (if you use non-lethal means to take down Jacob)

HENGSHA 2

S1 & S2 Corporate Warfare

Once you have made your way safely back into Hengsha properly for the second time, Hugh Darrow will contact you as soon as you enter the Youzhao district on your way to investigate Sevchenko's GPL device. Darrow is in need of your assistance, but refuses to go into further details as to what that entails; his only instruction is that you meet with an associate of his, Mengyao, on the rooftop above Yuanmeng Road.

» Meet Hugh Darrow's Contact

01 The rooftop you need to get to is located between two of the terminals you had to hack for Bobby Bao during the Bar Tab Side Quest. Climb up the ladder at **Position A**, and then go across the rooftops to the right to find the contact standing between two large skylights [→□ 1]. According to Mengyao, a group of terrorists have managed to get hold of some sensitive material relating to the Panchaea site, and they are looking to sell it to the highest bidder. Another associate of Darrow's has already set up a meeting with the terrorists, but Mengyao wants you to go in alone to retrieve the data chip. The primary reason for sending you in alone is that Darrow wants to ensure that there are no casualties, so that any terrorists can be questioned and prosecuted by the police.

Objective Completed	Objective Type	XP Reward	Add. Reward
Meet Hugh Darrow's Contact	Primary	100	–

» Go to the Meeting Location

02 The meeting is taking place in the open drain near the Alice Garden Pods, so you will need to travel back to the other side of Hengsha. Go down the same ladder you came up and then go through the tunnel opposite the ladders, once you reach street level to get back to the Kuaigan district. Follow the main street along past the Hung Hua Hotel and then turn left at the fork; after a short distance, take the alley to the right to start heading towards the drain. There will be a lot of Belltower guards in this area so make sure you keep moving quickly and don't stay in their field of vision for very long.

Objective Completed	Objective Type	XP Reward	Add. Reward
Go to the Meeting Location	Primary	100	–

Recommended Tranquilizer Rifle & Stun Gun

» Incapacitate the Terrorists
» Retrieve the Data Chip

03 Engaging the terrorists from above the drain is a very risky proposition because you can easily get spotted by the Belltower Guards; engaging them from within the drain is a much safer option. At the end of the alley, turn left and start heading up the path, and then cross the first bridge when you come to it. Double back on the other side of the drain and start heading towards the storage unit, where Ning was being held during the Rotten Business Side Quest.

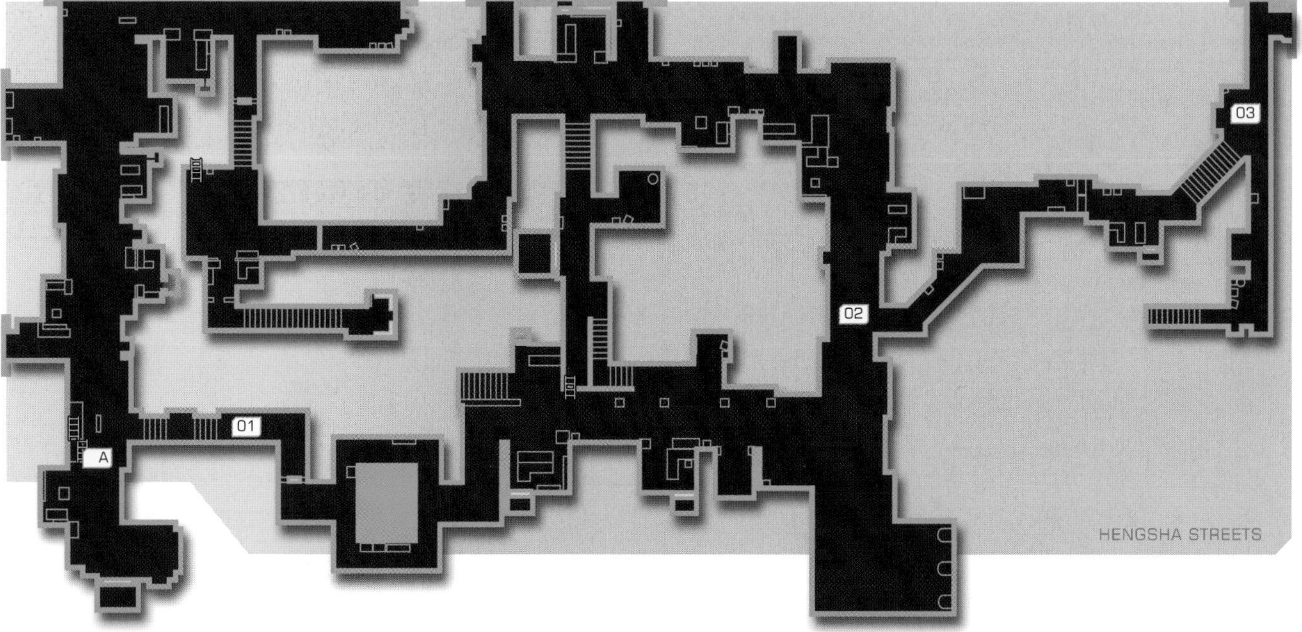

HENGSHA STREETS

Keep going down the stairs towards the drain but stop once you are about halfway down them, because one of the terrorists patrols the area below; wait to see if the area is clear and then continue down the stairs and take cover at **Position B**. There are five terrorists in total, so you will pay close attention to when, and in what order, you take them out so as not to alert them. Stay in this position until the patrolling guard makes his way back towards you, and then, when he stops nearby, move out quickly and use a Takedown to incapacitate him. [→☐ 2]

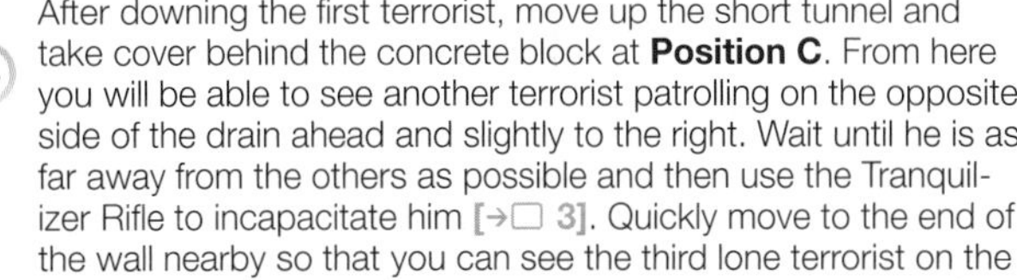

04 After downing the first terrorist, move up the short tunnel and take cover behind the concrete block at **Position C**. From here you will be able to see another terrorist patrolling on the opposite side of the drain ahead and slightly to the right. Wait until he is as far away from the others as possible and then use the Tranquilizer Rifle to incapacitate him [→☐ 3]. Quickly move to the end of the wall nearby so that you can see the third lone terrorist on the same side of the drain as you. As soon as you have a clear shot, incapacitate him using the Tranquilizer Rifle.

The body of the second enemy is usually obscured from the view of the third by the large central column, but you should try to take him down before he walks too far towards you, just in case. If the body does happen to get spotted, this area around the stairs provides excellent cover from where to keep trying to incapacitate the remaining terrorists. If you happen to have a Gas Grenade it can be extremely effective at taking them out, if you can lure them back into the tunnel.

The final two enemies are standing in the corner of the drain with their backs towards you, oblivious to what is going on behind them. Crouch down and move up quietly behind them, and then, when you are within range, use the Stun Gun to incapacitate one of them and instantly use a Takedown on the other. If you happen to have the Multiple Takedown Augmentation, that is also perfect for the job [→☐ 4]. Now that all the terrorists have been incapacitated you can safely retrieve the data chip from one of their bodies and bring it back to Mengyao on the same rooftop as where you met her.

Objective Completed	Objective Type	XP Reward	Add. Reward
Incapacitate the Terrorists	Primary	750	–
Retrieve the Data Chip	Primary	100	–

Recommended Social Enhancer

» Return to Mengyao

05 After starting a conversation with Mengyao you will have the option to inquire about the contents of the chip before handing it over to her; if you do not have the Social Enhancer Augmentation, however, she will not be forthcoming with any information. If you have it, try and Charm her Beta personality with Pheromones so that she tells you exactly what is on it. For your trouble, after handing over the chip, Mengyao will pass on an additional bonus from Darrow in the form of 1000 credits.

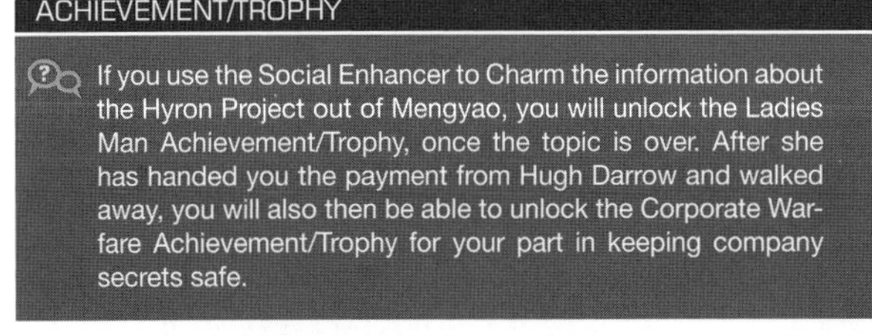

ACHIEVEMENT/TROPHY

If you use the Social Enhancer to Charm the information about the Hyron Project out of Mengyao, you will unlock the Ladies Man Achievement/Trophy, once the topic is over. After she has handed you the payment from Hugh Darrow and walked away, you will also then be able to unlock the Corporate Warfare Achievement/Trophy for your part in keeping company secrets safe.

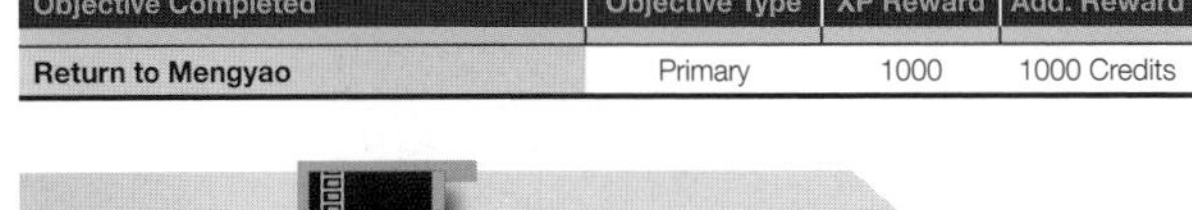

Objective Completed	Objective Type	XP Reward	Add. Reward
Return to Mengyao	Primary	1000	1000 Credits

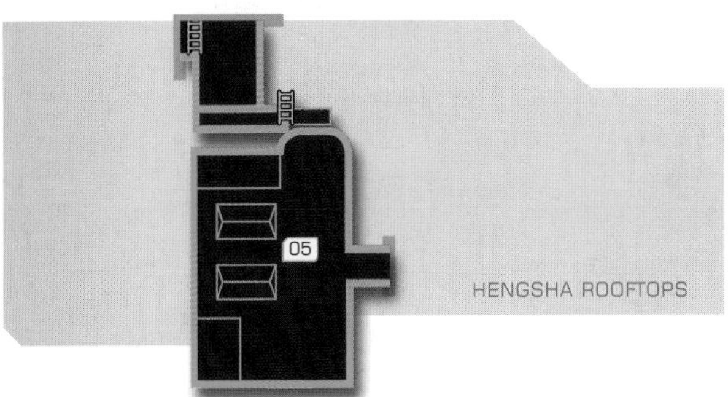

S3 Talion A.D.

Shortly after you exit the Construction Site you will get a message over the Infolink from Pritchard regarding the faulty biochips, and from that point on you can do this quest at any time. The person you need to speak to is called Doctor Wing, and you can find him in the waiting room of the Hengsha LIMB Clinic; even if you do not want to have your biochip changed you can still come here and accept the quest.

Doctor Wing heard about Jensen when a group of Belltower agents came into the LIMB Clinic looking for him, and from that he knows that Jensen has the skills needed to help him stop a dangerous Augmented soldier and his squad. The soldier's name is Michael Zelazny, and he has been Augmented with highly experimental, and illegal, technology at the hands of various LIMB Doctors, including Wing. Zelazny has now gone rogue, and has embarked on his own personal mission outside even Belltower's control. Wing's hope is that Jensen's unique background will allow him to reason with Zelazny and end the situation peacefully; if that is not an option, however, then at least he can get out alive.

» Locate the Butcher Shop Where Zelazny is Hiding

01 The first place you need to search for Zelazny is in a butcher shop that Wing suspects is a cover for Zelazny's staging area. The butcher shop is located near the Pandeng Road in the Youzhao district, and the quickest way to get there is to exit the LIMB Clinic and go through the metro station to the right. As you enter the metro station in the Youzhao district you will be on Pandeng Road; keep following the road and turn into the small alley at **Position A**. A short way into the alley you will need to hack your way past a security gate, but it only has a rating of 1, so you will not need any additional Augmentations. Go up the stairs on the other side of the gate and the butcher shop you are looking for will be directly ahead of you. [→□ 1]

Objective Completed	Objective Type	XP Reward	Add. Reward
Locate the Butcher Shop Where Zelazny is Hiding	Primary	100	–

» Enter the Back Room of the Butcher Shop

02 Go through the main area of the butcher shop and into the door at the back to reach a set of stairs that will lead you down to the secret back room that was suspected of being used by Zelazny. There is no sign of Zelazny in the room, however, so you will need to search it thoroughly for any evidence that might point you towards his current location. Signs of a struggle are everywhere in the room and you get the feeling that Zelazny's team pulled out in a hurry. So quickly in fact that they didn't have time to dispose of the body belonging to a Belltower operative who was sent to capture them.

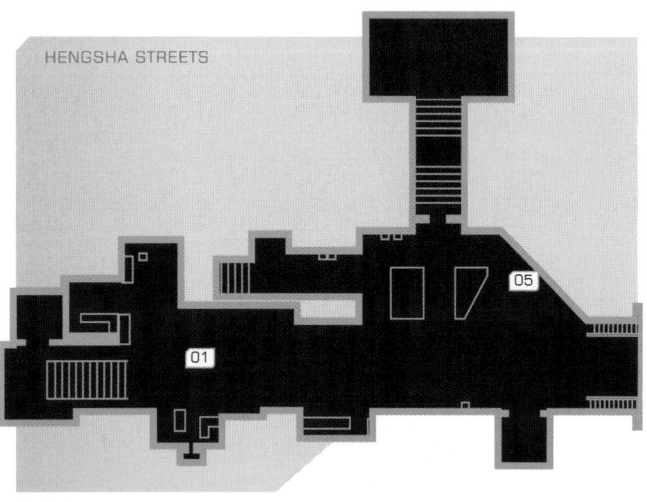

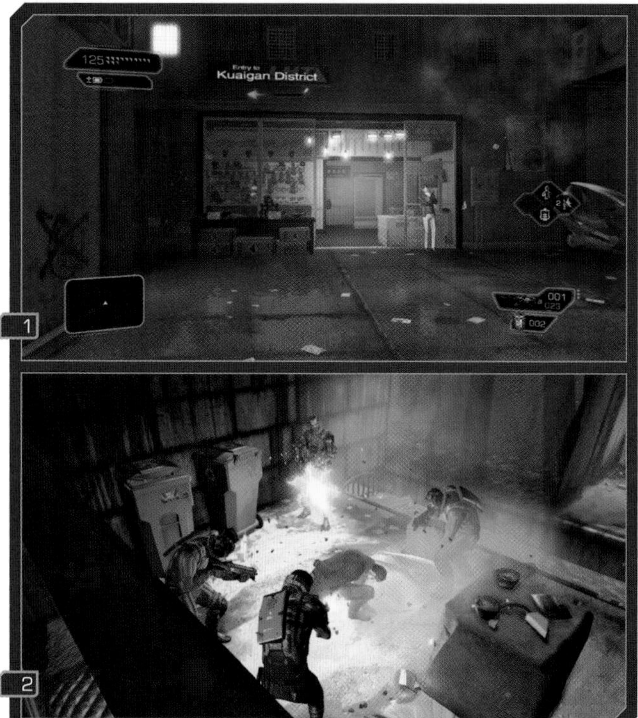

On the body you will find a Pocket Secretary that contains a hint pointing towards the sewers as the location of their next hideout. That is all of the information that is left in the room, so once you are done in the area, head back out of the butcher shop and go through the gate to the Kuaigan district.

Objective Completed	Objective Type	XP Reward	Add. Reward
Enter the Back Room of the Butcher's Shop	Primary	100	–
Find Information on Zelazny's Current Whereabouts	Primary	100	–
Read the Dead Agent's Pocket Secretary	Primary	100	–

» Locate Mike Zelazny and his Team

03 You have no objective marker to follow at this time, which means you'll have to venture down into the sewers without any guidance. The closest sewer entrance to Zelazny's position is the one near the open drain, so run along the main road and then take the alley at **Position B** to reach the drain. The sewer entrance can be found at **Position C** next to the drain.

Recommended Typhoon

Recommended Revolver/Frag Grenade (Lethal), Tranquilizer Rifle/Gas Grenade (Non-Lethal)

» Locate Mike Zelazny and his Team

04 As soon as you are in the sewers, move along the main tunnel until you round the first corner, after which you will see Zelazny and his team sitting around at the end of the tunnel at **Position D**. If you approach Zelazny you will automatically enter into a dialogue with him. Through the course of the dialogue with Zelazny, you will be able to uncover the truth about why he went rogue and started his own personal crusade, and at any time you can also choose to put an end to the conversation and fight him.

If you go through the whole conversation, trying your best to get Zelazny to see reason, and you have the Social Enhancer Augmentation, you will get the opportunity to try and influence him by using the Pheromones. Unfortunately, Zelazny is immune to the effects of the CASIE and knows you are trying to use it. Since Zelazny appears unlikely to simply surrender and let himself be taken in, the only options left for you are to either fight him straight away, or let him go so that he can continue his mission.

Choosing to fight Zelazny from within the conversation is a very dangerous idea (especially if you attempt to use firearms) because he and his men are well armed and they have you surrounded. If you are extremely quick you can run to the side and climb the nearby ladder to escape their gunfire, but fighting them from that position is very difficult. Another option is to immediately activate the Typhoon, if you have it, as it will allow you to take out the whole team instantly without risk [→☐ 2]. If you have sufficient Energy Cells you can also use a series of quick Takedowns on them; this is made even easier if you have the Multiple Takedown Augmentations, which also give you another non-lethal option.

If you do want to engage them with normal weapons, it is much better to do so without first talking to Zelazny. Go back along the tunnel and climb the ladder at **Position E** to reach a small platform overlooking Zelazny and his men. From here you can easily take all of them out with a well placed Frag or Gas Grenade, or you could get an early advantage by engaging them with firearms. Try to focus on Zelazny first, before his teammates, because his Heavy Rifle can be especially deadly if you leave him alive. After you have either killed or let Zelazny go, you will need to return to the LIMB Clinic to let Doctor Wing know the outcome.

Tip **If you choose to let Zelazny go, he will contact you when you exit the sewers, letting you know that he used his old contacts in Belltower to get patrols in the area reassigned, which will make moving about in the city easier for you.**

Objective Completed	Objective Type	XP Reward	Add. Reward
Locate Mike Zelazny and his Team	Primary	300	–
Deal with Zelazny and his Team	Primary	750	–

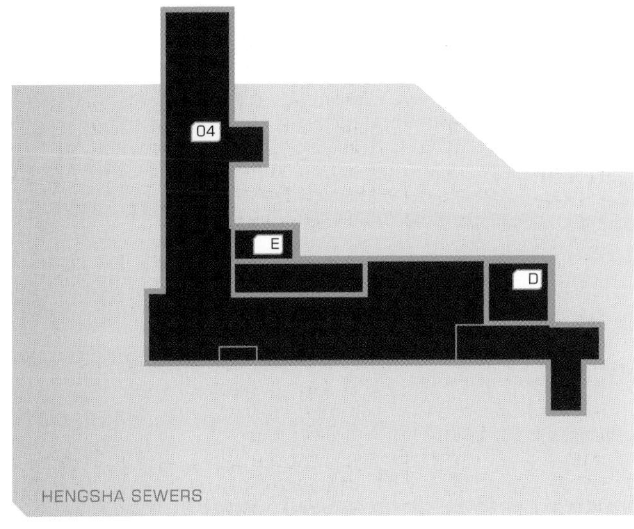

HENGSHA SEWERS

05 ›› **Return to Dr. Wing**

Dr. Wing is still in the waiting room of the LIMB Clinic. He is eager to hear about your investigation into Zelazny. Regardless of how you dealt with Zelazny, Wing will be largely happy with the result and will also hand you a Praxis Kit for looking into the matter for him.

ACHIEVEMENT/TROPHY TIP

As soon as your conversation with Dr. Wing is over, you will automatically unlock the Talion A.D. Achievement/Trophy.

Objective Completed	Objective Type	XP Reward	Add. Reward
Return to Dr. Wing	Primary	1000	Praxis Kit

HENGSHA STREETS

CH07 Extras

Here we'll provide a wealth of supplemental information about *Deus Ex: Human Revolution* that all true fans will appreciate. The game's countless secrets and references are revealed, and the Achievement/Trophy Guide makes unlocking everything easy. Everything you need to complete your knowledge of the game can be found right here.

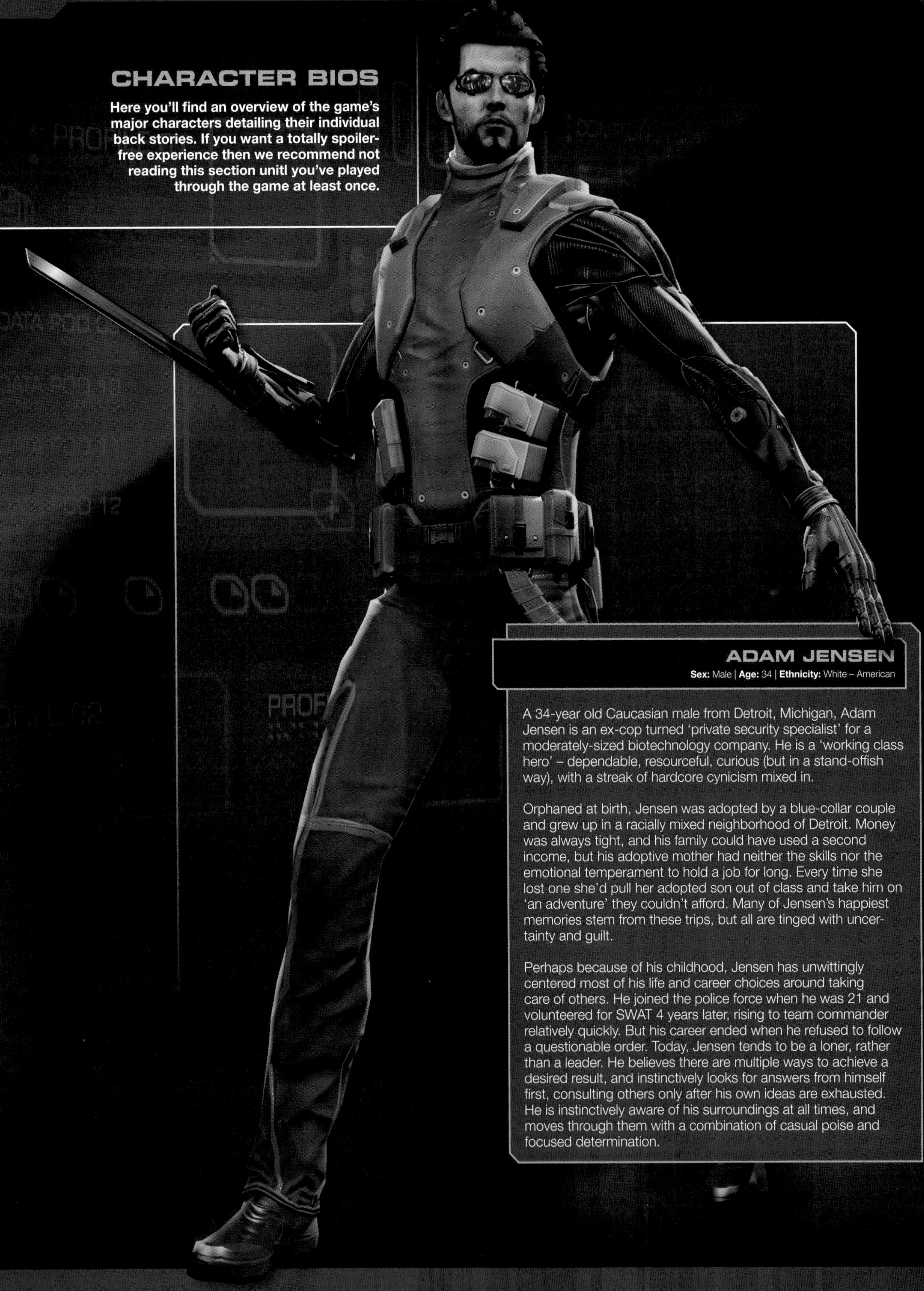

CHARACTER BIOS

Here you'll find an overview of the game's major characters detailing their individual back stories. If you want a totally spoiler-free experience then we recommend not reading this section unitl you've played through the game at least once.

ADAM JENSEN

Sex: Male | **Age:** 34 | **Ethnicity:** White – American

A 34-year old Caucasian male from Detroit, Michigan, Adam Jensen is an ex-cop turned 'private security specialist' for a moderately-sized biotechnology company. He is a 'working class hero' – dependable, resourceful, curious (but in a stand-offish way), with a streak of hardcore cynicism mixed in.

Orphaned at birth, Jensen was adopted by a blue-collar couple and grew up in a racially mixed neighborhood of Detroit. Money was always tight, and his family could have used a second income, but his adoptive mother had neither the skills nor the emotional temperament to hold a job for long. Every time she lost one she'd pull her adopted son out of class and take him on 'an adventure' they couldn't afford. Many of Jensen's happiest memories stem from these trips, but all are tinged with uncertainty and guilt.

Perhaps because of his childhood, Jensen has unwittingly centered most of his life and career choices around taking care of others. He joined the police force when he was 21 and volunteered for SWAT 4 years later, rising to team commander relatively quickly. But his career ended when he refused to follow a questionable order. Today, Jensen tends to be a loner, rather than a leader. He believes there are multiple ways to achieve a desired result, and instinctively looks for answers from himself first, consulting others only after his own ideas are exhausted. He is instinctively aware of his surroundings at all times, and moves through them with a combination of casual poise and focused determination.

DAVID SARIF

Sex: Male | **Age:** Late 50s | **Ethnicity:** White – American

David Sarif is the founder and CEO of Sarif Industries, a moderately-sized biotechnology company based in North America. He is a well-preserved male in his late 50s, of average height and build, in decent shape. His features are Mediterranean.

The son of an immigrant family from Boston, Sarif was brought up to understand the value of hard work and dedication, and from an early age his insight into machines set the tone for the man he would become. He worked his way through university and from there to a scholarship at MIT, getting a Master's and an MBA before entering the prosthetics field.

Sarif believes in justice, progress, science and technology, civilization, human endeavor, and people. He is direct when dealing with others and unafraid to show emotions. Some find him blunt or pushy, others refreshing, even invigorating. His sense of honesty applies only to his behavior - he has no aversion to keeping secrets when appropriate; usually his demeanor lets him get away with it.

MEGAN REED

Sex: Female | **Age:** Early 30s | **Ethnicity:** White – American

Megan Reed is a scientific genius, a leader in the field of human enhancement technologies, and the most prominent neuroscientist working for Sarif Industries, a Detroit-based biotechnology firm. She is in her early thirties; Caucasian; attractive in a simplistic, unadorned manner; and completely unaware of how good-looking she is.

Reed grew up in Seattle, the only child of two doctors who both decided early on that family life would never interfere with their careers. Left on her own more often than not, the young girl compensated by developing a rich inner life; today her fertile imagination enables Reed to connect information and extrapolate it toward a theoretical endpoint in great intuitive leaps. Unfortunately, she also has a tendency to become so focused on her thoughts that everything else fades in the background. Relationships with others have suffered.

One such relationship involves Adam Jensen, the ex-cop turned 'private security specialist' who's working at Sarif Industries. Reed and Jensen had a very intense 4-year relationship that both believed would end in marriage. She was leading an important research project at the time and, in a moment of desperation, used Jensen's genetic material without his knowledge to complete it. In the process she discovered that Jensen was a genetic anomaly, and became so focused on studying his genes that ultimately, she lost sight of their relationship. The couple grew distant; eventually Jensen ended the relationship.

Today, several years after the break-up, Reed's feeling for Jensen remain layered and complex. She still feels affection for him and perhaps, on some level, hopes for a second chance at love. But she's angered by his rejection and troubled at having stolen his DNA. She's tried to come clean several times but, unwilling to really face what the theft says about her as a person, has ultimately never succeeded.

FARIDAH MALIK

Sex: Female | **Age:** Late 20s | **Ethnicity:** White – American

A petite woman in her late-20s with Arabic features, Faridah Malik is the chief helicopter pilot for cybernetic manufacturer, Sarif Industries. She is a third-generation American born in Dearborn, Michigan.

Faridah likes a bit of danger, a touch of risk. She generally pilots her chopper faster – and closer to the ground – than necessary. When confronted on this, she will at first ignore the criticism, and when that no longer works, will feign innocence as a way of pushing social boundaries – again, to see what she can get away with.

Although in general an easy-going woman, it doesn't take much to get Faridah's back up. If she thinks she's been insulted, she'll cuss you out fit to turn a sailor's ears red. If she thinks you're being stupid, she won't hesitate to tell you so, possibly even striking you if she thinks you deserve it. She'll often regret it afterward, though, and she doesn't hold a grudge.

FRANK PRITCHARD

Sex: Male | **Age:** Mid 30s | **Ethnicity:** White – American

A Caucasian male in his mid-thirties, clean-shaven with a somewhat florid complexion and the characteristic 'monitor tan' of someone who spends most of his life in front of a screen, Frank Pritchard is Sarif Industries' head of Cyber Security.

Pritchard possesses a keen intellect and an ability to comprehend complex patterns (such as data sets) very rapidly, but often has difficulty 'thinking outside the box.' The very opposite of a man of action, at first sight he appears almost lazy, but in fact his behavior stems from his physical weakness. On some level he knows he is a weak man, but he overcompensates with the ferocity of his arrogance and his intellectual skills.

Having spent much of his formative years around those who were physically superior but intellectually inferior to him, Pritchard has developed an acerbic and arrogant manner toward all those he encounters. His default assumption is that everyone he meets is not as smart as he is, and he is completely unaware that his conceited behavior prevents him from making any real emotional contact.

ELIZA CASSAN

Sex: Female Artificial Intelligence | **Age:** 20s – 30s | **Ethnicity:** Projected Image Looks and Sounds Caucasian, Mid-Atlantic Accent

As far as the world is concerned, Eliza Cassan is a beautiful newscaster, somewhere between her mid-20s and 30s; a trusted 'friend' who is intelligent and sexy, eccentric and engaging all at once. In truth, she is a highly sophisticated Artificial Intelligence program that has only recently discovered itself to be sentient.

Eliza started out as a simple data-mining tool, written to help researchers at PICUS Communications (the global leader in news and entertainment production in 2027) sift and parse the endless tide of information being generated on the Internet. Her ability to see the spread of data as a whole eventually caused her to exceed her original programming; soon Eliza was not just gathering data for her masters, she was also somehow altering it, to enhance the emotional content. Picus' news ratings skyrocketed, so Eliza was encouraged to keep going.

Today, Eliza views her work at Picus as a kind of performance art. She's had no moral compass written into her, so while she understands on an intellectual level that what she's doing might be wrong, she isn't terribly concerned. You might say her personality is underdeveloped. In many ways, Eliza is just naïve and lacking in emotional maturity. The need to gather information colors everything she does, so in any situation, from commonplace to life-threatening, she will be looking to understand, to seek out new knowledge and hoard it. In the end, given her questing curiosity and sense of wonder about the world, Eliza comes across as trusting and rather childlike.

ZEKE SANDERS

Sex: Male | **Age:** Late 30s | **Ethnicity:** Hispanic – American

An Hispanic male in his late 30's, with a thin beard and a very close-cut, almost 'skinhead' haircut, Zeke Sanders leads a group of militant political extremists who believe that the human body is sacred, so science must never be used to change it. He and his followers vow to end all forms of bio-modification "without exception, without compromise, and without apology".

Of average height with a wiry, whipcord strength in his build, Sanders embodies both the passionate machismo of the Latino, and the honor and commitment to duty of the proud ex-Marine. He grew up in Los Angeles, the youngest of four in a blue-collar family, but left home at 17 to join the Corps. In 2009 in Afghanistan, shrapnel from a roadside bomb took out his left eye and ear, and should have sent him immediately stateside, but the US military had other plans. They offered to surgically replace his damaged organs with cutting-edge, technologically-enhanced mechanical ones, free-of-charge, provided that he re-enlist. Within a year Zeke was back on the front lines, seeing things and doing things with his augmented senses that still haunt him to this day.

Now, in 2027, Sanders is radically opposed to augmentations, having spiraled through a post-traumatic darkness following the war that nearly led to his suicide-by-cop. He has removed his enhancements, and covers his missing eye with a patch. Zeke also has a number of tattoos on his arms, including a United States Marine Corps sigil. He walks with a swagger and the air of a soldier.

BILL TAGGART

Sex: Male | **Age:** Mid 50s | **Ethnicity:** White – American

Bill Taggart is a political activist and the founder of the Humanity Front, a global, non-profit organization that believes the human body is sacred so science should never be used to change it. He seeks to abolish, or at least severely restrict, the use of human enhancement technologies for precisely this reason.

In his mid-50s, with a bearing and posture that make his thinning frame appear solid, Taggart is, by education, a psychologist. By nature, he's a consummate politician — one who radiates wisdom, dependability, calmness and strength, rather than aggressive power. In his heart of hearts, he knows he is one of a very small elite whose understanding of human nature and societal trends bestows upon him the right, and the obligation, to lead mankind down the path it must follow. But he also knows he must never express this truth directly to the masses.

Born into money, Taggart attended the best schools growing up. With his wife Marjorie's emotional support, he started a successful psychology practice after college and eventually published two books, one of which was a self-help bestseller. Then Marjorie was murdered by an augmentation addict suffering a psychotic episode – and Taggart's life and calling changed. He decided that human augmentation was a danger to mankind, and started the Humanity Front organization to pressure governments to put a stop to it.

ISAIAS SANDOVAL

Sex: Male | **Age:** Early 40s | **Ethnicity:** Hispanic – American

An Hispanic-American male in his early 40's, Isaias Sandoval is a doctor turned political activist. At a time (2027) when people are using cybernetic implants to alter and improve their mental and physical abilities, he believes that bio-modification is dangerous. And he's working as the second-in-command at a global, non-profit organization called the Humanity Front to have the practice outlawed worldwide.

A quiet but intense individual, Sandoval grew up in Los Angeles, the oldest of four in a blue-collar family. From the start, he was raised to be responsible; to take care of his younger siblings and to teach them, by example, the value of hard work and personal sacrifice. His decision to become an ER doctor was a logical extension of this. In his heart, Sandoval always believed that the plight of others had to be addressed, and he wanted to help where he could. It was in the ER that he first saw the dangers of bio-modification, as people whose bodies began rejecting their implants came in. Years later, the danger hit closer to home, when his younger brother Zeke, a mechanically-enhanced veteran of the Second Gulf War, went on a rampage in a shopping mall. Sandoval was unable to talk Zeke down but someone else could: Bill Taggart, the charismatic man who founded the Humanity Front. With no harm done and no loss of life, Zeke was taken into custody.

It was a life-changing moment for Isaias. Feeling a debt of gratitude he could never repay, he quit his job to work at the Humanity Front. Since then, he has offered Bill Taggart complete trust and loyalty, doing whatever the man asks without question. Safe in the knowledge that Taggart will always be there, campaigning on his behalf, Sandoval is able to quell any doubts and concentrate on the task at hand. Even if that task is ethically questionable. Sadly, Sandoval's faith in Taggart is misplaced. For when the shit hits the fan, he will find himself alone in the hot seat and faced by a very grim choice: expose Taggart's complicity as well, or fall on his sword and protect him.

LAWRENCE BARRETT

Sex: Male | **Age:** Mid 30s | **Ethnicity:** White – American

A White male in his mid 30s, Lawrence Barrett is part of a team of elite, special operations mercenaries working for Belltower Associates, a private military corporation. At first glance, he is the classic example of a US Marines poster boy: impeccable crew cut, muscular frame, a sense of coiled energy, and a machismo that just doesn't quit. At second glance, you'll quickly see that cruelty and opportunism live side-by-side in his eyes.

Barrett was born in a poor area of St. Louis, Missouri. His father was a cross-country trucker who was never at home, and his mother was a sporadic housekeeper addicted to Valium and booze. Bigger and stronger than other kids his age, he quickly became the schoolyard bully, using skills he would routinely perfect at home on his only brother. His favorite pastime was watching television and movies, especially martial arts and war stories.

Today, Barrett's bullying past is reflected in his domineering stance and methodical, lumbering movements. The man is a swaggering Midwestern carnivore, built like a brick shit house. He has mechanical enhancements up the ying-yang. Barrett lives for the moment when he's beaten his enemy into submission, and he's the type of man who will never surrender or retreat. As long as blood still flows in his veins, even if most of it is spilling onto the floor, Barrett will fight his enemies until he has defeated them or died.

YELENA FEDOROVA

Sex: Female | **Age:** 26 | **Ethnicity:** Black – Unknown

With an athletic build and statuesque, augmented height of 6'7", twenty-six year-old Yelena Fedorova is a trained assassin, part of an elite team of special operations mercenaries working for Belltower Associates, a private military corporation. A black woman with a cut of shoulder-length, spiky black hair, she's rarely seen out of her combat gear; her only affectation is a silver cross on a black steel chain around her neck, a family heirloom of great personal value.

Born in the former Russian state of Georgia in 2001, Yelena grew up as a rebellious child among a community of Ethnic Russians who opposed Georgia's independence. In 2016, while still a teenager, a series of clashes between Georgians and Ethnic Russians forced Yelena and her family to seek refuge in the hills. Unfortunately, militia groups from both sides were fighting over control of those hills – and in one terrible night, Yelena saw all of her loved ones ruthlessly attacked, raped, and murdered by soldiers. She was lucky to escape the carnage by hiding, but being forced to watch helplessly as those she loved were killed caused something inside of her to snap. Since that day, she has not uttered a word, preferring to let her actions and movements speak for her.

Today, Yelena is a ruthless and resourceful combatant, never choosing frontal assault when another approach will more easily destroy her enemies with less effort. When she moves, she does so with unexpected agility, speed, and grace – a sleepy-eyed cobra uncoiling rapidly as it strikes. Well aware of being one of few women in a man's world, Yelena has become adept at vigilance and is cautious of everything around her; she's not easy to sneak up on, and usually has a plan for every eventuality.

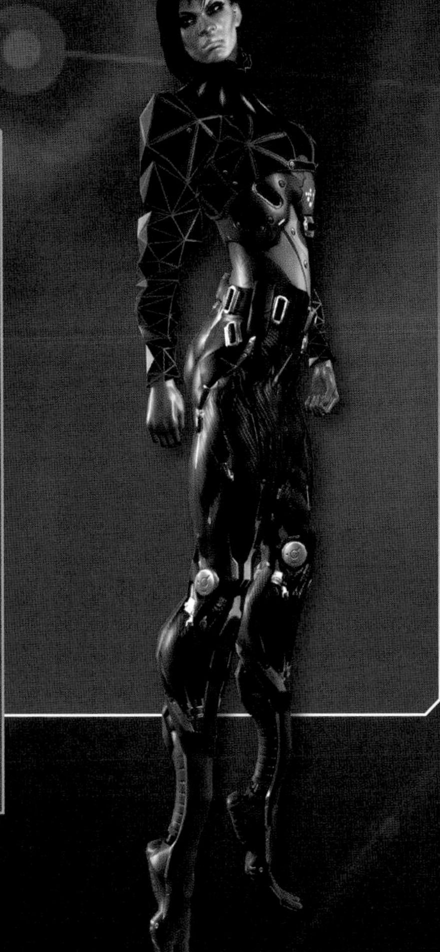

JARON NAMIR

Sex: Male | **Age:** Early 40s | **Ethnicity:** White - Middle Eastern

An athletic and well-augmented male of average height, Jaron Namir is the highest ranking special operations mercenary currently working for Belltower Associates, a private military corporation. He has dark brown eyes and an intense metered gaze. His hair is short and dark with some gray creeping in. While on duty, he wears his combat gear like a second skin, moving with the easy, lethal grace of a career killer.

Born in Haifa, Israel, Namir entered national service with the Israeli armed forces when he was eighteen, and later became a field agent in the Mossad. In 2022, when Israel was decimated by an Arab military invasion, Namir called in favors from global contacts to flee the Middle East with his wife and kids. One of the men helping him was Luther St.John-Ffolkes, a senior executive in Belltower Associates. In London, when St. John-Ffolkes offered him a job in the private military corporation's clandestine division, Namir recognized it as a lifeline. He accepted the position gladly, and has served Belltower with unswerving devotion ever since.

Today as he heads into his forties, Namir's face is all hard lines and firmness, as if it had been cut from sandstone. He is the consummate soldier, unswervingly loyal to his allies and ruthless with his enemies. Iron-willed and merciless, he is well accustomed to using secret and dirty means to achieve his ends. Yet he is not without some contradictions, for Namir is also a devoted father and husband. While he would never admit it to anyone, Namir has noticed that he is slowing down, that he is not the man he once was. His failure to terminate Adam Jensen when he had the chance plays directly into this fear, motivating him even more to undo his error.

TONG SI HUNG

Sex: Male | **Age:** Late 50s | **Ethnicity:** Asian – Chinese

To the outside world, Tong Si Hung is the assiduously discreet owner of a popular nightclub in Lower Shanghai called THE HIVE. But to those who really know him, he's the biggest crime lord in the city. Tong specializes in drug trafficking, gambling, and prostitution from inside the Hive, while on the other end of town, he runs a very successful black market operation in human enhancement technology through an augmented gang of street thugs known as 'Harvesters.' (So named, because they'll harvest cybernetic implants right out of you.)

A Chinese male in his late 50s, Tong knows most of what goes on in 'his' city, and is sometimes willing to provide that information to others, if he sees an advantage to it. He is highly intelligent and has an uncanny instinct for forging alliances that will inevitably profit him in some way. Exactly how he'll profit is rarely understood by anyone but Tong until after the deal is made. In a city that's ruled by a cutthroat multinational corporation and policed by rather brutal military contractors, Tong does what he has to, to survive.

He's therefore never afraid to get brutal. Tong will cut off a man's testicles and feed them back to him without qualms, if it will get his point across. Yet despite this, Tong sees himself as a man who lives according to a strong moral code. Nothing is more important to him than family and keeping one's word. He maintains an air of culture and outward civility at all times, and is even capable of genuine acts of kindness, should the situation allow it.

ZHAO YUN RU

Sex: Female | **Age:** Early 40s | **Ethnicity:** Asian – Chinese

A petite and elegant Chinese woman in her early 40s, Zhao Yun Ru is the president of Tai Yong Medical, a multinational biotech corporation that specializes in human enhancement products. Physically, Yun Ru moves with a careful, fluid grace that's almost cat-like, never making expansive or large gestures unless she is highly agitated. She is comfortable in both the severe lines of corporate power-dress and traditional Chinese garb. She is also multilingual; when speaking in English there is only a faint trace of Chinese in her accent.

Given all this, Zhao seems an unthreatening presence at first glance, an impression she does her best to further in order to wrong-foot her enemies. It's only her eyes, cold and hard like chips of sea ice, that betray her true character. Yun Ru is arrogant, manipulative, driven, and uninhibited. She plays the notes she must in order to draw the responses she needs, and feels no guilt at her behavior – merely contempt for those who fall for her wiles.

If Zhao does have an Achilles' heel, it's this: she's never had to confront real danger. For years, she's been skirting the edge of it, following the orders of men more powerful than she while silently chaffing under their restrictions. Zhao secretly fears that the day will come when their patience with her chaffing will be exhausted. On that day, she expects to know true terror once and for all.

HUGH DARROW

Sex: Male | **Age:** 54 | **Ethnicity:** White – British

54-year-old Hugh Darrow is a visionary and entrepreneur; the creative genius whose ground-breaking ideas about robotics, biotechnology, and human enhancement have enabled people (in 2027) to greatly exceed their bodies' natural capabilities using cybernetic implants. Unfortunately, a rare genetic disorder prevents him from ever doing the same.

Born and raised in Blackheath, South London as the only child of a Knighted media mogul and a Privy Councilor's daughter, Darrow grew up surrounded by extreme wealth and privilege. He developed an early fascination with robots and, intent on pursuing it, quit school before college to found his own company. Four years later, following a debilitating skiing accident that left him with a permanent limp, Darrow envisioned a technology that could strengthen and improve the human body. He immediately changed the focus of his company to create it. Over the next ten years, Darrow Industries' products would change the very fabric of society, by allowing men and women who could afford them to improve their minds and bodies at will. Sadly, Darrow himself would never benefit, thanks to a genetic incompatibility he only discovered after his body rejected its first implant.

Today, Darrow's public demeanor combines the superiority and entitlement of one born into great privilege, with the energy, passion, and spontaneity of the intuitive genius. Above all, he exudes an aura of intelligence and great competence – although at times, a darker emotion creeps in. For years, Darrow has been forced to sit by and watch as others around him use the technology he created to evolve, while he – the man who made self-evolution possible – gets left behind.

Furious that a man of his stature, power, and wealth can't get what he wants, (and secretly despising everyone else who can), Darrow has begun to question whether cybernetic implants should have been invented at all. He believes the only way to "uninvent" them is to set off a cataclysmic event of such magnitude that no sane person would ever willingly use them again. And he's become convinced that, as the "father" of augmentation technology, he's the man who needs to do it.

STORY

Here you'll find the story of the game. You can also find a version of this text in the game at the loading screens, however we present it here, with a few tweaks for clarity, so that you have the entire story, as told by the game, at your fingertips. Embrace your inner cyberpunk, and immerse yourself in the story of Deus Ex: Human Revolution!

Welcome to the Revolution

The year is 2027. Multinational biotech corporations specializing in human enhancement are vying for dominance in what has become a controversial field. Many engage in clandestine wars against each other, employing thieves, moles and hackers to steal their competitors' research. To protect its research, Detroit-based Sarif Industries has recently developed its own internal security force. Enter Adam Jensen, newly appointed head of Sarif Industries' Security.

Back in the Saddle

Six months have passed since mysterious Black-Op mercenaries attacked Sarif Industries, destroying labs and murdering the company's top researchers. Although nearly killed in the attack himself, Jensen has been called back to work in the middle of his post-op recovery. Seems his boss, David Sarif, needs the newly Augmented Jensen's skills to protect the firm from yet another crisis.

Sarif Under Siege

A group of anti-Augmentation extremists calling themselves "Purity First" have broken into Sarif Industries' manufacturing plant and taken hostages. Detroit SWAT teams are ready to storm in, but Sarif needs to keep them out until a top-secret military prototype can be hidden away. He's ordered Jensen to infiltrate the plant and retrieve the "Typhoon" swiftly, saving Sarif's workers if he can.

A Wolf Among Sheep

En route to recover the Typhoon, Jensen discovered a Purity First terrorist trying to steal it. But the so-called extremist was secretly Augmented and killed himself to avoid interrogation. Hoping to find answers, Jensen confronted Zeke Sanders, the Purity First leader, who swore up and down he didn't know his man was enhanced. Jensen let Sanders escape, determined to focus on the Augmented hacker.

Ghosts and Proxy Soldiers

Inexplicably denied access to the Augmented terrorist's corpse, Sarif sent Jensen to steal the dead man's Neural Hub from the Detroit Police Station Morgue. At the same time, Frank Pritchard, Sarif's Chief of Cyber-security, tried to figure out how the Augmented hacker had bypassed the company's firewall so easily. The hub Jensen steals provides his first clue: it turns out that a very talented hacker had been controlling the terrorist's actions remotely, possibly from somewhere in Detroit.

Moving Shadows

Decrypted data contained in the dead hacker's Neural Hub pointed Jensen to an abandoned factory complex in Highland Park. Flown there by Faridah Malik, Jensen sets out to investigate the area. Little does he suspect what he will find.

Maneuvers in the Dark

Sent to Highland Park to investigate a signal, Jensen discovered more than he bargained for: a secret FEMA facility temporarily occupied by Black-Op mercenaries, the same mercenaries who left him for dead six months ago. Forced into combat with a soldier named Barrett, Jensen proved victorious, emerging from the battle with a corpse on his hands and another possible lead: an apartment complex in China called Hengsha Court Gardens.

Black Market Deals

It appears that Jensen wasn't the only one interested in that Hengsha apartment: Belltower Associates, a private security firm under contract to the Chinese Government, was searching it when he arrived. Denied access to the building, Jensen found his own way in past Belltower security. Here he learned that Arie Van Bruggen, the criminal hacker who lived there, was now running for his life. Who better to help Van Bruggen escape justice than the triads? Confirming this meant a trip to The Hive nightclub, followed by a rendezvous at a capsule hotel known as Alice Garden Pods.

Corporate Warfare

Arie Van Bruggen had no qualms about admitting involvement in the attacks against Sarif Industries, and even gave Jensen the name of the woman that had hired him: Zhao Yun Ru, president of the Tai Yong Medical (TYM) Corporation. It seems that TYM wants to monopolize the Augmentation industry, and hired Black-Op mercenaries to destabilize its competitors. But to prove this, Jensen needs to infiltrate the biotechnology giant and locate recorded evidence that Van Bruggen stashed on the TYM servers.

White Noise

Shocking evidence pulled from the TYM servers revealed a more elaborate plot than expected: Sarif Industries' top research team didn't die six months ago; the attack was staged to cover up their kidnappings! Desperate to learn more, Jensen confronted TYM's president, Zhao, in her Penthouse, but she tricked him and escaped into a panic room. Nevertheless, what little she said before escaping directed Jensen to Picus Communications and the world's most famous newscaster, Eliza Cassan.

Truth and Lies

Eliza Cassan wanted to tell Jensen everything she knew about the kidnappings, but "someone" wouldn't let her. That someone turned out to be Fedorova, another of the Black-Op mercenaries. Jensen killed Fedorova in a tense, yet silent, fight, enabling Eliza to admit some truths. First: she, Eliza Cassan, the world's most famous newscaster, is actually a highly sophisticated Artificial Intelligence program. Second: David Sarif knows more than he's been telling Jensen. And third: Jensen hasn't seen the last of the anti-Augmentation extremists.

Peeling Back the Curtain

Jensen returned to Detroit, intending to confront Sarif and track down Eliza's second lead. But tensions between normal and Augmented humans had reached a flashpoint: riots had erupted in several cities, including Detroit, and the U.N. was being urged to intervene. When confronted by Jensen, Sarif admitted that the scientists were taken by the Illuminati, probably because of the research they had been conducting. After explaining this, Sarif urged Jensen to get his people back, handing him a ticket to a Humanity Front convention hosted by Bill Taggart.

Fallen Soldiers

Determined to locate Sarif's scientists, Jensen confronted Bill Taggart at the convention center and ascertained the location of Taggart's personal assistant, Isaias Sandoval. With this information, Jensen tracked down Sandoval and confronted him. Sandoval admitted to operating on the kidnapped scientists in the hope of disabling their implanted GPL tracking devices, but he refused to implicate his boss, Bill Taggart. Pritchard then traced one of the scientist's GPL signals back to China, thus sending Jensen and Malik scrambling to track down the missing scientist. Unfortunately, the conspirators were still one-step ahead.

Harvesting Hope

Shot down and ambushed by Belltower Associates, Jensen escaped into Lower Hengsha, still hoping to track Sarif's scientists. But the signal he was following ended up in the possession of Tong Si Hung, the leader of the infamous "Harvester" gang. Tong told Jensen that he had scavenged the Augmented arm of Vasili Sevchenko and was now "wearing" it. Tong further elaborated that Vasili was dead, and he had been given the corpse by Belltower for scavenging. Tong then directed Jensen to a seaport used by Belltower for human trafficking. With a bit of luck, and by doing Tong a favor, Jensen might end up where he most wanted to be.

Tripping Point

Several days after slipping aboard a Belltower ship, Jensen arrived at a remote laboratory complex called the "Omega Ranch" in Singapore. Sarif's scientists were there and were being forced to create a unique biochip that could prevent people from using their Augmented abilities. But millionaire Hugh Darrow, the father of Augmentation, owner of The Omega Ranch, and willing participant in the Illuminati plan, had a different use for the biochip in mind. Convinced that Augmentations would be the death of mankind, Darrow used the chip to drive Augmented people insane, thus setting off an event of horrific proportions that only Jensen could end.

Jensen used Darrow's Leo Shuttle to depart the Omega Ranch and reach Panchaea, Darrow's high-tech oceanic project designed to stop global warning. The signal that was driving Augmented people insane was being transmitted from Panchaea, and Jensen had to find a way to shut it off. This led Jensen to the base of the facility and the Hyron Project, the world's most advanced AI computer that used human subjects as processing units. Upon reaching the Hyron Project, Zhao showed up and tried to interface herself with Hyron so that she could control the signal. Unfortunately for Zhao, Hyron would not merge with her biochip, and she was taken over by the project. With no other choice before him, Jensen destroyed the Hyron Project and reached the broadcast room. Once there, Eliza Cassan contacted him and helped him not only to shut off the signal that was driving everyone crazy, but also to get a message of truth out to the people of the world.

ACHIEVEMENT/TROPHY GUIDE

We have taken a unique approach to the Achievement and Trophy guide for Deus Ex. This chapter will give you instructions on how to get 100% of all Trophies or Achievements in a single playthrough, with no need to restart or play the game through a second time just to collect something you may have missed. Of course, should you want to come back and get a Trophy or Achievement after you finish the game, or attempt them in a different order, we will cater for that too by offering detailed explanations on each one where necessary. But by attempting the Trophies/Achievements in a specific order and with our help, you can accomplish the impressive feat of unlocking them all during the normal course of play, and in record time.

//-CH 07 EXTRAS

GAME PROGRESSION

There are certain Trophies/Achievements that you will obtain naturally as you progress through the game. To ensure you get all of these on the first run, make sure you play on the Deus Ex difficulty from the beginning of the game, and don't change the difficulty at any point, as this will stop you from gaining certain Trophies/Achievements.

Achievement/Trophy Details

Name	Xbox 360	PS3	Description
Trooper	50G	Silver	Complete Deus Ex: Human Revolution.
Legend	100G	Gold	Complete Deus Ex: Human Revolution at its hardest setting.
The Bull	15G	Bronze	You defeated Lawrence Barrett, elite member of a secret mercenary hit squad.
The Mantis	15G	Bronze	You defeated Yelena Fedorova, elite member of a secret mercenary hit squad.
The Snake	25G	Bronze	You defeated Jaron Namir, Leader of Belltower's Elite Special Operations Unit.
The End	25G	Bronze	You defeated Zhao Yun Ru and destroyed the Hyron Project.

Trooper

This Trophy/Achievement is unlocked when you finish the game on any difficulty. You can alter the difficulty at any time and still unlock it when the game finishes, although doing so will lock the Legend Trophy/Achievement. So if you are aiming for a 100% Trophy/Achievement run in a single playthough, start on the Give Me Deus Ex difficulty and don't change it.

Legend

To unlock this Trophy/Achievement, you must have started a new game on the Give Me Deus Ex difficulty and never change it during the rest of the game. Completing the game on this difficulty from start to finish will unlock both this and the Trooper Trophy/Achievement. This is a tricky task, especially if you are also attempting to get every other Trophy/Achievement, but thankfully our walkthrough is written for this difficulty, so following it should get you through.

The Bull

This Trophy/Achievement is unlocked after you defeat Lawrence Barrett, the first boss.

The Mantis

This Trophy/Achievement is unlocked after you defeat Yelena Fedorova, the second boss.

The Snake

This Trophy/Achievement is unlocked after you defeat Jaron Namir, the third boss.

The End

This Trophy/Achievement is unlocked after you defeat the Hyron Project, the last boss.

Check out the Opponents Chapter for detailed strategies on how to beat each boss.

COMPLETIONIST

These Trophies/Achievements are optional and are usually unlocked when you go out of your way to complete a particular task. Many of these Trophies/Achievements must be unlocked as and when you encounter them. You can miss them and, once passed, cannot be unlocked unless you start a new game. They are presented in the order in which you can obtain them. Of particular note is the Old School Gamer Trophy/Achievement, which must be obtained in the very first room you start in, before you leave it. Don't miss it!

Achievement/Trophy Details

Name	Xbox 360	PS3	Description
Old School Gamer	10G	Bronze	You found all the hidden story items in Megan's office. Point and Click much?
Balls	5G	Bronze	Seems you like playing with balls, eh?
Good Soul	15G	Bronze	Against all odds, you saved Faridah Malik's life.
Hangar18	10G	Bronze	You found and read the secret message. Now you know too much...
Deus Ex Machina	50G	Silver	Experience all the different endings that Deus Ex: Human Revolution has to offer.
The D Project	15G	Silver	You watched the entire credit list and saw the surprise at the end.
Doctorate	50G	Silver	Read all 29 unique XP books within a single playthrough.
Unforeseen Consequence	15G	Bronze	You convinced Zeke Sanders to let his hostage go.
The Desk Job	15G	Bronze	You convinced Wayne Haas to let you into the morgue.
Yes Boss	15G	Bronze	You had an argument with your boss, David Sarif, and won.
Darker Shades	15G	Bronze	You convinced a fast-talking bartender to let you see Tong Si Hung.
The Throwdown	15G	Bronze	You convinced the smooth-talking politician Bill Taggart to tell the truth in public.
The Last Straw	15G	Bronze	You talked Doctor Isaias Sandoval out of suicide.
The Final Countdown	15G	Bronze	You showed millionaire Hugh Darrow that his logic was flawed.

Old School Gamer

When you first start the game, you will find yourself in Megan's office. Before you speak to her and start the automated sequence that will take you to Sarif's office, there are certain objects of interest in the room that you can interact with by highlighting them with your reticule and pressing the Use button. Doing this with all six items will unlock this Trophy/Achievement. The items are:

E-book reader: The first item is to your left, on the couch [→☐ 1]. Interact with the eBook reader and then move towards Megan's desk.

Newspaper: The first item on the desk is the newspaper on the left of it. [→☐ 2]

Megan's childhood picture: Next is a picture of Megan near the middle of the desk.

Megan's Computer: To the right of the picture is Megan's computer. Interact with it and make sure you open each of the emails.

Gray's Anatomy First Edition: Follow the desk all the way around and on the right side is a rare First Edition of Gray's Anatomy (the book, not the overrated T.V. show). [→☐ 3]

Matchstick box car: The final item is a toy car on a set of drawers to the right of where you found Gray's Anatomy, next to a printer. [→☐ 4]

Once you have interacted with every item, the Trophy/Achievement should unlock.

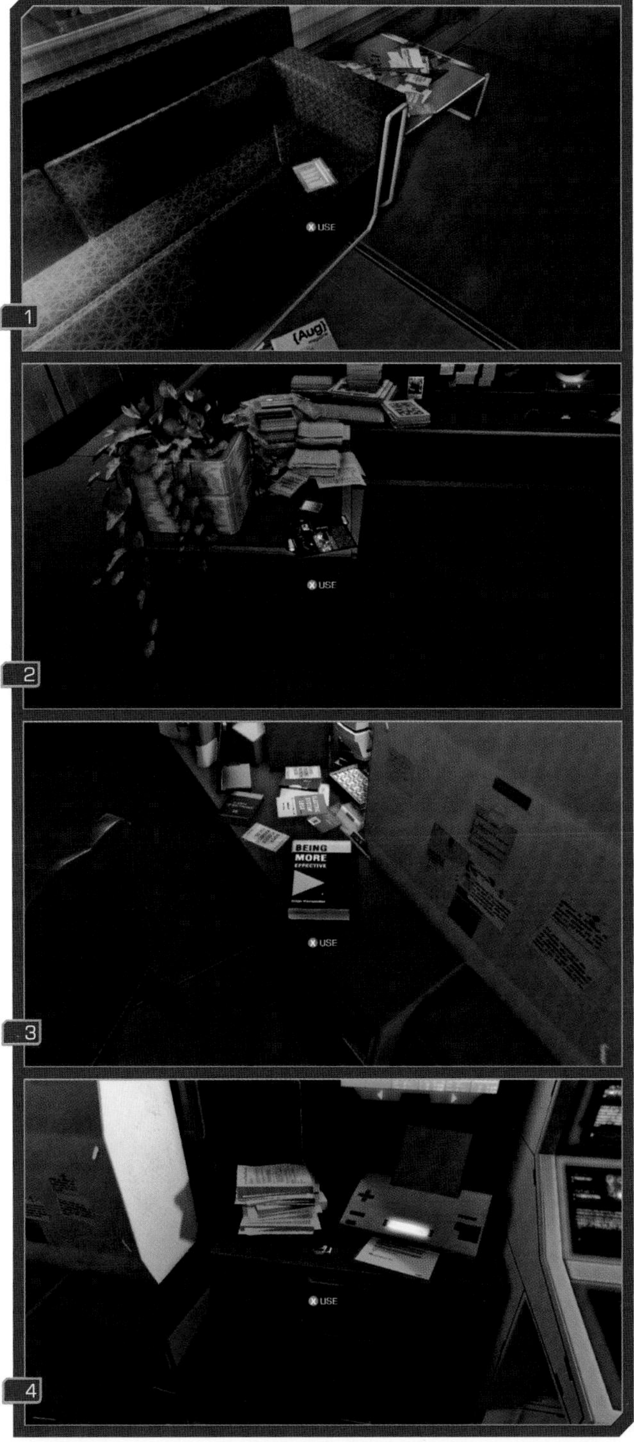

Balls

This fun little Trophy/Achievement is unlocked while you are in Detroit city, and you can get it as soon as you access the streets of the city. The actual basketball court is a little hard to get to. To the right of the LIMB clinic is a gas station, and to the right of that an alleyway that winds around the back. Follow the alleyway to the end, keeping generally to the right. Near the end is a boarded-up area on the right that has a gap in it. Go through this gap to find the basketball court. [→☐ 1].

Pick up the basketball and stand relatively close to the hoop, where the screenshot indicates [→☐ 2]. Look up and throw it almost straight up at the angle in the screenshot [→☐ 3]. If you have done it correctly, the basketball should come down through the hoop, unlocking the Trophy/Achievement. Try to do this before you get the Move/Throw Heavy Objects Augment, as the increased throw range you have will make things more difficult.

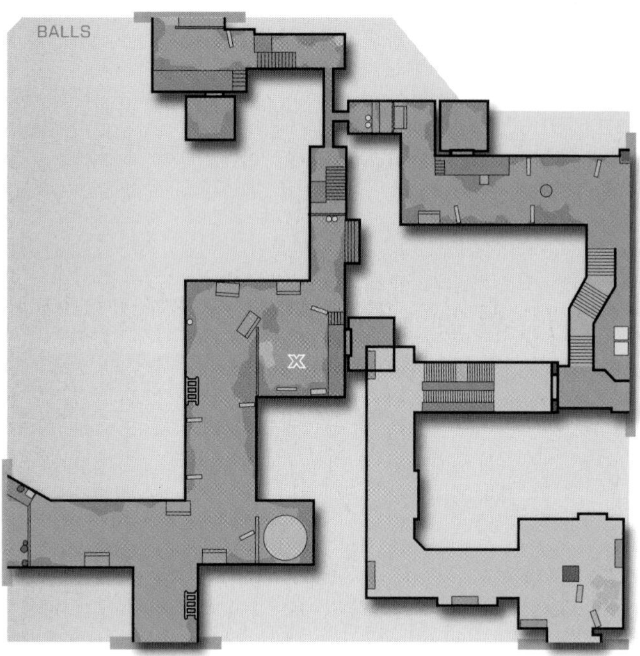

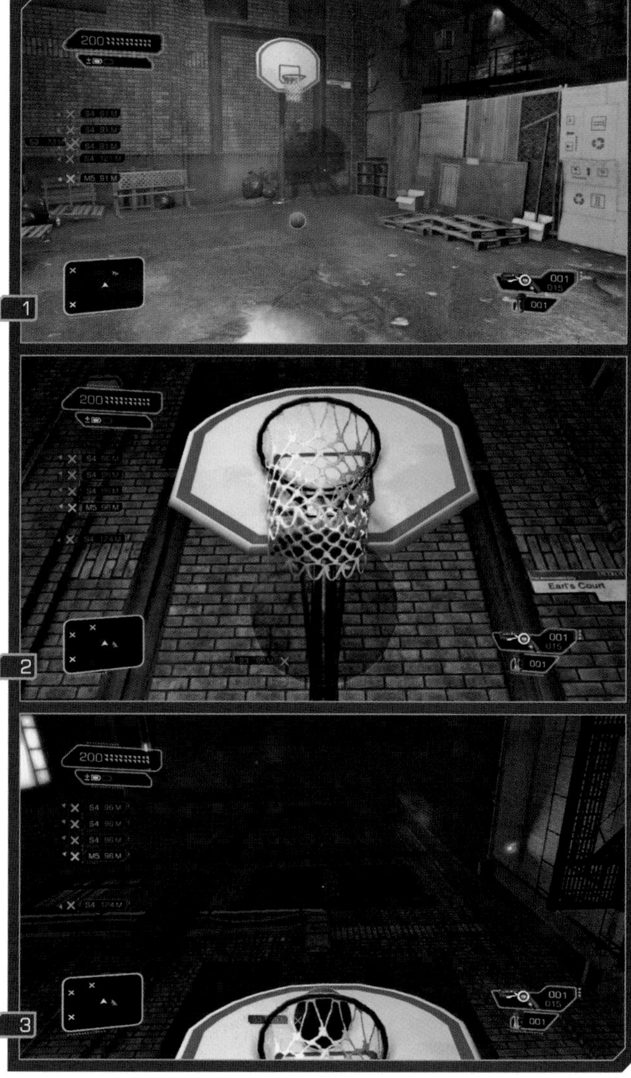

Good Soul

At the beginning of the construction complex area, where Malik's aircraft crashes, you have the option of staying to defend her as she repairs it or of leaving her. If you stay and successfully eliminate all the enemies in the area, you will unlock the Good Soul Trophy/Achievement. Also, if Malik's aircraft takes too much damage from enemy fire, it will explode and you will be unable to get the Trophy/Achievement.

Assuming you are playing this on the hardest difficulty, this can be the toughest Trophy/Achievement to get. Save it immediately, as soon as you have control of your character. Unless you start taking out every enemy very quickly, Malik will die in around 20 seconds.

You will need to be very well equipped to be able to pull this off. At the bare minimum, you should have at least two Frag or Gas Grenades (or a combination of both), and either the Typhoon Augmentation or an EMP Grenade. You should also have a decently powerful mid- to long-range weapon, and a powerful close-range weapon. The Sniper Rifle is a good alternative if you are low on grenades.

As soon as you have control over your character, save the game. To begin, shoot the explosive barrel on your left, near the second level of the building at the end [→☐ 4]. Then, jump down from where you are and run to the right, where you will find a red container with a ramp that you can run onto [→☐ 5]. Get onto it, then jump up to the higher

level. From here, you will see an enemy in front of you amongst the pillars. Take him out. Go to where he was standing, and look at the ground level to your left. You should be able to see an Ogre walking towards Malik. Throw a Frag or Gas Grenade at him, and then look to the back of the lower area [→☐ 6]. There's another Ogre here, so take him out with a grenade too. Proceed further along the top area, where you should encounter two more enemies firing at Malik. Take them out with Takedowns and then go down the stairs at the back of this area.

By this time, a Box Guard will have landed at the lower level. Use your EMP or Typhoon to take it out (the Typhoon will only weaken it, and so you will still have to finish it with other weapons) [→☐ 7]. Now there should only be a few stragglers left around the area. Move quickly and take them out, making sure not to forget the sniper at the very top of one of the buildings. [→☐ 8]

Hangar18

In the Omega Ranch, after you have defeated Namir and spoken to Megan, you are supposed to go to the hangar and press the button on the control panel to open the roof for Malik to fly in and pick up the scientists. After they have boarded the aircraft, the door to the room you are in will open. Go through the door and down the stairs, and go left at the bottom of the staircase [→☐ 9]. You will come to a dead-end that has a security door at the end. To the left of the door is a box in the corner. Move it out of the way. This reveals a secret room, which contains a computer [→☐ 10]. Hack it, and read the email. It contains the lyrics to a song call Hangar 18, by the group Megadeath. The song is well known for its references to conspiracy theories, a fitting Easter egg for a game like Deus Ex.

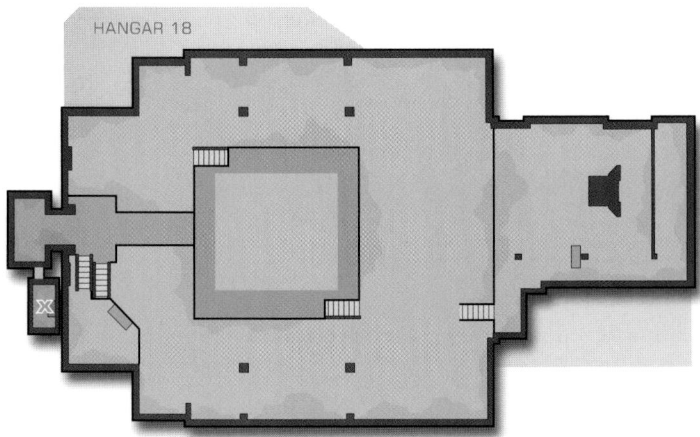

Deus Ex Machina

In the final room of the game, the Broadcast Center in Panchaea, you have a choice that determines which ending you will see. You can broadcast Darrow's message to the world, or you can choose to let the facility self-destruct. However, there are also two other options. If you find and talk to Sarif and Taggart in Panchaea, you will also have the option of broadcasting their messages in the final room, giving you a total of four different endings. Viewing all four will unlock this Trophy/Achievement.

Sarif can be found with other survivors barricaded in the Machine Room. Taggart is locked in the Server Room. Please refer to the Walkthrough Chapter for the exact locations.

Once you have spoken to all of them, have defeated the Hyron Project and are in the final room about to make your choice, simply save the game. Now you can pick each ending in turn by reloading your save file. You don't have to view each ending. As soon as it begins you can skip it, then skip the credits before loading your file again.

The D Project

To unlock this Trophy/Achievement, allow the credits to roll after you have finished the game and viewed the ending. It doesn't matter which ending it is. After the credits have finished rolling, an extra scene will play and, upon viewing it, the Trophy/Achievement will unlock. Don't skip the credits or you won't be able to see the extra scene.

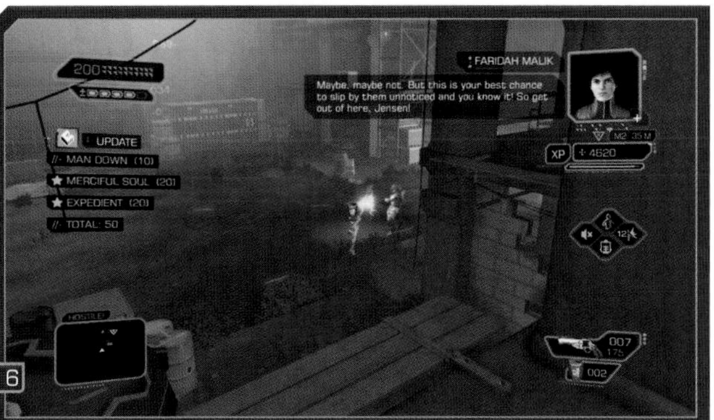

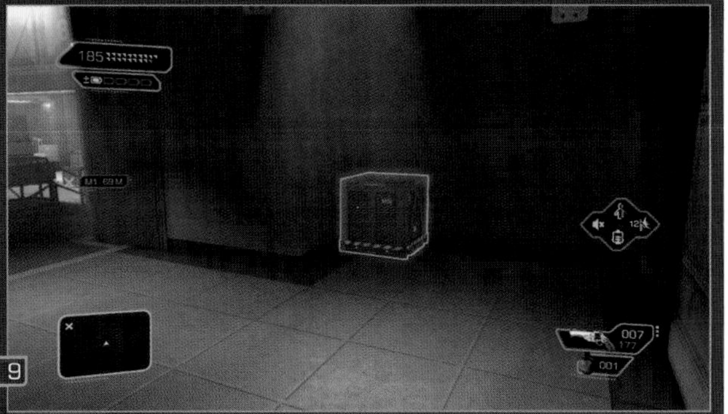

DOCTORATE

Unlock the Doctorate Trophy/Achievement by finding each of Hugh Darrow's eBooks, which are dotted about the game world. The table shows how many books are in each area of the game (if an area isn't listed, that area doesn't have any books). Remember that the exact locations of each eBook are shown on the item maps in the Walkthrough chapter.

Area	Books
Sarif HQ	3
Sarif Manufacturing	2
Detroit (first visit)	6
FEMA Camp	1
Shanghai City	6
Alice Garden Pods	1
Lower Tai Yong Medical	1
Upper Tai Yong Medical	2
Picus	2
Harvester Hideout	1
Detroit (second visit)	3
Omega Ranch	2

Sarif HQ

Book 1: The first book in Sarif HQ is located in Pritchard's office. You can obtain it early on when you have your retinal Augmentation repaired. It is located on the desk next to him. [→□ 1]

Book 2: On the second floor of Sarif HQ, the same floor that Pritchard's office is on, there is another office containing another book. It is in office 25, on a desk. [→□ 2]

Book 3: The final book in Sarif HQ is located in the office next to number 25, in office 27. [→□ 3]

Sarif Manufacturing

Book 1: The first book in Sarif Manufacturing is located in a room at the end of the corridor that houses the automated Turret. The book itself is under a cardboard box in the room. [→□ 4]

Book 2: You will find a desk in the left corner of the room where you encounter Zeke Saunders. The second Darrow book is on this desk. [→□ 5]

Detroit City Hub (First visit)

Book 1: The first book is available in Jensen's apartment room. It is on a dresser next to his bed. The apartment is located on the upper floors of the Chiron Building. [→□ 6]

Book 2: In the Detroit City Police Station, at the back of the morgue, is the coroner's office. On his desk is one of the Darrow books. [→□ 7]

Book 3: In the weapons dealer Seurat's apartment there is a Darrow book on his bed. His apartment is in the northernmost of the quartet of Downtown Apartment buildings, and the building must be accessed via a window. [→□ 8]

Book 4: In the westernmost of the Downtown Apartment buildings, you will find a locked apartment located on the second floor. This makeshift surgery contains a Darrow book on a desk that sits behind a secured door. [→□ 9]

Book 5: This book can be found in Greg Thorpe's apartment, which you will go to anyway during the One Good Turn Deserves Another Side Quest. If you wish to get it at a different time, his apartment is located in the southernmost of the Downtown Apartment buildings. [→□ 10]

Book 6: When you go into Derelict Row to deactivate the signal jammer, be sure to take a short detour and grab another Darrow book. It is located on a barrel deep inside their territory. [→□ 11]

FEMA Camp

Book 1: During your infiltration of the FEMA camp, you will come across the detention block. Just to the south of this area is a locked room; inside is a Darrow book on a desk. [→□ 12]

Shanghai City Hub

Book 1: In The Hive club, there is a book in the office of the bartender, Bobby Bao. It is located on the first floor, behind a few secured doors in the restricted area. [→□ 13]

Book 2: Again, in The Hive, is another Darrow book. This time it is located on the basement floor, in Tong's office. You must win the conversation with him while he is posing as a bartender, otherwise you won't be able to get in. [→□ 14]

Book 3: In order to get into Van Bruggen's apartment during your visit to Hengsha Court Gardens, you should take a short detour to get another book. Just to the left of the main entrance of the building is a locked apartment. Hack it to get inside and obtain the book. [→□ 15]

Book 4: In Youzhao District, in the Downtown Apartments near the south of the map, there is another Darrow book. To get to it, climb up to the rooftop using the ladder you find at street level, then head inside and go down to the second floor. The apartment here houses the book. [→□ 16]

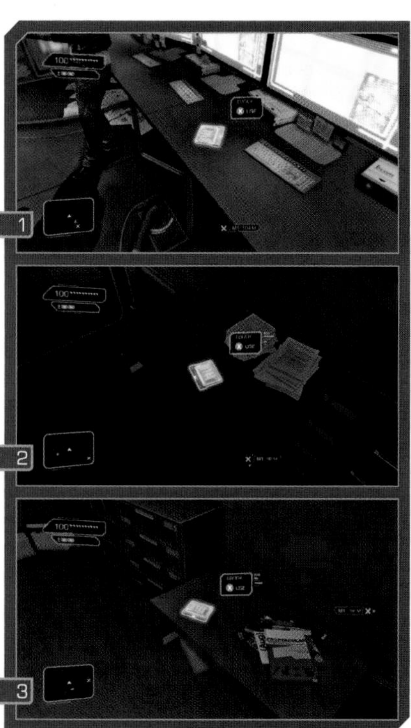
1
2
3

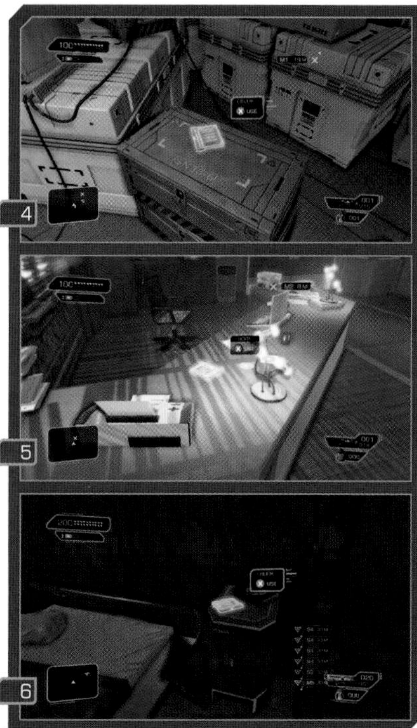
4
5
6

7
8
9

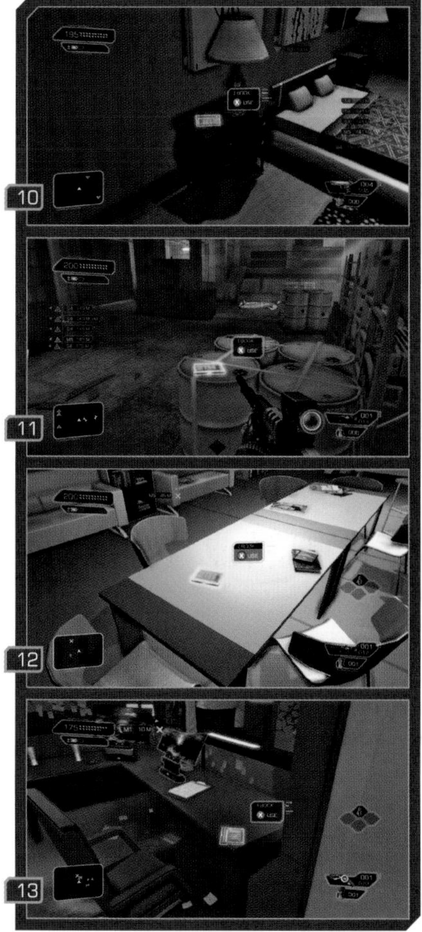
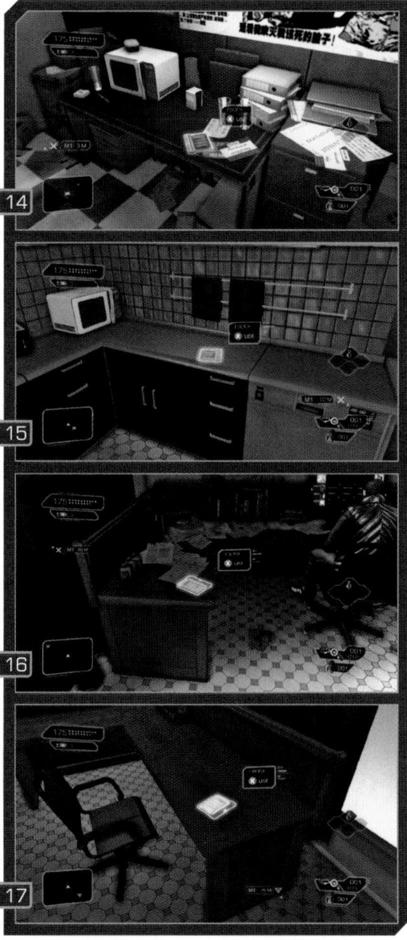
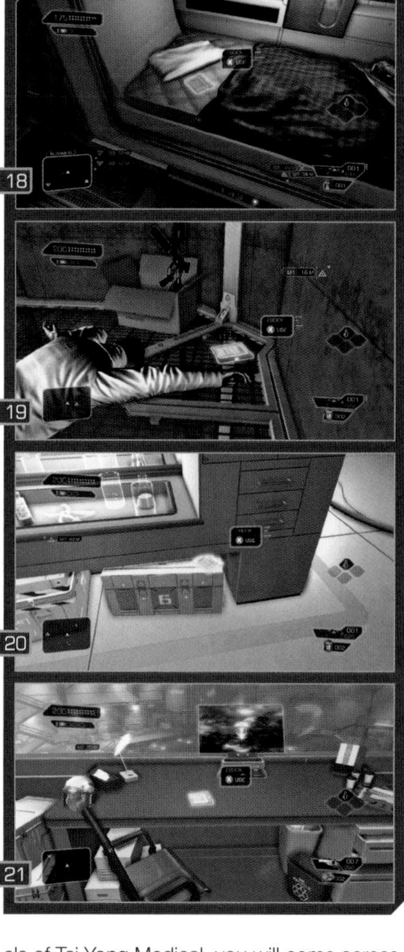

Book 5: While you are on the rooftop of the Downtown Apartments in Youzhao, look into the apartment room to the north on the rooftop. This room contains another book. [→□ 17]

Book 6: The next book is located in the Alice Garden Pods area. On the third floor, in pod number 143, you will find the book inside. This pod is located in the far northeast corner. [→□ 18]

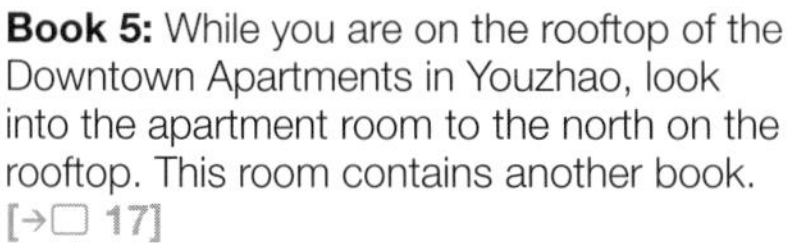

Lower Tai Yong Medical

Book 1: Just before you enter the upper levels of Tai Yong Medical, while you are on the highest level of the Pangu, you can find another book. Before you enter the elevator, look for a vent a little high up on the wall. Stack a few boxes to get to it, follow it and drop down to find a corpse and, next to it, a Darrow book. [→□ 19]

Upper Tai Yong Medical

Book 1: Soon after you reach the upper levels of Tai Yong Medical, you will come across the Lee Geng Memorial Laboratory. In the very centre of this room, on the lower shelf of a cabinet that contains beakers and other laboratory apparatus, rests a Hugh Darrow book. [→□ 20]

Book 2: In the Hangar, before you make your escape from Tai Yong Medical, head to the security room in the far southwest corner of the map. This room has a Darrow book on the desk. [→□ 21]

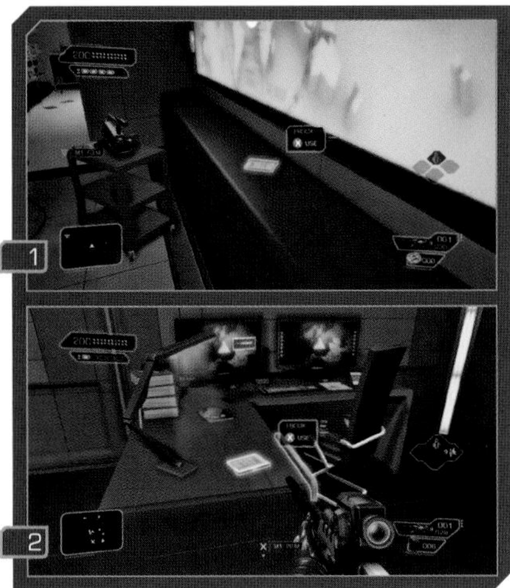

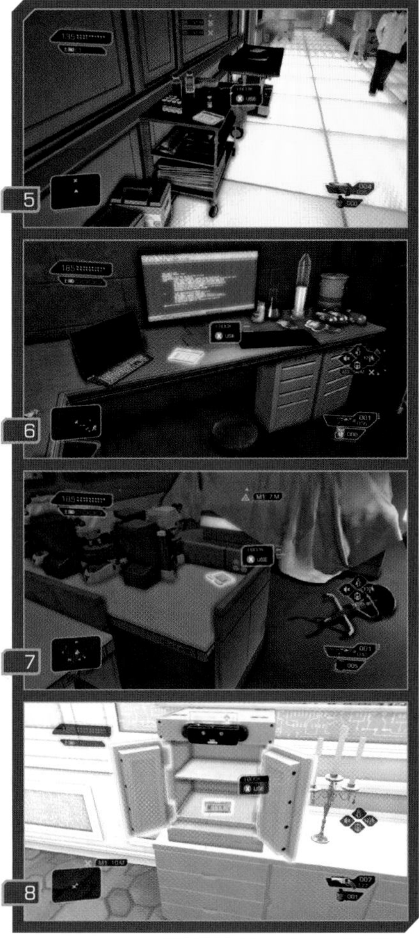

Picus

Book 1: After you escape the ambush by going down the elevator, find the staircase that leads to the fourth floor. On this floor is a locked broadcast room; get into it to find the book on a desk. [→☐ 1]

Book 2: Just before you head down to the basement level to find the source of Eliza Cassan's signal, there is a side room on the floor above it (floor 2). This side room contains another book. [→☐ 2]

Detroit City Hub (Second visit)

Book 1: In the backstage area of the Convention Center there is a room with Security Guards watching a TV screen. In the corner of this room is another book. Be sure to get this before talking to Taggart. [→☐ 3]

Book 2: After following Sandoval's trail down into the sewers and confronting him, investigate his desk closely. You will another book there. [→☐ 4]

Book 3: On your second visit to Detroit you should visit the LIMB clinic again. Check out the back rooms where the Augmentations are performed, and here you will find another book. [→☐ 5]

Harvester Hideout

Book 1: At the lowest level of the Harvester Hideout there is a gruesome autopsy room in the northwest corner of the map. This room holds a Darrow book. [→☐ 6]

Omega Ranch

Book 1: On the second floor of Omega Ranch there is a cold storage room that holds another Darrow book. The room is next to the elevator. [→☐ 7]

Book 2: After defeating Namir and speaking to Megan, stay in her room. Break into the safe on her desk and you will find the final Darrow book. [→☐ 8]

DIALOGUE TROPHIES/ACHIEVEMENTS

You will periodically encounter situations in the game in which you engage in a dialogue minigame with various characters to try to convince them to take a particular course of action. Each one of these 'Conversations' can be won or lost, and winning each one unlocks its corresponding Trophy/Achievement. Only the very first option you select in each conversation has a set win, loss or draw value attached to it. The direction the conversation takes, and the effect of every choice you pick from then on, is random. Every winning, losing or drawing option you select is tallied at the end of the dialogue, and your total score determines whether you win or lose. Using the Social Enhancer Augmentation can help you manipulate the NPC to allow you to win the dialogue more easily. [→☐ 9].

Unforeseen Consequence

This Trophy/Achievement is unlocked when you win the dialogue minigame against Zeke Sanders. The best first option you can pick is Empathize, after which the effectiveness of your answers will be randomized.

The Desk Job

This Trophy/Achievement is unlocked when you win the dialogue minigame against Wayne Haas. The best first option you can pick is Plead, after which the effectiveness of your answers will be randomized.

Yes Boss

This Trophy/Achievement is unlocked when you win the dialogue minigame against David Sarif. The best first option you can pick is Refocus, after which the effectiveness of your answers will be randomized.

Darker Shades
This Trophy/Achievement is unlocked when you win the dialogue minigame against Tong Si Hung. The best first option you can pick is Pinpoint, after which the effectiveness of your answers will be randomized.

The Throwdown
This Trophy/Achievement is unlocked when you win the dialogue minigame against Bill Taggart. The best first option you can pick is Confront, after which the effectiveness of your answers will be randomized.

The Last Straw
This Trophy/Achievement is unlocked when you win the dialogue minigame against Doctor Isaias Sandoval. The best first option you can pick is Tough Love, after which the effectiveness of your answers will be randomized.

The Final Countdown
This Trophy/Achievement is unlocked when you win the dialogue minigame against Hugh Darrow. The best first option you can pick is Extrapolate, after which the effectiveness of your answers will be randomized.

PERSISTENT

These Trophies/Achievements should be unlocked as you play, and you should constantly work towards them during the course of the game. There is no set time for when you must unlock them, so as long as you meet the criteria for each of them before the end of a single playthrough, you should unlock them.

Achievement/Trophy Details

Name	Xbox 360	PS3	Description
First Hack	5G	Bronze	Perform your first Hack successfully.
Hax0r1!	15G	Bronze	Successfully hack 50 devices within the same playthrough.
Up the Ante!	15G	Bronze	Upgrade your first weapon of choice.
Gun Nut	20G	Bronze	Fully upgrade one of your weapons.
Transhumanist	5G	Bronze	Fully upgrade your first Augmentation of choice.
First Takedown	5G	Bronze	Perform your first Takedown. Civilians don't count, so be nice.
Opportunist	15G	Bronze	Perform 50 Takedowns within the same playthrough. (Civilians don't count.)
Consciousness is Overrated	15G	Bronze	Knock out at least 100 enemies in a single playthrough.
Pacifist	100G	Gold	Complete Deus Ex: Human Revolution without anyone dying by your hand. (Boss fights don't count.)
Ghost	15G	Bronze	You made it through an entire hostile area without so much as a squeak.
Foxiest of the Hounds	100G	Gold	Complete Deus Ex: Human Revolution without setting off any alarms.

First Hack
This is as simple as it sounds, and simply requires that you win a hacking minigame. The hack must be successful, and it can be done on any device that is hackable. [→☐ 10]

Hax0r!
You are likely to unlock this Trophy/Achievement during the course of a normal playthrough, and probably won't have to take any special measures to ensure you unlock it. It is imperative that you get some of the Hacking Augmentations, particularly the different levels of the Hacking Capture Augmentations. As you progress further into the game and higher level security is more common, you will need these to perform hacks. The Hacking Stealth Augmentation is also very useful as it will help increase your chances of a successful hack, which are the only ones that count towards your total. Also, try to avoid relying too much on finding codes in Pocket Secretaries to get access to electronic devices, and instead try to ensure that you hack a device whenever possible.

Up the Ante!
You will inevitably unlock this Trophy/Achievement when you go for the Gun Nut Trophy/Achievement. The first time you attach any regular or unique upgrade to any gun, this will unlock. The Silencer and Laser Sight attachments do not count, so don't bother with those. [→☐ 11]

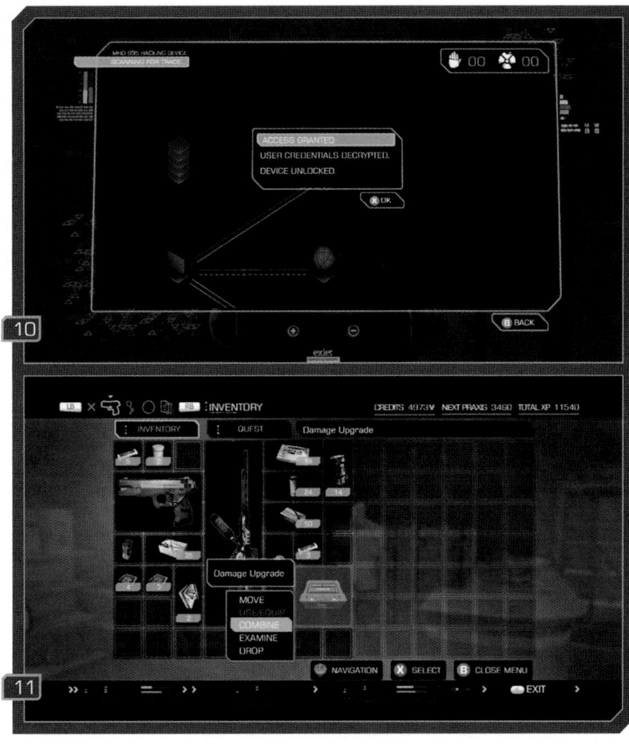

10
11

Gun Nut
To get this Trophy/Achievement, you will have to upgrade a weapon to its maximum level via regular upgrades, and the weapon's unique upgrade, if it has one. You do not need to add any attachments like the Silencer or Laser Sight.

There are two good ways of approaching this Trophy/Achievement. If your sole intention is to unlock it as fast as possible, you are best off upgrading the weapon that has the lowest maximum upgrade levels.

For example, the Rocket Launcher only requires four Reload Speed Upgrades and the unique upgrades before it is fully upgraded. Other easy weapons to upgrade are the Pre-Order weapons, the Crossbow and the Tranquilizer Rifle.

You should also consider simply using the upgrades on a weapon that you use often and is actually useful. If you are attempting to get every Trophy/Achievement in a single run, you will have to be careful where you spend your upgrades. Concentrate on your most used weapon first, fully upgrading it before moving onto other weapons. A good candidate for this is the Revolver, as you will get it early and it is very useful when fully upgraded.

Transhumanist

You should take a similar approach with this Trophy/Achievement to your approach with the Gun Nut Trophy/Achievement. Try to go for an Augmentation tree that is actually useful, one that you will be using often in the course of the game. Good candidates for this are the Hacking Capture and Hacking Stealth trees, as they will also help in the hacking-related Trophy/Achievements [→☐ 1]. Also, purchasing an Augmentation that only has one upgrade option, such as the Social Enhancer, does not count as an Augmentation tree and will not unlock the Trophy/Achievement. It must have at least two levels of Augmentation.

First Takedown

This will be unlocked after you perform your first Takedown on an enemy opponent, whether lethal or non-lethal. Only Takedowns performed on enemy combatants count, so no civilians. Remember to go for a non-lethal Takedown if you are also going for the Pacifist Trophy/Achievement. [→☐ 2]

Opportunist

This Trophy/Achievement will be unlocked when you have performed 50 Takedowns in the same playthrough. A Multiple Takedown still only counts as one, so try not to use this too much, no matter how cool it is.

There are a couple of ways to land Takedowns. Separating enemies from the rest of their squad is important in order for you to land a Takedown, so try to use thrown items, or opening a door in view of the enemy as a means of luring him into position. You can also use the sounds of a Crossbow bolt or Tranq dart hitting a surface as a way to lure enemies in. [→☐ 3]

The stealth-related Augmentations, particularly the Cloaking System, are vital in order for you to get close to the enemy unseen. If possible get the silent movement Augmentations as well. The Hyper Oxygenation Augmentations are good in conjunction with Silent Sprinting, allowing you to close the distance extremely quickly when performing a silent Takedown. [→☐ 4]

Consciousness is Overrated

The Opportunist Trophy/Achievement will contribute directly to this one, assuming you use only non-lethal Takedowns on your enemies. This is a broader Trophy/Achievement, however, and allows you to use other means to render your opponents unconscious.

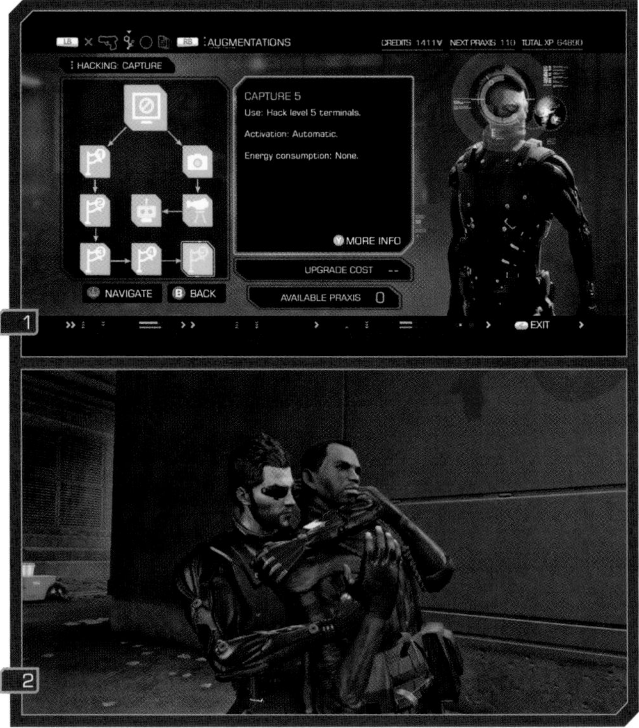

In addition to the aforementioned non-lethal Takedowns, you can also use the Stun Gun or Tranquilizer Rifle to render opponents unconscious [→☐ 5]. These will be your main means of accomplishing this Trophy/Achievement, and will be your most used weapons anyway when you are going for the Pacifist and Ghost Trophy/Achievements. You can also throw light objects, such as small ones, to render your foes unconscious. You'll have to be careful with this, however, as an object that's too heavy could kill them, ruining your chance of the Pacifist Trophy/Achievement.

Pacifist

This can be a very difficult Trophy/Achievement to win in certain parts of the game. The Trophy/Achievement will be unlocked if you complete the game from start to finish while registering zero kills. There are a couple of exceptions to this. You are allowed to kill Bosses, and any robotic enemies, such as Box Guards and Medium Sentries, can be destroyed without any negative repercussions. No NPCs, including any humanoid enemies and civilians, can be killed. [→☐ 6]

Much like the Consciousness is Overrated Trophy/Achievement, you will find yourself relying heavily on non-lethal weaponry, such as the Tranquilizer Rifle, Stun Gun, Peps and Gas Grenades. Gas Grenades especially will become your best friend, as they are very quiet, very fast-acting and have an effect over a huge area, helping to keep you stealthy and non-lethal [→☐ 7]. You should purchase as many of

these as possible from merchants whenever you can. Non-lethal Takedowns also work well. Your best ally in getting this Trophy/Achievement will be stealth. Avoiding confrontation is the best way to go, and while you will need to interact with enemies as a bare minimum to obtain the Takedown related Trophy/Achievements, you should try to do this only when it is a manageable situation, such a solitary guard or a patrolling guard who has strayed from the rest of the group [→□ 8]. Also, don't hack Turrets or Medium Sentries so that they attack other enemies. This will register as a kill. Make sure you don't knock enemies off large buildings either, as the fall will register as a kill for you.

Ghost

To get this Trophy/Achievement, you have to get the Ghost experience bonus. For this, you have to complete an objective without being seen by any enemy. Not every objective will grant you this bonus, but the ones that do will be listed in the table. The easiest way is by completing the first objective that lets you get the Ghost bonus, 'Enter the Manufacturing Plant'. [→□ 9]

Foxiest of the Hounds

The Foxiest of the Hounds Trophy/Achievement is awarded for getting the Smooth Operator experience bonus for every objective in the game, where it is possible to get it. The Smooth Operator bonus is granted for completing an objective without an alarm being activated during it. This differs significantly from the Ghost bonus, as even if you get spotted or an enemy is in the Alarmed state, you won't be in danger of losing the bonus, unless an alarm is actually activated. As long as you can stop the enemy from doing so, you can still keep the bonus intact. Being spotted by a camera or walking through a laser field will also activate an alarm, costing you the bonus. The alarm being scripted or triggered automatically by the game will not affect your Smooth Operator bonus. The table shows all the objectives where you will have to avoid setting off an alarm.

Area	Objective	Ghost	Foxiest of the Hounds
Manufacturing Plant	Enter the Manufacturing Plant	✓	
	Confront Zeke Sanders		
Detroit 1	Retrieve the Dead Terrorist's Neural Hub	✓	✓
	Locate and Shut Down the Antenna in Derelict Row		
FEMA Camp	Infiltrate the Mercenary Compound	✓	✓
	Locate the Mercenary Leader		
Hengsha 1	Investigate the Penthouse Apartment	✓	✓
	Find and Speak with Tong Si Hung		
	Escape the Alice Garden Pods Ambush		
Tai Yong Medical	Enter TYM's Tower by Passing through the Pangu	✓	✓
	Find and View Van Bruggen's Recording		
	Confront Zhao in the Penthouse		
	Escape and get to the Hangar		
	Open the Hangar Bay Doors		
Picus	Escape the Ambush by Reaching a Lower Floor	✓	✓
	Get to Funicular		
	Summon the Funicular		
	Get Inside Room 802-11		
Detroit 2	Go to the Convention Center and Obtain Sandoval's Location from Taggart	✓	✓
	Find and Confront Sandoval		
Hengsha 2	Escape the Construction Site	✓	✓
	Find Vasili Sevchenko's GPL Device		
	Rescue Tong's Son		
	Meet Tong in the Harvester Hideout		
Seaport	Retrieve Tong's Package from the Shed	✓	✓
	Place the C4 on Administrator Wang's Desk		
Omega Ranch	Disable the Signal Jammer	✓	✓
	Search for Signs of Megan's Team		
	Find and Speak with Nia Colvin		
	Find and Speak with Eric Koss		
	Find and Speak with Declan Faherty		
	Upload a Virus to the Security Computer and Enter the Restricted Area		
	Use the Leo Shuttle to Reach Panchaea		
Panchaea	Get Inside the Tower and Disengage the Lockdown	✓	✓
	Reach the Broadcast Center		

SIDE-QUESTS

These Trophies/Achievements are unlocked by completing certain special Side Quests. Some of them are also unlocked by fulfilling certain special conditions within the Quest. Remember that other persistent Trophies/Achievements such as the Ghost and Takedown related Trophies/Achievements are still at risk when completing these Side Quests, so be sure to save before attempting each one. The rewards in the tables indicate what you can get if you complete every objective available in the Side Quest, including secondary ones. Remember to refer to the Side Quests Chapter for more details on each Side Quest.

Achievement/Trophy Details

Name	Xbox 360	PS3	Description
Lesser Evil	10G	Bronze	Deal with Mr. Carella's indiscretion.
Motherly Ties	10G	Bronze	Put a grieving mother's doubts to rest.
Sentimental Value	10G	Bronze	You kept Megan's bracelet for yourself. Apparently, letting go really is the hardest part.
Cloak & Daggers	10G	Bronze	Deal with the man in the shadows.
The Take	10G	Bronze	Greedy bastard. You accepted O'Malley's blood money and let him go.
Smash the State	10G	Bronze	Help Officer Nicholas take out the trash.
Lucky Guess	10G	Bronze	Next time, Jacob better use a more complex code to arm his bombs.
Acquaintances Forgotten	10G	Bronze	Follow Pritchard's lead to uncover the truth.
Kevorkian Complex	10G	Bronze	You granted a dying man his final request.
Rotten Business	10G	Bronze	Help a lady in the oldest of professions clean house.
The Fall	10G	Bronze	You sent Diamond Chan on the trip of a lifetime.
Bar Tab	10G	Bronze	Help the Hive Bartender settle a tab.
Guardian Angel	10G	Bronze	You paid poor Jaya's debt in full. How very... humane... of you.
Shanghai Justice	10G	Bronze	It may take some sleuthing, but justice must be served.
Super Sleuth	10G	Bronze	You really nailed your case against Lee Hong.
Corporate Warfare	10G	Bronze	Protect a client's interests by performing a less-than-hostile takeover.
Ladies Man	10G	Bronze	You convinced Mengyao to spill the beans on the mysterious Hyron Project.
Talion A.D.	10G	Bronze	Descend into the bowels of an urban jungle and confront a warrior-priest.

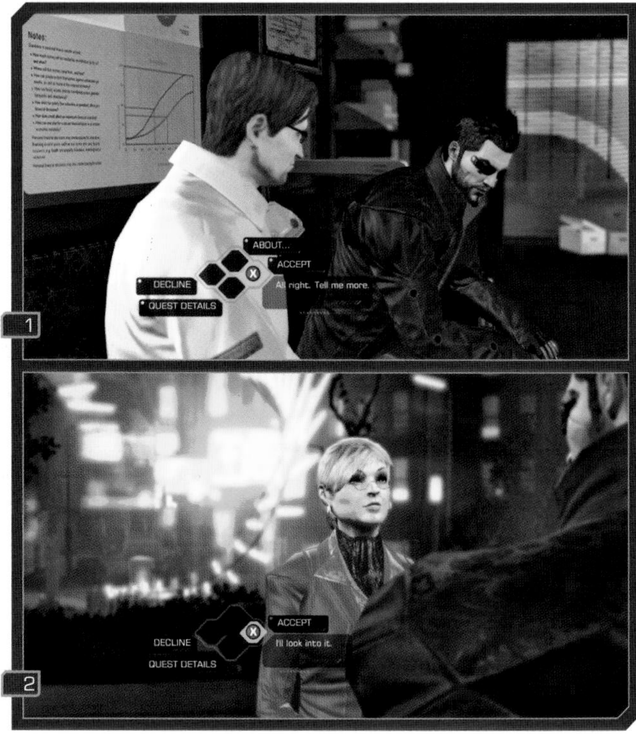

LESSER EVIL

Quest Details

Reward Type	Received
XP	3450
Credits	None
Items	Laser Targeting Mod

This Side Quest is the first one you can do, and becomes available after you return from Sarif Manufacturing. To accept it, you must go to your office after you hear the announcement over the PA system and then speak to Tim Carella [→☐ 1]. It concerns the recent Neuropozyne thefts happening at Sarif. Carella is being blackmailed by his partner Tindall, and wants you to retrieve the incriminating evidence Tindall has on him. Upon completing the Quest, you will unlock the Trophy/Achievement.

MOTHERLY TIES

Quest Details

Reward Type	Received
XP	3200
Credits	None
Items	None

After exiting Sarif HQ, Megan Reed's mother will approach you, giving you the option to accept the Side Quest [→☐ 2]. Mrs Reed wants you to investigate the suspicious circumstances of her daughter's death more thoroughly. The Sentimental Value Trophy/Achievement is also linked to this Side Quest.

Sentimental Value

During your investigation of the storage unit behind the Police Station, you will come across a safe. Hacking it will give you access to several items, one of which is a bracelet. Upon completing the quest and talking to Mrs Reed, you will be given the option of returning the bracelet. Keeping it will allow you to unlock this Trophy/Achievement.

CLOAK & DAGGERS

Quest Details

Reward Type	Received
XP	5650
Credits	4500
Items	Ammo Capacity Upgrade, Bottle of Great Wall Red Chardonnay Wine

Upon exiting the Police Station for the first time you will be contacted by Pritchard, who tells you that an ex-colleague of yours wishes to meet you on Grand River Road [→☐ 3]. Speaking to Jenny Alexander will give you the option of starting the Quest. The crux of this long quest is that you must gather evidence to bring down corrupt cop, Jack O'Malley. When finishing the Quest and speaking to Jenny for the final time, she will give you the option of confronting O'Malley to make the arrest yourself. Make sure to pick this option to get the second Trophy/Achievement that is tied to this one.

The Take

This Trophy/Achievement is directly linked to the conclusion of the Cloak and Daggers Side Quest. Upon choosing to arrest O'Malley yourself, head to his apartment to confront him. He will offer you a bribe if you allow him to escape. Accept this deal to unlock this Trophy/Achievement.

SMASH THE STATE

Quest Details

Reward Type	Received
XP	2800
Credits	1000
Items	Silencer

When you leave the Detroit Convention Centre after finding out Sandoval's location during the second Detroit section, you will be approached by a former colleague. This Quest requires you to investigate a potential bomb threat by searching various locations. This Quest also gives you access to the Lucky Guess Trophy/Achievement.

Lucky Guess

When you find the bomb, you can disarm it by entering a code. Believe it or not, the code for disarming it and foiling Jacob's master plan is 0000. That's right. [→☐ 4]

ACQUAINTANCES FORGOTTEN

Quest Details

Reward Type	Received
XP	5650
Credits	4500
Items	None

There are a few prerequisites for gaining access to this Side Quest. To begin with, when you return from the FEMA camp, Pritchard will ask to speak to you about Sarif. See him before talking to Sarif [→☐ 5]. Afterwards, speak to Sarif, and you will engage in a dialogue minigame with him. You must win this, so save the game before you attempt it. Once you do, Sarif will send you some emails. Go to your office and read them, and then Pritchard will come to speak to you as you go to leave your office.

Later, when you go to the Convention Centre to confront Taggart, Pritchard will contact you regarding the emails. He will give you a lead, namely to go and speak to Brent Radford [→☐ 6]. This signifies the beginning of the Side Quest.

Kevorkian Complex

This Trophy/Achievement is related to the "Acquaintances Forgotten" Side Quest. During your final conversation with Brent Radford, he will ask you to give him a final, lethal dose of morphine. Oblige him, and you will unlock the Kevorkian Complex Trophy/Achievement.

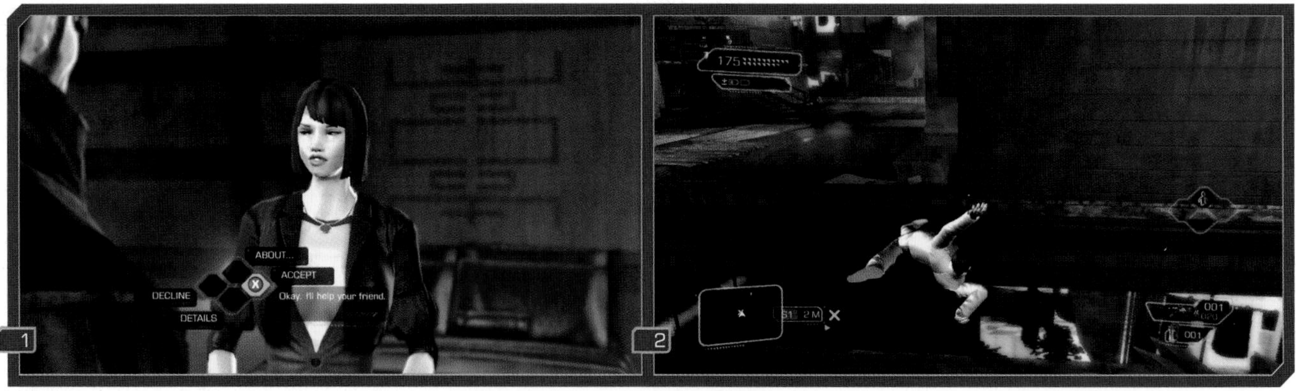

ROTTEN BUSINESS

Quest Details

Reward Type	Received
XP	5000
Credits	3000
Items	None

To access this Side Quest, you must find Mei Suen. She can be found in Hengsha, close to where you initially land. You will find a rooftop access door near here for the Hung Hua Hotel, go into it [→☐ 1]. Take the stairs to the fourth floor and enter the first room you come to to find her. Mei Suen wants you to find a kidnapped girl, who is to be Augmented against her will. The Trophy/Achievement The Fall is also tied into this Side Quest.

The Fall

This is a slightly complex secondary Trophy/Achievement to unlock. After finding Diamond Chan, save your game. Unlocking this Trophy/Achievement requires you to kill Diamond Chan, which will lock out the Pacifist Trophy/Achievement. Then, knock him out with a non-lethal Takedown (make sure you don't use any weapons fire). Once knocked out, drag his body over to the edge of the rooftop and throw it off, making it look like a suicide [→☐ 2]. This will unlock the Trophy/Achievement. Once it is unlocked, you can reload your save game, knock out Diamond Chan again and then plant the drugs on him to complete the Side Quest in a non-lethal fashion.

BAR TAB

Quest Details

Reward Type	Received
XP	3850
Credits	None
Items	Praxis Kit x 2

To gain access to this Side Quest you will need to speak to the bartender in the Hive Bar, Bobby Bao, after you have spoken to the manager [→☐ 3]. Bobby Bao wants you to track down and collect a debt for him. The Guardian Angel Trophy/Achievement is connected to this one.

Guardian Angel

Should you choose to pay off Jaya's debt yourself, you will unlock this Trophy/Achievement. This will cost you the steep sum of 5000 Credits however, so make sure you are adequately wealthy beforehand.

SHANGHAI JUSTICE

Quest Details

Reward Type	Received
XP	3900
Credits	None
Items	Praxis Kit

When you first head to the Alice Garden Pods to speak to the hacker Van Bruggen, you will be approached by Faridah Malik. She wants you to investigate the suspicious death of her friend. The Super Sleuth Trophy/Achievement is also linked to this one.

Super Sleuth

To unlock this secondary Trophy/Achievement, you must use every piece of evidence you can to outmaneuver Lee Hong in your conversation with him. To do so, you will need to know the facts behind the autopsy report, and to have found the four pieces of evidence in Lee's apartment [→☐ 4]. The evidence you need is: the answering machine message, the emails on Lee's computer, the antique clock on the dresser, and the baseball bat leaning against the wall. Once you have gathered all this evidence, you can begin the dialogue minigame with Lee. See the Side Quests Chapter for exact details on how win the conversation with Lee and unlock this Trophy/Achievement.

CORPORATE WARFARE

Quest Details

Reward Type	Received
XP	2050
Credits	1000
Items	None

On your second visit to Hengsha, when you are Sevchenko's GPL device, you will be contacted by Hugh Darrow. He will ask you to meet his assistant, Mengyao on a nearby rooftop. Darrow wants you to go in and retrieve some sensitive material regarding Panchaea that has been stolen by terrorists. The Trophy/Achievement Ladies Man is tied in to this one.

Ladies' Man

To unlock this Trophy/Achievement, you must have the Social Enhancer Augmentation, it is impossible to get it any other way. When you are about to complete the Quest and hand over the chip, you can enquire as to the contents of said chip. Mengyao will not be forthcoming with this information however, unless you use the Social Enhancer. Charm her with Beta Pheromones and she will spill the beans, and in the process you will unlock this Trophy/Achievement.

TALION A.D.

Quest Details

Reward Type	Received
XP	2450
Credits	None
Items	Praxis Kit

After exiting the Construction Site, you will be contacted by Pritchard regarding the faulty biochips. From then on, you can accept this Side Quest at any time by going to speak to Doctor Wing in the LIMB Clinic. The good Doctor is hoping you can find and reason with Michael Zelazny, a rogue Augmented soldier. Regardless of how you choose to deal with Zelazny, once you speak with the Doctor again and claim your reward this Trophy/Achievement will be unlocked.

TID-BITS

This section will detail many of the small references and Easter eggs that Deus Ex: Human Revolution is packed with.

An Anatomy Lesson

In several areas of the game, you'll see a picture of a few men crowding around a table with a corpse on it. That particular painting is a nod to Rembrandt's oil painting entitled "The Anatomy Lesson of Dr. Nicolaes Tulp", which was painted in 1632. One place to find and view this picture is in David Sarif's office. [→☐ 5]

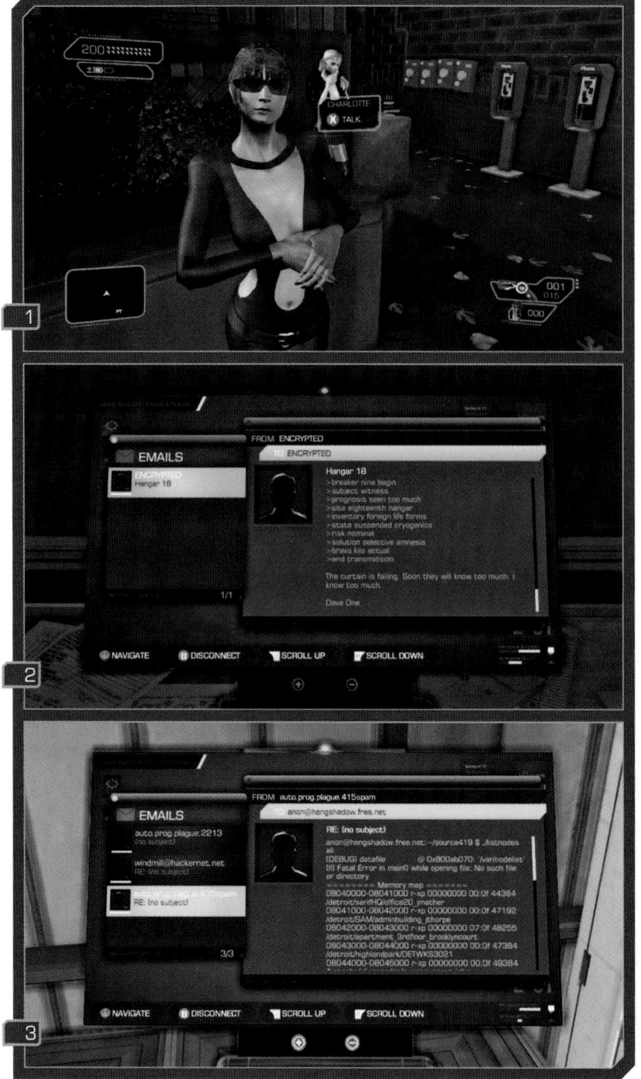

Daedalus and Icarus

There several nods and references to the Greek Myth of Daedalus and his son Icarus. In the Greek Myth, Daedalus, a skillful craftsman and artisan, made a set of wings for himself out of bird feathers that he gathered. When he saw that they worked, he fashioned a pair for his son. The feathers were held to the wing construct by string and wax. When Daedalus and his son took flight, Daedalus warned Icarus not to fly too high or else the heat of the sun would melt the wax. Icarus ignored his father's warning however, flew too high during the flight and the sun melted the wax. His wings came apart and Icarus fell into the ocean below and drowned.

In the original trailer for Deus Ex: Human Revolution, Adam Jensen is portrayed as Icarus with wings for arms and he flies too high causing the wings to burst into flames. This is Jensen's nightmare about the actual tragedy that befell him in Sarif Industries' labs that lead to his Augmentations.

In several places throughout the game, you'll see a picture that is a reference to Peter Paul Ruben's Painting "The Fall of Icarus" which was painted in 1636.

The Icarus Landing System Augmentation which allows you to fall safely from any height is obviously named after the Icarus Myth.

Tai Yong Medical's name means "Sun". David Sarif's last name (and thus, the name of his company, Sarif Industries) was chosen because of its similarity to Seraphim, or angels. Both symbols are references to the Icarus Myth.

Heavy Metal Working Girl

This one is a reference to the Heavy Metal band Iron Maiden.

There are plenty of "Working Girls" in Detroit, but only one is actually named. You'll find her in the same area that Jenny Alexander is located in, when you unlock the Cloak and Daggers Side Quest in Detroit. That particular Working Girl is named "Charlotte" which is a reference to an Iron Maiden song called "Charlotte the Harlot". This song tells the story of a prostitute and appears on Iron Maiden's self-titled debut album which was released on April 14, 1980. [→☐ 1]

In fact, Charlotte was something of a fixation with Iron Maiden, and she was referenced in three other songs which where "22 Acacia Avenue" from the album "The Number of the Beast", "Hooks in You" from the album "No Prayer for the Dying", and "From Here to Eternity" from the album "Fear of the Dark". It could be interpreted that Charlotte died in the last song " From Here to Eternity" thus ending her saga.

Heavy Metal Aliens

This one is a reference to the Heavy Metal band Megadeth.

In the Omega Ranch, at the end in Darrow's Shuttle Hangar where the LEO Shuttle is located, you can find a hidden PC. If you hack it and read the email, you'll unlock the Hangar 18 Achievement/Trophy. This Achievement/Trophy and the email on the secret PC both refer to Megadeth's song called "Hangar 18" on the "Rust in Peace" album. [→☐ 2]

Note that the Username of the secret PC is MSTAINE and the person that signed the email is named Dave. The lead singer of Megadeth is named David Mustaine.

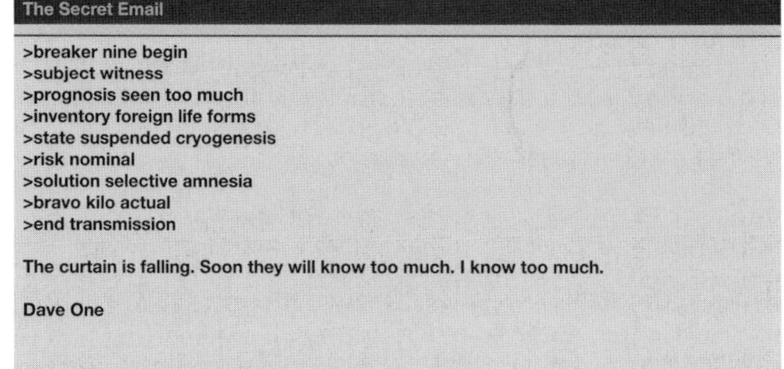

The Secret Email

>breaker nine begin
>subject witness
>prognosis seen too much
>inventory foreign life forms
>state suspended cryogenesis
>risk nominal
>solution selective amnesia
>bravo kilo actual
>end transmission

The curtain is falling. Soon they will know too much. I know too much.

Dave One

A Hacker's Paradise

If you go to Kuigan, Level 1, to the eastern end by the Metro Station, you'll find a locked storage unit that you can hack. Inside is a safe with a Revolver and some ammo. The combination to that safe can be found in a Pocket Secretary in the storage unit located underneath one of the large crates.

What's more interesting about this unit is that it is owned and used by an anonymous hacker, who apparently knows Van Bruggen. If you hack the PC in that storage unit, you'll find three emails. The first is a transcript of the dialogue for the opening scene of the game. The next is a brief email from Windmill (Van Bruggen) talking of his frustration with Nucl3arsnake (Pritchard). The last email looks like gibberish at first, but there is meaning in the madness.

That last email shows the location of every PC in the game that has the Nigerian Scam Email on it. The Nigerian Scam Email has been around for decades, and seems to still be going strong in the year 2027. The location of each PC that has a copy the scam email is divulged as follows. The locations are listed in Unix style directory format, and should be fairly obvious where they are. [→☐ 3]

Nigerian Scam Email Locations
/detroit/sarifHQ/office20_jmather
/detroit/SAM/adminbuilding_jthorpe
/detroit/apartment_3rdfloor_brooklyncourt
/detroit/highlandpark/DETWKS3021
/hengsha/alicegarden/guestsupport_jchou
/hengsha/TYM/archiveroom_fujiayi
/montreal/PicusWeb/jen_peacock
/detroit/conventioncenter_taggart
/hengsha/HarvHO/ZhengLiang
/singapore/GenLab/ccantrella

When you read the Nigerian Scam emails, note the address they come from which is "419@scowlingmask.ni". The 419 is a known designation for the Nigerian Scam and refers to the article of the Nigerian Criminal Code dealing with fraud; specifically, part of Chapter 38: "Obtaining Property by false pretences; Cheating".

Three Seashells

When you are investigating Van Bruggen's Penthouse, take a little time to go into his bathroom. In particular, look near the toilet. You'll find that there is no toilet paper, but instead his lavatories are equipped with Three Seashells. This is a nod to the science fiction movie Demolition Man. That movie was set in the year 2032, and according to the film, they no longer used toilet paper and instead used the Three Seashells. While that film never explained how those seashells worked, it appears Van Bruggen has figured it out! [→☐ 4]

Radford Is Loaded

In the "Acquaintances Forgotten" Side Quest where you deal with Brent Radford, you'll find three different references. First, Radford asks for morphine, and as Adam leaves to go find it, he says "I'll be back" thus referencing the movie The Terminator.

Next, when talking to Radford, he'll ask Adam for an overdose of morphine at the end to kill him. If you refuse to overdose Radford, he mentions "Asimov" and refers to the Law's of Robotics. This is a reference to science fiction author Isaac Asimov, and his collection of short stories which were published as a novel called "I, Robot" which was published in 1950. In particular, the short story "Runaround" which is the first appearance and clear definition of Asimov's "Three Laws of Robotics". [→☐ 5]

Asimov's Three Laws of Robotics
A robot may not injure a human being or, through inaction, allow a human being to come to harm.
A robot must obey any orders given to it by human beings, except where such orders would conflict with the First Law.
A robot must protect its own existence as long as such protection does not conflict with the First or Second Law.

Finally, when you go to investigate Radford's storage unit, you'll have to deal with four hostiles called "Men In Black Suits". If you incapacitate the leader and then search his body, you'll find a Pocket Secretary with the travel itinerary of a "Mr. Grey". The name of the four hostiles is a reference to the science fiction movie "Men In Black". The name of the mysterious "Mr. Grey" is a nod to Tarantino's crime film "Reservoir Dogs" in which six of the characters are named as follows: Mr. Blonde, Mr. Blue, Mr. Brown, Mr. Orange, Mr. Pink, and Mr. White.

What About Chocobos

In several areas of the game, you can find posters advertising a new RPG, and a rather famous one at that. The posters are advertising Final Fantasy XXVII (27). Apparently, the Final Fantasy franchise is alive and well in the year 2027. Naturally, we are left wondering if Chocobo Racing is still around in XXVII.

Ignore The Signs

When it is time to go to TYM, you have to first enter the TYM Employee Shuttle Station in Kuigan. Before getting on the shuttle, check the area for some signs. In particular, look at the trash cans! There you'll find a rather disturbing sign that reads "Please don't Pee into the garbage can". Next to that sign is a "No Smoking" sign. If you look on the ground below the No Smoking sign, you'll see a huge pile of cigarette butts. If everyone is ignoring the No Smoking sign, then you probably don't want to pick up those trash cans! [→☐ 6]

Identities Revealed

During the opening cinematic of the game, you'll see a man having a conference call with several others. The people he is talking to are disguising their voices to remain anonymous, and are listed only by their location with no identifiable picture or video of the person. So who are these mysterious people?

The man you see is Bob Page, a member of the Illuminati, and the main villain of the first Deus Ex game. Besides Bob, there are three others on the conference call that you'll recognize. [→☐ 7]

Location	Identity
New York	Bill Taggart
Singapore	Hugh Darrow
Shanghai	Zhao Yun Ru

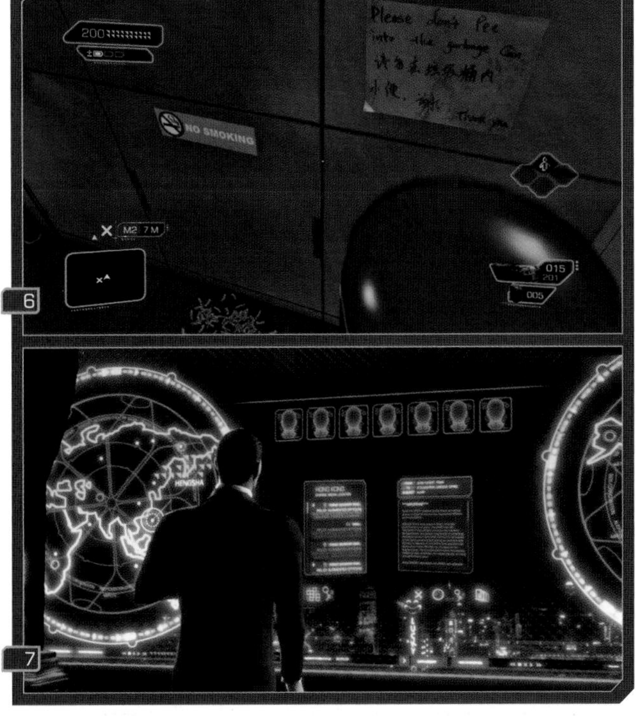

What's In A Name

The names of nearly everything in Deus Ex: Human Revolution have been carefully picked for a reason! Many have double meanings and/or are references to real people. Look around next time you play the game and see if you can spot these.

The TV Network Picus was named after the Roman god Picumnus. He is also believed to be Sterquilinus, the god of manure. An interesting choice, which insinuates Picus is spreading some BS around. Note: The meaning of Picus in the game is as described and should not be confused with the first king of Latium named in Roman Mythology as "Picus".

Eliza Cassan's office in Picus is Room 404, and 404 is the HTTP standard response code and error message for "File Not Found".

The room in which you finally find Eliza Cassan is "Data Storage 802-11". The 802-11 refers to the Institute of Electrical and Electronics Engineers (IEEE) 802.11 set of standards for implementing wireless local area network computer communication.

Almost all the people working at Sarif Industries (the names you see on doors of the offices) have been named after Renaissance scientists, although most names have been updated and "Americanized".

Most of the policemen working in the Detroit Police station are named after famous cyberpunk authors.

Most of the street names in Hengsha have double meanings in Chinese.

Get The News

Throughout the game, you'll find electronic newspapers lying about or in newspaper stands. These newspapers are not static and change frequently according to how you've played the game. For example, in Sarif Manufacturing, if you save the hostages, the newspapers will tell of how they escaped death,. However, if you let them die, the newspapers will reflect that grim fact as well. You should read the newspapers often to see how your playing style is affecting the news!

And speaking of news, pay close attention to the ticker tapes running across every TV news story. They contain references to Deus Ex and a few jokes, as well. When you find a TV, make sure to turn it on (if it is off), and then watch the screen! [→☐ 1]

1

Darrow's Leg

Ever wondered how Darrow injured his leg? You can find the answer in an eBook located in one of the locked apartments in Hengsha Court Gardens which is the same area in which Van Bruggen lives. The eBook to find is "Tomorrow's Man: The Hugh Darrow Story" and it reads as follows.

Adversity & Challenge

An ill-fated ski trip in 1995 left Darrow's anterior cruciate ligament in his knee ruined, and the failed attempts at allograft surgery left him debilitated; but for Hugh, it was the moment in which his visionary mind first drew a connection between robotics, prosthetics, and improving human capabilities to realize the transhumanist potential of mechanical augmentation.

Hugh returned to England in 1996, and at age 23 he purchased a struggling prosthetics research and manufacturing firm. Merging the lab with his robotics company under the new name of Darrow Industries, he completely changed the focus of both firms.

Over the next decade, Darrow would devote much of his personal time and resources to traveling the world, convincing many of the best and brightest biotech scientists and researchers to come work for him in the emerging field of human enhancement technology.

GOODS AND SERVICES

Throughout the game's environments, you'll find many a valuable item hidden away, tucked in a corner, under a box, or even lying out in plain sight. However, even though there are things that you can find just laying around, the most valuable items are often found in the possession of the various dealers and sellers. It takes a few credits to get the good stuff, but it's usually a wise investment.

About Weapon Dealers

Weapon Dealers not only Sell, but will also buy items from you. They will purchase nearly any item in your inventory, but at a price that is suitable to them. That is, they buy items at 50% of the retail price. So if you bought a Rocket Launcher for 4000, the resell value is only 2000. However, you can turn this to your advantage by picking up weapons and items you don't intend to keep. Why leave those items lying on the street when you can turn them into cold hard Credits!

When selling items, the dealers round up all percentages. So for example, if you are selling an item that retails for 25 credits, 50% of that is 12.5. The dealer will give you a break and round that up to 13 credits. As you progress through the game, the Dealers will update their inventory. So make sure to check back with them each time you revisit an area to see what new wares they have to offer.

2

About LIMB Clinics

All LIMB Clinics have the exact same inventory throughout the game, and they never update their inventory. Also, LIMB Clinics never buy items; they are sellers only. There is an upside to this though; the Praxis Kits. If you buy all the Praxis Kits they have available in an area, then when you revisit that area later, those Kits will have replenished meaning you can buy two more! So always buy both Praxis Kits each LIMB Clinic offers before leaving the area and progressing with the story. [→☐ 2]

MINOR SELLERS

Besides the Weapon Dealers and LIMB Clinics, you will encounter three unique characters that have some things to sell you. When you meet these characters, think wisely about spending your credits. It's always best to spend your credits first on Praxis Kits and then Weapon Upgrades. After that, have some fun with your Credits if you like.

3

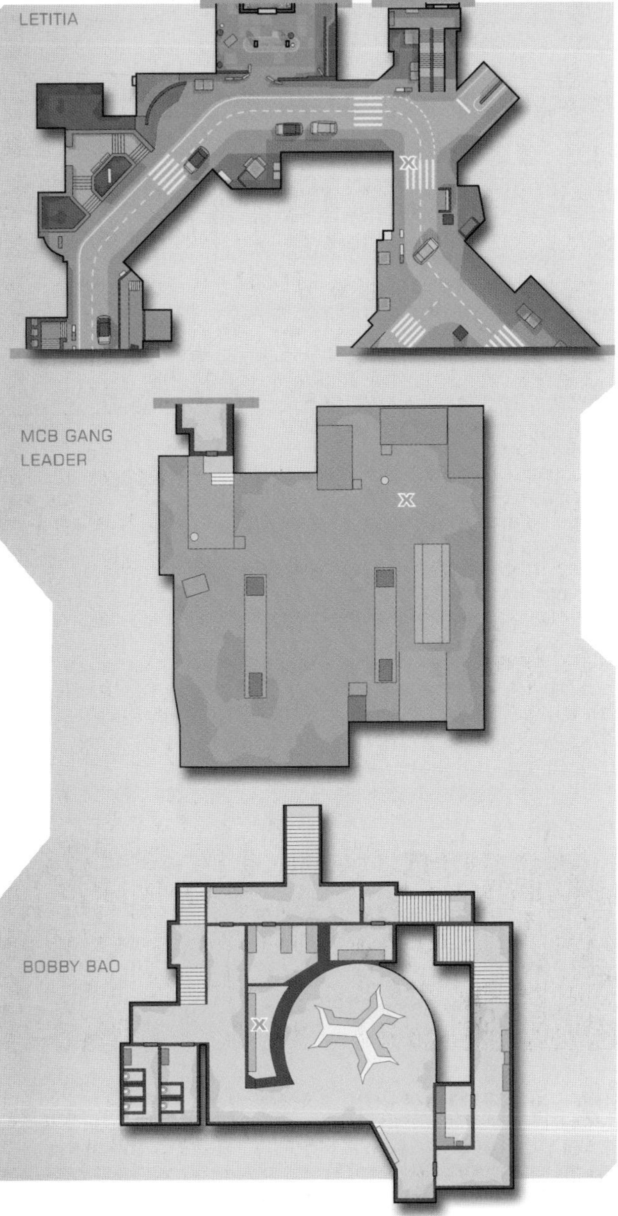

Letitia

Sex	Female
Age	Mid 30s
Ethnicity	Black - American

Letitia is a homeless woman who's willing to sell valuable codes, tips, and information about secret paths in Detroit for the right price. Despite her distracted air and addiction to Hop Devil Beer, she's one of Jensen's more reliable informants. [→☐ 3]

MCB Gang Leader

Sex	Male
Age	Early 30s
Ethnicity	Black - American

This guy is a strong, confident, and very amicable man who is more than willing to help out. He'll gladly offer you information for free, but he does have a few items that will take Credits to get if you decide you want them. Never one for the hard sell, he's definitely an easy going kind of guy with a live and let live kind of attitude.

Bobby Bao

Sex	Male
Age	Mid 30s
Ethnicity	Asian - Chinese

Bobby Bao is the bartender at The Hive, a popular Hengsha nightclub. He's every customer's best friend; always ready with a smile, a drink, a one-liner, or a sympathetic ear. But he also harbors a secret: under the watchful eye of his boss, Tong Si Hung, Bao helps manage a profitable black-marketeering operation. So just below the surface of his charm lie the smugness and arrogance that come from being the biggest fish in one's own tiny little pond.

MAJOR DEALERS

Grayson

Sex	Male
Age	Mid 40s
Ethnicity	White - American

A gun-runner and black marketeer who can be found selling his wares inside an abandoned Gas Station in downtown Detroit. Grayson most often speaks in a low, sleazy drawl that hints at innuendoes and seems always on the verge of emitting a private chuckle. [→☐ 4]

Seurat

Sex	Male
Age	Late 30s
Ethnicity	Eastern European

Another gun-runner and generally crooked type, Seurat can be found selling his wares from a two-bedroom apartment in Detroit. Seurat speaks very quickly in short, terse sentences that cut straight to the point.

6

When dealing with Seurat, if you complete the Thorpe Side Quest, Seurat will do you a favor since you know Mr. Thorpe and give you the "egghead" discount. This amounts to 24% off all merchandise!

Lin Fu Ren

Sex	Male
Age	Late 30s
Ethnicity	Asian - Chinese

Yet another gun-runner, Lin Fu Ren operates his business inside a notorious brothel in Lower Hengsha City, in China. [→□ 1]

Peng Xin Hao

Sex	Male
Age	Mid 30s
Ethnicity	Asian - Chinese

A notorious backroom weapons dealer, Peng Xin Hao can be found selling his wares in Hengsha's Capsule Hotel, and then later on the streets of Hengsha after Alice Garden Pods has closed. [→□ 2]

Lu Pin Rong

Sex	Male
Age	Late 30s
Ethnicity	Asian - Chinese

A gun-runner and Harvester loose cannon who can be found selling his wares in the sewers just outside the Harvester Hideout that lead to the Hengsha Seaport. [→□ 3]

Dr. Vera Marcovic (LIMB)

Sex	Female
Age	Mid 40s
Ethnicity	White - Russian

A Slavic woman in her 40s, with blonde hair, blue eyes, and a solid frame, Vera is, in a word, stunning. To those unfamiliar with her she appears to be a stereotypical Ice Queen, but up close there is a warm humor in her eyes, and an easy tendency to laugh with her whole body. She is intelligent, educated, and clever. Very little escapes her notice, and when it comes to her patients, nothing does. Her wit is quick and often acerbic, although rarely unkind. She does not suffer the company of fools.

Huang Ling (LIMB)

Sex	Female
Age	Late 20s
Ethnicity	Asian - Chinese

A receptionist at the Hengsha LIMB Clinic, Huang runs the front desk of the Clinic in Hengsha. When the biochips are recalled, she will also offer Jensen

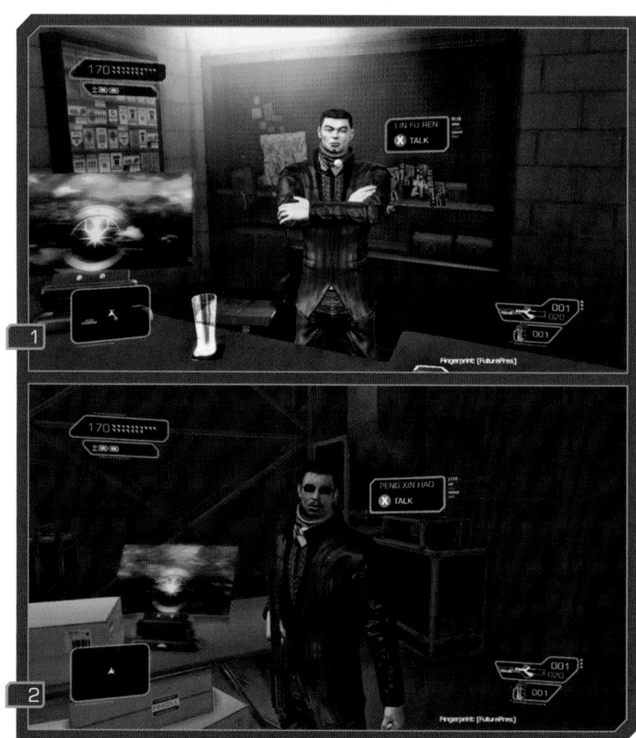

GRAYSON

SEURAT

LIN FU REN

PENG XIN HAO

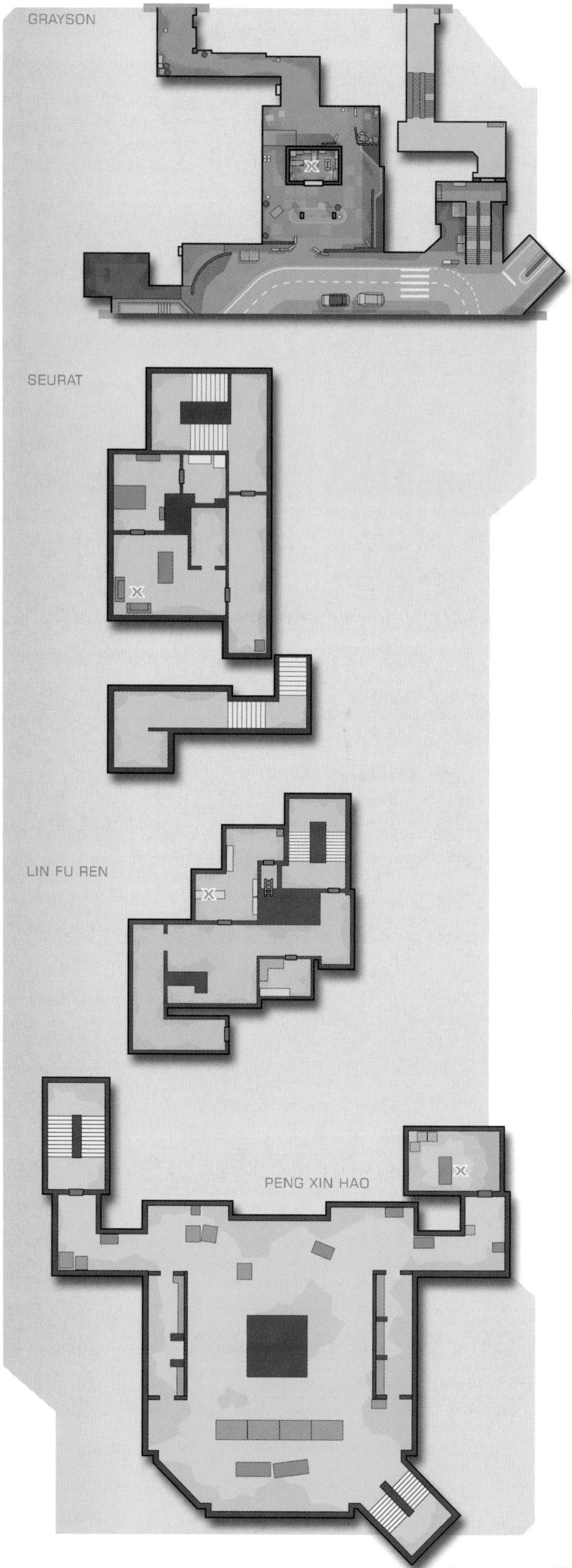

a chance to undergo a special surgery - the replacement of the defective biochip that has been causing him to experience momentary malfunctions in his heads-up-display.

Andrea Mantegna (LIMB)

A receptionist in the Detroit L.I.M.B. Clinic, Andrea runs the Front Desk of the Clinic when Dr. Marcovic is busy with other duties.

Sex	Female
Age	Mid 30s
Ethnicity	White - American

Gerta Mueller (LIMB)

Gerta is a no-nonsense German woman who runs the L.I.M.B. clinic in Panchaea, a deep ocean installation in the middle of the Arctic. Like all L.I.M.B. merchants, Gerta runs the front desk of the Clinic. However, when we meet her, augmented humans who are building Panchaea have gone insane and are attacking everything in sight, so she is a bit rattled and scared for her life. [→☐ 4]

Sex	Female
Age	Mid 30s
Ethnicity	White - German

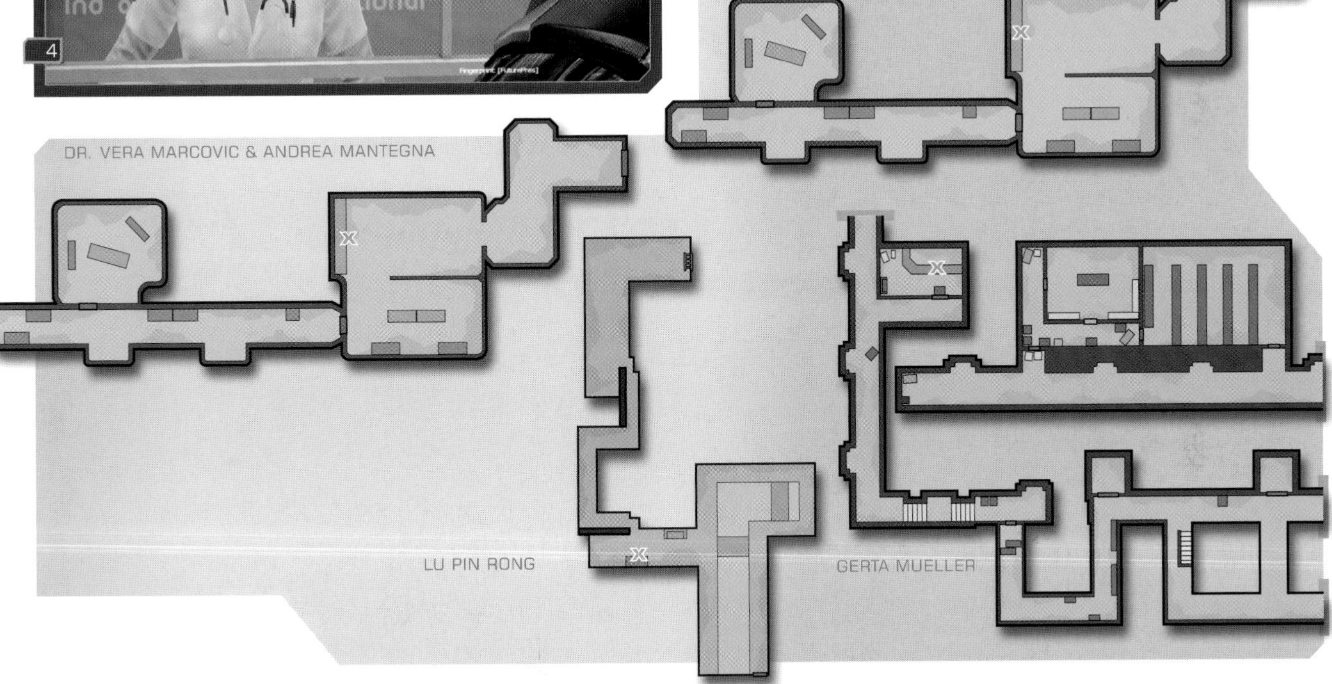

MINOR SELLER INVENTORY

Letitia

Located in Detroit, Letitia has a taste for Mahara Jah Hot Devil Ale. Give her four of them, and you'll get a reward. Other than that, it'll take credits to get anything else from her.

Quest Reward

Mahara Jah Hot Devil Ale (Beer)	Item Received.
Quantity = 4	Pocket Secretary with the Level 5 Hack code to the storage unit next to the basketball court in Detroit.*

*You can get this same Pocket Secretary from Seurat's safe in his bedroom if you can hack it, but he'll take his best shot at killing you if you try!

Information For Sale

Information Topic	Cost	Information Received
Weapons	500	Hint to go and check out an abandoned gas station nearby if you are looking to buy weapons.
	1000	Hint about a suspected assassination attempt from an elevated position near the LIMB clinic. Location of a Sniper Rifle and ammo cache on the roof of the gas station, access requires Capture level 4.
	2000	Password for the computer terminal controlling access to the armory in the Police Station. Password = patriotism
Secret Paths	500	Hint about items located behind weak walls in the sewers near the Police Station.
	1000	Code for the Police Station Sewer access door. Code = 2599
	2000	Hint about the location of weak walls and elevator shafts that can be accessed from the upper floors of buildings in DRB territory.
City Mood	Free	A warning that starting trouble on the streets (gunfire, takedowns, etc) in public will trigger a response from not only the Police, but the Punks on the streets as well.

MCB Gang Leader

Located in Highland Park near the Helipad. If you choose to Get Info, he'll tell you about the strange happenings in Highland Park involving the mercenaries - The same mercenaries that broke into Sarif Industries and nearly killed Jensen. The info is free, but if you want items, you'll have to fork over some credits.

Item	Price	Quantity
Tranquilizer Rifle Ammo (5 Pack)	250	1
Crossbow Ammo (5 Pack)	175	1
Shotgun Ammo (8 Pack)	280	1
Grenade Pack: 1 Gas & 1 EMP	400	1
Target-Leading System (Tranquilizer Rifle & Crossbow)	1500	1

Bobby Bao

Bobby is the Hive's Bartender, the real one, and he sells drinks that, believe it or not, are good for your health. Each offers a boost in HP coupled with a few seconds of blurry vision. Bobby can also offer you a Side Quest under the right conditions, so please refer to the Side Quests chapter for more information on that.

Drink	Price	Quantity	HP Boost
Slum Dog	10	1	15
Gut Punch	15	1	25
Phoenix	25	1	30

MAJOR DEALER INVENTORY

Detroit 1

Once you are done with Sarif Manufacturing, you will finally be able to leave Sarif HQ and venture out into the streets of Detroit. Once there, track down these dealers to sample there wares.

Dealer: Grayson

Item	Price	Quantity
10mm Pistol Ammo (5 Pack)	25	6
Shotgun Cartridges (5 Pack)	100	2
Tranquilizer Darts (2 Pack)	100	5
Tranquilizer Rifle	1500	1
Shotgun	1500	1
Damage Upgrade	250	1
Burst Round System (Shotgun)	1500	1
Mine Template	75	3

Dealer: Seurat*

Item	Price	Quantity
Machine Pistol Ammo (15 Pack)	120	5
Stun Gun Darts (5 pack)	50	5
Machine Pistol	750	1
Stun Gun	500	1
Silencer	500	1

*You get a 24% discount if you completed the One Good Turn Deserves Another Side Quest.

Detroit 1.2

You'll return from Highland Park and FEMA to Detroit, but nothing has changed since your last visit.

Henghsa 1

With the information that you ascertained from Barrett, Sarif decides to send you to Hengsha China to follow the leads. Once you are there, take a little time to look up these dealers and partake of their wares.

Dealer: Marcovic (LIMB Clinic)

Item	Price	Quantity
Typhoon Ammo	100	5
Hypostim	100	2
CyberBoost ProEnergy Jar	250	2
Praxis Kit	5000	2

Dealer: Lin Fu Rin (Hung Hua Hotel)

Item	Price	Quantity
Rockets (Single)	150	2
Machine Pistol Ammo (15 Pack)	120	5
Sniper Rifle Ammo (5 Pack)	150	2
Crossbow Arrows (2 Pack)	70	4
Rocket Launcher	4000	1
Machine Pistol	750	1
Sniper Rifle	3000	1
Crossbow	2000	1
Frag Grenade	150	2
EMP Grenade	200	1
Silencer	500	1
Laser Targeting System	500	1
Damage Upgrade	250	1
Target-Seeking System (Combat Rifle / Machine Pistol)	1500	1

Dealer: Ping Xin Hao (Alice Garden Pods)

Item	Price	Quantity
Revolver Ammo (5 pack)	130	2
Combat Rifle Ammo (10 pack)	100	4
Shotgun Cartridges (5 pack)	100	2
P.E.P.S. Energy Pack (Single)	50	5
Tranquilizer Darts (2 pack)	100	5
Stun Gun Darts (2 pack)	50	5
10mm Pistol Ammo (5 pack)	25	6
Revolver	600	1
Combat Rifle	1250	1
Shotgun	1500	1
P.E.P.S.	750	1
Tranquilizer Rifle	1500	1
Stun Gun	500	1
10mm Pistol	350	1
Mine Template	75	3
Gas Grenade	200	1
Concussion Grenade	60	2
Rate-of-Fire Upgrade	250	1
Exploding Rounds Package (Revolver)	1500	1
Stop! Worm Software	50	5
Nuke Virus Software	50	5

Dealer: Huang Ling (LIMB Clinic)

Item	Price	Quantity
Typhoon Ammo	100	5
Hypostim	100	2
CyberBoost ProEnergy Jar	250	2
Praxis Kit	5000	2

Detroit 2

After defeating Federova in Picus, you'll return to Detroit only to see the city is tearing itself apart with riots between Purists and the Augmented. Never fear though, even in adversity, the Dealers are there to meet your needs. On this trip, all shops have been update with new inventory. If you purchased both Praxis Kits at the LIMB clinic on your previous visit, then rush to the LIMB Clinic again as those Praxis Kits have been replenished and you can buy two more!

Dealer: Grayson

Item	Price	Quantity
10mm Pistol Ammo (5 Pack)	25	6
Shotgun Cartridges (5 Pack)	100	2
Tranquilizer Darts (2 Pack)	100	5
P.E.P.S. Energy Pack (Single) -New-	50	5
Heavy Rifle Ammo (25 pack) -New-	250	4
Revolver Ammo (5 Pack) -New-	130	2
10mm Pistol -New-	350	1
Shotgun	1500	1
Tranquilizer Rifle	1500	1
P.E.P.S. -New-	750	1
Heavy Rifle -New-	2500	1
Revolver -New-	600	1
Damage Upgrade	250	1
Laser Targeting System -New-	500	1
Reload Speed Upgrade -New-	250	1
Ammo Capacity Upgrade -New-	250	1
Burst Round System (Shotgun)	1500	1
Target-Leading System (Tranquilizer Rifle & Crossbow) -New-	1500	1
Cooling System (Heavy & Plasma Rifles) -New-	1500	1
Exploding Rounds Package (Revolver) -New-	250	1
Armor-Piercing System (10mm Pistol) -New-	500	1
Mine Template	75	3
EMP Grenade -New-	200	1
Concussion Grenade -New-	60	2
Stop! Worm Software -New-	50	5
Nuke Virus Software -New-	50	5

Dealer: Seurat*

Item	Price	Quantity
Machine Pistol Ammo (15 pack)	120	5
Stun Gun Darts (5 pack)	50	5
Rockets (Single) -New-	150	2
Crossbow Arrows (2 pack) -New-	70	4
Sniper Rifle Ammo (5 pack) -New-	150	2
Combat Rifle Ammo (10 pack) -New-	100	4
Stun Gun	500	1
Machine Pistol	750	1
Rocket Launcher -New-	3000	1
Crossbow -New-	2000	1
Sniper Rifle -New-	3000	1
Combat Rifle Ammo -New-	1250	1
Silencer**	500	1
Rate-of-Fire Upgrade -New-	250	1
Heat Targeting System -New-	1500	1
Target-Leading System (Tranquilizer Rifle & Crossbow) -New-	1500	1
Target-Seeking System (Combat Rifle & Machine Pistol) -New-	1500	1
Gas Grenade -New-	200	1
Frag Grenade -New-	150	2

*You get a 24% discount if you completed the Thorpe Side Quest.
**If you bought the Silencer earlier, it will not be for sale again here.

Dealer: Andrea Mantegna (LIMB Clinic)

Item	Price	Quantity
Typhoon Ammo	100	5
Hypostim	100	2
CyberBoost ProEnergy Jar	250	2
Praxis Kit*	5000	2

*Praxis kits have replenished since your last visit during Detroit 1.

Hengsha 2

Tracking Vasili Sevchenko's GPL leads you back to Henghsa as you close in on the signal. While you are there, turn to the streets and look up the Dealers once again. New inventory is available now, and the LIMB Clinic has also restocked its Praxis Kits. Take note though that since Alice Garden Pods has been shut down, Ping Xin Hao had to change locations. You can now find him at the most southern tip of the Youzhao District, just Southwest of the Downtown Apartments.

Dealer: Lin Fu Rin (Hung Hua Hotel)

Item	Price	Quantity
Rockets (Single)	150	2
Machine Pistol Ammo (15 Pack)	120	5
Sniper Rifle Ammo (5 Pack)	150	2
Crossbow Arrows (2 Pack)	70	4
Heavy Rifle Ammo (25 Pack) -New-		
Rocket Launcher	4000	1
Machine Pistol	750	1
Sniper Rifle	3000	1
Crossbow	2000	1
Heavy Rifle -New-	2500	1
Frag Grenade	150	2
EMP Grenade	200	1
Silencer	500	1
Laser Targeting System	500	1
Damage Upgrade	250	1
Target-Seeking System (Combat Rifle / Machine Pistol)	1500	1
Heat Targeting System (Rocket Launcher) -New-	1500	1
Cooling System -New-	1500	1

Dealer: Ping Xin Hao (Moved From Alice Garden Pods)

Item	Price	Quantity
P.E.P.S. Energy Pack (Single)	50	5
Tranquilizer Darts (2 Pack)	100	5
Stun Gun Darts (2 Pack)	50	5
Shotgun Cartridges (5 Pack)	100	2
Combat Rifle Ammo (10 Pack)	100	4
Revolver Ammo (5 Pack)	130	2
10mm Pistol Ammo (5 Pack)	25	6
P.E.P.S.	750	1
Tranquilizer Rifle	1500	1
Stun Gun	500	1
Shotgun	1500	1
Combat Rifle	1250	1
Revolver	600	1
10mm Pistol	350	1
Burst Round System (Shotgun)	1500	1
Target-Seeking System (Combat Rifle & Machine Pistol	1500	1
Exploding Rounds Package (Revolver)	1500	1
Armor-Piercing System (10mm Pistol)	1500	1
Mine Template	75	3
Gas Grenade	200	1
Concussion Grenade	61	2
Stop! Worm Software	50	5
Nuke Virus Software	50	5

Dealer: Huang Ling (LIMB Clinic)

Item	Price	Quantity
Typhoon Ammo	100	5
Hypostim	100	2
CyberBoost ProEnergy Jar	250	2
Praxis Kit*	5000	2

*Praxis Kits have replenished since your last visit during Hengsha 1.

Hengsha Sea Port

After chatting with Tong, you're heading to the Hengsha Seaport, but it's not a pleasant journey as you'll need to make your way through the sewers to get there! But there is a bright side to that little journey: a new Weapon Dealer has set up shop in the sewers, so pay him a visit on your way to the Seaport.

Dealer: Lu Pin Rong (New Dealer)

Item	Price	Quantity
Tranquilizer Darts (2 pack)*	100	5
Stun Gun Darts (2 pack)*	50	5
Heavy Rifle Ammo (25 pack)	250	4
Sniper Rifle Ammo (5 pack)	150	2
Machine Pistol Ammo (15 pack)	120	5
Heavy Rifle	2500	1
Sniper Rifle	3000	1
Machine Pistol	750	1
Reload Speed Upgrade	250	1
Ammo Capacity Upgrade	250	1
Cooling System (Heavy & Plasma Rifle)	1500	1
Target-Seeking System (Combat Rifle and Machine Pistol)	1500	1
Frag Grenade	150	2
Gas Grenade	200	1
EMP Grenade	200	1
Mine Template	75	3

*Even though he sells the ammo for these, he doesn't sell the weapon.

Panchaea

This is it, the last area of the game. If you've been hording your credits, then now is the time to use them. There are no weapon Dealers in Panchaea, but there is a LIMB Clinic, so spend all those credits like mad - you can't take them with you!

Dealer: Gerta Mueller (LIMB Clinic)

Item	Price	Quantity
Typhoon Ammo	100	5
Hypostim	100	2
CyberBoost ProEnergy Jar	250	2
Praxis Kit	5000	2

CODE MAPS

SARIF HQ

On the following pages you'll find maps that reveal the codes and passwords needed to access all terminals in the game. Maps only appear for areas that contain terminals that require a code or password. The information in this section is obviously a type of spoiler, so you shouldn't consult it unless you've either played through the game already or don't mind spoiling the experience of discovering the codes for yourself.

SARIF INDUSTRIES F2

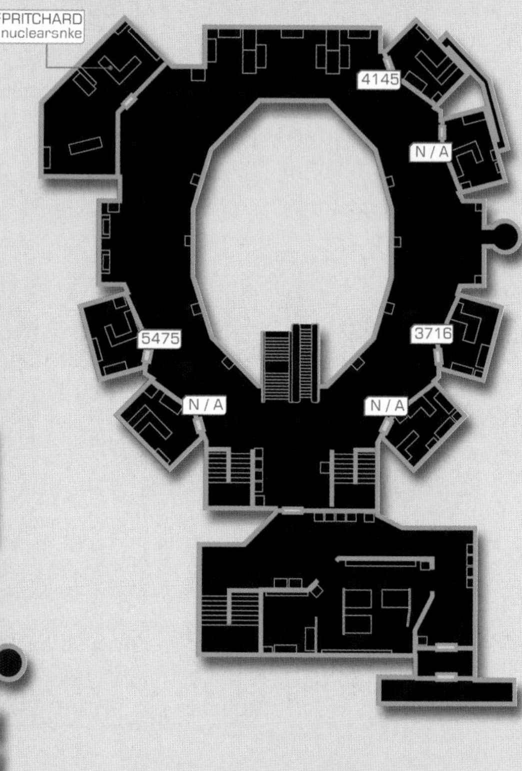

AMARGOULIS
gsspgirl

SARIF'S OFFICE

SARIF INDUSTRIES F3

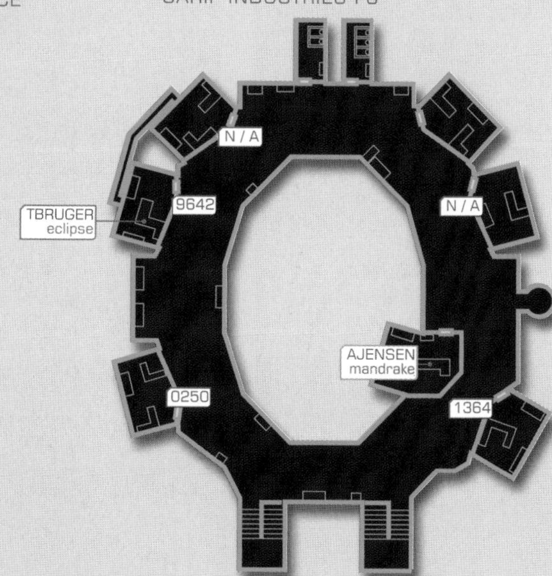

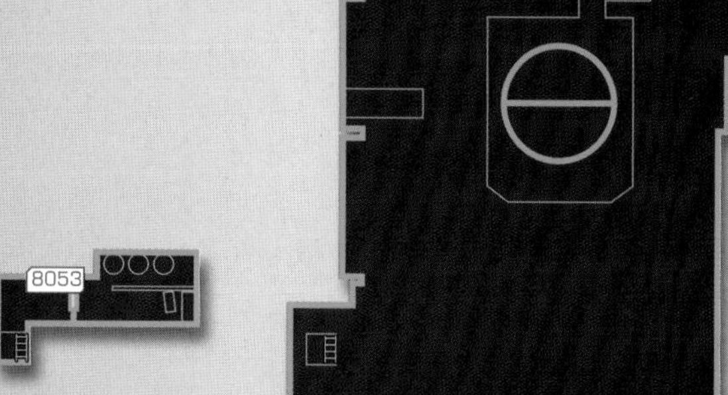

Username
Password

Security Panel

Security Terminal

Alarm Panel

Laser Grid Panel

Bomb Panel

Safe Panel

SARIF INDUSTRIES F1

SARIF MANUFACTURING PLANT

USERNAME
Password

Security Panel

Security Terminal

Alarm Panel

Laser Grid Panel

Bomb Panel

Safe Panel

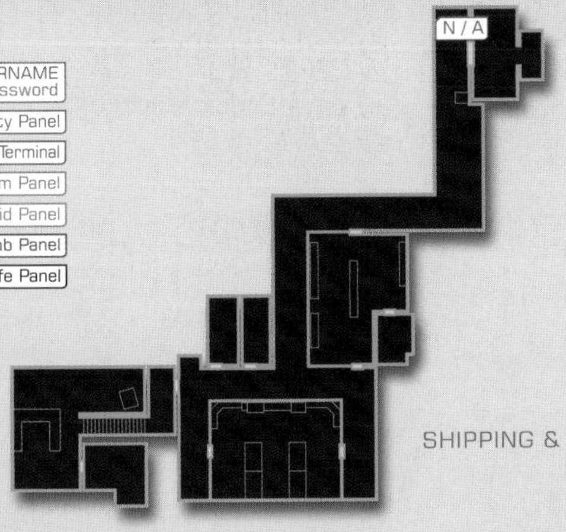

N / A

SHIPPING & RECEIVING F1

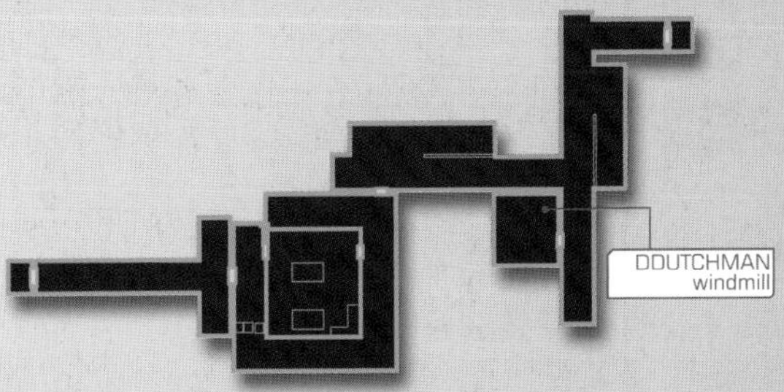

DDUTCHMAN
windmill

FACTORING LABS F1

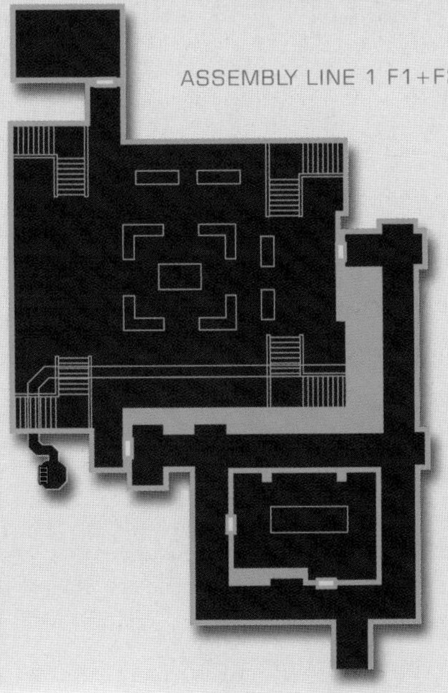

ASSEMBLY LINE 1 F1+F2

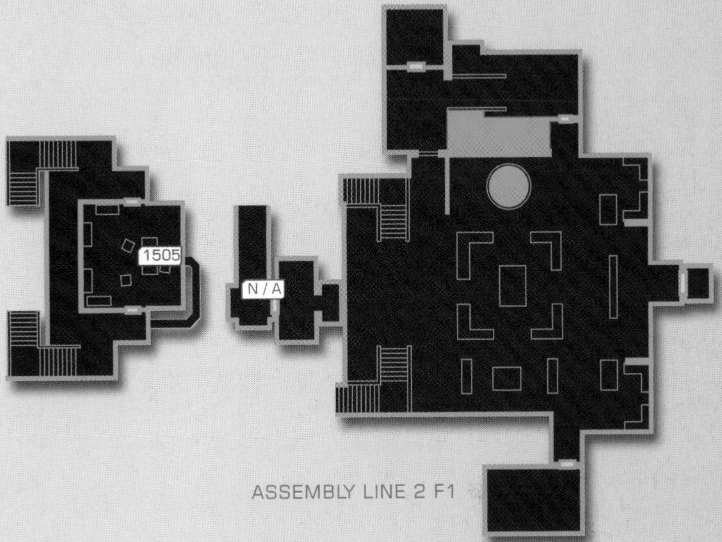

1505

N / A

ASSEMBLY LINE 2 F1

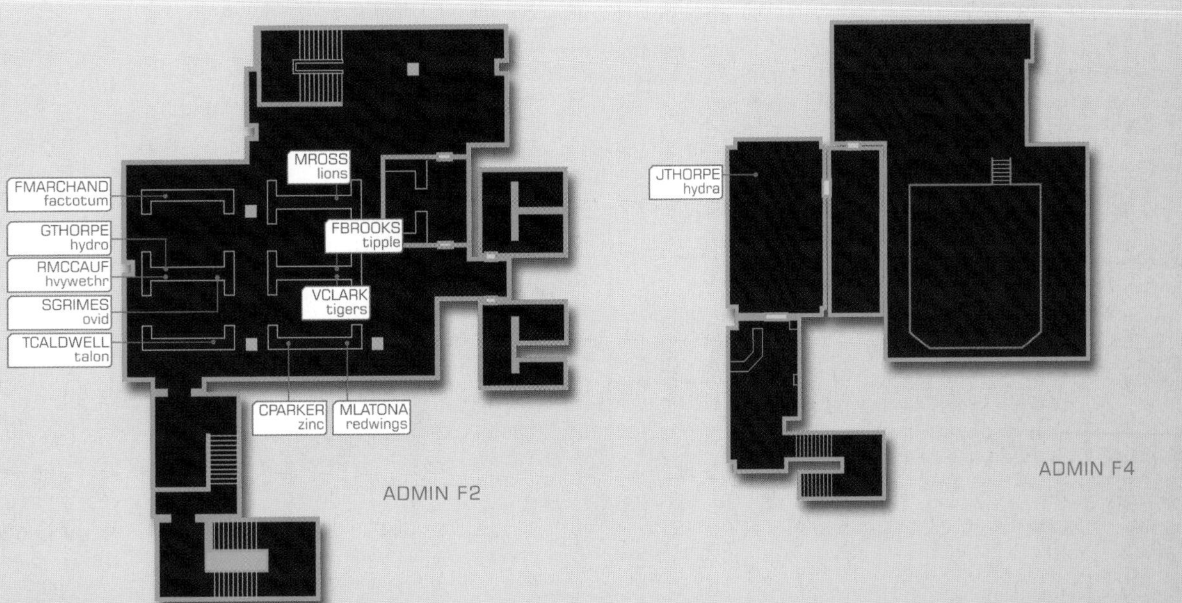

DETROIT CITY STREETS

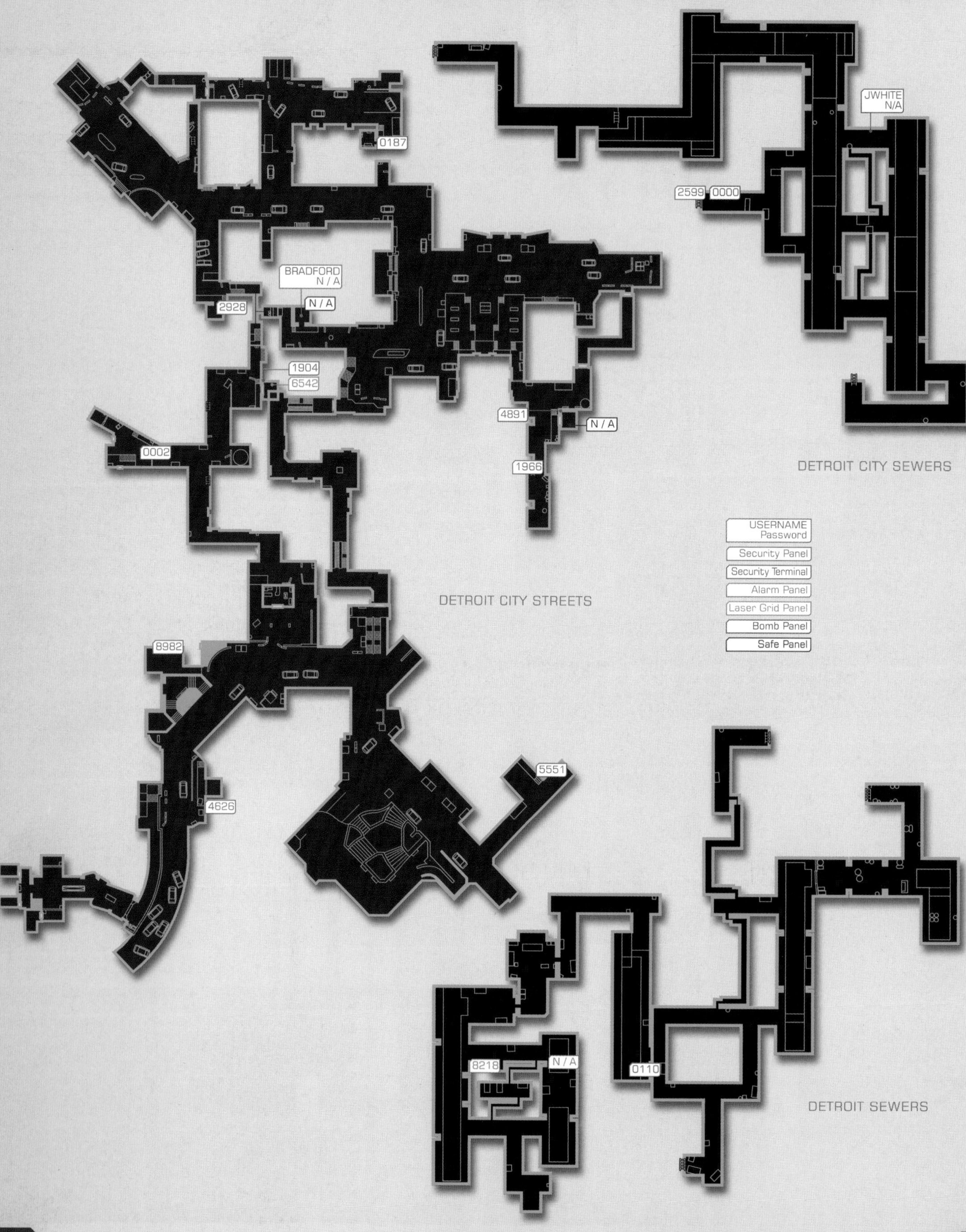
0187
JWHITE
N/A
2599
0000
BRADFORD
N / A
N / A
2928
1904
6542
4891
N / A
0002
1966
DETROIT CITY SEWERS
USERNAME
Password
Security Panel
Security Terminal
Alarm Panel
Laser Grid Panel
Bomb Panel
Safe Panel
DETROIT CITY STREETS
8982
5551
4626
8218
N / A
0110
DETROIT SEWERS

DETROIT INTERIORS

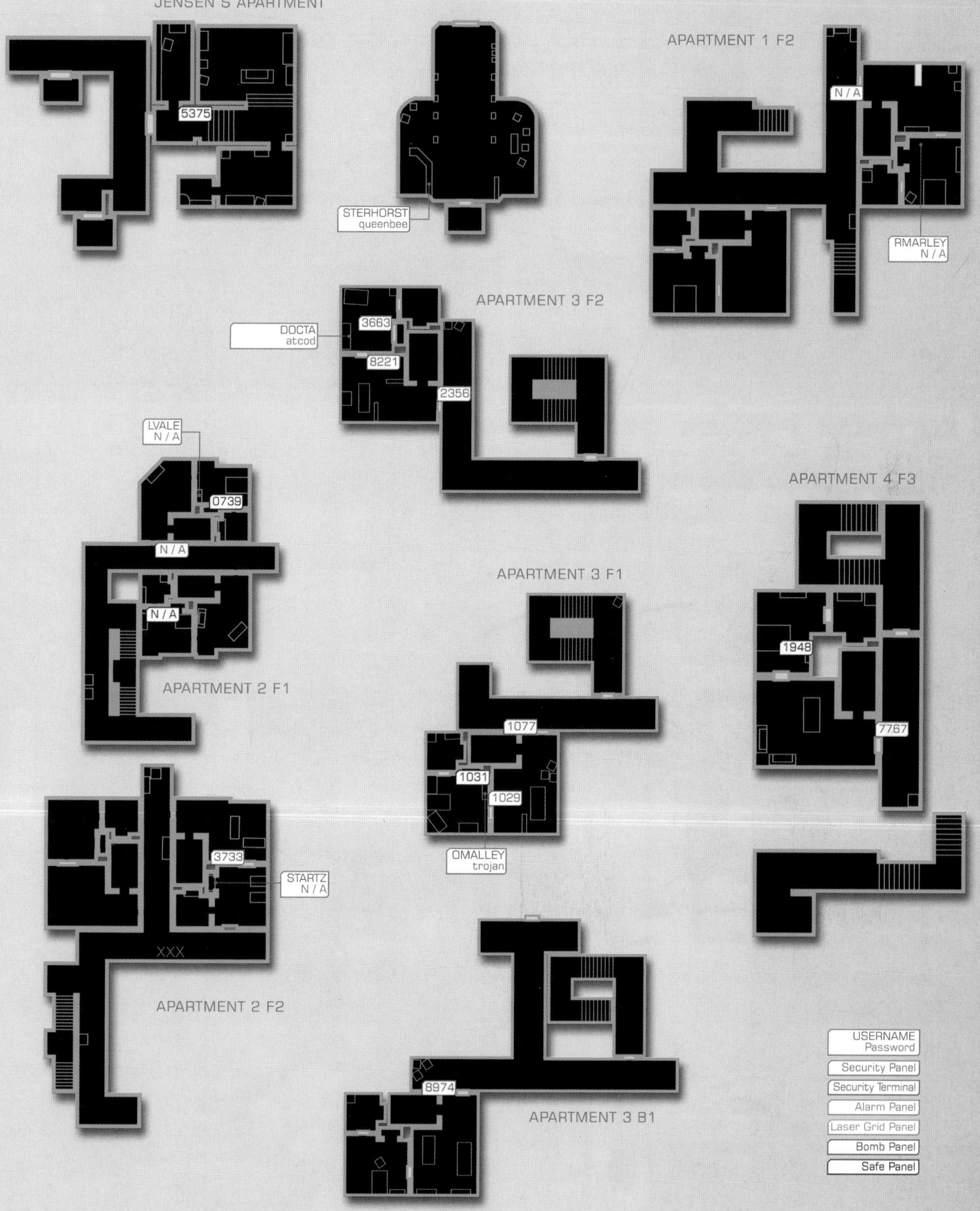
JENSEN'S APARTMENT
5375
STERHORST
queenbee
APARTMENT 1 F2
N / A
RMARLEY
N / A
APARTMENT 3 F2
DOCTA
atcod
3663
8221
2356
LVALE
N / A
0739
N / A
N / A
APARTMENT 2 F1
APARTMENT 4 F3
1948
7767
APARTMENT 3 F1
1077
1031
1029
OMALLEY
trojan
3733
STARTZ
N / A
XXX
APARTMENT 2 F2
8974
APARTMENT 3 B1
USERNAME
Password
Security Panel
Security Terminal
Alarm Panel
Laser Grid Panel
Bomb Panel
Safe Panel

DETROIT DERELICT ROW

DERELICT ROW F1

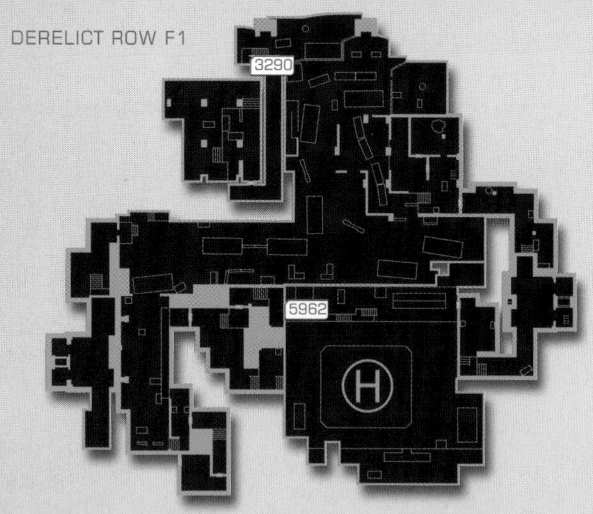

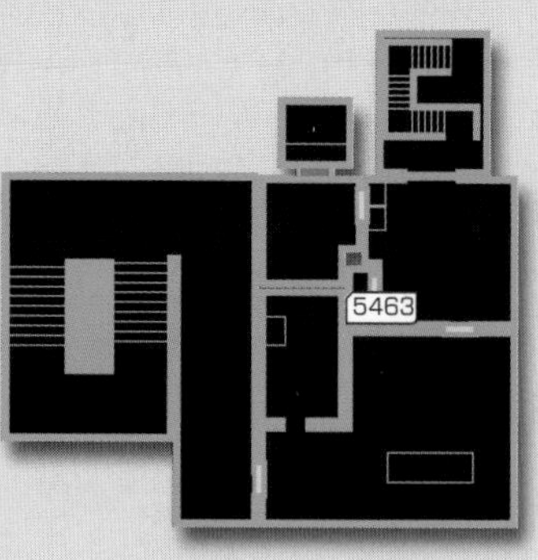

DERELICT ROW APARTMENT F3

DETROIT POLICE DEPARTMENT

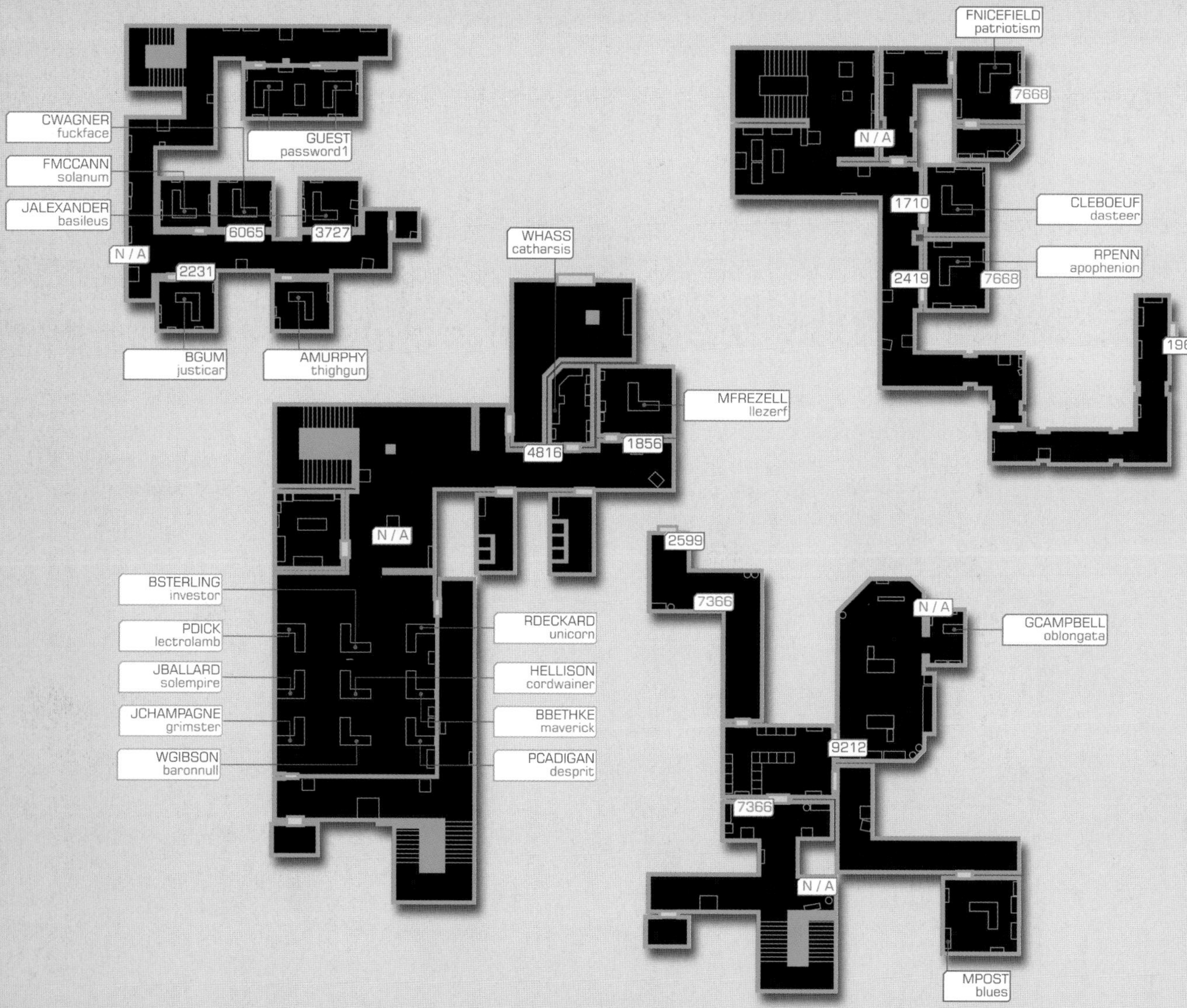

CWAGNER fuckface
FMCCANN solanum
JALEXANDER basileus
GUEST password1
N / A
6065
3727
2231
BGUM justicar
AMURPHY thighgun

FNICEFIELD patriotism
7668
N / A
1710
CLEBOEUF dasteer
2419
7668
RPENN apophenion
1966

WHASS catharsis
MFREZELL llezerf
4816
1856
N / A
BSTERLING investor
PDICK lectrolamb
JBALLARD solempire
JCHAMPAGNE grimster
WGIBSON baronnull
RDECKARD unicorn
HELLISON cordwainer
BBETHKE maverick
PCADIGAN desprit

2599
7366
N / A
GCAMPBELL oblongata
9212
7366
N / A
MPOST blues

FEMA CAMP

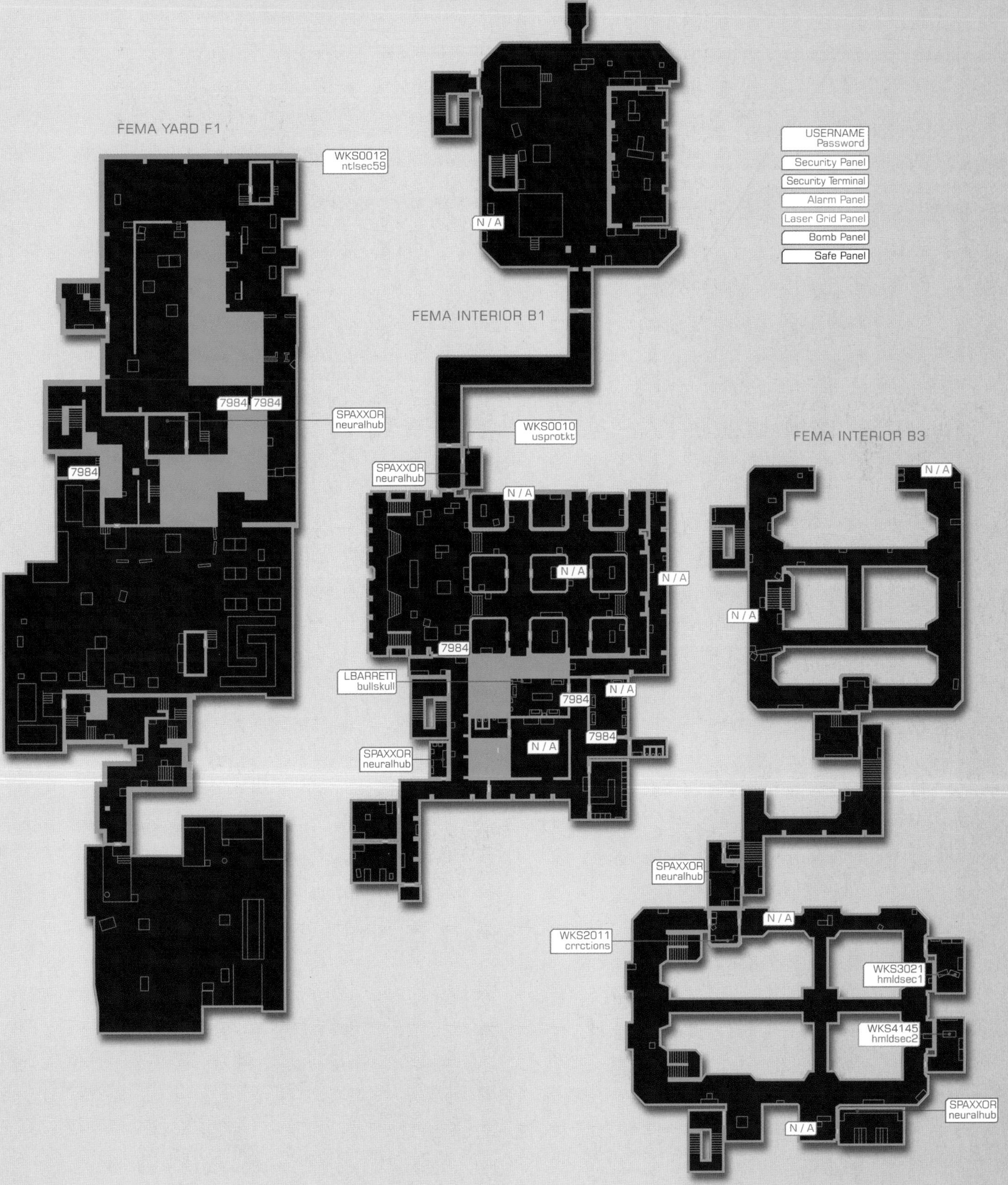

FEMA YARD F1
WKS0012
ntlsec59
7984
7984
SPAXXOR
neuralhub
7984
FEMA INTERIOR B1
N / A
WKS0010
usprotkt
SPAXXOR
neuralhub
N / A
N / A
N / A
7984
LBARRETT
bullskull
7984
N / A
7984
N / A
SPAXXOR
neuralhub
USERNAME
Password
Security Panel
Security Terminal
Alarm Panel
Laser Grid Panel
Bomb Panel
Safe Panel
FEMA INTERIOR B3
N / A
N / A
SPAXXOR
neuralhub
N / A
WKS2011
crrctions
WKS3021
hmldsec1
WKS4145
hmldsec2
SPAXXOR
neuralhub
N / A

HENGSHA CITY STREETS

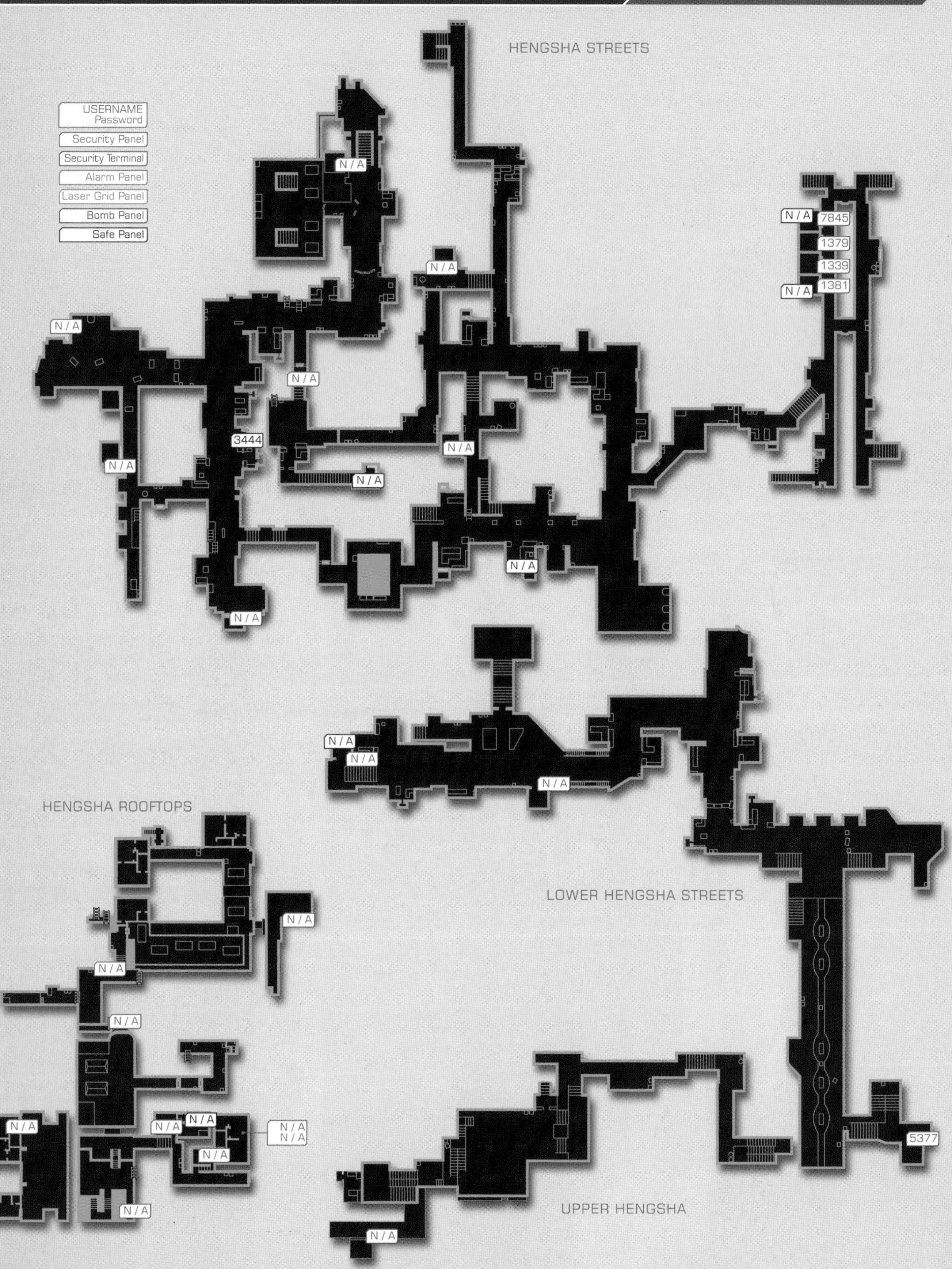

HENGSHA STREETS
USERNAME
Password
Security Panel
Security Terminal
Alarm Panel
Laser Grid Panel
Bomb Panel
Safe Panel
N / A
7845
1379
1339
1381
3444
HENGSHA ROOFTOPS
LOWER HENGSHA STREETS
UPPER HENGSHA
5377

HENGSHA INTERIORS

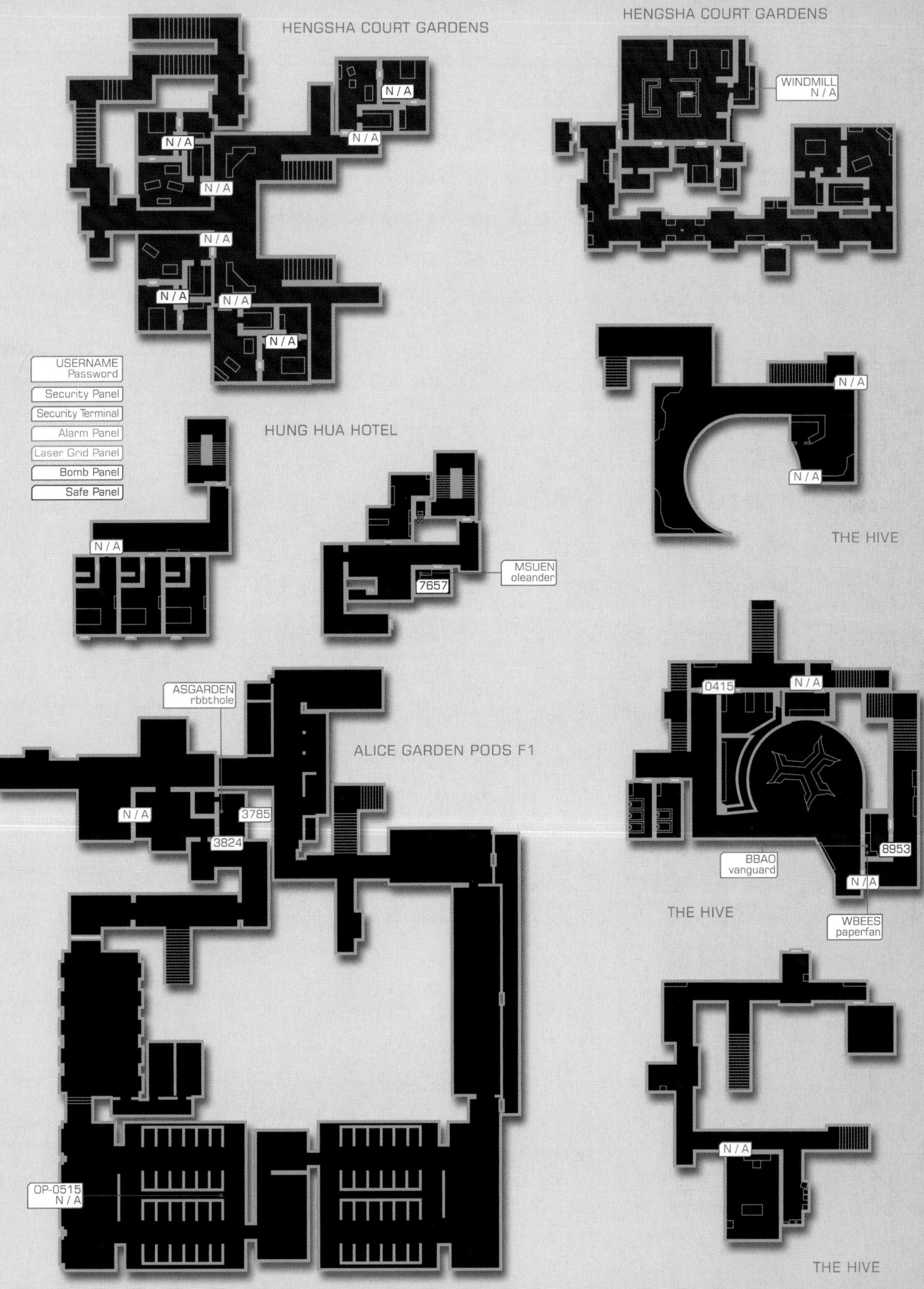

TAI YONG MEDICAL

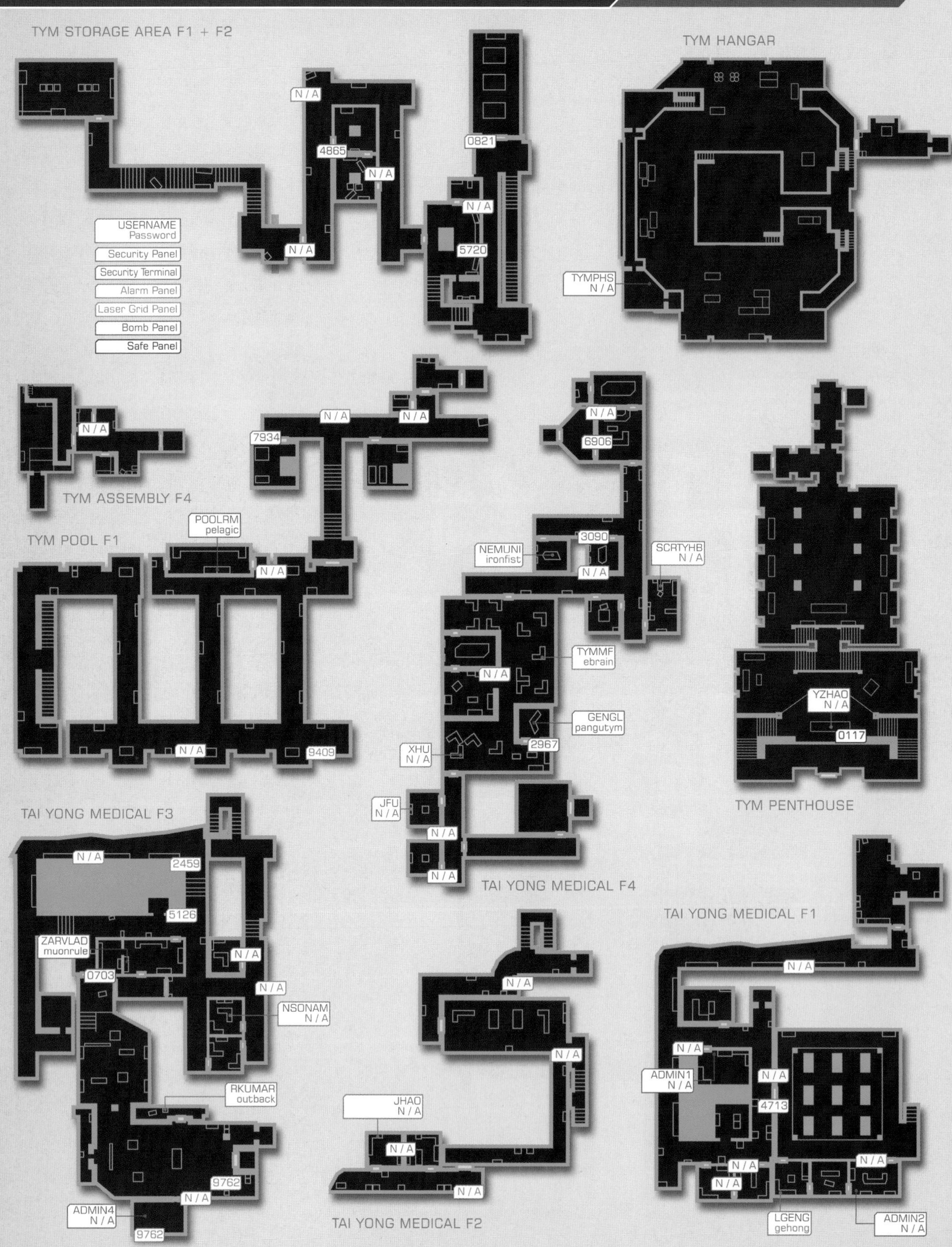

PICUS

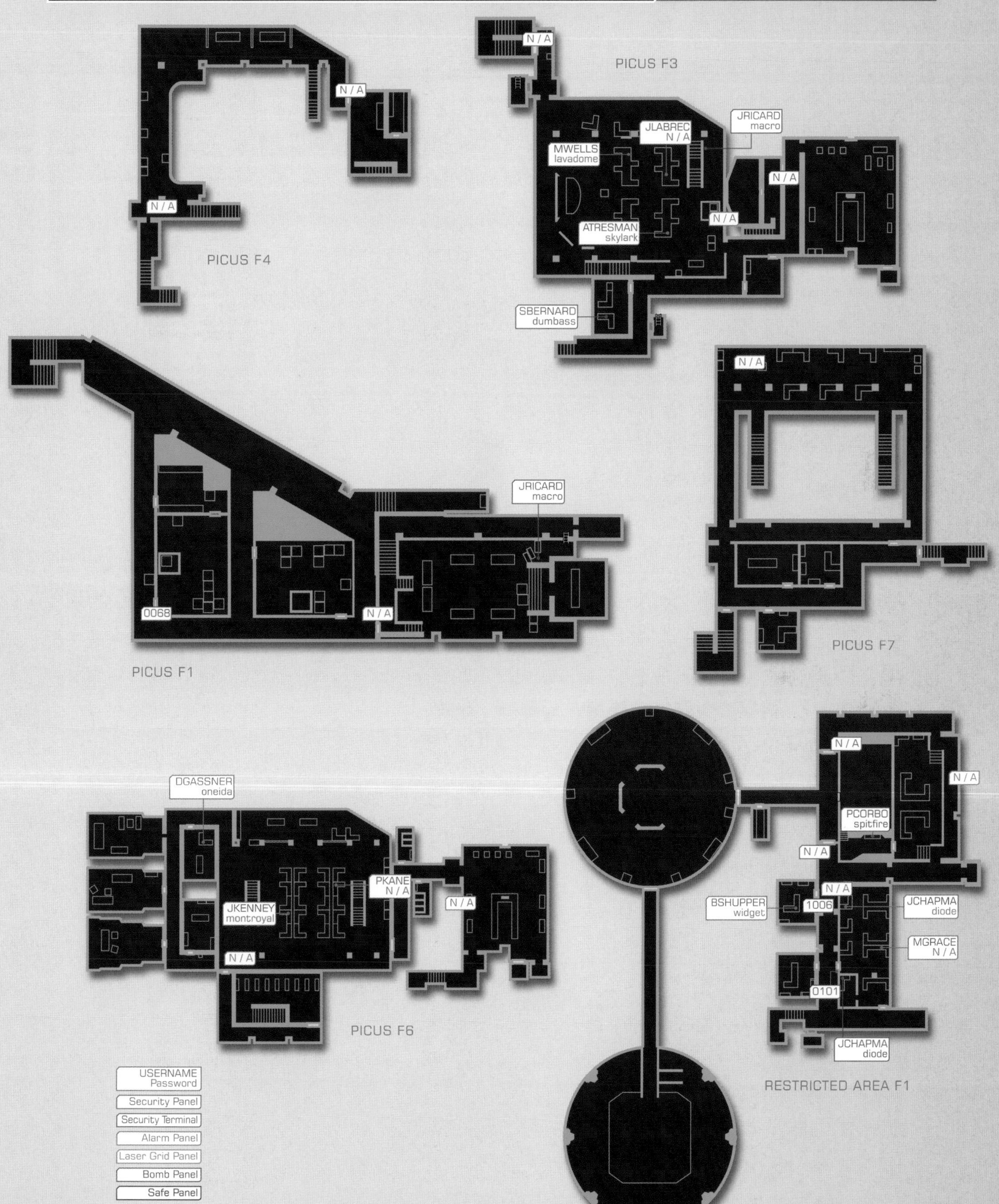

N / A
PICUS F4
N / A
PICUS F3
N / A
JRICARD
macro
JLABREC
N / A
MWELLS
lavadome
N / A
N / A
ATRESMAN
skylark
SBERNARD
dumbass
N / A
JRICARD
macro
0068
N / A
PICUS F1
PICUS F7
N / A
DGASSNER
oneida
PKANE
N / A
N / A
JKENNEY
montroyal
N / A
PICUS F6
N / A
N / A
PCORBO
spitfire
N / A
N / A
BSHUPPER
widget
1006
JCHAPMA
diode
MGRACE
N / A
0101
JCHAPMA
diode
RESTRICTED AREA F1
USERNAME
Password
Security Panel
Security Terminal
Alarm Panel
Laser Grid Panel
Bomb Panel
Safe Panel

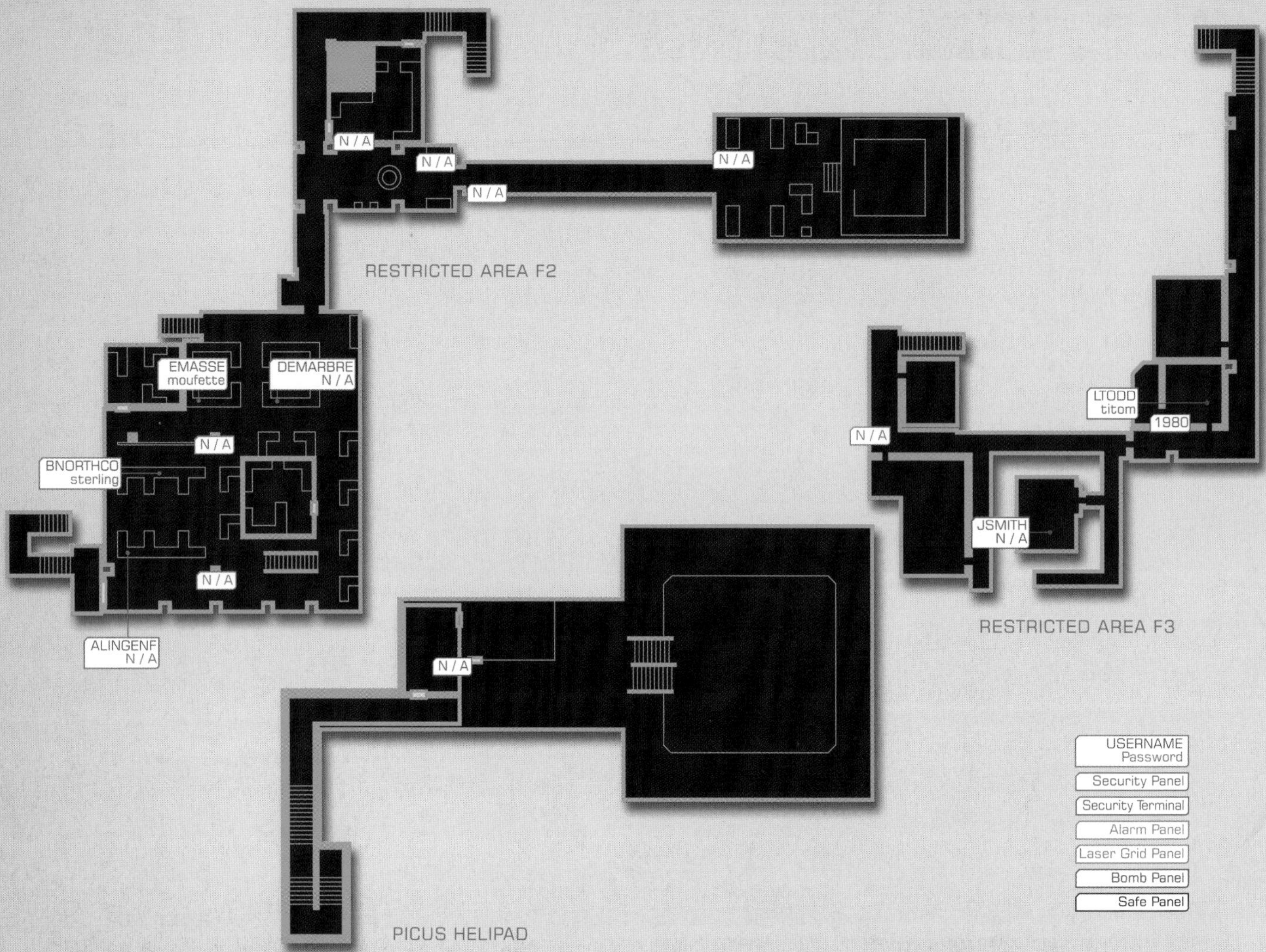

N / A
N / A
N / A
N / A
RESTRICTED AREA F2
EMASSE
moufette
DEMARBRE
N / A
N / A
BNORTHCO
sterling
N / A
ALINGENF
N / A
LTODD
titom
1980
N / A
JSMITH
N / A
RESTRICTED AREA F3
N / A
PICUS HELIPAD
USERNAME
Password
Security Panel
Security Terminal
Alarm Panel
Laser Grid Panel
Bomb Panel
Safe Panel

DETROIT CONVENTION CENTER

CONVENTION CENTER F1
N / A
N / A
N / A
CONVENTION CENTER F3
N / A
N / A
SECTOR12
N / A
WTAGGART
marjorie
USERNAME
Password
Security Panel
Security Terminal
Alarm Panel
Laser Grid Panel
Bomb Panel
Safe Panel

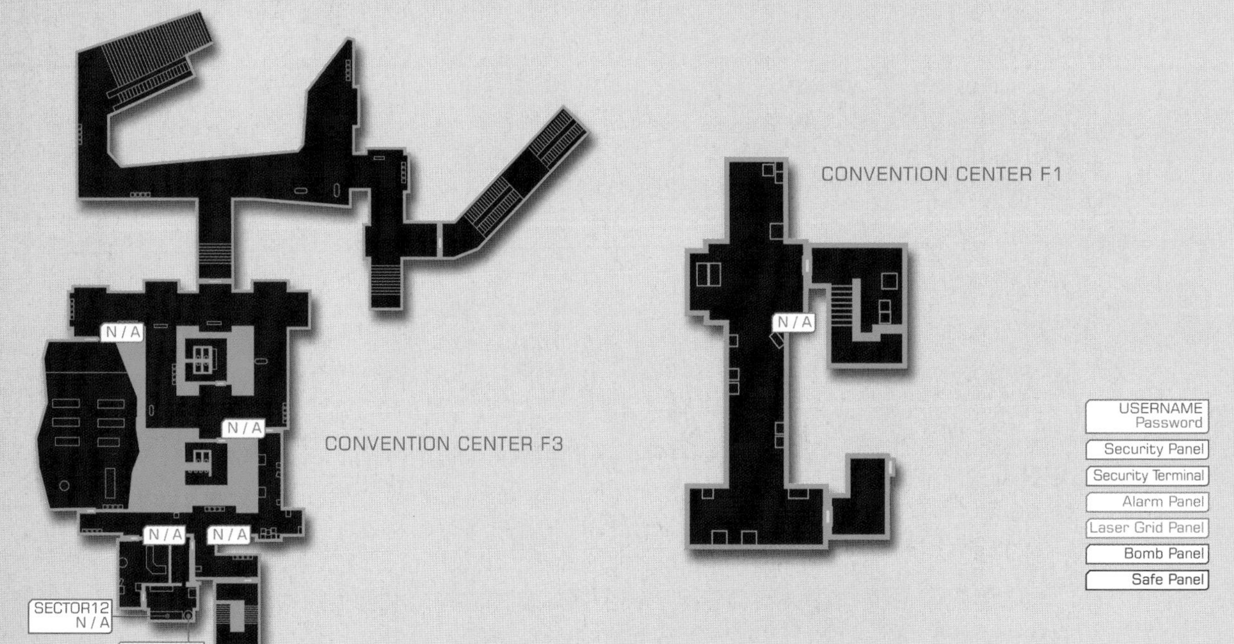

HARVESTER

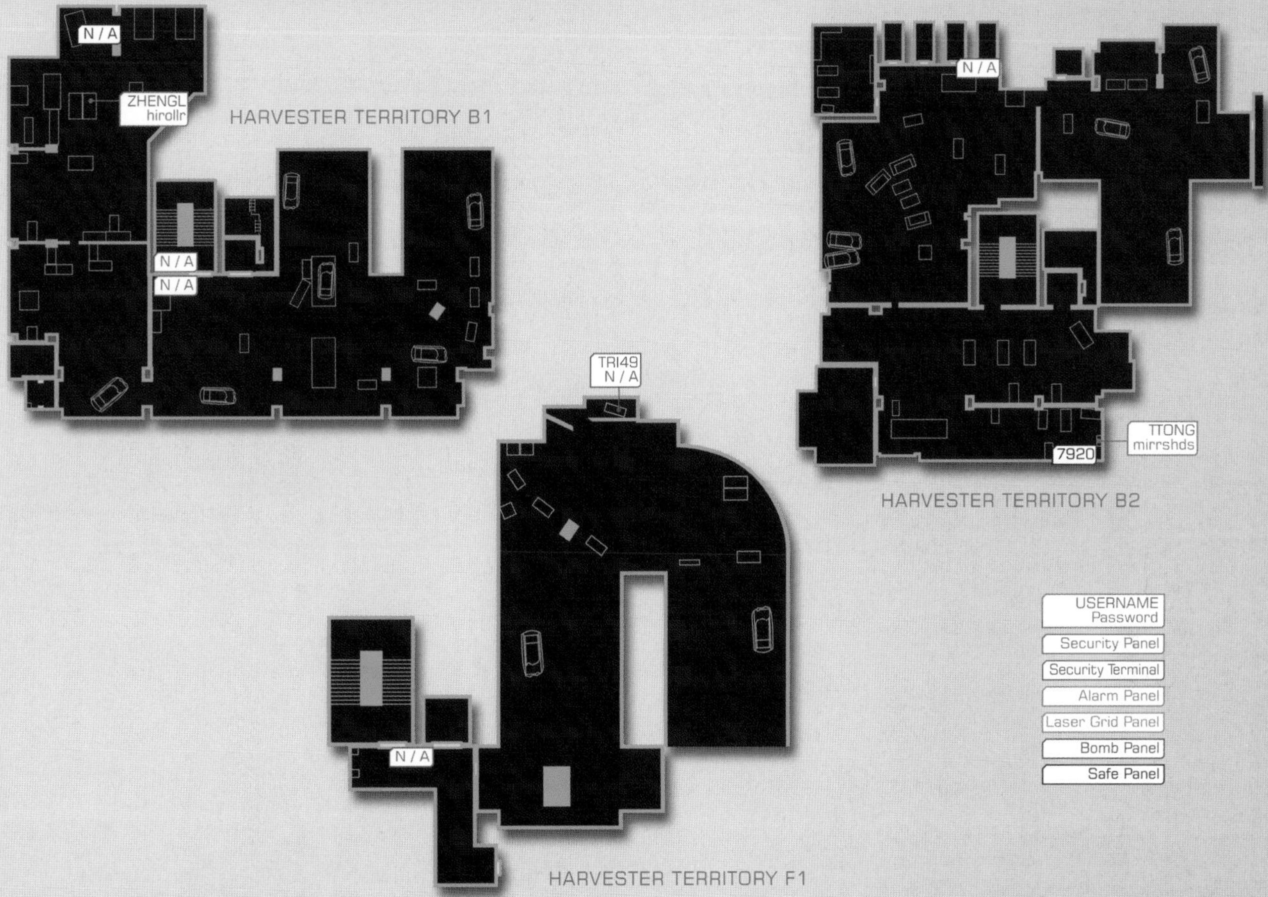

N / A
ZHENGL
hirollr
HARVESTER TERRITORY B1
N / A
N / A

N / A
TTONG
mirrshds
7920
HARVESTER TERRITORY B2

TRI49
N / A
N / A
HARVESTER TERRITORY F1

USERNAME
Password
Security Panel
Security Terminal
Alarm Panel
Laser Grid Panel
Bomb Panel
Safe Panel

HENGSHA SEAPORT

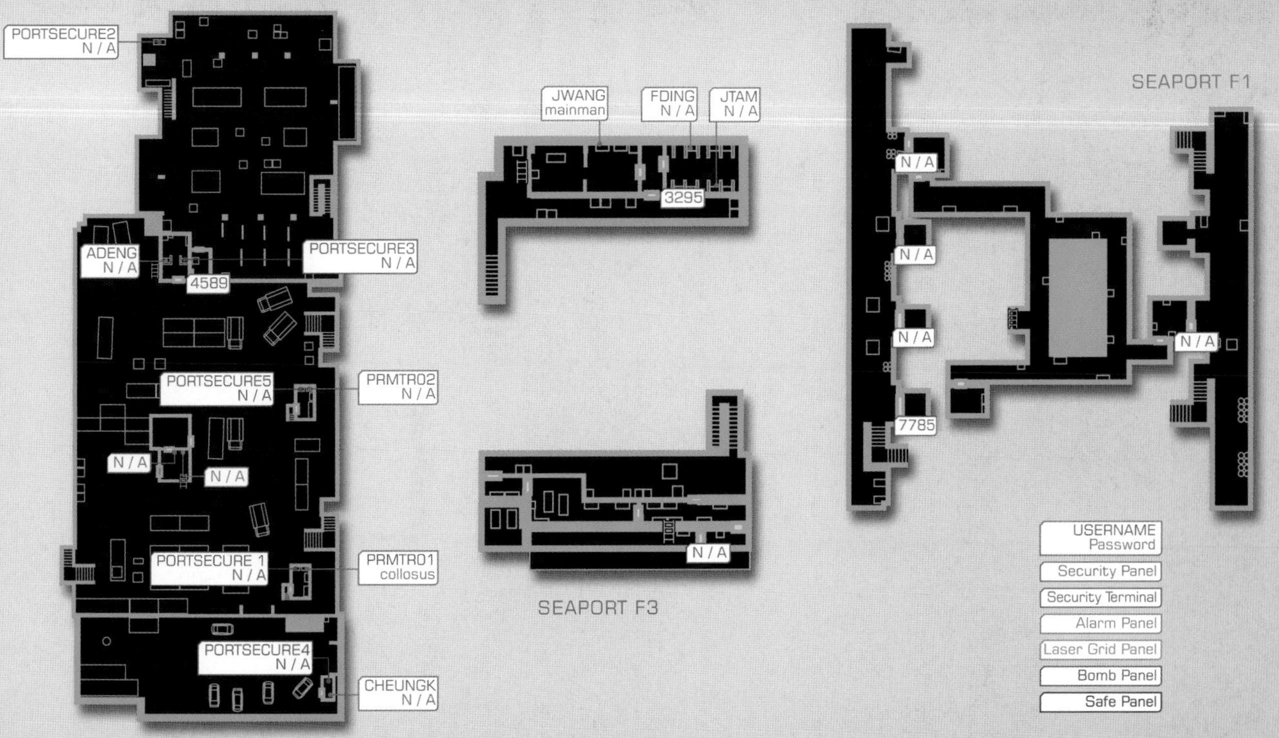

OMEGA RANCH

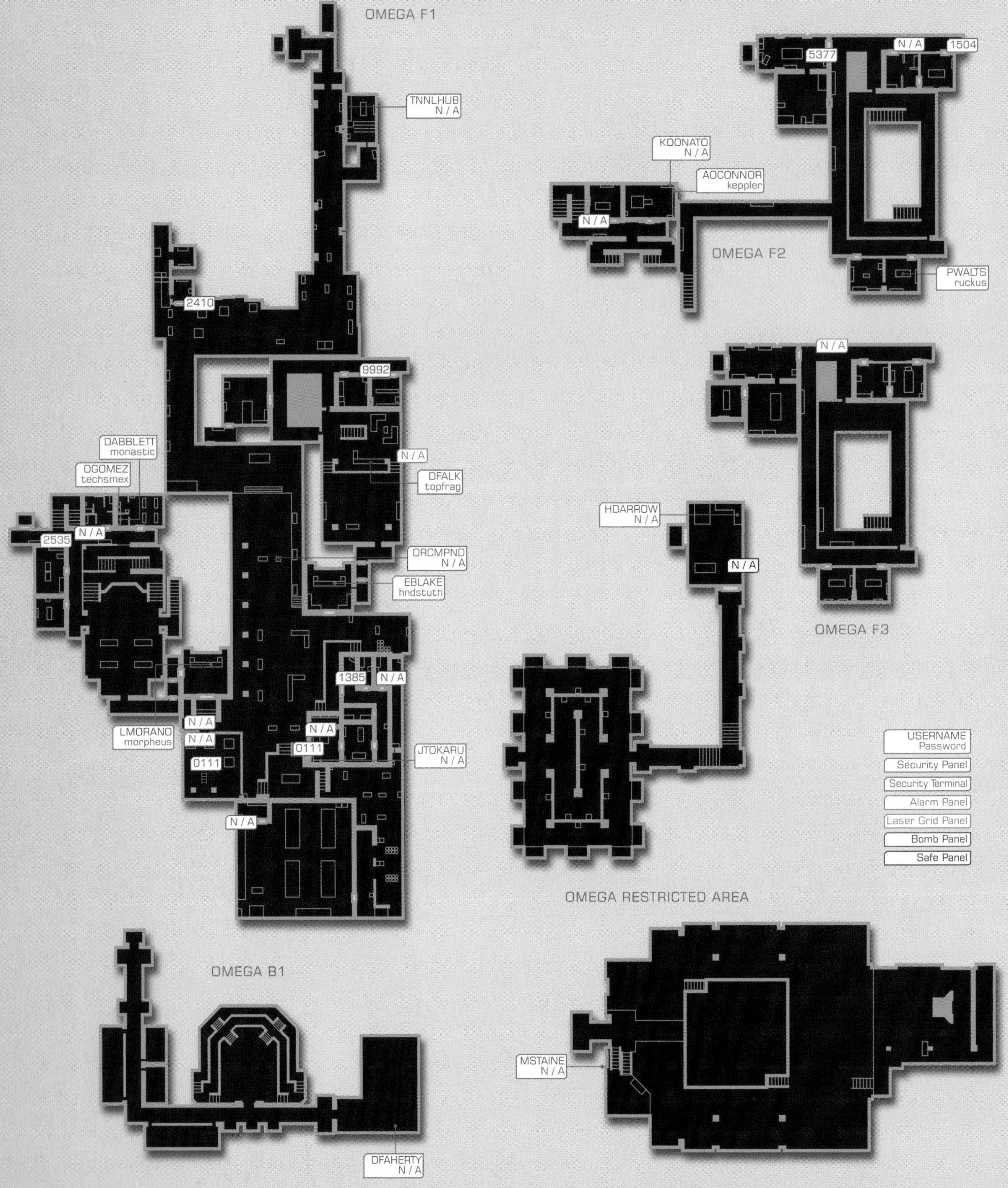
OMEGA F1
TNNLHUB
N / A
2410
9992
DABBLETT
monastic
OGOMEZ
techsmex
N / A
DFALK
topfrag
N / A
2535
ORCMPND
N / A
EBLAKE
hndstuth
1385
N / A
LMORANO
morpheus
N / A
N / A
N / A
0111
0111
JTOKARU
N / A
N / A
OMEGA F2
5377
N / A
1504
KDONATO
N / A
AOCONNOR
keppler
N / A
PWALTS
ruckus
N / A
HDARROW
N / A
N / A
OMEGA F3
USERNAME
Password
Security Panel
Security Terminal
Alarm Panel
Laser Grid Panel
Bomb Panel
Safe Panel
OMEGA RESTRICTED AREA
OMEGA B1
MSTAINE
N / A
DFAHERTY
N / A

PANCHAEA

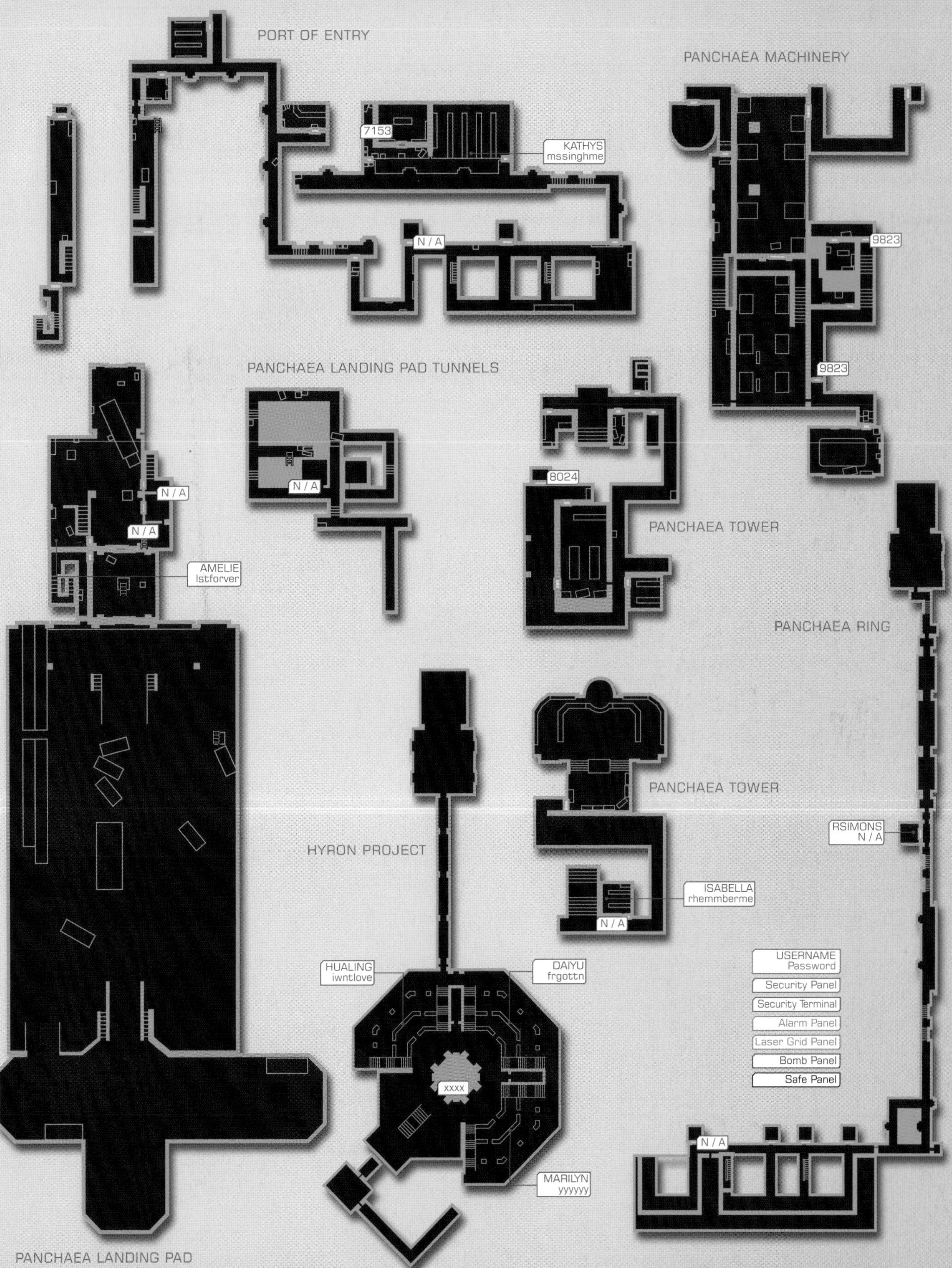

PORT OF ENTRY
7153
KATHYS
mssinghme
N / A
PANCHAEA MACHINERY
9823
9823
PANCHAEA LANDING PAD TUNNELS
N / A
N / A
N / A
AMELIE
lstforver
8024
PANCHAEA TOWER
PANCHAEA RING
PANCHAEA TOWER
RSIMONS
N / A
HYRON PROJECT
ISABELLA
rhemmberme
N / A
USERNAME
Password
Security Panel
Security Terminal
Alarm Panel
Laser Grid Panel
Bomb Panel
Safe Panel
HUALING
iwntlove
DAIYU
frgottn
xxxx
N / A
MARILYN
yyyyyy
PANCHAEA LANDING PAD

INDEX